JACOBITES

After Robert Mordon, *A chart wherein ... all the different rout[e]s of P[rince Charles] Edward in Great Britain*, engraving, *c.* 1747.

JACOBITES

A New History of the '45 Rebellion

Jacqueline Riding

BLOOMSBURY PRESS

NEW YORK · LONDON · OXFORD · NEW DELHI · SYDNEY

Bloomsbury Press
An imprint of Bloomsbury Publishing Plc

1385 Broadway   50 Bedford Square
New York   London
NY 10018   WC1B 3DP
USA   UK

www.bloomsbury.com

BLOOMSBURY and the Diana logo are trademarks of Bloomsbury Publishing Plc

First published in Great Britain 2016
First U.S. edition 2016

© Jacqueline Riding, 2016

ISBN: HB: 978-1-60819-801-6
ePub: 978-1-60819-804-7

Library of Congress Cataloging-in-Publication Data has been applied for.

2 4 6 8 10 9 7 5 3 1

Typeset by Newgen Knowledge Works (P) Ltd., Chennai, India
Printed and bound in the U.S.A. by Berryville Graphics Inc., Berryville, Virginia

To find out more about our authors and books visit www.bloomsbury.com. Here you
will find extracts, author interviews, details of forthcoming events, and
the option to sign up for our newsletters.

Bloomsbury books may be purchased for business or promotional use. For information
on bulk purchases please contact Macmillan Corporate and Premium
Sales Department at specialmarkets@macmillan.com.

For Jack, Pat, Haworth, Tom, Florrie, Ern & Nellie

'A romance of real life equal in splendour and interest to any which could be devised by fiction.'

Sir Walter Scott

'a noble attempt'

Dr Samuel Johnson

Contents

A Note on Dates

Until September 1752, Britain was still using the Julian calendar (Old Style or OS), while continental Europe had already introduced the Gregorian calendar (New Style or NS). As a result, during the eighteenth century, Britain was eleven days behind France, the Low Countries, Italy etc. In the main, the dates in the current history follow OS or NS depending on where the action is taking place, but when letters are being sent between Flanders and Britain for example, the authors invariably gave both dates for clarity, and this habit is continued here. At times, again for clarity and also when useful, the corresponding NS or OS has been included in brackets. The additional complication of the OS year traditionally commencing on 25 March, something England continued to do in our period but not Scotland (1 January), means that dates in January, February and March were invariably written with the old and new year included. So, 1 December 1745, would be followed by 1 February 1745/6, which would be followed, in turn, by 1 April 1746. The old tradition is used here throughout.

Prologue

Captain Richard Robinson's last voyage had not gone exactly to plan. His ship, the brigantine *Ann*, had set sail from Liverpool in late July 1745, bound for the Baltic port of Riga. The outward journey was uneventful and, having loaded his brig with a cargo of timber, the captain and his crew embarked for home. Navigating the treacherous seas around the British Isles was no simple matter. But while heading south past the west coast of Scotland, the unusually rough winds drove the *Ann* to seek refuge near the small Inner Hebridean island of Canna, located twelve miles off the south-west of Skye. And here she remained, until a sequence of disturbing incidents forced her captain to take his vessel back out into the open, stormy seas.

The *Ann* finally docked at Liverpool at around eleven o'clock at night on Thursday, 15 August and, early the following morning, Captain Robinson hastened to the chambers of the mayor, Owen Prichard.[1] Under oath, the captain recounted his story as a clerk scribbled down the particulars. The *Ann*, he recalled, had dropped anchor near Canna at about five o'clock on the afternoon of Saturday, 10 August. Soon after she had been joined by a snow brig under the command of Captain William Ross, another refugee from the storms raging to the west. According to its captain, the snow brig was carrying a small arsenal: a large quantity of small arms, twenty barrels of gunpowder, and twenty nine-pounder carriage guns that had been salvaged from a Swedish Indiaman wrecked off the Orkneys. Ross had been en route to Glasgow to deliver the cargo to its new owner. After this brief exchange, Captain Ross made his way to the island for provisions, but soon after landing he was taken hostage by a gang under the command of Donald MacDonald, known to the snow brig's captain as 'the Chief Man of the said island'. Now, with her master held captive, MacDonald sent a party of his men to the snow brig to search for arms but surprisingly (given what was on board) they came away empty-handed. Meanwhile, onshore, Ross' guards had become steadily drunk and rowdy, forcing their terrified captive at gunpoint to join them in a toast to King James VIII in Rome, the 'King over the Water'. Sometime later, after his guards had drunk themselves into a stupor, Captain Ross made his escape and arrived back on board the *Ann*, as Robinson recollected, 'in a great freight'. Both captains resolved to set sail at the first opportunity and at sunrise the two ships slipped out of their harbour, finally parting company off Kintyre at the mouth of the Clyde.

As described, Richard Robinson's time near Canna would have been eventful enough. But just after dropping anchor, and before the snow brig's arrival, a small rowing boat had come alongside the *Ann* carrying a passenger who urgently requested permission to board. This was a local Protestant schoolmaster who had been eagerly awaiting the arrival of a British ship. The schoolmaster informed Robinson that a foreign frigate of eighteen guns had recently arrived in the waters thereabouts, and only three days before he had seen a stranger, an uncommonly tall young man, on the mainland to the east of Skye. Since then, armed clansmen had started to gather: five thousand had already arrived and five thousand more were expected within the week. This young stranger, the schoolmaster continued, was referred to among the local Gaelic-speaking islanders as *Prionnsa Teàrlach*, Prince Charles.

As a loyal supporter of King George, the House of Hanover and the current British government, Mayor Prichard knew exactly who the tall young man was. But how long had he been lurking about Skye? Certainly long enough to gather the support of Donald MacDonald and his ruffians, plus ten thousand other Highland rebels. Whatever else was going through his mind, Mayor Prichard was certain of one thing: this was important, possibly vital intelligence and speed was of the essence. The statement was duly signed by Captain Robinson, countersigned by Mayor Prichard, enclosed with a covering letter addressed to the principal Secretary of State in London, and handed to an express rider.

Early on Sunday, 18 August Thomas Pelham-Holles, Duke of Newcastle and His Majesty's Secretary of State for the southern department, was asleep at his London town house on Lincoln's Inn Fields when the express from Liverpool arrived. His Grace was awoken by his manservant and emerged from his bedchamber unwigged and in his night shirt, housecoat and slippers as the express rider handed him the package of documents. Soon after Newcastle, now more formally dressed, arrived at his ministerial rooms in Whitehall where he hastily penned a response to Mayor Prichard.

'I R[eceived] very early this morning by Ex[pre]^ss the favour of [your] Letter of the 16, with the enclosed Information,' Newcastle scrawled. 'I shall not fail,' he continued, 'to lay it before the L[ord] J[ustices] who I am persuaded will greatly approve [of] your Zeal & attention; to His M[ajes]^ty service, in sending in the most exp[re]^s manner, an Intelligence which justly appeared to you of such great Importance.'[2] Rumours and counter-rumours had been circulating for months, but over the last week information coming from the north was beginning to align in certain crucial details. Only the day before, a short report (itself dated Whitehall, Saturday, 17 August) had been released by the government and published in the *London Gazette* which spoke of 'a French Vessel of 16 or 18 Guns' which 'had appeared on the West Coast of Scotland' and 'had there landed betwixt the Islands of Mull and Skie, several Persons' one of whom, 'there is the greatest Reason to believe is the Pretender's Son'.[3] The Duke of Newcastle was one of the few government ministers to have taken the rumours seriously. So, with the arrival of this statement from an independent witness, it seemed that his worst fears were confirmed beyond reasonable doubt: Charles Edward Stuart, son of James Stuart, the exiled claimant to the British throne, was in Scotland, and a new Jacobite rising had already begun.

Sir Godfrey Kneller, *Prince James Francis
Edward Stuart*, 1688.

Rome

'This Rebellion took its rise chiefly in Rome'

James Francis Edward Stuart, the only living legitimate son of King James II of England and VII of Scotland, resided with his small family and court in a palace in Rome rented on his behalf by the pope.[1] Located to the east across the River Tiber from St Peter's Basilica, and on the north side of the Piazza dei Santi Apostoli, the building was known locally as the Palazzo del Re (the King's Palace) in recognition of James' status in Rome since his father's death in 1701 as King James III and VIII, *de jure* monarch of England, Scotland and Ireland. Here the exiled Stuart court lived and operated within a conveniently located and suitably dignified setting. The pope had also graciously allowed James use of the Palazzo Apostolico in Albano, to which he and his entourage habitually retired during the sweltering Roman summers.

James Francis Edward had been in exile since he was six months old after his father, a convert to Roman Catholicism, had fled to France in 1688 to seek the protection and support of his cousin Louis XIV during the Protestant 'Glorious Revolution'. Long before this, attempts had been made in parliament to exclude James from the succession while he was heir apparent to his brother Charles II (the 'Exclusion Crisis'), who had no legitimate children. Even after his accession in 1685, there was a bid to remove James by armed rebellion led in the south-west of England by Charles' charismatic natural son, James Scott, Duke of Monmouth, and in Scotland by Archibald Campbell, 9th Earl of Argyll. Argyll was arrested and executed in Edinburgh on 30 June. The defeat of the rebels in the south-west at Sedgemoor on 6 July, followed by the execution of Monmouth and the savagery of the so-called 'Bloody Assizes' – many of the rebels were executed or transported as indentured servants to the West Indies – removed any real threat to James' rule for now. But it was the birth in June 1688 of a male heir from the King's second marriage, a child whom James was determined should be raised a Catholic, that was the pretext for his Protestant nephew and son-in-law, the Dutch prince William of Orange, to invade England at the invitation of the 'Immortal Seven', including the Earls of Danby, Shrewsbury and Devonshire. From William's point of view, he needed Protestant allies in Europe to counter the might of Catholic France, not a sequence of Catholic monarchs in Britain and Ireland who were close relatives (and therefore, he would say, subordinates) of the French king. Crucially, by the birth of this prince, William's Protestant wife and cousin Mary, James' eldest daughter by his first marriage, was no longer the heir apparent, and as a result William's influence would be dramatically reduced.

At home, the idea that a Roman Catholic could rule over the predominantly Protestant nations of Scotland and England, and be supreme governor of the established Protestant state church of the latter, was a circle many found impossible to square. James, too, had found this insufferable. He attempted, as had his brother before him, to intimidate and control the Presbyterian Kirk (a form of Calvinism) in Scotland, while introducing legislation across his domains to advance toleration for Roman Catholics, among others, which many within the British Isles viewed with alarm, as the first step towards the return of Catholicism as the state church with the pope at its head. There was also the troubling business of the 'Divine Right of Kings' – invariably accompanied, the opposition would argue, by its even uglier twin 'arbitrary government' – to which the Stuarts tended to cling, even when it was politically advantageous not to for the sake of a workable relationship with the English and Scottish parliaments: as James' father Charles I had found to his cost. On James' flight to France, the English parliament declared that he had abdicated and invited William and Mary to assume the throne as joint monarchs. The Scottish Convention Parliament preferred the term 'forfeited' – reiterating that James, indeed all Scottish kings, held the crown contractually, as set out in the Declaration of Arbroath (1320) – and then invited William and Mary to do the same in Scotland. The Presbyterian Kirk was now established as Scotland's national church.

When James' army was defeated in Ireland at the Battle of the Boyne in 1690, leaving him in exile near Paris for the time being, several attempts were made to restore him and the senior Stuart branch to the throne by his supporters, the Jacobites, deriving from the Latin for James, 'Jacobus'.[2] The movement gained significant momentum when James' Protestant second daughter, Anne, who had followed the childless and widowed William III in 1702, also died without any living offspring in 1714: for the queen a great personal tragedy, for the embryonic United Kingdom of Great Britain (since the Act of Union between Scotland and England in

1707) a potential disaster. Both William and Anne had considered naming James Francis Edward as their heir, on the condition that the young prince became a Protestant. Catholics had been excluded from the succession in England and Scotland since 1701 and 1704 respectively. But James' mother, Mary of Modena, and later James Francis Edward himself refused to accept such a deal. James, as his father before him, would rule as a Catholic monarch of all the Stuarts' territories, or not at all.

In 1714 the succession therefore passed to Georg Ludwig, Elector of Hanover, great-grandson of James I and VI, the Stuart monarch who had personally united the crowns of England and Scotland in 1603, bypassing fifty Catholic claimants in the process, including Queen Anne's half-brother. Within months of the arrival of George I, the Whig party (staunch supporters of the Glorious Revolution and the Protestant succession) won a resounding parliamentary election victory and, soon after, a rebellion in favour of the House of Stuart occurred. Jacobites – whether Scottish, Irish, Welsh or English, Episcopalian (effectively the Church of England in Scotland, re-established by Charles II, but since 1688 without bishops), Catholic, Anglican and nonjuring (the latter refused to swear the oath to the new Hanoverian monarch as head of the Church of England) – now had a variety of reasons for supporting a Stuart restoration: from belief in the indefeasible hereditary right of the Stuarts, whatever their religion, coupled with distaste for this foreign 'usurper', to the dismantling of the Act of Union, what could be called a Scottish nationalist strain, and toleration for Roman Catholicism. Indeed, from the onset it was in the Stuarts' interest to encourage any anti-Union grievances: fertile ground when Scotland's economy was ailing and the promised terms of the recent Union remained undelivered. In such circumstances the Stuarts could offer themselves as both an outlet for opposition and as a force for redress.[3]

Those firmly against the Stuarts, rather than neutral, were more focused in their reasons for preventing their return: the rejection of what they viewed as the French-style absolutist inclinations of the Stuarts, as most recently demonstrated by James II/VII, coupled with the preservation of the 1688–9 revolution principles, the Protestant settlement, the state churches of England and Scotland and the Union. All views – whether Jacobite or 'Georgite' (pro-Hanoverian), Tory or Whig – were spurred by a combination of patriotism, tradition, familial, social and cultural ties as well as religious, financial and political self-interest.

This latest Jacobite rebellion, known as the '15, was largely a Scottish, Highland rising led by John Erskine, 6th Earl of Mar, supported by France and with smaller rebellions in the west and north-east of England.[4] Despite initial success and even the arrival from France of James Francis Edward at Peterhead on the north-east coast of Scotland, the rising was effectively over when the Jacobite advance was arrested by an army commanded by Field Marshal John Campbell, 2nd Duke of Argyll and grandson of Monmouth's ally, at the Battle of Sheriffmuir. Mar fled to France. In the aftermath, huge fines were imposed and lands forfeited. Some of the leaders were executed, most notably the Englishman James Radclyffe, 3rd Earl of Derwentwater, while several of the clan chiefs, including Sir Ewen Cameron of Clan Cameron, went into exile. A disarming act came into force in November 1716, which outlawed unauthorised holding or bearing of arms in defined areas of Scotland. Despite these measures, the clan system and culture remained essentially undisturbed, although it is also true that the pro-Stuart Catholic or Episcopalian clans who had once been all-powerful in their regions, such as the MacDonalds and the Camerons, became increasingly poor and isolated from political influence, whether that of Edinburgh or London, while pro-Hanoverian clans, such as the Presbyterian Campbells, Monros (or Munros) and Sutherlands, grew more powerful and wealthy.

Another Jacobite attempt four years later, this time with the support of Catholic Spain and led by George Keith, the Earl Marischal of Scotland, William Murray, Marquess of Tullibardine and his brother Lord George Murray (sons of the Chief of Clan Murray, James Murray, 1st Duke of Atholl), all of whom had been exiled for their part in the '15, and Donald Cameron of Lochiel, grandson of Ewen Cameron (d. 1719), also failed. The 1st Duke of Atholl had been born into an Episcopalian family but had shown an inclination for the Kirk, had opposed the Treaty of Union but later proclaimed George I king at Perth: conflicting stances that are reflected in the different allegiances of his three sons. William and George had joined the Jacobite army against their father's wishes and his heir, William, was disinherited in favour of the pro-Hanoverian second son, also James.

Meanwhile, a treaty between Britain and France forced James Stuart and his courtiers to move out of France to Avignon, then within the Papal States, and later to Rome. But despite the failure of the '15 and the '19, the threat within Britain from Jacobite plots continued to plague the new British royal dynasty and its Whig government throughout the 1720s and 1730s. James' marriage to the Polish princess Maria Clementina Sobieska in 1719, the birth only a year later of a male heir, Charles Edward, Prince of Wales, and then in 1725 Henry Benedict, Duke of York, had given renewed focus and energy to the Jacobite cause.

For political expediency, the British Whig 'Prime Minister' Sir Robert Walpole declared publicly that the opposition Tory party in Britain was rife with Jacobitism, which in 1715 was not strictly speaking true: in fact some Tories were offered and accepted important positions of state. Many fervently believed in hereditary right regardless of the religion of the monarch. This could be fudged while a daughter of King James II and VII ruled and, in the case of Queen Anne, displayed an inclination towards the Tory party. But with the arrival of a distant cousin who was not just pro-Whig but avidly anti-Tory, for those isolated from power thoughts naturally turned to a Stuart restoration. If this was the position of a committed minority in 1715, then, as the years rolled on, with a change of monarch (George II r. 1727) and still no respite from effective exclusion from government and high office, it gained ground more generally within the Tory party as the only way out of this political wilderness. So among some (but not all) Tories, and even the Whig opposition to Walpole's government, who showed no sign of losing their grip on power, absence certainly could and did make the heart grow fonder.[5]

At the same time, the longer that James and his court remained in exile, the more difficult it must have been for them to sustain a sense of combat readiness for their crucial function within a Stuart restoration. During a previous exile, after the execution of Charles I (1649), the then Stuart court had been absent for only a decade. By 1740, James had been in exile for over fifty years and for the vast majority of his lifetime. Inevitably this situation had a significant impact on his character, manner and outlook. Each unsuccessful restoration attempt made it more difficult to dismiss the notion that the temporary stay in Rome might become permanent. And as the decades came and went, as the established order seemed more secure and the economy (including Scotland's by the 1730s and 1740s) more buoyant, there was the very real possibility that supporters, even ardent followers, would through necessity learn to live with and even thrive under the House of Hanover. Or just die out.

Considering the multitude of stresses he had to endure as best he could, it is not surprising that James is often described as having the air of a man burdened with care and even melancholic. Yet it is still the case that rather than being the decaying remnant of a hopeless cause, in the mid-eighteenth century the purpose of the Stuart court in exile continued to be what it had always been: the restoration of the Stuart dynasty in Britain and Ireland. Its fundamental role was as the central hub for what was an international Jacobite network, to maintain and coordinate existing supporters while encouraging new blood, to keep the pressure on sympathetic foreign powers to provide the money, arms and troops for an invasion of

Britain, and, despite the difficulties, to act as the core element of a court in waiting, prepared to transfer to London – potentially at a moment's notice – in the event of the restoration. Whatever the day-to-day activities of James himself, his household, pensioners and wider entourage, this was the ultimate, overarching goal and where, barring the usual internal disagreements and bickering, their energies were channelled. In the meantime many Scots, Irish, English exiles and their families, having settled in France while the Stuarts had resided at St-Germain-en-Laye, near Paris, now occupied influential positions at the court at Versailles, and held commissions or raised Scottish and Irish regiments within the French army.

Above all, James made the best of his time in Rome. In 1719, as befitted his position, the Palazzo del Re had been completely refurbished for its new occupant with all the paraphernalia associated with European royalty. The 'King's Apartment', where James lived, conducted his business and entertained publicly and privately, was on the principal (first) floor. Other rooms were occupied by leading courtiers and household staff, while the princes Charles and Henry had their own separate apartments on the second floor with adjoining bedchambers. The main access to the King's Apartment was via a grand staircase to the north, which led to a long sequence of connected rooms, moving from the more public areas via antechambers including a throne or presence chamber and a dining room, to the private rooms to the south: the bedchamber, gallery and closet or cabinet. The walls were lined with portraits of James' parents, James himself and his wife Princess Maria Clementina (who had died in 1735) and their handsome sons. Here also were two spectacular large-scale paintings of the marriage of James and Maria Clementina, and the baptism of Prince Charles, the focus of all future Jacobite hopes.[6]

James' household included his groom of the bedchamber, the Scotsman Captain William Hay, and his principal private secretary, another Scotsman, James Edgar. The latter occupied a room next to his master's bedchamber. The largest room in the private area, the gallery, had windows overlooking the piazza which were useful for viewing the comings and goings around this public thoroughfare, and a ceiling decorated with the longed-for Catholic Stuart restoration in mind: two plump putti holding the sceptre and crown of England, with other figures representing 'faith' and 'the Catholic religion'.[7] James was also attended by two physicians, Dr Robert Wright and Dr James Irwin, and a surgeon, James Murray – all Scots. Beyond this there was the usual panoply of *valets de chambre*, grooms and coachmen, cooks and washerwomen, all going about their business under the watchful eye of palace and royal bodyguards, also provided by the pope.

Regular visitors to the palazzo would have included the incumbent French and Spanish ambassadors in Rome, who advised James on the current state of play of both the local and international support for his cause. In addition, from 1739 his chief advisers were the French cardinal, Pierre-Paul Guérin de Tencin, and his nephew Jean-Louis Guérin, while the role of chief minister was fulfilled by another cardinal, Domenico Riviera. Such reliance on high-ranking foreign and Catholic individuals was inevitable given where the court resided, as well as the need for a foreign sponsor for any invasion of Britain. But one of the key figures within the exiled court was the protestant Scot James Murray, Earl of Dunbar. Until 1738 Lord Dunbar had had the important role of governor to Prince Charles, and as such had responsibility for his royal charge's education and development, in concert with an Irishman, Sir Thomas Sheridan, as under-governor. These two men were crucial in the forming of Charles' character. That his upbringing and education were not all that they should have been, as the future Jacobite leader and king, is stated by several contemporaries. During a visit to Rome between 1739 and 1740 the French writer Charles de Brosses met the princes and described them in a letter as 'amiable, polite and gracious; both of them have but a mediocre wit, and are less polished than princes should be at their age'.[8] One Stuart courtier in Rome said of Prince Charles that 'tis true his Education has not been in every particular such as a person of his rank is supposed generally to have', but loyally continues, 'yet by a good fund of sense people will see that nature has supply'd whatever may have been wanting in care and industry'.[9]

James Edgar, who knew the princes as well as their father (perhaps better), describes Charles as an avid sportsman, spending entire days hunting and shooting. Yet at the end of the day he 'diverts himself with musick for an hour or two, as if he had not been abroad, and plays his part upon the Bass Viol extremely well, for he loves and understands musick to a great degree'. Young Henry is less musical, 'but he sings, when he pleases, much better. En fin, were their friends to see them either at home or abroad, they could not but be infinitely charm'd with them both.' Edgar concludes, offering an indication as to the closeness of the brothers, 'thô of different turns and tempers, they agree very well together and love one another very much'.[10]

Of Charles' entourage, which in addition to Sir Thomas Sheridan included an equerry, the Englishman Francis Strickland, only Lord Dunbar was a Protestant. That the Stuart heir apparent was not only born and raised a Catholic in Rome, but was dominated by Catholics within the Stuart court itself, troubled some supporters in Britain. Many Protestant

Jacobites were happy for the Stuarts to return on any basis, as their God-given hereditary right should not be dismissed at the whim of parliament and ministers. However, some believed that James and his sons should convert. The French minister, the marquis d'Argenson, recalled a conversation at the palace of Versailles with an English Jacobite who insisted the Stuarts 'must be good Protestants' for the sake of their country, and that they 'should say, as our Henri IV did of the mass, "A crown is worth more than a sermon"'.[11] So for some supporters, their religion was not just one of many barriers, but the *only* barrier to the Stuarts being welcomed back to Britain with open arms. But this lack of cohesion concerning the dynasty's religion hints at inherent tensions within the Jacobite camp.

Dealing with the rivalries and personality clashes that inevitably existed among the Jacobite party, whether in Britain, Versailles or Rome, coupled with managing the expectations of James' faithful followers, was a wearying necessity. On this subject James was to advise Charles in a letter 'to be on your guard in such cases, since it is our business to favour & protect all good subjects without taking party in their little picques & animosities'.[12] Every new attempt that failed, every plot that was foiled, although evidence of a loyal and persistent Jacobite following, resulted in a new influx of exiles seeking refuge and support. Every prince should reward loyalty. But unlike the resources that King George had to hand, taxation in particular, James had to work within quite limited means, as his main income came from the pensions he received from France and the papacy, along with donations – large and small – from his devoted supporters. The business of spying and intelligence gathering cut both ways, inevitably requiring some financial incentive. On one occasion Francis, Lord Sempill, one of James' envoys to the Court of France, made a payment to a new informer, which James retrospectively agreed to 'thó,' James wrote, 'I am far from being flush of money at this time'.[13] Even if the money was tight, James did, however, have status, excellent connections and influence: as a European prince, an eminent Roman Catholic and, as some considered him, a rightful king. Riviera, James' chief minister, had been nominated to the College of Cardinals (from which a new pope was chosen) by James himself, an example of the influence he wielded as *de jure* King of England in the eyes of the papacy.

Despite its geographical distance from Britain and Ireland, which inevitably made coordinating Jacobite activity more difficult, the Stuart court in Rome had one crucial advantage. Rome was the key destination on the 'Grand Tour', a cultural rite of passage whereby young male Britons (a term which at this time embraced Irishmen), usually from wealthy, influential families, travelled through Western Europe seeking education, enlightenment and entertainment. Many of the young travellers had relations or associates who had participated in the '15, the '19 and later Jacobite plots and intrigues and who now lived either at, or within, the orbit of the Stuart court. Even if a traveller had no direct association, or was hostile to the Stuart cause, the ability to meet and socialise with fellow English, Welsh, Scots and Irishmen so far from home was very welcome indeed. Crucially, the Stuart court provided practical as well as social support to such travellers. While Britain had no official embassy in Rome – Queen Anne, George I and George II had not been recognised by the papacy – this role was effectively assumed by the exiled Stuart court.[14]

Those employed at the Palazzo del Re lived in rooms within it or in the surrounding area, or, as likely, near the Piazza di Spagna and its environs: the very neighbourhood where many British grand tourists and travellers took lodgings. If a British gentleman walked from the Piazza di Spagna to, let's say, the Forum, it is likely that he would pass the Palazzo del Re en route. He might therefore bump into a member of the Stuart household, or even see the 'King', 'Chevalier' or 'Pretender' (from the French 'prétendant', meaning 'claimant') himself. In fact, by 1740 James appears to have developed a daily routine, which, although bordering on the banal, certainly made him easy to locate from one hour to the next. Most remarkable were his public devotions. In the opinion of Charles de Brosses, 'He is excessively devout; he spends his mornings by his wife's tomb, praying to the holy apostles.'[15] In 1741 the artist John Russell wrote to 'Mrs R', 'Your curiosity, Madam, no doubt, will expect to find some-thing here concerning the Chevalier [a more polite term than 'pretender'], and his Two Sons.' Russell goes on that James 'passes all his time in a very regular manner : rising early, he spends the morning in business, hears Mass at a set hour, and dines at twelve. He often walks in the fine gardens at Rome, especially those of the Villa Borghesa: in the evening, he receives visits, sups at ten, and goes to bed about mid-night.'[16]

Such a regime jarred with a young man like Charles, who desired purpose and action. The regular hunting excursions would be normal behaviour for any prince or even nobleman. But with Charles, there is a sense that his devotion to such pastimes was a way of occupying himself physically and mentally for want of anything else. In 1740, in an important, some might say belated, move – for the sanity of his son as well as the future of the Stuart cause – James finally allowed the now twenty-year-old Charles to attend council meetings, and to share in the intelligence and correspondence arriving in Rome from all over Europe.[17]

James may have inclined towards a quiet, devout private life, which acted as the counterbalance to the stresses of his chief business. But he had a public duty and obligations, firstly to his host, the pope, and more broadly to the Roman nobility, who sustained and dignified his very existence within his temporary adopted city. Secondly, he had an obligation to the Jacobite cause itself. Maintaining visibility allowed the curious, like John Russell, as well as the faithful to observe and evaluate Britain's alternative monarch and his heirs. For a visiting Whig, Tory, Georgite or Jacobite, the exiled Stuarts held an obvious fascination.

Perhaps due to the danger and intrigue surrounding them, there was an avid, almost obsessive interest in James and his sons, and news of them was a conspicuous element of any travel journal or letter home. Every detail was recorded and reported on, how they looked and dressed, how they behaved, who they spoke to and where they went: whether at the opera, attending a ball, walking in the gardens of the Villa Borghese or at mass. Much of this was also useful intelligence for the British government. But such encounters served another purpose to the Stuart cause beyond gossip. The written reports back to friends and family, and the entertaining travel anecdotes at many a tavern gathering or supper party on return, kept the exiled Stuart dynasty alive in the minds of all Britons: whether as the true royal house, the almost legendary leading players of a turbulent recent past, or mythic national bogeymen.

To see and be seen, in addition to regular prayers and walks, James supported and regularly attended public musical concerts and the opera, often accompanied by his sons, and the family were usually present at the most lavish balls and festivals that Rome could offer. Such events were also attended by British travellers. During a tour of Italy, Joseph Spence, writing from Rome to his mother, Mirabelle, in Winchester on 13 January 1731, observed, almost casually, that at the opera, 'We are seated in the second Row of Boxes; &, whether by good or bad luck, in the very Box under the Pretender's. He was there last night, with his second son (the Eldest was gon[e] out on a Party of Hunting).' Spence continues, 'tho' I never make any Visit to my Neighbour above stairs, I went over to my L[or]d Stafford, who is opposite to us, to take a view of them'.[18]

The two princes were both well schooled in those accomplishments that were for public display and scrutiny. The playwright Samuel Crisp, writing to his friend Christopher Shute, describes a masked ball during the Carnival of February 1739 (NS) which was hosted by the Marchese Bolognetti and attended by James and his sons, who were, as usual, the highlight of the event for every one present. Unsurprisingly, Crisp has a keen eye for theatrical detail. Both princes, he recalls, were 'in Masquerade Habitts of two young shepherds wore rich white silk Hats with fine Diamond loops & buttons Bunches of White Ribbands at their knees & shoes their faces unmask'd'.[19]

Crisp watched James walk across the room to where a number of English gentlemen were standing, which the playwright believed he had done 'on purpose', although 'nobody took any manner of notice of him tho he talked English for half an hour together to one of his attendants; I was very next to him & he heard the English Gentlemen talking together, all round him'. Then the master of ceremonies 'came and askd him, by the name of Sire, if his Majesty had a mind to see the young Princes dance; to which he answer'd he should be very glad of it & accordingly the Eldest began'. Crisp recalled: 'I never saw any thing so genteel . . . his looks, his gesture, all was the finest, & most expressive that can be imagin'd.' Later both princes 'got up to begin English country Dances, which they have taught all the Roman ladies, who are much pleas'd with the fashion'. Crisp declares his amazement at hearing the tunes 'Butter'd Peas, Willie Wilkie struck up in a Roman Palace'. Even if they were already known in Italy, surely it was the handsome Stuart brothers who made these dances popular among the Roman nobility.

However, there was a strategy behind Charles being ordered to dance in front of the English visitors. Two years after Samuel Crisp, John Russell attended another Carnival ball at the Palazzo Pamphili in the Piazza Navona, attended by 'the chief Quality, who were all in masquerade'. At this event Charles 'was dressed in a Scotch Highlander's habit, with a bonnet, target, and broad sword; and adorned with jewels to the value of 100,000 Roman crowns. He opened the Ball, and was seconded by his Brother; they being Both respected here as persons of the first rank.'[20] The performing of English country dances and the wearing of Highland garb, particularly where Britons could see them, was a clear attempt to present the Stuarts as British. Yet, conversely, such attempts may have simply emphasised just how unBritish they now were – in appearance, manner, attitude and outlook – after a half-century in exile. Further, it is worth stressing that even James had little personal experience of the lands he felt destined to rule; the Jacobite Prince of Wales had none at all.

Viewing the Stuarts in public was one thing. Mixing with their entourage, or even visiting them at the Palazzo del Re, was quite another. The journal of Alexander Cunyngham of 1736–7, who was then travelling with the young artist Allan Ramsay, reveals how easy it was to move into the orbit of the Stuart court. Arriving in Rome at the end of October 1736, the young Scotsmen took lodgings in the Piazza di Spagna and almost immediately had regular visits from James' physicians, Dr Wright and Dr Irvine. On 14 November (NS) Cunyngham and Ramsay witnessed James at his prayers in the Jesuit church and four days later Cunyngham records that 'Dr Wright dined with me and gave me many diverting histories of the young Chevalier', of 'his willfulness and restlessness and hardiness, his quickness of capacity'.[21] After dinner they went to the Villa Ludovic where both young princes happened to be.[22] The day was concluded with a visit to a coffeehouse that was frequented by George Seton, Earl of Winton, who had been out in the '15 'and several other of their stamp and there fell a-singing old Scots songs and were very merry'.[23] And so the journal goes on – all innocent enough you might think. But both Cunyngham and Ramsay were members of the Jacobite Masonic Lodge in Rome of which Winton was master: another vital mechanism for this international network.[24]

As this suggests, the artistic and cultural attractions of Rome were a suitable ruse for any home-nation Jacobite, wishing to visit the Stuart court, to leave Britain or Ireland without drawing obvious attention to themselves. To give the full quotation from Sir John Clerk of Penicuik, Baron of the Exchequer for Scotland, 'This Rebellion took its rise chiefly in Rome, for some of the Highland chiefs and others, as they traveled into Italy, never failed of visiting the pretender's family, and chiefly made their court to the two princes, Charles and Henry, the sons of the s[ai]ᵈ pretender and the princess Sobieski, both in appearance handsome sprightly young men.'[25] It was treason for any British citizen to set foot in the Palazzo del Re, indeed, even to correspond with James and his family. So adjoining James Edgar's room, within the private area of James' grand apartment, was a small, secret staircase leading down to the palazzo's south entrance situated directly below the gallery (with its Stuart restoration ceiling) and located on the Piazza dei Santo Apostoli itself. The staircase allowed visitors to gain access to James and the princes without being seen, even by a majority of the staff and household, some of whom were almost certainly British government spies.

David, Lord Elcho, the young heir of the staunchly Jacobite Lord Wemyss, recounts this at length during his own travels in 1739–40. He was brought to the palazzo by James' groom of the bedchamber William Hay and entered through a little door that led into the cellars. Hay pointed towards a staircase or 'ladder' up which Lord Elcho was to climb. Having followed instructions, Lord Elcho emerged from the secret stair into James Edgar's chamber and was then shown into a suite of rooms. He was told that James was awaiting him in the fourth along. Lord Elcho 'duly found him there', the room no doubt dimly lit for this clandestine encounter, 'and after having kissed his hands he made me sit close to him before the fire'.[26] As Lord Elcho continues, James then 'told me that he knew that my father was very attached to him, and that this would be taken into consideration should he ever come to the throne'.[27] The exchange was as much to do with information gathering as encouraging the young man's continued loyalty. James then rang a bell to summon the princes, and Lord Elcho kissed their hands. James 'made me stand back to back with the elder, Prince Charles, who was a year older than I and much taller'. Lord Elcho was dismissed and concluded the episode with a 'supper tete a tete' with James Edgar, who 'told me that of all the British visitors, the Duke of Beaufort was the one who most often climbed the ladder'.[28] This was a group who needed to maintain a profile in Britain and to manage and expand their support base. Fostering greater loyalty by allowing young men from loyal families access to James and the princes, encouraging a sense of intimacy and exclusivity while also appealing to their sense of adventure, was absolutely vital.

John Murray of Broughton, another heir to a staunch Scottish Jacobite, travelled to Rome in about 1737 and in similar circumstances met James and his sons. According to a later memoir, Murray was brought into their presence 'to kiss their Hands', and then had a long discussion with Charles. As a result, the young Scottish gentleman was bewitched, as an adoring description of the prince written a few years later amply reveals. Charles was not only tall, physically perfect with refined features, pale red hair and stunning dark brown eyes, but had a dignity and 'an unspeakable Majesty diffus'd through his whole Mien and Air' which inspired awe in those who witness it, making him 'without Exception the most surprisingly handsome Person of the Age'. Furthermore, Charles was a happy combination of 'the good Nature' of the Stuarts with the 'Spirit' of his Polish Sobieski forefathers and therefore 'equally qualified to preside in Peace and War'.[29] Ignoring for a moment the gushing hyperbole, Charles still emerges as a young man who is not only charming and attractive, but one who can stimulate admiration and even adoration in his followers. Such traits might carry a determined and focused individual a very long way indeed.

So, far from moribund, the Stuart court, under challenging circumstances, kept the flame of Jacobitism very much alive in Great Britain. But James and all right-thinking Jacobites knew that whatever the strength of support for the Stuart cause at home, in addition, and crucially, they required the active military and financial support of a foreign power to achieve the longed-for restoration. In reality, by 1740, the only real contender was France.

A. Benoist after Blackey, *Louis XV*, 1741.
(BIBLIOTHÈQUE NATIONALE DE FRANCE)

2

Versailles

'this grand theatre'

Towards the end of her life, Jeanne Antoinette Poisson, marquise de Pompadour and *maîtresse-en-titre* to the King of France, recalled her first impressions of the French court, 'this grand theatre' as she called it, in residence at the palace of Versailles some ten miles from Paris. 'I thought myself amidst another species of mortals,' she wrote, 'their manners and usages are not the same; and that in regard to dress, deportment, and language, the inhabitants of Versailles are entirely different from those of Paris.'[1] The marquise describes a court living and working cheek by jowl, in claustrophobic isolation from the nation's capital, let alone the remainder of this sprawling and still largely agricultural country.[2] At the heart of Versailles' unwieldy assembly of aristocrats, ministers and administrators was the King of France himself, Louis XV. To the young newcomer, within the confines of Versailles, emotions and therefore behaviour become distorted and exaggerated.[3] In such a place the whims and inclinations of the king, coupled with the strengths and weaknesses of his character, dictated the nature and progress of all policy, and therefore when – or if – the causes of foreign princes were favoured and armies mobilised.

In 1715 Louis XV, an orphan since the age of two, had inherited the thrones of France and Navarre from his great-grandfather, Louis XIV. He was five years old. By that time France was exhausted and almost bankrupt from war. From 1715 until 1723 France was ruled by a regent, the king's great uncle, Phillipe Charles, duc d'Orléans. In 1718 France and the United Kingdom signed the Treaty of the Quadruple Alliance by which France agreed not to harbour James Francis Edward Stuart or any of his descendants. In fulfilment of the obligations set out in this treaty, Orléans had expelled James from French territory, hence his eventual move to Rome, and had been instrumental in the discovery and suppression in 1722 of the planned insurrection of the English Tories known as the

Atterbury Plot, named after Francis Atterbury, Bishop of Rochester and Dean of Westminster.

In 1723 Louis reached his majority (aged thirteen), which was quickly followed by Orléans' death. Louis Henri, duc de Bourbon and Prince de Condé, head of the Bourbon-Condé cadet branch of the reigning Bourbon family, became Louis' chief minister, and after offering a daughter of King George I the hand of his cousin in marriage (politely refused, as her conversion to Catholicism was a requirement) Monsieur le Duc negotiated for Louis to marry the Polish princess Marie Leszczyńska in 1725. Soon after, the duke was dismissed as chief minister in favour of Louis' tutor, mentor and surrogate grandfather, Cardinal André-Hercule de Fleury, Bishop of Fréjus. The dynamic between the child king and the cardinal was crucial to the former's intellectual and emotional development, and therefore his future conduct once in full possession of power. In fact the king remained submissive to the advice of his former tutor, and Fleury continued to dominate politics at Versailles throughout the 1720s and 1730s. Cardinal François-Joachim de Pierre de Bernis observed that, on the one hand, his fellow cardinal could be praised for instilling strong religious principles into his charge, but on the other he had made a prince 'born with intelligence, memory, accuracy in discernment, and a great desire to do well and to render everyone happy and content', frankly, a bit work-shy. Worse still, the 'Bishop of Fréjus inspired the king, unfairly, with an immense distrust of himself, and as great a distrust of others', keeping the cardinal very much in charge of public affairs.[4]

On occasion Cardinal Fleury showed interest in supporting the Stuart cause, but in the main continued the anti-Jacobite stance of the regency by upholding the stipulations of the treaty with Great Britain. His opposition in council to what became known as the Cornbury Plot of 1733–5 signalled the demise of yet another insurrection in England. What was more than evident was that while Cardinal Fleury lived, Louis was disinclined to show any interest in ruling himself and therefore James Stuart's cause, as far as France was concerned, was on hold. And, as a result of France's inactivity, during this period there was effectively a suspension of any hopes for a restoration.

Sixteen years after the king had come of age, the councillor of state, René-Louis de Voyer de Paulmy, marquis d'Argenson, would observe, with as much despair as Cardinal de Bernis before him, that 'Louis XIV made his reign felt by France when he was only twenty-one years old'. Louis XV on the other hand was nearly thirty, and yet still led 'the life of a dandy and a useless being'. The king 'takes much exercise to disperse his morbid humours' and 'tears himself from his frivolous occupations for one hour's work on his papers and books, and that is all; for what he does with his ministers does not count'.[5] Aside from the monarch's seeming lack of interest in hard work and governing, both Bernis and d'Argenson allude to Louis' compulsive pursuit of pleasure: a trait that achieved legendary status. Louis was charming, very handsome, dark-eyed and quite swarthy, not unlike his Stuart cousins and Charles II in particular. In the context of female company – as La Pompadour understood all too well – Louis was at once voracious and easily bored. This was hardly unusual behaviour for a male ruler of the *ancien régime*. Besides which, by 1740 Louis' queen had given him ten children and thus, having done her duty, had banned him from her bedroom.

However, at the same time as indulging his sexual appetite with an ever-changing parade of mistresses, the king was both religious and melancholic. These conflicting urges, from unrestrained self-indulgence to an almost pious self-loathing, resulted in an overwhelming and at times debilitating internal struggle. As a result, according to his intimate Pompadour, 'he is one of the most unhappy men in his kingdom'.[6] During moments when the royal emotional pendulum had swung towards contrition and even religious fervour – during a period of life-threatening illness, for example – Louis might look upon the restoration of the Catholic Stuarts, the true and divinely appointed kings of England, Scotland and Ireland as he would view them, as a way of easing his guilt, while demonstrating his piety and confirming his status as a true Christian, that is Catholic, monarch. As the early nineteenth-century historian A. E. Challice claims, here 'Louis found a secret solace for his troubles, and perhaps hoped to gain absolution for all his sins, past, present, and to come, in the belief that he was born to plant a crucifix on London Bridge'.[7] Self-indulgent, melancholic and pious (after a fashion) he may have been, but Louis was no fool. When the fog of deep despair had cleared, such personal desires would need to sit alongside more practical and political concerns. The Stuart cause could never take precedence over the needs of France. But when the needs of the two causes coincided – what, His Most Christian Majesty might ask, could be better?

In a journal entry of 1739 the marquis d'Argenson summarised the debate at Versailles regarding a Stuart restoration very succinctly. He lists among the 'pressing affairs', both domestic and foreign, of the State of France, Britain's commerce and excessive wealth.[8] In his opinion, the greedy, expansionist trading policy of the British was fundamentally out of balance and unfair, and therefore the chief reason for discontent in Europe. All France wanted, the marquis declares, was that Britain's commerce should not be excessive or 'rapine', to use his own phrase, and that Britain should not conquer North America (where both countries were battling over land and colonies), while he bemoans the power and strength of the Royal Navy.[9] The rivalry between France and Britain extended to the trade in lucrative commodities such as tobacco and sugar, produced in plantations along the east coast of North America and the West Indies, and dependent on enslaved African labour. Pondering the issue of the Stuart restoration within this national and international framework, the marquis considers 'what good will it produce for France and the world?' In fact, assessing from year to year or even month by month what benefit a Stuart restoration would bring to France would dictate whether Louis was stirred into action or remained aloof. D'Argenson first considers the internal destabilising effect that a restoration attempt would create: for surely, he poses, an 'English [sic] government a little tottering is perhaps a good thing'? (The use of 'English' throughout his journal – in 1739 the Union was only thirty-two years old – suggests that old habits die hard.) He immediately dismisses this as a temporary solution. Better, he observes, to assist in the establishment of 'a legitimate, tranquil king, reigning according to the laws of his nation, and having no foreign sovereignty like that of Hanover [King George maintained his position as Elector]' who would be less rapacious, and content himself with 'legitimate commerce'. Unlike, that is, 'Walpole and the Hanoverians' who are 'combining together for rapine, instead of suppressing it'. Certainly Sir Robert Walpole had always avoided war precisely because it was a significant drain on national finances (while increasing national debt) and bad for Britain's burgeoning Empire, trade and commerce. The expense of war also put pressure on Walpole to increase the Land Tax, something the cheerfully self-serving owner of the extensive Houghton Hall estate liked even less. So, as d'Argenson continues, 'If the Stuarts can bring about such times as these, let us favour their return, without, however, spending much effort or making many sacrifices for a result which, after all, is uncertain.' Yet, he concludes, 'if their restoration could produce the effect I have just mentioned, the obligation they would thus contract towards us would turn, I hope, to the profit of England and the world. We should, besides, gain this: that the Stuarts would have no duty to Austria, like the Hanoverians, and no son-in-law in the Prince of Orange [William IV, married to King George's eldest daughter Ann, Princess Royal].'[10]

In d'Argenson's opinion an invasion of Britain in support of the Stuarts, and the resulting domestic disruption, was, at the very worst, a way of distracting France's old enemy (formerly England, now Britain) and more importantly her military and financial resources, away from the European theatre of war, and even beyond, from their colonial activities in the Indian subcontinent and America. But France would not be simply creating a distraction. Nor would she be aggressively placing a usurper on the thrones of Great Britain and Ireland. Rather, France would be assisting in the return of the rightful monarch to a, presumably, thankful nation. In this sense, France would not be waging war on the United Kingdom, but the illegitimate House of Hanover and the usurping German Elector. Further, if the restoration of the Stuarts succeeded, the French would have a grateful, less commercially and colonially expansionist neighbour with no treaty or attachment to France's enemies. D'Argenson's hope that such a significant disruption to the European status quo could be achieved with as little effort or sacrifice from France as possible seems optimistic or naive: invading Britain has and always will be an expensive and risky business. However, France's finances had recovered since her nadir in the latter years of Louis XIV's reign. She was therefore well placed to take a few risks.

In October 1739, a month after d'Argenson was debating the Stuart issue in his journal, the whole situation in Europe transformed. Britain was at war with Spain (the War of Jenkins' Ear) who immediately began to consider supporting an invasion of Britain with the assistance of France. In the winter of 1740–1 Frederick II, 'the Great', of Prussia invaded the Austrian province of Silesia, eventually drawing Hanover, and therefore George II as Elector, into war with Prussia. Across the Channel, Sir Robert Walpole's grip on power was finally loosened (with the assistance of the Tory and Whig opposition, encouraged by James in Rome) and he was forced to resign in February 1742. After which, the pro-war members of King George's council bowed to the monarch's desire for British support for Hanover's interests, and sent British troops into the Austrian Netherlands (Flanders). France was already involved in support of her Prussian ally. This was developing into a confusing, piecemeal, Europe-wide conflict, which eventually became known as the War of the Austrian Succession. And it was now only a matter of time before France and Britain would be openly at war, which in turn immediately improved the prospects of a French-sponsored invasion in support of the Stuarts, for all the reasons d'Argenson had outlined. But the progress of the war in Flanders was France's overriding concern.

Sensing this change, British Jacobites considered the time was right for a new rising in support of their king. In May 1740, Cardinal Fleury was paid a visit by the veteran English Jacobite James Barry, 4th Earl of Barrymore, in an attempt to encourage support for an invasion of England. This came to nothing. Less than two years later, the cardinal was sent a letter declaring that a group of Scottish peers, known as the 'Association' or 'Concert', were ready to rise in favour of the Stuarts with French assistance. There would be '20,000 men on foot for the service of our true and only lord, King James VIII. of Scotland, as soon as it will please His Most Christian Majesty to send us arms and munitions'. That these Scottish peers were focused, in the first instance, on returning James to his Scottish kingdom – rather than the United Kingdom of Great Britain – makes clear that, in their minds, the reversal of the Union between Scotland and England (which some Scots still considered a betrayal) and the return of the Stuart dynasty were inextricably linked.[11] These 20,000 men would easily overcome the few troops currently in Scotland, and before British troops could be brought back from the wars in mainland Europe. Having returned Scotland to the authority of her legitimate king, they would then set about 'the recovery of these other States, which will be all the easier since our neighbours of England are not less wearied than we are of the odious tyranny under which we all equally groan'. Indeed 'we know that they are thoroughly determined to unite with us, and with any power whatever that would give them the opportunity they require to place themselves once more under a legitimate and natural Government. We are at present taking measures to act along with them.' The declaration was subscribed by James Drummond, Duke of Perth; Lord John Drummond, his younger brother (both Catholic Scots raised in France); Simon Fraser, Lord Lovat, Chief of Clan Fraser; Lord Linton, heir to the Earl of Traquair; Donald Cameron of Lochiel; Sir James Campbell of Auchlinbreck and William MacGregor [Drummond] of Balhady.[12] The latter was the named secretary of 'the Association'.

Cardinal Fleury's response to this extraordinary letter was essentially to do nothing. In Albano, James Edgar writing to Lord Balhady declared, 'It is a most sensible mortification to me that the worthy sages should be kept so long in expectation and suspence, but I would fain hope that the time is near when they will have occasion to try and show their skill.' He continues that 'Mr. Fisher', one of the code names for Prince Charles, 'told me t'other day that he longed to be with them, for that he was quite wearyed of this country, I don't wonder at it', for, as ever, 'his sole amusement here is to go out a shooting, to wch he has gone every other day during all this season before day break, whether fair or foul'.[13] That the elder Stuart prince was restless and in need of purpose is not a surprise. However, by now there were rumours concerning the health of Louis' octogenarian chief minister, which suggested that a change of personnel, and therefore Stuart policy, might soon occur at Versailles.

It was the general understanding within the Court of France that Cardinal Fleury would be succeeded in the role of principal adviser and minister to the king by none other than the new French ambassador in Rome and James Stuart's chief adviser, Cardinal Guérin de Tencin. Considering Tencin, like James' chief minister Cardinal Riviera, owed his elevation to the College of Cardinals to James, this was a significant development. It meant that, if all went to plan, James would have a first minister at the French court who was not only inclined to assist the Stuarts but honour bound to do so. It also meant that Cardinal Tencin would not fall back on supporting whatever was in France's best interests, regardless of how this might impact on the House of Stuart.

On Cardinal Fleury's death, however, in the January of 1743 (NS), what had seemed impossible happened, with Louis declaring to the amazement of his council, 'Messieurs, I am now prime-minister!' As the marquis d'Argenson wryly observed, 'Cardinal de Tencin and his party have had what is called a slap in the face'.[14] From past experience no one truly believed that Louis would apply himself to his new position. So, despite this apparent setback, Cardinal Tencin maintained to James and his emissaries at the French court, Lord Francis Sempill and Colonel Daniel O'Brien, that his position was still strong and that, when the time was right, he could manoeuvre the king and enough members of the Council of State to assist them in an invasion of Britain. But what Tencin and a majority of Louis' official ministers were unaware of was that the king, far from being an idle wastrel, had been preparing for his personal rule after Cardinal Fleury's death for years. By the 1740s Louis had in place what was called the King's Secret, an intelligence and administrative network that functioned, imperceptible to all but a chosen few, in parallel with (and sometimes in opposition to) the king's official council and court. As Cardinal de Bernis had observed, Louis was suspicious and guarded. But he was also clever.[15] Given this, it is not surprising that the Jacobite envoys at the French court had such difficulty comprehending what Louis was actually thinking: many of his ministers were in the same position.

In the spring of 1743, Lord Sempill brought a message to the Secretary of State for Foreign Affairs, Jean-Jacques Amelot de Chaillou, outlining the readiness of leading English Jacobites for a Stuart restoration assisted by the French, namely Henry Scudamore, 3rd Duke of Beaufort (he who had 'climbed the ladder'), who was one of the wealthiest men in the country, Lord Barrymore, Lord Orrery, Sir Watkin Williams Wynn (a Welshman), Sir John Hynde Cotton and Sir Robert Abdy. Meanwhile, John Murray of Broughton – a tireless Stuart agent since his encounter with Charles in Rome – arrived in France to follow up on the 'Association' letter sent to Cardinal Fleury. Now that Fleury was dead, he would attempt to get an assurance of support from Amelot. At their meeting in Versailles, Murray records that he asked a straightforward question, 'to know his Majesty's intentions, with what message would be proper for me to carry back'.[16] Amelot had been instructed by Louis to tell Murray that he could 'assure the party [in Scotland] of his [Louis'] friendly intentions towards the King [James] my Master, and as soon as the situation of his affairs would permit, he could give him all the assistance in his power': as Murray observed, a noncommittal assurance if ever there was one.[17]

Despite this discouraging exchange, the secretary of the associated Scottish Lords, Lord Balhady, accompanied John Murray on his return to England in June to see what could be arranged. As no one in England was willing to commit themselves in writing to treasonous acts, certainly not for the benefit of an ambivalent French king, Louis sent his master of horse, James Butler, the illegitimate son of the exiled Jacobite Irish peer James Butler, 2nd Duke of Ormonde (implicated in the '15, participant in the '19), on the pretence of purchasing livestock for the royal stables. In reality he was sounding out the mood in England and especially London. Louis told him to inform the English Jacobite leaders that they would get what they wanted as long as Butler could vouch for their commitment to a Stuart restoration. Butler initially spent time in London, including the City, and then travelled to the Lichfield races, an event attended by Tory gentlemen, where he met Sir Watkin and other leading Jacobites.[18] During this time James' 'friends in England' had been informed of an idea to put Prince Charles at the head of any potential expedition, and were 'so pleas'd with the proposal that Balhady perceives it has raised their spirits & will make the appearance for [your] M[ajes]ty more hearty & unanimous than it would be if none of the Royal Family were present'.[19] At the same time Lord Sempill also reported to James that, apart from Amelot, Louis was effectively directing operations himself and 'will not let the other Ministers into the secret'.[20]

In order to rise in support, the English Jacobites had requested 10,000 French troops and arms. It was vital that London was taken as a priority. Maldon in Essex was the chosen landing site – there were many leading Jacobites in the county, it was easily within striking distance of the capital and on the right side (i.e. north side) of the River Thames. They asked for Maurice de Saxe, the great French general of German descent and, crucially, a Protestant, to lead the French army landing in Essex, and the exiled Earl Marischal of Scotland, George Keith, to lead a separate invasion force of 3,000 men from the French army's Irish brigade in the Scottish Highlands.

Along with the demands of the English Jacobites, James Butler was also given two lists: the first noted the nobility and gentry 'who could be relied upon' within each of the counties of England, and the second listed the members of the Corporation of London ('The City'), marking against each whether they were 'Jacobite', 'Patriot', 'Hannoverian' or 'Whig'.[21] In the first, under Cheshire is listed, among others, Lord Barrymore, while Lancashire, considered 'of great size, containing a great number of very ancient families, is completely devoted to the true king's cause'. Under Derbyshire and Yorkshire is named one of the leading landowners and a Tory Member of Parliament, Sir Nathaniel Curzon of Kedleston Hall. In the second list there were a few marked as being 'indifferent' but, in the main, those listed come under the category of either 'J' or 'H'. Of the 236 members of the Corporation of London named, an astonishing 190 are listed as Jacobite, including the Lord Mayor himself, Robert Willimot, and Richard Hoare of the wealthy banking family on Fleet Street. From these extensive lists, it appeared certain that the House of Stuart had many staunch supporters throughout England as well as in the financial heart of the United Kingdom, the City of London, who were not just keen to see, but willing to assist in a Stuart restoration.

After several months in England, Lord Balhady sent James his personal musings on the state of Jacobitism in that country.[22] Previously he had assumed that support for the Stuarts was not deep rooted, that is, since James II's flight in 1688, but the result of recent disaffection towards George I and II. But he now realised that the support ran much deeper. Indeed, ever since 1688, three-quarters 'of the landed interest of England' and two-thirds of the City of London had been 'zealous for your Majestie's return'. Butler's lists supported this. The issue was, why had the existence of such a large group of well-affected Jacobite people not been obvious to James' agents, nor those foreign powers keen to assist in the Stuart restoration, in particular the French? Why, indeed, had they not shaken off their Hanoverian chains themselves? Balhady thought it a combination of an English distrust of and contempt for strangers, with the oppressive nature of their government, who 'since the revolution' had put in place many 'sanguinary penal laws . . . whereby the crime of jacobitism is renderd more horridly dreadfull in its consequences, than Murder, Witchcraft, or even open Deism [belief in God's non-intervention], or Atheism'. As a result 'a jacobite can never be discovered by his words, it must be his actions that decypher him; and these a Stranger is as little judge of; as he is of the reasons and circumstances they flow from'. Jacobitism in England was rife, then, but covert. Balhady may have been right. But with such high stakes, how many would be willing to turn an inclination – even a conviction – into positive action? The closer a Jacobite was to London, the more they could feel the British government's breath on the back of their necks. Finally Balhady recommended the ardent Lord Barrymore as the main contact and leader. To James in Rome, reliant on the advice and judgement of his emissaries, this was all extremely encouraging.

Meanwhile, James Butler had returned to Versailles clutching his lists and with a similarly positive message for his master. Louis required no further encouragement. By November plans for an invasion of England were already in train. Despite his past inactivity and procrastination, this time Louis was in earnest, and to confirm it he sent a letter to his uncle, Philip V of Spain, explaining what was about to happen. The fundamental purpose was not a Stuart restoration as such, but to destroy 'suddenly, and completely, the League of Enemies of the House of Bourbon'.[23] King Philip's letter in response was very approving of the enterprise.

Rumours reached James in Rome that France was at last contemplating a significant attempt on England, but there was a complication. In order to convince the English people that this was not an act of aggression by France masquerading as a Stuart restoration attempt, Prince Charles needed to be present with relevant documentation: a manifesto from James to his British subjects and a declaration confirming the prince was acting as regent on behalf of his father. But if the invasion was to stand any hope of success, it needed to be cloaked in secrecy – there was to be no warning or a French declaration of war on Britain. As Lord Sempill's letter to James confirms, Louis had even kept most of his own ministers completely in the dark, including Cardinal Tencin, and would continue to do so until the very last moment. So, the question was, when should the prince leave Rome?

What happened next is still a puzzle. It seems unlikely, considering the need for secrecy, that Louis would ever consider inviting his cousin to Paris until it was absolutely necessary. France was not officially at war with Britain and therefore assisting the Stuarts was in breach of the treaty Louis was still bound to. Charles' movements were constantly monitored by British agents and such was the journey time that his disappearance from Rome would certainly have tipped off the authorities in London that something was afoot, weeks before his arrival in Paris confirmed it.

So Lord Balhady was sent to Rome in December 1743 for one of two reasons. The first, which is Charles and James' version, was that Balhady was to invite the prince to come to Paris on behalf of the French king. However, there is another argument, that Balhady was sent to Rome with the impossible task of putting off James and his son from any immediate action, while at the same time extracting the signed documentation necessary for France to proceed with the invasion.[24] Knowing that James would need some indication that this was a genuine restoration attempt, Balhady had managed to ascertain when Charles' French passport would be valid: he was told it would be some time in January. Whatever the truth of it, Balhady certainly arrived in Rome in December. As predicted, James was not convinced by any of Louis' verbal assurances and even wrote to his Bourbon cousin hoping for some clarification.[25] Eventually, however, James allowed Charles to decide how to proceed, and, predictably, Charles was for action and as soon as possible.

Plans as to how and by what route Charles should travel to Paris were discussed. Eventually, as James writes to Lord Sempill at the very beginning of January (NS) 'we have at last settled all that relates to it . . . I have fixed on the road of Genoa & Antibes, as the least exposed to danger & accidents.' Lord Sempill had previously suggested that there was some request for a delay from the English Jacobite party, but James considered events had overtaken them, for 'matters are too far advanced now to go back or suspend, The King of France has called for The Prince, & he shall part, & by all I know or can observe The French projects are chiefly grounded upon an immediate expedition upon England'. If the English Jacobites buckled, then the French would have great reason to complain and may 'never more look upon us'. So their hopes now rested on 'the general good disposition of the nation' and that the arrival of troops 'will inspire courage unto the more timorous, where past doubts & fears will not hinder the success of the enterprize'. 'En fin,' he writes, 'I take the case to be now or never in relation to France, & therefore we must all act accordingly.'[26]

The prince left Rome early on the morning of 9 January 1744 (NS), accompanied by his brother, who at this point was also ignorant of the scheme, under the guise of a hunting trip to Cisterna. Later that day James wrote again to Lord Sempill, 'We have been at so much pains & contrivance to cover it that I hope the secret will be kept for some days, perhaps several.' Everyone in Rome thinks he is en route to Cisterna, James continues, and no one seems to have any inkling otherwise. Indeed 'the more I think on the matter, the more I am convinced of the bad & may be dangerous consequences of any delay in the great project, especially now that it must be soon known The Prince is on the wing.'[27] All appeared to be going to plan. On 17 January, James writes again to Lord Sempill, 'It is now eight days since The Prince left us, & I dont yet find there is any suspicion here of his not being in the country with his brother.' Still the English Jacobites appeared to be uncertain, to which James declares again that it was frankly too late, and besides which 'we think ourselves sure of the affections of the City of London, & of the generality of the people all over the island'.[28] This letter is proof that Lord Balhady's report of the buoyant state of English Jacobitism had been entirely believed by James. Four days later James observed to the Duke of Ormonde that, as far as he knew, no foreign ministers in Italy had managed to get sufficient information on the prince's journey 'to write about it to their respective Courts before Saturday last; it is very singular & very happy that this secret should have been kept so long'.[29]

He was absolutely right. On 22 January, two weeks after the prince left Rome, one such foreign minister, Horace Mann in Florence, wrote to Horace Walpole, youngest son of Sir Robert, that he had just sent word to the Duke of Newcastle 'that the Pretender's eldest son is departed from Rome, the notice of which has been sent to me by the expresses from thence'.[30] Mann's correspondence at this time reveals the confusion over what Charles' disappearance might actually mean and to what purpose. Was he going to join the French fleet at their base at Brest, then to make a descent on Scotland, or marry either a French or Italian princess? Either way, 'His appearance in the world will undoubtedly occasion a great alarm in England, though it must end in nothing, for it is not to be supposed that there is any considerable [number] of people either in England or in Scotland so mad as to espouse so foolish a cause.'[31]

Meanwhile, the English Jacobite leaders remained jittery. James wrote to Lord Sempill at the end of January that this 'is really unaccountable'. But France was determined to pursue the expedition regardless, and they 'will certainly have equally a War with England'. Besides which, the British government had apparently done so little to protect itself against the invasion that the French 'see they risque little for themselves in making the attempt' and 'the sooner they make it, the greater hopes there will be of success'. However the moment Charles' journey was known, 'that will give the general alarm'.[32]

After an extraordinary journey, via Antibes and Avignon, dodging British agents, storms and even the plague, Charles arrived in Paris on 8 February (NS).[33] Lord Elcho was in the city and recalled that Charles was lodging at Lord Sempill's house. Two weeks after his arrival, both the Earl Marischal and Lord Elcho had visited the prince, and the latter 'found the Prince all alone in his chamber, drinking tea. He opened the door for me and shut it himself, and seemed very uneasy because his arrival in Paris was not known.' Charles informed Lord Elcho that the King of France had invited him and 'had promised to send into England an army of 10,000 men, commanded by Marechal Saxe who was to assemble and embark them at Dunkirk'. He gave Lord Elcho, who had no military experience, the commission of a colonel of dragoons (mounted infantry). Meanwhile, the Earl Marischal, who had not been consulted up to this point, was given 'a patent to command in Scotland', after which they were both directed 'to appear at Dunkirk towards the end of the month of February 1744'.[34] Despite some misgivings, the Earl Marischal went to Dunkirk, and Charles travelled to nearby Gravelines at the most northerly tip of the French coast.

On 26 January, Admiral Jacques Aymar de Roquefeuil had left Brest with a squadron of twenty-two ships in order to lure the Royal Navy out of the way, so that Marechal de Saxe's invasion force could leave Dunkirk and cross the English Channel. But, despite all the secrecy, the British government had already been tipped off by their agent '101', the French ambassador in London, François de Bussy.[35] As a result Admiral Sir John Norris was cruising near Spithead to engage the invasion force. At Dunkirk there were 10,000 men ready to embark on transports, after which three battalions of the Irish brigade would move to Dunkirk to embark with the Earl Marischal for Scotland. But on 6 and 7 March (NS) a violent storm scattered Norris and Roquefeuil's ships and battered the transports at Dunkirk. Twelve vessels were lost. Four days later, another great storm hit.

Despite the devastation caused by the storms, later dubbed the 'Protestant wind', Charles remained on the coast at Gravelines convinced that this was a temporary 'retardment', and that the French king would continue with the invasion plans. In fact, far from considering recent events a disaster, Charles' letter to his father on 13 March was sanguine, even upbeat. Above all, he writes, 'a violent storm of wind, which thank God is at ane end, this gave me the greatest unease, yet I have reason to be thankfull to God for so signal a deliverance, for had not that Storm interposed to save us, I and all they [that] would have been with me, had been prisoners to Noris now in the Dunes, with a powerful squadron'. He continues, 'I find C.D.S [comte de Saxe] far from being discouraged by this unfavourable cercumstances, and all the other officers obstinat that the expedition goe on, which I hope a few days will put an end to, the weather now becoming favourable upon the change of the Moon.'[36] A few days later, however, the prince received a letter from the Earl Marischal at Dunkirk who was far from optimistic, having had no communication from the French court and nothing but bad news from the very nervous Jacobite party in England. 'I fear,' he writes, 'such a change as alters entirely the affair, and that untill there are new accounts from the party in England every thing will at least be laid aside for a time.' His assessment of the current situation made for grim reading. Firstly, habeas corpus had been suspended; that is, the British government was using the emergency measure of imprisonment without trial to remove from circulation the known Jacobite leaders in England. As a result the Earl Marischal had been informed 'that the principall people of the party are taken up'. This had had the added effect 'that many zealous people especially in Scotland have retired into hiding', albeit 'to keep themselves free to join upon a landing in England and Scotland'. Meanwhile, regardless of how this would impact on British Jacobites, the Earl Marischal feared that France would consider 'for views of interest visible enough' to continue to make 'a show of an expedition' upon which many across the Channel would be ruined unless they were warned.

With the British government alert to France's plan, Earl Marischal considered a strengthening of troops in England inevitable, via the sending of 6,000 Dutch troops, which, by an agreement with the Dutch Estates General of 1713, King George had at his disposal should his dominions be threatened, with additional British troops brought over from the conflict in Flanders, and others from Ireland. In short, the chance to catch Britain undefended had gone and a new plan was required. The Earl Marischal thought the immediate future looked bleak, and in his opinion 'the affaire for the King's cause has failed entirely for the present'. He warned Charles that he may now become a pawn rather than a protagonist in France's plans 'against which I hope your Highnesse will be on your guard'. It could be said that Charles had been precisely that all along. The seasoned Earl Marischal, for one, did not trust them. But he concludes, almost brightly, that he may be wrong and that 'new accounts from England may show Y[our].H[ighness]. and the court of France that the late retardment has not spoilt the affair'.[37]

There then ensued a flurry of letters between Gravelines and Dunkirk, which confirmed that the Earl Marischal's understanding of what was happening on both sides of the Channel, although patchy, was probably superior to the prince's. On 15 March Charles wrote to the Earl Marischal of the 'Unlucky Weather' that had impeded their plans, but that as far as he knew this had not caused a change of heart in England. On the suspension of habeas corpus and the Jacobite arrests he writes almost dismissively that 'some indeed may be taken up, which will be a misfortune'. But, he continues, this should not dissuade them from proceeding as planned. The real issue, he sensed, was that the fact of the expedition going ahead (despite recent events) had not been properly communicated to the English and Scottish Jacobites and if he could 'inform them, (as I am informed with assurances) that the french King is determined not to give up this expedition untill it is fully executed' then all would be well, 'unless our friends put a stop to it by their not concurring properly'.[38] Charles was receiving his information from Lord Sempill, whose 'advices must be from the Minister [Amelot]'.[39]

The Earl Marischal quickly disabused Charles of such notions. In his response the very next day he says that anyone assuring Charles that Louis was still keen on an invasion 'speak on very ill grounds'. He repeats his concern that France was using Charles 'to hurt your natural subjects, and that such snares will be laid for you, I can make no doubt'. Yesterday he had received an account, partly confirmed, concerning the arrest of several English Jacobites and the harassing of others. 'Sir,' he concludes, 'if the habeas corpus act is taken off or suspended, and your principal friends taken up, I see no possibility to do any thing right at present.'[40] The intelligence he refers to from 'Dr Cooper just come from England' states that 'Charles Weems', 'Ld John Drummon', 'Ld Lovat', 'Col. Cecil' and 'Ld Barrymore' have been arrested, 'Perth called up, by a messenger' and 'it is said that many people are retired and run away & messengers sent to most of the sea ports to apprehend suspected persons'.[41] Lord Barrymore had indeed been arrested.

The following day, the Earl Marischal wrote again to Charles, confirming that he had received word from Amelot inferring that even if a descent on England was now impossible, there might still be the chance of an expedition to Scotland. The Earl Marischal was having none of it, for 'as I am most fully convinced that none can be made at present into that countrey but for its destruction, tho perhaps it might make a usefull diversion for the interest of France, I am resolved emediately to leave this place'. He would spend a few days at his house in Boulogne, and perhaps meet up with the Duke of Ormonde en route to Paris. 'If,' he concludes, 'your Royal Highnesse has any commands for me, please let me know.'[42] Lord Elcho recalled that 'my Lord Marechal went to see Prince [Charles] Edward at Gravelines. The Prince proposed to him to hire a vessel and to go together to Scotland. This the Earl Marischal refused to do.'[43] On 26 March Charles wrote to his father that 'I am actually entierly in the Dark'.[44] Four days later, the invasion was officially abandoned and France declared war on Great Britain.

Charles-Nicolas Cochin, *The Masked Ball given by the King in the grand gallery of Versailles,* 1745.

3

Paris

'in the Dark'

Charles was now considered an embarrassment. Furious at his treatment, he put pressure on Cardinal Tencin, who was powerless. On hearing of the collapse of the expedition, James, bitterly disappointed himself, empathised with his son, but, knowing France was the only real hope for another attempt, advised Charles to comply with any demands from Louis, concluding, 'What has happend is a misfortune it is true, but I am far from thinking it an irretrievable one, except we should make it so ourselves, by pursuing precipitate & desperate measures, & undertake some rash & ill concerted project, which could only end in your ruin & in that of all those who joyn with you in it.'[1] Over the decades James had become conditioned to playing the longer game; Charles had not. He lacked his father's experience of anticipated success followed by setbacks and failure. James' stance was not simply astute diplomacy in order to keep the French king on side. It was vital for self-preservation. It is clear from this letter that James feared his son would be pushed into making a foolish attempt through sheer frustration. So, for moral support, James readily agreed to his son's request to have his old tutor, Sir Thomas Sheridan, join him in France.

Eventually, the prince bowed to the French Court's demands to leave Gravelines and to maintain himself incognito, but instead of compliantly disappearing to an obscure region of France as directed, he travelled in secret to Paris. Initially he enjoyed hearing from fellow travellers and passers-by that he had vanished, writing to his father (without mentioning a location) that 'everybody is wondering where the Prince is som[e] put him in one place and some in another, but nobody knows where he is really, and some times he is told news of himself to his face, which is very diverting'.[2] In reality, there is no doubt that Charles would have been followed from

Gravelines. Later, Louis' spies would have informed the king of his cousin's arrival in Paris, and then kept a close watch on his subsequent movements. Even so, the prince lived in Paris in disguise, writing a letter to his father on 24 April 1744, again with no location, 'I am entierly deprived of company and society, which obliges mee to read more then ever I have done in my life . . . Your Majesty will see by this choise of mine that I think of no thing but your service, and canste enjoy anything till the business is done.'[3] In another letter written a week later, still with no location, he jokes, 'I am in perfect good health, and am rather affred [afraid] of growing too fat, which will appear very surprising to you.'[4] At the same time, James wrote to his son that his 'darkness' and 'anxiety are great' and that 'I have nothing particular to say to you now, but to recommend to you to be very attentive & exact in complying with all The King of France may desire of you & to be solicitous to maintain his kindness towards you.' He endearingly signs off 'Dear Carluccio, whom I tenderly embrace'.[5]

By early May 1744, the French king was toying with the idea of Charles joining him on military campaign in Flanders. Apart from this, James (as he had already intimated) had no idea what was happening to his son and the Stuart cause. As he states in a letter to Lord Sempill dated 5 May 'in my darkness it seems odd to me that The Prince should be so shut up so long & that there should be so little discourse of his making the Campagne but I should suppose that those who direct all know what they do'.[6] Perhaps in the expectation of finally leaving Paris for Flanders, the prince announced his actual whereabouts to his father in a letter with the code name for Paris, 'Francfort'.[7] The talk of joining the French army was real progress from the prince's point of view. Charles writes in this heavily coded letter dated 11 May 1744 that Louis' 'kindness for me is very remarkable . . . saing that he regretted mitely that sircumstanses had not permitted him to see me hitherto' and, regarding Charles joining the French army, 'he said I will have him with me' and then 'another time that he was asked the same question he answered with an air as if it was not to be doubted (vreman setoit toujours mon intention de l'avoir opre de moi)'. And, the prince continues, 'it will certainly be so if Lord Marischal dose not hinder it'.[8] In fact the Earl Marischal had presented to Charles some very obvious disadvantages to the prince fighting alongside France in Flanders. Namely that 'it would disgust entierly the English, by serving in the same Army, that is to fite against them'. That Charles does not comprehend why the 'English', surely the British as a whole, would find the idea of the Jacobite heir fighting alongside their enemy unpalatable, hints at a shocking level of naivety on his part coupled with a worrying lack of political nous: a direct result, no doubt, of his closeted upbringing in Rome. On 18 May he wrote in relation to his incognito, 'I am still intierly hiden according to Mr. Adams [Louis'] particular dirrections and hope in a few days to be free of this lurking.'⁹ Charles adds in an almost jovial manner that he had hired a valet, who knew how to shave and dress a wig, but even after three months had no inkling who his master actually was.¹⁰

But the prospect of joining the French army was either wishful thinking on the prince's part or cynical delaying tactics by Louis, for all thoughts of Charles campaigning in Flanders alongside the French king were soon after abandoned. Cardinal Tencin was now excluded from discussions with the French ministers and Louis. The unsympathetic Philibert Orry, comte de Vignory, was put in charge of Jacobite affairs, although in Charles' presence at least he was encouraging. Lord Sempill had arranged a meeting between Charles and Orry in the middle of June at a secret location where 'he particularly recommended to me the Incognito & assured that it would finish, about the end of July, and that then, we would get what we wanted'. Charles concludes that 'Sr Thomas is very well, and came last night to live with me in my hermitage'.¹¹ Of this meeting Sir Thomas Sheridan, already suspicious of Louis and his ministers, wrote to James that Orry had 'seen The Prince himself & told him all he coud or at least thought fit to let him know'. Sheridan had updated James on Charles' new living arrangements, a pretty little house near Montmartre, and his changing appearance. Charles was healthy and appeared 'taller & broader than when I saw him last'. His increased height was explained by his heels 'wch he wears now of the usual size, whereas before he wore them remarkably lower than other People'. Charles was physically as well as metaphorically rising in confidence. Altogether he had 'a much more manly Air than he had when he began his travels'.¹²

In general, Louis and his ministers maintained that some form of undertaking was still possible, but no one seemed available to discuss the details of what that might be and when. Eventually Cardinal Tencin was put in charge of liaising with the Jacobites, but in reality Tencin was still the weakest and least consulted of Louis' ministers. After several months had passed, James was revealing deep concerns at France's treatment of his son. In a typical letter of August 1744, James writes to Lord Sempill, 'I don't see what end this incognito answers that can be for our advantage, for it cannot be supposed but that all the world knows that the Prince is somewhere in the French dominions . . . the Prince has manifestly been made a sacrifice of on this occasion.'[13]

It was at this moment, when the prince's position was at its most insufferable, that he had a visitor from Scotland: John Murray of Broughton. Back in Edinburgh, Murray had formed a drinking club that met once a week. Called the 'Buck Club', its members were supporters of the House of Stuart and only those elected by all the members could join.[14] According to one member, Lord Elcho, the group 'were very numerous' and included the Duke of Hamilton, the Duke of Perth, Earls Traquair and Nithsdale, Lord Nairne, Lord Lovat, Viscount Strathallan, Donald Cameron of Lochiel, MacDonell of Glengarry, MacDonald of Clanranald, MacDonald of Keppoch, Charles Stewart of Ardsheal, Lord Oliphant of Gask, James Hepburn of Keith and Alexander Forbes, Lord Pitsligo.[15]

John Murray recalls in his memoirs arriving in Paris in the August of 1744 and calling on the banker Aeneas MacDonald, brother of Donald MacDonald of Kinlochmoidart, and nephew of Lochiel. At this time Charles was living at MacDonald's house, and through him Murray arranged a meeting. One aim of Murray's trip (as he later stated) was to clarify with the prince the position in Scotland. He believed the likely strength of any rising, reported as 20,000 men, had been grossly exaggerated by Lords Sempill and Balhady, and explained this in their presence. In reality the prince should not depend on anything near that amount, at which the said lords initially looked disconcerted and then laughed at Murray's ignorance.[16] It was now evident that Murray did not trust Sempill and Balhady (and vice versa), and believed that what he considered their exaggeration of support, whether in England or Scotland, was injurious to the cause. For, without solid intelligence and information, the correct preparations for a successful rising could not be made.

At a second meeting, when neither Sempill nor Balhady were present, Murray recalls being plainer still as to the actual situation in Scotland. He also considered the current French military position in Flanders to be weak, suggesting that at this moment any assistance from that quarter, the redeployment of French troops for an invasion of Britain, for example, was extremely unlikely. Despite this the prince, utterly bored of procrastination, declared 'that at all events he was determined to come the following summer to Scotland, though with a single footman'. Taken aback, Murray responded that the prince 'could not come sooner to Scotland than would be agreeable to his friends there, but I hoped it would not be without a body of troops'. Charles was confident that assistance would be forthcoming and then repeated what he said before 'with still greater energy'. Murray concluded that 'he was really resolved upon it at any rate'.[17]

Despite the prince's apparent determination, Murray pressed him further by stating that although his resolve was laudable, yet the fact remained that he 'could not positively depend upon more than 4000 Highlanders, *if so many*'. In fact, even including the Western Highlands, which had seen the greatest concentration of support during the '15, only the Duke of Perth, Lochiel, Keppoch, Clanranald, the Stewarts, the MacDonells of Glengarry (part of Clan Donald), 'with Cluny [MacPherson] and Struan Robertson's people, were all he could rely upon with any certainty'. But even these loyal men would be 'sorry to think he should risk himself without foreign assistance, for though their attachment to his interest might induce them to join, yet it would be with regret'. Others like Simon Fraser, Lord Lovat, although professing great zeal now, might use a lack of French troops 'as a reason to sit at home'. In response Charles apparently said, 'that he would try every method to procure troops; but should that fail, he would, nevertheless pay us a visit'.[18] To which end the prince wanted to know what preparations should occur in Scotland for his arrival the following summer. Murray appears to have played along, while advising the prince not to come in isolation, as he later recorded, but only with French troops and financing. Even so it was agreed that the principal Jacobites in Scotland, in particular the Associators, should be warned of his imminent arrival and that they should build up arms in the Highlands. Lord Elcho and Lord Traquair were identified as the key figures in the Lowlands.

By Murray's own account he had hardly been encouraging. But others who were with the prince over the coming months believed categorically that it was John Murray's visit that confirmed Charles' resolution to go to Scotland the following summer, come hell or high water. In one close associate's opinion, who presumably got the information from Charles himself, Murray had assured the prince that he would be welcomed by the King's friends with open arms, and once they had taken the main forts in the Highlands he would be Master of Scotland without having to draw a sword. 'This,' the associate recalled, 'was certainly encouragem[en]t enough for a young Prince.'[19] John Murray may well have encouraged the prince during their private meeting and then retrospectively altered the facts in order to distance himself from what happened next. It is unlikely that he is unique among Jacobite commentators in doing this.[20] Alternatively, the positive assessment was simply what the prince wanted or chose to hear. The reality was probably a mixture of both. Either way, very soon such details would become irrelevant.

On 17 August, Charles wrote another heavily coded letter to James from 'Francfort', decoded on receipt, as usual, by James Edgar, which opens with a hint of the prince's sense of isolation and even loneliness: 'A few days ago their came letters from Room [Rome], but their was none for me, nor for any of my acquaintance, which gave me great pene [pain].' He continues that he understood very well that his father was against any attempt to land in Scotland alone, but if the French court offered to support, even in a small way, such an attempt, could he, Charles, in all conscience turn it down? The situation in England continued to be good and the Stuart supporters were bound to rise, 'the sword once drawn in ye Hand'. Surely then, France would be persuaded to give greater assistance. Charles would be aggrieved if he had to reject an opportunity, which would finally give meaning to the months he had spent in France and the risks he had already taken. Besides which, he certainly did not want 'to return to Rome with the melancholy prospect of spending my life there'.[21] Having implied that he would be foolish to reject an offer of French assistance (whatever form that might take) and being, besides, far from keen to return to the tedium of Rome, Charles informs his father of some disturbing news. While on campaign at Metz in August 1744, Louis XV had fallen ill, some thought gravely. Charles observes that it would be a terrible blow if Louis should die, for at this moment it was better the devil you know. In a postscript he says Louis is still desperately ill 'and it was sed this morning he was ded but hope it is only a faulth [false] alarm, what is certain is that he is in great dangir'.[22] In such danger, in fact, that in a flood of piety the king had dismissed his current mistresses. They had been accused of exhausting their royal lover and thus exposing him to the illness that now brought him to death's door.

Despite this, by September the king had rallied, but not before François de Fitz-James, Charles' cousin (Fitz-James' father, James FitzJames Stuart,

1st Duke of Berwick, was one of James II/VII's illegimate children), had attempted to extract some concessions on behalf of the Stuarts from the weakened French monarch.[23] When death seemed near, His Most Christian Majesty's thoughts and sympathies had turned once again to his poor dispossessed Catholic cousins. But on recovery, both the lusty mistresses and the king's ambivalence towards the Stuarts returned. Although Louis' behaviour since the failed invasion had been at best contrary, as Charles had rightly observed a change of monarch at this moment would not have served the Stuarts' purpose at all.

James responded to Charles' letter on 11 September (NS), saying it 'is true I have been all along, & am still against any faint attempt upon Scotland alone' while 'persuaded that honnour & interest will equally hinder Adam [King of France] from making any rash and in considerate attempt in our favour, since by it he would run a manifest risque of involving many of our friends in to ruin & perhaps loss [of] his own troops without being the better for it'. However, James acknowledges that he is not on the spot and therefore 'should be to blame to give you any particular advice or directions'. As a general rule he advises 'that whatever carries a reasonable prospect of success with it is to be accepted, whatever does not, is to be rejected'. Then, in a direct, fatherly riposte to Charles' disdain at the prospect of returning to Rome, James observes, 'it would certainly be much more melancholy to return then, however, after an unfortunate expedition & the ruin of a number of our friends who might not be able to remain at home, while we might not be able to subsist them abroad'.[24] Here James is allowing Charles to judge the merits of any opportunity for himself. But he is advising him, once again, not to act out of any personal feelings or frustrations he may have, and at the same time to consider the risk that he would be putting his supporters under. James also hints at the financial pressures incurred by any exiles after a defeat. These are wise words. But the line between daring and recklessness can be a very fine one. It is usually defined retrospectively, by the action's success or failure.

All this time Charles was running up enormous debts – there had been no expectation of a prolonged stay in France when he left Rome. Perhaps worse still, factionalism within the Jacobite party was becoming rife, as the antagonism between John Murray on the one hand and Lords Sempill and Balhady on the other had made clear.

In the meantime John Murray returned to Scotland in October and immediately reported back to the Buck Club. According to Lord Elcho, 'Mr. Murray told the members . . . that he had been at Paris, that he had seen the Prince, and that the Prince had said to him that he intended to come next summer and throw himself into the arms of his friends in Scotland, and he asked what was to be done under such circumstances.'[25] Again from Lord Elcho's recollections, at this point the opinion of the members was much the same as before Murray's visit. A majority, including Lord Lovat, thought that an express should be sent to the prince saying that if he arrived with 6,000 regular troops, with arms for 10,000 more and 30,000 louis d'or in cash, then by all means come and with their blessing. But if not 'they counselled him very strongly not to come, for his presence would only effect his own ruin, the ruin of his cause, and that of all those who embarked with him on an enterprise so dangerous'. The latter part of this statement echoes almost word for word James' fears of a 'rash' undertaking. However, according to Lord Elcho, and contrary to Murray's later recollections of his audience with Charles, at the club meeting Murray 'aimed at encouraging everyone to join the Prince, even if he came alone'. And he succeeded, with the Dukes of Hamilton and Perth, Lord Nairne, Viscount Strathallan, Donald Cameron of Lochiel, Glengarry, Clanranald, Keppoch, James Hepburn of Keith and Lord Pitsligo, among many others, promising to join the prince '*in any event*'.[26]

On 16 November, Charles wrote to his father that he had been searching for a new priest and had alighted on George Kelly.[27] He was an Anglican cleric of Irish descent who had been imprisoned in the Tower of London after the Atterbury plot of 1721–2 but escaped in 1736. He had been secretary to the Duke of Ormonde. Two weeks later Charles wrote again to his father stating that he was in good health, although 'that is the only thing that is good I have to say', but 'as long as there is life there is hop[e]s, ses the Proverb'. His problems continued to be, primarily, the treatment by Louis, who the prince now believes 'thinks very little of me', his 'imprisonment' and money. He then writes that he is plagued 'out of my life' with infighting. He had said to one Jacobite who was 'plaguing me with complaints' that whether he was right or not, such behaviour 'was cutting ower own throts'. He hoped to get some answer from the French court, but he concludes 'the more I dwell on these matters, the more it makes me melancholy'.[28]

By December, the situation in Paris was far from encouraging. On the 14th Charles wrote to his father, 'The Prince still remains in Prison living upon tick not getting any thing from The King of France, ether great or small.' He had been attending music parties at Colonel O'Brien's house, but was clearly bored and out of humour.[29] A week later Charles wrote again to James, stating that he was 'very much mortified to see plainly that [Louis] at present thinks so little of [Charles] and his lawsuit [the cause]'. The prince had agreed to go to a country house near Paris, i.e. out of harm's way, and spend the winter there. He had been informed that his pension had been augmented after much wrangling and that 'the last word has not been said [on the matter]'.[30] Charles dutifully moved from Paris to Fitz-James, his cousin's chateau in Picardy, 'for since there is no change to be made as to his way of living it is no ways decent he should remain in this Town'.[31]

In early January, the sense of despondency continued. Sir Thomas Sheridan declared to James Edgar, 'The French Court longs to have us gon.'[32] A week later, James was writing a letter to Lord Sempill setting out his assessment of the situation regarding Louis and the French court and his irritation at their continuing bad behaviour towards his son. The French court's silence regarding 'our great affairs' is ominous and their behaviour towards Charles even worse, as 'now they say they never sent for him' in the first place. His removal to Fitz-James for the winter makes what little money he has go further, for his private expenses at least, 'but can noways suffice for what may be called politick or publick expenses'. For, James astutely continues, unless there is some hidden explanation, the current policy 'rather seems to be to keep my son as cheaply & obscurely as they can somewhere within call' so that they can 'make use of him if they find it for their purpose, in the mean time as a rod over The Elector of Hannovers head, & then, if it serve their turns to drop him with less shame than they could have done, had he made a publick appearance amongst them'.[33]

At least Charles' personal situation had decidedly improved since the arrival in Paris from Rome of John William O'Sullivan. O'Sullivan was an Irishman and former staff officer in the French army, who had been sent to negotiate on behalf of the Stuarts with the French court and was then recommended to the prince's household. In 1745 O'Sullivan was in his mid-forties and a contemporary account declared that 'no one who knows Mr. Sullivan can deny his being one of the best bred, genteelist, complaisant, engaging officers in all the French troops'. In addition, 'To these external accomplishments were added . . . a sincerity of heart, and an honest freedom of both sentiment and speech, tempered with so much good nature and politeness as made his Conversation and friendship equally useful and agreeable.'[34] Here was someone whose company Charles enjoyed and whom he felt he could trust. In return, O'Sullivan was also unerringly loyal to the prince.

Despite no official invitation from Louis to meet or visit, Charles was entertaining himself by covert trips to Paris to see his extended family, and even venturing to the palace of Versailles itself. On 11 January 1745 (NS) Charles wrote to James from Paris that through Cardinal Tencin he was 'much plesed with making and receiving visits of all those that are anyways my relations' and that the previous night 'I went to the Opera Ball in mask' accompanied by his cousin the prince de Turenne.[35] A month later, during carnival, Charles writes that 'Tother day The Prince went to Paris and from thence in a Pot de Chambre for not to be suspected to Talbots [James Butler's] lodgings at Oporto [Versailles] where he Masqued and had the pleasure of seeing all The K of France's family.' This must have been an extraordinary adventure for the prince – not only to see Louis XV, his family and court, but to experience the magnificence of Versailles for himself. He believed that Louis was somehow involved, which he took 'to be a very good omen', despite the fact that James Butler said the king knew nothing about it.[36] In this instance it is probable that Butler was telling the truth.

The event appears to have acted as a lift to the prince, as only the previous week he had written to James that he believed the French king and ministers hoped to wear him down to the point that he would give up and return to Rome. They could then say to the world that he had come to France and then left again of his own volition, 'for which reason The Prince thinks it of the greatest importance that as long as the war lasts or that there is the least glimps of hopes; The Prince should stay in Norway [France]; coute qui coute [*coûte que coûte*, 'at all costs']'.[37]

Two weeks later Charles updated his father, writing from Paris that 'I have been so much hurrid between Balls and busines',[38] even attending an Easter service at Notre-Dame.[39] It is not certain whether Louis was complicit in any of Charles' adventures in and around Paris, or whether his behaviour was considered at best a nuisance, at worst highly provocative. After a tedious and frustrating year incognito, Charles required diversion, and enjoyed attending entertainments at Versailles, masked and apparently under the noses of the court, the ministers and even the king. But in reality such a harmless and even frivolous existence was a cover for far more serious activity.

Pierre Soubeyran after Charles-Nicolas Cochin, *The Battle of Fontenoy*, 1745.

4

Fontenoy

'the soldiers' Great Sir'

Since March 1745 the Captain General of the British forces in Flanders had been George II's son Prince William Augustus, Duke of Cumberland.[1] The duke had been born at Leicester House, located on the north side of Leicester Square in London, on 15 April 1721 (OS), the first surviving Hanoverian prince to be born in Britain. In his early years this and the name chosen for him seems to have made him a popular royal figure, locally at least, as the duke's early biographer Andrew Henderson recounts: 'He was baptized by the name of William, a name very propitious for England, for Holland, and in short for the protestant cause: the birth of a son born to the Royal family, and among ourselves, was singularly pleasing to the public, and the more so on account of the name given him.'[2] Unlike his grandfather and father, English was William's first language, but like most European princes the duke spoke several, including German and French. Contemporary descriptions of the young prince suggest a character that was naturally measured and not prone to impulsive reactions or responses.

Unlike his elder brother Frederick Louis, Prince of Wales, William was adored by King George and Queen Caroline and, as the relationship between Frederick and his parents disintegrated, so their younger son increasingly became the particular focus of their attention and love.[3] Many theories have been put forward as to why the Hanoverian monarchs invariably hated their heirs. The fact that Frederick had been left in Hanover on the accession of his grandfather in 1714 (he was only seven at the time) to act as the representative of the dynasty in their German domains is unlikely to have assisted familial bonding. He was only brought to London in 1728 – despite becoming the British heir apparent in 1727 – and as a result seems to have held a very bitter grudge against his father. Prince Frederick, also unlike his brother, became and in turn encouraged the perception that he was a safe focus for any opposition to his father: safe, in that anyone paying court to Frederick could not be accused of being anti-Hanover or a Jacobite, whether or not that is exactly what they were. As a result Frederick became the unlikely focus for dis-enfranchised Tories as well as the Whig opposition. Frederick appeared to delight in opposing the king in everything. It was reported by the courtier John, Lord Hervey, that on her deathbed in 1737 the queen took leave of all her children, excepting the Prince of Wales, and '"As for you, William," continued she to the duke, "you know I have always loved you tenderly, and placed my chief hope in you."' According to Hervey, the queen then urged her teenage son to

> show your gratitude to me in your behaviour to the King; be a support to your father, and double your attention to make up for the disappointment and vexation he must receive from your profligate and worthless brother. It is in you only I hope for keeping up the credit of our family when your father shall be no more. Attempt nothing ever against your brother, and endeavor to mortify him no way but by showing superior merit.[4]

However, despite his toxic relationship with his father, Frederick wanted to be seen to be British and patriotic. He was a great supporter of the arts, and it is to him that we owe the existence of the patriotic song, 'Rule, Britannia!', from the masque *Alfred*, the text by the Scotsman James Thomson set to music by the Englishman Thomas Arne.

Despite the extreme contrast in the widowed King's attitude towards his two sons, surprisingly perhaps this did not completely damage the relationship between the brothers – at least from the young duke's point of view. Certainly William had no thought of taking advantage of his father's partiality for him. Regarding Frederick's expected assumption to the throne, Horace Walpole later observed that the duke's 'strongest principle was the dignity of the blood royal, and his maxim to bear any thing from his brother . . . rather than set an example of disobedience to the royal authority'.[5] It seems he had indeed taken to heart his moth-er's dying wish. The duke's loyalty to the king, the Hanoverian dynasty and therefore the Prince of Wales was absolute. On Frederick's part, the resentment and even jealousy that he surely felt towards his younger brother must have reached new heights after the duke's dramatic rise in the military and the mark of particular favour King George had shown him.

The duke was four months younger than his Stuart cousin and inevitably, as the second surviving son (Prince George William having died in 1718), had been given the relative freedom to pursue his own inclinations. The duke was a fine horseman – as would have been expected from any man of his status – enjoyed hunting and had a passion for horseracing. From a very early age he had shown a desire to be in the armed forces. In 1740 he enlisted as a volunteer on the flagship of Sir John Norris, HMS *Victory*, but then committed to a future in the army when he became Colonel of the Coldstream Guards.

Three years later the duke saw action at the Battle of Dettingen alongside his father, during which he was wounded in the leg. His behaviour during and after the battle was widely reported and generally admired. Charles Lennox, 2nd Duke of Richmond (a grandson of Charles II through the King's mistress, Louise de Kérouaille), writing to the Duke of Newcastle, observed that 'by his brave behaviour upon the Day of Battle, by his love of the service, by his generosity & compassion to prisoners, & by all the good qualitys that ever a young Prince was endow'd with: he has justly got the love and esteem of every body'.[6] It was vital for Georgite Whigs, as well as the House of Hanover, that this still recently arrived and decidedly foreign royal family should have a rising British-born star in their midst. And the admiration was not only felt among political supporters. Voltaire recounted a story that occurred after the Battle of Dettingen, which the author felt offered an example of the duke's generosity, and therefore 'ought to be handed down to posterity'. While having his leg wound treated the duke saw a Frenchman named Girardeau, who had greater need of medical attention: 'Begin, said he nobly, with the wound of that French officer ; he is more dangerously hurt than I am, and stands in need of more assistance ; I shall as yet want none.'[7]

In 1745 William was unmarried, having recently avoided a political alliance to Princess Louise of Denmark. Besides, the bachelor life seems to have been the standard for high-ranking officers in the British army. The duke had pale blue eyes and mid-brown hair. He was handsome, tall and, like his mother, tended towards plumpness, but in his mid-twenties he was fit and energetic. Long after the wound itself had healed, the injury he received at Dettingen affected his gait, which was particularly noticeable when he was tired. As a result he preferred to ride. Indeed, on horseback, on his favourite Yorkshire hunter, he cut a very imposing figure. Andrew Henderson, admittedly a not unpartisan observer, offers a comprehensive description of the duke's bearing, character and, to an extent, appearance.[8] From this William emerges as no-nonsense, forthright, uninterested in either pomp or frivolity, charming and attentive if needs be but far from superficial or insincere. He certainly did not court the limelight, was neither hot-tempered nor reckless – a solid military man from head to toe. Above all the duke is shown as steadfast in his loyalties and perhaps therefore unforgiving, or at least unbending, in his attitude towards anyone who sought to undermine those he was loyal to. Inevitably, at the top of this list would be anyone hell-bent on removing King George and the House of Hanover from the British throne. But the duke was also mindful of who had been responsible for bringing his family to the throne and who was keeping them there: the Whigs. For as he wrote to the Duke of Newcastle, 'without them we should never have seen England, & without them I fear we should hardly stay'.[9] Of course, as ever in politics, there were Whigs, and then there were Whigs.

During the threatened invasion by France in 1744, the duke had been put in charge of defending London. But by early 1745 he had assumed his new command in Flanders. To support the prince in this role, Sir Everard Fawkener, then fifty years old, was appointed as personal secretary and Major Robert Napier took charge of the duke's military correspondence. The duke's aides-de-camp included William Kerr, Earl of Ancram, son of the 3rd Marquess of Lothian; George Keppel, Viscount Bury, son of the Earl of Albemarle and, through his mother Lady Anne Lennox, a great-grandson of Charles II; Charles Schaw Cathcart, 9th Lord Cathcart, Chief of the Lowland Clan Cathcart; and the Hon. Joseph Yorke, younger son of the Lord Chancellor, Philip Yorke, 1st Baron Hardwicke. The urbane and well-travelled Sir Everard was an interesting choice.[10] He came from an old gentry rather than aristocratic family in Leicestershire, and like his father had been a successful merchant. He was a member of the Levant Company and between 1716 and 1725 had resided in Aleppo, Syria. Through his regional knowledge and connections Sir Everard was later appointed as British ambassador at Constantinople. A close friend was Horatio Walpole, the diplomat brother of Sir Robert. Sir Everard was not only well connected, but he was also a cultured man. Voltaire had lived at Fawkener's house in Wandsworth from 1726 to 1728 and they became lifelong friends – if erratic correspondents. On hearing, rather belatedly, that Fawkener had become the duke's private secretary, Voltaire wrote a witty letter stating, 'How could I guess that your musulman person had shifted from Galata [an area of Constantinople] for Flanders? and had passed from the seraglio to the closet of the Duke of Cumberland?' If he had known that it was 'my dear sir Everard who was secretary to the great prince, I had certainly taken a journey to Flanders'.[11]

In Flanders, Sir Everard's new master was not only commander of the British forces but also the commander-in-chief of the Allied or 'Pragmatic' army, which was formed of Austrian and Hanoverian troops under Marshal Lothar Josef Dominik von Königsegg and the Dutch under Prince Karl August of Waldeck. The duke was brave but still inexperienced for such a command – a reminder that the British king still wielded great power and influence – although the duke's role was tempered by the presence of the other commanders, in particular Marshal Königsegg and the French-born British senior officer, Sir John Ligonier. Sir Everard travelled to Flanders in advance and, clearly relishing his new role, writes to the Prime Minister Henry Pelham on 19/30 (NS/OS) April 1745 from Brussels, 'I feel myself in a most happy situation, & shall always have in mind how much I owe to you for the part you so kindly took towards placing me in it.'[12]

The duke arrived in Flanders accompanied by Joseph Yorke. Lord Chancellor Hardwicke wrote to his twenty-year-old son 'Joe' on 15 April (OS) that 'it was with great joy' that news had arrived 'of yo[u]r safe landing at Ostend. May the same good providence attend you & yo[u]r master & bring you home in safety.' He concludes, displaying the concern of any father whose son has gone to war: 'Why should I tell you I love you, since you know it, & [that] it will always be a pleasure to me to hear from you.'[13] The duke and his entourage arrived at Brussels at the time Maréchal Maurice de Saxe was besieging Tournai, one of the principal strongholds in the Netherlands. On 24 April (OS), Lord Chancellor Hardwicke wrote to his son, 'Wee are told here Tournay is invested, but false news is so much in fashion, wee are at a loss what to credit, & I am told some of our millitary people are disposed to think The French have not troops enough in Flanders to form the siege of [that] place, & a covering army too.'[14] He goes on, 'The Parliament separates next week, & then the King leaves us [for Hanover]. God send him a prosperous journey & return, but such folk as I wish he stay'd here, since the greatest are not exempt from accidents, more than those of less consequence.'[15] He concludes, 'God Bless you, & send us a prosperous champaign, [that] wee may rejoine in safety next winter by the fire side, where I am like to spend many an hour by myself, wanting yo[u]r Company.'[16]

King George's habitual summer journeys to Hanover not only raised concerns among his ministers, fearing that a mishap during the voyage might bring the tricksy Prince Frederick to the throne earlier than was desirable, but raised eyebrows on the Continent. As the marquis d'Argenson wrote in his journal, 'The King of England has gone to Hanover, which astonishes all Europe and makes the lower English classes say that he abdicates, for whoever quits a country loses it.'[17] Perhaps he had James II in mind. In the King's absence, authority lay with the Lords Justices. This was effectively the cabinet acting in the manner of a regency, but, despite all being Whigs, it was a far from united group. Henry Pelham, the prime minister, his brother the Duke of Newcastle and the Lord Chancellor, Lord Hardwicke, were all protégés of Sir Robert Walpole, and even after Walpole's resignation were acknowledged as being part of the first prime minister's long 'reign' through the nickname the Old Corps. The Old Corps were distrusted by the king, who preferred the opposition Whig John Carteret, 2nd Earl of Granville, with whom he could chat away in German, much to the irritation of Walpole and his associates. But the Pelhams had one advantage, in that the Duke of Cumberland, the King's favourite son, supported the Pelham ministry and the duke's personal correspondence confirms that he tended to accept the counsel he received from the Duke of Newcastle in particular. Then there were the supporters of the King's favourite Granville: Charles Powlett, 3rd Duke of Bolton; Field Marshal John Dalrymple, 2nd Earl of Stair, since 1743 Commander-in-Chief of the Forces in 'South Britain' and John Hay, 4th Marquess of Tweeddale, Secretary of State for Scotland. Whether Britain was at war or not, internal politicking would continue as usual.

The Allies' strategy in Flanders was to relieve the siege of Tournai by forcing the French into a battle four miles away to the east, near the village of Fontenoy. The French and Allied armies were quite evenly balanced – between 50,000 and 60,000 men on each side. The French king was already in Flanders with his son, the fifteen-year-old Dauphin, also Louis. According to Voltaire, Louis' 'Royal Historiographer', the king and his son watched the battle from nearby, where Louis 'observed every thing with great attention'.[18] But as Cardinal de Bernis observed, 'Two bullets might have deprived France of her master and her hopes.'[19] Knowing the Allies' plans, Maréchal de Saxe had prepared a defensive position with a sequence of redoubts (enclosed gun positions located beyond the main defensive line), the strongest lying between Fontenoy and a wood called Barri or Barry, on a stretch of land that had a gentle incline. Here the guns were fixed in embrasures and manned by a battalion from the regiment of Eu under the command of the marquis de Chambona. As Voltaire describes it, the 'cannon of this redoubt, with those which were planted to the left-side of Fontenoi, formed a cross-fire sufficient, one would imagine, to stop the efforts of the most intrepid enemy'.[20] Running between Fontenoy and the town of Antoing were three further redoubts, each 'furnished with three batteries of cannon, one of eight pieces, the other two of four'.[21] The Allies planned for the Dutch and Austrian troops to attack between Fontenoy and Antoing while the British and Hanoverian troops attempted to pass between Barry wood and the 'Redoubt d'Eu'.

As the British and Hanoverian infantry advanced, the fire from this redoubt (as Voltaire had stated) was relentless. But despite this, the British and Hanoverian troops as a body continued to move methodically forward, and, having topped the ridge, the two opposing armies were suddenly very close. The French refused to fire first. Rather than gallantry, this was a lesson learned at the Battle of Lens of 1648, where they had wasted their ammunition by firing first while out of range. The British infantry proceeded to fire, as Voltaire recalled: 'lord Charles [Hay], turning about to his men, gave the word of command, in English, to fire! The English [sic] made a running fire ; that is, they fired in platoons, in this manner, that when the front of a battalion, four deep, had fired, another battalion made its discharge, and then a third, while the first were loading again.'[22] The French infantry, on the other hand, 'did not fire; it was single, and four deep, the ranks pretty distant, and not at all supported by any other body of infantry : it was impossible but their eyes must have been surprized at the depth of the English corps, and their ears stunned with the continual fire.'[23] Eventually the 'first rank being thus swept away, the other three looked behind them, and, seeing only some cavalry at the distance of above three hundred fathom, they dispersed . . . The English, in the mean time, advanced gradually, as if they were performing their exercise . . . Thus the English pierced beyond Fontenoy and the redoubt.'[24]

Joseph Yorke recalled, 'word was brought that the left had already entered the opposite side of the village of Fontenoy, and if we did but attack it on the right at the same time we should soon be masters of it'. As a result 'orders were immediately given by the Duke in person to the Highland regiment [the 43rd] to attack the village sword in hand and the two lines were ordered to follow 'em immediately' which they did in 'a spirit worthy of the nation and its Prince'. But in 'vain did our Highlanders twice enter the French intrenchments: 'twas but to get out again with loss' and rather than 'being supported by the Dutch Infantry, ordered for that purpose, the ancient honour of their Republic having forsook them, they basely turned their backs upon the foe and left some of their officers to fight alone'.[25] Captain Yorke concludes, 'It was a cruel massacre of brave gentlemen, but 'tis a fate prepared for us all; may we all submit to it as well! I can't say our spirits are at all dejected; for, to say the truth, both officers and men seem desirous to meet again on more equal terms.'[26]

James Wolfe was eighteen years old at the time of the battle and already an experienced officer, having fought at Dettingen two years before. His regiment, Barrell's, was at Ghent when the battle occurred, but he reported to his father that after the Dutch failed to support the British advance, 'The army made a fine retreat, in such order that the French did not think proper to pursue them. The Duke, I hear, has shown in this action most unparalleled bravery, but was very sensibly touched when he found himself obliged to give over the attack.'[27] The Dutch were universally blamed for failing to support the British and Hanoverian troops. And, despite it being a technical victory for the French, the British had other ideas. As Philip Yorke (Joseph's eldest brother) wrote to Horatio Walpole, 'I think you very right in your judgment, that the French were *only not beat.*' The other fact that the British seemed to be universally agreed upon was the heroic behaviour of the Duke of Cumberland. As Philip Yorke continues, echoing his brother's description, the duke scorned to expose his men to more danger than he was willing to suffer himself, which 'put them in mind of Blenheim and Ramilies' and the great English General John Churchill, Duke of Marlborough: 'in short, I am convinced, his presence and intrepidity greatly contributed to our coming off so well.' Another officer praised in dispatches was Sir John Ligonier, 'who, the duke writes, fought like a grenadier, and commanded like a general'. The duke, 'determined to keep up strict discipline . . . drew out a pistol upon an officer, whom he saw running away'. Meanwhile Königsegg 'was run over and bruised by the Dutch cavalry, in their flight; insomuch that when the army marched to Lessines, he was left at Aeth'. Philip Yorke concludes, 'I have not heard, as yet, that the French plume themselves much upon their victory. Their accounts run in a modester strain than usual. It was certainly a dear-bought advantage.'[28] It was indeed. According to Cardinal de Bernis, Maréchal de Saxe's comment to Louis after witnessing the carnage on both sides was, 'Sire, you now see on what the loss or gain of a battle hangs.'[29]

Some weeks later, Horace Walpole, writing to Horace Mann in Florence, observed, 'All the letters are full of the Duke's humanity and bravery: he will be as popular with the lower class of men, as he has been for three or four years with the low women: he will be the soldiers' *Great Sir* . . . I am really glad; it will be of great service to the family, if any of them comes to make a figure.'[30] It is not clear what the notoriously waspish Walpole means here by the duke's popularity among the 'low women', although the duke's first mistress is known to have been the actress Nanny Wilson. More importantly, Walpole senses that here is a member of the House of Hanover who has the potential to win the hearts of not only the British army, but the British people. This would no doubt be assisted by the broadsheets circulated in Britain immediately after the battle reporting that it 'lasted from Five in the Morning, till Five in the Afternoon', and that all the while 'his Royal Highness was constantly in the Heat, of the Action, encouraging the Men, rallying them when broken, leading them to the Charge, and at the same Time watching every Turn, and . . . making every Disposition that might procure him any Advantage', concluding, 'God be prais'd, his Royal Highness has not received the least Hurt.'[31]

From the British army camp at Ath the day after the battle, Joseph Yorke writes to his father observing, 'My handwriting is sufficient to assure you of my being alive with[ou]t saying it, but I ought to add, that the Providence of the Almighty led me thro' the utmost Perils in following my Royal master, without the least hurt.'[32] He reports that Lord Cathcart and Lord Ancram are wounded 'but will do I believe very well'. The former had been shot in the face and, once healed, would, with a breezy flourish, cover the scar on his right cheekbone with a small strip of black silk, earning him the nickname 'Patch' Cathcart.[33] Joseph continues, 'I wish it had succeeded better, our Captain deserves better fortune. He is a true Hero.' He concludes, 'I hope things will go better another time, but Tournay will certainly be taken.' In return, Lord Hardwicke expressed his relief, thanking God that his son was unharmed, yet 'Would to God our private Joy was not now damp'd by the public Calamity.'[34] He continues that the duke's behaviour 'is universally extoll'd. It is the universal Voice of all the Letters, as well foreign as national. Surely nothing can equal it. It is happy that you have such an Example of a young Prince before your

Eyes, whom I doubt not you will endeavour to serve & imitate in the best manner.' Finally, 'All our attention here is taken up in considerations how your Army may be reinforc'd & augmented. It is our misfortune that the King is upon the Sea, having embark'd on Friday noon, whereas the messenger [with news of the battle] arriv'd on Saturday morning.' He signs off, 'Don't be dispirited. Our Cause is good, & if not at first, at last Providence will favour it.'[35]

Despite the guarded optimism, after Fontenoy and the surrender of the citadel of Tournai that followed, events in Flanders had swung decidedly in favour of France. Regarding the situation with the Allied army, on 22 May (NS) the Duke of Cumberland had written to the Duke of Newcastle from the new British camp at Lessines that the 'whole strength of this army is not thirty thousand men, I mean that can fight, & that's but a poor army especially when the right wing has no sort of confidence in the left & for that reason can not be brought to exert their courage as the foot did last time'. Regular soldiers may believe in the cause for which they are fighting and if they admire and trust their leader they will certainly fight for him. But fundamentally they fight for each other. Confidence in the men either side of you in battle, as well as those within your regiment and beyond, is crucial. The duke continues 'this letter of ill tidings' by stating that he and Marshal Königsegg will endeavour 'to save what we can of these poor remains of the last warrs conquests' but 'how much that will be God allone knows'. He concludes, 'for my part thô I affect to be in spirits & talk of demollishing the French I shall be [contented] if we save Brusselles & Flanders'.[36] Sir Everard, writing in a letter marked 'private' to the Duke of Newcastle, states that, in regard to Fontenoy, 'The Duke bears it extreamly well & seems to turn his thoughts altogether forward . . . his preservation was a recompence to us, for our loss, We must all hope that nothing will induce Him to expose Himself so far again, & I wish your Grace wou'd say something to Him upon this occasion.'[37]

However, despite the personal success for the Duke of Cumberland, it was still the case that the French had now won the advantage in the war. And Maréchal de Saxe proceeded to make full use of it. After the capitulation of Tournai, under the terms of which the Dutch agreed not to fight for France's enemies, including King George, the city of Ghent fell, followed by Oudenarde, Bruges and Dendermonde. The vital ports of Ostend and Nieuwpoort remained in Allied hands and open to British ships. But if they too fell to the French, then Britain would have lost its vital transport and communications link to the Low Countries. As the duke had admitted, things were in a very bad way. Certainly what Britain did not need at this moment was a major distraction at home.

Nicolas Poilly after Domenico Duprà, *Prince Charles Edward Stuart*, 1746.
(NATIONAL PORTRAIT GALLERY, LONDON)

5

Brittany

'I shall chuse to leave my bones among you.'

In a letter to John Murray, written some time in mid-June 1745 (NS), Prince Charles wrote:

> you may well remember when I saw you last, I had no great hopes of procuring any Succours from the french, and ask'd you what we should do, if we could obtain none. your answer was, that then we should trust to Providence, and see what we could do for and by ourselves. upon which I gave you my word to do so, and pay you a visit this summer: It being at the same time agreed, that this resolution should be kept as secret as possible, and particularly from the King and Lord Marischall, the latter being never like to approve of, or the other consent to any such thing. I am now resolved to be as good as my word and to execute a resolution, which has never been a moment out of my thoughts, since I first took it in your presence.[1]

According to John Murray himself, he had argued consistently throughout his meetings with the prince in the late summer of 1744 that an attempt should only be made with the assistance of French troops from the outset, and that this would be the expectation of the loyal peers and clan chiefs in Scotland. Indeed in February 1745, one of the most prominent of these chiefs, Donald Cameron of Lochiel, had written to James in Rome, asking for clarification as to what was currently being planned in France, while offering to visit Charles and explain their position to him in person.

From the prince's point of view, however, if a French-backed invasion was 'plan A' then all possibility of it had now been exhausted. He was therefore compelled to move on to 'plan B', in his mind (as his letter suggests) an option agreed with Murray, which was a low-key descent on Scotland with no direct support at all from the French king or court. As the prince himself explains, neither the Earl Marischal nor his father were aware of these plans either. So, as far as Charles was concerned, all of the major players in Rome and France were currently ignorant of his imminent departure. As warned, the prince was throwing himself on the mercy of his loyal friends in Scotland, and Charles was convinced that an early success in the Highlands would undoubtedly spur France into providing the necessary troops and financial support he needed to escalate the campaign and bring it to a happy conclusion.

His reason for choosing to maintain secrecy was to prevent it being 'the Town Talk of Paris and Madrid', while his desire to proceed sooner rather than later sprang from a fear that any delay would allow time for a peace treaty between France and Britain. And to seal the treaty, Britain would insist on France expelling Charles from their territories, as they had done his father. Rather than return to the stultifying tedium of Rome (as he had hinted to James) Charles dramatically declares, 'I shall chuse to leave my bones among you.' The prince enclosed the Declaration and Commission of Regency, both documents produced for the failed expedition of the previous year, which Murray was to get printed up for mass circulation 'the moment hostilities are begun'. Charles then discloses some of the discussion that he had had with Sir Hector Maclean, the chief of the Macleans of Mull, who had recently visited Charles in Paris. Soon after, Sir Hector had been sent back to Scotland with an enigmatic letter from Charles stating that the bearer was not entirely party to a secret 'wch I have hitherto kept from the best and greatest of my friends on this side [of] the water'.[2] Maclean had recommended that the prince land near the 'Isles of Mull' (Charles clearly had no idea what these were) so 'you may therefore expect me at one or other of them'. Murray should prepare for his arrival and, once landed, advise him what the next steps should be. He then confirms that neither Lord Sempill nor Lord Balhady would be let into the secret. The package to John Murray also contained notes to the Duke of Hamilton, the Duke of Perth, Lord Elcho and Donald Cameron of Lochiel. Soon after, news of Sir Hector's arrest in Edinburgh, because of some letters found in his lodgings, and subsequent confinement in the Tower of London reached Charles and 'dispiritted the Prince's party',[3] but as the letters were suitably vague and Sir Hector not fully involved in the plan, the prince did not consider the arrest particularly damaging.[4]

As Charles' letter and package to John Murray make absolutely clear, far from whiling away his time attending masquerades waiting for the French court to leap into action on his behalf, Charles had been extremely busy indeed. By this time the prince had a secret store in Nantes, a major port on the Loire thirty miles inland from the Brittany coast, in which he had built up over several months a cache of arms for his expedition. The money to purchase these items had been borrowed from George Waters, the Stuarts' banker in Paris. As Charles acknowledges in another letter, this time to James Edgar dated 12 June, with this money he had bought over 1,500 'fuses' (muskets), 1,800 broadswords, 'a good quantity of Powder, Ball, Flints, Durks, Brandy &c', twenty small field pieces 'two of which a Mule may carry' and a modest war chest of 4,000 louis d'or.[5]

'It will appear strange to you,' he observes to Edgar, 'how I shou'd get these things without the knowledge of the F.[rench] C.[ourt] I employ'd one Rutlidge and one Walch, who are subjects [of France].'[6] Walter Rutledge was an Irish banker at Dunkirk who had introduced the prince to the staunchly Jacobite Antoine Walsh, a wealthy merchant, privateer and slave trader of Irish descent based at Nantes and St Malo. These two men were also providing Charles with his transport and an escort ship. According to the prince's letter to James Edgar, Rutledge had permission to use a French man o' war to cruise around the west coast of Scotland as a privateer, a standard redeployment of such vessels if they were idle, 'and is luckily obliged to go as far North as I do, so that she will escort me with out appearing to do it'. Which may explain how the minister who issued the grant, Jean-Frédéric Phélypeaux, comte de Maurepas and *ministre de la marine*, could have had no idea that the proposed journey of this ship, the *Elisabeth*, had a secondary purpose. After all French privateers regularly cruised in British waters attacking British merchant ships. However, Antoine Walsh was a former officer in the French navy and well regarded at the French court. Even if a majority of Louis' ministers were innocent of any involvement, the possibility that the king knew exactly what was going on, through his spies and the local officials, and was either covertly supporting it or just turning a blind eye is very likely. Whatever Louis' involvement, the prince himself would be travelling in Walsh's own ship, the *Dutillet*, also referred to as *Du Teillay* and 'Doutelle'.[7] All that was left for Charles to do was to await the message from Walsh that everything was ready, after which he must head straight to Nantes.[8]

Of the three men closest to Charles at this time, initially only Sir Thomas Sheridan and the priest, George Kelly, were party to the plan. But once the transport had been arranged, John O'Sullivan was let into the secret and, soon after, he received orders to purchase the prince's campaign equipage and to source as many arms as he could – all within fifteen days.[9]

O'Sullivan was fast becoming indispensible to the prince and 'had the honour of conversing daily' with Charles, 'who soon contracted such an esteem for him that he was never easy but when this agreeable Irishman was with him'.[10] O'Sullivan seems to have sourced some if not all of the broadswords itemised in the prince's letter to James Edgar. Among his papers are receipts and accounts from a variety of tradesmen and craftsmen, from swordmakers, such as 'Geraldins & Bougerès', saddlers and spurmakers, to tailors and apothecaries.[11] One apothecary, 'S^r. Geoffroy', supplied items such as 'Cheriaque', 'Confection d'Hyacinthe', 'Eau de Bellot' and 'Eau de luce', along with instructions listing what conditions they each treated, and how they should be administered.[12] The latter, a pungent ammonia-based liquid, could be used as smelling salts and to treat wounds.

The orders for Charles' personal requirements were sent from Sheridan to O'Sullivan in a letter from Fitz-James dated 2 May 1745 (NS) and included 'an Armor' or armoire, a travelling wardrobe or clothes chest, a 'field bed', plates, dishes, 'knives forks & spoons, with a soupe spoon & two cuielleres a ragout [stew spoons]'.[13] A single account from the celebrated Parisian silversmith Jacques Roettiers, which includes 'cuillieres a potage' and 'deux Chandeliere', amounts to a princely 13,698 livres.[14] Within a list of items sent by O'Sullivan from Paris to Nantes there is 'Un Lit de Campe de dammas', a damask cot or camp bed.[15] In a subsequent letter, Sheridan also mentions the design of a sword for Prince Charles, 'the blade . . . mounted in steel basketwork'.[16] The description of this sword is similar, but not identical, to the silver basket-hilt sword probably given to the prince by the Duke of Perth in 1740 and which Charles had brought with him to France.[17] Charles had also brought from Rome a solid silver and silver-gilt travelling canteen, made by Ebenezer Oliphant of Edinburgh, which neatly contained thirty-one pieces of dining equipment, including two cups, cutlery, a cruet set and a corkscrew/nutmeg grater.[18] This is how princes travel. Among O'Sullivan's books, packed and ready for delivery, are, intriguingly, 'l'art de la guerre par le marquis de Guise', the works of Machiavelli in eight volumes, and 'lettres Philosophiques de Volterre' or Voltaire's *Letters Concerning the English Nation* (first published in French in 1734).[19] O'Sullivan managed to gather together and then transport without discovery all these disparate items under the false name 'Champville', with the arms signed off as a 'paccodille' (or allowable trading merchandise for a captain), bound for the West Indies.[20]

Enclosed in Charles' letter to James Edgar dated 12 June was another much longer missive (eight sides of large sheets) addressed to his father, which finally explains or, rather, offers an interpretation of what had occurred over the previous months, particularly regarding his discussions with the Jacobites in Scotland and his motivation in attempting a landing and rising there first. He opens by saying, 'I believe your Majesty little expected a Courier at this time, and much less from me; to tell you a thing that will be great surprise to you.' That is, 'I have been above six months ago invited by our Friends to go to Scotland, and to carry what money, and Arms I cou'd conveniently get.' This was, they believed, 'the only way of restoring you to the Crown, and them to their libertys; that they were well enough informed how scandalous the F.[rench] C.[ourt] had treated me, which shewed but too plainly how little they thought of me, or my affairs'.[21] Charles states that he impressed upon his friends that the French court would help, when and if they could, but if any representation to this court in the near future did not succeed in advance,

> that in such a case I would approve of their Rising; and that after due consideration before they undertook this work they shou'd be still determined rather to Dye than Live longer in oppression, they might be well assured I wou'd not let them do anything without my presence and that I wou'd go even alone to head them, and so Conquer or Dye with them; that rising by themselves might be their ruin and as I looked upon my self to be in this world for their good and preservation; that my Friends might be assured my Resolution was already taken, to do so, iff I cou'd not do better [i.e. in his discussion with France].[22]

He then uses a very personal argument for grasping this opportunity: 'Your Majesty cannot disapprove a sons following the example of his Father; you yourself did the like in the year 15 but the circumstances now are indeed very different; by being much more encouraging, their being a certainty of succeeding, with the least help.'[23] And here he was absolutely correct in his perceptions, particularly with the French successes in Flanders making the withdrawal of British troops to deal with any domestic issues, at this precise moment, extremely unlikely. Charles then moves on to the lack of influence enjoyed by the Stuart cause at the French court, having tried every means to gain access to the king and his ministers 'without the least effect', not helped by the fact that Tencin 'is not much trusted or well look'd upon' by Louis, who is himself 'timerous, and has not resolution enough to displace him'. As a result, Charles has been 'obliged to steal off without letting the K of F[rance] so much as suspect it, for which I make a proper excuse in my letter to [him]'.[24] If Louis was indeed assisting Charles, then the prince shows no knowledge of it.

Charles must have spent many hours of the same day writing these letters, as the one to Louis, which opens 'dear Uncle', is also dated 12 June 1745: 'Having tried in vain by every means to meet Your Majesty in the hope of getting, out of your generosity, the help I need to enable me to play a role worthy of my birth, I have resolved to make myself known by my deeds and on my own to undertake a project which would be certain to succeed with a moderate amount of help.' After this optimistic start, Charles hopes that Louis' good intentions towards him have not changed since the failed attempt the previous year. He then refers to Fontenoy and the French successes that followed:

> Might I now not dare to say that the signal victory which Your Majesty has now gained over your enemies (for they are indeed mine too) will have changed matters and that I will be able to benefit from this new and glorious light that shines on you? I beg Your Majesty to reflect that in supporting the justice of my claim, you will put yourself in a position to reach a firm and lasting peace, the final conclusion to the war in which you are presently engaged.[25]

This 'signal victory' over Louis' and Charles' mutual enemy was, of course, over the British army, albeit led by a prince of the House of Hanover. The strategy was obviously to force France, through a combination of embarrassment and obligation, to do something, anything, to assist him. In this way Charles says, 'I cannot help thinking, I shall at least get the Irish Regiments [of the French army], which will make the work shure.'

Returning to the letter to his father, the prince here concludes, 'It is most certain, the generality of people will judge of this enterprise by the success, which if favourable, I will get more honour than I deserve, if otherwise, all the blame will be put on the F.C. for having push'd a young Prince to shew his mettle, and rather dye than live in a state unbecoming himself.' Charles was certain that 'Whatever happens unfortunate to me, cannot but be the strongest engagement to the F.C. to pursue your Cause.'[26]

Around the same time Lord Sempill, oblivious to what Charles has been up to, writes to James of new plans to resuscitate a French invasion. He begins by condemning the 'shameful animosities', by which he probably means the open divisions between the Jacobites at the French court, and even between himself, Balhady and the prince, which (in his opinion) had 'disgusted The K. of France & discouraged our friends in Brittain' and which have lulled the British government into a false sense of security. Otherwise how can one explain the departure of 'The D. of Hannover' abroad and the removal of so many troops from Britain? Whatever the reason, Sempill reports that Lord Balhady has gone to England at a very opportune moment, and 'he assures in general that there is no alteration in The Kings friends, but for the better'.[27] He concludes by saying, 'I have had today the great honour of a letter from the Prince, who is, I thank God! in perfect health, and much pleas'd with his new residence, where H.R.H. is pleas'd to tell me he has great pleasure in the Stag-hunting.' This new residence was the Chateau de Navarre at Évreux in Normandy, owned by Charles' cousin Charles Godefroy de La Tour d'Auvergne, duc de Bouillon. The prince had arrived here with Sheridan late on 29 May (NS).[28] Sempill concludes, 'I am just going to send H.R.H. my accounts from Walker [?] [Balhady].'[29] What Balhady was reporting back from England has a very familiar ring.

Two weeks later Lord Sempill, again writing to James, states that the situation in Britain was very encouraging indeed.[30] The Lords Justices were divided. King George had been so encouraged in his selfish foreign wars (among other things) by 'our friends in the administration' that the British nation, in its exasperation, was turning to thoughts of revolution. Further, the defeat at Fontenoy 'has enraged the middle & lower ranks of people'. From all this 'they conclude that there never was & never can be again such a favourable opportunity to attempt yr M[ajes[tys] Restoration'. In this climate, if the prince landed in England with ten battalions, or even less, 'there will be no opposition, but on the contrary that H.R.H. will be received with blessings & acclamations'. Certainly, to many in Britain, King George's absences abroad gave the impression that he cared more for the interests of Hanover than Britain, and was more than willing to use British money and spill British blood in pursuit of them.

Lord Sempill then reports to James what, in his opinion, is a very disturbing development. In the next letter from Balhady, Sempill learned that Sir Hector Maclean was back in Scotland and soon after Lord Elcho had travelled in some haste from London to the north, leaving Lord Traquair and Balhady in fear 'that something very weak & rash may be attempted & that some great misfortune will ensue'. They also believed that Sir Thomas Sheridan was behind it all and that only an intervention from Charles to John Murray 'can prevent the bad consequences of it'.

They therefore requested a letter from the prince desiring that all Jacobites should act with restraint, to remain quiet and give the British government no reason to suspect any plans were afoot until James ordered otherwise. Lord Sempill had received a letter from the prince about ten days previously stating that Charles would be in Paris imminently and would pay him a visit. Lord Sempill shows some concern that the Stuarts' banker, George Waters, had been told by the prince not to forward any letters to him until further notice. As Charles had explained to John Murray, the entire project had been conducted in the utmost secrecy. So secret, in fact, that Lord Sempill presumed that the prince was entirely innocent of any planning behind the scenes and that the mastermind was Sir Thomas Sheridan (of all people), who he believed was coordinating the activities of Sir Hector Maclean and therefore, by extension, Lord Elcho and John Murray.

In fact, by this time the men Charles had chosen to accompany him to Scotland had already travelled to Nantes independently to avoid suspicion. They were the three Irishmen Kelly, Sheridan and O'Sullivan. The only Englishman, Francis Strickland, had been the prince's equerry in Rome. William Murray, Marquess of Tullibardine, was very useful for his stalwart support of the Stuarts and his contacts in Scotland, particularly his ancestral lands in Atholl, Perthshire. After his attainder following the '15, Tullibardine had lived in exile, while his title and lands had passed to his brother James. Meanwhile his other brother, Lord George Murray, had been pardoned after the '19 and, with the encouragement of Duke James, had recently sworn allegiance to the House of Hanover. Aeneas MacDonald, brother of Kinlochmoidart, had been happy to assist in financing the project and to act as a contact in Paris, but had been less inclined to venture to Scotland himself. Eventually he was persuaded because his MacDonald contacts in the Western Highlands would be crucial to the initial success of the project. Finally, there was another Irishman, Sir John Macdonald, whom the prince considered loyal and personable. His history is vague, but he had led cavalry in the French army in Spain.[31] So, a motley group, but these men were loyal to the prince and willing to take the risk.

On 3 June (NS) Sheridan had written to John O'Sullivan from Navarre,

> Mr. Burnet [Charles] thinks you woud do well to set out about the time you proposed, because you may be of use towards spurring others on: but as the fat man & his comrade cannot be milling [?] without making a noise he thinks the longer they stay at Paris the better; & he woud have them

contrive it so as to be at the Rendezvous about the 13th, it being as he judges absolutely needless for them to be there sooner.[32]

Who Sheridan means by 'the fat man' or his 'comrade' is not clear. On arrival at Nantes, each man took up his lodgings in a different part of the town. Sir John Macdonald recalled that he arrived the morning of the 11th, sent word to Antoine Walsh and was then directed 'to an inn opposite the Recollets, beyond the bridges of the Loire, where I went to lodge and a few days later Sir Thomas Sheridan came to see me'.[33] Aeneas MacDonald wrote in his memoirs that, 'if they accidentally met in the street or elswhere they took not the least notice of each other, nor seemed to be any way acquainted, if there was any person near enough to observe them'.[34] While these men were at Nantes completing the preparations for the journey, Charles remained at the Château de Navarre (as he had informed Lord Sempill, who in turn informed James in Rome) for 'some days' diversion in hunting, fishing, and shooting'.[35] A similar 'smoke screen' letter also appears to have been sent to his father, as James later writes to the Duke of Ormonde that 'I have heard from the Prince from his new habitation from Navarre where he will probably stay the summer' if, that is, 'what we all wish for so much does not call him from thence'.[36] It was at Bouillon's estate that Charles wrote his letters to both James and James Edgar outlining his planned expedition.[37] There is another letter from 'Navar' (to Colonel Daniel O'Brien at the French court dated 14 June),[38] and soon after writing this, Charles must have received the signal from Walsh that all was ready and set out for Nantes.[39]

Nantes was the first stage of the journey. After rendezvousing here, the party were to travel together towards the coastal town of Saint-Nazaire. According to John O'Sullivan it was Antoine Walsh who suggested the prince should be disguised as an abbé.[40] Dressed in the black habit of a clergyman and acting the part of Sheridan's son, the prince arrived early in the morning at the quay at Nantes – the precise dating is confused, but some time late June NS – where he met his fellow travellers, including seven servants. They boarded two boats, set off down the Loire and arrived at Saint-Nazaire in the evening.[41]

By late June, Lord Sempill was perhaps beginning to realise that the prince was less innocent than he had thought. In a letter to James Edgar, Sempill writes that he believes the prince is well, 'but I am a little uneasy to have heard nothing of him these six days past'. He hopes 'no body will presume to lead H.R.H. into an unconcerted adventure or indeed into any important measure that is not digested and directed by H[is]. M[ajest]y's Royal wisdom'.[42]

Meanwhile, in a letter dated 'St. Lazaire [sic] at ye mouth of ye Loire ye 2nd July 1745 N.S [a Friday]', Charles writes again to his father (the previous letter of 12 June was still unsent and, according to Charles, sitting in Paris awaiting his departure): 'The Contrary winds that have been blowing hither to have diferd my Embarking, which will be this afternoon at seven, for to go to the re[n]devou[s] of ye man of war of 67. Guns [the *Elisabeth*]; and 700 men abourd as also a company of sixty Volontiers all gentlemen.' The presence of French-Irish troops, volunteers or not, confirms complicity on the part of the French king: whether proactive assistance, or simply passive non-interference. The rendezvous with the escort ship, the *Elisabeth*, was the island of Belle-Île located off the Brittany coast, due west of Saint-Nazaire. He continues, 'Wee have nothing to do now but to hope in ye Almighties favouring uss, and recompencing our troubles, which as you may see by the nature of ye thing were not small. I hope in God my next will bring comfortable news, In ye mean time I remain Laying myself at your Majestys feet most humbly asking Blessing.' It is signed 'From [your] moste Dutifull Son'.[43]

Captain Darbé of the *Dutillet* recorded in the ship's journal that he had left Mindin, lying on the Loire estuary to the south of Saint-Nazaire, at five o'clock in the morning of 2 July and dropped anchor at Saint-Nazaire 'to wait for the passengers, who arrived one after the other in large boats'. Then at seven o'clock in that evening, he sent a little boat to collect the final three passengers 'who had remained behind, who were H.R.H. the Prince of Wales, the Chevalier Scheriden, and Monsieur Walsh'.[44] Charles wrote another note to James Edgar, probably this time aboard the *Dutillet* one imagines, as the writing is very loose and large. Here he says,

> This being the Laste note I shall write this side of ye seas, I woud not faill to give you adieu in it making my Compliments to Lord Dunbar, and to as many of my Friends as you shall think convenient and proper. I enclose here two letters for King, and Duke [his brother Henry] which will go together with the great packet of ye 12th last, as soon as I am ferely sailed off from Belle Isle. I hope in God wee shall soon meet, which I am resolved will not be but at home.[45]

'Home' was, of course, Britain, a place he only knew second hand through letters, official reports, newspapers and travellers to Rome, as well as his father's fading recollections and the wistful tales of Jacobite exiles. According to her captain, the *Dutillet* raised her anchor on Saturday, 3 July and arrived at the 'roads of Belisle' at 5 a.m. on Sunday the 4th to await the *Elisabeth*.[46]

The second package of letters written by Charles had clearly not been sent from Saint-Nazaire, as the postscript to that addressed to James Edgar is dated 12 July from Belle-Île 'a La Rade', or the harbour. The arrival of the man of war *Elisabeth* had been delayed, leaving Charles plenty of time to kill. Aeneas MacDonald recalled that 'during the stay at this island, the Prince took great delight in fishing'. He adds that the 'better to conceal himself, he never would be shaved from his leaving Nantz to his arrival in Scotland'.[47] Disguise was a necessity, but Charles seems particularly attracted to it, to masking himself, being for a time someone else. It is reminiscent of his appearances at the Roman Carnival as the fey Arcadian shepherd and, later, as an adolescent Chief of the Clans. However, the postscript in the note to James Edgar suggests that Charles was not as relaxed as Aeneas MacDonald believed. These are the last words that the prince wrote before embarking. He scribbles in a more hurried and therefore less elegant manner than the original script written ten days previously, revealing his excitement and nervousness at what was about to happen:

> After having waited a week here not without a little ancyety [anxiety], we have at laste got ye Escorte I expected which is just now arrived . . . I am thank God in perfect good health, but have been a little sea sick, and expect to be more so, but it do[e]s not keep me much a bed, for I finde the more I strug[g]le against it the Better. Pray make my excuses along with moste humble duty to the King, for not wryting; not having anything more particular to add but what is here, I recconed it woud suffise, My excuses also to ye Dear Duke [Henry] with many compliments. My compliments again to all Friends, and give you adieu having nothing more to add, and being in a great hurry.[48]
>
> C[harles]. P[rincep].

Just before midday on Tuesday, 13 July (NS) the *Elisabeth* finally arrived in the roads of Belle-Île, her master one Captain d'O, and two days later, she and the *Dutillet* weighed anchor at about five o'clock in the morning, and set sail for the Western Isles of Scotland.[49]

Simon François Ravenet I after Arthur Pond, *Prince William Augustus,*
Duke of Cumberland, 1747.

6

Flanders

'a strange stir'

By early August, rumours regarding Prince Charles and an attempt on Scotland were circulating within the French army. The effect, particularly among the Scottish exiles, was electric. One prominent member was Lord John Drummond. His grandfather had been stripped of his title for his part in the '15. His elder brother was the titular Duke of Perth, a Jacobite title not recognised by the British government. Both were signatories of the Association and in 1743 Lord John had raised a regiment in the French army, the Royal Ecossais. On 6 August NS [26 July OS] from the French Camp at Aalst in Eastern Flanders, Captain James Hay wrote to Captain Alexander Baillie of the Royal Ecossais, 'We are in a strange stir here about the Prince of Wales who parted from Nantz [Belle-Île] the 15th last month we have no certain accounts of his landing in Scotland, but onely [only] hear say.' As a result 'we are strieving to obtain force from the Court to assist him. God knows what wil be the consequence. But one thing is certain that the Country is in Great Commotions especially at London.'[1] Similarly, a few days later, Baillie's commander, Lord John, wrote to James Edgar, 'You can not imagine how well is taken here the Princes Bravery and resolution, and they [the French] seeme to be resolved to sustean [sustain] it to [the] utmost, the more that they think it is [just] now ther interest.' 'It is not to be expressed,' he continues, 'the Joy that appears Here in the countinance not only of the Kings Soubjets but of evry french man, who ar persuaded of our success.'[2]

By this time, the Duke of Cumberland was at the new British army headquarters in Vilvoorde on the Brussels–Antwerp canal just to the north-east of Brussels. The British command were also aware that such an attempt may have been made, and in consequence that France was now potentially planning an invasion of Britain. On 3 August NS (23 July OS) Robert Trevor, British ambassador at The Hague in the United Provinces, wrote to Sir Everard Fawkener that 'I can pick up no decisive [descriptions?] of France's intended Invasion; & wish, that Panick may not lead us into false measures.' He then moves on to the issue of 'the young Pretender'. According to Abraham van Hoey, Dutch ambassador to the French court, 'the Pretender's Eldest son embarked, as long ago as the [15th of July?] last, at Nantes for Scotland, on board a French man of war, called the Elizabeth, & with a frigate in Company, laden with arms for [10,000?] men, Horse, & Foot'. Trevor had also been told that a man called 'Welch', an Irish merchant, 'is said to have begged these two ships of the French Court, & to have equipped them, himself, at his own expense'. Trevor concludes, 'you'll say this is a strainge story; but such as I hear it I give it you'.[3]

On 26 July OS (6 August NS) the Duke of Newcastle from Whitehall wrote two letters to the Duke of Cumberland stating confidently that France was planning an invasion of Britain, but at no point does he mention Prince Charles.[4] He also confirms that the land forces in Britain were too small to cope with such an invasion, and as a result the only hope lay with the Royal Navy, who had been ordered to direct their strength towards the south-east coast, in anticipation of movement from the French fleet at Brest as well as the ports of Boulogne and Dunkirk. By these means, 'we shall soon have a force, that will be superior to any thing, that can be brought against it'.[5]

Three days later Sir Everard sent a letter to Willam Stanhope, Earl of Harrington, who was with King George in Hanover, stating 'we have had several flying reports that the Pretenders son was landed in Scotland, it was said in the French Army, that [the] King had said at Table, he was gone ashore there with ten other Persons'. Dining in public was a ritual observed by Louis even when on campaign. During the meal, the French king might well let slip such a juicy titbit, for general and, more specifically, British consumption. But, Sir Everard continues, 'as there has not yet been any news from England relating either to Him or the attempt, I take the story of his being landed at least, to be quite without foundation'.[6]

In consequence of having heard no news from England, Sir Everard wrote to the Duke of Newcastle in London relaying the Duke of Cumberland's surprise 'that He has not yet heard from England of the Expedition of the Pretenders Son, considering how long it has been talkt of abroad. This & the variations about it here, lessens his credit to it.' Sir Everard then describes the curious circumstance by which word had first been received at the duke's headquarters. An enquiry had been made by Maréchal de Saxe's secretary to one of the British army cornets (the lowest rank of cavalry commissioned officer), which was then backed up by the pronouncements of Van Hoey, and later Louis' quoted comments at dinner. More recently it had been reported that one of the ships had been severely damaged during a battle with a Royal Navy man o' war, and had in fact returned to Brest.

According to this intelligence, Charles had continued on his journey 'with one of the small Vessels'.[7] But since this, nothing further had been heard.

In his letter to Lord Harrington, Sir Everard had repeated the details of the current understanding of the expedition as set out in the letter to Newcastle adding, in regard to the French and the ship that had reportedly returned to Brest, 'tho they don't own He was aboard that Ship, yet they say He has not been heard of since the Engagement'.[8] The following day Robert Trevor updated Sir Everard: 'Having given you already an account of the extravagant Enterprise of the young Pretender, I must now give you news of its success . . . the young gentleman is said to have gone on board the Frigate, & to have pursued His voyage, tho that Lord knows where.'[9]

In response to the various letters from Sir Everard, expressing surprise that not a single word concerning Charles had been reported from London, the Duke of Newcastle finally wrote from Whitehall on 2 August 1745 (13 August NS) that 'all the accounts from France agree, That the Pretender's Son embarked at Nantes [Belle-Île] on the 15th past N.S., and, as is confidently given out, for Scotland'. There had been, as yet, no word of such an attempt or a landing from government officers and supporters in Scotland itself. But orders had been sent to Sir John Cope, commander-in-chief in Scotland, and His Majesty's servants in that country, that such an attempt might be made. Either way, the Lords Justices had ordered a proclamation 'offering a Reward of Thirty Thousand Pounds for apprehending the Pretender's son, in case He shall land, or attempt to land in any part of His Majesty's Dominions'.[10] So Prince Charles now had a considerable bounty on his head.

Newcastle enclosed another letter, this time addressed to Sir Everard Fawkener, in which he confirms the news of Charles' journey and that preparations were being made to bring a detachment of British troops back from Flanders.[11] On the same day, Lord Harrington writes to the Duke of Cumberland from Hanover that, regarding the expedition, 'the Court of France would have the World believe that they have no share in [it]', despite the fact that King George had 'certain knowledge of the contrary'.[12]

The king, his ministers in Hanover and the Lords Justices in London believed that France was not only involved in Charles' expedition, but was already preparing for an invasion to support it. They were also aware that Charles had left France via Nantes, but although a bounty had been advertised for the capture of the Stuart prince, and the relevant officials in Scotland had been warned, no measure beyond this would occur until there was concrete intelligence that the Stuart prince had actually landed in Scotland. And this could only come from Scotland itself.

John Faber Junior after Jeremiah Davison, *Lord President Duncan Forbes of Culloden*, 1748.

7

Edinburgh

'when so much is at stake'

In early August 1745, Duncan Forbes, the 5th Laird of Culloden (b. 1685) and since 1737 Lord President of the Court of Session, was in his chambers at Edinburgh, finishing off official business, before preparing for the journey north to his beloved Culloden House near Inverness. This fortified stone building (also called Culloden Castle), a 'plain four-storied edifice, with battlemented front and central bell-turret',[1] lay on the south shore of the Moray Firth, and from his commodious first-floor bedchamber (facing north-east) the Lord President had spectacular views over a conifer wood to the Firth and, further still, to the distant mountains of the 'Black Isle' peninsula. Seven sisters had married advantageously and, with an extended network of blood relations, the Lord President was connected to many eminent families throughout Scotland: a fact that was to have great bearing on his influence in the Highlands and beyond.[2] The Marquess of Tweeddale was Secretary of State for Scotland, but in reality the administration on the ground was managed by four men: Lord President Forbes, the Lord Justice Clerk Andrew Fletcher of Milton, the Lord Advocate Robert Craigie and the Solicitor General Robert Dundas. Both Forbes and Fletcher owed their positions to John Campbell, 2nd Duke of Argyll (died 1743), whose family had by recent tradition overseen the government's affairs in Scotland. As previously observed, the current duke's grandfather, the ally of the Duke of Monmouth, had been executed by James VII/II and his lands confiscated. His father, the 1st duke, had supported the succession of William of Orange, for which the family lands were restored to them, and was his chief adviser in Scotland. Later he had helped to forge the Union between Scotland and England. The 2nd duke, the elder brother to Archibald the 3rd and current duke, had come out on the Hanoverian/government side during the '15. The Argyll dukes, their descendants, extended clan – among them the Earl of Loudoun and Major

General John Campbell of Mamore – in tandem with other Presbyterians and sincere believers in what would become constitutional monarchy, such as Forbes and Tweeddale, were certainly no friends of the Stuarts.[3]

Rumours of an imminent rising had been circulating for some years now, but they had been vague and had come to nothing. Besides, in the first few months of 1745 the Lord President had had more pressing family concerns. His son, John, or Jock, was a lieutenant in the Horse Guards and was currently fighting in Flanders. Forbes' wife, Mary Rose, had died soon after John's birth in 1710. In May, the Lord President had received a letter from Lieutenant Colonel John Monro of Newmore containing a personal account of a recent battle just outside the little village of Fontenoy. During the battle, Monro had been a captain (since promoted) in the 43rd (later 42nd) Highland Regiment or 'Black Watch' formed from Independent Highland Companies raised from Clans Monro, Grant, Fraser and Campbell (at the instigation of the Irish-born British army field marshal, George Wade, in 1725) to 'watch' or police the Highlands. Their distinctive uniform, approved of and much admired by King George in 1740, was a plaid of dark green tartan gathered and belted at the waist with the remaining length pinned on the left shoulder, a red coat with buff facings, a red waistcoat and a blue bonnet with black cockade. The regiment's Lieutenant Colonel at Fontenoy was John Monro's cousin Sir Robert Monro, Chief of Clan Monro (the Monros were also related to the Forbes family), who had since been promoted to the colonelcy of the English 37th 'North Hampshire' Regiment of Foot, now, according to tradition, renamed 'Monro's' after their new commanding officer.

Lieutenant Colonel John Monro immediately allays the worst fears of this anxious father by informing him that John 'is in good Health, and suffered nothing but the loss of his horse, who was shot in our retreat'. The letter offers a brief account of the battle itself, which Monro describes as 'the bloodiest, as to Officers, that happen'd to the British in the memory of Man'. Among the Scots casualties named are 'poor Charles Ross of Balnagown', who died from a musket-ball wound to the stomach, General Sir James Campbell, who 'lost his leg, but is not yet dead' and Captain John Campbell of Carrick, who had been decapitated by a cannon ball. Lieutenant Colonel Monro has no admiration for either the Dutch 'who in their usual way were very dilatory', or the French, who 'never appeared out of their trenches but once; and, to tell the truth, they made but a poor stand'. But the Hanoverian troops 'behaved most gallantly and bravely' and the British 'behaved well'. The Duke of Cumberland is singled out for particular praise: 'I cannot fail telling you, that the Duke shewed as much real courage and temper as ever Caesar or Hannibal did.' Colonel Monro continues, 'we the Highlanders were told by his Royal Highness, that we did our duty well'. In a postscript Colonel Monro states with military brevity that, 'Since writing, Gen Campbell is carried by here in a cart, dead.'[4]

On 1 July, the Lord President had received a letter which informed him that a rumour was abroad of a Jacobite rising, and, being a prudent man, he immediately informed Sir John Cope, since February 1743/4 the British army's commander-in-chief in Scotland.[5] Sir John in turn informed the Marquess of Tweeddale. Talk of an imminent invasion from France was widespread in London by late July, followed by the news of Prince Charles' reported departure from Nantes. The Lord President had given little credence to the rumours, based on his thorough and intimate knowledge of the clans, whether loyal or not to the House of Hanover or Stuart, and his own dedicated work over many years in convincing erstwhile Jacobite chiefs and waverers – whose traditional ties pulled them one way, their reason or sense of preservation the other – of the futility of another rising for the Stuart cause. If such clans would not go so far as to support the current government and King George, he felt certain that a majority would at least remain neutral, should temptation in the guise of a Stuart prince come calling. The Lord President was also profoundly aware that major events of – at the very least – European significance were being played out in Flanders, and he was of the opinion that Scotland's current and future success lay as an active part of a victorious and dynamic United Kingdom of Great Britain and Ireland under the protestant House of Hanover, not as the grateful and pliant Stuart satellite of a dominant and colonially avaricious France. Any Scots patriot of sense and ambition would surely see this.

It was, as the Lord President himself described it, 'in a state of profound tranquillity' that he wrote to Henry Pelham on 2 August that 'we have been alarmed with advices, which are said to have been received at London, of intended invasions; and particularly of a visit which the Pretender's eldest son is about to make to us, if he has not already made it'. Such information, and 'particularly as to the visit just mentioned, I must confess, have not hitherto gain'd my belief. This young gentleman's game seems at present to be very desperate in this country; and, so far as I can learn, there is not the least apparatus for his reception, even amongst the few highlanders who are suspected to be in his interest.'[6] The Lord President's assessment is far from complacent, although he appears to be accusing the citizens of the British capital of unnecessary gullibility and even hysteria. Despite his 'tranquillity' in the face of these rumours from London, Forbes was circumspect enough not to dismiss any murmurings out of hand, for 'when so much is at stake, no advice, how improbably soever, is to be neglected'. He would journey to the north early to show support to the friends of the government and 'prevent the seduction of the unwary, if there should be any truth in what is reported'.[7] At Culloden he would be closer to his contacts within the Western Highland clans and be able to test the mood for himself.

The Lord President was still in Edinburgh on 8 August when he wrote to the Marquess of Tweeddale, confirming the advice received by the government that Charles had boarded a ship at a French port and was bound for Scotland. This, he considered 'highly improbable', although he also believed his own presence in the north to be important 'should the Report . . . have any foundation in Truth'. The Lord President sets out the reasoning for doubting that any success could be achieved, even if the young Stuart had ventured to Scotland. 'I am confident,' he writes, 'that Young Man cannot with Reason expect to be joined by any considerable Force in the Highlands.' Perhaps some 'loose lawless Men, of desperate Fortunes, may indeed resort to him', but 'I am persuaded that none of the Highland Gentlemen who have ought to lose will, after the Experience with which the Year 1715 furnish'd them, think proper to risque their Fortunes on an attempt which to them must appear desperate; especially as so many considerable Familys amongst themselves have lately uttered their sentiments'. The situation would, however, be worrying if any attempt were supported by a foreign power and accompanied by an invasion. And considering 'it is of consequence to France to create Confusion in Britain at any Expence it behoves every Dutiful Subject to be attentive to such Reports, however improbable, and to leave nothing undone that might be fit to be done, in Case they should, contrary to Expectation, prove true'.[8] In fact, there was nothing amiss in the Lord President's assessment of the situation. But he may have been underestimating the allure of a Stuart prince when actually present on Scottish soil – an event not witnessed since 1715.

The Lord President then asks if 'Your Lo[rdshi]p will pardon me if I fling out a few hints which my former Experience suggests may deserve the Consideration of the Government, if there is any thing real in the Rumours that are spread'.[9] After which he makes three observations with corresponding suggestions as to what action should be taken. The first concerns the lack of a 'Lawful Authority' such as Lieutenancies within the Highlands (as had existed in 1715), which could coordinate the call to action by the loyal friends of King George and the government in that region. The second, that in 1715 the government's friends – who were far fewer in number then – were armed, which at present they are not while 'the loose Banditti of that Country [the Highlands], are; and there can be no doubt that, if any Enemy from abroad land, plenty of Arms will be brought alongst'. In the greatest of ironies, due to the disarming acts passed after the '15 and the '19, loyal clans had complied and disarmed, but the Jacobite clans had not. In response, Forbes suggests that arms should be sent to the main Highland forts, Forts George, William and Augustus, 'with Directions to whom, & by whom, they may be delivered out'. And finally, as ever, there was the issue of money, or lack of ready cash provided by the government to pay for supplies, intelligence and arms, which in 1715 had been a great hindrance in suppressing the rebellion. Supporters had dug deep to cover this lack but as few had been reimbursed, much less rewarded, it was unlikely that they would be so eager again. The Lord President suggests 'at this Juncture to lodge with some proper person, or persons, Money or Credit sufficient to answer such Occasions, and to be accounted for'.[10] It is depressingly familiar that a British government, which had everything to gain from showing gratitude to its loyal friends in the Highlands, chose instead to display such disregard and even distrust. In fact, regardless of their loyalty, within the British government (specifically the English contingent), there was a singular lack of trust in the Scots in general. Forbes must have hoped that sense, gratitude and even honour would this time prevail.

The Lord President offered the government, through Lord Tweeddale, sensible suggestions, as well as sound and well-informed advice. No doubt Lord Tweeddale would prove as sensible and do all in his power to convince the government of their utility, as well as the necessity of putting them into immediate action. Having dispatched his thoughts to the marquess, the Lord President was now ready to travel northwards. At Culloden he would be better placed to coordinate a campaign against a potential rising gaining any meaningful foothold in the Highlands and Islands.

H. Moll, *Scotland divided into its Shires*, 1745.

8

Eriskay

'a role worthy of my birth'

The *Elisabeth* and the *Dutillet* left Belle-Île with 700 volunteers from the Irish Regiment de Clare (raised by Charles O'Brien, 6th Viscount Clare), 20 small cannon, 11,000 arms, 2,000 broadswords and gunpowder. Among the party were Charles' seven close companions: two Scots, William Murray, Marquess of Tullibardine and Jacobite Duke of Atholl, and Aeneas MacDonald; one Englishman, Francis Strickland; and four Irishmen, Sir Thomas Sheridan, George Kelly, Sir John Macdonald and John William O'Sullivan. In addition to these seven, the small party included Antoine Walsh, Duncan Buchanan (a clerk associated with Aeneas MacDonald), Abbé Butler (related to the Duke of Ormonde and acted as chaplain, who would return to France with Walsh), Michele Vezzosi (Italian follower of James and Charles) and Duncan Cameron, former servant of the Camerons of Lochiel and a native of the Outer Hebridean island of Barra. Such were the humble beginnings of this extraordinary enterprise.

For Charles, the relief must have been overwhelming. This was the very purpose of his life and upbringing. He was, after all, the Jacobite Prince of Wales and true heir to the throne. With no prospect of an imminent restoration, and, worse still, no attempts to bring about such an outcome, his existence was arguably meaningless. His focus, drive and, crucially, his sense of destiny had finally succeeded in forcing the issue, and whatever happened over the coming days, weeks and months the impact of his actions would be far-reaching: potentially profoundly so. As far as Charles was concerned, he – the talisman of a Jacobite rising and Stuart restoration – was fulfilling his promise to come among his father's loyal Highland subjects: undoubtedly they in turn would act as promised.

For now, though, the most important task was getting both ships safely to harbour in the Western Isles. But very soon they encountered an obstacle.

As reported later in Flanders, on 9 July (OS, 20 July NS) as the two vessels skirted the Lizard Peninsula off the south-west of England, another ship was sighted.[1] This was the Royal Navy warship HMS *Lion*, commanded by Captain Percy Brett. As described by O'Sullivan, 'the English man of War, the *Lyon*, was a fine light Ship of 64 Guns' whereas, in contrast, *Elisabeth* was 'a he[a]vy log'.[2] At 5.30 p.m. the *Lion* came alongside *Elisabeth* and, now within pistol shot, the two ships engaged, pounding each other relentlessly. The *Dutillet* twice attempted to rake or fire at the *Lion* through her stern, but was beaten off by the *Lion*'s stern gun (or chase). The *Dutillet* then lay out of range, with its passengers and crew observing the action. According to Aeneas MacDonald, who was standing on the *Dutillet*'s upper deck, the two ships 'fought with equal bravery for several hours, but the British sailors showed superior skill and dexterity, which was highly praised by all on board the *Doutelle*, as well French as Scotch men'.[3] Yet by sunset, with the *Lion*'s masts shot away 'so that she lay muzled in the Sea', forty-five men killed and 107 wounded, the *Elisabeth* might have claimed a marginal victory.[4] Captain Brett himself was one of the wounded, along with all his lieutenants. His sailing master's right arm had been shot off. But such a victory was to prove Pyrrhic. As the *Lion* turned homeward to Plymouth to refit, it was clear that her opponent had suffered enough damage and loss of life to force her immediate return to Brest. Among the dead were the captain and his brother. Given that the *Elisabeth* carried the vital arms and regular troops for the campaign, this was devastating.

Observing the *Elisabeth*, which was now listing so badly that no attempt at safely transferring its cargo of men and arms could be made, Aeneas MacDonald recalled that 'some of the passengers of the Doutelle [*Dutillet*] endeavoured to prevail upon the Prince to return also till another convoy could be prepared, or the same [i.e. *Elisabeth*] could be refitted'. This may have been the sensible approach, but from a psychological point of view it was absurd. If they had turned back, Charles' supporters and detractors alike could be forgiven for observing that here was yet another Jacobite attempt, and yet another failure. The prince would have appeared ridiculous. And Charles had already waited well over a year for this attempt, such as it was. There is a moment when prudence borders on timidity, a trait that could not be applied to the young architect of this particular adventure. Unsurprisingly, then, a return was something Charles could not countenance and he 'resolved to proceed on his voyage'.[5] The *Elisabeth* limped home to France, and the *Dutillet* continued alone on her original course for the Western Isles.

The *Dutillet* encountered several violent storms en route. But when a calm settled and they were finally within reach of the Isle of Barra, virtually the last piece of land between Scotland and North America, the ship is said to have been guided towards the island by an eagle, hovering above the prow. The Marquess of Tullibardine turned to Charles and declared that 'the king of birds is come to welcome your royal highness upon your arrival in Scotland'.[6] As they steered past, Captain Darbé noted in his journal that Barra was 'a big island, very high, and steeply cut into peaks on every side, behind which on the great island are houses'.[7]

Captain Edmund Burt, an English military engineer, observed in the late 1720s that the Highlands were so little known to Lowlanders, that they

> have ever dreaded the Difficulties and Dangers of Travelling among the Mountains; and when some extraordinary Occasion has obliged any one of them to such a Progress, he has, generally speaking, made his Testament before he set out, as though he were ent[e]ring upon a long and dangerous Sea Voyage, wherein it was very doubtful if he should ever return.[8]

However, the English, in Burt's opinion, had hardly any experience of the Highlands at all. In fact, he continues, more books were published on the West Indies, India and the Far East than this area of the British Isles.[9] Furthermore, the people of the more remote Highland regions were considered by many in the remainder of the country to be savage and uncivilised: and such an opinion existed as much among some of the Lowland Scots of East Lothian as the British government in London. Conversely, post-Union, the Highlander was also viewed (again by some) as the living embodiment of a pure, pre-Union Scotland.[10] After the Act of Union, England and Scotland maintained separate and distinct legal systems, as well as mechanisms for local government, although English laws on treason extended to Scotland under the 1709 Treason Act. But despite concerted efforts since James VI [and I] to bring the area within the reach of Lowland government, it was grudgingly accepted that the Highlands and the Western Isles in particular effectively lay beyond common law and governance, and were steeped in old traditions and loyalties – including for many a veneration of the ancient Scottish Royal House of Stuart – to which they instinctively adhered. Cattle-thieving rather than commerce was seen as their chief means of survival: one reason for the existence of the Black Watch.[11] The life was certainly tough, but the people were resilient and hardy.

As previously noted, Scotland also had a distinct Protestant state church, the Presbyterian Kirk, which offered a particular 'democratic' idea of civil society and the relationship between the people, church, state and monarch, which adherents certainly considered worth defending against Jacobitism, with their lives if necessary. Many Church of Scotland ministers played a crucial role in supporting and in turn encouraging support for King George and the British state, as the best hope of the Kirk's survival. Religious affiliation among the West Highland and Island clans tended to be Roman Catholic and Episcopalian, as well as Presbyterian. The area could not be described as uniformly Jacobite. The Episcopalian church, unlike the Presbyterian Kirk, was a hierarchical form of Protestantism reintroduced into Scotland after the Stuart restoration in 1660 and was now closely associated with the exiled house. The more radical presbyterians (known as Covenanters, derisively nicknamed 'whiggamores' or 'cattle drivers' from where the term 'Whig' probably derives) had refused to support the reintroduction of Episcopalianism, while many Presbyterian families (such as the Forbeses of Culloden), during the seventeenth-century civil wars, had supported the Parliamentarians against Charles I, and then Oliver Cromwell's Commonwealth: as a result all had suffered greatly at the hands of Charles II and then James VII after the restoration of the monarchy.

The clan system whereby the clan chief had fundamental power over each and every clan member still existed, although in practice it was by no means as clearcut or universal. And it cannot be said that the clans were so steeped in their ancient, semi-feudalistic social and cultural systems that they were resistant to new ideas or change. Many of the clan chiefs, like Donald Cameron of Lochiel, were educated, sophisticated men, who were balancing the introduction of modest reform and modernisation within their lands, in tandem with the old traditions and deep bonds of kinship so characteristic of Highland society.[12] The situation was made more complex still by inter-clan blood relations, friendships, rivalries, animosities and outright warfare, stretching back hundreds of years. However, it was generally presumed that, among the people of the Western Isles and adjoining mainland, the Stuart prince would inevitably find a deep and sincere welcome.

The *Dutillet* proceeded to the small island of Eriskay, which lies between Barra (to the south) and South Uist (to the north). Aeneas MacDonald recounted, 'They were scarce arrived when they spied two sails which they apprehended to be ships of war, and therefore got all their money, arms, and ammunition on shore as fast as they could. All went ashore except the Marquess of Tullibardine, who was laid up in the gout and could not stir.'[13]

Charles first set foot on Scottish soil around three o'clock in the afternoon of Tuesday, 23 July OS on a stretch of coastline now called *Cladach a' Phrionnsa*, 'the Prince's Strand'. Captain Darbé observed, 'It was terrible weather.'[14] This land was Clan MacDonald of Clanranald country, the most powerful of what remained of the Catholic clans and vehemently Jacobite. At the beginning of the century, the local-born author Màrtainn MacGilleMhàrtainn (Martin Martin) described the land of 'Erisca' as 'partly heathy, and partly arable, and yields a good produce. The innerside hath a wide Anchorage. There is excellent Cod and Ling in it.'[15] The Clansmen spoke 'Erse' or Gaelic 'more perfectly here, than in most of the other Islands; partly because of the remoteness, and the small number of those that speak English, and partly because some of 'em are Scholars, and versed in the Irish Language.'[16] Martin also states that 'the more Ancient People continue to wear the old Dress, especially Women'.[17] The traditional dress of the male Highlander, as also seen in the uniform of the Black Watch, was the belted plaid or great kilt, a long woollen, tartan cloth, which was gathered and wrapped around the waist, with the spare length thrown over the shoulder, although the short kilt or 'philibeg' was becoming increasingly popular. Both garments were now often worn with a shift or shirt, waistcoat and coat (or jacket).

As Martin Martin's remarks suggest, a greater contrast to cosmopolitan Rome and Paris would be difficult to find. Charles, of course, was undaunted. Now full-bearded, as a result of the resolution he had taken in Nantes, still disguised in a clergyman's habit and somewhat unkempt from a difficult voyage, the prince was unrecognisable from the primped, silk and lace sophisticate of European elite society. He had never been to London or Edinburgh, let alone the remote Hebridean islands. And he was revelling in it. Aeneas MacDonald recalled that on that first night, with the rain thundering down, they stayed in a 'mean low hut', probably, as described by Martin Martin, 'a little Stone House under Ground' which 'is very low and long, having an entry on the Sea side',[18] and for their first meal Duncan Cameron 'stood cook', roasting over coals the flounders that they had caught nearby. Charles, meanwhile, 'sat at the cheek of the little ingel, upon a fail sunk [turf seat], and laughed heartily at Duncan's cookery, for he himself owned he played his part awkwardly enough'.[19]

The prince's disguise during these first days on British soil provides some further anecdotes. The host in their 'mean low hut' was a straight-talking tacksman or principal tenant by the name of Alexander MacDonald. Aeneas MacDonald says that 'they were all refreshed as well as the place could afford' and 'they had some beds, but not sufficient for the whole company, on which account the Prince, being less fatigued than the others, insisted upon such to bed as most wanted it. Particularly he took care of Sir Thomas Sheridan, and went to examine his bed and to see that the sheets were well aired.' That Charles was too excited to sleep is understandable, and he was obviously mindful of his frail former tutor. The host, however, observing the clergyman, as he thought, inspecting the bed and declaring 'he would sit up all night', took umbrage with this high and mighty individual and declared 'that it was so good a bed, and the sheets were so good, that a prince need not be ashamed to lie in them':[20] no doubt to the amusement of the prince's close companions. The little house had no windows and was heated by burning peat. The prince, 'not being accustomed to such fires in the middle of the room, and there being no other chimney than a hole in the roof, was almost choaked, and was obliged to go often to the door for fresh air'. The host called out with tangible irritation, 'What a plague is the matter with that fellow, that he can neither sit nor stand still, and neither keep within nor without doors?'[21]

However, it was from their host that Charles and his companions received the vital information that Ranald MacDonald, 18th Chief of Clanranald, and Alexander 'Mor' MacDonald of Boisdale, his half-brother, were both on the island of South Uist, a mere two miles away, and that Ranald MacDonald or young Clanranald, the chief's eldest son and heir, was at Moidart on the mainland. Early on the morning of 24 July the party returned to the *Dutillet* 'wet through by the rain'.[22] Charles immediately set about contacting the chiefs who had declared allegiance to him. A message was sent to Boisdale on South Uist, whose support was considered crucial because of his influence with his half-brother and nephew. Boisdale was the first to be received on board the *Dutillet*. John O'Sullivan, who was present, later recalled that Boisdale refused to join the prince himself, adding that he would do everything in his power to discourage his brother and nephew. He then stated 'there was nothing to be expected from the contry, [that] not a soul wou'd joyn wth him, & [that] their advise was [that] he shou'd go back & wait for a more favorable occassion'. To be absolutely clear, Boisdale said that he had recently seen Norman MacLeod, Chief of Clan MacLeod (of Dunvegan, Skye), and Sir Alexander MacDonald of Sleat, both of whom were unwilling to join the campaign and required Boisdale to inform the prince of their resolution. Unsurprisingly, as O'Sullivan wrote, in response to this news, 'Every body was strock as with a thunder boult . . . especially from MacCloud, who was one of those [that] said, he'd be one of the first [that] wou'd joyn the Prince, in case even he came alone.'[23] It is during this tense interview that Boisdale is said to have told the prince to return home, to which Charles replied, 'I am come home, sir, and I will entertain no notion at all of returning to that place from whence I came; for that I am persuaded my faithful Highlanders will stand by me.'[24] Ignoring this heartfelt declaration and having delivered his crushing message, Boisdale took his leave.

Charles must have been, momentarily at least, severely shaken by so negative a response to his arrival in Scotland, having been convinced of a deep devotion to his father's cause and unquestioning support in returning the Stuarts to the throne, even with so few men and arms. But despite this he remained undeterred. The same could not be said for all his companions. According to John O'Sullivan, all but Walsh and himself argued for an immediate return to France.[25] In reply to this, Sir John Macdonald states that Charles 'supported his opinion with admirable reasoning and greatness worthy of a Prince capable of great and perilous enterprises . . . and H.R.H. having decided, every one followed him'.[26] However, it was clear that the situation was nowhere near as promising as had been intimated and the prince had hoped for. In defence of these loyal Jacobite chiefs, they had made it abundantly clear that a rising should only occur with significant support of men, arms and money from France. Charles' father clearly thought so, too. But, unwilling to rely on the opinion of one man, albeit one as important as Boisdale, Charles sent a messenger to Sir Alexander MacDonald direct, requesting, if not his presence, then his support, and Aeneas MacDonald travelled to the mainland to find his brother, Donald MacDonald of Kinlochmoidart.[27] Furthermore, they could not remain at Eriskay as there was insufficient food and the Royal Navy were patrolling.

On the evening of 24 July the *Dutillet* set sail, and the following day it entered the bay of Lochnanuagh, anchoring near Borrodale in Arisaig. Captain Darbé noted, 'A fine plain with a few poor houses and a great many cattle.'[28] Charles stayed in the house of Angus MacDonald, the tacksman of Borrodale, and remained in the neighbourhood, either on land or on board ship for two weeks. Soon after the prince took up residence, Kinlochmoidart arrived and was then sent to inform Lochiel, since his father's attainder effectively Chief of Clan Cameron, the Duke of Perth, John Murray of Broughton, among others, of Charles' arrival.

While travelling to Edinburgh on this vital errand, Kinlochmoidart encountered his kinsman Hugh MacDonald, brother to the Laird of Morar and another member of the extended Clanranald family, who was travelling in the opposite direction.[29] Hugh MacDonald recalled Kinlochmoidart asked him

'What news?' 'No news at all have I,' said Mr. Hugh. 'Then,' said Kenlochmoydart, 'I'll give you news. You'll see the Prince this night at my house.' 'What Prince do you mean?' said Mr. Hugh. 'Prince Charles,' said Kenlochmoydart. 'You are certainly joking,' said Mr. Hugh, 'I cannot believe you.' Upon this Kenlochmoydart assured him of the truth of it. 'Then,' said Mr. Hugh, 'what number of men has he brought along with him?' 'Only seven,' said Kenlochmoydart. 'What stock of money and arms has he brought with him then?' said Mr. Hugh. 'A very small stock of either,' said Kenlochmoydart. 'What generals or officers fitt for commanding are with him?' said Mr. Hugh. 'None at all,' replied Kenlochmoydart. Mr. Hugh said he did not like the expedition at all, and was afraid of the consequences.

Hugh MacDonald then recalls that, in reply to his justifiable concerns, Kinlochmoidart said, almost with a wry shrug, 'I cannot help it . . . If the matter go wrong, then I'll certainly be hanged, for I am engaged already. I have no time to spare just now, as I am going with a message from the Prince to the Duke of Perth.' They then took leave of each other and parted.[30] In many ways this conversation, recalled only five years after the event, encapsulates the dilemma facing the prominent clansmen who held varying degrees of sympathy or loyalty to the House of Stuart. Surely every clansman, excepting perhaps Boisdale, had had such a discussion either with family members, close friends or even with himself. It also sets out the arguments for and against such an enterprise as dictated by the head (Hugh MacDonald) and the heart (Kinlochmoidart).

Meanwhile, Charles had sent a message summoning the young Clanranald (whose father, the chief, refused to take part but had allowed his eldest son to join), who then arrived and boarded the *Dutillet* accompanied by Alexander MacDonald of Glenaladale and Aeneas MacDonald. Young Clanranald had been educated in France and he and Charles were known to each other. As recalled by one member of the Clanranald party (now identified as the celebrated Gaelic poet Alexander MacDonald), 'our hearts were overjoyed to find ourselves so near our long wished for P[rin]ce'.[31] Alexander MacDonald then describes the scene. On the deck of the ship was 'a large tent erected with poles . . . and well furnished with variety of wines and spirits'. The party were welcomed 'most chearfully' by

Tullibardine, whom some of them had known from the '15, and, as they talked together, young Clanranald was summoned to Charles' cabin. After this conference with the prince, which lasted some three hours, young Clanranald returned to the tent or 'pavilion' on deck, upon which, 'in about half ane hour after there entered the tent a tall youth of a most agreeable aspect in a plain black coat with a plain shirt not very clean and a cambric stock fixed with a plain silver buckle, a fair round wig out of the buckle, a plain hatt with a canvas string having one end fixed to one of his coat buttons; he had black stockins and brass buckles in his shoes'. Clearly presuming this young man was Charles, Alexander MacDonald writes, 'at his first appearance I found my heart swell to my very throat'. But the prince was still incognito (although apparently now shaved) and to prevent any unguarded slip which would expose his true identity, 'we were immediatly told . . . that this youth was also ane English clergyman who had long been possess'd with a desire to see and converse with Highlanders'. To pass without question as an English clergyman, the prince must have spoken English not only extremely well, but with little or no trace of a foreign (or rather non-British/Irish) accent. Certainly throughout his young life there had been a large number of English-speaking natives of Britain and Ireland at the Stuart court.

Language and accent is one thing. How people behaved around an actual clergyman, rather than a prince dressed as one, was quite another. So to continue the ruse, when this young man entered, those who were seated were forbidden to rise, and Alexander MacDonald 'presumed to speak to him with too much familiarity yet still retained some suspicion he might be one of more note than he was said to be'. During this affable conversation, Charles interrogated Alexander on the intriguing subject of Highland garb – was it cold, restricting, how did you sleep or fight in it? – no doubt with a view to wearing it himself once he could get rid of his clerical disguise. After which, 'rising quickly from his seat he calls for a dram, when the same person whisper'd me a second time, to pledge the stranger but not to drink to him, by which seasonable hint I was confirm'd in my suspicion who he was. Having taken a glass of wine in his hand he drank to us all round, and soon after left us.'[32] After this meeting young Clanranald was sent to Skye to try once more to summon Sir Alexander MacDonald and MacLeod of MacLeod, and Glenaladale was charged with assembling Clanranald's clansmen, who would act as guard to the prince.

Yet, despite the successes, there was still a general sense of unease, and even open opposition, among the leading clansmen. MacDonald of Scotus

(on behalf of Glengarry), MacDonald of Keppoch and MacDonald of
Glencoe also visited the prince during this time and, like Boisdale, advised
him to return to France. Hugh MacDonald, who had been informed of
Charles' presence in Scotland by his chance meeting with Kinlochmoidart,
arrived at Kinlochmoidart itself, where he was told by Aeneas MacDonald
that he could meet the prince the following day, but to be aware of his disguise 'as he was known to none of the crew'. After travelling the short distance, Hugh MacDonald, in the company of Aeneas, boarded the *Dutillet*
and immediately met the prince, who was on deck. As counselled, Hugh
MacDonald greeted him as a clergyman, and then proceeded airily by 'welcoming him to Scotland [and] asking how he liked the country'. Having
realised Hugh MacDonald's family connection to Morar, Charles asked to
see him in his cabin, declared himself and then explained his plans. Hugh
MacDonald 'paid his respects to him as to a prince, and begged he would be
exceeding cautious and keep himself private, as the garrison at Inverlochie
[Fort William] was not far off, and the Campbells in the neighbourhood
thereof, who (all of them) would be too ready to take him, and give him
up to his enemies. Etc.'[33] The prince apparently responded, 'I have no fear
about that at all'. Hugh MacDonald, as so many before him, then advised
that a return to France to await a more favourable opportunity and French
troops might be an appropriate plan. To which Charles replied that 'he did
not chuse to owe the restoration of his father to foreigners, but to his own
friends, to whom he was now come to put it in their power to return'.[34]
Here the prince is clearly being disingenuous, considering the previous
assistance given by France and his expectations for further assistance in the
not too distant future.

Soon after, young Clanranald returned from Skye with another refusal
from Sir Alexander and MacLeod. As a result, according to the contemporary historian John Home, young Clanranald was understandably disheartened and even reluctant to proceed. Home states that the prince had
been 'almost reduced to despair in his interview with Boisdale', although
this was not reported by those who had been present. Home goes on to say
that to have Sir Alexander and MacLeod's rejection confirmed by young
Clanranald, and as a result to have the latter falter in his support for the
campaign, was more than Charles could bear. Whether true or not, Home's
account does offer a detailed version of one of the most famous stories
relating to the '45. He states that Clanranald's news was delivered in the
presence of Kinlochmoidart and, standing to one side, the latter's younger
brother Ranald MacDonald of Irine. Charles implored young Clanranald

and Kinlochmoidart to help him 'in his utmost need' but they refused, for, without support, it 'was to pull down certain destruction on their own heads'. Charles 'persisted, argued, and implored'. The whole time they were passing up and down the deck. Young Ranald 'gathered, from their discourse, that the stranger was the Prince of Wales: when he heard his chief and his brother refuse to take arms with their prince, his colour went and came, his eyes sparkled, he shifted his place, and grasped his sword.' Charles observed this 'and turning briskly towards him, called out, Will not you assist me? I will, I will, said Ranald, though no other man in the Highlands should draw a sword, I am ready to die for you. Charles, with a profusion of thanks and acknowledgments, extolled his champion to the skies, saying, he only wished that all the Highlanders were like him.'[35] Thus shamed by the youthful verve of Ranald, the two elder MacDonalds declared that they also would join. It is disputed whether Kinlochmoidart was actually present. Certainly his conversation with Hugh MacDonald – that he was too involved already to pull back – does not suggest any lack of commitment on his part. This story at least serves to present the older, more senior clansmen as sensible individuals, mindful of honour and allegiance, but more mindful still of the logistics of such an enterprise and its risks. The romantic recklessness springs from a younger, less experienced man, who is dismissive of the obvious dangers. Not unlike the prince himself.

Meanwhile, the British government had discovered Lochiel had been in communication with James Stuart, and had already issued a warrant to arrest him. Lochiel, like others in the Buck Club, considered the prince's presence in Scotland with no French troops as futile. And fearing he would be persuaded to join this dangerous campaign through his natural loyalty to the Stuarts, Lochiel sent his brother Archibald Cameron, a physician, to urge the prince to return to France. Charles responded, perhaps sensing Lochiel's ploy, by sending messengers to entice him 'to do his duty'. En route to his interview with the prince, Lochiel visited another brother, John Cameron of Fassifern, who apparently said, 'this Prince, once sets his eyes upon you, he will make you do whatever he pleases'.[36] The traditional telling of their encounter follows John's fears: that is that Lochiel's defences collapsed on seeing the Stuart prince. The reality was probably a little less romantic. Lochiel attempted to persuade Charles to return, and finding him resolute – no comment is required regarding Charles' resilience against any opposition – said he would raise his clan, but on two conditions. Firstly, 'that the prince give security for the full value of his estate should the attempt prove abortive', and, secondly, on John MacDonell of Glengarry's undertaking – in writing – to raise his clan. Charles agreed to the first, and Glengarry's clan was raised under the command of his second son, Angus, and his kinsman Donald MacDonell of Lochgarry.[37] Of course, at this vital moment, Charles would agree to anything as long as they joined him. In his *Memoir*, Lochiel simply states 'after making fruitless attempts to persuade H.R.H. to go back to where he came from, Lochiel was in the end alarmed at the dangerous position in which His Royal Person was placed' and therefore brought out his clan.[38]

After this, with the crucial support of Lochiel and his Camerons, arrangements were made for the raising of the Stuart standard at Glenfinnan, on Loch Shiel's most northern and inland edge, on Monday, 19 August. To confirm there was no going back, the baggage, stores and armaments were removed from the *Dutillet* on 4 August, and then Walsh and the ship left Lochnanuagh – returning only to deliver the welcome spoils from some local privateering. On 7 August, Captain Darbé and Antoine Walsh went ashore to wish Charles success and then left him 'with two of the gentlemen who had crossed over with him, and not more than twelve men for company'.[39] Walsh was given a note by Charles thanking him once more for his loyalty and assistance, and stating, 'if ever I reach the throne, to which my birth calls me, you will have occasion to be as pleased with me as I am with you'.[40] By this time, as he no longer required a disguise, Charles changed his dress into a form of Highland garb.

Just prior to the *Dutillet* leaving, the prince wrote a letter to his father, to be delivered to him through Antoine Walsh. In it Charles writes, 'I am thank God arrived here in perfect good health but not with little trouble and dangir, as you will hear by the Bearer who has been along with me all along.' He continues,

I am joyned here by Brave people as I expected, as I have not yet set up the Standard I cannot tell ye number, but that will be in a few days as soon as ye armes are distributed at which wee are working with all speed. I have not as yet got the return of ye Message sent to ye low Lands [to John Murray, Perth and others] but expect it very soon [. . .] The worst that can happen to me iff France do[e]s not succo[u]r me, is to dye at the head of such Brave people as I finde here, iff I shoud not be able to make my way, and that I have promised to them, as you [k]no[w] to have been my resolution before parting The French Courte must now necessary[i]ly take of[f] the maske or have an Eternall sheme [shame] on them, for at present there is no mediom [i.e. no middle way], and wee what ever happens will gain an immortall honour by doing what wee Can to deliver our Country, in restoring our Master, or perish with S[w]ord in hand.

The remainder of the letter challenges the idea that Charles cared very little for the opinion of his father regarding this adventure: 'Your Majesty may esely conseive the aneyety [anxiety] I am in to here [hear] from you.'[41] It is a timely reminder that, for all his confidence and spirit, Charles is still a twenty-four-year-old who had barely left his father's sight since the day he was born, and was perhaps feeling a little lonely and not a little daunted; something he dared not reveal to his companions, but could at least hint at in a private letter to his father.

John Faber the Younger after Allan Ramsay,
John Campbell, 4th Earl of Loudoun, 1755.

9

Culloden House

'this mad Rebellious attempt'

If the Lord President's resolve for an early journey to his house in the Highlands was driven by mere caution on 2 August, it was an absolute necessity a week later. On 6 August copies of a letter written by the Duke of Argyll's steward to the Deputy Sheriff of Argyllshire (dated the 5th) were forwarded by the latter to the Duke of Argyll and Andrew Fletcher, Lord Justice Clerk. It stated that a vessel had arrived at Arisaig carrying 'the Pretender's Eldest son, General Kieth [sic], and old Lochiel' and that part of Clan MacDonald was already in arms. The author thought the source unreliable, but 'it is Fact that something uncommon was expected'. The Deputy Sheriff had added in his covering letter that if men had indeed landed, it was likely that they would spread the rumour that General Keith, the Earl Marischal, was with them, 'as He is a man of character, and a person that Party has for some time considered as their Hero, & firm friend, which may encourage People to join them'.[1] The Earl Marischal was, of course, still in France. The Duke of Argyll forwarded the various letters to the Duke of Newcastle, with the comment that he had been warning that such an attempt was likely, and 'if others had given the same attention to the advice I so often humbly offered, as your Grace did, I should not now have been reduced to the necessity of writing so disagreeable a letter'. He observes that, if true, the landing place was well chosen for such an expedition, and that he must now leave Argyllshire for Edinburgh, for, if he remained, 'I shall do little less than surrender myself prisoner.'[2]

At the same time the Lord Justice Clerk alerted Sir John Cope of the likely landing of Prince Charles in Scotland. This was then corroborated on 9 August, when the following letter arrived at the Lord President's Edinburgh abode. The letter begins: 'To my no small surprise, it is certain that the Pretended Prince of Wales is come on the Coast of South Uist and Barra, and has since been hovering on parts of the Coast of the main Land

that lies betwixt the point of Airdnamurchan and Glenelg.' The author
continues: 'he has but one ship, of which he is aboard; she mounts about
16 or 18 Guns. He has about thirty Irish or French officers with him, and
one Sheridan, who is called his Governor. The Duke of Athol's brother
is the only man of any sort of note (that once belonged to this Country)
that I can hear of that's alongst with him.' The author observes, 'His view,
I need not tell you, was, to raise all the Highlands to assist him, &c.'[3] The
author was Norman MacLeod of MacLeod, one of the clan chiefs of Skye,
and the very man whom Charles had been attempting to recruit. The letter
was actually dated 3 August, but had taken much longer than was usual to
arrive in the Lord President's hands. MacLeod continues,

> Sir Alex. Macdonald and I, not only gave no sort of Countenance to these
> people, but we used all the interest we had with our Neighbours to follow
> the same prudent method; and I am persuaded we have done it with that
> success, that not one man of any consequence benorth the Grampians will
> give any sort of assistance to this mad rebellious attempt. How far you think
> we acted properly, I shall long to know; but this is certain, we did it as our
> duty and for the best; for in the present situation of Affairs in Europe, I
> should have been sorry to see any thing like disaffection to the Government
> appear, tho' ever so trivial; or that there was occasion to march a single
> Company to quell it, which now I hope and dare say there is not.[4]

Sir Alexander was the other Skye clan chief whom Charles had been
desperate to contact. MacLeod makes it clear that the war in Flanders, as
well as domestic concerns, had persuaded him to oppose the activities of
the young Stuart. In the postscript MacLeod writes, 'Young Clanranold
has been here with us, and has given us all possible assurances of his prudence, &c.' Perhaps unbeknown to the Lord President, both MacLeod of
MacLeod and Sir Alexander MacDonald of Sleat are named by Lord Elcho
as not only members of John Murray's Buck Club but as having both
pledged the previous winter to support Prince Charles, 'in any event'.[5] But
for now, they seemed determined to remain aloof, and even join the Lord
President in dissuading their neighbours from rising. Despite their efforts,
young Clanranald had since joined the prince.

After calling on Sir John Cope, Lord President Forbes crossed from
Leith to Kinghorn and Falkland, where he chanced to meet Lord Elcho,
himself en route to his family seat at Wemyss Castle 'to be within better
reach of news'. Lord Elcho later recalled that during their encounter the

Lord President informed him of Charles' arrival and that he 'was very sorry nevertheless, because the Prince (in his opinion) would merely kindle a fire of straw, which would be quickly put out by the energy of General Cope, and would end in the ruin of many very honourable gentlemen, whose prospective fate he deplored'. He 'referred sadly' among others 'to the Duke of Perth and Mr. Cameron of Lochiel'. He concluded by telling Lord Elcho that General Cope was even now preparing to march to the north with 2,500 infantry. Lord Elcho had already received word from Duncan Buchanan, who had carried a letter from John Murray of Broughton, informing him that Charles was at Lochaber. Lord Elcho had then met up with Murray before the latter had set out to join the prince. But as it was clear that Charles had arrived without the troops and support that the Buck Club members and Associators had originally asked for, Lord Elcho had decided to bide his time, to 'watch the progress of events and not to join the Prince till he was near Edinburgh'.[6]

Presumably with no knowledge of any of this, Lord President Forbes continued on his journey, spending the night at Blair Castle, the seat of James, Duke of Atholl (the younger brother of Tullibardine), and arrived at Culloden House on 13 August. Awaiting him was a letter dated two days earlier from Sir Alexander MacDonald, who writes, 'you'll have heard, before this reaches you, that some of our neighbours of the main land have been mad enough to arm and join the Young Adventurer . . . Your Lordship will find our Conduct with regard to this unhappy scrape such as you'd wish, and such as the friendship you have always shewed us will prompt to direct.' Indeed, the bond of kinship, friendship and deep admiration for the Lord President was a formidable barrier to many clan chiefs joining the prince, and therefore in turn the success of Charles' campaign. Sir Alexander continues, 'Young Clanranold is deluded, notwithstanding his assurances to us lately; and, what is more astonishing, Lochiel's prudence has quite forsaken him. You know too much of Glengarry not to know that he'll easily be led to be of the Party; but as far as I can learn, he has not yet been with them.' Lochiel was indeed a personal blow. There is an equal mix of concern and exasperation in Sir Alexander's letter. Between him, MacLeod and Forbes there is a sense, almost an inevitability, that the rising will fail, and therefore incredulity that their neighbours would risk everything – again. There is also a corresponding apprehension as to what to do next. That 'we will have no connection with these madmen is certain', yet MacLeod and Sir Alexander were 'bewildered in every other respect till we hear from you'. The lack of arms to defend themselves was a particular worry.[7]

The Lord President immediately set about writing to the chiefs, advising them what to do. Through Alexander Brodie of Brodie, the Lord Lyon King of Arms, he heard of Cosmo George Gordon, Duke of Gordon's 'great desire of knowing what truth was in the various reports that were flying about, to the end he might take the proper measures for showing his zeal for the Government'.[8] In response the Lord President informed his Grace that,

> as it is made in the King's absence, probably with intent to divert the atten-
> tion of the Government from the affairs on the Continent, & thereby to
> make some diversion in favours of the ambitious views of France, it would,
> in my apprehension, be of great service to the publick, & could not fail of
> being exceedingly well taken at present, if men of fortune & figure were to
> show their dislike to this attack (I may say) upon the libertys of Europe, as
> well as the libertys of this country, by putting themselves & their follow-
> ers in such a posture as should leave no hopes of success to those rash
> adventurers.[9]

To Sir John Cope, the Lord President writes, 'That Lochiell should play the madman in this manner surprises me; & I have still some faint hopes it is not true, tho' I have been by some well-wishers of his informed that he has absconded for some time, upon hearing that a warrant was out against him. I wish no such warrant had ever been granted.'[10] In the same letter the Lord President confirms that Simon Fraser, Lord Lovat (known as the Old Fox), Forbes' near neighbour, had recently dined with him. Despite the fact that he was somewhat disgruntled with the government, Lord Lovat 'said, he had heard with uneasiness the reports that were scattered abroad; but that he look'd on the attempt as very desperate', although nei-ther sentiment would lead him to be presumed a supporter of the British government. However, the Lord President believed 'his wishes still being, as well as his interest led him, to support the present Royal Family'. Lovat had apparently ventured to Culloden House to ascertain from the Lord President 'what was proper to be done on this occasion'. It is clear from such comments that Lord President Forbes was undeniably seen as one of the leaders of the pro-government faction in Scotland at this time, if not the pre-eminent one. His advice and good opinion was being sought by many individuals. But in the face of a rising all about them, and with so lit-tle leadership evident from London, it was to Forbes that they all turned.

The Lord President states in his letter to Sir John Cope that until they had a greater sense of how the rising might progress or not, his advice to

Lovat was to gather as much intelligence as he could while preventing 'his kinsmen from being seduced by their mad neighbours'. So Lovat was to gain intelligence for Forbes and keep his clan out of the rising, 'which he readily promised to do'. The Lord President may or may not have believed Lovat, known to be slippery – in Forbes' own words, a master of 'shilly-shally'[11] – of changeable loyalties and ultimately self-serving, but it was important to encourage Lovat to hold off joining the rising for as long as possible, if, that is, the Old Fox was simply biding his time before declaring for Prince Charles. Lovat was after all a signatory of the Association. That there was a genuine affection, despite this, between Lovat and Forbes is undeniable.[12] The Lord President concludes his letter by observing to Cope that as 'the Highlanders who have joined the Adventurer from France are beginning to use threats to compel their neighbours to join them, it will naturally occur to you that the immediate presence of the troops is necessary'.

News of a likely event at Glenfinnan was circulating by 17 August. Meanwhile, Forbes had received a response from Lord Tweeddale, then at Whitehall, acknowledging that the Lord President's early move northwards was 'extremely necessary and useful' all things considered, although 'I own, I have never been alarmed with the Reports of the Pretender's Son's landing in Scotland. I consider it as a rash and desperate attempt, that can have no other consequence than the ruin of those concerned in it.'[13] He goes on, 'I am sensible of the want of a legal authority in the Highlands to call forth the King's friends to action, in case there should be occasion for them; but your Lordship will remember the difficulties that occurred about naming Lord Lieutenants of certain Counties at the Time of the last Invasion, which were the reasons that prevented any Nominations being made at that Time.' Not, one might think, a wholly satisfactory response. He then says that arms had already been ordered to Inverness (Fort George) and a credit had been sent to Sir John Cope. Regarding money for the Lord President to buy 'Intelligence, and other Services to the Government, Mr Pelham assured me, that whatever Sums you advanced he would certainly repay'.[14] In the meantime, the indefatigable Lord President had confirmed the support of the leading lords Sutherland and Mackay, the Grants of Grant, Kenneth Mackenzie, Lord Fortrose, the Clan of Monro, and had begun recruiting for the Highland regiment under the command of General John Campbell, 4th Earl of Loudoun. It was a good start. But the Lord President may well have asked himself, was it good enough to nip this rebellion in the bud?

Artist unknown, *Prince Charles Edward Stuart.*

Glenfinnan

'the sword once drawn in ye Hand'

After the *Dutillet* departed, Charles took up residence in Borrodale. While he was here, Alexander MacDonald recalled that he and his people gave the prince as hearty a welcome as they could muster. On one occasion Charles was seated at the head of a table surrounded by locals of all ages and status, with everyone crowding in to get a glimpse of this exotic, to some sacred, figure. After the meal the prince said grace in English, a language some of the gathering understood, but Alexander 'presumed to distinguish myself by saying audibly in Erse (or highland language) *Deochs laint-an Reogh*'. Charles realised that he had drunk 'the King's health', and asked him to repeat the phrase so that he could memorise it. This pleased the company. As Alexander MacDonald was fluent in the language of the Highlands, 'H.R.H. said I should be his master for that language, and so was made to ask the healths of P[rince]. and D[uke of York]'.[1]

While here, Charles continued to send messages to known supporters, including George Mackenzie, 3rd Earl of Cromartie. The prince also set about drilling his new personal guard, twenty men from the Clanranald MacDonalds. John O'Sullivan recalled his amazement at the level of secrecy they had managed to maintain over several weeks and under the very noses of the British army and government. Fort William, one of the main garrisons in the Highlands, was less than a day's ride away.[2] The credit for this must go to the local people. On Saturday, 10 August, the same day that the Liverpool brig, the *Ann*, dropped anchor near Canna, Charles and his entourage travelled the short distance to Kinlochmoidart. Four days later Charles sends from 'Kinloch' more standard letters, informing the known loyal clan chiefs and lairds of the imminent raising of the standard at Glenfinnan. He appreciated that this was short notice, 'but I hope you will not fail to join me as soon as possible: you need not doubt of my being always ready to acknowledge so important a service, and giving you proofs of my sincere friendship'.³ On 18 August, John Murray of Broughton arrived at Kinlochmoidart, becoming the prince's principal private secretary, and, soon after, Charles set off for Glenfinnan. By this stage he had heard of the £30,000 bounty on his head.

The prince and his entourage were rowed up Loch Shiel and lodged at Glenaladale. Here Charles was joined by John Gordon, Laird of Glenbucket in Aberdeenshire, and one Captain John Sweetenham of the British army's 6th Regiment of Foot, who, on the 16th, had left Fort Augustus with a small guard to gain intelligence of the rumoured rising, entered an inn and was immediately surrounded by eight 'rebels', as he later reported, 'and conveyed a prisoner to the Young Pretender's camp'.⁴ The captain and his men would soon be in the extraordinary position of witnessing the raising of the Stuart standard and the official beginning of the rebellion.

On the morning of 19 August, Charles and his companions continued to the northern point of Loch Shiel, first landing at the head of the loch at one o'clock in the afternoon. The route was practical, as this long stretch of water allowed the party to penetrate a great distance inland. For drama and beauty, however, a better spot could not have been chosen for so auspicious an event. The imposing mountains rising up on three sides of the loch dwarfed the men as they clambered on to the shore. But the scale of the mountains, accompanied by an eerie silence, simply emphasised the fact that no one else was there. It was now a matter of waiting to see if anyone would arrive. Charles settled himself in a small house or 'little barn'⁵ at the loch head and took some refreshment while he waited. At this time, he was accompanied by 300 of Clanranald's men. About two hours later, first came the distant sound of pipes and then, gradually, several hundred Camerons under Lochiel and 350 MacDonalds under Alexander MacDonald of Keppoch could be seen descending the mountains in a zigzag path. Watching them advance towards the loch, John O'Sullivan recalled they 'made a very good appearance & began to raise every body's spirits'.⁶ Some, he noted, were 'clivor fellows' but many were badly armed. Sir John Macdonald declared, 'Never have I seen anything so quaintly pleasing as the march of this troop of Highlanders.'⁷ The immediate response was surely profound relief. Charles ordered the standard to be carried to the place chosen for the ceremony – probably on the raised ground behind the church – and there the silk standard, a simple white square on a red background, was unfurled by the Marquess of Tullibardine.⁸ John Home adds the detail that 'when displayed [it] was about twice the size of an ordinary pair of colours'.[9] With the standard aloft and the clansmen gathered around it, as well as a large number of onlookers (both ladies and gentlemen), James Stuart was proclaimed king, his manifesto and declarations were read out, and the assembly cheered.[10] Charles declaimed that he had come to this region knowing that the brave men here would follow the 'noble example of their predecessors', and being 'jealous of their own and their Country's honour' would 'join with him in this glorious enterprise'. With their help, and 'the protection of a just God' he 'did not doubt of bringing the affair to a happy issue'.[11] The Prince then ordered that brandy should be distributed to the men to drink the King's health. Perhaps here, as a popular gesture, Charles demonstrated his recent grasp of Gaelic.[12] This was undoubtedly an extraordinary and emotional occasion, although the unfortunate Captain Sweetenham and his men must have been suffering from extreme emotions of a very different nature. But, despite all the discouragements, Charles and Charles alone had driven the enterprise forward to this modest but promising phase. The charisma that John Murray had described, coupled with his unswerving focus on what he knew to be his destiny, had persuaded the likes of Lochiel – against their better judgement, despite their deeply held loyalty – to risk everything once more for the Stuart cause. And as a result, the euphoria must have been tinged with uncertainty as to what would happen next, and how this rising would end. But one thing was certain: there was no going back.

After the ceremonials, the focus became the business of building a force good enough to beat one of the best-trained armies in the world. The gathering of around one thousand clansmen was certainly a promising start, and some were fit, fighting men, or, as O'Sullivan described them, 'clivor'. But, as O'Sullivan also observed, many were undisciplined (that is untrained) and unarmed.[13] They were also formed into groups of varying sizes according to their clans, rather than organised as a regular army would be, with companies of equal numbers of men and officers. The prince remained in Glenfinnan to distribute arms and ammunition, to give time for the expected clansmen to join and to begin forming up and training the Highlanders, which, according to O'Sullivan, was desperately needed, 'for all was confused'.[14] Sir John Macdonald also commented on the need for a second in command to the prince, in order to 'see to the details of guards, marches etc. and to avoid confusion', and states that, after a few days, the role of Adjutant General was given to John O'Sullivan.[15] On the face of it, it was a sensible choice, as O'Sullivan was one of the few within the Jacobite ranks who had any experience of the organisation of a

regular army. Yet it should be noted that the overall impression of 'confusion' among the Highland troops is a judgement based on this particular
experience. For at this juncture O'Sullivan and John Macdonald (both
Irish) had little knowledge and no understanding of Highland society or
military culture. As if to illustrate this, O'Sullivan immediately proposed
that the army form into companies of fifty men each, commanded by a
captain supported by one lieutenant and four sergeants. But, sadly, this
'cou'd not be followed, they must go by tribes ; such a chife of a tribe had
sixty men, another thirty, another twenty, more or lesse ; they wou'd not
mix nor seperat, & wou'd have double officers, [that] is two Captns, & two
Lts, to each Company, strong or weak. That', O'Sullivan pithily observed,
'was uselesse.' This irregular, clan-focused arrangement was both a strength
and a weakness of this embryonic army. Many of these clansmen had been
called out, not because they necessarily believed in the Stuart cause and
were willing to abandon their homes and families to fight for it (although
some clearly did), but because their chief had claimed his ancient right to
do so. As the Lord President had stated, some had been bullied and threatened with violence against their homes, their livelihoods and loved ones.
However although 'They wou'd follow their own way' eventually, little by
little, O'Sullivan observed that the clansmen 'were brought into a certain
regulation'.[16]

Despite the challenges in arming and training the clansmen, the Jacobite
cause was gaining in heart and strength. In contrast there was growing anxiety among the supporters of the government and House of Hanover. The
very day of the raising of the standard, Ewen MacPherson of Cluny, technically a Jacobite but at this moment somewhat ambivalent, was writing to
Lord President Forbes fearing that the growing army at Glenfinnan would
inevitably proceed south through his country, 'and if the Government does
not forthwith protect us, they must either be burnt or join'. At the same
time, he had heard that Sir John Cope was at Stirling, which was no use
to his people, being too far east, 'and what to do, so as to save this poor
country from immediate ruin, is a very great question to me'.[17] If the government acted swiftly to such pleas for help, then another clan would be
kept out of the rebellion. For the time being, Cluny accepted a commission in Lord Loudoun's Highland regiment.

Meanwhile, Lord Lovat, writing to the Lord Advocate Robert Craigie,
begins by stating that nothing 'can alter or diminish my Zeal and
Attachment for his Majesty's Person and Government. I am as ready this
day (as far as I am able) to serve the King and Government as I was in the

Year 1715.' And yet, 'my Clan and I have been so neglected these many
Years past, that I have not twelve stand of arms in my Country, tho' I thank
God I could bring twelve hundred good Men to the field for the King's
Service, if I had arms and other Accoutrements for them.' Lovat also con-
firms that Charles, 'that Mad and unaccountable Gentleman has set up a
standard at a place called Glenfinnon Monday last'.[18]

Less than a week after the Stuart standard was raised, a council of war
was called at Glenfinnan and, soon after, the small Jacobite army began its
march south-east towards the Scottish capital.

Paul Sandby, *Horse Fair on Bruntsfield Links, Edinburgh,* 1750.

Auld Reekie

'Royal City'

Daniel Defoe described Scotland's capital as 'a large, populous, noble, rich, and even Royal City'.[1] The ancient heart of modern Edinburgh, the 'Old Town', is built on a long, narrow crag that lies on a roughly west–east axis. In 1745 the city extended not much further than this imposing geological feature. In fact it had changed surprisingly little over the previous one hundred years, with a majority of the development occurring to the south. Perched on the westerly tip is the Castle. The road called the West-bow curls down from Castle Hill Street to the open 'square' called the Grassmarket to the south, and at its western edge is the West port, one of six gates within the city's old wall – the latter now in a patchy state of repair and, according to one contemporary, fit only for policing local smugglers.[2] To the south and within the southern section of the wall lies George Heriot's Hospital, built in the seventeenth century, with its elegant inner court, cloister and formal parterre gardens. To the east, set against the wall, can be seen the adjoining quadrangles of King James' College. Further on is the Royal Infirmary and finally Surgeons Hall, where the wall turns due north parallel to the Pleasance (which leads to St Mary Wynd) and continues through the city, defining its eastern border and separating it from Canongate. This large suburb spreads out eastwards, with the Royal Abbey and Palace of Holyroodhouse at its furthest edge.

This mid-eighteenth-century city is bordered to the north by a marsh, the Nor' Loch and Lang Dykes and Carltoun Craigs to the north-east. To the south-east, just beyond the Abbey and Palace, sit two further volcanic outcrops, Salisbury Crags and Arthur's Seat, and nestling on the far side of the latter is the village and loch of Duddingston. Domestic and agricultural buildings dot the landscape around the city, and from the Castle's lofty vantage point the village of Corstorphine and the hump-backed Colt Bridge, lying four miles due west and two miles north-west respectively, and the hamlet of Slateford, two miles to the south-west, are visible. The port of Leith lies a mere two and a half miles to the north-east on the shore of the Firth of Forth and at the mouth of the Water of Leith.

From above, the city has the appearance of a large, half-consumed 'fish-bone'. The Castle, the fish's head, sits on the highest point of the crag and is surrounded on three sides by a sheer drop, described by Defoe as 'a frightfull and impassable Precipice'.[3] As this comment suggests, the Castle is considered almost impregnable. The obvious weakness is the eastern wall, which overlooks a narrow thoroughfare leading to the city itself. This thoroughfare, Castle Hill Walk, begins the gradual downward slope – along the fish's spine – via Castle Hill Street and the Landmarket (now Lawnmarket) directly through the city, passing the Church of St Giles, Parliament Close, the ancient 'mercat' or 'market'-cross and the Tron Kirk, to Netherbow Port, the main port or gate within the east wall. This imposing port, with its tall central clock tower, straddles the road, and is the main access point between the city proper and its Canongate suburb. Progressing on, through the gate, the road continues in a direct line, passing the house of sixteenth-century firebrand John Knox (founder of the Presbyterian Kirk), and further on to the Canongate Kirk, built by order of James VII in 1688. Finally, it arrives at the old porch of the Palace of Holyroodhouse: the fish's tail.

This 'long continuous street' measuring an old Scots mile (longer than its English equivalent) is justly acknowledged by Defoe and countless other observers to be 'the most spacious and best inhabited in *Europe*'.[4] As well as the buildings fronting the entire length of the main thoroughfare, there are emanating due north and south from this 'spine', like the ribs of the fish, the wynds or allies, lining which are narrow, multi-storey apartment build-ings. The English military engineer Captain Burt described these buildings as of 'Eight, Ten, even Twelve Stories' and that every storey 'have each a particular Family, and perhaps a separate Proprietor'.[5] As a warning to the traveller, Defoe observes that walking to and from and even around the city was not for the faint-hearted, for 'which way soever you turn, you go down Hill immediately; which is so steep, that it is very troublesome to those who have not very good Lungs'.[6]

As a suburb located on the lower lying land and unconfined by the city wall, Canongate has a different appearance and character to the remainder of the city. Here the houses are less crowded together, many being inde-pendent residences rather than apartment blocks, and very few rise above four or five main storeys. Defoe remarks that it is further distinguished by 'several very magnificent Houses of the Nobility, built for their Residence when the Court was here'.[7] The ancient royal land entailed the palace, abbey and the 'King's Park' that surrounded them.

Besides the looming presence of the Castle, since Charles II a garrisoned fortress, the defence of the city proper would have depended largely on the strength of the wall which surrounded it on three sides and which varied in height from ten to twenty feet. To the recent divinity graduate and later historian John Home, it was 'no better than a garden wall, or park wall of unusual height'.[8] Even so, Canongate, in comparison, was very exposed. Beyond this, the crucial factor was the number of regular soldiers currently stationed within the city, the Trained Bands, Town and City Guards (under the command of Edinburgh's civic head, the Lord Provost), combined with what support could be raised either from outside, through the timely arrival of regiments of local militia and – preferably – the British army, and, from within, the mobilisation of the citizens themselves into volunteer companies.

The city had had warning, some weeks before, that trouble was brewing to the north-west. The Lord Provost Archibald Stewart received a letter from the Marquess of Tweeddale, dated Whitehall, 13 August, stating that 'the Lords Justices, having received intelligence that the Pretender's son is already landed, or intending to land in Scotland, have recommended it to me to give you notice thereof; that you may exert your care and vigilance on this occasion'. The Lord Provost and city council – much like the rest of Great Britain – were not unduly alarmed by this news. In his response, dated four days later, the Lord Provost declared that 'this town was never better affected, nor more peaceable [than] at present'. He also assured the marquess, that 'Nothing shall be neglected on my part, to preserve the people in their duty towards their king and their country; and we trust in God that no threatened danger shall ever reach us.' At the same time we 'will keep a watchful eye, in order to prevent, as far as it is in our power, everything that may disturb the peace of this place'.[9] Four weeks later, however, they had ample cause for alarm.

During the last week of August Edinburgh had received little news of the whereabouts of either the Jacobite army or Sir John Cope and his 2,500 troops. It was presumed that Cope was in the process of arresting the former's advance. Any news that arrived in the city, whether first hand via expresses and letters, or second hand through the London press, was immediately published in the Edinburgh newspapers, and then read in homes, taverns and coffee houses the length and breadth of the city. On 20 August the *Caledonian Mercury* published the full proclamation by the Lords Justices (dated Whitehall, 1 August), offering a reward of £30,000 'to any Person who shall seize and secure the Eldest Son of the Pretender, in case He shall land, or attempt to land, in any of His Majesty's Dominions'.[10] Two days later the newspaper printed letters from Inverness 'with Accounts of what has been lately transacted in the West Highlands'. One letter, dated the 16th, confirmed that the Camerons and MacDonalds were in arms, 'but thank God there is no Foreign Forces or Councils among 'em; so that any Commotion these mad Men occasion, must very soon be quashed'. The letter also reported that Sir Alexander MacDonald had dined the previous Monday with the Lord President and the Laird of MacLeod, and that Sir Alexander 'has given all Assurances, That neither he nor any of his People shall aid or abet the Invaders of our Country. On the contrary.' This edition included the following line concerning events at Glenfinnan, that 'they have erected a Standard, the Motto, *Tandem Triumphans* [at last triumphant]'.[11] There was also welcome news of local activity from the Royal Navy, that HMS *Fox* and *Happy Jennet* were steering north to join two other warships 'to act in concert against the Insurgents in the North-west'.

On 27 August, the *Caledonian Mercury* published on its front page letters from The Hague which stated, 'There is nothing so much talked of here as the Expedition of the Son of the Pretender. This is the Subject of all Conversations.' It is then recounted that the French minister at The Hague, the Abbé de la Ville, had produced letters from France and England proving that there was considerable support for 'the young Pretender' in Ireland and Scotland and 'that there are likewise in England and even in the City of London, such Numbers, were they known, of Malcontents, who only wait for a favourable Opportunity of rising'. In response, the British ambassador at The Hague, Robert Trevor, reportedly described such assertions as false and 'chimerical', and yet another ploy by the French court to divert the British government's attention from French and Spanish activities in the American colonies. Here was a hint to the people of Edinburgh that their current situation was not simply the result of local or domestic interests.

Closer to home, the newspaper announced that the city magistrates had ordered the searching of all printing houses, as well as the homes of publishers and printers, for various papers entitled 'a *Declaration*, an *Act of Regency*, a *Manifesto, &c*', which had allegedly been sent to Edinburgh from the north.[12] Two days later, the readership learned of the recent arrival in town of Captain John Sweetenham, who was on parole courtesy of 'the young Chevalier'. And the paper also announced the imminent arrival, not before time, of King George in London. If the delay hinted that the situation had been, initially at least, of little concern to His Majesty, his early return from Hanover declared how serious it had now become.

However, on 31 August (the day the king actually arrived) intelligence was received that Sir John Cope had not engaged with the Jacobite army, nor was he on his way south to Edinburgh. Rather, he was heading north to Inverness, while the Stuart prince and his Highlanders were advancing south, and at speed. On 3 September the *Caledonian Mercury* reported, rather airily considering, that the previous Saturday (i.e. 31 August) an advance guard of Highlanders had arrived at Blair Castle, the seat of the Dukes of Atholl, 'where the young Chevalier dined with several Gentleman in Lowland Dress; at least it is informed, that a very agreeable and handsome Youth dined there, and so called, that Day. They expected another Body of their People that Night or Sunday.' The proprietors of the newspaper certainly appeared to be very well informed, and their true allegiance, disguised up to this point, was becoming more and more apparent as the 'agreeable' youth and his troops drew nearer and nearer. That the prince had reached Blair Castle was confirmed by the sudden arrival in Edinburgh of the Duke of Atholl himself, Tullibardine's younger brother James Murray, on 1 September. The report goes on to say, 'We have nothing certain from General Cope, only 'tis firmly believed he got safe in to Inverness last Saturday.' This would have been no comfort to those in town who feared the presence of an occupying army, particularly the Highland contingent, in their midst. Meanwhile, the textile merchants Gardiner and Taylor on the Landmarket, apparently catching the mood of its Lowland Jacobite clientele, were advertising a 'great Choice of TARTANS, the newest patterns'.[13]

Five days later, the newspaper announced, 'An express has brought Advice, That 400 Highlanders took Possession of the Town of Perth last Tuesday Night' and that 'Bodies of them are coming down into Fife, and that they have sent Letters to several persons requiring them to attend their Standart; so that several People are retiring hither with their Effects, while others are said to have joined the Highlanders.' Perth was just sixty miles away, and this information was now three days old. The Edinburgh citizens could only assume that the main body of the Jacobite army had since arrived at Perth and potentially already moved on: but to where? The newspaper helpfully reported that they had all left Blair Atholl, 'but whither is not positively said; some pretending to the South, other to the North, &c'. To which news was added a letter from a citizen of Glasgow (lying to the west of Edinburgh) imploring the recipient to 'Write me all your News; all ours is Fears of the Highlanders crossing the Upper-Forth, and coming up to us. We are naked and defenceless, and have not yet resolved to arm, in Defiance of the Laws.'[14] Another indication that the terms of the various disarming acts were coming back to bite the British government.

On 9 September, the newspaper continued reporting the triumphant advance of the Jacobite army by confirming 'the Chevalier' was proclaimed king and his son regent at the cross at Perth the previous Wednesday, and that 'the young Chevalier entered Perth two Hours after the Ceremony; and that he was seen next Morning in Highland Dress'. It was also reported that Cope and his army were now heading for Aberdeen (one hundred miles to the east of Inverness) and were expected there the previous Saturday. Once at Aberdeen, Cope and his men would embark for Dunbar to the south, on transports sent from Leith, in order to head off the Jacobite army before it could take Edinburgh. But given the scale of the journey Cope and his men were now attempting, and the proximity to Edinburgh of the Jacobite troops, it was generally thought that the 'Highlanders', like Hannibal, would be at the gates before Cope had even landed.

At the beginning of September, and despite the urgency of the situation (as relayed via the local press), little had been done to prepare the city for a likely visit from Charles and his men, and on the 2nd of that month a group of twenty gentlemen 'of known good affection to his Majesty and the Government' gathered at the popular Luckie Clarke's tavern in Writer's Close to consider the matter. Among this group was the renowned chair of mathematics at the College (later University of Edinburgh), Colin Maclaurin. Maclaurin recalls, 'It was complained of in this meeting that the application which had been made a week before to his Lordship [the Lord Provost] had not met with due encouragement but that the persons who waited on his Lordship and their zeal had been ridiculed and made the subject of insipid jokes.'[15] As Maclaurin's entry suggests, there were mutterings among those loyal to King George and the present Government that Lord Provost Stewart was either not taking the situation seriously enough or, worse, had ulterior motives for not arranging the necessary improvements to the city's defences. Eventually, after several petitions and the submission of a plan of emergency works, Maclaurin was put in charge of the fortification of the wall, which commenced, slowly in his opinion, on 8 September. Three days later some ships' cannon arrived to be sited at strategic points along the wall and work continued. But on 13 September all activity, inexplicably given the circumstances, ground to a halt because of some local elections.

While the work proceeded on the wall, albeit at a snail's pace, hundreds of Maclaurin's like-minded citizens had begun volunteering to form independent companies to act as support to the Town Guard and the Castle garrison. The Castle itself was under the command of the doughty octogenarian Lieutenant-General Joshua Guest, a Yorkshireman who had been stationed in Scotland during the '15. With him was the former Deputy-Governor and fellow octogenarian General George Preston, a member of the Scots gentry who had accompanied William of Orange to England in 1688 and had commanded Edinburgh Castle during the '15. Both had seen action under the Duke of Marlborough at the beginning of the century. Now in their dotage, Preston reportedly in a wheeled chair, it had been a fair assumption that the posting to Edinburgh would result in a gentle, uneventful retirement. But in the eighteenth century British army officers never really retired.

Despite the evident disadvantages, many inhabitants like Colin Maclaurin believed that the city could, and should, hold out against the Jacobite army, to provoke Prince Charles into an attempt to besiege the city and starve them out. A siege would be problematic for the Jacobite army due to their lack of heavy artillery and cannon. More to the point, the longer the city held out, the longer Sir John Cope had to bring his troops back south to defend them. Certainly the Grassmarket saddler and ironmonger Patrick Crichton of Woodhouselee, who was also a fervent Whig and Presbyterian, was confident that the city would be defended. As he noted in his journal, at this time 'Edinburgh had a good dale of zeale and spirit'. In addition to the 800 volunteers, all armed from the Castle, a full Town Guard and permission from the king to raise a further 1,000 men, Crichton recorded that 'the walls were put in better order', barricades of turf were constructed at the gates of the city and cannon planted along the wall. All this, plus two regiments of dragoons who were heading towards Edinburgh, 'might have resisted and probable defeat fowr thowsand or a few more ill armed ill accowtered fatigued Highlanders'.[16] Sir John Cope was expected daily, and, in the meantime, the city's hopes rested, as Crichton observed, on the promise of these two dragoon regiments.

However, these mounted infantry regiments numbered only a few hundred men. One was under the command of Colonel James Gardiner, born at Carriden near Linlithgow and now owner of nearby Bankton House, close to the village of Prestonpans. Gardiner had joined the army at the age of fourteen. At eighteen he had been shot through the mouth during the Battle of Ramillies (1706) and then taken prisoner. Gardiner also served in the British army during the '15. Alexander Carlyle, who was the son of the Presbyterian minister at Prestonpans, recalls that in 1719, after reading 'Gurnhalls Christian Armour, which his Mother had put in his Trunk many Years before', Gardiner 'Left off all his Rakish Habits, which Consisted in Swearing and Whoring (for he never was a Drinker) and the Contempt of Sacred Things, and became a serious Good Christian ever after'.[17] Colonel Gardiner and his regiment of dragoons had retreated before the Jacobite army from Linlithgow to Corstorphine, where the colonel had resolved to make a stand. To that end, Gardiner was to be joined by Hamilton's Dragoons, an Irish regiment, and overall command of both regiments would be given to Brigadier Thomas Fowke, who had himself only recently arrived at Leith. These were the only regular cavalry regiments in the whole of Scotland. To bolster their numbers it was resolved to summon the Guard and some of the volunteer companies.

One such volunteer was the twenty-three-year-old Alexander Carlyle, who had hurried back to his father's house from Moffat, arriving at Prestonpans on Thursday, 12 September. Here he was informed that Edinburgh was preparing for the imminent arrival of the Jacobite army. The following day he walked to the city, where he discovered his fellow students and young professionals were forming into volunteer companies.[18] However, Carlyle recorded a great deal of confusion and dissension among the citizens as to whether they should risk the ire of the Jacobite army and their leader by defending the city at all. In regard to loyalties within Edinburgh, 'besides the Two parties of Whigs and Jacobites, of which a well inform'd Citizen told me, There were two Thirds of the Men in the City, of the First Description or Friends of the Government, and of the 2^{d} or Enemies to Government, two Thirds of the Ladies'. Further dissension existed between those who were keen to defend the city and those who were not. Of the latter, Carlyle believed Lord Provost Stewart was the most prominent. In fact, the Lord Provost's behaviour was such that the local Whigs suspected that he favoured the Stuart cause, and 'there were not a few who suspected that his Backwardness and Coldness in the Measure of arming the People, was part of a plan to admitt the Pretender in to the City'.[19] Although it is clear from both Maclaurin and Carlyle's statements that Lord Provost Stewart's evident tardiness was considered among the Whigs as highly suspicious, even treasonous, it

should be observed that arguing against defending the city, and allowing the Jacobite army to enter it peacefully, did not automatically make
the Lord Provost a rampant Jacobite. Lord Provost Stewart probably had
Jacobite sympathies, but his hope may have been that the city and occupants would be better treated, with less damage to property and life, if
they did not resist. Whereas defending the city, particularly one so vulnerable (except the Castle), could be viewed not only as futile, but as
likely to encourage less sympathetic treatment, even retribution, by way
of plunder, pillage and worse.

On the morning of Sunday, 15 September, Patrick Crichton was attending a service at Glencorse Kirk, south of Edinburgh, when a messenger
arrived for Mrs Philp from her husband John, a director of the newly
incorporated Royal Bank of Scotland (1727). Crichton writes, 'we were
allarmed with accownt Prince Charles and his Highland bandits were at
Corstorphin two miles from Edinburgh and three from us at Woodhows
Lea'. Regardless of this disturbing news, the minister, Mr John Wilson,
continued to preach, which Crichton 'had not patience to hear owt,
considering the enemie was at the gaits'.[20] Mrs Philp, who 'was in owt-
most terror and amazement', promptly left to join her husband and child
in Edinburgh, quickly followed by George Straiton, 'by his Master Mr
Mowbry's warning', in order to drive his master's horses into the hills and
out of harm's way. Mr Wilson rambled on, but Crichton had had enough
and left with his family.[21]

Meanwhile, in the city itself, where Crichton's fellow citizens had also
gathered for divine services, as Carlyle recalled, news arrived that the
Jacobite army had been at Linlithgow the previous night and was now
marching straight for Edinburgh. 'This,' he observed, 'alter'd the Face of
Affairs, and made thinking people Fear that they might be in Possession
of Edinb[r] before Cope arriv'd.'[22] Colin Maclaurin wrote in his journal
that at this crucial moment 'a most unlucky signal was pitched on' to
gather the Town Guard and volunteer companies, that is the ringing of
the Fire bell 'which never fails to raise a panic in Edinburgh'. The alarm
occurred during the church service, after which the congregations were
hastily dismissed, 'in confusion and terror and this was the first appearance of fear in the place and this signal ought not to have been proposed
or allowed by the magistrates in such a time of the Rebels not being far
from us'.[23] In unison with Maclaurin, Crichton described the Fire bell
as 'a dismall signall'.[24] The use of it was another black mark against Lord
Provost Stewart.

On the alarm, Carlyle and his fellow volunteers gathered in the College Yards before ten o'clock and were addressed by Captain George Drummond, who encouraged them (as Carlyle recalled) to 'expose our Lives in Defence of the Capital of Scotland, and the Security of our Country's Laws and Liberties . . . he Hop'd his Company would Distinguish themselves by their Zeal and Spirit on this Occasion.'[25] This rousing speech was 'answer'd by an Unanimous Shout of Applause'. Drummond, who had been Lord Provost, was a staunch opponent to Jacobitism and a vehement adversary of Archibald Stewart. The group was then marched up to the Landmarket, but already some of their company had refused to move. At this moment Carlyle recalls that Hamilton's Dragoons marched past on their way to join Gardiner's regiment at Colt Bridge, and 'We cheer'd them in Passing with an Huzza'. The dragoons responded with like shouts of encouragement and clashing of swords. Carlyle concludes that 'the Spectators began to think at last, that some Serious Fighting was likely to Ensue, Tho' before this Moment, many of them had laugh'd at and Ridiculd the Volunteers'.[26] Having escaped the tedious sermonising of Mr Wilson, Patrick Crichton had climbed to the top of Leepshill with his two children. Before him lay Edinburgh itself and through his telescope he could see the two dragoon regiments gathering at the west end of Corstorphine.[27]

Back in Edinburgh, the divided loyalty within the citizens and the mob became more apparent as the volunteers were awaiting orders at the Landmarket. For 'an Hour, the Mob in the Street, and the Ladies in the Windows, treated us very variously, Many with Lamentation and even with Tears, and some with apparent Scorn and Derision'.[28] Carlyle vividly describes the fear and courage evident among the volunteers, none of whom were trained soldiers but, like him, students and young professional men, including Carlyle's friend John Home. All were in anticipation of an enemy whose ferocity and, many believed, brutality was legendary. In the following passage, which describes the volunteers moving down to the West Port in order to march out to join Colonel Gardiner in his stand against the Jacobite army, it is clear that a gamut of emotions from incredulity and incomprehension to panic and despair was beginning to overwhelm the very people the volunteer company had formed to defend. It also reveals that the volunteers were better versed in classical texts than warfare:

In marching down the [West] Bow, a Narrow Winding Street the Scene was different, for all the Spectators, were in Tears and uttering Loud Lamentations; Insomuch that, M[r] Kinloch a Probationer, the son of M[r]

Kinloch one of the high church Ministers who was in the 2^d Rank Just behind Hew Ballantine, said to him in a melancholy tone, Mr Hew, Mr Hew, Does not this Remind you of a Passage in Livy when the *Gens Fabii* March'd out of Rome to prevent the Gauls Entering the City, and the Whole Matrons and Virgins of Rome were wringing their Hands and Loudly Lamenting the Certain Danger, to which that Generous Tribe was going to be expos'd. Hold your Tongue says Ballantine, otherwise I shall complain to the Officer, for you'll Discourage the Men. You must recollect the End of all Mr Hew, *Omnes ad unum perieri* [they perished to a man]. This Occasion'd a Hearty Laugh among those who heard it. Which being over, Ballantine Half Whisper'd Kinloch, Robin, if you're affraid you had better steal off when you can find an opportunity; I shall not tell that you are Gone till we are too far off to Recover you.[29]

Again, much to the amusement of some of the onlookers, as they marched to the West Port the brave group of volunteers began to dwindle, with members disappearing off down the narrow lanes, and at last, when their commander George Drummond had passed through the gate and turned around, he was astonished to find only twenty men left in his corps. Those few who remained stood by the West Port and were served bread, cheese, strong ale and brandy by some sympathetic Grassmarket brewers.

At this moment, Alexander Carlyle's younger brother Will appeared. In his concern for his brother he had walked to Edinburgh from Prestonpans and, hearing he was one of the volunteers charged with going out to meet the dreaded foe, had hastened to the Grassmarket to find him. Carlyle took his brother to one side and attempted to calm him by saying it 'was only a Feint, to keep back the Highlanders'. He then gave Will a 'Portugal piece' and '3 Guineas that I had in my Pocket' at which Will burst into tears because he must be lying, 'otherwise I would not so readily part with my Money'. Alexander recalls that he comforted his brother, taking back the coins, and arranged to meet him that evening.[30] Meanwhile, the dwindling volunteer company was treated to a deputation of clergymen, including Dr William Wishart who begged them 'to Desist from this Rash Interprise', which he said, with some justification, 'was exposing the Flower of the Youth of Edin^r and the Hope of the Next Generation, to the Danger of being Cut off or made Prisoners, and Maltreated without any Just or Adequate Object'. Despite acknowledging that Dr Wishart's point was a good one, and a few armed students would be no match for one Highlander, 'Youthfull Ardour, made us Reluctant to abandon the

prospect of shewing our Prowess'.[31] Patrick Crichton, who had walked up
to his town house on the Landmarket, declared that 'All was confusion'
among the volunteers, who were 'raw men' who had been 'betrayed, by
the Kings liftenent the cheif magistrate',[32] that is, Lord Provost Stewart.
The volunteers were dismissed, but told to rendezvous in the evening at the
College Yards for night guard duty on the city wall.

On Monday, 16 September, with no more than a few hundred of the
Town Guard and a handful of volunteers, the two dragoon regiments retired
slightly eastwards from Corstorphine towards Edinburgh and encamped at
Colt Bridge. By all accounts neither regiment was fit for combat, having
been, in Colonel Gardiner's opinion, 'harass'd and fatigued for eleven Days
and eleven Nights, little or no Provision for the Men, or Forage for the
Horses'. He feared that if they engaged the enemy, the king would, without doubt, lose two regiments of horse.[33] Patrick Crichton had risen early
at his house, and passing down to the Grassmarket and through the West
Port he walked to Colt Bridge. He spoke with Colonel Gardiner, who was
visibly unwell, and whose regiment appeared ill equipped for an imminent
encounter with several thousand Jacobite troops.[34] He adds, 'The foot,
[infantry] near the east end of the bridge, they looked licke men for the
purpose but they were a handfull.'[35] Crichton remained with the dragoons
until about three o'clock in the afternoon, 'when one of the scowts came
in and said that 400 of the Highland advance gaird was on the north east
poynt of Corstorphin Hill. I took leave of Gardener and retired cross the
fields and saw the dragowns mount.'[36]

No doubt Patrick Crichton thought, as he ambled across the fields from
Colt Bridge, that the dragoons were mounting to make their stand. But
soon after, the advance guard from the Jacobite army had fired on the small
rearguard of the dragoons left at Corstorphine by Colonel Gardiner, who
promptly 'without returning one shot, wheeled about, and rode off'. In
the meantime, having received the news of the Jacobite advance, the dragoon officers at Colt Bridge had decided to retire to Leith Links and await
Cope and his troops. But with the rearguard suddenly joining the main
body in something of a panic, 'General Foukes and the two regiments of
dragoons set off immediately, and between three and four o'clock in the
afternoon, passed on the north side of the town by the Long Dykes . . .
in full view of the people of Edinburgh.'[37] No matter how sensible their
retiring was in the circumstances, the dragoons appeared to have abandoned the city to its fate. The event was soon after disparagingly styled the
'Canter of Coltbridge', and despite Brigadier Fowke's attempts to define it

as a strategic and orderly withdrawal, even Colonel Gardiner described it as a 'retreat, I may say run a way'.[38]

The effect on the already tense populace was predictable. Watching their only immediate relief and hope disappearing out of sight, 'Instantly the clamour rose, and crowds of people ran about the streets crying out, that it was madness to think of resistance, since the dragoons were fled.' They beseeched Lord Provost Stewart 'not to persist in defending the town, for if he did they should all be murdered'.[39] Patrick Crichton compared Edinburgh at this time to the biblical Babel, stating, 'To notice all the particulars in a distracted city were impossible,' and describing the inhabitants in a deranged state 'run[n]ing owt runing in and runing abowt was all was done'.[40] The alarm rang out once more, and a meeting of the magistrates and town council was hastily called in Goldsmith's Hall near St Giles. Messengers were sent to the Lord Justice Clerk, the Advocate, and Solicitor, 'to entreat that they would come and assist the Council with their advice. The deputies returned, and reported that all these gentlemen had left town.'[41] The captains of the volunteer companies, who had now mustered again in the Landmarket, were also called, but apparently could not offer any advice one way or the other.

The tension in the Goldsmith's Hall was unbearable. John Home reports that as each person said their piece for and against the defence of the city, it was 'not without reproach or abuse on both sides'.[42] The room became so crammed with agitated citizens that they had to move to the New Church Aisle within St Giles, which was immediately filled with people, 'the most part of whom called to give up the town; that it was impossible to defend it. Those who attempted to speak against the general opinion, were borne down with noise and clamour.'[43] At the height of this anxious meeting a messenger arrived. According to John Home, Deacon Orrock was handed a letter which he opened, no doubt to a now silent, nervously expectant gathering, and announced that it was signed 'Charles Prince Regent'. In one account of this event, the Lord Provost declared that he could not listen to the contents of the letter, no doubt fearing that it was treasonable to even hear the words read out, and left. The letter read:

From our Camp, 16ᵗʰ September 1745

Being now in a condition to make our way into the capital of His Majesty's ancient kingdom of Scotland we hereby summon you to receive us, as you are in duty bound to do. And in order to it, we hereby require you, on receipt of this to summon the Town Council and take proper measures in it for securing the peace and quiet of the city, which we are very desirous to protect. But if you suffer any of the Usurper's troops to enter the town, or any of the canon, arms, or amunition now in it, whether belonging to the publick or to private persons, to be carried off, we shall take it as a breach of your duty and a heinous offence against the king and us, and shall resent it accordingly. We promise to preserve all the rights and liberties of the city, and the particular property of every one of His Majesty's subjects. But if any opposition be made to us we cannot answer for the consequences, being firmly resolved at any rate to enter the city, and in that case, if any of the inhabitants are found in arms against us, they must not expect to be treated as prisoners of war.[44]

On the strength of this apparently reasonable, but in substance threatening, summons, and as the senior legal men and government representatives had all retired from the city, it was decided that resistance was useless, and the only thing that could be done was to delay the surrender of the city for as long as possible. To that end four men, Gavin Hamilton, John Yetts, David Inglis and Jamie Norrie, were to be sent by coach to the Jacobite army's camp to negotiate terms – in effect to play for time.

Meanwhile, Alexander Carlyle and the volunteers, now stationed in the Landmarket, were eagerly awaiting orders from the Lord Provost. At that moment, as Carlyle reports, 'a Man on Horseback whom nobody knew came up from the Bow, and, Riding at a quick pace along the Line of the Volunteers, call'd out that the Highlanders were at hand, and that they were 16,000 strong. This Fellow Did not stop to be examin'd, but made off at the Gallop.'[45] This figure appeared around the time that the summons was delivered to the Lord Provost and council, suggesting that he was the messenger from the encamped Jacobite army. Whoever he was, the stranger's announcement to the volunteers stating the large number of Highlanders advancing towards them was clearly intended to shake their resolve. And it seems to have done the trick, for soon after, with no orders from the Lord Provost and after some discussion between Captain Drummond and his fellow officers, the volunteers delivered their arms to the Castle 'as no good could be done by keeping them, for the town was to be given up'.[46] John Home continues, 'The sun was setting when they laid down their arms; many of them with visible reluctance, and some of them with tears.'[47] He also observes that on 16 September 1745 OS 'the sun sets 54 minutes after five o'clock'.[48] As day turned to night, Alexander

Carlyle recalled that he and his companions were glad to deliver up their weapons, but, at the same time, they were 'not a little asham'd and afflicted at our Inglorious Campaign'.[49] As the volunteers sloped off, relieved and embarrassed, to supper and then bed, the delegation from the council had clambered into a coach and were now trundling towards the Jacobite encampment.

Robert Strange, *Lord George Murray, c.* 1746.

Perth

'a large, well ordered family'

The day after the raising of the Stuart standard at Glenfinnan, the prince and his small army began their march south. This would not be without difficulty and hardship. Some of the guns brought on the *Dutillet* were buried and ammunition abandoned.[1] On 23 August, the prince lodged at Fassifern, the house of Lochiel's younger brother, John, who was not there to act as host, unsurprisingly perhaps. They then passed through the Great Glen, at which time they received intelligence that Sir John Cope and his troops were heading for Inverness.[2] While the main army marched south, a detachment attacked the garrison at Ruthven Barracks, but to little effect, other than the loss of some precious Jacobite troops. On the 29th the army reached Dalwhinnie and the head of 'the Chain' to the south (the network of roads and forts built by Field Marshal George Wade after the '15 and now, ironically, assisting the Jacobite advance), and two days later they arrived at the Marquess of Tullibardine's ancestral seat, Blair Castle in the Vale of Atholl. Here the prince was joined by William Drummond, 4th Viscount of Strathallan, Laurence Oliphant, Laird of Gask and his son (also Laurence), the Hon. William Murray of Taymount, appointed Chamberlain of the prince's household, and John Roy Stuart. The latter was a seasoned officer and participant at Fontenoy, who had travelled to Scotland directly from the French army camp in Flanders.

Roy Stuart arrived with a verbal message of support from Maréchal de Saxe as well as various letters, including one from Charles' cousin, the duc de Bouillon, dated 10 August (NS, 30 July OS).[3] Bouillon writes that, after receiving confirmation of the prince's expedition, 'I flew to the King, and with tears in my Eyes conjur'd him to support your generous Resolution.' Louis assured him 'he had your Interest at heart' and that 'I might assure you That he would serve you in every thing that you might stand in need of for the Interest of your project'. Bouillon had demanded of the king's

ministers that 'they should send you Troops', to which their response was
that 'they must have assurances of your being landed before they could
send off anything. That then it would be your business to ask for what
you should think necessary or usefull for carrying on your Designes.'⁴
Another letter was from the prince of Campo Florida, Spanish ambassador to Versailles, who states, 'Wee waite here with the greatest impatience
for the news of your Royall Highness's landing.' He confirmed that the
French king 'did not hesitate to promise an immediate assistance of Armes
& money and gave orders to prepare both' and then wrote immediately to
the King of Spain 'to informe him of this Resolution, and [I] can assure
your Royall Highness that his Catholick Majesty will conforme himself to
the dispositions of the most Christian King his Nephew, and will assist you
in an equall proportion. These are fixed resolutions on which your Royall
Highness may lay your account.'⁵ Excellent news indeed.

To keep out of harm's way the Marquess of Tullibardine's younger
brother, Duke James, was then travelling from the family's other residence, Tullibardine in Dunkeld (where Lord George Murray and his family lived), to Edinburgh. Meanwhile the marquess had written ahead to
his widowed cousin nearby, the Hon. Mrs Robertson of Lude, known as
Lady Lude, to make ready the house for the prince's imminent arrival and
to prepare to take on the role of hostess. Such an honour could not have
been bestowed on a more eager recipient. A witness to the prince's arrival,
Thomas Fraser, described Lady Lude as kneeling before the prince on the
castle green, although he was not close enough to see whether she kissed
his hand or not.⁶ Meanwhile, Duke James' steward, Thomas Bissett, wrote
to his master from Blair Castle, 'The young Pretender, your Brother, and
the Highlanders, came here about three o'clock in the afternoon this day.
They all as yet behave verry civilly, and I expect they'l continue so dureing
their stay here, which will be till Munday morning. From this they are to
go to Perth by way of Dunkeld.'⁷ Thomas Bissett goes on to explain that
he had discussed matters with the chiefs and had arranged quarters for
their men in the surrounding countryside. He then informs Duke James,
'The Highlanders doe not yet exceed in number 2000, and they'l scarce be
so much, two thirds of which are the poorest naked like creatures imagin-
able, and verry indifferently armed; I doe not think the one half of their
guns will fire. Some of them have guns without swords, and some swords
without guns.'⁸ He now moves on to consider the new house guests. 'The
young Gentleman himself,' he says, 'seems to be good natured, but I doe
not think that he hath verry much in him.' Tullibardine 'is still the old

man as he was', indeed he looked ten years older than he should, and was keen to know where the guns were kept. Then there are the 'five or six gentlemen, that came over in the ship with them, old aligrougus [alla-grugous, i.e., grim] like fellows as ever I saw'. Bissett had a cow and a large sheep slaughtered for them and assured Duke James that he would make daily reports. He concludes, 'I thought there had been pine aples in Italy, but it seems not, for we hapened this day to get one up from Dunkeld, whereof the young gentleman did eat, and said that it was the first that he had ever seen.'[9] In a postscript he observes, 'Lady Lude is here with them, & behaves like a light Giglet [a giddy girl], & hath taken upon her to be sole mistres of the house.'[10]

Meanwhile, on Monday the 2nd, Charles visited 'the house of Lude, where he was very cheerful, and took his share in several dances, such as minuets and Highland reels. The first reel the Prince called for was "This is no mine ain house," and a Strathspey minuet.'[11] Thomas Fraser also recalled that 'the Pretender's son and several of the rebel Gentlemen [were] Entertained by the Lady Lude at her house of Lude with Dinner and with Musick and Dancing after Dinner', and, he observed, in tandem with Thomas Bisset, 'Lady Lude [was] so elevate while she was about the Young Pretender at that time that she looked like a person whose head had gone wrong.'[12]

The following day the army marched to Dunkeld, where Charles was once more the guest of the Murray family. The next day he dined at Lord Nairn's house (John, 3rd Baron), and the conversation turned to Charles' father in Rome, who at this time (the party thought) must be concerned for his son's 'dangers and difficulties' and 'upon this account he was much to be pitied, because his mind behoved to be much upon the rack'. Charles replied 'that he did not half so much pity his father as his brother. "For," said he, "the king has been inured to disappointments and distresses, and has learnt to bear up easily under the misfortunes of life. But poor Har[r]y! his young and tender years makes him much to be pitied, for few brothers love as we do."'[13] Here Charles was joined by his host Lord Nairn, who was made a brigadier general, and his brother the Hon. Robert Nairn. The Nairns were related to the Murrays of Atholl. From Dunkeld, the Marquess of Tullibardine wrote a letter to Baron Reid and other 'Vassals' (dated 4 September), stating, 'As I understand that you and the rest of my Vassalls and tenants do not bestir y[r]selves' in a manner 'that becomes Loyal Subjects for the King's Service', and having 'warned you of the dangerous consequences of disobeying my commands as y[r] Superior', the marquess desired and required them 'to raise

in arms all the men you can, and meet at Pitlochrie against the time formerly
conserted, & joine the King's standard with all speed.'[14] If not, he would be
obliged to 'call for a strong detachment from his Royall Highness, to use you
with that hostile rigour that all Rebells & disafected people to their King &
country deserve'. It seems that Tullibardine was having some trouble getting
his local clansmen to rise in support of the Stuarts. So encouragement, by
way of threats, was needed. Soon after Tullibardine returned to Blair to over-
see the recruitment himself.

Meanwhile, in Edinburgh, Duke James received a letter containing very
bad news – far worse than his elder brother's arrival at Blair Castle. It was
from his sister-in-law, Lady Amelia Murray, dated 5 September, and contained a letter from her husband, Duke James' younger brother, George,
whom he had hoped might have become reconciled to the House of
Hanover. Lady Murray wrote that she was deeply concerned by what Lord
George had done, 'but as it comes ill from a wife to blame her Husband, I
must endeavour patiently to suffer what I cannot help'.[15] Having read this,
Duke James must have turned to the enclosed letter with great trepidation.
It was dated from Tullibardine (Lord George's residence), 3 September
1745, 'Six at Night'. In it Lord George states, 'I never did say to any person in Life that I would not ingage in the cause I always in my heart
thought just & right, as well as for the Interest, good, & Liberty of my
country', and though 'what I do may & will be reccon'd desperate', 'may
very probably end in my utter ruen. My Life, my Fortune, my expectations, the Happyness of my wife & children, are all at stake (& the chances
are against me), & yet a principle of (what seems to me) Honour, & my
Duty to King & Country, outweighs every thing.' If he hesitates, it is only
with respect for his brother James, for 'I ow obligations to no body else
(I mean the Court of London), & if you find you cannot forgive me, yet
sure you will pitty me.' His wife's support, against her own inclination,
'makes so deep an impression upon me, that nothing but so strong an
atatchment as I have to the cause I am to imbark in, could make me do
what in all appearance must disturb her future quiet & Happyness'. The
likelihood of dying for the cause does not deter him.[16] This letter reveals
the struggle that Lord George had endured in the years following the 1719
rising, which had now come to a head on the arrival of his elder brother
Tullibardine, whom neither James nor George had seen for many years,
the Jacobite Prince of Wales, and a growing Jacobite army.

Lord George's act of conscience was considered, unsurprisingly, as particularly treacherous by those around the government who felt he had been

given a second chance after his involvement in the '19. Philip Yorke wrote on 19 September, 'I am greatly shocked at the ungrateful behaviour of Lord George Murray. Besides his being pardoned for the last Rebellion, the King had just given his son a commission in the new Highland regiment.'[17] Lord George's son, John, was sixteen years old and then at Eton. In a letter to his uncle James, whom John describes as his 'best friend', he states that he had borne as best he could the news of his family's misfortunes since the landing of the 'praetender', but 'a late peice of news has quite shook me, and I am no longer able to bear up against it, which is that my Father has declared for the praetender, which of all things I was most afraid of'. But as Duke James was for King George, and with his recent captaincy within Lord Loudoun's Highland regiment (in the event he did not serve), 'I shall lay down my Life and shall spend the last drop of my Blood in his service.' John then pleads to be allowed to come home: 'for I don't dout but that I could handle a broadsword or a musket well enough, for there are a gret many younger than I am who are both fighting in Flanders & else whare, and what I want in strenth I shall make up in willingness.' He concludes, 'for though I love my father as well as it is possible for any one to love his parent, yet it is impossible for me to think that he has acted Right in this particular'.[18]

Lord George Murray joined the prince at Perth, which the advance party had reached on 3 September – proclaiming Charles' father King James VIII and III, as the *Caledonian Mercury* later reported – and then the remainder, including the prince, arrived on 4 September. Here, too, James Drummond, Duke of Perth, also joined the prince, and he and Lord George were appointed lieutenant generals. As the leading commanders of the Jacobite army, they, as much as Charles himself, held the success or failure of the entire venture in their hands. To what extent these three men trusted each other, and how well they worked together, would be crucial. According to James Johnstone, son of a Jacobite merchant in Edinburgh who joined the prince at the same time as Lord George (becoming one of his aides-de-camp), his senior officer possessed 'a natural genius for military operations; and was indeed a man of surprising talents, which, had they been cultivated by the study of military tactics, would unquestionably have rendered him one of the greatest generals of the age. He was tall and robust, and brave in the highest degree.'[19] Lord George had some solid military experience. He had held a commission under the Duke of Marlborough prior to the '15, and had then participated in two Jacobite Risings. He was therefore (at this time) one of the most experienced men in the army. This would in turn create issues, as few were capable of advising him on military matters. 'However,' Johnstone continues, 'with an infinity of good qualities, he was not without his defects': 'proud, haughty, blunt, and imperious, he wished to have the exclusive disposal of every thing; and, feeling his superiority, he would listen to no advice.' Turning to the remainder of the army, Johnstone observes, the Highland chiefs and clansmen 'possessed the most heroic courage; but they knew no other manoeuvre than that of rushing upon the enemy sword in hand, as soon as they saw them, without order and without discipline'. Only Colonel John O'Sullivan, in Johnstone's opinion, possessed some, although limited, experience of a regular army, and 'We can hardly, therefore, be astonished that Lord George, possessing so many of the qualities requisite to form a great general, should have gained the hearts of the Highlanders; and a general, who has the confidence of his soldiers, may do wonders.' In this sense, the relationship forged between Lord George and Colonel O'Sullivan, Charles' confidant, the Jacobite army's adjutant general and now quartermaster general, would be as crucial as that between his lordship and the prince. Lord George possessed 'the art of employing men to advantage, without having had time to discipline them, but taking them merely as they came from the plough', as indeed some of the Jacobite army had, and that 'Nature had formed him for a great warrior; he did not require the accidental advantage of birth.'[20] The Duke of Perth, on the other hand (Johnstone was later a captain in his cavalry regiment), is described as 'though brave even to excess, every way honourable, and possessed of a mild and gentle disposition, was of very limited abilities, and interfered with nothing'.[21]

Another important recruit at Perth was Ewen MacPherson of Cluny. After his anxious letter to the Lord President, and having taken a commission in Lord Loudoun's Highland regiment, Cluny was reportedly kidnapped by his cousin Lochiel and held prisoner until he agreed to join the prince.[22] According to Glengarry junior (Glengarry's eldest son), 'Cluny Macpherson, junior, made the same agreement with the Prince before he would join in the attempt with his following, as young Lochiel had done . . . which the Prince accordingly consented unto.'[23] The manner of his joining hints at his ambivalence towards the current rising. However, the Jacobite army would now include the Clan MacPherson.

At this time, Charles is described in a letter by a witness as marching 'the whole day on foot, and every river they have to cross, he's the first man that leaps into it. He dines with his soldiers in the open field.' By such behaviour, 'The Pretender makes himself greatly popular'. He wears 'a Highland coat of fine silk tartan, red velvet breeches, and a blue velvet bonnet with gold lace round it, and a large jewel and St Andrew appended'. This witness describes him as at least six feet tall, 'walks well and straight, and speaks the English or broad Scots very well'.[24] Reporting on the prince's appearance and behaviour was on one level simply satisfying the curiosity of the letter's recipient. On another, it was vital intelligence that could be passed around locally and then on to other cities that might or might not lie in the Jacobite army's path. This particular description was sent in a letter from Dundee to Newcastle upon Tyne in north-east England, and was then published in the *York Courant* on 17 September. While Charles remained at Perth, he visited 'the House of Scone, where formerly the Kings of Scotland were Crowned'.[25] Despite the fact that the town of Perth was 'not well disposed' to the Stuart cause, Colonel John O'Sullivan recalled that they had received some good intelligence from local sympathisers.[26]

The Jacobite army remained in Perth until 11 September, which provided vital time to give the troops some training in basic duties, such as mounting guard.[27] The day before the army left, Charles also wrote to his father stating that 'love and harmony' reigned in his 'little army' and that it was 'a large, well ordered family, in which every one loves another better than himself'. He goes on to state, 'I keep my health better in these wild mountains than I used to do in the Campagnie Felice, and sleep sounder, lying on the ground, than I used to do in the palaces at Rome.' In one thing only has he had a disagreement with his 'faithful Highlanders', and that is over the £30,000 bounty and a corresponding 'price upon my kinsman's head'. Charles thought it amusing but beneath his dignity, indeed the dignity of any prince, to respond in kind, but his men 'flew into a violent rage, and insisted upon my doing the same by him. As this flowed solely from the poor men's love and concern for me, I did not know how to be angry with them for it.' However, 'nothing I could say would pacify them. Some went even so far as to say, – "Shall we venture our lives for a man who seems so indifferent of his own?" Thus have I been drawn in to do a thing for which I condemn myself.'[28] The prince concludes this long letter by regretting two things: that 'the brave Lord Mareshall is not with me' for his 'character is very high in this country' (a change of heart since his evident irritation with the Earl Marischal while in France), and that the Duke of Argyll could not be persuaded to side with the Stuarts, because the 'hard usage which his family has received from ours has sunk deep into his mind. What have these princes to answer for, who by their cruelties have raised enemies not only to themselves but to their innocent children?'[29]

This letter is so balanced, fair-minded, even magnanimous, and frankly better phrased and spelt than Charles' usual letters (certainly those quoted from France), that one can imagine it was written with the aid of another and with a much broader audience in mind than his father.[30]

And contrary to the letter's assertions, not all was rosy in the Jacobite camp. At Perth Sir John Macdonald recalled that, a few days after Lord George's arrival, a woman of the MacDonalds accompanied by a man from Clan Cameron came to see him 'to warn H.R.H. that Lord George was one of his greatest enemies'. Her proof was that she had heard some of the Athollmen had been told by Lord George that they were to fight for Sir John Cope, which they refused to do. Any suspicion that Lord George was an enemy to the prince runs counter to Lord George's obvious loyalty to the Stuart cause, as expressed in his letter to his brother James. In fact, in this letter he not only sets out what he is risking by joining the Jacobite army, which is everything, but appears to have no real hope of success. It is simply the honourable thing to do. But based on the hearsay of this woman and her companion, Sir John Macdonald 'gave this warning to the Prince, as I thought it my duty to do, with the less scruple as I had never yet spoken to Lord George, since it was only 3 or 4 days previously that I had ever heard of him'.[31] The prince's immediate reaction to this 'information' is not recorded. But Lord George himself later recalled an incident with Sir John Macdonald, after the army left Perth on the 11th, whereby a drunken 'which was frequently his case' and belligerent Sir John made an offensive remark to Lord George. Keppoch, who was present, 'said he believ'd Sr John must either be drunk or mad, if not both, & it was best taking no notice of him'.[32] Rather than a loving, unified family, then, the Jacobite command was already beginning to show signs of distrust and division.

After leaving Perth, the army reached Dumblaine by 12 September, and the following day passed the Ford of Frew 'without any opposition from the Dragoons that had been encampd att Stirling'. As they passed the river, Charles 'expressed a good deal of surprise to find that he had mett with no opposition, and demanded what for officers they had gott in Brittain, who were cappable of abandoning so advantageous a post'.[33] The army halted at Lecky. On Saturday the 14th Lord George recalled 'they march'd early, & pass'd by Stirling, holding about a mile to the south side, not to be in reach of the cannon of the Castle'. The Castle was held by the British army under the command of the Irishman General William Blakeney. As the vanguard marched through the nearby village of St Ninian, 'the Castle fired some Cannon at the Royall Standard, which was in the Center, but did no hurt'.[34] They continued to the east of Falkirk where the army encamped, Charles staying with William Boyd, 4th Earl of Kilmarnock, at Callander House. By all appearances Kilmarnock was a staunch supporter of King George and the current government, although his pension had been stopped after Sir Robert Walpole's fall in 1742. Since then he had certainly been open to persuasion, as he lived in a constant state of financial embarrassment, with the added pressure that his wife's father, James Earl of Lithlithgow, had been out in the '15. Kilmarnock entertained the prince but at this point remained aloof from the rising. As Colonel Gardiner's dragoons retreated, the Jacobite army took possession of Linlithgow. Here Dr Stuart Threipland of Fingask Castle near Rait in Perthshire joined the army, along with his brother David, and was appointed as physician to the prince. They informed Charles that, according to the advice from friends at Edinburgh, the prince should march swiftly on and take the city.[35]

The following day they continued their march in the expectation of an imminent attack from the British army dragoons. Arriving at Todshall or Foxhall, 'a gentleman's (Mr. Horn) seat upon Newliston River', the army halted for two hours while a party was sent out to reconnoitre the location of the dragoons. This advance guard, which, according to John Home, was no more than 'some young people, well mounted'[36] were soon to frighten off the dragoon rearguard at Corstorphine by firing their pistols at them (rather than simply observing them), thus causing the infamous 'Canter of Coltbridge'. The main army reached Corstorphine at about two o'clock, where a number of local people had gathered to see them 'chiefly from curiosity'.[37] According to John Home, a Mr Alves was passing the Jacobite army at about this time on his way to Edinburgh. Being acquainted with the Duke of Perth, who 'after having asked a young man, whom he called the Prince, if it was his pleasure; to which he seemed to assent', Alves was handed the summons for delivery to the Lord Provost.[38]

Charles and his army finally encamped less than an hour's march to the south-east of Corstorphine at Slateford on the Water of Leith. Edinburgh Castle was now just over two miles away and in plain sight. The plan was that the city should be surrendered without prevarication or a bullet fired, but, if the surrender of the garrison had not been secured, then the army would march around the south of the city, maintaining a suitable distance from the Castle's guns, and arrive at the Palace of Holyroodhouse to the east. Despite all their successes since Glenfinnan, the army still numbered no more than 2,000 men.

Domenico Duprà, *David Wemyss, Lord Elcho*, c. 1740.
(PRIVATE COLLECTION)

Gray's Mill

'to dallie of the time'

While the men bedded down in the fields around Slateford, Prince Charles took up residence in the modest two-storey house next to a flourmill called Gray's Mill, then leased by David Wright.[1] Visitors to the mill for the next 150 years would be shown to a very small room, which by tradition was known as Charles' private chamber.[2] Here at Slateford the prince now awaited confirmation from the Lord Provost that the city had capitulated. While waiting, a very welcome recruit arrived. Having written to John Murray and been assured in return that the army was 6,000-strong (with more expected) plus the services of a Spanish colonel (apparently Sir John Macdonald) and an Irish 'French General' (John O'Sullivan), Lord Elcho had decided now was the time to join the rising. On 11 September Lord Elcho with his servant Tiddeman left his father's residence, Wemyss Castle, located on the cliffs across the Firth of Forth from Edinburgh. Lord Elcho states that his father 'approved of my decision very strongly . . . charged me with his respects for the Prince' and confirmed that 'the Prince might count on his attachment to the royal House of Stuart'.[3] On the 12th, Lord Elcho arrived at Preston Hall, where the following day he was present at his brother Francis' marriage to Catherine, the sister of the pro-Hanoverian Duke of Gordon. Before leaving his brother, Lord Elcho told him what his current purpose was, at which Francis gave him 1,500 guineas. Lord Elcho already had 1,000 guineas of his own money.

Lord Elcho wrote in his journal, 'On the . . . 16 September 1745, I joined the Prince at Gray's Mill near Edinburgh. It was night when I arrived. The Prince, whom I had known at Rome and Paris, received me very politely and appointed me first aide-de-camp.'[4] Rather more ominously, he continues that the prince 'talked with me a long time, and told me, among other things, to be on my guard and not to speak of his affairs before my Lord George Murray, because he knew that Murray had joined him to betray him. The Prince was extremely credulous and readily believed whatever was told him by those that he had confidence in.'⁵ Unfortunately, in Lord Elcho's opinion, chief among these was John Murray, the prince's secretary, who, again according to Lord Elcho, had covertly undermined the prince's confidence in Lord George Murray chiefly because he favoured the Duke of Perth as sole lieutenant general of the army. Such were the prince's fears concerning Lord George, stoked by Sir John Macdonald and Secretary Murray, and so early in the campaign, that he apparently felt compelled to share them with a newly arrived recruit. It seems strange that the prince chose this moment, when all was going so well, to openly air such concerns – if he had them. Lord Elcho's observations were made some years after the event, but he had no reason to lie about the substance of his conversation with the prince. In any event and despite any concerns, Lord Elcho was doubly welcome because he had arrived with 2,500 guineas, of which the cash-strapped prince was in desperate need. According to Lord Elcho, Charles confided that 'he was in the greatest distress for want of money, not having the wherewithal to pay his army' and in response, that evening Lord Elcho handed over the 1,500 guineas his brother had given him.⁶

The four civic representatives from Edinburgh arrived at Gray's Mill some time after eight o'clock in the evening. Secretary Murray recalled that he met them on their arrival. They said that they had come 'to know what was expected from them', to which Murray plainly responded 'that his Master required no further than that they should open their gates to his army and delivre up the arms of the Town and garrison, with the ammunition and Military Stores than [then] in the Town'. If this happened the 'liberties of the Citty should be preserved, and all necessary protection given them'.⁷ The delegation responded that they had no control over the arms of the militia, those being the responsibility of the Castle garrison, 'but upon the whole desired time to return and consult with their brethern'. Secretary Murray reported back to the prince, who 'aggreed that they should have two or three hours to bring back an answer, but grant them no further respite, having good intelligence that they desired no more than to dallie of the time till they saw how far it was possible for them to be relieved by Gn. Cope'.⁸ Lord Elcho recalls that the delegates were ushered into the presence of the prince and, 'after they had kiss'd his hand', Charles told them that 'he was going to send of a detachment to Attack the town and lett them defend it at their peril; that if they did the Consequences would be bad, and if they did not he intended no harm to the old Metropolis of his Kingdome'.[9] The delegation then left the mill two hours after they arrived, clutching a letter, which reiterated that the manifesto and declaration of regency 'are a sufficient capitulation for all his Majesty's subjects to accept of with joy. His present demands are to be received into the city as the son and representative of the king, his father, and obeyed as such when he is there.' Charles presumes that no one has removed or is concealing arms or ammunition and that 'he expects a positive answer to this before 2 o'clock in the morning, otherwise he will find himself obliged to take measures'.[10]

Despite the Lord Provost's reputation as a staunch Jacobite among sympathetic and unsympathetic observers alike – Lord Elcho described him as 'a zealous supporter of the Prince'[11] – his delaying tactics certainly did not please the prince and tried the patience of his officers. Having already warned the city delegation that he was sending a detachment, after they left (suspecting they were playing for time) he ordered Lochiel to arm his men and be ready to march towards Edinburgh with Secretary Murray as guide. They were given strict orders to behave with moderation towards the inhabitants, that they should not partake of any spirits, and were to pay for provisions, 'promising them two shillings each so soon as they rendered themselves Masters of the place'.[12]

Several more hours passed and the two o'clock deadline had come and gone. In fact the council had since regretted sending any delegation to the prince, as confirmation that Sir John Cope was nearing Dunbar had finally arrived. However, another delegation was sent to Gray's Mill, namely Provost Coutts and Robert Baillie. By this time the prince's patience had been exhausted. This delegation was not received by him, but simply handed a curt summary of the previous note.[13] Thus dismissed, this second delegation returned to their coach and began the journey back to Edinburgh with all speed. But by now, silently moving towards the city were Lochiel, Colonel O'Sullivan, Secretary Murray and their detachment of Camerons.

They were in luck, for as Alexander Carlyle recalled, that night 'there was no Moonlight'.[14] After his earlier heroics, Carlyle had decided to leave Edinburgh with his young brother Will for the relative safety of Prestonpans. The two brothers passed 'thro' the Croud at the Head of the Cannongate, who were pressing both ways to Get out, and in'. They walked on to the Abbey and then beyond, 'meeting hardly a Mortal the whole way'.[15]

A Highlander of the Jacobite army, contemporary drawing from the
Penicuik Collection

Netherbow Port

'hardly a Mortal'

The Highlanders took the road to the south of the city 'by Merkistown and Hopes Park', where, as Secretary Murray recalled, they passed without being seen or heard by the Castle garrison, 'tho so near as to hear them distinctly call their rounds'. They then moved up the Pleasants, along the eastern city wall towards the Netherbow Port, without meeting a soul, and although they could see the wall at the Pleasants and St Mary's Wynd was mounted with cannon, again no one appeared.[1] The men gathered quietly around the gate, and Lochiel sent a single man to attempt to gain entrance by pretending to be a servant. According to Colonel O'Sullivan this man was in 'Lowland Cloaths' and told the guard at the gate that he 'was a servant belonging to an officer of the Drago[o]ns',[2] but, with the city in a skittish state, such a ruse was unlikely to succeed. Daylight was now coming on and it was decided that they should retire to nearby St Leonard's Hills and await further orders from the prince. Then something at once ordinary and extraordinary happened.

Someone alerted the Highland party that a coach was coming towards them, and Secretary Murray recognised it as the very same which had carried the second deputation to Gray's Mill. Having dropped them off, it was now making its way down from the Landmarket en route to Canongate. The men were ordered to keep quiet, and, as the guards opened the gate, Lochiel rushed in, with his men close behind, as the guards fled.[3] Whether by error or design, it was the second delegation of the town council who would be the means of allowing the Jacobite army to enter Edinburgh as planned: without a shot being fired. Watching from a window nearby was Richard Jack, a volunteer, who confirmed that 460 men entered at the Netherbow Port, 'none being there to oppose them', although some were unarmed, while others were carrying broadswords and even corn forks. Many had muskets without locks. In short, 'the Number of Guns that reasonably might be supposed could fire, did not exceed two hundred'.[4] Despite this the detachment now set about taking possession of the city. Colonel O'Sullivan states that at this time the Lord Provost and magistrates were assembled nearby at Luckie Clarke's tavern to hear the prince's response to the second delegation. O'Sullivan joined this meeting, to the surprise of the Lord Provost and his companions, and he held them there until they informed him what had happened at Gray's Mill. O'Sullivan, by his own admission, 'spoke to 'um a little high [handed], for having offer'd such conditions as they did to the Prince' but then assured them that they would be treated in a manner as befitted King James' loyal subjects, if they behaved as such from now on. O'Sullivan then told them 'in the Kings name' to give orders that there should be no unrest in the city. If a shot was fired from a window, O'Sullivan warned, he would set fire to the house. Butchers and bakers should continue their trades in order to supply the army, which would begin arriving later that day, and bread and beer should be delivered immediately to the detachment currently keeping guard in the city.[5]

Colonel O'Sullivan then sent a messenger to Gray's Mill to tell the prince of their success, and continued to secure the city by posting guards at all the city gates, closes and at the former Parliament House. In addition he put a guard as near as possible to the Castle, at the Weigh House or Tron at the western end of the Landmarket. The remainder, as recalled by Secretary Murray, were drawn up at Parliament Close awaiting the arrival of the key to the Parliament House, their new quarters, as well as straw to sleep on 'and tho they remained there from Six till eleven in the morning under arms, after the fatigue they had undergone' they were well behaved and 'so far from committing abuses that they took nothing but what they paid for'. Locals brought them plenty of bread and drink, but as ordered they did not touch any liquor.[6]

The Camerons, tired but fed, now awaited the arrival of Prince Charles.

A Highlander of the Jacobite army, a contemporary drawing from the
Penicuik Collection.

John Slezer, *The North Prospect of the City of Edenburgh from 'Theatrum Scotiae'*, published 1719.

15

Canongate

'rather like a dream'

Patrick Crichton heard the news that Edinburgh had fallen to 'the scurlewheelers' at his house in Woodhouselee, and, fearing his horse would be taken, he immediately set off on foot towards the city. En route, on the 'Lintown rod', he came across the Jacobite army's camp followers and baggage train. This caused him anxiety, as there might be some among them who would incline to be rough with a lone stranger.[1] He continued walking, encountering a farmer from Colinton whose house had been plundered and horses taken by the Jacobite army. Crichton then took the by-road to Braid, and walking down to 'Canaan muir' (now Morningside) he recalled seeing, at a distance, 'a politer sight', that is, 'the pretended Prince his retenew and gardes', with 'all the hillskipers in rank and file'.[2] A local man told him that the prince was in Highland dress with a velvet bonnet, both ornamented with gold lace. What Crichton was witnessing, from a distance, was Lord Strahallan leading, Prince Charles behind on horseback – a bay gelding, which had been a gift from the Duke of Perth – flanked by Lord Elcho and Perth, and the remainder of the Jacobite army marching in an orderly fashion behind them, with Lord George Murray on foot at the head of the infantry. All were progressing in a long column at some distance around the southern side of Edinburgh towards Holyroodhouse.

It was Charles' first sight, close to, of the entire southern length of the Scottish capital. The conquered city, perched on its crag, with smoke from the chimneys puffing up into the clear blue sky, must have looked glorious to him in the morning light. And although the conversation between the prince, the Duke of Perth and Lord Elcho is unrecorded, some comments and observations to that effect must have passed between them, with detailed descriptions for the prince's benefit of the buildings lying nearby – Heriot's, the Surgeon's Hall – as well as the church towers and steeples which punctuated the skyline above. In addition to the view, the prince was welcomed by curious locals and supporters, both eager to see at close hand this famous young man, and, if so inclined, to cheer him on his way. As Lord Elcho recalled, 'When the Army Came near town it was met by vast Multidudes of people, who by their repeated Shouts & huzzas express'd a great deal of joy to See the Prince.'[3] Aside from this, the issue of how to deal with the threat posed by the Castle, still under the command of Generals Guest and Preston, would have been a subject of particular discussion and debate on the march to Holyrood.

The view looking down from the battlements, towards the distant, snaking column of the Jacobite army, would have been far less appealing. While the army was in full view, the garrison commanders decided to give Charles and his troops a different sort of welcome. As Crichton observed, 'the Castle fyred three cannon shott which made them start and halt'[4] although they were well out of range. The army was maintaining roughly a mile distance from the Castle, along the road to Duddingston. Even Patrick Crichton, clearly no admirer of Highlanders, grudgingly gave the Jacobite army some credit for their orderly approach, 'for to give them there due never did 6000 [sic] theiving naked ruffiens with uncowth wappons make so harmeless a march in a civilised plentifull cowntry'.[5] Crichton, with a degree of incredulity, continues, 'on they came with there bagpipes and plaids, rusty rapiers, matchlocks, and fyerlocks, and tag rag and bob taile was there'.[6] However, Patrick Crichton had significantly exaggerated the Jacobite army's numbers.

The prince marched on, according to Crichton, stopping at Grange House to the south-east of the city, where he 'drunk some bottles [of] wine'.[7] Lord Elcho, who remained at Charles' side throughout, declared, 'When they Came into the Suburbs the Croud was prodigious and all wishing the Prince prosperity; in Short, nobody doubted but that he would be joined by 10,000 men at Edinburgh if he Could Arm them.'[8] Likewise, Colonel John O'Sullivan recalled, 'the most part of the inhabitants of the Town & Subborbs went to meet him. The demonstrations of Joy [that] both gente[e]l & simple shewed him, cant be expressed, the roads were so crouded for near upon a mil before he came to the Cannegate [that] he cou'd hardly make his way.'[9] The prince and his retinue continued to the south-west of Salisbury Crags, and then made their way through the hollow between the Crags and Arthur's Seat, all the while avoiding the Castle's fire.[10] According to Patrick Crichton, who must have heard this from an eyewitness, as they turned by the western border wall of the old royal hunting park, the 'King's Park', within which Salisbury Crags and Arthur's Seat are located, the prince was informed that Sir John Cope and his 2,500 troops had landed at Dunbar, to which Charles apparently replied, in a well-timed display of regal insouciance, 'Is he by God?'[11]

Lord Elcho, still riding by the prince's side, noted that near Duddingston the army entered the King's Park at a breach made in the wall, and the prince continued on horseback 'always followed by the Croud, who were happy if they could touch his boots or his horse furniture'. As he made his way down through the steepest part of the park, Charles dismounted and walked on, 'but the Mob out of Curiosity, and some out of fondness to touch him or kiss his hand, were like to throw him down'. So, as soon as he arrived at the bottom of the incline, he remounted his horse and rode on through St Anne's Yards.[12] The Edinburgh High School master and later biographer of the Duke of Cumberland, Andrew Henderson, also witnessed the event, writing, 'He made his Entry to the Abbey, thro' the Road that leads by St. Anthony's Well',[13] a natural spring on the slopes lying to the south of the Abbey and Palace grounds. He then reveals his sympathies by stating, 'he alighted and walked some few Steps, where halting, several of the Disaffected fell down upon their Knees and kissed his Hand, at which he frequently smiled. Here was raised the first general Huzza.' As Lord Elcho had recalled at St Anne's Yards, Charles remounted his horse.[14]

The prince then apparently paused for a few minutes, and 'seem'd very thoughtful'. Lord Strathallan and Secretary Murray rode up to him, and they agreed that the troops should encamp in the park, while he and his officers advanced to the palace. Having received another cheer, 'and the Gates of the Park being opened, he rode to the Abbey, amidst repeated Acclamations, which he received with a continued tho' irregular Smile'.[15] Henderson had been close enough to observe that Charles' 'Speech was sly, but very intelligible; his Dialect was more upon the *English* than the *Scottish* Accent, seem'd to me pretty like that of the *Irish*, some of whom I had known'.[16] Here 'sly' means soft or low.

Andrew Henderson also recalls his first impression of the prince's appearance, as 'a Slender young Man, about five Feet ten Inches high, of a ruddy Complexion, high nosed, large rolling brown Eyes, long Visage; his Chin was pointed, and Mouth small, in Proportion to his Features; his Hair was red, but at that Time wore a pale Peruke'.[17] As observed before, he 'was in Highland Dress', red velvet breeches, a bonnet with a white Cockade, and 'being in his Boots I could not observe his Legs; he had a Silver-hilted broad Sword, and was shewn great Respect by his Forces'.[18] John Home, who was also standing in the King's Park, considered the 'figure and presence of Charles Stuart were not ill suited to his lofty pretensions'.[19] According to Home, while Charles stood in the Duke's Walk (named after his grandfather), 'one of the spectators endeavoured to measure shoulders with him; and said he was more than 5 feet 10 inches high'.[20] This hints at a degree of crowding in and jostling of the prince, which chimes with Lord Elcho's description, that while dismounted he was so hemmed in by the crowds kissing his hand and touching him that he had to remount his horse. Home continues, he 'was in the prime of youth, tall and handsome, of a fair complexion; he had a light coloured periwig with his own hair combed over the front: he wore the Highland dress, that is a tartan short coat without the plaid, a blue bonnet on his head, and on his breast the star of the order of St. Andrew'. Having stood in the park, 'to shew himself to the people', he then 'mounted his horse, either to render himself more conspicuous, or because he rode well, and looked graceful on horseback'.[21]

The prince and his retinue continued down through St Anne's Yards, which lay to the south of the Abbey and Palace of Holyroodhouse (locally 'the Abbey' signified both), according to Lord Elcho, 'Amidst the Cries of 60000 people, who fill'd the Air with their Acclamations of joy. He dismounted in the inner court.'[22] Lord Elcho can be forgiven for exaggerating the numbers outside the palace. In reality the total population had barely reached that figure by 1751. In his journal, Lord Elcho expands on this account, by stating, 'The court of the palace was filled with the people who showed their satisfaction by cries of "Long live the Prince and the royal House of Stuart".'[23] Alexander MacDonald wrote, 'indeed the whole scene, as I have been told by many, was rather like a dream, so quick and amazing seemed the change, tho no doubt wise people saw well enough we had much to do still'.[24]

The palace, standing on the east side of the outer courtyard where these crowds had gathered, was described by Daniel Defoe as 'a very handsome Building, rather convenient than large'.[25] In structure, the palace is four connected wings around a square, inner court. The façade fronting the outer courtyard is a long block of two main storeys (as opposed to three in the remaining three sides) punctuated with tall windows on the principal floor and with two turrets at each end. The north turret was built by James V in the mid-sixteenth century. Charles' great-uncle, Charles II, had ordered a major remodelling of the building in the 1670s by the architect William Bruce, which included the western frontage, the addition of the turret to the south and lavish new royal apartments within. As a result, the palace that the prince now looked upon as he walked towards the main entrance had some remains of the sixteenth-century palace, but was predominantly seventeenth century in design and structure. From the outside at least, the palace had changed very little since his grandfather, James VII, when Duke of York, had resided there. Jutting out from the north side, and slightly disturbing the elegant symmetry of the front façade, was a later extension built by the Dukes of Hamilton, who were now both the main occupants and hereditary keepers. Behind this 'Hamilton Wing' sits the ancient, now partly ruined Abbey. In the centre of the front façade is the entrance, in Defoe's opinion 'majestick' and 'adorned with Pillars of hewn Stone, under a Cupola in the Form of an Imperial Crown, balustraded on each Side a-top'.[26]

If Charles had thought at all about how he would approach and then enter the ancient palace of the Stuart kings of Scotland, it is evident that he had decided against any pomp or rousing speeches. Nobody mentions pipes or trumpets. The prince simply walked across the courtyard, to the cheers or silence of the thousands that had turned out to see history in the making. At least one person standing within the crowd felt that something more heroic was needed to mark the occasion. John Home recalled that as the prince was nearing the door, which stood open to receive him, James Hepburn of Keith (one of the Associators), stepped out of the crowd, drew his sword, and, raising it aloft, walked before the prince: an improvisation which lent the moment some chivalric dignity or antiquarian pantomime, depending on the viewer. James Hepburn of Keith had been a fervent Jacobite since 1715. Yet, according to Home, and as an indication of the complex reasons that attracted different people to the Stuarts and Jacobitism, Hepburn 'disclaimed the hereditary indefeasible right of Kings', and even condemned the government of James VII/II. But he considered the Union between Scotland and England 'as injurious, and humiliating to his Country', and which, from his own experience, 'had made a Scotch gentleman of small fortune nobody'. As a result, Hepburn declared that 'he would die a thousand times rather than submit to it'.[27]

Despite his triumph, according to some witnesses, Charles himself did not appear in any way jubilant. Andrew Henderson gives the impression that he had an uneasy, fixed smile throughout the entire final stages of his journey to the palace. John Home observed that the 'Jacobites were charmed with his appearance: they compared him to Robert the Bruce, whom he resembled (they said) in his figure as in his fortune'.[28] Comparison to the Bruce, the fourteenth-century warrior king of the Scots, may have been a little premature, as Charles and his army were yet to prove themselves in battle. And it would soon become clear whether Charles would be satisfied with restoring his family to the Kingdom of Scotland alone. The loaded reference to Robert Bruce also recalls the ancient lineage of the House of Stewart in Scotland (the surname later became 'Stuart', the French spelling favoured by Mary, Queen of Scots and her second husband Henry, Lord Darnley), through Walter Stewart's marriage to Robert Bruce's daughter Marjorie. Their son Robert II (r. 1371–90) founded the dynasty.

However, and as John Home continues, the 'Whigs looked upon him with other eyes'. They accepted that he cut an impressive figure, and had achieved much in a short time, but also observed, 'that even in that triumphant hour, when he was about to enter the palace of his fathers, the air of his countenance was languid and melancholy'. In fact, they stated, 'he looked like a gentleman and a man of fashion, but not like a hero or a conqueror'. No one could deny that Charles was resourceful, persuasive and driven by an absolute belief in the legitimacy of his cause. But he had little experience of the world, of leading and managing individuals who had differing views and expectations, and even less experience of warfare. How good a judge of character and situation was he? How he handled the brusque, self-righteous, but ultimately dedicated and loyal Lord George Murray would be an indication. But would Charles be willing to seek out and even bend to the counsel of more experienced men? The opposition were taking courage, even in their darkest hour, for 'they formed their conclusions that the enterprize was above the pitch of his mind; and that his heart was not great enough for the sphere in which he moved',[29] solely, it should be noted, from his appearance and manner at this auspicious moment. However, Duke James of Atholl's steward had also come to that opinion, that is, as quoted earlier, 'I doe not think that he hath verry much in him.' This might have been wishful thinking on their part, or an indication that Charles was not very good at hiding his feelings; perhaps a bit of both. Regardless of his inner turmoil, Charles needed to look and act as both a hero and a conqueror – and fast. And yet, whatever the future might hold, as he entered the Palace of Holyroodhouse, no one could deny the enormity of his achievement so far.

Richard Cooper, *Charles Edward Stuart, 'The Wanted Poster'*, 1745.

The Mercat Cross

'Thus the winds blew'

Among the men who joined the prince at this time were Alexander Erskine, 5th Earl of Kellie, Arthur Elphinstone, later Lord Balmerino, James Hepburn of Keith (he with sword aloft), George Lockhart the younger of Carnwath,¹ as well as John Hay of Restalrig and Andrew Lumisden, the last two becoming treasurer and undersecretary respectively within Charles' personal household. Having entered the palace, Charles ordered that his father be proclaimed King James VIII and III. As the Heralds and Pursuivants had been gathered for the purpose, at midday the people of Edinburgh witnessed the proclamation at the Mercat Cross, followed by the reading of the Commission of Regency and Declaration (which, Home pointedly states, were 'dated at Rome, in December 1743'), followed by the manifesto in the name of Charles Prince Regent, 'dated at Paris, 16ᵗʰ of May 1745'. As Home continues, an 'immense multitude witnessed this ceremony . . . The populace of a great city, who huzza for any thing that brings them together, huzzaed; and a number of ladies in the windows strained their voices with acclamation, and their arms with waving white hankerchiefs in honour of the day.' Home concludes that such demonstrations of joy among the well-to-do were chiefly confined to the women, for few gentlemen were to be seen on the streets, or even at the windows, and 'even amongst the inferior people, many shewed their dislike by a stubborn silence'.² In contrast, inevitably, Colonel John O'Sullivan declared that all the windows at every floor, the entire length of the main street, were full of both men and women, the latter waving handkerchiefs 'like so many colours'. Considering the height of these buildings, that must have been an impressive sight. There was 'a continual cry of "God blesse the King" from both sexes'.³

Patrick Crichton was also in the crowd. After viewing the prince's advance around the southern side of the city, he entered Edinburgh by the Bristow Port, 'which I saw to my indignation in the keeping of these caterpillars'. He goes on to describe them. One, a boy, 'stood with a rusty drawen sword and two fellows with things licke guns of the 16th centuries sat on each syde the entry to the poors howse', all of which, 'were catching the vermin from ther lurking places abowt ther plaids and throwing them away'. Crichton asked the Revd John Jardine, minister of Liberton, who was passing, 'ar these the scownderalls have surprised Edinburgh by treachery?' Jardine answered, 'I had reither seen it in the hands of Frenchmen, but the divell and the deep sea are both bad.'[4] Crichton then climbed up the steep stairs to Parliament Close, pushed his way through the throng, and eventually witnessed what he describes as 'this commick fars or tragic commody' from a window on the north side of the main street. While awaiting the ceremony at the Mercat Cross, he observed that the attendant Highlanders were a mixed bag of varying ages, from very young to very old, some armed with guns of different sizes, some swords but no guns, others pitchforks, and even some old Lochaber axes.[5] Another local described how he talked 'with some of the Ruffians, as I could speak their Language a little . . . One of the Fellows had the Impudence to tell me, it would not give him the least Pain to cut all our Throats. You may believe I did not like this, and made the best of my Way out of their Reach.'[6]

The cross was covered in a large 'Persian' carpet, brought from the Royal Household for the purpose, and the heralds were standing about 'in their formalities' with a single trumpeter.[7] The pipes were also playing. As Crichton continues, 'All the streat and the windows and forstairs were crowded and silence being made the manifesto was read',[8] followed by the declaration. Another witness, Magdalen Pringle, wrote to her sister 'Tib' (Isabella, the letter dated Wednesday, 18 September) that after this the group immediately around the cross, which included James Hepburn, 'threw up their hats and huzz'd in which acclamation of joy they were joyn'd by all ye crowd which was so great I incline almost to call it the whole Town'. Magdalen also describes the ladies at the windows, waving their hankies and clapping, 'and show'd great loyalty to the Bonny Prince'.[9] Magdalen, from a staunch Whig family, concludes, 'Don't imagine I was one of those Ladies. I assure you I was not.' Another witness states that the Tory and Catholic ladies present 'shew'd a great deal of Zeal', but 'not a Gentleman could I see worth Two-pence; no, not One'.[10] Of course, gentlewomen, unlike their menfolk, would not be subjected to the full force of the law should the rising fail, and when such behaviour, no matter how minor or trivial, would have the air of treason. Printed copies of the various proclamations were then dispersed among the crowd.[11] 'Thus,' observes Crichton, 'the winds blew from Rome and Paris were to work owr thraldom.'[12] Crichton concludes ruefully, 'The honest partie had no human refuge to look to but Generall John Cope and his batalions, and the two dastardly Irish regiments of dragowns.'[13] In contrast, according to Lord Elcho, that evening and throughout the night a large crowd was gathered in the courtyard of the Palace of Holyroodhouse, who cheered energetically whenever the prince appeared at the window.[14]

The people of Edinburgh, should they have required reminding, awoke on 18 September to the latest edition of the *Caledonian Mercury*, which declared, courtesy of its Jacobite-leaning proprietor Thomas Ruddiman, now very much emboldened, 'Edinburgh, Sept. 17. Affairs in this City and Neighbourhood have taken the most surprizing Turn since Yesterday, without the least Bloodshed or Opposition; so that we have now in our Streets Highlanders and Bag pipes, in place of Dragoons and Drums.'[15] To residents, the transformation must have seemed swift and startling. The paper then proceeds to describe in painful detail the attempts to defend the city, the entry of about '1000 resolute, hardy-like Men' at the Netherbow, that the 'Prince lay in his Cloaths two Hours that Night at Slateford' (only two days before he had been 'the Young Chevalier', before that 'the Young Pretender'), and how, at about midday, he took possession of Holyroodhouse, 'accompanied by several Nobility, [and] Persons of Distinction'.[16] Magdalen Pringle, writing again to her sister that afternoon, describes the occupying army as being 'as quiet as lambs, civil to everybody and takes nothing but what ye pay for'.[17] James Maxwell of Kirkconnell, who joined the army at Edinburgh as an officer in Lord Elcho's Life Guards, recalled that 'tradesmen were employed day and night in preparing military accountrements; but all was quiet and orderly in the City, and people had the pleasure of seeing the whole apparatus of war without feeling the effects of it'. Lochiel had been put in command of guarding the town.[18]

But the presence of what was, predominantly, an ill-trained and in many ways alien army among urban civilians, no matter how quiet and polite, brought its own dangers. Magdalen goes on to inform her sister of an incident that had occurred that morning, involving 'poor Madie Nairn', who had been looking out of a window. Standing on the street opposite were a 'Highlander' and a boy, the latter holding a gun that suddenly went off, shooting poor Madie in the head. Thankfully 'the strength of ye ball had been spent by its Grazing on ye wall so that it struck and did not go through her skull or she must have Died instantly'. The doctor, Mr Ratray, 'has taken out ye Ball and sow'd up her wound he thinks her safe if she keeps free from a Fever'. Prince Charles had sent messages to enquire after her, 'which has help'd not a little to support her spirits under ye Pain of her sore wound'. In the wake of this gallantry Magdalen concludes, 'All ye Ladies are to kiss ye Prince's hand – I've an inclination to see him.'[19]

In the following days, Patrick Crichton observed, 'The Prince was in the Abby of Holiroodhows and his Hieghland gang spread in Sant An's yeards and towards the brea face or brow of the descent under Salesburg [Salisbury Crags]. The Prince had read his demand upon the town on Wednesday September 18, 1000 tents each to hold 6 men, pans for readying ther victwals 6000, and shoes and stockings.'[20] According to another resident, 'They made a Barracks of the New Assembly Room, the New and Old Churches, and the Parliament House. I think we may really say our Churches are now made a Den of Thieves.'[21] However, Secretary Murray stated, 'No more men were quartered in Town than were necessary for its preservation, and a small gaurd att the Palace, the rest of the Army was quartered att Duddingston, to be ready to march to G[n]. Cope so soon as his motions were known.'[22]

Meanwhile, news of the fall of Edinburgh to the prince and his small Jacobite army had reached London. The Marquess of Tweeddale, writing to the Lord Justice Clerk from his ministerial office in Whitehall, observes with tangible incredulity, 'That 2000 men, and these the scum of two or three Highland gentlemen, the Camerons, and a few tribes of the Macdonalds, should be able in so short a time to make themselves masters of the town of Edinburgh, is an event which, had it not happened, I should never have believed possible.' He concludes,

'Some satisfaction, however, it gives to us that from Sir John Cope's landing the troops at Dunbar, and being joined by the two regiments of dragoons, we may hope soon to see the face of affairs in our country changed for the better.'[23]

His letter was dated 21 September.

Detail from George Bickham the Younger, *A Race from Preston Pans to Berwick*, 1745.

Prestonpans

'On Gladsmoore shal the Battle be'

'Is he by God?' was Charles' reported response to the news that Sir John Cope and his troops had landed at Dunbar, thirty miles due east of Edinburgh.[1] Charles had barely had a moment to enjoy his army's occupation of the city when it became clear that the long-awaited military encounter was close at hand. The night of 19 September the prince rested at a tavern on the causeway at Duddingston. Here the Grants of Glenmoriston joined the Jacobite army and at first light Charles and his men began the march east towards Dunbar. Secretary Murray recalled that 'the Chevalier putt himself att the head of his small army, drawing his sword, said with a very determined Countenance, Gentlemen, I have flung away the Scabbard, with Gods assistance I dont doubt of making you a free and happy people, Mr Cope shall not escape us as he did in the Highlands'.[2] Colonel O'Sullivan adds more detail, and less elegance, to this moment. As he recalls, Charles rallied his men and put them in order of battle to the wail of pipes. When all was ready, he gathered the clan chiefs around him and declared they knew what they had to do, everything depended upon it, that his wish and his father's was to save them from the slavery they were under. The cause was good, and the enemy would be so troubled by their consciences (for fighting against their King and Country) that they would be halfway defeated before a shot was fired. 'So,' he said, 'God will protect us.' After which, 'he drew his Sword, "Now Gents" says he, "the Sword is drawn, it wont be my fault, if I set it in the Scabert, before yu be a free & happy people. I desire yu may retire to [your] postes, inform [your] men of what I said & march".' There must have been a short delay as the chiefs bellowed out the prince's words in Gaelic for the benefit of some of their clansmen, after which 'all the Bonnets were in the Air, & such a Cry, [that] it wou'd be wherewithal to frighten any enemy'. Charles made a signal, and the army marched.[3]

Sir John Cope, meanwhile, had begun his advance on Edinburgh the previous day. Having spent the night in a field to the west of Haddington he and his 2,500 troops (many recent recruits) were approaching Tranent, a village eleven miles east of Edinburgh, as night fell. Alexander Carlyle, John Home and some others from the student volunteers had joined the British army as it marched from Haddington. Carlyle recalls conversing with Major Richard Bowles of Hamilton's Dragoons, who 'was completely Ignorant of the State of the Country, and of the Character of the Highlanders. I found him perfectly Ignorant and Credulous, and in the power of every person with whom he Convers'd.' Carlyle queried this lack of discipline, which allowed the people to talk to the soldiers as they wished, and 'by which means their Panick was kept up, and perhaps their principles corrupted'. Carlyle believed Jacobitism was rife in East Lothian, and that the 'Commons in General as well as two thirds of the Gentry . . . had no aversion to the Family of Stuart, and could their Religion have been Secur'd [that is, Protestantism], would have been very glad to see them on the Throne again'.[4] As a result, in Carlyle's opinion some of the soldiers, and even the officers of the British army, were beginning to get disheartened by both the lack of support they encountered among the local people, and the descriptions of the fierce Highlanders they would soon encounter.

On 20 September, the Jacobite army arrived at Musselburgh, six miles east of Edinburgh. On hearing of the British army's position, and presuming Cope's plan was to engage them on the moors west of Tranent, they continued at a much greater speed. This took Cope by surprise. As described by an anonymous British army officer to a friend, 'we had frequent intelligence brought, that the rebels were advancing towards us with their whole body, with a quick pace. We could not therefore get to the ground it was intended we should, having still some miles to march through.'[5] Carlyle, who obviously knew this countryside well, observed that Cope's troops began their march too late, and by the time they had reached St Germains, the Seton family house, their scouts were returning with the news that the Jacobite army was well advanced. Rather than turning south, when 'they might have Reach'd the high Ground at Tranent before the Rebels',[6] Cope turned north and came to a halt on land, described by Carlyle, as an open field two miles long and over a mile wide, which stretched from Seaton to Preston (a village near Prestonpans), and from the meadow at Tranent to the sea.[7] Having judged that they could not reach their preferred ground in time, the

British army officer continues in a positive way, stating that the troops proceeded to the first piece of open land they could find (the recently harvested field as described by Carlyle), which lay within a mile south of the village of Prestonpans, and 'a better spot could not have been chosen for the cavalry to be at liberty to act in'. They arrived 'just in time before the enemy got up to us'.[8]

General Cope was forming his line of battle as the Jacobite army came into view about a mile away to the south-west. Seeing them, Cope's troops shouted a feisty greeting. Then, as the Jacobite army advanced towards Tranent, Cope shifted his line a little to the east, so that his troops were now facing them full on. According to Carlyle, all this manoeuvring had occurred by one o'clock in the afternoon.[9] The unnamed officer believed that, by this time, Cope's troops were ready either to wait for the Jacobite army to advance to meet them, or to make the attack themselves. While the British army watched the enemy advance, 'we exchang'd several huzzas with them, and probably from their not liking our disposition they began to alter their own'.[10] Standing in battle order in this flat, open land, General Cope, echoing his officer, considered that there 'is not in the whole of the Ground between *Edinburgh* and *Dunbar* a better Spot for both Horse and Foot to act upon'[11] and Captain James Johnstone, now aide-de-camp to both Lord George and Prince Charles, obviously agreed with him, writing, 'We spent the afternoon in reconnoitring his position; and the more we examined it, the more our uneasiness and chagrin increased, as we saw no possibility of attacking it, without exposing ourselves to be cut to pieces in a disgraceful manner.'[12] The Jacobite army finally encamped to the other side of a marsh, which was now the only obstacle that separated the two armies.

In the British army camp, Alexander Carlyle visited Colonel Gardiner, who was still unwell but prepared for battle the following day. Carlyle recalled that the colonel declared 'he could not wish for a better night to ly on the Field, and then call'd for his Cloak, and other Conveniences for Lying down, as he said they would be awak'd Early enough in the Morning, as he thought by the Countenance of the Enemy'.[13] In the meantime, a very dark, moonless night had settled around the two armies and despite British army patrols continuing to venture out until three o'clock in the morning, no movement could be seen or a noise heard from the Jacobite encampment.[14]

Far from still, the Jacobite commanders were now aware that they were not at such a terrible disadvantage as had been supposed. Rather than facing an expanse of impenetrable bog, they discovered there was a route through the marsh that offered the opportunity for a surprise attack. There is some discrepancy between contemporary witnesses as to who received this crucial information. John Home states that it was Lord George Murray – corroborated by Lord George himself who says, 'I knew the ground myself, and had a gentleman or two with me who knew every part thereabouts'[15] – whereas in Captain Johnstone's account, the land-owner called Robert Anderson of Whitburgh 'came to the Prince in the evening, very a-propos, to relieve us from our embarrassment'.[16] Anderson knew a path through the marsh, which he often used while hunting. Better still, 'General Cope, not deeming it passable, had neglected to station a guard there'.[17] This seems odd, given that one of Cope's officers, Colonel Gardiner, had been resident in the area for many years. However, as a result of this discovery, Secretary Murray recalled that the prince 'kept in very high Spirits the rest of the night, laying on the ground without any Covering but his plaid'.[18] Then, about an hour before daylight, the first troops, led by the Duke of Perth with Lord George behind, entered the marsh in silence, picked their way through, and formed their battle lines as they emerged out on to the field. The second line, led by Charles himself, then followed. Captain Johnstone noted that between the marsh edge and the field of battle there was a deep ditch, which was about three feet wide, and in attempting to leap over it Charles landed on his knees on the other side. Johnstone grabbed his arm and pulled him up. But on 'examining his countenance, it seemed to me, from the alarm expressed in it, that he considered this accident as a bad omen'.[19]

Despite this apparently portentous incident, Captain Johnstone then recalled that the second line had not fully arrived on the field, 'when the enemy, seeing our first line in order of battle, fired an alarmgun'.[20] Lord George 'did not give the English [sic] time to recover from their surprise',[21] and while Cope's men were forming up, the cavalry on either side of the infantry, Lord George ordered his men to charge. Captain Johnstone admired Lord George's ability in leading the army's Highland contingent by example, 'in the most heroic manner', rushing forward sword in hand, and crying "'I do not ask you, my lads, to go before, but merely to follow me'", which was 'a very energetic harangue, admirably calculated to excite the ardour of the Highlanders'.[22] According to Johnstone the strategy was to attack the cavalry first by aiming at the horses' heads, which 'would cause them to wheel around and then throw a whole squadron into such disorder, that it is impossible afterwards to rally it'. The troops 'followed this advice most implicitly, and the English [sic] cavalry were instantly thrown into confusion'.[23]

Accounts from the British army's side affirm that, despite attempts to calm and rally the dragoons, nothing could be done to prevent the disorder from spreading through the squadrons. The attack with broadswords, along with gunfire, 'struck such a panick into the dragoons, that in a moment they fled' leaving Colonel Gardiner, alone and exposed, demanding in vain that they return and make a stand. Lieutenant Colonel Whitney attempted an attack, but 'received a shot which shatter'd his arm' and, like Gardiner, was abandoned by his squadron. After the flight of the dragoons, the infantry, originally located at the centre, was left to take the full brunt of the Highland attack, which now surrounded them on three sides, and they in turn became 'possess'd with the same fatal dread, so that it became utterly impossible for the general, or any one of the best intentioned of his officers, either to put an end to their fears, or stop their flight'. One such officer, Colonel Charles Whitefoord of Cochrane's Marines, had, along with Major Eaglesford Griffith, almost single-handedly fired the ten British army guns on the field and then, having been abandoned, attempted to fight on alone.[24] In this way, the officers 'exposed themselves in such a manner to the fire of the rebels, that I cannot account for their escaping it any other way, but that all of it was aimed at the run-away dragoons', who did not stop to view the devastating effect of their flight on the remainder of the army.[25] Indeed, some did not pause until they arrived in the English border town of Berwick-upon-Tweed, fifty miles away to the south. When he realised all was lost, having attempted to rally both the dragoons and the foot, General Cope soon followed.

After his meeting with Colonel Gardiner earlier that morning, Alexander Carlyle had returned to his father's house and instructed a maid to wake him as soon as the two armies were forming up on the field of battle. As it was, he was unexpectedly awoken only a few hours later, by the first blast of British army cannon. He ran into the garden and clambered on to a rise from which he could see the battlefield, and 'Even at that time, which could hardly be more than Ten or 15 Minutes after Firing the First Cannon, The Whole Prospect was fill'd with Runaways, and Highlanders Pursueing them.' Carlyle saw many of the runaways had turned their coats to signal their surrender, but were still fleeing towards the town with Jacobite troops in pursuit. Those men that could not be outrun were fired at, 'and I saw two Fall in the Glebe'.[26] As Carlyle's description suggests, the

effect of the Highlanders rushing at Cope's cavalry and then infantry was
swift and devastating. Even a few years later, Captain Johnstone's observations are tinged with incredulity for the 'panic-terror of the English [sic]
surpasses all imagination'.[27]

Carlyle had no time to pause for breath, when he was surrounded by
Jacobite soldiers, and an officer 'whom I knew to be Lord Elcho pass'd with
his Train, and had an air of Savage Ferocity, that Disgusted and alarm'd'.
Lord Elcho then 'enquir'd fiercely of me, Where a publick House was to
be found; I answer'd him very meekly, not Doubting but that If I had
Displeas'd him with my Tone, his Reply would have been with a Pistol
Bullet'.[28] From this description we get a hint of the feverish state of someone just emerging from a fierce and bloody encounter, and Lord Elcho
had even less experience of warfare than his royal commander. Soon after
his exchange with Lord Elcho, Carlyle was witness to the impact of war
on the defeated, as the crowds of wounded and dying approached. But
'their Groans and Agonies were nothing compar'd with the Howlings and
Cries and Lamentations of the Women, which Suppress'd Manhood and
Created Despondency'.[29]

Inspecting the field of battle soon after, Captain Johnstone observed
that it 'presented a spectacle of horror, being covered with heads, legs, and
arms, and mutilated bodies; for the killed all fell by the sword'.[30] Andrew
Henderson, now a volunteer in Cope's army, supports Johnstone's description of the battlefield as a slaughterhouse: 'The private Mens Heads were
almost cut through; the greater Number were cut in the back Parts; some
had 7 or 8 Wounds; Noses, Hands, Arms, Legs, &c. were promiscuously
to be seen in some Places of the Field.'[31] His statement that many of
the men were cut in the 'back Parts', pointedly draws attention to the
fact that they were attacked while fleeing the field, rather than standing
and fighting. The front line, he goes on, 'was miserably massacred by the
Rebels. Such as threw down their Arms, and begged for Quarters upon
their Knees, were cut inhumanely; yea such as fled into the Inclosures
were pursued and murdered, but the great Carnage was at the *Grange*
Park-Dyke.' Here, the men attempting to climb over a high wall were
attacked, and 'twenty were killed by the Sword, for one who fell by a
Bullet'.[32] According to Henderson, it was the Duke of Perth and Lochiel
who ordered the slaughter to cease. The British army casualties are estimated at around 300 killed, up to 1,500 taken prisoner, of which 500
were wounded, including Lieutenant Colonel Whitefoord and Major
Bowles.

One of the most senior officers to fall during the battle was Colonel Gardiner, who, on being abandoned by his cavalry, and having then (according to one account) taken command of an infantry company, was struck down within sight of his own house. James Ray, who joined the British army volunteers a few months later, wrote that the colonel was on foot, fighting at the head of this company, when 'he was brought down by three Wounds, one in his Shoulder by a Ball, another in his Forehead by a Broad Sword, and the third, which was his mortal Stroke, in the hinder Part of his Head, by a *Lochabar* Ax', the latter a wound 'given him by a Highlander, who came behind him, while he was reaching a Stroke at an Officer with whom he was engaged'. Ray concludes, 'that he finished a worthy and exemplary Life, with a most honourable and heroic Death; for he very easily might have escaped with the rest, if like them, he would have deserted his Duty'.[33] It is too simplistic to view this image of an educated Lowland Scot, who was also an integrated member of both the modern British state and its armed forces, being finished off by a Highlander wielding an antiquated weapon, as part of a symbolic struggle between Scotland's past and future. Contemporaries certainly viewed it as a civil war, whether between Britons or Scotsmen. But, at the very least, the fact that Scots fought on opposing sides counters the belief – propagated by contemporaries like Captain Johnstone, and still in circulation today – that this campaign was the latest in the centuries-long struggle between Scotland and England.

Secretary Murray, on the other hand, considered the descriptions of Gardiner's death to be not just exaggeration (to encourage distaste for the brutishness of the Highlanders, and therefore the Jacobite army as a whole), but utterly false. He argues that far from being heroic, it was pique or even vanity that led Gardiner to place himself in the situation that caused his death.[34] This does not chime with the many descriptions of Gardiner's character: fatalism perhaps, vanity surely not. However his attendant, on seeing his master fall, ran to a mill two miles away and then returned some hours later with a cart to carry away Gardiner's body. By this time the battle was all but over. Arriving on the field, he discovered his master 'not only plundered of his Watch and other Things of Value, but also stripped of his upper Garments and Boots; yet still breathing', and adds, 'tho' he were not capable of Speech, yet on taking him up he opened his Eyes.'[35] According to the same account, Colonel Gardiner was carried to the Tranent Manse where he lingered, in agony, until the following morning. It is said that he died cradled in the arms of the minister's daughter, Beatrix Jenkinson.

Andrew Henderson chanced upon Charles just after the battle and reported – in very unsympathetic terms – the prince's appearance and manner. He pointedly attributes the ordering of surgeons from Edinburgh, for the benefit of the fallen British army troops, to the Duke of Perth rather than the prince and then describes Charles himself:

> He was clad as an ordinary Captain, in a coarse Plaid and blue Bonnet, his Boots and Knees were much fouled; he seemed to have fallen into a Ditch, which I was told by one of his Lifeguards he had; he was exceeding merry. Speaking of his Army, he said twice, *'My Highlandmen have lost their Plaids.'* At which he laughed very heartily. When talking of the Dead and Wounded, he was noway affected, there were seven Standards taken, which when he saw, he said in *French*, a Language he frequently spoke in, *We have missed some of them*; which was the only Interruption of his Jollity. Thereafter he refreshed himself upon the Field, and with the utmost Composure eat a Piece of cold Beef, and drank a Glass of Wine, amidst the deep and piercing Groans of the mangled Patriots, who had fallen a Sacrifice to his foolish Ambition.[36]

This account contradicts the descriptions from Jacobite observers, who are at pains to present their prince as a just and caring 'father' of his people. Henderson had no such aim. Writing only a few years after the event, he represents 'the Chevalier' in victory as callous, somewhat juvenile, and, worse still, unashamedly foreign.

Secretary Murray countered this by describing Charles as very concerned for the care of the enemy wounded, even to the detriment of his own men, 'who from being neglected till most of the troops were taken care of, their wounds festered, being all gun Shott and mostly in the legs and thighs'. He admits that Charles 'breakfasted on the field', but not as Henderson describes 'amongst the dead and within hearing of the groans of the wounded, as has been falsely asserted by little ignorant Scholl master who has pretend to write the history of an affair of which he could be no judge'.[37] The 'ignorant Scholl master' directly berated here is obviously Andrew Henderson. It is not unlikely that, to a degree, both reactions occurred. This was Charles' second taste of war (the first, as an observer, was during the siege of Gaeta in 1734), but the first time he had witnessed the horror of hand-to-hand fighting at close quarters. Not only was there a lot riding on this encounter, but it had been months, years, in the waiting. It is therefore not difficult to imagine the prince's euphoria, mixed with relief, at the success of his army – and achieved at such speed, and with so little immediate impact on his own troops. In fact, in contrast to the utter destruction of General Cope's army, the Jacobite casualties were incredibly light: just seventy injured, and thirty dead, although among the latter were Rob Roy Macgregor's son James and David Threipland. If he had, for a few moments, openly revelled in his victory, then this indicates his lack of experience and maturity, rather than his callousness. As the euphoria subsided, when he came to his senses, he can be credited with behaving in a manner better suited to his position, both as victor and, in his opinion, true prince of his people – which, technically, included Cope's vanquished troops.

Meanwhile, Alexander Carlyle was in a nearby house assisting the Edinburgh surgeons Cunningham and Trotter, who were attending to the British army wounded. The contrast between the cosy domestic interior, now a makeshift hospital, and the battle-bloodied injured and dying is marked. Here Carlyle 'observ'd a very Handsome young Officer Lying in an Easy Chair in a Faint, and seemingly Dying. They Led me to a Drawers Head, where there lay a Piece of his Skull about 2 Fingers Breadth and an Inch and an Half Long.' Startled, Carlyle cried 'this Gentleman must Die. No said Cunningham [the surgeon], The Brain is not affected, nor any vital part. He has Youth and a fine Constitution on his Side, and could I but get my Instruments there would be no Fear of him. This Man was Capt. Blake.'[38] Later, Carlyle saw 'the wounded officers were all Dress'd, Capt. Blake's Head was Trepan'd, and he was Laid in Bed'.[39] Carlyle also witnessed some of the many British army officers (now prisoners) walking on the seashore near Prestonpans. 'Then,' he says, 'saw I human Nature in its most Despicable abject form, for all most every aspect bore in it Shame, and Dejection and Despair.' They were horrified that they had been outwitted by such an irregular and badly armed enemy (as they thought), and unsurprisingly anxious about whether they would be treated as prisoners of war or rebels.[40] This was an important distinction. By convention, prisoners of war were protected; rebels, and particularly spies, could be summarily executed.

Later that day, at between eleven o'clock and midday, Alexander Carlyle and his father rode through the battlefield where the dead were still lying, mostly stripped of their clothes and belongings. Carlyle counted about two hundred bodies, besides which, 'There were only slight Guards, and a Few Straggling Boys.'[41]

Lord Elcho believed that the 'Prince from this Battle entertained a mighty notion of the highlanders, and ever after imagin'd they would beat four times their number of regular troops'.[42] Indeed, Charles had much to be pleased about. As Secretary Murray observed, 'the Success of that day having rendered the Chevalier entire master of that Kingdom, save the forts of Ed[inbu]r[gh] and Stirling, with the four small garrisons in the north'.[43] The garrisons in the north were Fort George in Inverness, Fort William in Lochaber, Fort Augustus (built by Marshal Wade between 1729 and 1742) and Ruthven in Badenoch (built in 1719). In addition to the weapons and cannon retrieved from the battlefield and beyond, Cope's baggage train had been captured, which included a war chest of above £2,000. This would fund the prince's campaign a little while longer. Charles' men had succeeded against a regular army that included artillery and cavalry – something the Jacobite army had lacked. This could now be addressed. On the field of battle, Charles gave Lord Elcho a commission as colonel of the prince's Horse Guards, and, as he proudly recalled, 'I raised a squadron of gentlemen, whose uniform was a blue coat and a red vest and red cuffs.'[44]

Later on the day of the battle, from nearby Pinkie House (the residence of the Marquess of Tweeddale, now also used as a field hospital), Charles immediately wrote to his father. Since his last letter from Perth, 'it hath pleased God to prosper your Majesty's arms under my command with a success that has even surprized my wishes'. Firstly, the fall of Edinburgh 'sword in hand', yet without shedding 'one drop of blood, or to do any violence'. And then, more amazing still, 'this morning I have gained a most signal victory with little or no loss'. If he had had cavalry 'to pursue the flying enemy there would not one man of them have escaped; as it is they have hardly saved any but a few dragoons who, by a most precipitate flight will, I believe, get into Berwick'. 'If,' he continues, 'I had obtained this victory over foreigners my joy would have been compleat. But as it is over Englishman [sic], it has thrown a damp upon it that I little imagined.' Yes, they were James' enemies, 'but they might have become your friends and dutiful subjects when they had got their eyes opened to see the true interest of their country which I am come to save, not to destroy. For this reason I have discharged all publick rejoicing.'[45] Knowing how bad Charles' English spelling tended to be, although not unusual in the mid-eighteenth century, here is another letter, attributed to the prince, that appears to have been finessed by another, possibly Secretary Murray.

When news reached Edinburgh, the Jacobites were jubilant. Patrick Crichton, on the other hand, noted that this 'was a melancholy day to those that love peace and qwiet for the Highlanders returned towards Edinburgh'. The main body of the army encamped once again at Duddingston. Prince Charles left Pinkie House on the Saturday night, and processed back to the Palace of Holyroodhouse, arriving on the Sunday evening, 'with bagpips playing'.[46]

Thomas Hearne, *Holyrood Palace*, 1778.

Holyroodhouse

'Splendour and Magnificence'

It is not surprising that the presence of a Stuart prince in Edinburgh, and specifically one in residence at the Royal Palace of Holyroodhouse, should have stimulated such rejoicing among the Jacobites in the city and its environs. Staunch Whigs like Patrick Crichton were immune to the young prince's charms, but, at the same time, Charles' arrival clearly stimulated interest, even excitement, in citizens who were no supporters of the Catholic Stuarts – Miss Magdalen Pringle for one. The last royal occupants of the palace had been the prince's grandfather and grandmother, when Duke and Duchess of York, during James Stuart's three-year rule as his brother's viceroy in Scotland. Prior to that, since James VI had united the crowns of Scotland and England, and, soon after, moved to London (returning once in 1617), the Stuart kings were very much absent Scottish monarchs.

In eighteenth-century Britain, the king in council remained one of the key mechanisms of government and, as court historian Clarissa Campbell Orr argues, the British court continued to be at the centre of political and national life.[1] The presence of a monarch and their court, as seen at St James's in London, brought ceremonials and entertainments, bustle and activity. It became the focus of news and gossip and, on a more practical level, generated employment and wealth through increased trade in everything from everyday foodstuffs to luxury goods. On a less tangible but still fundamental level, the presence of royalty put the heart and soul into what was otherwise a large, ornate, empty building. And 'kingship' – whatever you thought of the present incumbent – had its own magnetic appeal. All this lent James Stuart's residence in Scotland a particular and enduring aura. As the period was just within living memory, many could still recall the glittering royal court 'at the Abbey' and such tales passed on from parent to child to grandchild. It should also be noted that, after the Union,

Edinburgh had also lost her Parliament and the associated activities and ceremonials, most notably the annual riding ceremony and viewing of the regalia or Honours of Scotland: a loss the locals continued to mourn.[2] In 1745, then, like the fictional Edward Waverley, the intrigued citizens of Edinburgh, as well as the loyal Jacobites, awaited to be 'dazzled at the liveliness and elegance of the scene now exhibited in the long-deserted halls of the Scottish palace. The accompaniments, indeed, fell short of splendour, being but such as the confusion and hurry of the time admitted; still, however, the general effect was striking, and, the rank of the company considered, might well be called brilliant.'[3]

As Sir Walter Scott's description suggests, in the intervening years since Charles II's major redevelopment of the palace, followed by his brother's occupancy, the condition of the palace, abbey and environs had visibly declined. It is tempting to see it as a manifestation, in crumbling stone and plaster, of the attitude towards Edinburgh and even Scotland of a frankly uninterested, London-centric Stuart and later Hanoverian monarchy. With no prospect of a royal visit, the care and maintenance that did occur was chiefly for the benefit of certain high-ranking noble families, who over time had been granted large areas of the palace as their main abode in the Scottish capital. One of the few people who were in residence in the autumn of 1745 was John Campbell, 2nd Earl of Breadalbane and Holland (b. 1662) also known as Lord Glenorchy. He was, perhaps, too old to find himself conveniently absent like his neighbours. Some of the apartments came with an official position, such as that of the Duke of Argyll, who was Heritable Master of the Royal Household at Holyrood. In this instance it had been reported in the local press that the duke had 'set out from Holy-rood-house for London' on 21 August.[4] But the chief resident of the palace was the Duke of Hamilton and Brandon as hereditary keeper, who occupied what had been the Queen's Apartments, as designed for Charles II, within the front or western range of the building.

Where was the current hereditary keeper, James George Hamilton, 6th Duke of Hamilton and 3rd of Brandon? The duke was an unmarried twenty-one-year-old who had inherited the title from his father in March 1743 OS. The 5th duke had been made a Jacobite Knight of the Garter, a secret honour reserved for only the very loyal.[5] But he had later protested to George II that he had been barbarously 'misrepresented' by rumours 'of my having been to see the Pretender under the disguise of an Abbys Dress'.[6] During the autumn of 1744, Lord Elcho states that he and his brother-in-law visited the new Duke of Hamilton, who they found to be 'a very zealous partisan of the House of Stuart'.[7] It should be recalled that His Grace was also a member of the Buck Club. As a result, the duke had received one of Charles' rallying letters to the loyal clan chiefs and Scottish aristocracy delivered via Secretary Murray in June 1745.[8] However, the duke was not in residence when the prince arrived, nor was he in Edinburgh. On Monday, 5 August, the *Caledonian Mercury* had announced that 'Friday last the Duke of Hamilton set out hence for London, and we hear his Grace will soon after his Arrival there go abroad and compleat his Travels.'[9]

Although the current duke was unavailable to welcome him, it was in the Hamilton apartments that Charles now lived, conducted business and held court. As the Jacobite Prince Regent, even during a perilous military campaign to restore the House of Stuart, Charles must be seen to be the dignified physical and symbolic presence of his royal father, and, as such, maintaining a court, with all the trappings and events associated with it, was crucial. But such things needed organisation. The duke of Hamilton's housekeeper, possible the 'Ro'son' mentioned in the palace documentation, would have maintained the rooms whether the duke was resident or not.[10] Besides which, it is likely that the prince's own servants, accompanied by a guard and an aide-de-camp, would have hurried to Holyrood from Slateford on hearing of the occupation of Edinburgh, in order to inspect the prince's accommodation, including the auxiliary areas (such as the kitchens and laundry), and then prepare the rooms for the prince's arrival. If word arrived at Gray's Mill within an hour of the Highlanders entering the Netherbow Port, then Charles' advance entourage would have had about six hours to get to Holyrood and make the necessary arrangements. From his time in Edinburgh onwards, the logistically complex task of managing the prince's domestic needs – at a time when he and a sizable entourage of cooks, valets and aides-de-camp was constantly on the move from place to place and from building to building – was in the hands of James Gib, who entered the prince's service at Edinburgh as 'Master-Houshold and provisor for the Prince's own Table'.[11] Gib's household accounts provide a glimpse into how such behind-the-scenes activity operated.

The vacated Hamilton apartment was accessed, as Charles had done, through the main entrance to the palace, turning right through a colonnade, to a door, which opened on to William Bruce's majestic staircase. Above is an ornate, coffered ceiling. Having arrived on the first or principal floor, at the top of the stair (which turns back on itself), the vestibule leads on to the immediate right to the 'King's apartments' (the

south wing), now, in 1745, in a particularly dilapidated state. But walking directly forward, the visitor entered the Hamilton apartments – a different prospect altogether. Fortuitously, only a few years before Charles'
arrival, some areas of the palace and particularly the Hamilton apartments had received a significant upgrade and refurbishment. It was by
this quirk of fate that the prince could not only conduct himself in a
manner befitting the Stuart heir apparent, but also had the surroundings to support it. These apartments, formed of an enfilade of connected
rooms, ran from the main staircase (described above), to James V's north
turret and then beyond into the later extension. By tradition, royal and
aristocratic apartments were set out so as to move from what were considered public, to increasingly private spaces – as seen at the Palazzo
del Re in Rome. In this way, the first two rooms leading from the main
staircase would be seen as relatively open spaces, accessible to the public. As sizable rooms they could accommodate large numbers of people,
simply milling about, or awaiting an audience with the prince. The next
(or third) room along continued to act as an anteroom before the visitor
entered the prince's private rooms immediately ahead and from this lobby
you could view, through a doorway to your immediate right, the entire
length of the Long Gallery within the northern range of the palace. This
oblong room was described by Daniel Defoe as 'very remarkable, being
adorned with the Pictures of all the *Scots* Kings from *Fergus* I. to *James*
VII. inclusive, by masterly Hands. Those Kings that were eminent, and
all the Race of *Stuarts*, are in full Length.'[12] In the autumn of 1745 this
memorial to Scottish kingship, real and mythical, was where the evening
entertainments occurred.

   Continuing forward from the lobby into the first room next to James
V's turret, the visitor entered what was originally the 'Queen's antechamber', used by Charles as a dining room.[13] To the left off the dining area was
a door leading to the 'Queen's bedchamber', now the prince's withdrawing
room and council chamber, and the two smaller 'turret' rooms at the outer
corners were possibly used by Charles as a 'closet' or study, and a plan
room.[14] But walking straight on through the little dining room, the visitor
passed, via another doorway, into the extended area of the Hamilton wing,
within which was another antechamber (the Duchess' dressing room), and
finally a room originally assigned as the Duchess of Hamilton's but now the
prince's bedchamber. These two rooms were the princely inner sanctum.[15]

   The refurbishment of these interiors by another great Scottish architect, William Adam, from 1738 to 1742, had been extensive.[16] It included

new wooden flooring, sash windows, plaster ceilings, wall panelling and wall hangings (certainly a rich silk). In the Duchess' dressing room and bedchamber, both with windows overlooking the outer, front courtyard and the gardens to the north, there were white or dove-coloured marble fire surrounds and ornate looking-glasses provided by Francis Brodie of the Landmarket. In the alcove of the bedchamber was a magnificent, carved-wood canopied bed, covered in crimson silk damask with matching drapes. The drapes or curtains could be pulled around to enclose the ornately carved headboard and back cloth, also covered in crimson silk, the bed base or stock with feather mattress, pillows and fine (probably linen and silk) sheets. To complete the sense of opulence, lying over the sheets and pillows was a crimson silk damask coverlet. It was in this beautiful bed that the prince slept.

Aside from furniture and furnishings, the apartment would have been equipped with items such as silver cutlery, glassware and porcelain dining services. But this did not prevent some of the local Jacobite ladies from leaving gifts intended to make the prince's time at Holyroodhouse more comfortable: as Samuel Boyse writes 'Several Ladies of his Party furnished him with Plate, China, and Linnen for his Apartments'.[17] By tradition, some of the interiors in the palace were hung with large tapestries, and one of the dining rooms (possibly in the King's Apartments) housed some fine Arras tapestries depicting the History of Troy.[18] Similar Arras tapestries were also on view in the Hamilton apartments. In addition (presuming there had been no time or need to remove them) the Hamilton apartments were hung with hundreds of paintings – modern and old masters. A mid-eighteenth-century inventory of the pictures, probably connected to the William Adam refurbishment, offers an indication of what, or, rather, who would have been staring down at the prince, his companions, guests and visitors in 1745.[19] The 'Battle of the Boyne', if recognised, may have been removed for delicacy's sake. Located among the seascapes, landscapes and representations of Christ, the Madonna and various saints, and in addition to the 141 Scottish monarchs lining the Long Gallery, there were portraits of all the late Stuart kings from James VI via Charles II (by Sir Peter Lely) to James VII (by Sir Godfrey Kneller and Nicolas de Largillière) as well as images of Philip II of Spain, Henry VIII of England and his queens Katharine of Aragon and Anne Boleyn. If Charles had wanted, or needed, reminding of the vicissitudes of kingly rule, he could gaze upon several portraits of his great-grandfather, the executed king and later Anglican martyr, Charles I, or indeed those of his grandfather, James VII – all given greater poignancy and resonance located within the ancient palace of the Stuarts (now, technically at least, Hanoverian), rather than their seat of exile in Rome. In a similar vein, the prince could also have climbed the narrow James V turret staircase to the rooms above his council and dining rooms (also part of the Hamilton suite), which were once occupied by his other 'martyred' ancestor, Mary, Queen of Scots.

In Sir Walter Scott's *Waverley*, the prince is described as walking from the Long Gallery or ballroom 'to another suite of apartments, and assumed the seat and canopy at the head of a long range of tables, with an air of dignity mingled with courtesy which well became his high birth and lofty pretensions'.[20] Of course, Scott, writing at the beginning of the nineteenth century, knew the Palace of Holyroodhouse intimately. The room so lightly described may be the prince's dining room, but, crucially, the idea that the prince sat on a chair of state and beneath a canopy may not be pure novelistic fancy. A palace inventory of 1714 – the last year of Queen Anne's reign and the first of George I's – lists a number of state chairs, footstools, cloths and canopies in varying states of repair, all upholstered in crimson, black or blue velvet, and decorated with gold and silver thread. Some of these must have remained in the palace as symbols of the royal presence and authority, in tandem with the current monarch's state portrait. The portraits of George I and II, which would have undoubtedly graced the King's Apartment for this purpose, may have been hastily removed to the attics, along with the 'Battle of the Boyne'; unless, of course, Charles had a fancy to look upon the life-size, full-length image of his 'usurping' cousins. The inventory of furnishings was in the possession of James Steuart, who was Keeper of the King's Wardrobe in Scotland in 1745.[21] It is not known whether Steuart had remained at the palace, or made himself scarce before Prince Charles arrived. One of Steuart's assistants, Patrick Lindesay, was certainly in Edinburgh and even joined the Jacobite army, so it is likely that Lindesay at least was on hand to make the prince's stay not only comfortable but regal.[22] Such items, the chairs of state with accompanying canopies and cloths of state (with royal insignia), denoted authority, precedence and status, and could easily have been removed from the dilapidated King's Apartment and placed in one of the prince's chambers, to add a touch of majesty to these sumptuous but essentially aristocratic rooms.

None of this detail, the fabrics, the paintings, the furniture, is trivial. Arguably Charles, like his grandfather before him, was residing at Holyroodhouse in the capacity of regent in the absence of the king. Such regal accoutrement would be seen as a visible statement of that reality. Lord

Elcho recalled that the prince lived at Edinburgh 'with Great Splendour and Magnificence'.[23] It is clear that as a self-conscious display of 'royal' government, and even majesty, the prince's time at Holyroodhouse not only aimed to establish him as a fitting, legitimate claimant or, indeed, the true heir apparent to the British throne, but, more fundamental still, it acted as an indication, or dress rehearsal, for a restored Stuart dynasty.

Pierre Charles Canot, *Scotch Female Gallantry*, 1745/6.

The Abbey: Part One

'Heaven's Darling'

On the evening of Sunday, 22 September the prince returned to Holyroodhouse, as Patrick Crichton had observed, 'with bagpips playing'.[1] There had been no divine service in the city that day, except at the West Kirk 'just in the eye of the Castle',[2] where Mr McVicar led his congregation in the following prayer: '*Bless the King, thou knows what King I mean; may the Crown sit long easy on his Head, &c. And for this Man that is come amongst us to seek an earthly Crown: We beseech Thee, in Mercy, to take him to thyself and give him a Crown of Glory.*'[3] Charles does not seem to have taken such matters very seriously, and on 25 September he reiterated the pledge, via the *Caledonian Mercury*, 'That no interruption shall be given to publick Worship; but, on the contrary, all Protection to those concerned in it'.[4]

There is no reference to Charles himself attending divine service at any time while he was in Edinburgh. The Abbey church was no longer in use, while the local Canongate Kirk was now full of the lower ranks of British army prisoners of war, whom Charles was honour bound to maintain, but were a considerable drain on his limited resources. It was even beginning to circulate that Charles was quite flexible in his approach to religion. One citizen of Edinburgh observed, 'I assure you the Papists about Town were the first that paid their Compliments to the young Gentleman. None of his own People ever pretend to say he is a Protestant. They always endeavour to shift this Question, when put to them, by saying, he is quite indifferent to all Religion.'[5] This is quite a statement, considering what his grandfather and father had sacrificed for their Catholicism. As a result, the question of Charles' attitude towards religion is a crucial one. According to the diary of John Campbell, a director of the Royal Bank of Scotland, on Friday, 27 September he, Campbell, 'Went to the Abbey to see Earl Breadalbane [Campbell's relative] who told me the Prince was visiting him last night'.[6] During one such meeting between the aged earl and the prince, the following conversation apparently occurred and was later reported by Charles Yorke (Lord Chancellor Hardwicke's second son) to his younger brother, Joseph:

> Earl said, 'Sir, I believe I am the oldest peer in Scotland and the only one who remembers your royal grandfather in this palace.' *Y. Pretender.* 'Do you remember him my Lord; pray how did you like him?' *E. of B.* 'In some respects Sir, very well; in others I had great objections in him.' *Y. Pretender.* 'Perhaps you did not like his religion.' *E. of B.* 'No Sir, it did not suit with Britain.' *Y. Pretender.* 'That might be an objection to my grandfather in those days; but at present princes as well as private men have too much sense to suffer any impediments from religion in the pursuit of great views.'[7]

If this is true, it is another hint that Charles was not aiming to plant a crucifix on London Bridge. In fact, if the prince considered his father's dedication to Catholicism as an 'impediment' in the pursuit of his 'great view' (the Stuart restoration), then, when the time was right, might Charles, like France's Henry IV before him, convert for his nation's sake? Clearly not while he was in need of Louis XV's assistance. But it was certainly part of Charles' personal public relations campaign to support his father's declared intention, when restored, 'not to impose upon any a Religion which they dislike'.[8]

One of Charles' first acts on returning to Holyroodhouse was to send out an official response to the recent battle. A proclamation was given at the palace on Monday, 23 September and then published two days later on the front page of the *Caledonian Mercury*, now effectively the organ of the Jacobite cause. After declaring 'the greatest fatherly Love and Compassion to all our Royal Father's Subjects', as well as concern for their oppression 'during this long Usurpation' for which Charles undertakes 'this present Enterprize; which it has pleased Almighty God to favour, by granting us hitherto a most surprizing Success', he then considers the request to publicly celebrate 'our late Victory at *Gladsmuir*'.[9] Although a gratifying indication of support, nevertheless this victory 'has been obtained by the Effusion of the Blood of His Majesty's Subjects', and has caused calamity for many. Therefore 'We hereby forbid any outward Demonstrations of publick Joy; admonishing all true Friends to their King and Country, to return Thanks to God for his Goodness towards them, as we hereby do for ourselves by this our publick Proclamation.' This measured, reconciliatory proclamation is similar in tone to the letter Charles produced at Pinkie House a few days before. His sense of decorum may have been assisted, in part, by the threat from the Castle commanders that any public celebration – the ringing of bells, for example – would be met with a cannon blast. But this proclamation challenges an oft-quoted assumption that, after the battle, a ball was held at Holyroodhouse specifically to celebrate the victory. It is even said that a fan was produced, depicting the victorious prince in armour and surrounded by allegorical figures, which was handed out to the ladies who attended. Examples of such a fan certainly exist.[10] But if this event did take place, it must have occurred on the night of Sunday, 22 September (Charles was at Pinkie House the night of the battle), otherwise the proclamation of the following day advocating restraint would have been very hypocritical. A 'Victory Ball' on the Sabbath seems a stretch, and no such event is mentioned by any of the key contemporary sources.

However, the inhabitants of Prestonpans and surrounding villages were apparently troubled by this announcement for other reasons. As the prince's proclamation illustrates, the recent victory had been immediately dubbed by the Jacobites as the Battle of Gladsmuir in response, it was said, to the prophecies of Sir Thomas of Erceldoune, a thirteenth-century laird from Berwickshire also known as 'the Rhymer', or the legendary Arthurian wizard Merlin, or one 'Berlington'. In his *Memoirs*, Sir John Clerk refers to the Battle of Prestonpans, 'which the Rebels affected to call Gladsmoor, to make it quadrat with a foolish old prophecy of Thomas the Rhymer, "In Gladesmoor shall the Battle be" but,' continues Sir John, 'Gladesmoor happens to be at least two miles from the field of Battle.'[11] Some time during 1745 – probably soon after the battle – Thomas Lumisden and John Robertson published in Edinburgh what were alleged to be the prophecies of Thomas the Rhymer. The book was dedicated to Charles' father. The relevant prophecy, as quoted in this new publication, states that, 'Of Bruces Left-side shall spring out a Leafe,/As near as the ninth Degree', that this descendant of the Bruce would arrive from France, 'With hempen Helters and Horse of Tree', and that, soon after, 'On Gosfoord Green it shal be seen/On Gladsmoore shal the Battle be'.[12] In reality, according to the local antiquarian James Miller, the prophecy was a little less emphatic and even less reflective of recent events than Lumisden and Robertson suggest, stating that 'The corbie-craw would drink blood out of a *frugh-stane* in Gladsmuir churchyard', and that the 'Gine-burn would run red'.[13]

The villagers of Prestonpans itself and the surrounding area profoundly disagreed with the Jacobites and a petition on their behalf (possibly satirical) was published in *The Scots Magazine*. It argued that since antiquity battles were named from the fields on which they were fought, or from some town or village nearby. As a result the area became 'remarkable in the maps, and recorded in history'. They pointed to the small village of Dettingen, which no one had heard of until the battle fought there a few years before. Therefore, the battle fought on 21 September ought to be named accordingly. The author observes that 'even the conquerors themselves have no right, after a battle is once fought, to determine that it was fought on any other field than where it really was', and that such untruths 'can be inforced by nothing less than the late fashionable arguments of *military execution*'.[14] As history can relate, the villagers got their way – eventually.

The following day, Charles issued another proclamation, which was also placed on the front page of the *Caledonian Mercury* of 25 September. This concerned those who had formed associations or had taken up arms against Charles, many of whom had since fled. The proclamation continues, 'that Mercy and Tenderness' is 'the distinguishing Characteristic of our Family', and therefore a full pardon would be given for any treasons – not just those against Charles and his father, but stretching back to the time of the prince's grandfather – on the proviso, that the culprits present themselves at the Palace of Holyroodhouse within twenty days, and 'with a Declaration that they shall live for the future as quiet and peaceable Subjects to Us and our Government, otherwise these Presents to be of no Effect to them'.[15]

On hearing of the proclamation, Alexander Carlyle left Prestonpans for Holyroodhouse, as much out of curiosity as anything else. Carlyle recalls visiting the palace twice, at midday, so that he could see the prince riding out to the Jacobite army encampment at Duddingston. At close quarters, Carlyle observed that he 'was a Good Looking Man', tall, his hair 'Dark Red and his Eyes Black'. By now Charles' face was 'much Sunburnt and Freckled', but, not for the first time, Carlyle observed 'his Countenance Thoughtfull and Melancholy'. Charles obviously had a lot on his mind and this description – a favoured trope among his critics – seems aimed at making Charles closer in character to his father than observers of him in Rome or even later in France (where he had much to be melancholy about) were apt to be. Carlyle also counted no more than 400 people in the crowd, believing this proved, 'By that time Curiosity had been Satisfy'd.'[16]

Still, as Carlyle's description suggests, the prince's days at the Abbey followed a routine that made him easily available to his admirers and the curious alike. John O'Sullivan recalled that Charles was up every day before daylight, and was immediately delivering orders and writing letters.[17] He then held a levee at nine o'clock, an hour-long reception for his officers in his private rooms, after which the council gathered in the adjoining chamber. The discussion in council was bound to be robust, given the current lack of any clear forward plan, as well as the urgency of expanding, training and funding the Jacobite army. Charles also had hundreds of prisoners in his care. Eventually he had to release many of them on parole for want of cash. In retrospect Lord Elcho described these council meetings, which continued long after the army left Edinburgh, as dysfunctional from the start. The prince would first announce what he thought should happen, after which he would ask everyone present, in turn, for their opinion. According to Lord Elcho, one-third of the council believed 'that Kings and Princes Can never either act or think wrong, so in Consequence they always Confirmed whatever the Prince Said'. The Duke of Perth would certainly be included in this first group, along with (according to Lord Elcho) the Irish contingent, notably Charles' closest advisers, Sir Thomas Sheridan and John O'Sullivan. Lord Elcho goes on:

> The other two thirds, who thought that Kings and Princes thought sometimes like other men and were not altogether infallible and that this Prince was no more so than others, beg'd leave to differ from him, when they Could give Sufficient reasons for their difference of Opinion. Which very often was no hard matter to do, for as the Prince and his Old Governor Sir Thomas Sheridan were altogether ignorant of the Ways and Customs in Great Britain, and both much for the Doctrine of Absolute monarchy, they would very often, had they not been prevented, have fall'n into Blunders which might have hurt the Cause.[18]

Lord Elcho and Lord George Murray would certainly be included in this second group, along with some, but not all, of the clan chiefs. In fact, continues Lord Elcho, the prince could not bear hearing an opinion different from his own, disliked anyone who opposed him, and 'had a Notion of Commanding this army As any General does a body of Mercenaries, and so lett them know only what he pleased, and they obey without inquiring further about the matter.'[19] The very existence of the council, a forum where discussions occurred and opinions were sought, suggests that this could not be (completely at least) the case. And even the most even-handed and inclusive of leaders would still be required to make the decisions themselves – otherwise they would simply be a figurehead and no more. Whether Lord Echo liked it or not, Charles wanted, expected, to be much more than a rallying point.

And then Lord Elcho arrives at what lay at the heart of his issues with the prince and what he calls Charles' favourites. The prince's expectation of unchallenged obedience 'might have done better had his favourites been people of the Country, but as they were Irish And had nothing at Stake, The People of Fashion', including Lord Elcho and Lord George, 'that had their all at Stake, and Consequently Ought to be Supposed to Give the best advice they were Capable of, thought they had a title to know and be Consulted in what was for the Good of the Cause in which they had so much Concern.'[20] Further, Charles preferred the Irish because 'these gentlemen were of his own religion, and having nothing to lose flattered him at all points'.[21] So, in Lord Elcho's opinion, the Irish, with (according to him) nothing to lose but their lives, were inevitably obsequious, gung-ho risk takers. And, at the same time, Charles was not listening to Lord Elcho and his fellow Scots, nor was the prince showing enough gratitude for what they were risking by joining his campaign.

In opposition to Lord Elcho, James Maxwell of Kirkconnell gives the prince the credit for having 'always consulted the principal people of his army upon every emergency, and nothing of consequence had been done but with their consent'. This process was formalised at Edinburgh and, as the campaign moved on, the colonels of all the regiments were also admitted. To Maxwell, who was not a member, the issue was not whether the council was consulted, which clearly it was, but the quality of the counsel that the prince received within this forum. As he goes on to say, 'I must acknowledge that very few of the Members of this Assembly were either able statesmen or experienced officers.' Even so, Maxwell believed that things would have proceeded much better, if within the council there had been 'as much harmony and union as the importance of the affair required'. But Maxwell observes, even while in Edinburgh, an ill-timed rivalry 'soon crept in, and bred great dissension and animosities; the Council was insensibly divided into factions, and came to be of little use when measures were approved of or condemned, not for themselves, but for the sake of their author'.[22]

James had advised Charles on how to deal with such infighting, and the prince had openly despaired of the self-destructive behaviour displayed by some of the Jacobite party in France. This division within the council, obviously, did not bode well and it would require great strength, energy and shrewdness from the prince – preferably with the personal support of a wise, objective inner circle – to manage and temper the effects of such division, while at the same time keeping everyone focused on the great prize. Charles had a supportive inner circle, Sir Thomas Sheridan and Colonel John O'Sullivan, but they were far from objective: in fact, for Lords George and Elcho, their influence over the prince was a major problem in itself. But by far the greatest issue facing the Jacobite command was that at this stage Charles had not fully communicated to his predominantly Scottish council what, in his mind, the great prize was. At this moment he was arguably master of Scotland. With an expanded army coupled with the long-promised support from France, he could secure Stirling and Edinburgh castles plus the garrisoned forts and then, if he wanted to, fully establish himself as regent in Holyrood, while awaiting the formal return of his father as King James VIII of Scotland. Such considerations would make anyone thoughtful.

After the council meeting, the prince would dine in public. In so doing, Charles was self-consciously aligning himself with the courts of Europe, and Versailles in particular. Even if there was no direct interaction between the prince and his audience, as seen with King Louis in Flanders, every comment made to companions would be heard, recorded and circulated. Such a circumstance was recounted by Andrew Henderson, who stated that 'to win the Hearts of the Populace, he admitted all to see him dine, during which Time he frequently said, "if I succeed, *Scotland* shall be my *Hanover*, and the Palace of *Holyroodhouse* my *Herenhausen*."'[23] On the face of it, this reference to King George's routine visits to his German domains appears to confirm Charles' desire, if successful, to spend the majority of his time in London, but with the promise of regular, extended visits to Scotland and Holyroodhouse. Of course, an advance into England was another option for the prince and his army.

As seen by Alexander Carlyle, the prince would then ride out to Duddingston at midday, where the majority of the army was encamped and where, as Colonel O'Sullivan recalled, 'he employed the rest of the day, in exercising the men, makeing 'um march, seeing the Guards mounted, made several General revews, in short every

thing, [that] cou'd contribute to form 'um'. Rather than always returning to Holyroodhouse, Charles often slept in a tent within the camp,
partly to encourage his army's Highland contingent. But, according to
O'Sullivan, the Highlanders 'did not like the Tents, found it too troublesome to pitch 'um'.[24] That Charles was taking his present circumstances
and the task in hand very seriously is more than evident from the various descriptions of him at this time. As with his dining, the prince's
daily ride to the camp was a spectacle for the curious. Take Magdalen
Pringle, a teenager in 1745 and, it should be recalled, the daughter of a
staunchly Whig family.[25] On 13 October, she writes to her sister Tib, 'O
lass such a fine show as I saw on Wednesday last.' Magdalen had gone
to the encampment and, along with other ladies, encircled the entrance
of the prince's tent in order to gaze at him. When he emerged, 'with a
grace and Majesty that is unexpressible', he saluted the ladies 'with an
air of grandeur and affability capable of Charming ye most obstinate
Whig'. While they were nearby, the prince mounted his horse, 'and in
all my Life I never saw so noble nor so Graceful an appearance as His
Highness made, he was in great spirits and very cheerful; which I have
never seen him before'.[26] This adoration, welcomed at first, must have
become very wearisome over the weeks after Prestonpans. But despite
the pressure Charles was under, and again to his credit, he maintained
an air of affability and politeness, which, as Magdalen writes, could
charm the most obstinate of his opposition: even to the extent that they
would describe him as 'His Highness'. No longer in Highland garb, the
prince now wore 'a Blue Grogrum Coat' trimmed with gold lace, a red
waistcoat similarly decorated, and breeches. He was also wearing the
Garter Star and a sword with a silver basket hilt. His hat, which had
replaced the blue bonnet, had a white feather in it, a white cockade, and
was also trimmed with gold lace. Nor was he riding the bay on which
he had entered Holyrood, but another horse, 'black and finely bred (it
had been poor Gardners) . . . I don't believe Cesar was more engagingly
form'd nor more dangerous to ye liberties of his country than this Chap
may be if he sets about it.'[27] Magdalen then observes, 'he looks much
better in Lowland than in Highland Dress'. In being seen in both styles,
Charles was clearly aiming to appeal to as broad a Scottish following
as possible. He was also aligning his chivalric orders according to his
dress: the Scottish Order of the Thistle, reconstituted by James VII in
1687, patron saint Andrew, with Highland garb; the English Order of

the Garter, created by Edward III, patron saint George, with 'Lowland' dress. Also, as Magdalen informs her sister, Charles was now openly riding Colonel Gardiner's horse, which presumably had been taken on the battlefield as a spoil of war. Magdalen would not be the last to draw attention to it. The symbolism that could be derived from this is obvious: horsemanship, whether good or bad, was not only a metaphor for military prowess but also statecraft.

According to Lord Elcho, after reviewing his troops the prince returned to the Abbey 'where he received the ladies of fashion that came to his drawing room. Then he Sup'd in publick, and Generaly their was musick at Supper, and a ball afterwards.'[28] Some of Charles' immediate circle, Colonel O'Sullivan in particular, showed concern for his punishing daily regime, believing that he required some temporary distractions. To this end, and 'as a great many Ladys us'd to come & pay their Court, when he suped at the Abbey, they propos'd a Bal to those Lady's, thinking the Prince wou'd take pleasure in it wch he consented to'. The ball was arranged, during which the prince admired the dancing, paid his compliments and retired. Not quite the reaction that was planned. Some gentlemen followed him, '& told him, [that] they knew he loved dancing, & [that] the Ball was designed for him to amuse him; "Its very true," says the Prince, "I like danceing, & am very glad to see the Lady's & yu divert y[ou]rselfs, but I have now another Air to dance, until that be finished I'l dance no other."' O'Sullivan, who may have accompanied the prince on his covert visits to the masquerade balls at Versailles, and certainly witnessed his love of hunting and shooting, observed that it 'is very strange [that] a Prince of that age who really liked danceing, & fowling, never thought of any pleasures, & was as retired as a man of sixty'.[29] But this, again, reveals his level of commitment. In tandem with his reported vow of chastity, believed to have been sworn when he was young, Charles appears to have made a mental pact with himself, and even with God, to devote himself solely to his primary task in exchange for His blessing and success.[30]

The Revd John Jardine, a friend of John Home who would also plan a 'History of the Rebellion', observed of Charles, perhaps ironically, 'various remarks were soon made upon him and at last it was discover'd that there was something about him more than Human'.[31] As the various descriptions and particularly Magdalen Pringle's account reveal, Charles certainly had a pronounced impact on women. Soon after the Battle of

Prestonpans, Miss Christian Threipland (sister to David and Stuart) hastened to Edinburgh. At forty-five, she was a relatively mature member of
this staunch Jacobite family from Fingask Castle near Perth. In a letter to
her friend Lady Geddes, dated some weeks later, she writes that on her
arrival, 'I found my eldest Brother had fallen a Victim to the merciless
Rage of his Enemies.'[32] Lingering for a moment on the circumstances
of David's death during the Battle of Prestonpans, she moves swiftly on
to the actual subject of her letter, or, as she describes him, 'the blessed
Object', Charles Edward Stuart. 'O!', she cries, 'had you beheld my
beloved Hero, you must confess he is a Gift from Heaven', and that 'he
is the *Top of Perfection* and *Heaven's Darling*', concluding, 'he continues
to make Friends wherever he comes, and has got the better of his Ill-
wishers, and is like to have more Friends than he can well employ . . . O
would [to] God I had been a Man, that I might have shared his fate of
Well or Wo, never to be removed from him!'[33] As we have seen, Christian
was by no means the only woman (or indeed man) to fall under Charles'
spell. She was, however, unfortunate enough to not only have this letter
intercepted, but published as a broadsheet: a truly underhand act which
aimed, no doubt, to pour scorn upon the conspicuous ardour that the
prince appeared to stimulate in his many female followers and therefore,
by association, to pour scorn upon the prince himself. For a conquer-
ing hero might enjoy the love and admiration of his people, but only a
preening fop would encourage such girlish giddiness from an apparently
sensible, mature woman. In consequence, the family attempted to buy
up and destroy as many copies of the broadsheet as they could lay their
hands on.[34]

Whether they were concerned at the time or not, some of Charles' followers were at pains to distance the prince from his female admirers. Most
famously, Lord Elcho stated, 'At night their came a Great many Ladies of
Fashion, to Kiss his hand, but his behaviour to them was very Cool: he had
not been much used to Womens Company, and was always embarrassed
while he was with them.'[35] Such diffidence towards women was recorded
by Alexander Carlyle, who observed that at Edinburgh in 'the House where
I Liv'd they were all Jacobites, and I heard much of their Conversation',
but in his opinion, 'they had less Ground for being so Sanguine and uppish
than they Imagin'd'. As he goes on, 'The Court at the Abbey was Dull and
Sombre, the Prince was Melancholy. He Seem'd to have no Confidence

in any Body, Not even the Ladies who were much his Friends.'[36] Charles might not have realised it yet, but he could ill afford to dismiss his female admirers out of hand: they might not be able to bear arms themselves, but they could raise money and even men. Some, if the need arose, would be willing to risk their lives.

Artist unknown, *The Mitred Champion, or, The Church Militant*
[Archbishop Thomas Herring], 1745.

The Abbey: Part Two

'ye Happy day of meeting'

While Charles maintained his court at Holyroodhouse and visited the army at Duddingston, a crisis in relations with the garrison – since the occupation confined to the Castle – was developing. On 29 September, a letter was sent to the Lord Provost stating that if communications between the city and the Castle were not opened up, then the Castle would fire on the Highland guard and, failing that, the city itself. To which Charles responded that if these threats were carried out, then General Preston's house, Valleyfield, would be likewise 'distressed'. The general's immediate riposte was that he would order the guns of the *Fox* man-of-war, now cruising in the Firth of Forth along with the sloops the *Hazard* and the *Happy Jennet*, to turn on Lord Elcho's ancestral home, Wemyss Castle.[1] A six-day truce was negotiated, which then broke down on 1 October when the Highland guard at the Weigh House fired on a group carrying provisions to the Castle. The Castle commanders responded by firing at the houses on Castle Hill that were occupied, or believed to be occupied, by the Highlanders. According to Patrick Crichton one of these houses, called the 'Goose Pie' and owned by the poet Allan Ramsay (father to the painter), was badly damaged.[2]

On 2 October, Charles declared that the Castle would be sealed off from the city, and no communication should occur between them on pain of execution.[3] From then on, there was constant firing from the Castle down the main street towards the Highland guards 'when any of them dars peep owt'.[4] Patrick Crichton recalled the 'great guns demolishing and burning howses in Livistons yeard upon the Castle hill, and fyring down the street', and 'many of the Prince's party killed and some innocent persons did not keep owt of the way'. He counted, on some days, over sixty cannon shots 'and mustkets withowt number, volys, platoon shot, and droping shots as they hoped to do execution'.[5] This was now an urban street battle between the garrison and the Highland guard. As Magdalen Pringle writes to her sister, 'The Castle (that "damned angry Bitch" as ye Highlanders calls her) has been quiet since Saturday last on which day it had done a great deal of mischief having fir'd down ye Streets and kill'd and wounded some people.'[6] Archibald Hart confessed to his friend William Innes, a merchant in London, that 'never was there a time of greater calamity than when the castle fir'd on the town . . . your sister hart is staying at Leith till once this confusion is over because in our house we are much expos'd. there was a [cannon] ball come threw Mr Cunninhames into mine which alarmed us not a little'.[7] Finally, on 5 October Charles relented because of 'the many Murthers which are committed upon the innocent Inhabitants of this City, by the inhumane Commanders and Garrison of the Castle of *Edinburgh*'. The communication for provisions was opened up once more, and the advertised punishment suspended.[8] In reality, if Charles had committed himself to starving the garrison into surrender, it would have been a long drawn-out affair, because, unbeknown to the prince, the Castle had enough provisions and ammunition to hold out for months.

Soon after the situation with the Castle was resolved, Charles publicly reiterated Stuart opposition to the Union of Scotland with England. On hearing that the British parliament at Westminster had been recalled for 17 October, Charles issued two proclamations on the 9th and 10th which were then published in the *Caledonian Mercury*: the first warning and commanding 'all His Majesty's Liege Subjects, whether Peers or Commoners, to pay no Obedience to any such Summons',[9] declaring it an act of treason and rebellion to do so, 'the pretended Union of these Kingdoms being now at an End'. In the second he goes further, by setting out his father's opposition 'to the pretended Union of the two Nations' as partly in response to 'repeated Remonstrances against it from each Kingdom', but mainly because its 'principal Point' was 'the Exclusion of the Royal Family from their undoubted Right to the Crown'. Furthermore, in answer to the British government and their supporters' anti-Jacobite propaganda – as Lord Hardwicke had observed to the Archbishop of York, Thomas Herring, 'representing the Pretender as coming (as the truth is) under a dependence upon French support; I say stating this point, together with Popery, in a strong light, has always the most popular effect'[10] – Charles dismisses as pure fantasy the 'dreadful Threats' currently thundering out from pulpit and newspaper alike 'of Popery, Slavery, Tyranny and arbitrary Power, which are now ready to be imposed upon you, by the formidable Powers of *France* and *Spain*'. Indeed (and a little disingenuously) his 'Expedition was undertaken unsupported by either'. Here Charles seems to be specifically responding to Archbishop Herring's now famous barnstorming sermon, delivered on 23 September in response to Hardwicke's hint and immediately published and circulated, which itemised these exact threats (as he saw them) to British sovereignty and the Protestant settlement, as currently embodied by the House of Hanover.[11] But, Charles continues, rather cleverly, as the foreign allies (including the Dutch and Hessians) are rallying to protect the Elector of Hanover and his government against King James' subjects, 'is it not high Time for the King my Father, to accept also of the Assistance of those who are able, and who have engaged to support him?'[12]

At the time of the proclamation, Charles could not have known that more French support was finally about to arrive. On Thursday, 17 October John Campbell wrote in his diary, 'ship landed at Montrose, one of distinction from thence lodges in Abbey'.[13] This 'one of distinction' was Alexandre de Boyer, marquis d'Eguilles of Aix-en-Provence, a lawyer by profession and a protégé of the marquis d'Argenson, who had arrived at Holyroodhouse on 14 October as an envoy and observer from the French Court. Antoine Walsh had returned to Versailles by late August confirming that Charles had indeed landed, and recounted the prince's early successes while also pressing for greater assistance from Louis to advance the prince's campaign. Walsh also sent the Abbé Butler to Rome to deliver the prince's letters, while stating to James in a private letter, that, although the prince had experienced great difficulties, he was sure to increase his army 'especially if the people of Scotland see that they can rely upon the help of France'.[14] The immediate result of Walsh's arrival at the French Court was the dispatch of the marquis d'Eguilles on board the small Dunkirk privateer *L'Espérance* with some men, arms and a modest sum of money. Other ships (all privateers), carrying volunteer Irish officers from Lally's and Fitz-James' regiments, plus more arms, guns and ammunition, would embark a few days later.

Crucially for Charles, the marquis d'Eguilles' arrival confirmed that French ships were not only attempting to run the gauntlet to the east coast of Scotland, but were actually managing to elude the Royal Navy. To signify the official or legitimate nature of Charles' court, the marquis was from the onset described by the Jacobites as the French ambassador, although this status was not recognised by Louis until later. Understandably d'Eguilles' arrival caused great excitement. To her sister, Magdalen Pringle confirmed that there was 'not much here stirring . . . except ye arrival of an Envoy from ye King of France to Prince Charles . . . I was at ye Abbey yesterday seeing ye Prince dine but I did not see ye Envoy.'[15] In a letter to Colonel Daniel

O'Brien at Versailles, John O'Sullivan writes optimistically (partly for the benefit of the French court), 'Our army increases daily. We are expecting the Duke of Atholl [Tullibardine] who is 3 days march away from us with two thousand of his people.' Many more are on the march, O'Sullivan reports, 'so that our army will soon be at least 12,000 men'. This number was certainly optimistic. With a sly reference to King George's imminent birthday (30 October) O'Sullivan continues, 'If our friends the French would hurry up we should take the cake for the King at London.' And then in relation to the newly arrived marquis, 'Monsieur de Boyer is a great success. The Prince loves him and all appreciate him. He dresses like a Highlander!'[16] In his later account, O'Sullivan elaborates on the importance of the marquis d'Eguilles' arrival when he says that the assurances of an imminent French embarkation 'set every body in high sperits, & I believe determined more & more the Princes resolution of going to England'.[17] However, delays in recruitment and the need to replenish a dwindling war chest had extended the stay in Edinburgh. In fact under threat of their property being 'distress'd', John Campbell and his fellow directors at the Royal Bank of Scotland eventually began releasing money which had been taken to the Castle for safe keeping, effectively financing the Jacobite army.[18]

On arrival, the marquis presented to Charles a short letter from Louis himself, where the king states 'I am sending M. d'Eguilles to you, whom I have charged with explaining my sentiments', with confirmation of his great affection for his young Stuart 'brother'.[19] D'Eguilles also delivered a package of letters containing several from the prince's father. One, written while Charles was still in France and dated 26 June (NS), concerns Charles' frustrations at that time with the French Court. But, despite this, James tells his son that 'you do well to shut your eyes often, & to keep your thoughts to yourself', that he should be on his guard, but not to be secretive, and always 'endeavour to maintain & support that character of candour & veracity which I & indeed every body, have always remarked in you'.[20] Charles immediately replied to both Louis and his father. These letters were to be delivered in person by George Kelly via d'Eguilles' ship, L'Espérance, still moored at Montrose. To Louis, 'Mon Oncle et mon Cousin', he writes:

> It has made me impatient to see the results of your Majesty's generosity towards me. It is true that I have recently received arms and money . . . But these do not nearly fulfil my needs, and time is short. My enemies have gathered their forces and have brought in as many troops as they need from

overseas, while I have not been sent a single regiment. If we still aim to make the most of such a good opportunity, there is not a moment to lose. I myself am resolved to push on and to risk undertaking another battle soon. Fate, which has smiled on me through great danger, and the bravery of my troops give me hope of great success. But this does not stop me from entreating the Prince's help, upon which I have so many reasons to depend.[21]

In the letter to his father, Charles declares, 'I have at laste had the Comfort of receiving Letters from you, the letest of which is of ye 7[th] September N.S. I am confounded and penetrated with so much goodness and tenderness y[ou]r Majesty expresses to me in all y[ou]r Letters.'[22] During an interview with the marquis d'Eguilles, Charles had stated that he wanted Prince Henry at the head of any French invasion of England. To his father he writes, 'I wish to god I may find my Brother Landed in England, by the time I enter it which will be in about ten days, having then with me near 8,000 men and 300 Hors at lest.' However, 'I cannot Enlarge on this subject as in many others for want of time becose of such a multiplicity of things, which [h]ourly occors for ye cervice of ye Affair.' These letters confirm that Charles had no thought of establishing himself in Edinburgh. The great prize was London.

Charles then notes the arrival of the marquis, 'who brought me y[ou]r Letters', and who will send Louis 'notice of anything that I may want, which as he says will be done immediatly'. To that end he has written several expresses, and 'what is sed is very short, pressing to have succor in all heste, by a Landing in England, for that as matters stand I must either conquer or perish, in a little while. Thank God I am in a perfect good health, but longing much for ye Happy day of meeting.' As the ship was ready to leave he concludes, 'I have only time to enclose here a [scrall?] of ye account of ye Battle which I in a hurry writ some days ago.'[23] This last is not the letter (already quoted) apparently written on the day of the battle while at Pinkie House, but another description written several weeks after (on 7 October), which presents a very different attitude towards 'one of ye moste surprising actions that ever was', and particularly the vanquished:

Wee gained a Complete Victory over General Cope who commanded 3,000 fut and to Regïments of ye Best Drago[o]ns in ye Island, he being advantagiosly posted, with also Baterys of Cannon, and Morters, wee having neither hors[e] or Artilery with us, and dering to attack them in their post,

and obliged to pas before their noses in a defile and Bog. Only our first line
had occasion to engage, for actually in five minut[e]s ye fild was clired of
ye Enemy, all ye fut killed, wounded or taken prisoners, and of ye horse
only t[w]o hundred eskap'ed like rabets [rabbits] one by one, on our side
wee only losed, a hundred men between killed and wounded, and ye Army
afterwards had a fine plunder.[24]

The 'fine plunder' included stripping the dying Colonel Gardiner. If
contrasted with the other letter, dated 21 September, which was transcribed by the fervent Jacobite Robert Forbes several years after the event
(a copy of which is not in the Stuart Papers or the Captured Stuart Papers),
one explanation is that Charles had someone producing official responses
which were not intended for his father, but for local and national consumption. Either way, Charles displays his true, unguarded feelings in the
letter of 7 October: a letter his father did receive.[25]

About this time, an unnamed Englishman from York arrived in
Edinburgh with the purpose of finding out about the prince and his forces.
In a letter outlining his observations he states, 'I was introduced to him
on the 17th; when he asked me several questions as to the number of the
troops, and the affections of the people of England. The audience lasted
for a quarter of an hour, and took place in presence of other two persons.'
The author then creates a familiar pen portrait, starting with his unusual
height, then stating that he 'wears his own hair, has a full forehead, a small
but lively eye, a round brown-complexioned face; nose and mouth pretty
small; full under the chin; not a long neck, under his jaw a pretty many
pimples.' The prince, 'is always in a Highland habit, as are all about him'.
The Englishman notes the daily public dining and that Charles 'constantly
practices all the arts of condescension and popularity – talks familiarly
to the meanest Highlanders, and makes them very fair promises'.[26] This
is not simply a description for the interest of the recipient. The author
may have been one of the first Englishmen actually to meet the prince
before his likely advance into England. Samuel Boyse observed of Charles
that 'Balls and Assemblies were held, at which he appeared in the English
Dress, with the Blue Ribband, Star, and other Ensigns of the Garter', while
at 'other Times he was seen in the Highland Habit' and the Cross of St
Andrew, as previously described.[27] By this description, Charles appears to
have maintained decorum and changed from his Highland garb and riding boots, to the fashionable attire of a European prince for the evening
entertainments.

In fact it was as a European prince, rather than as a Highland chief, that Charles chose to have himself painted while in Edinburgh. On 26 October, Allan Ramsay, the now famous London-based portrait painter (who happened to be in Edinburgh at this extraordinary time) received the following note from Colonel John Roy Stuart: 'To Mr Allan Ramsay, Painter. Sir, you are desir'd to com to the Palace of holyroodhouse as soon as possible in order to take his Royal Highnesses Picture so I expect you'll want no further call.'[28] The portrait is almost certainly the painting in the Wemyss family collection at Gosford House near Edinburgh, or, at the very least, a lost painting from which the Wemyss portrait was copied.[29] What is immediately striking is that in contrast to the image produced to coincide with the £30,000 bounty, and the countless eyewitness descriptions of him in Highland garb, Charles is here immortalised as a European, or perhaps more accurately, British prince, in a pale lilac velvet coat with silver lace, the hint of a gold waistcoat, a red velvet train trimmed with ermine draped over his left arm, a blue Garter sash with Garter star, his wig neatly 'buckled', powdered and tied with a ribbon from which white curls tumble down his back. This is no Highland laddie. The pale, refined, almost delicate face, with pink cheeks, is made manly by just the shadow of a moustache and beard. The very dark brown eyes are also mentioned in the eyewitness descriptions. The other curious aspect to this portrait is his expression – hovering somewhere between aloof and apprehensive.[30] Certainly not melancholic but, as might be expected, pensive.

John Pine, 'His Majesty's First Regiment of Foot Guards', from
The Cloathing Book, 1742.

Vilvoorde

'the bursting of a cloud'

On 4 September Lord Harrington had written from London to the Duke of Cumberland, at his headquarters in Flanders, stating, 'We are informed that there are actually in the Port of Dunkirk three or four French Men of War, with thirty large Merchant men appearing to be design'd for Transport Ships; The Irish Regiments are known to be ordered down to the Coast.' Charles Louis Auguste Fouquet, duc de Belle-Île and Maréchal de France (grandson of Louis XIV's finance minister), had reportedly arrived at Ostend. This, and 'Mr. d'Argenson at Dunkirk, give the greatest Reason to believe that the French Court has taken her Resolution to push this Enterprize upon His Majesty's Dominons with the utmost Vigour'. He continues, 'the King can no longer deferr to strengthen his hands at home, by a Detachment from the Army under your Royal Highness' Command', for the 'Dangers with which his Kingdoms are threatened from Foreign as well as Domestick Enemies make it indispensable, at the same time that it is a measure universally and earnestly insisted on by his faithful subjects'.[1] The duke had already prepared for such a scenario, with transport ships ready to sail ten battalions back to England, as soon as the wind would allow it. A week later, and ten days before the fateful Battle of Prestonpans, the Duke of Newcastle had written a personal letter to the duke, stating that though 'I have constantly seen the reality & Danger of this attempt to invade His Majesty's Dominions', yet 'I own I did not imagine that in so short a time the Pretender's Son with an Army of 3000 men would have got between the Kings Troops [Sir John Cope's army] & England, & be within a few days march of Edinburgh, where some think we shall soon hear that he is'. Some believed that Charles would reinstate the Scottish Parliament (as a statement of intent for the eventual dismantling of the Union) but 'others rather suppose, he will proceed w[it]h his army towards England, where there are no regular troops to oppose them, 'till he comes towards

London'.[2] Astonishingly, despite recent events, the sense of urgency was only being felt among the Pelhamite ministers. Horace Walpole writing to Horace Mann from Westminster on 20 September states that 'Lord Granville and his faction persist in persuading the King 'tis an affair of no consequence', while the Duke of Newcastle 'is glad when the rebels make any progress in order to confute Lord Granville's assertions'.[3] Lord Chancellor Hardwicke had observed that this misjudgement of affairs by some of the King's ministers had contributed to 'a strange lethargy and deadness' among the people as a whole, and therefore 'the spirit of the nation wants to be roused and animated'.[4]

This all changed a few days later. Sir John Ligonier had been sent ahead with the first detachment of troops from Flanders, and wrote to the Duke of Cumberland from Lord Stair's London house on 24 September (the day after his arrival in the capital) that 'this morning came an a[c]count of the intire defeat of Sr John Cope, with the loss of artilery bagage & his troops behaved extreamly ill'. He hopes that 'your R H will excuse me from [relaying?] as a most disagreable subject', but 'the affair by this Grows Serious, and I fear it will end in sending for more of the forces under your R H as soon as the [Flanders] campain is near over'.[5] In turn, on 25 September, both Lord Harrington and the Duke of Newcastle wrote to the duke at Castle Vilvoorde. The first letter confirmed the defeat at Prestonpans and the arrival in England of the ten battalions from Flanders, eight of which were Dutch, as the Earl Marischal had predicted the year before.[6] The second letter, supporting Ligonier's view of the situation, observed that 'had not the Reinforcements, providentially arrived, the day before the news came of Sr J. Cope's Defeat, the Confusion in the City of London would not have been described; and the King's Crown, (I will venture to say), in the utmost Danger'.[7] This sense of general alarm was reiterated in Lord Harrington's letter from Whitehall to Robert Trevor in The Hague (dated two days later) in which he states that 'by the unfortunate Defeat of the King's small army on the 21st inst[ant], near Edinburgh, the Rebels being become in a manner masters of the whole kingdom of Scotland', the Jacobites 'are according to our freshest advices, preparing to assemble the States in Parliament, where their first steps will be doubtless dissolving the Union, renewing the old alliance with France, & calling in a French army, to their assistance, under colour of the National Authority'. As to whether Charles and his men would now march into England, Harrington declares, 'we are yet uncertain'. Harrington continues that it is now necessary to recall more troops from Flanders, not least because 'what has happened in

Scotland having already struck so general a Damp & Consternation into people's minds here, that the Bank [of England] has been for some Days crouded with Multitudes demanding payment for their Bills, & the run is so great that the Publick Credit cannot be supported but with the utmost difficulty'. Therefore, 'the cry of all Ranks of People for the Return of a greater part of our national forces, and the reproach upon the Government for not having immediately recalled them, are the strongest that can be imagined'. He concludes that these are 'very critical, dangerous, & distressful circumstances'.[8]

Bad news from Britain continued to arrive in Flanders. On the same day as Lord Harrington was penning his letter to Robert Trevor, Sir John Ligonier wrote to Sir Everard Fawkener, 'acounts are since come that the Rebells increase, and some make them amount to 16000 men, that they have sumon'd a Parliament at Edinbourg, to declare that kingdom separate from England under the Protection of france, & so that this thing is now Grown very serious'. He seems amazed that 'the Rebells to the Great Dishonour of Scotland having taken Possession of it with three or 4,000 Begarly Bandity', and that as a result (and as Lord Harrington had already declared), 'the Cry of all here Great and smal is for our forces Coming Home, and who dares resist the [torrent?] when every man seems to think the kings person & crown in Eminent [sic] danger'.[9] The recalling of the Scottish Parliament was in fact incorrect, but such reports reveal the genuine anxieties and confusion around the intentions of the 'young Pretender', the disruption already caused to the stability of the United Kingdom coupled with (and more important still) the fears of an imminent French invasion in support of this Jacobite rising. Ligonier also reports, 'I hear the Resolution was taken last night to send for eight Battalions more to be transported to Newcastle and so put out this Infernal flame at once', while Marshal George Wade marches north with more men including the Dutch regiments. He continues, 'tho the People all Roar for the Duke the fear of dispiriting Entirely the Remains of His weak army I hear keeps HRH there [in Flanders]. I can express to you my uneasiness for His situation, what can He do with His handful of men against those numbers.'[10]

The removal of most of the troops from Flanders may have been an over-compensation to make up for the government's relative inactivity up to this point. Whether it was actually necessary to quell the rebellion is debatable, but something was needed to allay public concern and to dispel what could otherwise become a financial crisis. Ligonier concludes in a manner which indicates the high standing of the young Hanoverian prince among his senior officers: 'for all our sakes finish your Campain Bring our duke home safe putt me at His feet as one that Loves him (if I dare use that expression)'.[11] If one good thing came out of this fiasco, it is that King George was now (at last) convinced that he and his crown were at risk. As Revd Thomas Birch wrote to Philip Yorke, a week after Prestonpans, 'His Majesty is now at last awakened into a sense of his danger and, I hope, into a distrust of those who have taken such pains to amuse and deceive him.'[12] Two days later, Charles Yorke wrote to his brother Joe in Flanders that it was extraordinary to him 'that the work of so many wise and honest men, of so many parliaments of fifty seven years', indeed, 'that a fabric of so much art and cost as the [Glorious] Revolution and its train of consequences, should be in danger of being overwhelmed by the bursting of a cloud, which seemed, at first gathering, no bigger than a man's hand'.[13]

Soon after, on 1 October, Lord Harrington sent the duke confirmation of the king's orders to detach a further eight battalions: preferably British infantry but, failing that, Hessians. He also confirmed that it was now the general expectation among the government ministers that the Jacobite army would begin its march south to England imminently. Just prior, according to a letter dated 1 October, the duke had received Harrington's letter of 25 September containing 'the most mortifying news I could hear', that is, of course, Cope's defeat at Prestonpans. The duke writes that he will soon confirm the infantry and dragoon regiments that will form the second detachment, but then observes that 'the British forces in this Country will be reduced to 12 broken Battalions & twenty Squadrons [cavalry]', and as 'every thing is prepared & ready for Winter quarters, I beg your Lordship to use your utmost interest that his Majesty may permit me to return to England, where there is now the greatest prospect of my being able to render Him service'.[14] By 9 October the Duke of Newcastle (at least) could write with more optimism that 'we shall now soon have troops enough at home, to quash our intestine Rebellion: and to Discourage our foreign neighbours from making any attempt upon us'.[15]

As the duke's comment regarding 'Winter quarters' reveals, by mid-October (NS) the campaign in Flanders was drawing to an end for the winter. By this time, France had taken the whole of Austrian Flanders, with troops stationed at Ghent, Termonde, Bruges and Ostend and artillery at Tournai and Valenciennes. The few British troops left were centred on Antwerp, while Brussels, Mons, Charleroi and the strongholds of Brabant and Hainault were held by the Dutch, Hanoverian and Hessian armies. On 3 October OS (the 14th NS), the duke wrote to Lord Harrington setting out the timetable for departure of the various allied troops, and asking for his father's permission 'to employ my Duty & affection to His Majesty & my Country, where they now seem most to be call'd for', stating, with some impatience, that 'it would be the last mortification to me when so much is at stake at home, & brought to the decision of Arms, to be out of the way of doing my duty there'.[16] Four days later, the duke confirmed that Henry Hawley and Lord Crawford would stay at Antwerp for the time being with the remaining British troops, and that his brother-in-law, Prince Frederick of Hesse, was aware of King George's request to deploy Hessian troops, but as they were not currently needed they would remain at Antwerp in readiness. He also had intelligence that the Irish brigade of the French army was currently marching to Dunkirk. Finally, and with even less patience than before, he writes, as 'I can be of no further use here, I hope his Majesty will be pleasd to give way to my immediate return'.[17] Three days later, the duke sent an update on the transports, declaring, 'I wait every hour with impatience to receive my orders to return to England'.[18] This letter crossed in the post with one from Lord Harrington, bringing the longed-for order that, when the armies had gone to winter quarters, he was at liberty to return home.[19] On 18 October (OS) the Duke of Cumberland arrived in London.

The Pretender.

Attributed to Robert Strange, *Charles Edward
Stuart 'The Pretender'*, 1745.

22

South

'conquer or perish'

By the end of October, Charles and his army had been in Edinburgh and its environs for almost six weeks. Lord Lovat was still procrastinating, encouraged by Lord President Forbes. Kinlochmoidart had been sent north to finally get the Old Fox to raise his clan, but was arrested soon after. In fact, the Lord President's activities were considered so damaging that a warrant had been issued to Lord Lewis Gordon, younger brother of the Duke of Gordon and until recently in the Royal Navy, now stationed in the strong Jacobite area around Aberdeen, to arrest him for 'rebellious practices against the King our Royal Father by seducing or endeavouring to seduce the subjects from their alledgeance and to take up arms gainst him'.[1] Lord Lewis was to 'search for seize and apprehend the person of the said Duncan Forbes whom you are to bring Prisoner to our Camp'. The prince and his commanders were also concerned that the army, particularly the Highland contingent, encamped at Duddingston would lose patience due to the extended inactivity and start returning home in dribs and drabs. In fact, many had already wandered off with their booty after Prestonpans. Every day, the prince hoped to hear of his brother and a French invasion force arriving in the south-east of England. But, in the meantime, Charles had received intelligence that the veteran Field Marshal George Wade, former commander-in-chief in Scotland and famed builder of the Highland roads after the '15, was making his way north to command an army gathering at Newcastle upon Tyne, while a detachment under Lieutenant General Roger Handasyde was at Berwick-upon-Tweed. The first was made up of 4,500 Dutch and Swiss infantry, 5,000 British infantry and 1,500 British cavalry.[2] The second was what was left of Sir John Cope's defeated army. Sir John himself was in London, not knowing if he was to be court-martialled for the humiliation at Prestonpans.

Charles appointed Viscount Strathallan as governor of Perth and commander-in-chief of the Jacobite forces gathering in Scotland, with responsibility for further recruitment. Other governors were appointed for Dundee and Aberdeen. The prince reviewed his troops towards the end of October and councils of war were held on the 30th and 31st attended by, among others, Tullibardine, Perth, Lord George, Lord Elcho, Lord Pitsligo, Lochiel, Keppoch and Clanranald.[3] By this time, Lord Kilmarnock had decided to nail his colours to the Jacobite mast and, along with Lords Elcho and Pitsligo, had been charged with raising a cavalry regiment. He, too, joined the prince's council. During these meetings, Charles imparted the intelligence concerning Marshal Wade, along with the other preparations against them occurring in England, and asked the opinion of everyone present.[4] Charles was for entering England at Berwick, and then marching to Newcastle upon Tyne to give Wade battle.[5] The reasoning was, according to Secretary Murray: first, that these troops would be at their most fatigued having just arrived from Flanders; second, Prestonpans was a recent bad memory and the troops would be demoralised; third, Wade's numbers were not so great as the Jacobite army, and there was the issue around whether the Dutch troops accompanying him would fight once France was openly involved (as dictated by the Treaty at Tournai); fourth, marching to Carlisle in the northwest of England would be dispiriting to the Jacobite army, as it looked as if they were running away from Wade; and, last, the advantages of winning a major victory near Newcastle upon Tyne would be immense – not only occupying the wealthy city itself, but also the county of Northumberland. This would surely act as encouragement to the prince's friends in the west of England, particularly the well-affected counties of Cheshire and Lancashire, as well as Yorkshire, the county to the immediate south of Northumberland. The taking of a prominent English city such as Newcastle upon Tyne would be a serious blow to unnerve the government in London. Charles feared Marshal Wade could feasibly march to Carlisle faster than the Jacobite army and therefore block their passage over the River Esk into England.[6]

Lord Elcho puts a different emphasis on the prince's argument, stating that 'he was sure all the Country [of England] would join him', because 'in his Youth his Governors and Flatterers amongst his Fathers Courtiers had always talk'd of the Hanover Family as Cruel Tyrants hated by every body', they 'enslaved the poeple', and 'that if he or any of his Family were ever to appear in Britain that they would flock to him & Look upon him as their deliverer and help him to chase away the Usurpers family (as they call'd him)'.[7] His reception at Edinburgh and the defeat of Cope 'not only

Confirm'd him in all the ideas he had when he came into the country, but he likewise now believed the regular troops would not fight against him, because of his being their natural Prince'. As a result of such wild arguments, according to Lord Elcho, there was open opposition within the council to proceeding into England.[8] Captain Johnstone (no Anglophile) considered the prince to be the victim of an inexplicable family obsession with England, 'having inherited the sentiments of his ancestors, who always entertained an extravagant attachment to the English people', and this, Johnstone continues, despite everything the English had done to them, including civil war, *coups d'état* and regicide. In fact, the prince 'was occupied only with England; and he seemed little flattered with the idea of possessing a kingdom [Scotland] to which, however, the family of Stuart owes its origins and its royalty'.[9] Johnstone goes so far as to say, 'Some of the chiefs even told him, that they had taken arms, and risked their fortunes and their lives, merely to seat him on the throne of Scotland; but that they wished to have nothing to do with England.'[10]

Meanwhile, with reference to the march into England, and as a further hint of the increasing division between the prince's Scottish and Irish officers, Sir John Macdonald offers a completely different account, recalling that 'the Scots were determined to conquer England (a thing which seemed to them so easy that they scarcely troubled to consider how it was to be done) without any one not a Scot to have the least share in the profit or the glory of the conquest', and, allegedly quoting Lord Elcho, that 'many of them wished to have the Prince in the same dependence on them as their ancestors had done with Charles II'.[11] A majority of the accounts, however, agree that the Scottish commanders were not only against the march into England (at this moment at least) but believed that consolidating Scotland was not only achievable, but, as it currently stood, the only sensible option.[12] Lochiel considered that, over time, they could 'arm all the loyal Highlanders, summons the Estates of the realm, and put an army together which could defend itself, or even help the English shake off the usurpers yoke.'[13] At this opposition, the prince appeared to shift course, suggesting that they march to the border to entertain the troops (which everyone, according to Lord Elcho, agreed upon) only to shift again, stating, 'I find, Gentlemen you are for Staying in Scotland and defending Your Country, and I am resolved to Go to England.'[14]

A compromise was reached whereby the army would enter England from the northwest (Cumberland), a mountainous terrain Lord George considered much better suited to the army's Highlanders than Northumberland.[15] Colonel John Roy Stuart, who was not present at the meetings, considered entering England with such a small army, and with no confirmation of a French landing or an imminent English rising, as 'unaccountable' and a 'great error'.[16] Colonel O'Sullivan later observed that the army at this time 'was, it's most certain, not sufficient to Conquer England' but 'the hopes [that] the English wou'd joyn' and a French landing, plus being unable to raise enough money 'to entertain his Army in Scotland . . . determined the Prince to undertake what he did'.[17] Nevertheless, the prince had got his way and the army was mobilised. To overcome such strong opposition suggests a very persuasive and resilient individual: an individual who had (once again) galvanised support, even against the inclinations and better judgement of those around him. Charles had the encouragement of the marquis d'Eguilles, who apparently supported the prince's scheme to his face, while informing Lord Elcho and others in private that King Louis was happy to put James Stuart on the throne of Scotland, but 'it was all one to France whether George or James was King of England'.[18]

As recalled by James Maxwell, on 31 October the 'Prince set out from Holyrood House in the evening; there was an infinite crowd of people assembled to bid him a long farewell'. Maxwell believed that their 'concern was now as remarkable for the Prince's departure as their joy had been formerly for his arrival; they were affected with the dangers they apprehended he might be exposed to, and doubtful whether they should ever see him again'.[19] Others were not so sad to see the prince and his army leave. In an unsigned letter to 'Miss Barclay' dated the day after Charles left, the author writes, 'Ah, Peggie, what think you will become of all this? Our present prospect is extremely dismal – to be sure there must be a date of bloodshed, and probably at the very gates of Edin[bu]r[gh]. War at any rate is terrible but a civil war a hundred times more so than any other.' The author concludes, 'We hear the Highland army intends to march southward. I sincerely wish it may be so that the scene of Action may be a little removed.'[20]

The Jacobite army had completely evacuated Edinburgh by 4 November, all moving towards Dalkeith en route to England. Just prior to leaving, Henry Patullo, muster master, reviewed the troops and calculated that there were 'a few above 5000 foot, with about 500 on horseback, mostly Low-country gentlemen and their servants, under the names of guards, hussars etc.'[21] As Patullo's reference to 'Low-country gentlemen' makes clear, recruitment since Glenfinnan had changed the composition of this army. It was no longer an exclusively Highland force, yet many observers, Peggie's correspondent quoted above included, would continue to describe it as such. And despite all efforts to the contrary, the army's long stay in the environs of Scotland's capital had apparently left behind a ravaged land. Captain James Murray wrote to Duke James of Atholl, 'Our nighbours of East Lothian, and indeed all the country within thirty miles of Edinburgh, have suffered as much as if it had been conquered by a set of Turks.' He continues, 'the rebells have fallen into a down right rage, spare nothing, take even the working horses out of the ploughs, a specimen of the government is to be expected from them, and which Scotland will not forget for a couple of generations to come'. As a result, he believed they 'have given a more effectual cure to Jacobitism than the lenity of a fifty seven years administration could effectuate'.[22]

By this time Charles had received word of pro-Hanoverian 'disorders' in Perth, instigated by local celebrations in honour of King George's birthday, and had written to Lord Strathallan stating that he should keep 'the ringleaders of the late Riot . . . in close confinement till farther orders'.[23] Indeed, only a few days after Charles had left the Palace of Holyroodhouse, John Campbell noted in his diary that he had received an alarming message from Earl Breadalbane, declaring that 'the mob had got up in the Abbey, were opening doors, and like to destroy the house and every thing in it'. The Earl begged that General Guest should immediately 'send down a guard to the Abbey to protect it'.[24] What a contrast to the cheering crowds thronging the palace courtyard less than six weeks before.

Soon after, Lieutenant General Handasyde marched north towards Edinburgh with two regiments of foot and two of dragoons, and entered the town on 14 November without opposition.[25]

J. Daullé, *Prince Henry Benedict Stuart, c.* 1746.
(BIBLIOTHÈQUE NATIONALE DE FRANCE)

Fontainebleau

'make haste'

W hen Henry was finally told that his brother was in fact travelling to Paris in early 1744, he immediately put pen to paper, declaring: 'I can assure you Dear Brother that I am here with out you like a fish out of water', and confirming the 'respect, love and tenderness I have for you' which 'I can assure you Dear Brother (were the King but to permit me) wou'd make me fly through fire and water to be with you'.[1] Twenty months later, as soon as confirmation of Charles' landing in Scotland reached Rome, Henry was finally given an opportunity to do just that.

From late July 1745, when letters began trickling and then flooding into Rome from France and Flanders informing James of Charles' embarkation from Brittany and congratulating him on his son's daring and bravery, James was agog. But by early August, he was able to send a measured letter to his envoy Lord Sempill at the French Court, where he states that 'I know not particularly the grounds he goes upon, but I am affrayd there is little room to hope he will succeed, except he be vigourously supported by The Court of France'. Therefore, 'we must all of us in our different spheres leave nothing undone for that office'. James had already written to Louis, Maurepas, Orry, the brothers d'Argenson and the duc de Noailles, and he advises Sempill – and by extension the bickering Jacobite party at the French Court and beyond – that they must 'look forward, & not blame what is past'. For although 'Tis true I never should have advised The Prince to take such a step, but since it is taken it must be supported'. James even believes, regardless of the outcome, that 'it will certainly turn much to The Prince's personal honor' and that his treatment by Louis, coupled with 'the dread of Peace' between Britain and France, would have been 'strong motives to push him on a rash undertaking'. Besides, James continues, 'who knows but what he has done may in some measure force The Court of France out of shame to support him'. Finally, he hopes Charles' example

will encourage 'our friends in England', for 'he has ventured generously
for them, & if they abandon him they themselves, & indeed our Country
will be ruined'.²

As late as 20 September (NS, 9 September OS) James wrote to the
Duke of Ormonde that he still had not heard from Charles himself – the
prince's letters, carried by Antoine Walsh, had not yet been delivered –
although the existence of various reports that he had indeed landed in
Scotland meant 'that I think no further doubt can be made of it'. His
greatest fear at this time was that Louis and the French Court's removal to
Fontainebleau for the hunting season would result in nothing meaningful being decided upon until they returned to Versailles.³ Lord Balhady
then wrote to James on 19 October (NS, 8 October OS), stating that
recent reports from Scotland concerning Charles indicated 'that the whole
Kingdom was in Motion to join him', and 'that he behaves with so much
spirit and courage, and at the same time with so much humanity that he
captivates every mortall's heart'.⁴

By this time, Henry had already been tasked to act as his brother's chief
envoy and agitator at the French Court. Along with additional money
donated to Charles' campaign by Pope Benedict XIV, Henry left Rome
at the end of August (NS), in the first instance for Avignon (where he
fell very ill with a fever), finally arriving in Fontainebleau on Sunday, 24
October (NS, 13 October OS), under the guise of the comte d'Albany.
He discovered a court divided in its reactions to the Stuart prince's success. Cardinal Tencin and the marquis d'Argenson were for an immediate
French landing in Scotland, while Maréchal de Saxe believed no further
support was required at present, as the Jacobite advances had already been
useful for France's position in Flanders. This latter perception is the key.
True to form, King Louis had stalled making a final decision regarding a
full invasion attempt by sending the marquis d'Eguilles as a special envoy
to Holyroodhouse, where he was expected to report back on the current
state of play and particularly the prince's intentions regarding an advance
into England. In fact, the decision to send d'Eguilles had been made before
the French Court had heard of the Battle of Prestonpans.

After news of that 'astonishing' (as Louis reportedly described it) victory reached France in early October, the French king began to plan in
some earnest. Louis had already decided to send Lord John Drummond
and his regiment, the Royal Ecossais. His full intentions were finally
and formally ratified in the secret Treaty of Fontainebleau, signed on 24
October by Colonel Daniel O'Brien and the marquis d'Argenson. Here,

Louis committed himself to assist Charles 'in all possible ways'[5] against their common enemy, the Elector of Hanover. Henry arrived on the same day and was granted an immediate audience with Louis – something Charles had singularly failed to achieve during an entire year in France. Henry, writing to his father a week later, described the difficulties he was encountering due to the divisions within the Jacobite party at court and the lack of concerted action by the French ministers. He confirmed that an English Jacobite, Sir James Harrington, was expected from England, but until he arrived, 'I see nothing is to be done' regarding the invasion, but when he does 'I am persuaded if The Prince can but maintain himself as he is at present every thing will be very soon ready'.[6] A week later Lord Balhady wrote to James from Fontainebleau stating that he had brought recent editions of the *Caledonian Mercury* back from England the week before and that Lord Sempill had translated these for 'The King of France and his court, who are extremely fond of them'. Indeed, these reports had had 'the desired affect', for France was now determined to send 12,000 troops into England. And 'they have been busy about it in their own way', that is, sadly, 'postponing the most essential and pressing affair to what they judge their own private interest, so divided that nothing can go on to purpose'. However, Louis' 'fix'd resolution, I may say zeal to support your m[ajes]tys cause, is the only sure foundation for our expectation and the real cause of what is done already'.[7] On the same day, Lord Clancarty (another Jacobite emissary to the French Court) wrote to James from Paris that Sir James Harrington, who had 'great Weight, and Interest' among the English Jacobite party, was expected in France in three weeks' time and, regarding the troop transports for the invasion, 'so soon as he arrives I hope we shall Embarque'.[8]

By mid-November (NS) Lord John Drummond and his men were ready to embark in the French navy frigate *La Fine*, accompanied by another frigate and six privateers as transports for more detachments from the Irish regiments in the French army. On 25 November (NS), Sir John Graeme, a former secretary to James in Rome and now resident in France, reported that George Kelly, Charles' priest, had arrived in France via Holland, where, prior to his arrest, he had been obliged to burn the papers he carried from Charles to the French king. However, Kelly had verbally summarised what the prince had requested from Louis – in particular an invasion force in England sufficient to stir the English Jacobites – and stated that when Kelly left the prince, he was at Duddingston with eight or nine thousand men (an inflated number to encourage the French).[9] In response, Henry had written a long letter to Louis asking him to provide Charles with everything he had asked for and to 'smooth away all the difficulties your majesty's Council has successively found in the way of this expedition',[10] while Kelly, Earl Marischal, Lord Clancarty and Colonel Daniel O'Brien had gone to the French Court to press them to 'make haste'. For, in Sir John Graeme's words, although the senior French general Louis François Armand de Vignerot du Plessis, duc de Richelieu, 'was nam'd last week to command the embarkation for England yet I don't see things advance so fast as would be requisite'.[11]

However, by 26 November (NS, 15 November OS), Henry could state in a letter to Charles, 'Things [are] going here even better than I well expected.'[12] Irish regiments of the French army, to be commanded by Maréchal Richelieu, were gathering on the north-west coast and Antoine Walsh was coordinating the assembly of an invasion flotilla, made up of everything from fishing boats to coastal craft, in order to land the troops on the English coast.[13] By far the best news was that the marquis d'Argenson had allowed Henry to inform his brother that 'ye King of France was absolutely resolved upon ye Expedition into England, qu'il y avoit mis le bon, and [that] you might count upon its being ready towards [the] twentieth of December new stile'.[14] In private, the marquis hoped that the Jacobite army's advance through England would not be too swift, giving the French as much time as possible to prepare. But in any case, if all went to plan there would be a French invasion force with Charles' brother at its head – and with an elegant new manifesto written by no less a personage than Voltaire – landing in south-east England soon after 9 December OS.[15]

Anonymous, *The plagues of England
or the Jacobites folly*, 1745.

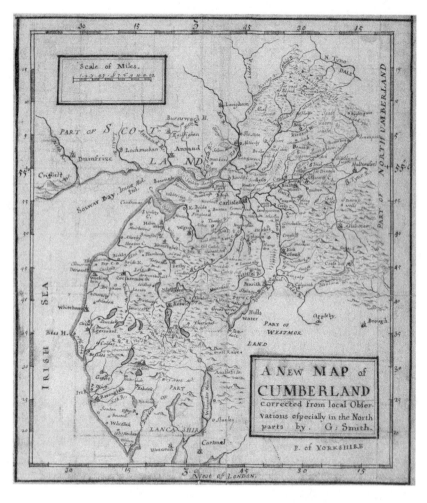

Anonymous, *A New Map of Cumberland*, 1745.

24

England

'our danger is now at the height'

In recent times, and certainly after the Act of Union, the border citadel of Carlisle, still essentially a castle and town lying within late medieval walls, was no longer required as England's most northwesterly defence.[1] The garrison was now made up of two companies of Invalids, mainly veterans of Marlborough's wars, numbering about eighty men in total. From the late 1730s one of the company officers was the kindly Lieutenant John Bernard Gilpin. As the garrison was now effectively used for guard duty and little else, the soldiers and townspeople mixed together very affably with many of the men residing with their wives and families beyond the castle's walls. By 1745 the population of Carlisle was about 4,000. Lieutenant Gilpin enjoyed a reasonably leisured life, filled with painting and fishing. In the meantime, little effort had been given to the maintenance of the fortress. When the governor of the castle, Lieutenant General John Folliot, inspected the defences, he found them 'in a very weak condition'.[2] The town walls were little better and some of the dilapidated sections had already been pulled down for reasons of public safety. Beyond the town, the outworks (ditches and trenches) that had once prevented attackers marching up to the walls had fallen into disrepair. All in all, the situation would be grave indeed should Prince Charles decide to cross the border into England from the north-west.

Still, little was done by the British government to rectify this. In a letter dated 9 September 1745 the Lord Lieutenant of Cumberland, Henry Lowther, 3rd Viscount Lonsdale, had written to the Duke of Newcastle, informing him that the people in this area of England were sufficiently alarmed at what was happening to the north that he was now raising the Cumberland and Westmoreland militias.[3] He blamed the local inactivity, thus far, on a naive acceptance of the reassurances from London that the rebellion was nothing to be concerned about. The local citizens volunteered to the number of about 580 and a bullish loyal address was sent to King George confirming the town's commitment to His Majesty, the House of Hanover and the Protestant settlement. The citizens appeared confident that Carlisle could, and would, defend itself against any advance by the Jacobite army. This confidence was partly encouraged by the fact that, in 1715, the Scottish army had passed Carlisle by, aiming instead for a fast march to Lancashire, a county with strong Stuart loyalties.

Two weeks later, Cope's troops were defeated at Prestonpans. Dr John Waugh, Chancellor of the Diocese of Carlisle, writing to the Duke of Newcastle stated that the town would be ready to defend itself against an 'irregular mob', as the Jacobite army had been previously deemed, but 'they could not consider the Rebels who had defeated one of the King's armys in that light' and he feared the inhabitants' nerve would falter unless they had some assistance.[4] Although the government was still reticent about committing regular troops to help defend the town, Lieutenant Colonel James Durrand was sent to Carlisle, arriving on 11 October to take command of the garrison, boost morale and prepare it for an attack. What he found was a town 'in a very weak and defenceless condition' with 'no ditch, no out-works of any kind, no cover'd way, – the walls very thin in most places'. But, in agreement with Lieutenant Gilpin, it was decided that they should not 'mention our opinion of the weakness of the place for fear of discouraging the Militia and inhabitants; but on the contrary, to speak of it as a strong place and very tenable'.[5] The garrison Invalids he described as 'very old and infirm' and even when bolstered by the militia and volunteer companies, he considered it 'too weak a garrison for a town and castle'. However, attempts were now made to build up the defences, which included ordering additional guns from the coastal town of Whitehaven, walling up the 'Scotch' and 'Irish' town gates and patching the walls.[6]

On 17 October, Dr Waugh reported on recent intelligence he had received from Edinburgh to Dr John Bettesworth in faraway Canterbury, Kent. The Jacobite army, he wrote, had increased and 'others are come and coming, who seem to be very resolute to die or conquer'. Lord Lovat, Dr Waugh continues, has apparently stated he can do nothing about his son (also Simon, Master of Lovat) and Clan Fraser rising; meanwhile other clans are arming. He quotes one unnamed author, who states that, 'We have yet no certain account when the army will march, or the route they will take to England; they are in daily expectation of a landing of the Irish brigade and other regiments from Dunkirk.' The said author continues by confirming the arrival of the French envoy, the marquis d'Eguilles, with 'several of the officers having landed last Monday at Montrose, and with them a great many arms, ammunition, &c.; and it is believed, money'.[7] Just over two weeks later, on 2 November, Dr Waugh, writing again to Dr Bettesworth, enclosed a letter detailing the movements of the Jacobite army around Edinburgh. According to this author 'the Baggage, Artillery, Ammunition, &c., were upon Waggons and Carts going to Dalkeith, and . . . the whole army were in motion and preparing to march Southward; . . . they gave out they were to go by Kelso, and were resolved to meet Marshall Wade and give him Battle.' From this Waugh concluded 'our danger is now at the height'.[8]

Over the next week, Dr Waugh received a barrage of letters and enclosures from Dumfries, Peebles, Moffat, Annan and Jedburgh, all detailing the onward movement of the Jacobite army. In Dumfries, George Bell forwarded an account (which had also been copied to Marshal Wade in Newcastle upon Tyne) outlining a variety of conversations and intelligence gathered by two unnamed men. The provost of Peebles, for example, had been told by the Jacobite quartermasters to prepare 'meat, drink, and lodging' the night of Saturday, 2 November for 1,800 men and a further 4,000 for the following day. Meanwhile, 'great preparations were also that night making at Broughton', Secretary Murray's house near Peebles, 'where some persons of distinction were arrived, escorted by 60 horse'. There is no doubt that Prince Charles was one of these guests. The baggage, arms and ammunition that had arrived at Montrose was now at Perth, and horses pressed 'under pain of fire and sword' to carry it to Alloa, a town lying the furthest inland on the north bank of the Firth of Forth and close to Stirling. Apparently accompanying the baggage were twenty-four engineers with the intention of capturing the Castle of Doune (near Stirling). However, General Blakeney at Stirling Castle, seeing this advance, dispatched Captain Abercrombie with some soldiers and countrymen to attack the rear, wounded some, took several prisoners (including Highland 'wives'), plus baggage, arms, money and letters, 'which it's supposed will afford Genl. Blakeney some useful discovery'.[9]

All the intelligence received by Dr Waugh was uncertain as to whether Carlisle was on the Jacobite army's route, until, on 5 November, the Provost of Dumfries (only thirty-three miles away to the north-west) sent notice that he had heard from Moffat, that a Jacobite quartermaster had arrived at one o'clock demanding quarters for '4,000 Foot and 600 horse, and the mess[enge]r says he saw them within half a mile of the town before he came away. We expect them or a part of them this way to morrow. I beg you will dispatch expresses to Penrith, Kendall, Lancaster and Whitehaven.'[10]

The towns named, except Whitehaven, were all lying on the route south of
Carlisle. Dr Waugh's last correspondence to Dr Bettesworth in Canterbury
simply states, 'they advance this way very fast. Send no letters.'[11]

At Dalkeith the prince was rejoined by the Marquess of Tullibardine
and about 1,000 men (Athollmen, Menzie's men, Grandtully's and
MacPherson's), plus six Swedish cannon from the armaments lately arrived
at Montrose. Here, the army split into two main columns, each then moving in different directions: the first led by Prince Charles and Lord George
moved to the south-east via Lauder potentially towards Berwick-upon-
Tweed (and therefore Newcastle upon Tyne) and the other, under Perth
and Tullibardine (with the artillery) moved south-west via Peebles and
Moffat towards Carlisle, 'the view of keeping the enemy, by this stratagem,
ignorant of the place where the Prince intended to enter England'.[12] A
stratagem that had obviously worked very well, as the exchanges between
Dr Waugh and his contacts in Scotland makes clear.

On 6 November, Charles passed the Tweed at Kelso, after which a
detachment of Lord Elcho's lifeguards was sent on a middle route towards
England via Hawick and Langholm. Charles and his troops now switched
to a south-westerly direction, following the River Teviot via Jedburgh passing 'by terrible mountains, very bad roads, & worse quarters'.[13] On Friday,
8 November, Charles crossed the River Esk into England, just south of
the town of Canonbie, accompanied by the Camerons, and sent Hussars
ahead to reconnoitre. The other regiments remained on the Scottish side
of the river. Secretary Murray recalled, 'It was remarkable that this being
the first time they entered England, the Highlanders without any orders
given, all drew their Swords with one Consent upon entering the River,
and every man as he landed on tother Side wheel'd about to the left and
faced Scotland again.'[14] Captain John Maclean of Kingairloch (in Lord
Nairn's regiment) recalled: 'Our Army Gave a Huza Saluting the English
ground.'[15] For his first night on English soil, the prince lodged at a farm
called Reddings or Riddings, owned by David Murray, near Longtown. The
following day (Saturday the 9th), the entire column crossed and the prince
moved on, eventually arriving that evening at the village of Moorhouse,
four miles to the west of Carlisle. According to Captain Johnstone, secrecy
'was so well observed, that hardly any person in our army had the least idea
of the place where the junction of the three columns would take place' and
therefore 'we were very much surprised on finding ourselves all arrive, on
the 9th of November, almost at the same instant, on a heath in England,
about a quarter of a league from the town of Carlisle'.[16]

That afternoon, the advance party had arrived outside Carlisle at Stanwix Bridge lying to the north, but as it was Martinmas Saturday (one of two annual fairs) and the roads were heaving with locals travelling to and from the town, the garrison was unable to fire immediately on these outriders. From their vantage on the north bank of the River Eden at Stanwix Bridge, Major Baggot could see the castle on a rise to his right and the cathedral on another rise in the centre of the town before him. As Charles had decided to lay siege to Carlisle and while the castle guns were silent, locations for trenches and batteries were considered. Major Baggot returned to Moorhouse, informing the prince that from Stanwix Bridge 'he could see a good many people upon the walls, that they seemed very alert, and that they had no Sooner observed them upon the Bridge than they fired Some of their guns from the Castle, but without doing any execution'.[17]

At Moorhouse village Charles lodged at Stonehouse, then owned by a Quaker called Jonathan Ostell. In one of the main rooms, a sobering inscription on the stone mantel over the fire read 'HERE WE RESIDE, OUR NEXT REMOVE SHALL BE FROM TOILSOME TIME TO VAST ETERNITY'.[18] Colonel O'Sullivan recalls that the prince was in his chamber with Sir Thomas Sheridan and Lochiel, when 'they heard something gro[a]ning under the Bed'. The mistress of the house was summoned, who then begged the prince to spare her child, after which the said offspring was pulled out from under the bed.[19] The woman apparently believed that the child 'wou'd be set upon the Spit, as there was not much to eat in the house' because, again according to O'Sullivan, British government agents had encouraged the idea that the Highlanders 'murdred, ravished, burnt & destroyed all [that] come in their way, eat or lived upon human flesh'.[20] This notion was not just circulating in Cumberland. As O'Sullivan continues, 'it passed so currant in England [that] the children were alwaise set out of the way, & [that] a great many in our roads abandoned their houses'.[21] O'Sullivan's observation is supported by an extraordinary story which ran for several days in the *Reading Journal* and was then reported in the *Westminster Journal or New Weekly Miscellany* on 5 October. The editor of the London paper considered the account 'so incredible' that enquiries were made. It was discovered that a mother of three (aged six, three and one), of the parish of Radnage in Buckinghamshire, had visited a neighbour's house 'when the Discourse happened to turn chiefly upon the Pretender's Invasion'. She left one of her children with the neighbour, returned home, 'went up Stairs' and 'cut the Throats of her other two poor innocent Babes, laid them out one by the other on the Floor with Pillows under their Heads, and then came down Stairs, cut her own Throat, ript her Belly open, so that her Bowels came out'. It was in 'that frightful Condition' she was found, 'to the Astonishment of all who beheld her'.[22] If anti-Highlander propaganda was being spread by the government and then exaggerated by a fearful populace, then as this example shows it was likely to backfire with tragic consequences. In the case of the woman at Moorhouse, Sir Thomas Sheridan was able to allay her fears that the child would be eaten, after which the local villagers 'came to see the Prince, being at supper', laden with bottles of local beer.[23]

During the morning of Sunday, 10 November, as the three divisions of the Jacobite army converged on the town 'there was such a fog, [that] day, [that] a man cou'd hardly see his horses Ears',[24] which also obscured the size of the approaching army from the lookouts on the castle's battlements. At midday this fog cleared, revealing the gravity of their situation. Tullibardine had volunteered to raise a battery to attack the 'Irish' gate, located in the west wall of the town. But Colonel O'Sullivan considered the attempt to lay siege foolhardy, as 'we had no other Artillery but our swedish pieces of four pounders, wch wou'd hardly beat down a barn', plus the small one-pounders captured at Prestonpans. However, Perth's troops and the Athollmen were chosen to prepare for the attack, as the inherently impatient Highlanders were deemed unsuitable for siege warfare.[25] The chosen location for the battery was unfit, in O'Sullivan's opinion, as 'it was w[i]thin a smal musquet shot of the Castle', which was located at the north-west corner of the citadel. Nor did they have 'a picaxe, Shouvel or facine to raise a Battery, & if there were, it wou'd signify nothing wth our Artillery'.[26] The garrison immediately began to fire and the Jacobite army retired back, well out of range.

The Jacobite troops were then ordered to reassemble the following day and a better location was found to raise the battery that was 'not at all exposed to the Castle'.[27] At three o'clock Thomas Pattinson, Deputy Mayor of Carlisle, received a proclamation from 'Charles P. R.' stating,

> Being come to recover the King our Father's just Rights for which we are arrived with all His Authority, we are sorry to find yt you should prepare to obstruct our passage, We therefor to avoid the Effusion of English Blood hereby Require you to open your Gates, and let us enter as We desire in a Peaceable manner, which if you do we shall take care to preserve you from any Insult and set an Example to all England of the exactness with which we intend to fulfill the King our Father's Declarations and our own. But if

you shall refuse entrance we are fully Resolved to force it by such means as Providence has put into our hands, and then it will not perhaps be in our power to prevent the dreadfull consequences which usually attends a Towns being taken by assault. Consider seriously of this and let me have your answer within the space of two hours, For we shall take any farther delay as a peremptory Refusal and take our measures accordingly.[28]

According to O'Sullivan the core message was capitulate, or Carlisle 'wou'd be set to ashesses, wth red hot bullets'.[29] In his proclamation, Charles seems to be suggesting that he would be unable to restrain his troops – already believed by some locals, as we have seen, to be capable of inhuman acts of violence and terror even against children – resulting in unspecified 'dreadful Consequences'. Here any sensationalist government propaganda was being cleverly turned against itself. But the only response from Carlisle was another blast from the castle guns.

That night Charles lodged at Blackhall farm, a large building with a clear view towards the south-west of the town. Soon after arriving, the prince received intelligence that Marshal Wade was either marching or preparing to march out of Newcastle upon Tyne towards Carlisle. Charles immediately ordered that the army should be ready by morning to march to the town of Brampton to the east, and quartermasters were sent out to demand billets for 8,000 men the following day. Secretary Murray recalled 'it is almost impossible to describe the joy that was in every body's face upon the news of Wade's aproach'. The prince 'expressed the utmost Satisfaction, as he was now likely soon to be able to execute the plan he had formed to himself at Ed[inbu]r[gh] by the reduction of Newcastle, which inevitably must have followed a victorey'. The Highlanders, too, were 'pleasd to think that they now had not taken that rout to Shunn him', that is, to avoid Wade, 'but for reasons they could not comprehend'.[30]

On Monday, 11 November the prince marched with the majority of his troops to Brampton via Warwick Bridge to await the marshal's arrival there. As O'Sullivan observed, 'That country was looked upon to be a very proper place to wait for Wade (his horse cou'd be of no manner of use), & very fit for high-landers – Hillocks, morrasses, & passes, he [Wade] cou'd hardly find a place to set himself in battle, & there we expected to give a good acc[oun]t of him.'[31] At Brampton, Charles took lodgings on High Cross Street. From here on the same day he wrote a letter to Lord Barrymore, the leading English Jacobite lord whose country house was at Marbury in Cheshire:

My lord, This is to acquaint you the success we have had since our arrival in Scotland, & how far we are advanced without Repulse We are now a numerous army, & are laying siege to Carlisle this Day, which we are sure cannot hold out long. After That we intend to take our Route streight for London, & if things answer our Expectation we design to be in Cheshire before the 24 of this Instant. Then I hope you & all our Friends in that Country will be ready to join us: For now is the time or for ever. Adieu. C.P.R.[32]

The letter was handed to two messengers for safekeeping.

During the two days they were at Brampton the army had received conflicting news of Marshal Wade's movements, but, after a heavy fall of snow, it was considered most unlikely that the Marshal would now leave Newcastle upon Tyne. O'Sullivan recalled, 'We had scouts out dayly. Our men were well enough in their quarters ; there fell such a quantity of snow, [that] we cou'd not imagine [that] Wade wou'd undertake such a March, in such weather, since he had not already begun. Upon this the Prince call'd a Counsel, to see what cou'd be undertaken against Carlille [Carlisle].'[33] Although there were murmurings about whether advancing further into England was such a good idea, a compromise was reached whereby the Duke of Perth would return to Carlisle with troops to undertake the siege, while the remainder with the prince would continue at Brampton, monitoring the activity of Marshal Wade. Lord George had admitted he had no experience of preparing for a siege, but, with some well-chosen regiments, he would cover those who undertook the work.[34] Lord George and the Duke of Perth began the march back to Carlisle on Wednesday, 13 November.

Meanwhile, in Carlisle itself, on Monday, 11 November the sight of the majority of the Jacobite army apparently retreating suggested that, against all the odds, they had succeeded in repelling the enemy. To that end, Thomas Pattinson wrote a euphoric letter to Lord Lonsdale: 'we have outdone Edinburgh,' he declared, 'nay all Scotland.'[35] Lord Lonsdale had duly forwarded the letter to the Duke of Newcastle who in turn showed it to King George, who heartily thanked the magistrates and officers of Carlisle for their 'loyalty and courage'.[36] Newcastle congratulated Pattinson on the 'great Honor, the Town of Carlisle has gain'd by setting this Example of Firmness, and Resolution; which, it is to be hoped, will be follow'd in other Places, should the Rebels attempt to advance further'.[37] But on the 13th, before Newcastle had even written his reply, the townsfolk of Carlisle watched in despair as the Jacobite army returned and began to dig trenches on the east side of the town (between the Scotch and English gates) and away from the castle and its guns at the north-west corner. Lord George was in charge of the blockade. The Duke of Perth led the preparation of the siegeworks by example, in the trenches digging, stripped down to his shirtsleeves, all the while being fired at from the town. Cannon was then brought up 'more to intimidate than from any hopes that they could peep upon the walls'[38] and trees were cut down to make scaling ladders.

But, even so, the increasingly bad weather, marshy terrain, onerous labour and the constant fire from the town were chipping away at morale. In a letter to his brother at Brampton, dated 'Harbery' (his headquarters near Carlisle) 5.00 a.m., Thursday, 14 November, Lord George writes 'notwithstanding all the pains taken by the Duke of Perth, who is indefatigable in that service, and who meets with unnumberable difficulties, I suspect the place pitched upon will not answer'. But, if they must continue, 'the men posted upon the blockade of Carlisle will not expose themselves, either in trenches, or all night in the open air, within cannon shot, or even musket shot, of the town, except it be in their turn with the rest of the Army, and that to be decided by lot who to mount that guard, first night, second, and so on'. To that end, Lord George proposed that detachments be sent in rotation from the troops in Brampton, so that each took their share of this dangerous duty.[39] The reply, after a council of war held at Brampton (also dated 14 November) and in Secretary Murray's writing, read: 'So soon as the whole body that now forms the blockade has taken their turn of the guards, the division of the army now here will march in a body and form the blockade; but no detachments can be sent from the different corps, nor do they think it fair to require them to do so, as they had all the fatigue and danger of the blockade in Edinburgh.'[40] This response was unlikely to please Lord George, who would have taken the refusal to accept his recommendation as a direct and personal affront.

However, morale was collapsing faster within Carlisle itself than in the cold, muddy trenches beyond the walls. Colonel Durrand received a letter dated 10 November from Marshal Wade, saying he was having difficulty getting to Carlisle in time to relieve it, and that they should hold out as best they could. Then, on the morning of 14 November, the colonel received a message from the officers of the militia, acquainting him 'that having been lately extremely fatigued with duty, in expectation of releif from his Majesty's Forces', but as relief was not imminent 'and not being able to do duty or hold out any longer, they were determined to capitulate'.[41] Colonel Durrand immediately attempted to persuade them to hold

out. He observed that the Jacobite entrenchment, in his opinion, was too
far from the citadel to do any real harm. Indeed, 'as it was not usual to
carry on works in the day time, I imagined it was only done to intimidate
the Garrison'. Further, if they stood together, the town and castle could be
defended 'for some considerable time longer, against the whole force of the
Rebels, as by the best accounts we had of them, they had no Cannon large
enough to make a breach'.⁴² In fact, he was absolutely right, for according to Captain Johnstone the Jacobite artillery 'did not discharge a single
shot, lest the garrison should become aquainted with the smallness of their
calibre'.⁴³ Yet, according to Colonel Durrand, the militia 'still continued
fixed in their resolution', fearing that if they delayed the town would be
stormed that night and everyone put to the sword, as threatened.⁴⁴ The
militia officers then contacted the mayor to ask him whether he would join
them. He in turn contacted Colonel Durrand, who reiterated his determination to defend the town and castle, to which the mayor agreed that
he and the townsfolk would hold fast with him. However, in response, the
militia stated, 'they would send and Capitulate for themselves, upon the
best terms they could get',⁴⁵ with the inevitable result of striking panic in
the townspeople. A meeting was held, at which the majority of the people
agreed to defend the town – but even this was not enough for the militia.
So eventually, the townspeople agreed to join the militia and capitulate.
The garrison, commanded by Lieutenant Gilpin, protested and then with
Colonel Durrand (who in the meantime had had the cannon on the town's
ramparts nailed up) 'retired into the Castle, with the two Companys of
Invalids and about 400 other men, who all then said they would join
with me in defending the Castle to the last'.⁴⁶ But by eight o'clock the
next morning (Friday, 15 November), as Colonel Durrand recalled, 'they
changed their resolution, as all left us to a man'.⁴⁷

Later that morning the principal inhabitants and militia officers arrived
at the castle. Their capitulation had been refused. The Duke of Perth had
answered that 'the Town & Castle must surrender, or else [that] the Town
wou'd be in ashesses the next day' which, observes Colonel O'Sullivan, 'God
knows, he was not in condition to perform'.⁴⁸ It was either the castle and town
surrendering together, or nothing: the Jacobite army had learned its lesson
from Edinburgh. If the castle held out then the town would be destroyed,
while the Highlanders 'put all the inhabitants and Militia, without distinction to the sword'.⁴⁹ If they surrendered, the garrison would be allowed to
leave with all military honours, and all would be at liberty to go wherever
they wanted. As Colonel O'Sullivan had admitted, this was a bluff.

Within the castle, Colonel Durrand called a council of war. The situation was grave. The militia had refused to assist in the defence of the town and castle, the garrison consisted of only eighty predominantly infirm men who could not manage the guns, much less man the walls as well.[50] Then there was the threat 'to destroy both Town and Castle, with fire and sword unless the Castle surrendered'.[51] The war council considered that as the defence of the castle was not tenable, then 'it is for his Majesty's service, that it be abandoned, as it will be absolutely necessary, for the preservation of the lives of his Majesty's subjects, who would otherwise be exposed to inevitable ruin'.[52] Both castle and town capitulated. There had been only one casualty during the entire episode, as Lord George recalled (with a touch of gallows humour), 'an Irish officer, standing out of the Trench saing they could not fire cannon like guners from the Town. At the very time a Cannon Ball went thro' his throt.'[53] An express was sent to Charles at Brampton and the Duke of Perth entered the town in triumph with all his troops. The Jacobite army was now in possession of everything stored within the castle including firearms, gunpowder and 120 horses. In response to a letter from Secretary Murray, dated 15 November, Lord Strathallan in Perth wrote to Lord Lewis Gordon, who was still raising troops in Aberdeenshire, informing him of the fall of Carlisle 'after a vigorous defence' and 'that the whole army was in good health and top spirits'. It was now the prince's earnest wish 'that his friends on the North side of Forth use the utmost dilligence to joyn him' in England and therefore Lord Lewis should 'come up here as soon as possible with all the men you have conveened and any spare Arms'. The onward march should be kept secret, but 'your lordship will not faile to bring up all the money that can possibly be levied as the want of it will be our greatest hardship'.[54] Charles wanted his army together for the push forward through England, and he desperately needed cash.

At some point on this same day Lord George resigned his commission in favour (in the first instance) of Lord Elcho. Angry at the prince's refusal to rotate troops during the blockade, his stated reason was that 'I cannot but observe how little my advice as a General officer has any weight with your Royal Highness.' But, 'as I ever had a firm attachment to the Royal Family, and in particular the King, my master, I shall go on as a Volunteer, and design to be this night in the trenches as such, with any others that will please to follow me'.[55] Colonel O'Sullivan described this letter as 'very high'.[56] Certainly, Lord George's reference to 'the King, my master' established to whom his lordship felt ultimately responsible. In the section of his memoirs covering the siege of Carlisle, Sir John Macdonald refers to hearing from Francis Strickland about a letter written by Lord George to the prince, which he considered 'impertinent'. It is not clear whether Macdonald is particularly referring to Lord George's resignation letter, or an earlier missive (possibly that dated 14 November requesting the detachments from Brampton), but both thought such insolence (as they deemed it) offered 'a good occasion to get rid of this dangerous man, suspected by all the army except Sheridan and 3 or 4 others whom he had persuaded of his ability and honesty'. That the whole army suspected Lord George of being a danger to the cause is demonstrably untrue, but Macdonald and Strickland's pernicious bias against him is more than evident.

On Saturday, 16 November, the Duke of Perth proclaimed King James, attended by the mayor and civic officers in their robes and carrying the town's sword and mace. Their behaviour was noted. More damning still, soon after the mayor and corporation travelled to Brampton to present Charles with the keys of the town, reportedly on their knees. On Sunday, 17 November, as recalled later by Alexander Blair of the Life Guards, 'the Prince made his publick entry into Carlisle, attended by his Guards, when the Cannon of the castle and small arms from the Town were fired, and loud Huzzas as he passed along the streets, which were lined with the Highlanders, the Bells ringing all the time'.[57] According to George Mounsey the prince rode a white horse and was preceded by 'not less than an hundred pipers'.[58] The main army was now cantoned in the villages around the town.

The Duke of Perth, hearing of Lord George's resignation, had a private audience with Charles during which he resigned his own commission as lieutenant general, resolving to serve only as commander of his regiment. Despite the plotting of Strickland and Sir John Macdonald, Lord George resumed his commission now as sole lieutenant general and commander of the army. A council was held at Carlisle during which, once again, it was argued by some not to march any further into England: at least until some sign of a rising among the local Jacobites was evident. Some even argued for a return to Scotland; others, including Charles, were for continuing the advance into England regardless. Lord George, now wary of appearing wilfully obstructive, as he later recalled, 'stated the advantages and disadvantages of each of the different opinions, and concluded, that for myself I could not venture to advise his Royal Highness to march far into England, without more encouragement from the country than we had hitherto got'. Yet, now aware of the suspicions that circulated about him, 'I was persuaded, if his Royal Highness was resolved to make a trial of what could be expected, and would march south, his army, though but small, would follow him.'[59] The resolution was passed to advance further into England. Colonel John Hamilton was left as governor of Carlisle with about 100 men to act as garrison. The remainder prepared for the long march via Lancashire towards London.

John Faber Junior after Johan van Diest, *Field Marshal
George Wade*, 1736.

25

Newcastle upon Tyne

'this rigorous season'

Prior to Field Marshal Wade's arrival, on 6 October John Hixton, an innkeeper at Perth, had been captured as a spy in Newcastle upon Tyne and had attempted to cut his own throat. A paper from Charles was discovered in his glove, which ordered Hixton to contact the English Jacobites (particularly those in the north and north-west) with news of the Jacobite army's 'wonderful success' and of Charles' plans to move forward from Edinburgh in a few days. Charles states that 'it will be inexcusable before God & man if they do not do all in their power to assist and support me in such an undertaking'. The prince ordered that they should gather provisions and money for the army's march, and that they must understand, 'there is no more time for deliberation, now or never is the word, I am resolved to conquer or Perish if this last shou'd happen let them consider what they & their posterity have to Expect'.[1] This intelligence would explain the assumption made by Lord Harrington, among others, that the Jacobite army's move from Edinburgh would occur at the beginning of October. However, the prince and his men had remained *in situ* for several weeks more.

On 30 October, Marshal Wade arrived at his new headquarters in Newcastle and issued a proclamation which was printed up and 'great numbers of these are sent to be distributed amongst the Rebels' presumably, in particular, those still encamped near Edinburgh. The proclamation observed that some of King George's subjects 'have been seduced, by Menaces and Threatnings of their Chiefs and Superiors, to take Arms, and enter into a most unnatural Rebellion'. Therefore 'His Majesty hath authorised me to assure all such, who shall return to their Habitations, on or before the 12th Day of November next, and become faithful to his Majesty and his Government that they shall be Objects of his Majestys Clemency.' But 'if, after this his most gracious Intention being signified, they shall continue in their Rebellion, they will be proceeded against with Rigour, suitable to the Nature of their Crime'.[2]

The following day Marshal Wade wrote to the Duke of Cumberland, who was making preparations in London to travel north, that 'the poor soldiers, from long marches, and bad roads, are many of them barefooted, though we have taken all possible pains to provide them, with what shooes the Country can afford'. The seventy-two-year-old concludes, 'My age and infirmitys render me incapable of writing to Your Royal Highness in my own hand.'[3] News arrived that the Jacobite army had in fact moved towards the north-west of England and later that Carlisle was threatened. On 16 November, under very difficult circumstances, due to severe weather including heavy snow (as Colonel O'Sullivan had observed), the marshal began to move his ill-equipped troops westward to relieve the town. He had got no further than Hexham by the time intelligence arrived that Carlisle had fallen. George, Earl of Cholmondeley, Lord Lieutenant of Cheshire, confirmed to Sir Everard Fawkener (on 23 November from Chester) the desperate situation Wade's army was in, having received a letter from his brother, Brigadier James Cholmondeley (dated Hexham, 19 November) stating, 'I think it is impossible for Wade to follow the Rebells'. His men 'are so harrassd & such little provision made when they arrive att their Ground, yt what with the roads before him which are very Bad & the severity of the weather, I plainly foresee they must return to Newcastle or halt for some time where they can be well provided & taken care of, before it is possible for them to advance'. As Marshal Wade and his men were for the time being out of action, another army under Sir John Ligonier (then in the West Midlands) 'is all we have to depend on' and 'the old corps', that is the experienced soldiers rather than recent recruits, along 'with the artillery must decide our Fortune'.[4]

By the time Lord Cholmondeley was writing this, Marshal Wade and his beleaguered army had already returned to Newcastle upon Tyne. In response to a letter from his lordship, Wade confirms that 'the unexpected surrender of both town & Castle [at Carlisle], in a shameful manner and without the least resistance, put a stop to our proceeding further'. The lack of artillery to retake the city, the impassable roads due to heavy snow-fall, coupled with the presumption that the land around Carlisle would be plundered by the occupying army, and therefore provide no food or shel-ter for his own troops, were other crucial factors in his decision to retreat. However, on returning to Newcastle, the army had received some wel-come kindness from the civic leaders and townspeople who, Marshal Wade relates, 'in compassion to the sufferings of the poor soldiers, have permitted the whole body of the Foot, to take shelter here in Publick Halls, Glasshouses, malthouses, & many private houses' which has 'probably saved the lives of a great many of our men, who were half perished by lying in Camp in this rigorous season'.[5] Wade's many problems, from poor kit to lack of forage and all exacerbated by dismal weather conditions, indicate why military campaigns at this time rarely occurred during the winter.

At least the marshal would have also arrived back at his Newcastle headquarters to some good news, courtesy of a letter from his dear friends Lord President Duncan Forbes (still, despite Charles' order for his arrest, at large) and the Earl of Loudoun, updating him on their recent activities around Inverness. Between them they had enlisted 700 Highlanders, albeit with some difficulty, with several hundred more promised, and with whom they would endeavour to persuade the clansmen who had yet to come out 'to stay at home'. They aimed to open up the communication with Fort Augustus and Fort William immediately, after which they would march some troops to Banff and around Aberdeenshire 'to obstruct effectually the recruiting of Lord Lewis Gordon for the Pretender's Service, which goes on but heavily at present'. After this 'we shall be ready to do what further appear necessary and be within our Power, for putting an End to the present Rebellion'. In a postscript dated 17 November, Lord Loudoun and the Lord President confirmed that MacLeod of MacLeod 'with 400 of his kindred joind us' which gave them hope of preventing 'the March of the Frazers who are not yet gone – There is a great fall of snow on the Ground.'[6] That last detail must have stimulated a wry smile.

THE
JACOBITEs JOURNAL.

By J O H N   T R O T T-P L A I D, *Esq;*

After William Hogarth, *The Jacobites Journal*, Number 6, 1748.

26

Lancashire

'like Bees'

Through the late summer and early autumn of 1745, Richard Kay, a young surgeon from Baldingstone near Bury (seventeen miles south of Preston), noted in his diary little more than local events and his day-to-day professional engagements.[1] However, on 24 September the surgeon recorded, 'About 6 Weeks or 2 Months past we have been often hearing of a Rebellion in Scotland in favour of a Popish Pretender; our Government have sent a Body of Men to disperse them and we hear this Evening that our Forces have engaged them and are defeated by them, at or near Edinburgh in Scotland.'[2] This was three days after the Battle of Prestonpans, indicating the speed with which news travelled in 1745. In many ways the lack of interest – or at least concern – displayed by Richard Kay, before news of the battle arrived in Baldingstone, reflects the general perception in 'South Britain' that the insurrection, although shocking, was fundamentally a Scottish issue to be contained and dealt with within Scotland. It is also a reminder that, for the British populace in areas where the rebellion had had no direct impact, life went on as if nothing out of the ordinary was happening at all.

But now something extraordinary had happened. The Jacobite army had achieved the impossible, and, in the process, dealt a significant blow not only to the prestige of the British army, but also to public confidence in the troops within Britain who had been expected to defend them. Further, the government in London was now all too aware that the quashing of this rebellion would be no simple matter. To the civilian population, the concept of a belligerent army full of reportedly terrifying Highlanders rampaging through England had transformed overnight from impossibility to probability, and, as a result, the 166 miles as the crow flies between Edinburgh and Kay's little village in the north-west of England must suddenly have seemed no distance at all.

On 25 September Richard Kay records, 'We are hearing much News from the Rebellion in Scotland, but hear very little good News.'[3] However, references to the rebellion disappear completely from the surgeon's diary for the remainder of September and throughout October, that is, during Charles' extended sojourn in Edinburgh.[4] This suggests that the Jacobite army's prolonged period of relative inactivity, certainly a period where the element of surprise was gradually dwindling, meant that for Richard Kay nothing was occurring worthy of note. There is, perhaps, even a presumption that the rebellion would indeed remain in Scotland.

But, further afield, Richard Kay's neighbours in Lancashire were far from complacent. In Preston itself, Richard Shepherd wrote on 7 October to John Nourse, the bookseller at Temple Bar in London, that 'Affairs in Scotland have taken such a turn and the Rebells have had such surprising success that all business in this Part is now at a Stand'. He and his fellows 'are arming ourselves in the best manner we are able', but, 'if they should venture to take their rout[e] this way before the arrival of the King's Forces and tho' we are at no little distance from Edenborough we are under no small apprehensions from the number and progress of [them]'. As a precaution, Shepherd's 'last effects are removed to the Mountainous parts of the Country excepting my Books'.[5] A few weeks later the Jacobite army had left Edinburgh and begun its advance towards the border. But at the beginning of November the crucial question was, which way would they go: to the north-west and Lancashire via Carlisle, or to the north-east and Yorkshire via Newcastle upon Tyne? The clever feint of dividing the army into two columns, apparently heading in different directions, kept the northern counties of England guessing for a while, but after Carlisle surrendered the towns and cities lying on the Jacobite army's western path southwards, including Penrith, Lancaster, Liverpool and Chester, were on high alert. The north-west of England and particularly Lancashire was viewed as an obvious place for the Jacobite army to gain recruits (being a strong Catholic and nonjuring area) and was an easy distance to the counties of northern Wales, another region sympathetic to the Stuart cause.

Eight days after the Jacobite army began to move off from Edinburgh (8 November, the day before Carlisle got its first glimpse), Lord Cholmondeley reported from Chester to Sir Everard Fawkener that he had managed to raise 600 volunteers, 'a success I did not expect, as I have met with innumerable difficulties from the stories that have bin raisd and propagated by the disaffected in this county & the northern part of Wales, to deter men from Inlisting'. Indeed, the local Tory gentlemen 'have done all in their

Power in a clandestine manner to prevent their Tennants & Dependants from Entering'.[6] This observation confirms that English and Welsh Jacobite sympathisers were (if not keen to engage directly themselves) at least willing to assist the prince's advance, by discouraging local recruitment for the new British army regiments and militia. Lord Cholmondeley concludes, 'should the Rebells think of advancing either to Staffordshire or to this county & the Northern Provinces of Wales, In either case I but too much apprehend their being joind by great numbers.'[7]

Three days later Lord Cholmondeley again writes to Sir Everard, now clearly exasperated by the lack of communication from any quarter and with a hint of despair, as 'it is impossible for us in this part of the world to think of doing any thing towards stopping or impeding their march which you will find is pretty rapid', he will do what he can but without orders 'upon this pressing & dangerous conjuncture I fear if they bend their course this way that they must soon be masters of all of the Towns & Country'.[8] The situation regarding the garrison and fortifications at Chester is now a familiar one. So little had been done to prepare the town for its own defence, coupled with the speed of the Jacobite advance, that it was the opinion of both Lord Cholmondeley and Brigadier William Douglas, the officer now entrusted with organising these defences, that it was, alas, useless to try. As Douglas reports to the Duke of Cumberland, 'with the tools we have to work with I pronounce the place quite Defenceless'. Apart from the dilapidation of the ramparts, or 'walls I should call em', the castle itself is 'a very weak place and tho it has some guns, not a gunner that can point one'. Douglas then elaborates on the quality of the manpower, 'a parcel of ragged youths and some old men', who had been given guns, but so recently that 'they don't at all know the use of 'em'. In fact, 'I am thoroughly convinced if an Enemy shoud appear they woud throw them away.' Another regiment was expected soon, but 'are not better and are not all arm'd yet'.[9] In summary, Brigadier Douglas declares, 'I assure your Royal Highness that with such tools and such a Place no defence can possibly be made nor indeed do I find any Body sanguine enough to think of any.' He then asks, almost pleadingly, to be returned to his brigade 'where I may be of some use I am sure I can be of none here'.[10]

About this time, Lord Cholmondeley received a package of documents concerning two men currently held at Chester Castle on suspicion of 'treasonable acts'. They were Peter Pattinson and John Newby, the two messengers sent by Prince Charles from Brampton to Marbury Hall to deliver his letter into the hands of Lord Barrymore. But discovering that the earl was in London, Pattinson was brought before his son, James Barry, Viscount Buttevant. According to Lord Buttevant himself, Pattinson declared that he 'had a letter to any man of honour in Cheshire who co[ul].d be trusted and he hoped he was not deceived in his Lordship'.[11] The letter, a small piece of paper 'sealed up with a wafer', was handed to Lord Buttevant but, unfortunately for Pattinson, his Lordship – unlike his father – was no Jacobite; in fact he was a staunch supporter of King George. Having read the contents, Lord Buttevant threw the letter in the fire, perhaps not wishing to further incriminate his father, and then arranged for his servants to escort Pattinson and Newby to a nearby house, where he then had them seized. It was also said that Pattinson had boasted that the 'Chevaliers son' or 'Prince Charles' had 16,000 infantry and 4,000 horse all of which were 'better than any of the Kings men', and even advised the British army officers he had met 'to join them, for they must succeed it was impossible they sho[ul].d be resisted'. Such numbers were a gross exaggeration. Finally, Pattinson, who seems the chattier of the two messengers, declared that the Jacobite army 'wo[ul].d be at Manchester in ten days'.[12] With the interception of Charles' letter, coupled with the arrest of John Hixon in early October at Newcastle upon Tyne, it appeared that at this crucial stage in his campaign (whether he realised it or not) the prince was in the precarious position of having made no direct contact whatsoever with any of the leading Jacobites in England.

On 20 November Mr Cowper was standing in the main street of Penrith (twenty miles south of Carlisle) observing the arrival of the Jacobite army. In a scrawled note to Mr Lamb the postmaster at Brough (a village located twenty-two miles to the south-east from where he was standing) Cowper writes, 'The Highland Army is swarming in here all this Day like Bees' and 'Those we had last night are all gone the Lancashire Road'. He recognised Lord George Murray, Lord Elcho, Lord Nairne, Glenbucket and the Duke of Perth, 'who I have just now been with'. The prince was expected at any time and was to be quartered at 'F. Simpsons'. Further, all 'publick Money [has been] demanded under pain of Military Execution. They have received the Excise. The whole Body is undoubtedly moving this Way. Thier's all forced Marches numbers never stop. Emont Bridge will bring me their whole number: near two thousand have passed there already.'[13] Eamont Bridge lies just to the south of the town, on the boundary of the ancient counties of Cumberland and Westmoreland.

Later that day, at midnight, Cowper writes again to Lamb: 'The Highlanders have been coming in here, ever since Four this morning to

Nine. Some houses have 100 a piece. The whole Body, we have good reason to believe, is moving Southwards. We have Three Thousand in Town, what in the neighbourhood we cannot yet Judge. Tomorrow is to bring us several Thousand more.'[14] This intelligence was copied and then delivered by express rider to various commanding officers in the towns lying to the south of Penrith, including Sir John Ligonier, now at Lichfield, and the Duke of Newcastle in London.[15]

Further intelligence from a 'Mr Gillison' at Penrith – which was delivered to the Post Office in Liverpool by Christopher Jameson and eventually made its way to Ligonier – reads, 'The Pretender with his household came at the head of a Regim[en]t of foot abt. 3 in the afternoon.' Gillison goes on, the 'body of the Regular force very inconsiderable as yet; Abt 30 Hussars besides those wch marched with the Van Guard yesterday to Kendall. Carlisle is left only with 100 they talk of great numbers to come up, what has appeared taking the whole body together is not above 6000 besides women & boys.' He notes the women of rank accompanying the army to be 'Lady Ogilvie and Secretary Murray's lady'. Glenbucket had already advanced and Lord Elcho, the Duke of Perth and Tullibardine were in town. Other commanders were 'Ogilvie, Nairn, Murray, Pitsligo, Dundee'.[16] At Penrith, the High Constable received an order from Prince Charles to cause the shoemakers 'within the Village of Penrith and Neighbourhood' to deliver all the men's shoes they had by six the following morning 'for which they shall receive the usual prices'. This 'our order you and the said shoemakers are to obey under the pain of Military Execution to be done against your and their persons and effects'.[17]

On 21 November, in another quickly scribbled note, Walter Chambers, Recorder at Kendal (a town about twenty-seven miles due south of Penrith), writes: 'Part of the Scots amounting to about six score are just now ent[e]ring this Town', and then at the base of the note is written in another hand, that of John Wilson Chancellor of Kendall, 'Theres about 120 Horse come into town & only about 112 men being several 100 Horses they talk yt 2000 foot is to come in to night commanded by L.[d] Geo Murray.'[18] Such intelligence, recorded at the very moment that the events described were occurring, was once again copied and circulated to the British army commanders, as well as the civic leaders on the presumed Jacobite army's route. The combined information received from Messers Cowper, Gillison, Chambers and Wilson confirmed that between 20 and 21 November, the Jacobite army stretched all the way from Carlisle to Kendal, a distance of about forty-seven miles.[19] This was partly due to the need to billet and feed thousands of men at once and in increasingly inclement conditions, but in so doing it made this army very vulnerable.

At midnight on 24 November, John Beynon wrote an express from Preston, detailing the arrival of the Jacobite army into Lancaster (twenty-three miles south of Kendal and twenty-five north of Preston).[20] The intended recipient did not actually read the letter as it was intercepted by Jacobite outriders. Even so, it provides a detailed picture of the gradual arrival of the army into the town and the process of occupation, including the billeting of officers and troops. It displays the sense of urgency in relaying the details as accurately as possible, as well as the high level of risk taken by those who were required to linger in one location for long enough to gather such information together – the risk being either turned in or captured, and then executed as a spy. That day at noon, a quartermaster, six Highlanders wearing blue bonnets and white cockades, plus six more gentlemen wearing blue coats with scarlet linings, and two servants in attendance, came into Lancaster. The quartermaster 'lighted & went to the Town Hall & immediately issued out an order for the payment of the Excise & Customs, windo[w] & Land Tax by 12 o'Clock on Monday . . . & that order was declared in evry Street by the Belman'. Collecting local taxes was vital. With his war chest dwindling, it was the only way for the prince to pay his men, as well as reimburse locals for their quarters and provisions. Then, 'a Body of 30 horse more came in & rec'ed Billets' and the next order 'was that all Butchers, Bakers, Farmers etc sho'd follow their Employment & bring in Provisions for P.C.R [Prince Charles Regent's] Troops upon pain of military Execution'. Between two and three o'clock, Lord Elcho and 200 infantry arrived with bagpipes playing, followed by about 120 cavalry. Lord Elcho handed Beynon a declaration, 'for wch I thank'd him'. But, despite having disguised himself 'by wearing very bad Shoes tattered Stockings & hat slouched', Beynon writes, 'a damn'd Papist had blown me as a Spy', after which he made his escape at night arriving in Preston at ten o'clock. Beynon concludes:

This will be the last post night at Preston. The Rebels will be here Monday night. As they advance all Intelligences will be at an End. I assure you I have taken all the pains I could to give you the earliest Intelligence. I beli[e]ve I must buy a Horse for all the Common Horses are pressed for his Majesties Service & all Gent[leme]ns Horses are sent out of every Town. Bed is almost a stranger to me these 3 nights. I shall avoid falling into Company wth the Rebels any more. Most of the Highlandrs have 2 pistols on each side of their

Breast & a Musket slung over their Shoulders & a Broad Sword which they
carry from the time they get up till they go to Bed.
Yours etc. John Beynon.
N.B. I had convers'd with 'em some time before I had idea to go.[21]

James Ray, who had been a British army volunteer since the fall
of Carlisle, was now reconnoitring the Jacobite army and at Lancaster,
observed that the last column did not enter until 26 November and then
'in such Haste, that they only stayed to eat some Bread and Cheese standing
in the Streets'.[22] Both Beynon and Ray give a hint of the massive impact of
an army marching through, and temporarily residing in, what were small
towns and villages: from providing accommodation, stabling, food and
clothing en masse, to gathering campaign supplies and the enforced collection of large sums of money through taxation and fines – all under the
threat of military execution (martial law).

The twenty-two-year-old John Daniel recalled seeing Charles 'like a
Cyrus or a Trojan Hero, drawing admiration and love from all those who
beheld him',[23] in the midst of his army on the road between Lancaster and
Garstang (Garstang is at the mid-point between Lancaster and Preston).
At the time, Daniel was drinking with friends in a public house at the
roadside, when the Duke of Perth halted for refreshment. Perth enquired
about the local feeling for the Stuart cause, to which Daniel's companions responded, 'they believed it to be much in the Prince's favour'. Perth
then invited John Daniel to join him, which Daniel did with evangeli-
cal zeal. He set off into the surrounding countryside, to Ecclestone and
Singleton, causing Prince Charles' father to be proclaimed king, dispers-
ing manifestos and, echoing the contents of such Jacobite propaganda,
attempting 'to shew the people the misery and oppressions of tyranny and
usurpation, which like oxen yoked down to the plough, they seem to labour
under'. The prince was here to free them, so they should 'rise up and, like
lions . . . shake off the infamous yoke which too long had galled the necks
of free-born Englishmen . . . prove to the world, that they remained true
English hearts'.[24] Daniel then states, somewhat dejectedly, 'But alas! notwithstanding all our proposals and exhortations, few of them consented to
join the Prince's army.'[25] However, in John Daniel we have an example of
an Englishman with deeply held Jacobite views and the inclination to turn
this stance into active support. From John Daniel's testimony it appears,
with some notable exceptions, that few of his fellow Lancastrians were
willing – so far at least – to follow his example. However, Captain John

Maclean recalls on the Garstang–Preston road, 'we met two violers with their fiddles playing the King Shall Enjoy his Own Again. They were no Losers for severall of our officers threw money to them.'[26]

On 26 November, Lord Elcho had been the first to arrive in Preston, the location chosen for the main army and the vanguard, which had been separated by a day since Carlisle, to be brought together. Lord Elcho was followed by Lord George with the majority of the vanguard. Preston was famed for being the furthest south that the Scottish army had reached during both the 1648 (civil war) and 1715 campaigns. Lord George, mindful of the impact this would have on his troops, marched them straight through the town without stopping, and then on to Ribble Bridge, located one mile due south, 'to convince them that the Town Should not be their *ne plus ultra* for a third time, which seemd to give them a good deal of Satisfaction'.[27] This served to break the spell of 1715, while achieving a strategic benefit: the bridge was the key approach to the town from the south. Charles arrived with the remainder of the army that night and lodged at Edmund Starkey's house on the north side of Mitre Court. Lord Elcho writes, 'The poeple of Preston show'd more joy upon seeing the Prince Than they had done any where else, and their were for the first time in England several huzza's, and next day when the manifesto's were read the people ask'd for them and seemed keen to read them.'[28] This is supported by Secretary Murray who states, 'the Chevalier was mett by a great course of people and welcomed with the Loudest Shouts and acclamations of joy'.[29]

But both men also observe the lack of recruits, despite the apparent enthusiasm of the onlookers, as does, in turn, Colonel O'Sullivan, who recalled: 'It cant be expressed wth what demonstrations of joy the Prince was rec[eive]d here, bells ringing, bon-fires, all the houses illuminated, such croudes of people, [that] the guardes cou'd not keep them of[f]; every body, man & woman must tutch him.' Indeed, there was 'such a continual cry of "God blesse the King and the Prince,"' that 'it was thought they wou'd all follow & bring him directly to London. A great many of them took party, but did not follow.'[30] At Preston Charles was joined by two Welsh gentlemen, William Vaughan and David Morgan (a lawyer), both of whom entered Lord Elcho's Life Guards. Lord Elcho later wrote, 'The Prince road through the town of Preston with his guards dress'd in Lowland cloaths in order to Show himself to the people. Usualy he wore the highland habit.'[31] This change in appearance, as seen in the Lowlands, was intended to appeal to an English audience.

The disappointing recruitment from an apparently well-affected town worried some of Charles' officers, who began to voice the opinion (once again) that they had gone far enough.[32] But 'upon the Prince Assuring them they would be joined by all his English friends at Manchester, and Monsr de Boyer [d'Eguilles] offering to lay considerable wagers that the French were either landed or would land in a week, these discourses were laid Aside'.[33] The expectation of an imminent French landing, robustly supported by Louis' own man, was a crucial if not *the* crucial weapon in Charles' argument for an advance. While there was no solid evidence to the contrary, the arguments against would always falter. And the hope of an English rising was still alive, if dwindling. Meanwhile, Lord George sent men out to get intelligence of Marshal Wade and Sir John Ligonier's movements. The first returned with the information that Wade 'had march'd his army straight south upon the London Road, to Doncaster, and that their were rumours of his marching across the country into Lancashire'. The second reported that Ligonier was forming an army of 10,000 men around Lichfield and Coventry, and that the Duke of Cumberland was expected there any day to take over command.[34]

In addition to Morgan and Vaughan, and, in Secretary Murray's words 'some few Common people',[35] at Preston, Charles was joined by one of his most experienced recruits. Francis Towneley, who had been in the military service of Louis XV, came from an old Lancashire family near Burnley and was a Roman Catholic. Towneley himself explained his reasons for joining the prince's army. He did not 'wantonly or wickedly seek to disturb the Peace of my Country. My Situation in Life, added to the Tendency of those Principles of Government which I imbibed in my Education, induced me to stir in the [Prince]'s Behalf.' Indeed, he 'had no particular Aversion to the present Government. *England* was always dear to me; I took no Pleasure in disturbing her Peace', and, 'could the Pretensions of that Family . . . have been prosecuted any other Way than by Violence and Bloodshed, I should gladly have let my Sword grow rusty in its Scabbard, or have employ'd it in some other Service; any War would have been more welcome to me than a Civil War'.[36] However, Catholicism – even allowing for the fact that this repressed minority could expect greater freedom under a Catholic monarch – did not guarantee active Jacobitism and, unlike Towneley, the vast majority of local Catholics followed the recommendation of their clergy by remaining aloof to the current rebellion. This was no doubt encouraged by the British government's proclamations against Catholics (restricting movement, disarming them and so on) as well as the stoking up of any

residual anti-French/anti-Catholic feeling within the broader public, by
denouncing, as Archbishop Herring had done, this 'popish pretender' supported by England's old Catholic enemies France and Spain. Only a week
after Towneley joined, as events were coming to a crisis, King George was
waited upon at St James's by the Duke and Duchess of Norfolk, the most
senior members of the English nobility and the leading Roman Catholics
in the country. Given this, as the *True Patriot* observed, 'the Season which
they have chosen to express their Attachment to his present Majesty,
should silence the Clamours of hot-headed Men, who cannot separate the
Ideas of a Roman Catholic and a Rebel, tho' it be a notorious Truth, that
not one single Man of Consequence, who is a Professor of that Religion,
hath taken the Opportunity, of these Times of Danger and Confusion, to
express Marks of Disaffection to the Government, or to endeavour molest-
ing it.'[37]

According to Sir John Macdonald, Towneley appears to have had little
support from some of his fellow Jacobite officers: 'Young Townley however
joined and raised a troop of loyal people of the town and neighbourhood
in spite of the Scotch who treated him most disdainfully. This Townley was
a gallant and loyal gentleman, who had been for some years an officer in
France.'[38] This may be as much a reflection of the Irishman's attitude to the
Scots officers in the Jacobite army, as the Scots officers' attitude towards
the Englishman. Certainly, it is yet another indication that the Jacobite
command was far from unified.

According to a tradition retold in Edward Jeffery's *The history of Preston
in Lancashire* (published 1822), while the Jacobite army rested in the town
'a buxom, handsome young woman' called Peggy from the village of Long
Preston, near Settle in Yorkshire, 'anxious to see the Pretender and his
army', went to Preston in Lancashire for that purpose, a distance of about
thirty-eight miles, and after gratifying her curiosity, and staying some time
in or near the rebel camp, returned to her native village'. Her exploits
became so famous that a ballad was written about them. The gentleman
who had provided Jeffery with the anecdote, knew 'Long Preston Peggy'
and, even twenty-five years after the event, 'has frequently heard her sing
the very song, of which she herself was the subject'. Edward Jeffery concludes, 'The strains of "Long Preston Peggy to Proud Preston went,/To see
the bold rebels it was her intent" was seldom carolled from her lips till she
had been treated with half a dozen or more glasses of spirits.'[39]

While Long Preston Peggy was satisfying her curiosity, the Jacobite army
was preparing for its march to Manchester via Wigan. Captain Johnstone

remembers a sergeant 'named Dickson, whom I had enlisted from among the prisoners of war at Gladsmuir, a young Scotsman, as brave and intrepid as a lion, and very much attached to my interest'. The evening before the Jacobite army was due to leave Preston, Dickson independently left the town en route to Manchester, accompanied only by his mistress and a drummer.[40]

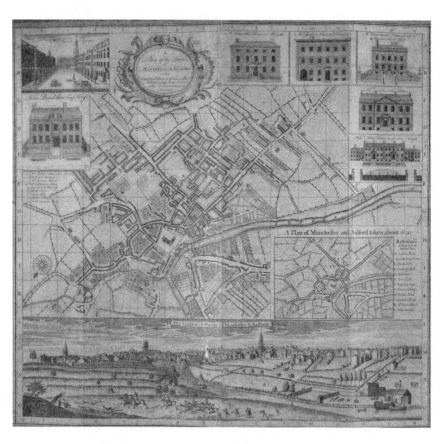

B. Cole, *A Plan of the Towns of Manchester and Salford,* 1751.

Manchester

'who Pretender is, or who is King'

The town that these unlikely conquerors were marching towards had been described by Daniel Defoe in the mid-1720s as 'one of the greatest, if not really *the* greatest mere Village in England'.[1] By 1745 Manchester was far from a village, with a population of under 20,000. Manchester's expansion over the first half of the century was due to the wealth derived from its cotton and weaving trades. The fashionable centre of the town had gravitated away from its ancient heart around the Anglican Collegiate Church, Hanging Ditch, the Shambles and Market Place, the site of the Old Cross, where the houses were built predominantly in wood and plaster or wattle and daub, to the newly developed area located around St Ann's Church (completed 1723) with its fine stone or brick town houses, adjoining gardens on wide streets (such as King Street and Ridgfield), spacious squares including St Ann's Square itself and the Jacobite-named St James's Square (laid out in 1739).[2] A narrow footpath and nearby cart way linked the two areas. But the inns and taverns of the old town, such as the Bull's Head and the Angel, continued to be the haunt of the local civic leaders and party rivals. The recently built Exchange (1729) and The Conduit, or public water supply, were also located at the southern side of old Market Place.

Manchester was linked to Salford, lying just to the north-west, by a single bridge over the River Irwell, the 'Old' bridge, and, despite the new development, the lanes and streets in both Manchester and Salford were rarely paved. Manchester had only two street lamps – one at the Old Bridge and the other at the Old Cross – although complete night darkness was lifted a little by the oil lamps that hung in front of some of the private houses. Essentially Manchester was an affluent but small market town with no 'city' wall or defences. It has been estimated that a pedestrian could walk across it, end to end, in ten minutes.

James Maxwell believed that Charles decided on this route through the north-west of England 'because he had been assured that Manchester was well inclined, and that an insurrection was as likely to begin there as in any town in England'.[3]

Like Richard Kay, the twenty-three-year-old Elizabeth Byrom, known to her family and friends as Beppy, was writing a journal from her home on Hanging Ditch.[4] Unlike the surgeon, Beppy displays from the onset sympathy, if not enthusiasm, for the Jacobite cause. She notes Sir John Cope's defeat two days after Richard Kay and then, under 8 October, she writes of a trip to her uncle's house at Baguley, then in Cheshire, where she cheerfully recalls 'everybody in hiding for fear of the rebels'.[5] After some discussion on the local Manchester 'Presbyterian' clergymen at St Ann's Church preaching against the rebellion – the church had been built as a pro-Hanoverian counterpoint to the Jacobite sympathies of the Collegiate Church frequented by the Byrom family – she records in almost light-hearted defiance, 'I bought a blue and white gown off Mr. Starkey, gave 12s. for it.'[6] Miss Byrom had clearly heard about the blue bonnets and white cockades sported by the bonnie prince and his men. Beppy concludes this entry by recording, 'The Presbyterians are sending everything that's valuable away, wives, children, and all for fear of the rebels.'[7]

Reflecting the confusion over the exact whereabouts of this rapidly advancing army, on 12 November Beppy writes 'an express [has] come that the rebels are coming, and another that they are not, and so on'.[8] She then observes the arrival on the 14th of 'my Lord Derby' (Edward Stanley, 11th Earl of Derby, the Lord Lieutenant of Lancashire) and that two days later 'an express is come to him that Carlisle is surrendered to the rebels'.[9] By the 25th Beppy records the delivery of 'an express that they are at Lan[caster]' and that a 'letter from Penrith says the rebels are but 7,000 men, but other accounts say they are 25,000 or 30,000'.[10] Beppy's account emphasises the reliance on both the regular and express posts for news of the rebellion, and equally how rumour and false information, as well as reliable fact, was relayed from town to town and from region to region.

The following day Beppy notes that 'they are at Preston this morning, came in there at ten o'clock, behaved very civilly'. Civil or not, this meant that the Jacobite army was a mere twenty-six miles from Manchester. Unsurprising then, as Beppy recounts, 'everybody is going out of town and sending all their effects away, there is hardly any family left but ours and our kin; they have sent away their shops and shut up shop, and all the warehouses in town almost are empty'.[11] Beppy quotes the opinion of a local physician and government loyalist, Dr Peter Mainwaring, who stated that 'the rebels have done nothing but what a rabble without a head might have done'.[12] Voicing such disdain for the Jacobite army was either brave or foolhardy given the circumstances. Yet, unlike many of his fellow 'Georgite' Whigs, Mainwaring had at least remained to face the imminent and, in his opinion, hostile occupation of the town. Among the people who had fled were the local magistrates, who knew all too well the form taken during occupation, via the reports received from other towns and cities to the north (particularly Carlisle), and did not wish to wait around to be coerced into acts of treason. The paucity of loyal citizens in Manchester was pointed out by the author of a communication sent to the Duke of Cumberland, who observed, 'I do not see that we have any person in town to give intelligence to the King's forces, as all our men of fashion are fled, and all officers under the government.'[13]

Prior to the arrival of the Jacobite army, several meetings were arranged by the local constables, Thomas Walley and William Fowden, firstly with the Justices of the Peace for the County of Lancashire, James Chetham and Robert Booth, at their meeting house in the aptly named 'Dangerous Corner', and then with other principal inhabitants of the town at the Old Coffee House, the Bull's Head and the Angel, in order 'to Consider w[ha]t was best to be done'.[14] It was acknowledged during the meeting with the Justices, that 'whatever they forced the Constables to do we must be obliged to observe . . . we strictly perform'd and by force obeyed'.[15]

By 27 November such was the mass movement of people out of Manchester that Beppy could recount, 'To-night there's not above four women hardly left in the Square.'[16] This depletion of the Whig or pro-Hanoverian opposition would inevitably increase – in relative terms – the proportion of Jacobite sympathisers. This, in turn, would distort the positive impression given to the Jacobite army by the remaining people of Manchester and Salford. Beppy also reports that the local militia was a disappointing defender of the town: 'Yesterday the militia was all discharged and sent home, but just in time before the Highlanders come, – well contrived.'[17] This corresponds with Lord Elcho's derisive assessment that it 'must be observed that the English militia is the most cowardly body of troops in the world. Forty or fifty Cavaliers of the Prince's army would suffice to make 1,000 of them afraid. Nowhere did they stand firm.'[18] News of the prince's entry into Preston arrived in Manchester the same day. Beppy wrote in her journal, 'the postmaster is gone to London to-day, we suppose to secure the money from falling into the hands of the rebels; we expect a party of them to-morrow. The P[rince] lay at Lawyer Starkey's at Preston last night; he has marched from Carlisle on foot at the head of his army.' Beppy then continues, 'he was dressed in a Scotch plaid, a blue silk waist-coat with silver lace, and a Scotch bonnet with J.R. on it'.[19]

Finally, after days, if not weeks, of anxious anticipation, the first sign of the imminent arrival of the Jacobite army in Manchester occurred on the afternoon of Thursday, 28 November. Not, however, the usual vanguard, nor even the outriders and quartermasters searching for suitable billets. To the palpable astonishment of everyone present, including Beppy Byrom,

> about three o'clock to-day came into town two men in Highland dress, and a woman behind one of them with a drum on her knee, and for all the loyal work that our Presbyterians have made, they took possession of the town as one may say, for immediately after they were 'light they beat up for volunteers for P[rince].C[harles].: 'All gentlemen that have a mind to serve HRH P C with a willing mind, &c., five guineas advance,' and nobody offered to meddle with them.[20]

Beppy's father, John Byrom, whose Jacobitism – unlike his daughter's – appeared to be somewhat tepid, later described the scene with significantly less enthusiasm and triumphalism. As it turned out, John recalls, false intelligence had arrived that the Jacobite army had gone to Liverpool, for that same day 'I beheld this extraordinary event of two men and a half taking the famous town of Manchester without any resistance or opposition, which I suppose the apprehension of the rest being at their heels might inspire us, however courageous, with the prudence not to make.'[21]

This eyewitness account of the taking of Manchester is challenged by Captain Johnstone whose sergeant, Dickson, was the hero of the drama. Johnstone states that 'having marched all night he arrived next morning at Manchester . . . and immediately began to beat up for recruits for "the yellow haired laddie"'. No one responded at first, but, realising the remainder of the army was not immediately behind, some locals surrounded Dickson 'in a tumultuous manner, with the intention of taking him prisoner, alive or dead'. Dickson in response 'presented his blunderbuss, which was charged with slugs, threatening to blow out the brains of those who first dared to lay hands on himself or the two who accompanied him', and, 'by turning round continually, facing in all directions, and behaving like a lion, he soon enlarged the circle, which a crowd of people had formed round them'. Dickson was then rescued 'from the fury of the mob' by several hundred local Stuart sympathisers, who 'dispersed the crowd in a very short tim[e]'. Finally, 'Dickson now triumphed in his turn; and putting himself at the head of his followers, he proudly paraded undisturbed the whole day, with his drummer, enlisting for my company all who offered themselves.'[22] Captain Johnstone was not actually present at the time, unlike John Byrom and his daughter, and only had the word of Dickson, the drummer and their female companion to count on. Certainly their bravery in arriving in the town alone was lessened by the passive response of the people who crowded the streets to witness this surprising turn of events. To the gathered Mancunians, it must have seemed as if some mock-heroic throwback from a distant, darker age had suddenly thrust itself into this gently urban and essentially 'modern' mercantile town.

In Johnstone's retelling, Dickson's adventures made Manchester a laughing stock and, further, the 'circumstance may serve to show the enthusiastic courage of our army, and the alarm and terror with which the English were seized'.[23] His account of Dickson's courageous stand against a crowd gripped with terror, as his comment reveals, conveniently and disdainfully sets up a contrast between Johnstone's undaunted countrymen and the timid locals. In unison, Lord Elcho stated that many of the townspeople displayed enthusiasm for the new arrivals out of fear.[24] Some clearly did fear the arrival of the Jacobite army but, in the main, the reaction appears to range from enthusiasm to mild interest to apathy. As both Beppy and John Byrom's calm reporting suggests, many of the fearful had already left town.

The intelligence dated 28 November which was sent to the Duke of Cumberland appears to corroborate the Byroms' version of events: 'These two men and the Woman without any others came into the Town amidst thousands of spectators.'[25] The author's choice of wording is interesting. It is as if the people who remained within the town had come out to play the intrigued audience to a piece of absurd theatre. But this was no travelling troop of players and far from an amusing entertainment. James Ray, as expected, offers a different, partisan spin on the event as well as some further details. The three 'rode up to the *Bulls-Head* on Horses with Hempen Halters on (a just Emblem of what they deserved [i.e. hanging]) where they din'd after Dinner, they beat up for Recruits, and in less than a Hour, listed about thirty'.[26] The recruits were handed a white cockade.[27] And among them were young men known to Beppy and named by her in the journal, including the barbers James Bradshaw and Thomas 'Tom' Syddall. The latter's father had been executed after the '15. Despite having a wife and children and, as Tom later recalled, 'far from being over confident of Success', he none the less resolved 'to contribute what Assistance lay in my Power' and thus 'freely abandon'd a good Shop and full Business, to follow the Fortune of a [Prince] for whose Interest I also joyfully hazarded my Life'.[28] Other recruits included Thomas Theodore Deacon and his brothers, Robert and Charles, who were the sons of Dr Thomas Deacon the nonjuring Bishop of Manchester. Finally, Beppy lists George Fletcher, a linen draper, and Tom Chaddock or Chadwick, a chandler's son from Staffordshire. Curiously, Beppy fails to mention at any point her kinsmen who also enlisted, John Beswicke or Berwicke, a linen-draper, and James Dawson. James, the son of an apothecary, a student of St Cyprian's of Salford Grammar School and later St John's College, Cambridge, was expelled from university and subsequently thrown out by his father. He came from a family that 'professed [Glorious] Revolution Principles' but having clearly fallen on hard times and with the encouragement of one Peter Moss, he joined the prince.[29]

According to Beppy eighty men had enlisted by eight o'clock that evening, at which time Pitsligo's Horse arrived, numbering over one hundred men. She and her father went to the market cross to see them, on what was 'a very fine moonlight night'. Beppy goes on to observe, 'the streets are exceeding quiet, there is not one person to be seen nor heard'.[30] Apparently stimulated by Lord Pitsligo's arrival, John Byrom and his brother consulted 'with Mr. Croxton, Mr. Feilden and others how to keep themselves out of any scrape, and yet to behave civilly'.[31] So here, in the case of John Byrom, is at least one sympathetic resident who, when push came to shove, was determined to sit on the fence. His Jacobitism was of the sentimental variety. Indeed, for the man who coined the phrase 'tweedle-dum and tweedle-dee', there were arguments for and against both sides, and he speaks for all ambivalent Britons with his ironic epigram 'Intended to allay the Violence of PARTY-SPIRIT':

> GOD bless the King, I mean the Faith's Defender;
> God bless – no harm in blessing – the Pretender;
> But who Pretender is, or who is King,
> God bless us all – that's quite another Thing.[32]

The two constables, who had been left to deal with the new arrivals attempted to lie low in the hope that their identity would not be revealed. Constable Fowden resisted an initial order to come before Lord Pitsligo at his headquarters, the Bull's Head tavern, but eventually he was discovered and escorted there by an armed guard.[33] On arrival, Fowden, in a display of bravery or foolhardiness, 'demanded by what authority he was sent for', to which, in response, Pitsligo 'drew his sword and sayd, "Damn you – by this"'.[34] Fowden was informed that he was required to obey all orders given by Prince Charles on pain of military execution.

The following day, Friday, 29 November, Beppy writes, 'they are beating up for the P[rince]; eleven o'clock we went up to the Cross to see the rest come in; there came small parties of them till about three o'clock, when the P[rince] and the main body of them came, I cannot guess how many'.[35] There had been little success in recruitment since Preston. Lord Elcho recalled that the road between Preston and Wigan en route to Manchester was crowded with people watching the army go by 'and they generaly all that days march profes'd to wish the Princes army Success'. Yet, if any were offered arms and encouraged to join the prince, 'they all declined, and Said they did not Understand fighting'.[36] As Charles had ridden through Salford he met the Revd John Clayton of Salford Grammar School accompanied by his students. Clayton reportedly dropped to his knees, to which the prince responded by doffing his bonnet. According to another eyewitness, Clayton then cried out, 'God bless your Royal Highness Prince Charles.'[37]

Intelligence sent to the Duke of Cumberland (dated 29 November) recorded, 'They do not appear to be such terrible fellows as has been represented. Many of the foot are diminutive creatures, but many clever men among them. The guards and officers are all in a Highland dress, a long sword, and stuck with pistols; their horses all sizes and colours.'[38] John Byrom later described Charles' entry into Manchester: 'The Prince (for so he has been called in all places when present, or near it, but, at a proper distance, Pretender) came in about noon, walking in a Highland habit, in the middle of a large party, and went to Mr. Dickenson's house, which his [men] had that morning ordered for his lodging after viewing some others, which, for some reason or other, they did not like so well.'[39] John Dickenson's house on Market Stead Lane (which lay to the south-east corner of Market Place) was a fine, freestanding town house of stone, set back from the street and surrounded by formal gardens. It would now be known as 'the Palace'.[40]

At the same time, another observer, sent to gain intelligence for the British army, was watching the prince and his entourage process through Manchester, while attempting to calculate the full strength of the Jacobite army. But 'what number in a regim[en]t I cannot learn, for they don't come in together, besides there are such crowds of people there is no counting them – they give out they are 10000 fighting men, and about 5000 more

that are not so well disciplined, and which they say they don't trust . . .
they are going directly to London as they say'.[41] As this comment suggests, a marching army was also a magnet for beggars, thieves and desperadoes. Meanwhile both constables had refused to assist in the billeting of
the army. Constable Walley had been ordered to meet Colonel O'Sullivan
at the Saracen's Head for that purpose, but had contrived to 'mistake' the
order, much to the colonel's fury. However, John Marchant in his *History of
the Present Rebellion* states: 'Most Persons entertain'd the Rebels, especially
those who call'd themselves Officers, of which there were great Numbers, in
a very handsome Manner, and few private Houses took any Payment.'[42]

While standing at the market cross, Beppy and her family were handed
copies of the manifesto and other declarations by an officer. This being late
November, the light would have started to dwindle by mid-afternoon, during which Beppy recalls, 'the bells they rung, and P. Cotterel made a bon-
fire, and all the town was illuminated, every house except Mr. Dickenson's
[the prince's], my papa, mamma and sister, and my uncle and I walked
up and down to see it'.[43] The likely reaction from every member of the
Jacobite army after the disappointing recruitment in Lancashire so far was
surely elation mixed with relief. As John Daniel, now a captain in the
Duke of Perth's regiment, recalled, 'The ringing of the Bells, and the great
rejoicings and salutations with which we were welcomed, gave us mighty
expectations.'[44] Of his entry into Manchester, James Maxwell wrote enthusiastically, 'The Prince had met nothing like this since his reception at
Edinburgh'[45] but then, given the muted response in England so far, that
was relative. Marchant, like Lord Elcho, believed this was a forced display,
for the 'Bellman went round the Town again, to order the Houses to be
illuminated which was done, and Bonfires made. The Bells also were rung.
No doubt many of the ignorant Scots swallow'd this forc'd Meat for a Dish
of Loyalty.'[46] The Irishman Sir John Macdonald certainly did, recalling,
'We found many adherents at Manchester'.[47]

At the same time as the Byrom family were witnessing the arrival of
the main army at the Old Cross, the hapless Constable Fowden was being
escorted to the Saracen's Head 'where was six or eight rebel officers with
their pistols and swords drawn', and the commanding officer repeated the
threat of military execution should the constable refuse to obey the orders
of Prince Charles: as Fowden himself recounted, 'if you refuse any of them
you are a dead man, and we'll lay your house in ashes and take your family prisoners. The first is, you are to read up Prince Charles's proclamation
at the market cross, and to search for arms, and swear the inhabitants

wherever you go.'[48] To which Fowden, apparently, responded, 'I have taken the oaths to King George and cannot do it.' The officer replied, 'If you mention George of Hanover in my presence, I'll stab you dead.'[49]

However, the constables' greatest show of resistance occurred in public during the proclamation of 'King James' later that same day, an event that had, according to Fowden's description, little of the pomp or gravitas the Jacobite officer in charge might have hoped for. In fact, as each constable in turn made an excuse for being unable to read out the proclamation, any hint of solemnity swiftly descended into farce. The constables were marched under guard to 'the Palace', and then at three o'clock, marched on to the market cross, 'where a rebel officer tendered the proclamation unto Mr. Whalley, who absolutely refused to read it'. The proclamation was then offered to Fowden, 'who gave a like refusal, but, upon being pressed he told them he could not see without his spectacles'. Then Whalley, 'being demanded to repeat the proclamation after one of the rebel officers, said he had a hesitation in his speech and could not, upon which they obliged Mr. Fowden to repeat after them, which he did very unwillingly and in great fear'.[50] John Byrom also witnessed the proclamation, saying, 'the two constables were forced to be there, and one of them to repeat the words. I came by as they were at it but, there was no great crowd or hurry about it nor any soldiers, only an officer or two, who I suppose performed this ceremony wherever they came.'[51] In fact, from John Byrom's description we can surmise that the proclamation had become less outwardly ceremonial – as seen at Edinburgh – and was simply required to be read out by a constable. If under duress, there was the bonus that it was a means of humiliating the civic representatives of the enemy.

After watching the proclamation, Beppy visited her aunt where she made 'St. Andrew's crosses' for the Jacobite army until two in the morning.[52] That evening the landlord of the Spread Eagle gave a dinner for the Jacobite officers and Charles held the first of two evening receptions at 'the Palace'. As an indication of the prince's high spirits, Lord Elcho recalled Charles was so taken by the welcome he had received in Manchester 'that he thought himself sure of Success, and his Conversation that night at Table was, in what manner he should enter London, on horse-back or a foot, and in what dress'.[53] The prince's household accounts for Manchester, meticulously recorded by James Gib, list the purchase of twenty-seven pounds of veal, two rabbits, two geese, 'a pigge and potted widcocks [woodcocks]', twenty chickens, six pounds of sausages, four pigeons, wild fowl, 'trips of bife', eggs, flour, apples, ten pounds of butter and eighteen pounds of candles.[54]

Some of this would be stocking up for the onward journey. But a prince would be expected to keep a princely table, even while in transit, so much of it would have been consumed by Charles, his large household, entourage and guests over the two days he spent in Manchester.

The following day was 30 November, the Scottish patron saint's day, for which Beppy and her companions had been so feverishly making 'crosses' until the early hours. Beppy noted 'more crosses making till twelve o'clock'.[55] While she was busy stitching at her aunt's house, her father was at home receiving a Highland visitor bearing a note from 'James D' of 'Morton Hall' dated 4 November 1745, which read: 'These do certify that the bearer, Alexander Macdonald, was a guard to my house at Morton Hall till this day, and is desirous to be directed forward to his country people wherever they are, because he cannot speak English.' John Byrom's memorandum continues that this 'note I copied from a paper which the little Highlander who came on Saturday morning to roast a piece of flesh by our fire had by him, he had three guineas quilted in the flap of his waistcoat, and one he showed me, asking if it was a good one as well as he could for he had but very few English words'. This young lad 'lay in the stable, behaved very quietly, so we let him stay, said he would call upon us at his return from London'.[56]

After completing her cross-making, Beppy continues, 'then I dressed me up in my white gown and went up to my aunt Brearcliffe's, and an officer called on us to go see the Prince, we went to Mr. Fletcher's and saw him get a-horseback, and a noble sight it is, I would not have missed it for a great deal of money'.[57] Beppy continues her description of the prince in a manner now all too familiar. Charles' horse 'had stood an hour in the court without stirring, and as soon as he gat on he began a-dancing and capering as if he was proud of the burden, and when he rid out of the court he was received with as much joy and shouting almost as if he had been king without any dispute, indeed I think scarce anybody that saw him would dispute it'.[58] Secretary Murray recalled on 30 November the cavalry, quartered at and around Stockport, patrolled the countryside to find out what preparations were being made against the Jacobite army to the south, while others were dispatched to gain news of Marshal Wade. An order from Charles was also issued stating that no soldier or officer under field officer, quartermaster or adjutant should ride, and, in an attempt to instil some discipline, that all officers were required 'to cause put away all the Disorderly Women', probably prostitutes, 'that follow the respective Battallions and that no women on any accoᵗ. whatsomever be allowd to follow the Army Excepting those who are married & who's husbands are alongst'.[59]

Meanwhile, in Manchester itself, as Secretary Murray recalled (echoing Beppy), 'The Chevalier got on horse back in the afternoon, and rode through the Town to view it by way of amusement, attended by the principle officers of his Army, when he was followed by vast Croweds of people with loud huzzas and all demonstrations possible of their zeal for his Success.'[60] John Byrom observed how easy it was for anyone 'friend or foe that was curious enough to see the Prince, to have an opportunity', and that 'whatever his pretensions may be, he makes a very graceful and amiable appearance; he is fair complexioned, well shaped, has a sensible and comely aspect'.[61] Thus publicly exposed, as seen elsewhere, it is perhaps surprising that no one attempted an assassination. But then again, the retribution would have been swift. Marchant offers a different perspective on this parade, stating that Charles 'had the Mortification to be convinced, that, in general, Manchester had been misrepresented', for the people of Manchester 'almost universally, shewed by their Countenances, (and the Pretender shew'd it by his that he read their Temper of Mind there) that they disaprov'd of and abhor'd him, and his barbarous, rapacious, slavish Crew'. Marchant goes on, 'Many of the Officers indeed declar'd, to Gentlemen where they were quarter'd, they [had] expected the whole Town would join them.'[62]

However, Beppy Byrom for one was having the time of her young life. On returning home after watching Charles parade through the town, where she 'eat a queen cake, and a glass of wine, for we gat no dinner', the attentive but unnamed Jacobite officer accompanied Beppy and her family to the army's encampment.[63] That evening Beppy, her father and his brother walked to Mr Fletcher's house. Here they remained, until the moment came for the highlight of the entire adventure. While the prince was at supper at Mr Dickenson's House,

> the officer introduced us into the room, stayd a while and then went into the great parlour where the officers were dining, sat by Mrs. Stark[ey]; they were exceeding civil and almost made us fuddled with drinking the P[rince's]. health, for we had had no dinner; we sat there till Secretary Murray came to let us know that the P. was at leisure and had done supper, so we were all introduced and had the honour to kiss his hand; my papa was fetched prisoner to do the same, as was Dr. Deacon; Mr. Cattell and Mr. Clayton did it without; the latter said grace for him; then we went out and drank his health in the other room, and so to Mr. Fletcher's, where my mama waited for us (my uncle was gone to pay his land-tax), and then went home.[64]

Beppy gives the impression that this was all harmless fun, but her father – who was 'fetched prisoner' into the prince's presence – understood what risks he and his family were taking. While the Byrom family were enjoying their royal introduction, Alexander Blair of the Life Guards was supping with the whole regiment at the invitation of Lord Elcho and 'being St.e Andrews day, when we drank a Health to all our Friends in Scotland'.[65]

Despite the support shown to the Jacobite army during their time in Manchester, the fact still remained that as preparations were made for their imminent departure, no more than two, perhaps three hundred men had volunteered in Lancashire. As Captain Daniel wrote in his journal, 'too true is the saying: *Parturiunt Montes, nascetur ridiculus mus*'.[66] (Horace, *Ars Poetica*: 'The mountains will be in labour, and a ridiculous mouse will be brought forth.') In addition to Francis Towneley and the more affluent shopowners, businessmen and former university students, the recruits were tailors, shoemakers, weavers, carpenters, joiners and labourers.[67] James Ray, unlikely to be sympathetic, described them as 'of desperate Fortunes . . . mostly People of the lowest Rank, and vilest Principles' which, according to Ray, 'occasioned him who called himself the Duke of *Perth* to say, "That if the Devil had come a recruiting, and profer'd a Shilling more than his Prince, they would have preferr'd the former"'.[68] Lord Elcho goes further, considering the prince had been duped by the English Jacobites, and 'relying on assurances that all his English supporters would join him in the county of Lancashire, he persuaded the army to advance' all the way from Penrith to Manchester, but in 'all these towns the people did not appear to be much interested in the Prince's Cause, indeed quite the contrary'.[69] Colonel O'Sullivan offered a more likely explanation as to why the majority, which included loyal supporters, chose not to enlist: 'We expected [that] at least 1500 men wou'd have joyned us here, for the whole Contry is well inclined, but very few joyned, the raisons [that] peoples [that] cou'd be of service did not joyn, was [that] wch hindred others, [that] there were no foreign forses.'[70]

The lack of any sign of the French invasion was compounded by the presence of the two armies, one led by Marshal Wade to the north, the second now led by the Duke of Cumberland to the south, between which the north-west of England could become effectively sandwiched. In such circumstances, the Jacobites of Lancashire and Wales were even less likely to come out in public support.[71] In many ways, such inactivity among English and Welsh Jacobites, so far, makes the volunteers that chose to enlist even more extraordinary. There has been a tendency to measure the importance of the English volunteers by their numbers. But at Prestonpans, Keppoch's regiment was of a similar size (about 250 men). Some, it is clear, needed paid employment and enlisted out of desperation, considering their lives a fair risk. Others, like the Deacon brothers, Tom Syddall and Francis Towneley, were risking everything for their principles. And for such volunteers, like their Scottish comrades who did not hold French commissions and therefore would not be considered foreign troops and prisoners of war, should the rebellion fail, these men would be treated as British rebels with a rebel's dismal fate – something Tom Syddall knew from personal experience.

A council meeting had been held on the Saturday afternoon, where it was decided that the recruits raised during the march through Lancashire would be called the Manchester Regiment. After some discussion, it was the Frenchman, the marquis d'Eguilles, who suggested Francis Towneley as colonel. D'Eguilles reported back to the French Court that 'of all the men who surround the Prince he has the greatest intelligence and prudence',[72] a sentiment shared by Sir John Macdonald but not, according to Macdonald, by Lord Elcho and his fellow Scots. Following the appointment of Colonel Towneley, Tom Syddall was named as adjutant, Peter Moss, James Dawson and George Fletcher as captains, Thomas and Robert Deacon, John Berwick and Thomas Chadwick as lieutenants, and the fifteen-year-old Charles Deacon as ensign (second lieutenant).[73] After this, the Manchester officers stayed a further day to raise more volunteers. As John Daniel wrote, 'I was as credulous as they.'[74]

James Maxwell considered 'the Prince's reception at Manchester and this new regiment gave great encouragement to the army in general'. Yet, as he continues, 'there were nevertheless a few who had still a very bad opinion of the affair'. Some of Charles' officers at Preston, as stated by Lord Elcho, had thought they had come far enough into England already. Maxwell recalled, 'I have been very well informed that a retreat was talked of at Manchester, and I believe Lord George Murray had it all along in his view, if there was no insurrection in England and no landing from France.' Indeed, 'One of his friends, that knew his mind', Lord Elcho perhaps, 'told Lord George Murray at Manchester, that he thought they had entered far enough, since neither of these had happened.' However, 'Lord George said they might make a farther trial, and go the length of Derby, and if there was not greater encouragement to go on, he would propose a retreat to the Prince.'[75] Whether Charles was aware of it or not, many of his officers already considered the small county town of Derby as the line in the sand between the onward march to London or retreat.

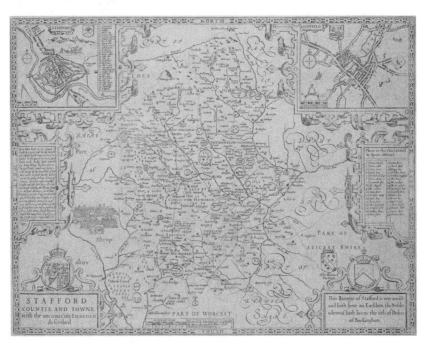

J. Speed, *A Map of The County of Staffordshire*, 1714.

Lichfield

'none of us know what rest is'

O n 23 November from Lichfield, lying to the south-west of Derby, the Duke of Richmond, now a lieutenant general and cavalry commander, wrote to Sir Everard Fawkener: 'Wee are all overjoy'd at the thoughts of his Royall Highness The Duke's commanding us in person, & are very impatient for his arrival.'[1] The same day Richmond also sent an express to the Duke of Newcastle, containing a less than enthusiastic assessment of the current command at Lichfield and the British army troops in the vicinity. Lieutenant General Hawley (who had returned from Flanders) 'is equall to any body, & will speake his mind', while 'Leg [Ligonier] is a good man butt in my poor opinion too complaisant, besides that, one of his legs was numb'd the other day, & I dont thinke his life to be depended on'. He cautions that 'this is only between you & I, butt pray make good use of my hint. I am sorry to say wee are in a strange irregular way.' Richmond then concludes, hinting at the exhausting pace being set by the Jacobite army, 'It is necessary to hurry on our troops else they'l be in London before us, & yett there dreadful fattiguing marches, will make them incapable of fighting. wee none of us know what rest is.'[2] Certainly, the British army was engaged in a race where the Jacobite army's ultimate destination seemed clear enough, but the route to it less so.

The following day, as the Jacobite army arrived in Lancaster, the Earl of Derby (Lord Lieutenant of Lancashire) wrote to the Duke of Richmond from his Knowsley estate (near Liverpool) with more depressing news.[3] If the British army had arrived in Lancashire in advance of the Jacobite army, writes the earl, the local militia might have assisted 'towards preserving of this county from the Ravages, & Desolation to which it will now be exposed'. But alone, 'it can scarce be expected by anybody that a raw undisciplined Militia consisting of Foot, without any one that knows how to command, shou'd be able to prevent the advance of an army seven or eight times their number'. This, rather than cowardice, was the reason the local militia did not make a stand against the Jacobite army. And apparently it was the opinion of several deputy lieutenants and officers 'who happen to be now with me'. The port of Liverpool 'is certainly not tenable', nor was there a stronghold for them to retire to. The situation at Carlisle and Chester was far from unusual. Colonel Graham had been ordered to pull down Warrington Bridge on the orders of Lord Cholmondeley, which, while impeding the Jacobite advance or retreat, also happened to be 'the pass for us from these parts towards Stone & Litchfield as well as Chester'. However, after this Colonel Graham 'will retire to reinforce the Garrison at Chester'. As Lancashire was effectively lost to the Jacobites, the earl intended to go to Manchester (as later recorded by Beppy Byrom) en route to London 'not seeing how it is any way in my power or of any of the Friends of the Government to be longer serviceable to the Country, in which my fortune lies or the nation in general'. Therefore he considers he is 'at liberty to save myself from the hands of those whose Religion of course make them enemies to the constitution under which they live [by which he means Catholics and nonjurors], with which sort of persons this County does but too much abound'.[4]

On 25 November the Duke of Cumberland received his instructions from his father King George: 'you are immediately to take upon you the Command of Our said Troops, and to march with them'; 'You are to be very attentive and vigilant, with regard to any Tumults, or Insurrections in any Parts within reach of Our Army under your Command'; you will 'gain information of suspected persons and seize and secure them if cause found'; to provide intelligence and information and be in constant contact with the principal Secretary of State; to be in constant correspondence with Marshal Wade at Newcastle upon Tyne, concert together as necessary, 'whether, when and where It may be advisable for the two Armies to join'; when united, the duke would have overall command; 'you shall have a view to the Cutting off the Retreat of the Rebels'; 'You may, as you shall find fitting occasions, give assistance to the proper Officers for the Disarming Papists, Non-Jurors, and other Persons dangerous to Our Government'; and, in the King's name, promise rewards to 'good subjects' performing 'signal service to us, and Our Government. And we do hereby empower you to promise Our Pardon to such Deserters from the Rebels, as may surrender Themselves to Our Forces under your Command.'[5]

When the official handover of command from Sir John Ligonier to the Duke of Cumberland occurred at Lichfield on 27 November, the British army troops in this West Midlands area of England were cantoned, housed rather than encamped, from Tamworth lying to the south-east of Lichfield to Stafford to the north-west, with the cavalry stationed at Newcastle-under-Lyme (to the north of Stafford), a total distance as the crow flies of thirty-four miles. Yet, on the day of the handover, it is clear from a letter written by Major General Humphrey Bland at Newcastle-under-Lyme to the Duke of Richmond, that some British army officers believed that the Jacobite advance might soon run out of energy. 'By the slowness of the march of the Rebels,' states Bland, 'I am still of the opinion they wont venture to pass the Mersey, as I should imagine they must be inform'd of the number and march of our troops and H.R.H. at our Head.' However, he continues, 'as their whole proceedings appear the Effect of Madness, rather than Reason, they may possibly be actuated by the same Phrenzy and push forward to their total destruction, which can't fail of happening soon after the junction of our forces.'[6]

The Duke of Cumberland arrived at Lichfield late on the 27th, writing the following morning to the Duke of Newcastle: 'The Journey hither was a little fatiguing & tho I stop'd no where from my first setting out, I was one & thirty hours coming hither', a straight distance of 104 miles. By the current cantoning arrangements, he continues, 'We endeavour to be equally at hand for the preservation of Darby or Chester.' The duke confirms that he had already written to Lord Cholmondeley asking him, despite the obvious difficulties, to hold the town and castle of Chester. The duke then summarises the current position: 'by our latest advices the Rebels who were already advanced as yesterday to Preston, & who seem to have a mind to remain there, may give us time to collect our whole body together, & then to advance directly up to them.' If this happens, 'I flatter my self the affair would be certain in our favour'. However, 'should they be mad enough to March forward to Manchester & Stockport, then it will be impossible to say how soon there may be an affair [battle] as I must move forward to hinder them slipping by me either way.'[7] Regarding Marshal Wade, 'I hear he is advanced no further than Persbridge today', Piercebridge being a village about thirty-three miles south of Newcastle upon Tyne. As a result 'it is probable this affair may be decided before his Corps can come up'.[8] The same day the duke wrote to Marshal Wade himself, saying 'the Kings intentions are that the Rebels should not return home, but I am in the greatest uncertainty here, as I have no news from you'.[9] Two days later Wade replied from Ripon in North Yorkshire: 'I perfectly agree with Your Royal Highness in Your sentiments of avoiding [a] decisive blow 'till you are joined by all Your force, considering the great consequence of an unsuccessful action.' Something Sir John Cope would have some sympathy with. Wade observes from recent intelligence, that the Jacobite army appears to be aiming for Derbyshire, in which case the marshal would have to move towards Doncaster as the only route where he could follow them with artillery. But the marshal could only confirm that once more certain information arrived concerning the 'enemy's' movements. Wade concludes, 'I can only assure your Royal Highness, that I will lose no time in advancing as fast as this severe season of the Year, and the excessive bad roads will permit.' He aimed to be at Wetherby on Tuesday to receive a delivery of bread at Borough bridge, as well as the distribution of 3,000 pairs of shoes and stockings 'of which we stand in great want'. But, in regard to a speedy advance, 'I am not sure if we shall not be obliged to halt there one day, on that account.'[10]

The Duke of Richmond, who was still at Lichfield but soon to move with the cavalry to Newcastle-under-Lyme, wrote to the Duke of Newcastle on Saturday, 30 November, St Andrew's Day, admitting, 'Now as to our scituation here at present between you & I, I don't much like it.' He goes on, 'nor shant be quite easy 'till munday is over, for the whole Rebel army is by our intelligence now at Manchester, & wee are not all yett so cleverly together as I could wish', although he also confirms the happy arrival that day of the first battalion of Foot Guards. The reference to the following Monday reflects the general expectation among the British army command of a battle with the Jacobite army on that day.

At this point in time, Richmond considers the Jacobite army have five options. The first, to attack '& if wee are together I wish they would, for then I am sure wee may do what wee please with them'. The second, to march into Derbyshire, which 'would be the next thing I could wish'. The third, to march to Chester and besiege it. The fourth, to push for North Wales without attacking Chester at all, and the fifth '& last thing which would be the worst of all, would be their going quite back again to the Highlands'.[11] By returning, the Jacobite army could sit out the winter in the mountains, where the British army, for obvious reasons, would be reluctant to follow, while awaiting the French invasion in Scotland or the south-east of England. If this happened, at best the rebellion would drag on for months.

Richard Rider, a Justice of the Peace for Staffordshire, wrote from Congleton to the Duke of Cumberland (letter dated 1 December) regarding the behaviour of the Jacobite army in Manchester: 'They behave hitherto ('tis said) civilly & have all along since they came from Carlisle paid their Quarters. I hear of no Complaints of misbehaviour where they are; on the contrary the people (the mob I mean mostly) are so fond to see 'em.' Concerning numbers, 'they give out, that 5000 are in the western skirts of Yorkshire, collecting the King's Revenue of Land tax, window money & excise for the last half year, which 'tis said, they do, wherever they can find it, but they don't plunder', although 'some of the Rabble that follows them are not over nice, where they meet with any thing they like in their way'. But he believed that the Jacobite commanders had dealt with such people 'since they came into England by firing at 'em to disperse 'em'.[12] In addition to prostitutes, the Jacobite army was still having problems with undesirables accompanying them on their march. Such people used the universal fear of the Highlanders among the unprotected local people, some of it justified, to attack, rob and pilfer them in turn. Such behaviour was certainly not encouraged by Charles and his officers, whether by hangers-on or the rank and file, as they were extremely keen to give a good impression for the sake of the Stuart cause.

Returning to Manchester, Richard Rider recounts, 'The people that have been to see 'em at Manchester tell me, they are a mixed medley, some very young, some very old. But others are lusty souldier like men. They seem to be in good spirits, and talk as if they disregarded Gen[eral] Ligonier and his Forces, or Marshall Wade.'[13] Meanwhile, Lord Chancellor Hardwicke, having read the Duke of Cumberland's updates from Lichfield, observed to the Duke of Newcastle that His Royal Highness was obviously in some doubt as to which way the Jacobite army was now moving (having turned off from Warrington to Manchester), for from here they could continue towards Chester or march to Buxton '& so to Derby, & avoid both the Duke's & Marshal Wade's Armies, & push directly for London'. 'If,' he continues, 'this last is their Scheme, & they are really no stronger than we have been inform'd, it is certainly a very extravagant & desperate one.'[14]

As Hardwicke's letter makes clear, no one could quite allow themselves to believe that this small army was going to risk everything and make a dash for Derby and then London. But, then, they clearly had no idea what the intentions of Charles and his men were anyway. All the while the government was keeping a nervous, watchful eye on the north-west coast of France, and Dunkirk in particular.

John Slezer, *The Prospect of the town of Montrose from 'Theatrum Scotiae'*, published 1693.

Montrose

'so Just and indisputable a Title'

On 14 November six French transport ships, accompanied by two frigates, had sailed quietly out of Dunkirk, heading across the German Ocean (or North Sea) towards the north-east coast of Britain. Their orders were to arrive somewhere between Berwick and the small harbour of Montrose. Aboard one frigate, *La Fine*, was Lord John Drummond with 300 men from his regiment, the Royal Ecossais. The remainder of the regiment was aboard the second frigate, *La Renommeé*. The convoy also carried detachments from Irish regiments in the service of France. In addition to men and a large quantity of ammunition and arms, the French ships were transporting heavy guns, two eighteen-pounders, two twelve-pounders and two nine-pounders, the type of cannon that would be useful in the event of a siege as well as a battle. However, such guns were difficult to move any distance over land, and inevitably slowed down an army on the march.

With Admiral John Byng and the Royal Navy on patrol nearby, this expedition (in advance of the main invasion planned for mid-December) was, as ever, a risk. However, a timely storm dispersed Admiral Byng's squadron. The main casualty was HMS *Fox*, which ran aground at Dunbar with the loss of all hands. Meanwhile, HMS *Hazard*, commanded by Captain Thomas Hill, had anchored for safety within the channel leading to Montrose's harbour basin.[1] This channel was notoriously difficult to navigate. Further, while HMS *Hazard* lay nearby, the town of Montrose was overrun by Jacobite troops.

Although the storm had luckily removed the immediate threat of encountering the Royal Navy in open sea, the *Hazard*'s location was at this time unknown, and the French convoy had also been dispersed. However, on 24 November the first French ship, *La Renommeé*, sailed past the *Hazard* and into Montrose harbour. The men and cannon were landed and then batteries were formed around the channel, with the guns directed towards the Royal Navy ship. The *Hazard* surrendered and was provocatively renamed *Le Prince Charles*.

Another of the French transport ships, *L'Esperance*, was taken by HMS *Sheerness* on 25 November, but the following day Lord John Drummond and his men on board *La Fine* were safely landed on a beach near Montrose. *La Fine's* captain then anchored his ship just outside the channel to Montrose harbour.

But the French ships were still in danger. On the 27th, HMS *Milford* came into view, having had word of Captain Hill's predicament, and sailed straight towards *La Fine*. The latter's captain decided to risk it and make for the harbour, but having entered the channel she ran on to a gravel bank. In pursuit, HMS *Milford* too ran aground – demonstrating the vital importance of local pilots – but was hauled off while the tide was still high enough. As Captain Thomas Hanway watched from the deck, the back of the stranded *La Fine* dramatically broke, in marine terms 'hogged'. As he sailed out again into open sea, it may now have dawned on the Royal Navy captain that more French ships were likely to follow. And so it was. On the 28th Captain Hanway captured another of the transport ships, the *Louis XV*, with about 180 officers, non-commissioned officers and men from various French-Irish regiments, and, with his prize, set sail for Leith. As HMS *Milford* disappeared from sight, the crew of the wrecked frigate *La Fine* boarded the newly christened *Le Prince Charles* and in turn made for open sea. The loss of a Royal Navy ship was embarrassing enough – its new name added salt to the wound.

By this sequence of events, Lord John Drummond's force was now reduced to about 800 men. But a majority of them had landed safely and the cannon, arms and ammunition would be very welcome to the gathering second Jacobite army in Scotland, under the current command of Lord Strathallan. The occupation of Montrose was a significant fillip to the Jacobites as it was one of the few harbours on this stretch of the east coast that offered protection from Royal Navy patrols. It now became the prime destination for any French ships transporting men and arms to Scotland. Lord John Drummond immediately printed and distributed a declaration dated Montrose, 2 December, which confirmed, as 'Commander in Chief of his most Christian Majesty's Forces in SCOTLAND', that Lord John and his men 'are come to this Kingdom, with Written Orders to make War against the King of ENGLAND, Elector of HANOVER and all his Adherents'. In addition, anyone who did not join in assisting Charles, the

Prince of Wales and Regent of Scotland, England etc., would be considered an enemy and dealt with accordingly. France, with the agreement of Spain, aimed 'to Support in the taking Possession of SCOTLAND, ENGLAND, and IRELAND . . . to which three Kingdoms, the Family of STEWART, have so Just and indisputable a Title'.[2]

As this declaration makes plain, French troops were now in Britain as a support to the Stuart prince's cause and at the behest of the French king; whether Louis, at this moment, wanted to openly admit this was another matter entirely. On the face of it, by the terms of the treaty at the surrender of Tournai, the Dutch troops under Marshal Wade could no longer equivocate and must withdraw immediately from supporting King George – Charles' and therefore France's declared enemy. Lord John's arrival with French troops, money and arms also clarified beyond any doubt the purpose of French naval activity along the north-west coast of France. A full invasion attempt was now expected, sooner not later.

Antoine Benoist after Thomas Smith of Derby, *A Prospect in
Dove-Dale 3 Miles North of Ashbourne*, 1743.

Derbyshire

'our Frights and Fears'

In late September William Cavendish, 3rd Duke of Devonshire and Lord Lieutenant of Derbyshire, had called two meetings to prepare for the defence of the county should the advancing Jacobite army venture that way. The *Derby Mercury* reported that the duke and his eldest son William, Marquess of Hartington, 'came to the George Inn in this Town, to meet the Gentlemen of this County', where 'there was the greatest Appearance of Gentlemen ever seen here, who having enter'd into an Association, cheerfully sign'd the same'. A grand entertainment was given for them at the George Inn, 'the Expence of which was generously defray'd by His Grace'. After the dinner, 'a Subscription was begun, and sign'd by the Gentlemen present, which amounted to a considerable Sum; and many more have since subscrib'd'.[1] A similar event was held at the King's Head with equal success, whereby 'it was agreed to raise immediately 600 Men, form'd into two Regiments; of which the Marquiss of Hartington, and Sir Nathaniel Curzon, Bart. [of Kedleston Hall] the two Knights of the Shire in Parliament, were appointed Colonels'.[2] Nathaniel Curzon was one of the Tory gentlemen considered in 1743 a 'Jacobite', according to James Butler's list.

Over the subsequent weeks, terms and conditions were agreed for the newly formed militia – called 'The Derbyshire Blues' – including the pay for each rank, while officer commissions were sent out and arms ordered. Some commissions were refused. Meanwhile, the Duke of Devonshire was kept abreast of events to the north by Lord Lonsdale, who forwarded several expresses from various contacts in the towns lying in the Jacobite army's path. One, dated 17 November, summarised the state of play at Newcastle upon Tyne and Carlisle, including Marshal Wade's march towards Carlisle and the subsequent surrendering of the town and castle. The next, from Samuel Lowthion at Penrith dated 18 November, stated,

'None of the rebels have yet advanced thus far' and that 'we now begin to pluck up our Spirits, hoping we shall be happily delivered from a visit, By the near approach of M. Wade's army'.³ Another from Lancaster, dated 19 November, put paid to the optimism of the previous note, by stating that 'Jon[atha]n Holland is just come hither, he left Penrith ab't 6 yesterday Evening and cam 5 miles on foot, he said he saw L'd Elcho march into Penrith with ab't 200 Horse'. Accompanying this note was yet another copy of Mr Cowper's letter to the Post Master of Brough describing the Jacobite army at Penrith as 'swarming in here all this day like Bees'.⁴ A clergyman from near Derby wrote to his brother in London, recounting 'the Hurry, Confusion, and Frights we have been in in these Parts'⁵ as such reports of the swift approach of Prince Charles and his army began to circulate. Local fears, as seen in Carlisle, seemed to have been exacerbated by reporting in the London newspapers of 'such dismal Accounts of their Plundering, Pillaging, and barbarous Practices wherever they came'.⁶

The Jacobite army left Manchester on Sunday, 1 December and, contrary to Major General Bland's prediction, forded the Mersey near Stockport, with the artillery and baggage crossing further up river on a makeshift wooden bridge near the village of Cheadle. They were now moving through the county of Cheshire. Here Philip Stanhope, Viscount Mahon, recalls an anecdote told to him by Lord Keith. Having crossed the Mersey, Charles encountered a welcome party of local gentry, including Mrs Skyring, 'a lady in extreme old age'. As an infant she had witnessed Charles II's landing at Dover in 1660, but her Royalist 'cavalier' family 'had afterwards to undergo, not merely neglect, but oppression, from that thankless monarch'. Yet, Mrs Skyring's parents remained deeply loyal to the Stuarts 'and their daughter grew up as devoted as they'. On James II's exile 'all her thoughts, her hopes, her prayers, were directed to another Restoration. Ever afterwards she had with rigid punctuality laid aside one half of her yearly income to remit for the exiled family abroad.' These donations to the Stuart court in France and then Rome were sent anonymously to save Stuart blushes at the treatment of her family. By early December 1745, Mrs Skyring had 'parted with her jewels, her plate, and every little article of value she possessed; the price of which, in a purse, she laid at the feet of Prince Charles', and 'while, straining her dim eyes to gaze on his features, and pressing his hand to her shriveled lips, she exclaimed with affectionate rapture, in the words of Simeon, "Lord! now lettest thou thy servant depart in peace!"'. Lord Mahon concludes, 'Such, even when misdirected in its object, or exaggerated in its force, was the old spirit of loyalty in England! Such were the characters which history is proud to record, and fiction loves to imitate.'[7]

The main army halted at the market town of Macclesfield, while Colonel Henry Ker (or Kerr) of Graden was sent towards Newcastle-under-Lyme (lying to the south-west of Macclesfield) to gain intelligence of the British army, thought to be in the vicinity. Here, Ker surprised a party of British army dragoons, and at the Red Lion at Talke (north of Newcastle-under-Lyme) he captured the government spy, Captain John Weir or Vere, who was recognised by some of the Jacobite army as having been in Flanders. According to James Maxwell it 'was proposed to hang him immediately in punishment of what he had done, and to prevent the mischief he might do in case the Prince did not succeed; but the Prince could not be brought to consent; he still insisted that Weir was not strictly speaking a spy, since he was not found in the army in disguise.' Maxwell concludes, 'it was his constant practice to spare his enemies when they were in his power'.[8] Weir was then tied to a horse's tail, and dragged along, barefoot, from town to town.

At this point Colonel Ker could also confirm that the British army command had now been transferred from Sir John Ligonier to the Duke of Cumberland, and that they were quartered at Lichfield, Coventry and Stafford, as well as Newcastle-under-Lyme. Battered and bruised, Captain Weir happily provided his captors with information, which in reality inflated the size of the duke's army. Lord George recalled that as a result of the combined intelligence received, they resolved to march for Derby, lying to the south-east of Macclesfield, 'and to cover our intentions, I offered to go with a column of the army to Congleton [to the south-west], which was the straight road to Litchfield'. By this feint it was hoped that the Duke of Cumberland, at Lichfield would believe that the Jacobite army was coming straight for him and would in turn, as a result, gather his army together and advance along the Lichfield–Congleton road to meet them. However, before this could happen, Lord George would switch direction 'so that we could get before them to Derby'.[9]

On Tuesday, 3 December the column that had duly advanced to the Cheshire town of Congleton switched direction and continued instead into Derbyshire, via Leek in Staffordshire, to Ashbourne, thirteen miles north-west of Derby, while Charles, with the remainder of the army, marched directly from Macclesfield to Leek. Here, due to the distance between the two columns, 'he thought his situation somewhat ticklish'. The prince therefore left Leek at midnight in order to bring the two columns together at Ashbourne for their onward march to Derby. Katharine Thomson, in her *Memoirs of the Jacobites of 1715 and 1745*, states, 'The inhabitants of the district retained some portion of their ancient loyalty to the Stuarts'[10] and according to James Maxwell, from 'Manchester to Derby the country seemed pretty well affected. As the army marched along, the roads, in many places, were lined with numbers of country people, who showed their loyalty by bonefires, acclamations, white cockades, and the like.' As a result, 'One would have thought that the Prince was now at the crisis of his adventure; that his fate, and the fate of the three kingdoms, must be decided in a few days.'[11] Certainly the proximity of the Duke of Cumberland's army strongly suggested that a battle was imminent. In contrast to James Maxwell, Lord Elcho recalled, 'All betwixt Maclesfield and Ashburn the people seemed much afraid of the Princes army, and the tops of the hills were crouded with men on horseback, who were often pursued but never came up with as they were well mounted.'[12] These observers were reporting back to the Duke of Cumberland the location, size and route of the Jacobite army.

Towards the end of November, as announced in the *Derby Mercury*, the Duke of Devonshire and his son left Chatsworth and arrived at the George Inn in Derby in order to coordinate the new militia companies in defence of the town.[13] He reviewed these men on Tuesday, 3 December, who 'went thro' their Exercise to the great Satisfaction of all present'. On this day the people of Derby were 'all in high Spirits by some Advices just received that the Duke of Cumberland's Army was near the Rebels, and 'twas expected a Battle would ensue the next day'. These high spirits did not last long, for an hour later news arrived that the Jacobite vanguard was at Ashbourne.[14] The local clergyman, already quoted, wrote, 'you may be sure our Frights and Fears returned upon us strongly' and that 'to terrify the People, it was said, that a numerous Rabble of Women and loose disorderly People followed them, and plunder'd all before them, which some doubted, more believed, but most feared. Then it was said the Rebels had fired upon them and dispersed them, which I hope is true.'[15]

Meanwhile, in Derby itself, the consternation of the local people was increased, as the *Derby Mercury* reported, by the militia receiving 'immediate Orders to march out of Town' after which 'nothing but Distraction was to be read in every Countenance'. Valuables and other vulnerable property, such as horses and livestock, had already been removed from the town or hidden some days before. But now 'most of the principal

Gentlemen and Tradesmen with their Wives and Children were retiring as fast as possible'.[16] At ten o'clock that night, the new militia companies were gathered in Market Place and being 'drawn up, they all march'd off by Torch Lights towards Nottingham [lying to the south-east] headed by his Grace the Duke of Devonshire'.[17] Once again, the townspeople were left to fend for themselves.

Detail from Samuel and Nathaniel Buck, *The East Prospect of Derby*, 1728.

31

Derby

'a fine Town'

The market town of Derby is located within the heart of 'the *Peak*', a landscape described by Daniel Defoe as 'inhospitable, rugged, and wild'. In contrast the town, lying on the west bank of the River Derwent, is 'fine, beautiful, and pleasant'.[1] Derby is populated by 'Gentry, rather than Trade', but what trade exists 'is chiefly in good Malt and good Ale'.[2] John Macky observed that the local ale was very strong, quoting Henry III's ribald poet laureate who likened it to '*the* Stigian *Lake*' and that, '*They drink it thick, and piss it wondrous thin*'.[3] Derby held a weekly market on Fridays and seven fairs a year in the centrally located Market Place. On the south side of this square was the Town or Guild Hall, built in 1730, and at the north-east corner (near Full Street) was the Assembly Room, where, in more settled times, 'the Ladies from the Neighbourhood, on Assembly-Days' make the town 'very agreeable to Strangers'.[4] Located north of Market Place is All Saints Church, the Perpendicular Gothic tower rising over 200 feet above the town. However, the great wonder of modern Derby was the imposing Silk Mills: the first was opened in 1717, located on the river 'all done in the *Italian* manner, both in Architecture and way of working the Silk'.[5] According to Defoe a single 'Engine' could work '73,726 Yards of Silk-thread, every time the Water-wheel goes round, which is three times in one Minute'.[6]

The Jacobite army left Ashbourne for Derby early on Wednesday, 4 December. As they marched, Captain John Maclean noted 'at severall houses we saw White flags hanging out Such as Napkins and white Aprons, and in the Gavels of Some houses white Cockades fixed'.[7] A detachment was sent ahead to the village of Swarkestone, four miles south of Derby, there to secure the bridge over the Trent and the onward passage towards London. Initially, two officers arrived in Derby at about eleven o'clock in the morning, and rode up to the George Inn, now, apparently, renamed 'the King's Head'[8] for obvious reasons. Here they asked for the magistrates, to which they were told the said magistrates had fled. They then ordered billets for 9,000 men.[9] This is now the familiar pattern, which was immediately reported – but by now simultaneously discredited – in the intelligence sent out by the government and British army observers. The quartermasters were joined by thirty hussars under the command of Arthur Elphinstone, soon to become Lord Balmerino. As ever, this first rousing display made the right impression on the local populace. The *Derby Mercury* grudgingly reported, 'the Rebels Van Guard rode into Town, consisting of about 30 Men, cloath'd in Blue, fac'd with Red, most of 'em had on Scarlet Waistcoats with Gold Lace, and being likely Men made a good Appearance'.[10] Having completed their task, the hussars sat silently on horseback in Market Place for several hours, awaiting the arrival of the main body of the army. The *Derby Mercury* stated that while the hussars remained – in a somewhat menacing manner – in the square, 'the Bells were rung, and several Bonfires made, to prevent any Resentment from 'em, that might ensue on our shewing a Dislike of their coming among us'.[11] Such published reports of the Jacobite army's occupation, as seen elsewhere, are understandably keen to stress that any appearance of celebration at the arrival of the Stuart prince was a charade enacted under duress.

Then, as the *Derby Mercury* continues, at about three o'clock in the afternoon Lord Elcho with his Life Guards, accompanied by many of the officers and chiefs, also arrived on horseback (numbering about 150) mostly dressed like the hussars: 'these made a fine Shew, being the Flower of their Army.'[12] Certainly 180 horsemen, dressed in bright red and blue with gold lace and gathered in a small market square, would have been a spectacular sight. Another observer, Hugh Bateman Esq of St Mary-gate, a signatory of the Derby 'Association', noted, 'They were fine figures, well dressed; but their horses were jaded.'[13]

Then followed the main body, marching six or eight abreast. As seen on their entry into every town and city, the army marched in an irregular manner to confuse those who stood at strategic points along the route attempting to estimate their numbers. The army now included its English 'Manchester' regiment, so efforts would be made to encourage locals to view it as not simply Highland or even Scots but a British force, in order, finally, to achieve the local recruitment they so desperately needed.[14] However,

Thomas Drake, a town constable who was intelligence gathering, observed, 'There are about 56 Lankashire Persons who was Distinguished by a Sash of Pladd,'[15] which is clearly a reference to the Manchester Regiment. The wearing of plaid, whether a Highlander or not, created a symbolic visual connection across all the regiments and in the process established this as one of the signifiers of the Jacobite army and movement as a whole. Drake also provides some idea of the artillery, baggage and the general paraphernalia that accompanied these troops, which included thirteen cannon, half of them of French manufacture, twenty covered carts and many wagons and carriages. The colours and standards he describes as 'some White some Quarter'd White and red, and some had their Commanders' Arms on them, but I Cou'd never Observe the Pretender's Coat of Arms, not even on his Coach'. Some items, Drake observed, were marked with the monogram 'P.C.'.[16]

The flashy uniforms and striking appearance of the Life Guards and hussars inevitably contrasted with what followed, and as the remainder of the army began to enter the town, there was an odd mixture of disappointment and something like sympathy, as well as relief in the testimonies of those watching. The clergyman informed his brother that almost all were dressed 'in Plads, some very well clad, others half naked, as they go, I suppose, in the Highlands'. Yet, though they were 'so indifferently cloathed, they were lively and well, regarded no Weather'. The curious from his parish 'and from all neighbouring Towns went to see them, and all came home mightily pleased with the Civility and Regularity of their Behaviour', and 'tho' the Town was so full of them, it is said (after they were in their Quarters) the Town was as still and quiet as if there was but a Hundred of them'.[17] This is difficult to believe. The report in the *Derby Mercury* was less generous, arguing that 'most of their main Body a Parcel of shabby, lousy, pittiful look'd Fellows, mix'd up with old Men and Boys; dress'd in dirty Plaids, and as dirty Shirts, without Breeches, and wore their Stockings made of Plaid; not much above half Way up their Legs'. Some were shoeless while many were so 'fatigu'd with their long March, that they really commanded our Pity more than our Fear'.[18]

Yet the sound of the bagpipes that accompanied their march must have been unnerving and exhilarating by turns to the more inquisitive of the locals who gathered to watch them. As Hugh Bateman recalled, 'They were ushered in by the bag-pipes, that ancient Northern music,

which raises the spirit of the martial Highlander.'[19] Bateman also noted
that they were 'a mixture of every rank, from childhood to old age, from
the dwarf to the giant, chiefly in deranged dresses, marked with dirt
and fatigue'.[20] There is, of course, no direct correlation between a smart
appearance and the ability or spirit to fight, something the British army
had discovered at Prestonpans. It should also be noted that this was
almost certainly the first time that many, if any, of the inhabitants of
Derby had come face to face with a Highlander. Mr Bateman and the
local journalist in their neat wigs and tricorn hats, fine wool or velvet
coats, waistcoats and breeches, stockings and buckled shoes, would have
had little idea what to make of Highland 'dresses', deranged or not. Still,
the Jacobite army had marched many hundreds of miles since its long
stay in Edinburgh, and the season was becoming more and more severe
as the days shortened. This would concern the Highlanders in particular far less than the rank and file of the British army, who were not used
to campaigning in the winter months. But the forced marches had no
doubt taken their toll.

While the bells rang and the bonfires added a welcome glow and
warmth to the dwindling daylight, Charles and his father were publicly
proclaimed before the Town Hall on Market Place, now overwhelmed by
the occupying army. As no magistrate was available, the common town
crier did the honours, according to the *Derby Mercury*.[21] However, Hugh
Bateman recorded that the Jacobite officers had 'seized upon Alderman
Cooper, too lame to run away, and obliged him to proclaim the Prince'.[22]
After this, as Bateman continues, at 'dusk the Prince arrived on foot
with his guards. He was tall, straight, slender, and handsome', dressed
in Highland plaid and carrying a broad sword.[23] Colonel O'Sullivan
recalled, 'his Royal Highnesse was parfectly well rec[eive]d. Bon-fires on
the roads, the Belles ringing ; we arrived a little leat, it was really a fine
sight to see the Illuminations of the Town.'[24] Charles' late arrival was
due to a detour to Radbourne Hall, the house of German Pole, a leading
local Tory. Perhaps he hoped to stir a local dignitary, well known to have
Jacobite sympathies, to make a public show of support. By local tradition,
the prince was also expecting to collect a sizable sum of much-needed
cash, which had been donated by local sympathisers. In both cases, nothing was forthcoming.[25]

Back in Derby, Hugh Bateman observed, 'The chief officers chose
the best gentlemen's houses' many of which were located in Market

Place.[26] Charles himself walked along Friar Gate (the road into Derby from Ashbourne), passed the George Inn (or King's Head) on Iron Gate, crossed Market Place and into the lower end of Full Street.[27] Here he lodged at Exeter House, a large, handsome, essentially mid-seventeenth-century brick building of three main storeys owned by Brownlow Cecil, 8th Earl of Exeter (previous earls had been Jacobite sympathisers), then also owner of Burghley House near Stamford, where he and his countess had only recently retired. Exeter House lay to the south of the famed Silk Mills and was later described by Katharine Thomson. It stood slightly back from Full Street, with a triangular entrance courtyard leading to the main west front. Once inside, 'a wide staircase, rising from a small hall, leads to a square, oak-panelled drawing-room, the presence chamber . . . On either side are chambers . . . One of these served the Prince as a sleeping-room.'[28] Adjoining the east or river front was a long formal garden with parterres and a fountain enclosed by high walls, which continued down to the edge of the Derwent. The prince's hostess was the widowed Mrs Ward.

Meanwhile, the army continued to arrive over many hours: 'Every House almost by this Time was pretty well fill'd, (tho' they kept driving in till 10 or 11 at Night) and we tho't we should never have seen the last of 'em.'[29] Hugh Bateman recalled, 'Many of the inhabitants had forty or fifty of various ranks quartered upon them, and some a hundred.'[30] The general reception, as reported, was the usual resigned acquiescence with some muted enthusiasm. Katharine Thomson, however, records 'the tendency of the town of Derby to Jacobite principles' at least among the upper orders, and recalls a tradition in her own family regarding her grandmother. The ladies of Derby (as seen elsewhere) 'vied with each other in making white cockades, of delicate and costly workmanship, to present to the hero of the day. To some of these admiring votaries he presented his picture . . . One of these Jacobite ladies is known by her family to have kept the portrait of the Prince behind the door of her bedchamber, carefully veiled from any but friendly inspection.'[31] Charles probably had a supply of portrait engravings to dispense to any supporters or admirers en route to London, possibly a mezzotint by Robert Strange, who had joined the prince in Edinburgh, hastily produced after the recent portrait by Allan Ramsay. As in the case of Katharine Thomson's grandmother, such images became the Jacobite version of household gods.

That first night, the entire army at 'their coming in they were generally treated with Bread, Cheese, Beer and Ale, whilst all Hands were aloft getting their Suppers ready; after Supper, being weary with their long March, they went to rest, many upon Straw, and others in Beds'.[32] In a letter from an unnamed member of the Jacobite army to 'Miss H', the author writes, 'This Derby is a fine Town & has a great many Inhabitants in it, it has in its neighbourhood severall People about Litchfield that are no great Friends to one another but may be reconcild soon, for their Law-suit will be determined with one hearing.' This is obviously a reference to the Duke of Cumberland and an imminent battle. He continues, 'All here are in perfect Health and greater Spirits' and concludes that he and his companion 'are just now going to attack a fine piece of Roast Beef having been a horseback since 3 in the morning'.[33]

That evening Charles dined with his principal officers at Exeter House. According to Colonel O'Sullivan, Lord George retired early to discuss with his host, Samuel Heathcote, the lists of subscribers to the Derby Association (including Hugh Bateman) in order to extract similar sums for the Jacobite army. A local tradition has it that, during the prince's meal, the Mayor of Derby, Robert Hague, returned to town and having entered Exeter House and mounted the stairs, attempted to 'speak to the Pretender'. At which Mayor Hague was immediately thrown down the said stairs by an angry Highlander, and told 'if you want to see a Pretender, you should go to St. James's'.[34] It is difficult to imagine a sensible civic leader, in an occupied town, acting so foolishly. Alternatively, to deflect any potential reprisals from the British government, this scene may have been contrived by the mayor in order to demonstrate he was no collaborator. Either way, at this moment in time, the Stuart prince could not have cared less about any triv-ial insult. As seen at Manchester, Charles is described on this first evening in Derby as extremely cheerful. And he had every reason to be. After all, his prize, the great metropolis of London, was only 120 miles away.

A Hussar of Murray of Broughton's regiment, a contemporary drawing
from the Penicuik Collection.

A British army grenadier, a contemporary drawing from the
Penicuik Collection.

Stafford

'our all is at stake'

The Duke of Cumberland moved his headquarters from Lichfield to Stafford, to the north, and on Monday, 2 December he wrote a quick note to the Duke of Newcastle, updating him on the current situation. He had visited Stone, to the north of Stafford, to find a suitable battlefield and 'where there is a very good one', but no sooner had he returned to his quarters and finished his meal than 'we had news that the Rebels were advancing towards us & that they were within nine miles of Newcastle [-under-Lyme] where the Duke of Richmond is with M[ajor].G[eneral]. Bland'. Even as he was scribbling down this note the 'assembly is beating & I must mount'. Before hastening out of the room he says, 'pray let my sisters know I am very well, but cant write to them now' and then 'P.S. We all join a little beyond Stone'. This proved to be a false alarm, as Lord George had switched his route and was now moving towards Derby. Another feint had succeeded. A problem for the British army commander-in-chief was the accuracy of the intelligence he was receiving, much of which was coming from well-meaning civilian volunteers. As Sir Everard Fawkener observed to the Duke of Newcastle, 'what is most apt to perplex is, that often, People who give intelligence, mistake a small party for the [main] Body'.[1]

The same day, the Duke of Cumberland received a letter from the Duke of Newcastle marked private and dated Whitehall, 1 December. It concerned a person called 'Broadstreet', who would be setting out the following day for the Jacobite headquarters, wherever they may be, 'and will send me constant accounts, by the name of Oliver Williams'. Newcastle asked the duke to send 'in a countryman's coat, any person you can depend upon . . . to the Head Quarters of the Rebels, and enquire for Mr. Broadstreet, an Irish gentleman and when he sees him, in private to speak to him by the name of Oliver Williams'. 'Broadstreet' would then share what he has discovered regarding the plans of the Jacobite command. Newcastle concludes, 'Tho' I am far from being sure, that this will be of any service to your Royal Highness; at a Time like this, nothing [ought] to be omitted, that has the least appearance of it.'[2] Newcastle was in the mood to try anything once. The Duke of Cumberland obviously felt the same way, as a few days later he replied, 'As to the affair mentioned in your secret & separate letter, I have a Person whom I propose to employ on that service, & shall let you know the success.'[3]

On Wednesday, 4 December the Duke of Cumberland wrote to Marshal Wade (from Stafford) updating him on the Jacobite army's movements. The duke admits he had expected them to continue south, but instead 'they not advancing & turning short to Ashborn & Darby, where I fear their Avant Garde is as [of] tonight'. As the duke's troops are 'tired wth continued forced marches these last ten days', he had halted the night before, and then that day marched back to Stafford and Lichfield 'from whence we shall march without any halt to Northampton where we hope to be able to give them battle, as it is an open Country'. He then states 'all the Foot about London ought to be encamped on Finchley Common, where at all Events I can be wth the Cavalry'. He concludes, 'I give you this Intelligence that you may know how affairs are here, with out which you might continue your march too much Westwards', whereas, the Jacobite army's route 'now seems to be for Darby & straight for London'.[4] Northampton is located between Derby and the capital, with Finchley Common, over 1000 acres of heath, lying just north-west of the villages of Highgate and Hampstead.[5]

The same day, the Duke of Cumberland also wrote to the Duke of Newcastle that 'certain advices came, that they had turn'd short & were gone for Leek & Ashburn, which is the direct road to Darby'. Regarding his own troops, if they had 'been as able as they seemd to be willing, I should have march'd directly for Derby'. But as they 'had scarcely halted six hours these ten days', 'had been without victuals for twenty four hours, & had been exposed to one of the coldest nights I ever felt without any shelter, for the country produced not straw sufficient for two Battalions', we were 'not able to march without a halt & provisions'. As a result 'we immediately came to a resolution of intercepting them at Northampton'.[6] So, the revised plan was to rest the troops at Stafford, while the Jacobite army entered Derby and then, with forced marches, the duke's army would head straight for Northampton. There, the duke planned to do battle with the Jacobite army, with the aim of ending the rebellion before they could get within sight of London. The contingency, if no battle at Northampton occurred, would be the troops at Finchley Common, which the duke could quickly join with the cavalry, rather than the foot, to defend the capital.

The duke also sent a private letter to the Duke of Newcastle stating, 'I am heartily sorry for this advance of the rebels as it will expose these counties & will perhaps (thô without reason) allarm people in town [meaning London] for I am certain we must reach them at Northampton.' He then refers to Marshal Wade and what appear to be rumours that the marshal will be given command of the army in Scotland, 'a country', the duke admits, 'I am totally ignorant of'. In this instance 'experience every day show us his insufficiency & it is of infinite consequence that some one more able be sent there besides I hope he wont accept it knowing his state of health', adding, 'for God sake let this be private'. He continues, but 'if he must go he should take all but the Dutch & march strait back for else he will have the whole Island to march over again with his batter'd forces & that will quite destroy them'. Finally, he declares, 'I am so fattigued & hurt to see an other town plund[e]red, before I can demollish these wretches.'[7]

The following day, Thursday, 5 December, Sir Everard Fawkener sent an update to the Duke of Newcastle, stating that the Jacobite army had taken possession of Swarkeston Bridge, and that the Duke of Cumberland was proposing to encamp his men the following day on Meriden Common, between Coleshill and Coventry, and then the next day near Northampton, 'by which means We shall be again before the Rebels, & in a condition to prevent any Alarms to Lon[don] in case they should attempt to push forward that way'.[8]

By the Friday, the Duke of Richmond had moved on from Newcastle-under-Lyme and was now at Coventry, due south of Derby. But he had lost all contact with the Duke of Cumberland and had no recent update on the movements of the Jacobite army. In a letter to the Duke of Newcastle, he complains that the Duke of Cumberland, four miles away, was getting all the intelligence '& wee have hardly any here'.[9] He continues, 'butt by all I can find you may be easy in London as to any approach of the Rebells, that way, for as they halted at Derby wee had got the lead of them here; butt as they are continually altering their motions, wee are obliged to do the same.' He then writes, with some exasperation, 'What in the name of wonder is become of Marshall Wade? some say he is now at Newcastle'; if Richmond means 'under-Lyme', then Wade was nowhere near, but 'if so I hope he will advance by Derby, & then the rebells retreat that way'. 'All I fear,' Richmond continues, 'is they may still slip back to their own damn'd country by Manchester, & Lancashire, & I dont see how wee can prevent it. butt I really thinke wee can cutt them off from Wales.' Considering the citizens of the British capital, he says, 'I dare swear thousands in London now sett upon their arses & say why does not the Duke march up to them. & if it was all hounslow heath [i.e. flat open land] between us, it would be a shame if he did not'. 'Butt,' he concludes, 'it [is] not to be conceived what a cursed country this is for marching & wee can move butt so slowly, that I fear, they will allways have time to escape.' From this and the Duke of Cumberland's previous comments, the British army command appeared confident that, somehow or other, between them they could head off any attempt by Charles and his men to advance into London, with the troops at Finchley Common as the final barrier. The citizens of London, on the other hand, may not have been so confident.

What the British army commanders were particularly exasperated about was the Jacobite army's ability to march faster than they could. This meant that the Duke of Cumberland and his officers were constantly under pressure to use any Jacobite army halts as an opportunity to move their men forward to block them. Yet, as Richmond had already stated, by far the worst development was not an advance to London, but Charles and his men retreating to the Highlands, and at a speed that a regular army would find impossible to outstrip. However, despite this, the greatest concern was not the Jacobite army, whose successes were more a frustration and an embarrassment to the British army than anything else, but the imminent arrival of a large French invasion force, which, by all accounts, was massing around Dunkirk: a French invasion would change everything. As Richmond continues, 'I make no doubt butt this embarcation will go on at Dunkirke. are ye all mad? that you don't send for ten thousand more foot, be they Hessians Hanoverians or Devills, if they will butt fight for us . . . indeed the whole kingdome is still asleep. our cavalry cant be here before Febru[ary] & the Pretender may be crown'd at West[minster] by that time.' Realising, perhaps, that Newcastle might take this outburst as a personal criticism, Richmond concludes 'dont be angry with me, butt our all is at stake'.[10]

Joseph Wood after Peter Tillemans, *The view [of London] from One-Tree Hill Greenwich Park*, 1744.

33

London

'in full March hither'

By the beginning of December, the largest town or city that the Jacobite army had occupied had been Edinburgh, a contained urban centre with a population of less than 50,000. And in the five or so weeks that the army had been in occupation, they had not been able to secure the Castle. By the mid-eighteenth century the population of London, the capital of England and the United Kingdom, was at least thirteen times greater than that of her sister in the north. These 660,000 souls lived within an estimated 124,000 dwellings and, rather than contained, the city sprawled from Tothill Street in Westminster to the west, to Limehouse in the east (roughly seven and a half miles), and from St Leonard's Shoreditch in the north to the southern end of Blackman Street in the borough of Southwark to the south (two and a half miles).

Just to the north of the city, the new Foundling Hospital, whose governors included the Dukes of Cumberland, Richmond and Newcastle, was being built in open fields, with the ancient parish church of St Pancras lying nearby. To the west of this was Tottenham Court turnpike with its taverns and brothels – almost the last buildings between London and the villages of Hampstead and Highgate on the hills to the north. Southwark was the main urban area located on the south bank of the Thames and was connected to the City of London (a distinct area within the metropolis of London) on the north side by the only bridge within London itself, the Old Bridge. A new bridge at Westminster was under construction. The Tower of London, still the main Royal Arsenal, lies on the eastern edge of the City. The village and common of Kennington (the latter, after Tyburn, one of the main sites of public execution) lay south of the river, between Southwark in the east and Lambeth Palace to the west. Located directly across the river from the Archbishop of Canterbury's London residence is the Abbey and Palace of Westminster, the seat of the British parliament.

Further west, the Thames hooks round towards the villages of Battersea and Chelsea.

In many ways, London's sprawl made it difficult to defend, should an army advance to its outskirts. The City of London was slightly different. This densely populated square mile still had gates on the main thoroughfares (much like Edinburgh's Netherbow Port) including the ancient Ludgate near St Paul's Cathedral. Although the Jacobite army was a small force, 6,000 determined men and boys could still wreak havoc among an undefended, unorganised civilian population. However, the intention was not to wreak havoc, but to restore the House of Stuart. This meant occupying, in as fast and as orderly a manner possible, all the key government, administration, legal and financial buildings at Whitehall, Parliament, the Inns of Court and the City (including the Bank of England), as well as the Royal Court at St James's. Not all of these vital institutions were conveniently located in one area. To take and then hold them would certainly require assistance from within London itself – preferably a combination of the mob and Jacobite-leaning civic and political leaders. If the lists of Jacobite supporters given to Louis XV in 1743 were correct, then the nation's financial centre, the City of London, should be secured relatively easily. And when parliament was recalled in October, many of the leading Jacobite members and lords would be conveniently in town. It can be assumed that one topic for debate at any council of war in Derby, in addition to outrunning or defeating the various armies converging on them, would be how Charles and his men were planning to coordinate all this with, or without, French assistance.

In mid-September Horace Walpole informed Horace Mann, in Florence, that by this time it had been expected that the Jacobite army would have entered England. But his uncle, Horatio, had just received an express confirming that they were at Edinburgh which had fallen, albeit 'the castle [was] impregnable, and in our possession'. Horace Walpole is incredulous that the English would be more disaffected than the Scots, and so far 'both nations seem to profess a neutrality'. Neither, at this time, had the French apparently stirred. However, referring to the Jacobite army, 'what can't any number of men do, that meet no opposition'? He observes, 'if we get over this, I shall believe that we never can be hurt; for we never can be more exposed to danger. Whatever disaffection there is to the present family, it plainly does not proceed from love to the other.'[1]

By October the shock defeat at Prestonpans, coupled with the now tangible threat of invasion from France, had instigated the withdrawal of troops from Flanders. These men continued to arrive in the capital and

its environs, which, as reported by Ligonier and Newcastle, had helped
to allay any local fears, for now. Charles' extended sojourn in Edinburgh
certainly, and unexpectedly, gave the British government time to organise itself, particularly in regard to the defence, if necessary, of London. In
addition to the return of troops from Flanders, over the following weeks
volunteers were being raised by subscription to supplement existing regiments in the British Army (such as the regiments of Foot Guards) both to
create additional companies and, if needs be, to act as the guard within the
capital to free up regulars for battle.[2]

But while such preparations were occurring, life carried on in the
metropolis and the theatre in particular was becoming the focus of any
pro-Hanoverian spirit. In late September, the *General Advertiser* revealed
that Mr Lacey, 'Master of his Majesty's Company of Comedians' at the
Theatre Royal Drury Lane 'has applied for Leave to raise 200 Men, in
Defence of his Majesty's Person and Government; in which the whole
Company of Players are willing to engage'.[3] That evening, after a per-
formance of Ben Jonson's *The Alchemist*, three famous soloists, Susannah
Cibber, John Beard and Thomas Reinhold, all favourites of the naturalised
Briton George Frideric Handel, stepped forward. Accompanied by a male
choir, they began to sing a traditional anthem, arranged by Thomas Arne
and with new words, to which the audience 'were agreeably surpriz'd', and
the 'universal Applause it met with, being encored with repeated Huzzas,
sufficiently denoted in how just an Abhorrence they hold the arbitrary
Schemes of our invidious Enemies, and detest the despotick Attempts of
Papal Power'.[4] Observing the popularity of this new anthem, Benjamin
Victor, writing to the theatrical impresario David Garrick two weeks later,
describes how Drury Lane and Covent Garden theatres are demonstrably
'the most pious, as well as the most loyal place in the three kingdoms', and
that 'Twenty men appear at the end of every play: and one, stepping forward from the rest, with uplifted hands and eyes, begins singing, to an old
anthem tune.' The words were:

> God bless our noble King,
> God save great George our King,
> God save the King.
> Send him victorious,
> Happy and glorious,
> Long to reign over us,
> God save the King.[5]

The musicologist Dr Charles Burney recalled 'Old Mrs Arne', mother of Thomas Arne and Susannah Cibber, assuring him 'at the time' that this anthem had been composed 'for King James, in 1688, when the Prince of Orange was hovering over the coast'.[6] She remembered hearing it sung in the playhouses and even in the street. Now, it had been appropriated as the rallying cry for supporters of King George. Susannah Cibber reported to Garrick that the 'Rebellion is so far from being a disadvantage to the play-houses, that, I assure you, it brings them very good houses'. Cibber had used this pulling power to raise money to support the defence of London. At her instigation, Covent Garden Theatre put on three benefit perform-ances of the crowd pleaser *The Beggar's Opera* with Cibber in the lead role of Polly Peacham. The proceeds amounted to a tidy £602.7s.[7]

Life also went on at court, where every effort was made to show sup-port to the king and to present an unflappable as well as an unusually united royal family. On 30 October, King George's birthday, and as the Jacobite army was preparing to leave Edinburgh, there was a levee at St James's Palace, which the Revd William Harris attended. He afterwards reported back to his sister-in-law 'some little account of the birthday fin-ery'. Princesses Amelia and Caroline were in white and pink flowered silk respectively, while Lady Cardigan, although dressed in a simple white and scarlet striped damask robe, 'excelled as to jewels, having on a magnificent solitaire, and her stomacher all over diamonds'. The Venetian ambassadress 'drew most people's attention' with her French manners, and sporting a flouncy pink and silver-fringed confection. The Prince of Wales was in light blue velvet, laced with silver, and the Duke of Cumberland 'was in scarlet and gold, and it seemed to be pretty much the same as his ordinary regimentals, only with rather more gold'. King George himself 'dresses in his usual way, without aiming at finery of any sort; and so he was now, having on a deep blue cloth coat, trimmed with silver lace, and waistcoat the same'. According to William Harris, the king 'seemed in very good humour, and behaved very graciously to all about him'.[8] That evening the *St. James's Evening Post* reported 'there was a ball at St. James's: The Quality, who were very numerous appear'd in a very splendid Manner. His Majesty came into the Ball-Room soon after Nine o'Clock, and withdrew about Twelve; and the Ball ended at One.' The Duke of Cumberland and his niece Princess Augusta 'open'd the ball with a Minuet'.[9]

On 7 November, from his chambers in Lincoln's Inn (lying just within the western edge of the City of London) Thomas Harris, brother to William and cousin to Anthony Ashley Cooper, 4th Earl of Shaftesbury, wrote to another brother, James, at Salisbury, outlining the confusion over the Jacobite army's intentions. 'I don't hear of any fresh Intelligence concerning ye Rebells to be depended on,' he wrote, 'only several people seem apprehensive they may get by Marshall Wade into England by marching Westward towards Carlisle, in wch case its said [that] Wade can't cross [the] Country to stop [them].' While others say, reports Thomas, that 'if they do this it will be fatal to them, for it will be deserting their advantages gaind in Scotland, & leaving a powerful army at [their] Backs, wch will be certain Ruin except they meet more friends in England than I hope they have any Reason to expect'.[10] The same day, the Earl of Shaftesbury also wrote to his cousin James, stating that he had no doubt the army intended to march into England. Most people, including the Earl of Stair, agreed with him 'but there are a great many persons in employments, as well as others, who ridicule this opinion as wild and absurd'. These 'persons' included the King's favourite, Lord Granville. Shaftesbury continues, the Jacobite army could pass into England via Carlisle 'and find scarce any interruption from our forces; for the crossroads are almost impassable, and besides such light-moving men as they can easily outmarch a regular army'.[11] How right he was.

A few days later Thomas Harris updated his brother on recent events in the House of Commons, where there had been a move for an enquiry into how Charles and his men had managed to achieve so much in Scotland, universally presumed to be an attack on the Marquess of Tweeddale 'and some other Scot[c]hmen'. One speaker bewailed the hardships that Scotland had been subjected to, and 'cry'd up their loyalty & said they were abandoned'. Although Prime Minister Pelham and his fellow ministers had decided not to challenge the proposed motion, yet the 'House exerted itself & after debate till 7 o'clock ye motion was rejected, 194 to 112, wch I am very glad of'.[12] Like Thomas Harris, Horatio Walpole considered the attempt to force an enquiry – at this time at least – into the causes and progress of the rebellion in Scotland a major distraction from actually getting on and dealing with it, and would have simply 'led us into divisions and party faction'[13] at precisely the moment when such things should be set aside. Perhaps that was the intention.

Yet the more successful the Jacobite army was, the more the fears of Henry Pelham and his brother, the Duke of Newcastle, appeared to be well-founded and therefore their warnings and advice adhered to. However, it was clear to Henry Fielding, at least, that the Pelham administration required some tangible display of support. At the same time, he obviously felt that the loyal population of London needed to be shocked into action.

To that end, he began to publish on a weekly basis a journal entitled *The True Patriot*. It was a mixture of fresh information, reports from other newspapers over the previous week, letters (apparently from patriotic readers) and editorial comment on the present situation. In his third issue (dated 19 November), the author and magistrate shared with his readership – and in graphic detail – a dream or vision that he is alleged to have had several weeks before. The scene is London, now overrun by marauding gangs 'in Highland Dresses'.[14] The author is dragged through the streets of the metropolis en route to trial and summary execution, where he sees 'Houses burnt down, dead Bodies of Men, Women and Children, strewed every where . . . great Numbers of Highlanders, and Popish Priests in their several Habits'. A 'Lady of Quality' is beaten and raped: only one example of 'the Cruelty which now methought raged every where, with all the Fury which Rage, Zeal, Lust, and wanton Fierceness could inspire into the bloody Hearts of Popish Priests, Bigots and Barbarians'. Finally, as the executioner places the rope around his neck, the author is awoken from this terrible dream by his little daughter, who informs him that the 'Taylor had brought home my Cloaths for his Majesty's Birth-day'. He concludes: 'The Sight of my dear Child, added to the Name of that gracious Prince at once deprived me of every private and public fear.' What the citizens of London were supposed to make of this is hard to say. But that Fielding's audience was not confined to the metropolis is evident from the Derbyshire clergyman quoted previously, who recalled the 'dismal Accounts of their Plundering, Pillaging, and barbarous Practices' printed in London newspapers.

On the same day (19 November), Thomas Harris reported the fall of Carlisle and that Marshal Wade was marching across the country towards the 'Rebells', whose 'designs I don't find any Politicians here able to penetrate'.[15] Eleven days later, referring to 'these troublesome times', Thomas confirmed that there was still no idea, among the powers that be, what exactly the plans of the Jacobite army were. Last heard they were in Preston and he believed they would hardly march further south, but, rather, turn back the way they came or retire north through Yorkshire and 'so plunder from York to Durham & to Scotland [that] Road: But this is all conjecture.' He then mentions the French ship that had been part of Lord John Drummond's convoy and which had been taken on 25 November by HMS *Sheerness*. It was reported that on board was the son of the late Lord Derwentwater (executed for his role in the '15) along with 'sev[era]l others to whom reports give great names, but ye best Politicians I have talkd with today, don't pretend to know' although, he continues, it was still suspected that a young man among them 'who goes by the name of Manley is ye Pret[ende]rs 2d son'.[16] This rumour that Prince Henry Benedict was among those captured continued for several weeks.

Writing to the Revd William Warburton, Charles Yorke declared that during his recent rambles from London he had 'fancied myself in Flanders' because of the mass movement of troops and baggage trains that he had happened across, also observing that into 'all the countries whither the Rebels advance the people fly before them with their families. In a word, the present confusion and terror everywhere are what we rarely feel in England.'[17] A timely reminder that in this sense the English people, indeed Britons as a whole, enjoyed a very different experience from most European civilian populations, for whom the confusions and terrors of war were all too familiar. A week later he wrote to his brother Joe, who was with the Duke of Cumberland (now free of court duties) at Lichfield:

> You say the terror which the Rebels carry with them spreads all over the country as it prevails here. The roads in Nottinghamshire within these three or four days, we are told, were crowded with gentlemen and ladies and all the considerable families of the country flying from it so that the inns could not contain them, and many were obliged to sit by the fireside all night for want of beds.[18]

In the light of the current disposition of the British army in the West Midlands, Lord Chancellor Hardwicke wrote to the Duke of Newcastle at the very beginning of December (regarding the defence of the capital), 'I presume our Reliance must be, for some time, on the Troops about London', currently under the command of the Earl of Stair, in which case, he asks, should not immediate orders 'be given for drawing these Troops together at some proper place of Rendezvous, so as to be properly posted to stop their Progress; and, in the mean time, to procure some Quiet to the minds of People here, & prevent that prodigious Harm & confusion, which otherwise would distract this Capital, & affect all Commerce & Credit'.[19] What he is particularly referring to is a potential run on the Bank of England, which had already been fended off at least once over the previous months. In fact, in the short term, if public credit and the financial system in general collapsed, the government and by association the Hanoverian dynasty could, technically, be crippled and then toppled through economic means alone.

Like Lord Chancellor Hardwicke, on 3 December John Montagu, 2nd Duke of Montagu was jotting down some recommendations.[20] Addressing the Duke of Newcastle, Montagu states by his calculations, within the regiments of Guards, there was not 'above 1200. old soldiers amongst them, all the rest are recruits lately furnished by the Parishes'. He understood that two battalions were to remain in the capital and that the other two battalions, who were to march out to meet the Jacobite army, would number 700 men each and be drafted from the best men available. This being the case, all that would then remain for the defence of London would be the recent recruits. He also rightly observes that, surely, the Jacobite army would not dare to advance on the capital unless they were certain of a rising within the city to support them, and, as a result, the troops left to defend London should not be cantoned as far out as Hampstead, Highgate and Islington, but, rather, 'in the suburbs of London', for, if they are too far away 'a suden Rizeing of disafected people in the night must carry their point, even before the troops coud be alarmed, assembled, and march to the Releef of the Town'. In fact, so far at least, there had been very little evidence of popular support in London for the Jacobite army, nor any anti-Hanoverian demonstrations (in contrast to the years 1715 and 1719), but the situation might yet change as Charles and his army advanced.[21] Montagu also observes, reiterating the importance of horsepower at this time, that if a rising in London was about to occur, then the first thing they would do was seize all the horses in all the stables about the city, as 'this was their proj[e]ct in the year 15'. Therefore, pre-empting this, all the hackney-coach horses in London should be gathered together and then 'mount the coach men & stable men that belong to them', while arming this improvised cavalry with cutlasses from the Tower. Although 'this woud be but an indiferent body of horse, yet it woud be nombers that myte be very troublesome to the enemy'.[22] The mobilising and arming of hundreds of coachmen and grooms is an original and (given the emergency) sensible suggestion.

By the beginning of December the available troops in the vicinity of London was about 6,000 foot, which included seventeen grenadier companies of the Foot Guards and 700 cavalrymen (not all mounted).[23] This meant that, numerically at least, this army was about 1,000 stronger than the Jacobite army then at Derby. Should a battle occur, these troops – some, as Montagu observed, recent volunteers – would at least be well rested, unlike Charles' men who would have been force-marched over one hundred miles (estimated as taking at least five days, using their speeds so far). As the Duke of Cumberland had recommended, Finchley Common was the site of rendezvous for these troops, which was located about twelve miles north-west of the most northern edge of the capital.

William Harris, writing again to his sister-in-law on Thursday, 5 December, declared the court and town were anxious about 'what news we should receive from the Duke of Cumberland. The express that arrived here last Monday evening brought word he had got within five miles of the rebels, so that an engagement was hourly expected.' But, 'after all, it seems they have given the King's army the slip, declined fighting, and are gone towards Derby. This account came last night. What course the rebels intend to take is uncertain.' Despite the fact that 'they do not appear to proceed on any settled plan', and as they 'are a parcel of mere desperadoes, one does not know but that, if opportunity offers, they may not boldly push on this way to try their fortune near the capital; though such a rash venture must, I should think, prove inevitable ruin to them'.[24] The *Daily Post* for Friday, 6 December reported the news from Derby, now three days old, that 'A Party of the Rebels are at Ashbourn, 15 Miles from hence, and the Remainder at Leek.' In the same paper there was an announcement from Whitehall, dated the previous day, stating that 'Letters from Edinburgh of the 30th past and 1st Instant mention, that the Rebels at Montrose had got Possession of his Majesty's Sloop the Hazard, and imprison'd Capt. Hill and his Crew.' This news was now at least five days old.

In another report, it was announced that 'Yesterday thirty Field-Pieces were mounted on Carriages at the Tower, for the Army that is to rendezvous on Finchley Common; and we hear Orders are actually issued for getting ready his Majesty's Field Equipage and Baggage.' Far from preparing for his escape aboard a yacht moored at the Tower of London (a rumour favoured among Jacobites and still repeated), King George was actually preparing to travel north to Finchley Common personally to lead the army gathering there. Prior to his Guards regiments leaving the capital for the encampment, the king held a military levee at which he is reported to have said, 'Gentlemen, you cannot be ignorant of the present precarious situation of our country, and though I have had so many recent instances of your exertions, the necessity of the times, and the knowledge I have of your hearts, induce me to demand your services again.' He then requested that 'all of you that are willing to meet the rebels, hold up your right hand; all those who may, from particular reasons, find it inconvenient, hold up your left hand'. Right hands were immediately and universally raised, a response which King George (clearly under great stress) found so affecting 'that in attempting to thank the company, his feelings overpowered him, he burst into tears and retired'.[25]

Meanwhile, on Friday, 6 December, the Duke of Newcastle wrote to the Lord Mayor of the City of London, who at this time was Richard Hoare, another gentleman marked as a Jacobite in James Butler's list of 1743. The Lord Mayor had jurisdiction within that particular area of the capital second only to the monarch, and would therefore be a key individual for a vital Jacobite rising in London. Newcastle informed Lord Mayor Hoare that His Majesty had that day received the news that Charles and his army were at Derby 'in their way, as they give out, towards London'. Newcastle assures the Lord Mayor that, in response, the Duke of Cumberland and his army will move towards Northampton and in such time as to be between this Jacobite army and the capital. But, to maintain law and order in the City at this difficult time, His Majesty had commanded Newcastle to recommend that immediate provision should be made to augment the guard within the City and that the Trained Bands should patrol day and night, being at the same time vigilant 'in preventing, or supporting any Disorders, or Tumults; and to sieze any Person, that may be assembled together, in a riotous manner: and also that a Guard may be constantly posted in the Squares, and open Places of the City'. Suitable signals, such as the firing of cannon, should be defined in the event of 'commotions', and alarm posts appointed within the City and its suburbs. The Lord Mayor should report back immediately, setting out how and when additional manpower for the guarding of the City would be in place.

In the meantime, King George was pleased to hear 'that a considerable Number of His good Subjects, Inhabitants of the City, out of zeal for His Majesty's Service, and for the Preservation of our Excellent Constitution, are desirous of appearing in arms, on the present occasion'. King George was very agreeable to such plans, and if the Lord Mayor provided a list he would immediately arrange the proper authority to allow them to proceed. Newcastle concludes:

> The zeal, which your Lord[shi]p, and the City of London, have shew'd for
> the Defence of His Majesty's Person, and Government, and the abhorrence,
> and Detestation you have express'd, for the present unnatural Rebellion,
> give His Majesty the strongest assurance, that you will exert your utmost
> Endeavours, in opposition to the bold, and dangerous attempts, now
> making by the Pretender, and His adherents; which threaten the Peace, and
> Tranquility of this great; and flourishing City.[26]

One such zealous group were the lawyers located around the Temple who, according to Thomas Harris (writing to his brother James), had called a meeting for the following Saturday which the Chief Justice to the Court of Common Pleas, Sir John Willes, had attended. The Chief Justice informed the group that the king was leaving in three days to take his place at the head of his army, now assembling at Finchley Common, and that he would take all his Guards with him, except those necessary to mount guard in London. To free up his regulars, the king would be very pleased if the gentlemen of the law formed into a regiment, in order to undertake guard duties at St James's and the Prince of Wales' residence, Leicester House (among other places), with Chief Justice Willes as their colonel. This was agreed. Thomas concludes, 'so by this you may imagine we are in real apprehens[io]ns'.[27] Once formed, the Associated Regiment of Law paraded daily in Lincoln's Inn.[28]

Thomas Harris then reports to his brother that the last intelligence received stated that on Wednesday, 4 December, the duke was at Stafford and the Jacobites at Derby. Therefore it appeared that the Duke of Cumberland had been outwitted by the rebels, who 'were then nearer Lond.[on] than He, and every body thinks They are in full March hither'. Therefore all hopes were now pinned on the duke's immediate march to Northampton, with his cavalry harassing the Jacobite army. However, if not, then 'we expect them here in a day or two, or at least a Battle very near this place'. Not everyone was girding their loins for a Jacobite advance on London. It is clear, as Henry Fielding later sarcastically described it, that on 'the Alarm of the Rebels having given the Duke the Slip, and being in full March for this Town', together with the information that the French had actually landed on the east coast of England (which, soon after, proved yet another false alarm), 'struck such a Terror into several public-spirited Persons, that, to prevent their Money, Jewels, Plate, &c. falling into Rebellious or French Hands, they immediately began to pack up and secure the same'. They then 'began to prepare for Journies into the Country; concluding, that the Plunder of what must remain behind in this City would satisfy the Victors, to prevent them at least for a long time from pursuing them'. However, while they 'were thus taking care of themselves, another Spirit hath prevailed amongst the Men, particularly in the City of London, where many Persons of good Fortune having provided themselves with the Uniform, were on Saturday last inlisted as Volunteers in the Guards'.[29] It was also reported that 'at a parade at St. James's, the city corps marched past the king, accompanied by their wives and children, as a proof that all they had was risked in the cause'.[30]

It seems that, rather than a universal panic, and as seen in Edinburgh, reactions from 'every man for himself' on the one hand, and a sense of urgency coupled with a calm civic resolve on the other, existed in the British capital in equal measure. But, whether the impulse was to flee or to fight, everything now depended on what the Jacobite army was planning to do next.

Anonymous, *Satirical Print of Charles Edward Stuart, c.* 1745.

34

Exeter House

'like a Romance'

O n Thursday, 5 December, the day after their arrival, the mood among the Jacobite troops was very upbeat. James Maxwell recalled, 'It was observed that the army never was in better spirits than while at Derby.'[1] While Captain Johnstone asserts, the 'Duke of Cumberland being only a league from Derby, our army employed the 5th in making preparations for giving battle to him next morning'. Despite the disproportion of numbers, 'the inequality was balanced by the heroic ardour of the Highlanders, animated, on that occasion, to the highest pitch of enthusiasm, and breathing nothing but a desire for the combat'. They were 'to be seen during the whole day, in crowds before the shops of the cutlers, quarrelling about who should be the first to sharpen and give a proper edge to their swords'.[2] Several intercepted letters, written by members of the Jacobite army on 5 December, refer to the 'good health' and 'greatest spirits' of the officers and troops.[3] Peter Ouchterlony, for example, formerly a coffee house keeper from Dundee, wrote to his wife Jeanie:

> We arrived here last night, amidst the acclamations of the people and publick rejoicings which wee have had in Several places and we are now within a hundred miles of London without seeing the face of one Enemy. so that in a short Time I hope to write you from London where if wee gett Safe the whole of our Story, and even what has happned already must appear to posterity like a Romance than any thing of truth.[4]

Alexander Blair of the Life Guards, also writing to his wife, stated, 'I hear General Wade is behind us, and the Duke of Cumberland and General Ligonier upon one hand of us, but we are nearer London than any of them and it is thought we are designed to march straight there, being only 90 Miles from it.' Even if 'both these Forces should unite and attack us, we do not fear them, for our whole Army is in top spirits, and we trust in God to make a good Account of them'.[5]

The *Derby Mercury*, inevitably, described the mood and behaviour of the occupying army from the perspective of the local townspeople, who would have been unused to a large military presence, still less thousands of Highlanders, as James Johnstone describes them, with their blood up. After a night's rest, 'they were very alert the next Day, running about from one Shop to another, to buy or rather steal, Tradesmen's Goods, viz. Gloves, Buckles, Powder-Flasks, Buttons, Hankerchiefs, Shoes, &c. and the Town being fill'd with 'em, look'd like some Fair in the Highlands'. The newspaper even reports that shoes were being taken from people's feet, and that the 'longer they stay'd the more insolent and outrageous they grew, demanding every Thing by Threats, drawn Swords, and Pistols clapp'd to the Breasts of many Persons, not only by common Men, but their Officers; so that several Persons were oblig'd to abscond to preserve their Lives'.[6] Hugh Bateman is more measured when he observes, 'If they took people's shoes, it was because they had none of their own; and no voice speaks so loud as that of necessity: if they omitted payment, it was because they had no money.'[7]

One very reluctant host who had six officers and forty private men billeted at his house, plus six 'shabby Horses', was so upset by the experience that he wrote a letter to the *Derby Mercury* and demanded it be published. By their appearance, the author thought them 'so many Fiends turn'd out of Hell' armed with 'Butchering Weapons'. He feared for the safety of his wife and family, but his guests 'being fatigued with their long march from *Leek* on *Wednesday* . . . stuffed themselves well with Bread, Cheese and Ale, and then about 20 of them, before a great Fire in my Hall order'd by 'em call'd for a large Quantity of straw, and nestled into it for Repose'. The remainder bedded down in a similar fashion before two fires in a large laundry room. The collective odour, certainly far from fragrant after weeks of forced marches, was 'as if they had been so many Persons in a condemn'd Hole'. The author was no more impressed by the officers who took possession of his house. They 'commanded what Supper and Liquor they would have, and expected me, my Wife and whole Family, to wait on 'em, as if they had been so many Petty Princes'.[8] Even if such rough behaviour did occur, it is difficult to imagine the likes of Peter Ouchterlony, a middling-sort tradesman from the Lowlands, or Alexander Blair being anything other than civilised guests – whether part of an occupying army or not. However Hugh Bateman, in tandem with the *Derby Mercury*, recorded other activities likely to leave a bad impression. Clothing was in some instances bought, but more likely taken. Those who had associated and subscribed for the support of the government, Bateman included, were 'obliged to pay the same sums to them. They demanded the landtax, excise, &c. and actually received about £.2,500.' When a demand for £100 from the post office was refused, they simply took one of the coaches.[9]

Attempts were made to counter such negative impressions. Lord George recalled 'at Derby the day we halted, as a battle was soon expected, many of our officers and people took the sacrament'.[10] Captain John Maclean, too, noted in his journal that 'we were Ordered to goe here prayers in the handsome Church of All saints where there is a very fine new Organs'.[11] It is said that at Derby, as well as Lancaster, Thomas Chadwick of the Manchester Regiment entertained some of the Jacobite officers by playing 'The King shall enjoy his own again' on the church organ. This song was written originally in about 1643, later revived on the return of Charles II from exile in 1660, and then revitalised as a Jacobite song after 1689.[12] Captain Maclean concludes his diary entry by stating, with a hint of disappointment, 'I missed the Seeing of a Curious Silk Manufactory which is at Derby which had (as I was told) more than ninety thousand motions.'[13]

Hugh Bateman recalled the Jacobite army's attempts to recruit, beating up for volunteers 'at five shillings advance, and five guineas when they arrived in London'. But, according to Bateman, only three people volunteered: Cook, a travelling journeyman blacksmith, Edward Hewit, a butcher, and James Sparks, a stocking-maker, all 'men of degraded life and sullied character'. Sparks was particularly eager, crying, 'This is the day I have long wished for'. Sparks usefully provided information on the inhabitants, friend or foe, and therefore 'who was to be favoured, and who oppressed'. He also 'guided the out parties to the seats of the neighbouring gentry, among others, to that of Hugo Meynell, Esq. at Bradley; where, making free with the liquors, he was left in the cellar completely intoxicated; the rebels themselves declaring, "he was not worth their regard"'.[14] Despite being sympathetic to the Stuart cause, which does not appear to have protected him from plunder, Squire Meynell had apparently taken the precaution of burying his silver in the garden of Bradley Hall.[15]

Captain Johnstone noted that, as the Jacobite army prepared for battle with the Duke of Cumberland next morning, an express arrived from Lord John Drummond. The contents brought welcome news concerning Lord

John's safe arrival at Montrose with his regiment and the picquets of the Irish brigade, and the imminent landing (if they had not already done so) of more troops, both Irish and French. Furthermore, he 'informed the Prince, at the same time, that he had a force of three thousand men, partly composed of the troops brought by him from France, and partly of the Highlanders who could not join the Prince before his departure for England'.[16]

A full council meeting was then called at Exeter House, in the oak-panelled drawing room on the first floor, with all regimental colonels present.[17] Although dissension within the leadership had been more than evident before this meeting, and no doubt opinion had been canvassed in advance of it, this forum was where their current situation was to be openly discussed, arguments made as to how to proceed and a decision taken. In the various accounts of this meeting – some by actual witnesses and participants to the discussion, others derived from second-hand information – who exactly said what and precisely when, and even exactly who was for or against which proposal, becomes slightly confused. But such confusion is an indication of the high stakes involved and therefore the conduct and progress of the debate: each argument was followed by counter-argument and, as the debate became more heated, there were interruptions, raised voices and accusations. As Captain Johnstone recalled, 'The council sat a long time, and the debates were very keen.'[18] There is even disagreement about whether the full council met once or twice during the course of the day. John Hay declares that no such meeting occurred at all.[19] However, most accounts confirm that the council did meet, while also agreeing on the substance of the arguments presented, and the result.

According to James Maxwell and Lord Elcho, and not unexpectedly, Lord George opened the proceedings by rehearsing the reasons why, in his opinion, an advance further into English territory was no longer an option. They had marched from Carlisle to Derby expecting at every stage a local rising and the swelling of their ranks with fresh recruits. Neither had happened. This English rising was to have been accompanied by the long-promised French landing in the south-east; thus far, this had not happened either.[20] As a result (as Lord Elcho recalled), Lord George concluded from this, and speaking for every Scotsman present, that 'the Scots had now done all that could be Expected of them'.[21] Yet, if the prince could produce 'any letter from any person of distinction in which their was an invitation for the army to go to London, or to any other part of England, . . . they were ready to go'.[22] Charles had to admit that no such letter or proof of encouragement was forthcoming.[23] The news that the prince had entered so far into England, without recent confirmation of support from the leading Jacobites, was apparently greeted with incredulity.

Moving on, in Lord George's opinion the most compelling reason for retreat was the two armies now converging upon them: the Duke of Cumberland's located to the south-west, and Marshal Wade's marching towards them from the north-east. As it stood, if they retreated now there was a clear run back up through the north-west of England. If they waited any longer, they risked being cut off by Marshal Wade before reaching Carlisle. In addition, Lord George stated, 'we knew that an army, at least equal to any of these, would be formed near London'.[24] Lord George's reference to a third army appears to be directed at the troops gathering at Finchley Common. Sir John Macdonald's account, however, suggests that their intelligence of what was converging on them, and from which direction, was sketchy: 'All we knew of the enemy was very vague, being only founded on reports or on their own published reports in the papers.' The British army 'were in three corps of unknown strength', that is, according to Macdonald, 'Wade's at Newcastle, Oglethorpe's at Yorkshire', and a 'third commanded by Prince William, the strength of which was not known to us, was on our route to London. It was therefore impossible to judge of the possibility of our advance.'[25] If the Jacobite army could not outrun or avoid them, Lord George continued, then they would have to defeat each opposing army in turn, and each time they fought they would be depleted by death, injury and desertion. Even if the Duke of Cumberland and his men were defeated, what was left of his army would regroup with the third army outside London, leaving Marshal Wade still at the rear. And, just supposing the Jacobite army could march straight to London, and then beat the troops located there, what impression would this battered corps make as it entered the capital? Not a sight to encourage a great flow of support.[26] And two enemy armies would still be in the field. Indeed, as Lord George concluded, if the Jacobite army was defeated at any point, the victorious army and the local militia would block the roads and surround them, and therefore 'it could not be supposed one man could escape'. As a result, 'the whole world would blame us as being rash and foolish, to venture a thing that could not succeed, and the Prince's person, should he escape being killed in the battle, must fall into the enemy's hands'.[27]

According to James Maxwell, 'The Prince, naturally bold and enterprising, and hitherto successful in every thing, was shocked with the mention of a retreat. Since he set out from Edinburgh he had never had a thought but of going on and fighting every thing he found in his way to London.'[28] In a similar vein, Lord George later recorded 'His Royal Highness had no regard to his own danger, but pressed with all the force of argument to go forward. He did not doubt but the justness of his cause would prevail, and he could not think of retreating after coming so far.'[29] Charles' reported counter-arguments suggest he simply repeated the claims he had made during the council of war in Edinburgh.[30] According to Lord Elcho, the prince was, apparently, still convinced that many from the British army would desert and even join the Jacobite ranks rather than fight against him, 'as he was Their true prince'.[31] Charles was also convinced that a French invasion of England was imminent. He may also have observed, again an argument made prior to the advance into England, that the 'Highlanders' were unbeaten and that morale within the 'Elector's army', where the memory of Prestonpans was still very fresh, would be low. To retreat at this juncture, he might conclude, would be to lose (at the very least) credibility, morale and discipline.

Lord George countered this by saying that Lord John Drummond's arrival in Scotland indicated that the French focus was there, and not in the south-east of England. Besides which, French aid in Scotland would be totally ineffectual if the main Jacobite army was defeated in the south. The current Jacobite forces in Scotland would double the army now in England. Therefore, a retreat to Scotland to bring the two armies together was more logical than an advance.[32] Finally, he repeated that an advance was only feasible if the English Jacobites rose, or the French landed in the south-east (preferably both): thus far (as established) neither had happened, nor was there any expectation in the very near future. Again, Lord Elcho seems to speak for a majority of the Scottish officers present when he says that Charles 'knew nothing about the country nor had not the Smallest Idea of the force that was against him, nor where they were Situated'. Lord Elcho blamed the prince's 'Irish favourites' who 'to pay court to him had always represented the whole nation as his friends, had diminished much all the force that was Against him'. As a result 'he always believed he Should enter Sᵗ James's with as little difficulty as he had done Holyrood house'.[33]

Recollections differ, but it is likely that Charles had only one open supporter at this crucial time, the Duke of Perth.[34] Lord George recalled that Charles 'was so very bent on putting all to the risk, that the Duke of Perth was for it, since his Royal Highness was'.[35] Others report that Perth had listened quietly as Lord George spoke, all the while leaning his head against the fireplace.[36] But even his resolve was buckling under the strength of Lord George's argument, which was clearly supported by a vast majority of the council. This was surely unsurprising, given the weight of opinion, voiced at the Edinburgh council of war, against entering England in the first place. Perth then suggested a compromise: a march to Wales. This was again opposed by the majority, who believed that they could be as easily cut off there as in England. Lord Elcho records that the 'Prince heard all these arguments with the greatest impatience, fell in a passion and gave most of the Gentlemen that had Spoke very Abusive Language, and said that they had a mind to betray him'.[37] Secretary Murray later stated that he accidentally entered the room, was in the process of leaving, when Charles told him to stay 'and told him, in some heat, that he was quite scandalised, for they were pressing him to go back to Scotland, instead of marching directly on London as had been intended'.[38] That the prince was overwhelmed by frustration and disappointment is certain. Charles himself stated that he had 'endeavoured to persuade some of them to join with him, but could not prevail upon one single person'.[39] Thus, as James Maxwell concludes, 'finding the far greatest part of the Council of Lord George's opinion', he 'yielded at last, but with great reluctancy; and the retreat was resolved upon'.[40] Even Colonel O'Sullivan believed that 'according to all the rules of War, & prudence, it was the only party to be taken'.[41]

Knowing that maintaining discipline within a retreating army was more difficult than within an advancing one, Lord George volunteered to take responsibility for the retreat. It was also agreed to keep the decision secret, partly to delay the inevitable response from the Highlanders, who were keen to do battle, and partly to confuse the British army command. Flexible orders were issued to the troops – which neither confirmed, nor denied, an advance or retreat. However, for now, all activity by the remainder of the army was predicated on the idea of an advance, with scouting parties sent out to that end. As a result, the citizens of Nottingham expected to be overrun by Highlanders at any moment. It seems that up to this point Prince

Charles was either oblivious to the level of opposition within his council, or wilfully ignoring it. He had, after all, time and time again overcome Lord George's arguments against the march to London, whatever the odds and whatever the dangers. Lord George had made it clear that the Jacobite army's penetration into England had only occurred in order to give the English and Welsh an opportunity to rise. At Manchester he had vocally opposed an onward march, but had acquiesced because, at Manchester at least, there had been some sign that the English Jacobites might finally stir. By the time they had arrived in Derby, the likelihood of gaining sufficient support from this quarter appeared non-existent.

Despite the decision to retreat, Lord Elcho recalls that the prince continued 'all the day positive he would march to London; the Irish in the army were always for what he was for'.[42] If, prior to Derby, there had been a split between the Irish and Scots, it was now a chasm. Supporting Lord Elcho, James Maxwell wrote that after the council was dismissed 'some of those that had voted against the retreat, and the Secretary [Murray], who had spoken warmly for it in private conversation with the Prince, condemned this resolution, and endeavoured to instil some suspicion of the courage or fidelity of those that had promoted it'. In turn, and unsurprisingly, Charles required little persuasion to convince himself that he had been too quick and compliant in agreeing to a retreat, although he would not go back on his word unless he was able to change the minds of those who were for it. And he now had hopes of achieving this, as Secretary Murray had already done so.[43] Lord George also recalls that some 'seeing the Prince so much cast down about the retreat, to ingratiate themselves, blamed the resolution', despite, that is, having agreed to it before. They excused their previous agreement 'because they knew the army would never fight well when the officers were against it. Sir Thomas Sheridan, and his Royal Highness's secretary, acted this part.'[44] As a result of this crack appearing in the resolve to retreat, Charles is reported to have spent the afternoon attempting to persuade some of the council members to change their minds, and argue instead for an advance. The Marquess of Tullibardine had not been present at the council of war and so, not knowing the specific arguments that had been presented, was easily brought around for the advance.

Lochiel had kept silent in the meeting, in deference to the Prince, but had said afterwards that he supported Lord George and a retreat. During the afternoon, Lord George, Keppoch and Lochiel were sitting together and talking over what had occurred, when they were interrupted (according to Lord George) by a drunk and angry Sir John Macdonald, 'who railed a great deal about our retreat: "What!" says he to Keppoch, "a Macdonald turn his back!" and to Lochiel, "For shame! A Cameron run away from the enemy! – go forward, and I'll lead you." This gentleman was old, and had dined heartily, for he was much subject to his bottle.'[45] Despite the provocation, Lochiel responded in a calm manner: 'If you knew all, you would agree with us.'[46] It is true to say that many of those who favoured an advance were not members of the council, and, as Lochiel's comment suggests, were not in possession of all the information available. Sir John Macdonald told David Morgan that he held Lords George, Elcho and Ogilvy personally responsible for the retreat. They were 'weary of the affair . . . they were for quitting him [Charles] and betraying him'.[47] According to Lord George, when these officers realised that an attempt was being made to reverse the decision to retreat, 'They told his Royal Highness, that they valued their lives as little as brave men ought to do, and if he inclined to go forward they would do their duty to the last; but desired that those that advised his Royal Highness to march forward would sign their opinion, which would be a satisfaction to them.' This bluff worked, as no one was willing to put their resolution to advance in writing, let alone sign it, and this 'put a stop to all underhand dealings'. In regard to the retreat, when Tullibardine 'heard others upon the subject' he 'was fully satisfied as to the necessity of the measure'.[48]

At about seven o'clock that evening, fresh intelligence was received from an English lord who had just arrived in Derby. This gentleman had requested that he should remain anonymous, for fear of being exposed in the London press. He stated that in addition to the Duke of Cumberland's army gathering around Lichfield, there were another eight or nine thousand troops at Northampton under Hawley or Ligonier. This information would have simply confirmed that their knowledge of the various armies gathering against them was inconsistent at best, and that an orderly retreat was the only option. Secretary Murray, writing two weeks later to Lord Lewis Gordon, states that he had sent a full explanation of the decision to retreat to Lord John Drummond, but that, in short, the prince had resolved upon it 'after hearing of the French landing [at Montrose] not judgeing it proper to fight the Duke of Cumberland as he must have had some loss and probably more than he could well afoord as he must have engaged Mr Wade afterwards'.[49]

That same evening, according to Captain John Daniel, a reception for the townspeople was held. This was after the decision to return to Scotland had been made, but before the majority of the army or any of the local people were aware of it. Captain Daniel recalled that a 'Great number of People and Ladies (who had come from afar to see the Prince), crowding into his room, overturned a table, which in falling over turned and broke the Royal Standard – soon after our return [or retreat] was agreed upon – so I leave the reader to judge and make his reflexions on this'.[50] That night, according to Lord Elcho, Charles sent for his Scottish officers 'and told them he consented to go to Scotland, And at the same time he told them that for the future he would have no more Councills, for he would neither ask nor take their Advice, that he was Accountable to nobody for his Actions but to his Father'.[51]

Meanwhile, the unwilling host and family were experiencing a second day with their guests. The master of the house recorded that the situation was actually worse than the day before, possibly because the officers (rather than the private men) knew of the retreat back to Scotland, and therefore were even less inclined to be courteous. The host described the officers and their men as 'more bold and insolent' in ordering their food and drink and, if they were not served immediately, 'some of them would surround you with fierce and savage Looks, as if they had been . . . so many Mutes appointed to strangle, or some other way assassin you'.[52] No doubt this family was not unusual in wanting to see the back of the Jacobite army. In two days their unwanted guests had eaten, or taken, 'near a side of Beef, 8 Joints of Mutton, 4 Cheeses, with abundance of white and brown Bread, (particularly white) 3 Couple Fowls, and would have Drams continually, as well as strong Ale, Beer, Tea, &c.'.[53] These items are the provisions intended to feed a large family in the middle of winter. They are not easily, or cheaply, replaced.

It was, then, with some relief that the townspeople of Derby bid farewell to the prince and his men. As the *Derby Mercury* reported, 'Early on Friday morning their drums beat to arms, and their bag pipers play'd about town; no one knowing their route, but most people imagined they would march to Loughborough for London, their advanced guard having secured the pass at Swarkstone bridge.' But then, to everyone's surprise, they returned 'marching off about 7 o'clock in the morning. The reason for their return back was not known.'[54] The anonymous and very unhappy host, in his angry letter to the *Derby Mercury*, declared that his guests had left several presents on departure, namely 'a Regiment or two of Highland lice, several Loads of their filthy Excrements, and other Ejections of different Colours, scatter'd before my Door, in the Garden, and elsewhere about my House', along with 'Wishes for a speedy meeting again at DERBY, with their Prince crown'd with Victory and Peace. – A true Portrait of those who would be our Rulers!'[55] The Highland troops, according to James Johnstone, were clearly in very good spirits, because they still believed they were marching onward to London and glory. But in no other town, where they had been quartered so far, were complaints made of them randomly defecating in the houses and gardens. It is possible that such things had happened before but remained unreported, or no complaints made, for fear of retribution. Lord George admitted that the 'taking of horse for carrying their baggage, or for sick men, was what the Highlanders committed the greatest excess in' and 'To be sure, there was some noted thieves amongst the Highlanders, (those called our Huzzars were not better;) what army is without them? But all possible care was taken to restrain them.'[56] It is also possible that isolated examples of bad behaviour was being exaggerated for propaganda purposes, intended to tap into widely held prejudice against the Highlanders, which was now swiftly turning into prejudice against the Scots in general.

The clergyman, writing to his brother in London on 9 December, recalled that it 'was thought they would set out in the Night, as soon as the Moon was up, but it seems, they were in no such Hurry', for they stayed until morning 'and then after making a Feint, as if they would march for Loughborough, as they all along gave out, in order, as it is guessed, to deceive Spies and Messengers, they turned back again to Derby, which at last, to no little Joy of the frighted Inhabitants, they left about Nine on Friday Morning last'.[57] Charles had had an entire night for his frustration, bitterness, sense of humiliation and betrayal to fester. He had reportedly wept when all hope of an advance had gone.[58] Colonel O'Sullivan observed that 'I never saw any body so concerned as he was for this disapointm[en]t, nor never saw him take any thing after so much to heart as he did it.'[59] Rather than displaying the usual buoyant camaraderie by walking at the head of his troops, he left Exeter House at about nine o'clock, several hours after the army had begun its feint towards Loughborough, 'mounted upon a Black Horse, (said to be the brave Col. Gardner's,) . . . and riding cross the Market-Place went thro' the Rotton-Row, then turn'd down Sadler-gate towards Ashburn, preceded and follow'd by the main Body of his Army'.[60] John Hay appears to explain this change of behaviour as a sort of psychosomatic response to the retreat: Charles 'was obliged to get on horseback, for he could not walk, and hardly stand (as was always the case with him when he was cruelly used)'.[61] Either way, as the *Derby Mercury* concludes, 'We were rid of them all (except a few Stragglers) by 11 o'Clock.'[62]

The response from those not present at the council meeting, and therefore not party to the reasoning behind the decision, was marked. The retreat had begun in the dark to confuse the men. The Jacobite army as a whole, but particularly the Highland contingent, according to Captain Johnstone, 'conceiving at first that they were on their march to attack the army of the Duke of Cumberland, displayed the utmost joy and cheerfulness'. As soon as it was light enough to recognise their surroundings, and finding 'we were retracing our steps, nothing was to be heard throughout the whole army but expressions of rage and lamentation. If we had been beaten the grief could not have been greater.'[63] To an extent, the prince's inability to mask his disappointment – one might better call it despair and sense of betrayal – did nothing but harm to the general morale of his army. The council members could point to their own sober reasoning and, furthermore, their desire to secure a stronghold in Scotland. Yet in this instance we can see how crucial Charles' personal behaviour was. No matter how much his manner was justified as an individual, as a leader it reveals a desperate naivety on his part. For the mettle of a leader becomes evident not when all is going well, but in adversity. Appearances in this instance really counted.

If billed as a retreat, rather than strategically retiring, then this action could have been seen, and would be promoted by the opposition, as a massive failure of nerve. One key element of the mythology of this army was that, against all reason, it had achieved one extraordinary success after another. Whether a tactical manoeuvre or not, without the element of surprise there was an even greater need for an English or Welsh rising – and neither was evident. It seems that the Jacobite commanders might now agree with James Ray's assessment: 'Upon the Whole, it may be said of the *English* Jacobites, no People in the Universe know better the Difference between drinking and fighting.'[64] It was one thing to toast the King over the Water, quite another to take a risk and put your life on the line for him. The Scottish commanders, particularly those who had argued against the advance into England, must have considered that they had given the other kingdom more than enough encouragement and opportunity. Now, they could return to their own lands, join the second army amassing near Perth and consolidate their successes. This alone would not be an easy task, as they had now been absent from Scotland for a month. And their greatest gain, Edinburgh, was now under the protection of the British army. Further, the towns and cities of Scotland were no longer devoid of those representatives of the current regime and supporters of King George, who had thought it prudent to depart before the Jacobite army arrived. These people had returned, and whether through embarrassment at the ease by which their towns had capitulated, or with greater knowledge of the manner and strength of the Jacobite army, they would not again be so easily overwhelmed or so compliant. Ultimately, in marching so far south, many of the prince's commanders had expended a lot of time, energy and resources chasing Charles' great prize, not their own.

Hubert Gravelot, *Headpiece to Paul de Rapin-Thoyras's*
'The History of England', 1744–47.

Packington

'flying back'

On Friday, 6 December the Duke of Cumberland was at Packington, thirteen and a half miles due south of Derby. He writes to the Duke of Newcastle, updating him on the British army's advance to Northampton) and now confirming that the cavalry, artillery and some battalions had already arrived in Coventry. By this movement, and as planned, the duke believes 'we had gaind a march on the Rebells, & had it in our Power to be between them and London'. But he continues, revealing mild astonishment, 'of a sudden they quitted Derby & are gone to Ashbourn with great precipitation'. This retreat suggested that there had been little, if any, coordination between the French invasion force gathering across the Channel and the advancing Jacobite army. But this was not the duke's immediate concern. The race was now on to cut off Charles and his men from the north while pursuing them from the south. To that end, the Duke of Cumberland had immediately dispatched Colonel Conway to Marshal Wade at Doncaster, with orders for the marshal to march north-west into Lancashire, in order to intercept the Jacobite retreat into Scotland 'which other wise they might probably succeed in'. For now, the duke's own troops were in no condition to pursue, as he affirms: 'Since Monday that we first march'd from Litchfield to this day We have marchd more hours than there had been daylight, & tho the Troops hitherto supported with a most surprising cheerfulness & health yet they can hold out no longer without some Rest.' The duke also admits that this situation is very new to him 'as this is my first Winter Campain' and therefore 'I can only judge by what others of more experience say, & by what I have read'. The early winter 'has been as severe as it is possible to conceive', and the marching back and forth to block the Jacobite army's advance had meant that 'every man has worn one if not two pair of shoes'. As a result, 'I have been forced to promise them this day a pair of stockings & shoes each Man, which I hope the King will not disapprove of.'[1]

Over the following days the duke received various pieces of intelligence concerning the events at Derby and the subsequent movements of the Jacobite army. One, dated 6 December, stated that the observer, Mr Lydall, 'saw them or went with them three miles from Derby towards Ashborn & that they tooke the direct road thither'. Lydall also recalled that 'they marched very fast & that the horses which drew their artillery & Baggage went upon a trot'.[2]

The following morning the Duke of Devonshire, then at Pontefract in Yorkshire, sent a note to the Duke of Cumberland, enclosing several pieces of information that had arrived at Chatsworth during the night, which confirmed that the Jacobite army had left Leek. According to his intelligence, they had marched out of Leek at three o'clock that afternoon for Macclesfield, 'so I think it cannot be doubted, but that they will go back for Scotland if practicable'. William Hudson, his Grace's servant, 'brings me this account, who has now been with them constantly for six days, he says there are not 4000, fighting men, amongst them, & those so miserably harassed that they seem totally dispirited'.[3] Devonshire's covering letter also observes, 'I believe at Macclesfield they [the Jacobite army] have a tollerable good road towards Chester.'[4] The inference being that they could either retrace their steps through Manchester, Preston, Lancaster, Penrith to Carlisle, or follow a slightly different route via Chester.

From 'T Furnivall' at Congleton, also dated 8 December, the Duke of Cumberland was informed, 'I have heard that they passed through the hills and went forward in the Night towards Manchester which I give some credit to, for now of those that went to observe them at Macclesfield are returned.' He goes on, 'five in their Scotch Dress were a few days ago in a village near this town and said they had deserted and they expected many of the others would soon do the like. If I find any they shall be secured.'[5] Meanwhile, Lord Halifax forwarded a letter from John Stephenson, a woollen draper in Stafford, which stated that the Jacobite army was at Leek preparing to march in three parties to Macclesfield, Congleton and Newcastle-under-Lyme en route to Scotland, and that they had taken all the horses and men's shoes that they could find. An unnamed Jacobite captain had told Stephenson's brother (in confidence) that 'there was 9 ships comen from ffrance with 9000 men in them which where to joyne these & then they would return to England & go directly for London'. Although the British army commanders would be immediately suspicious of any information so readily offered by a Jacobite officer to a complete stranger – they were by now familiar with such exaggeration and bluff – none the less, a quick return to England in order to finally join up with a French invasion force was still plausible. Stephenson concludes, 'it was reported some of them [were] very ill'.[6] Such reports encouraged the idea within the British army command that the Jacobite army was in utter disarray, despite the success and speed so far of their retreat north.

In response to the letter from the duke, dated 6 December, and intelligence that the Jacobite army had already moved through Ashbourne and Leek for Macclesfield, Marshal Wade called a council of war at Ferrybridge on Sunday the 8th, where it was resolved to march to Lancashire with all haste. But having been informed by the Quartermaster General and 'commissary of Wood and Straw' that they would not be prepared for a march for another two days, it was decided 'that the army shall begin their march on Tuesday morning to Wakefield, the next day to Hallifax and continue the march with all possible expedition for the purpose aforesaid'.[7] Colonel Conway was dispatched with a letter for the Duke of Cumberland informing him of their delay. This apparent lack of urgency was unlikely to please the British army commander-in-chief.

Of the five options open to the Jacobite army, as set out by the Duke of Richmond as they advanced south, the worst option from the British army's point of view was happening. From the British government's point of view, however, the situation looked much brighter. The Jacobite retreat not only suggested that there had been no coordination with the French, but also took the pressure off dealing with them as part of a two-pronged attack on London and the south-east of England. Despite this, as there was still every expectation of an imminent embarkation from Dunkirk, or at least from somewhere on the north-west coast of France, the priority for those in London was not the pursuit of the Jacobite army, but focusing resources on defending the south-east of England. At a cabinet meeting on 8 December attended by the Lord Chancellor, Lord Privy Seal, Lord Chamberlain, the Dukes of Bolton, Argyll, Montagu and Newcastle, Earls Stair and Harrington, Viscount Cobham and Henry Pelham, it was decided, 'considering the great fatigues The Duke's Army has undergone', coupled with the fact that there was no certain information about the Jacobite army's intentions, and in light of accounts that the long expected French invasion was about to occur, that the duke should halt his army at Coventry, and only move further away from London if Chester was attacked.[8]

The following day, unaware of these new orders, the Duke of Cumberland wrote to the Duke of Newcastle from Lichfield, updating him on what was a rapidly changing situation. On the Jacobite army's retreat, he had ordered Major General Bland with two dragoon regiments to advance to Lichfield, while the Duke of Richmond with the second division of cavalry was moving to Stafford via Birmingham. The duke had since joined Lieutenant General Hawley and Major Bland at Lichfield 'with a thousand foot Volunteers of whom I had mounted as many as we cou'd procure horses for'. These 1,000 mounted infantry, along with the dragoons, were going to pursue the retreating army. But, 'I fear our Chace will be fruitless for they march at such a rate that I cant flatter my self with the hopes of overtaking them, tho I set out this Morning upon a march of at least thirty measured miles.' The duke had also ordered Sir John Ligonier to move the encamped battalion on Meriden Common into billets within the town, and to keep the infantry there and at Coventry until further orders. He then observed that now 'the scene is so entirely changed & that the Rebels are now flying back towards Scotland' he required new orders as soon as possible, because otherwise 'I shall continue to pursue with this flying Corps, til I shall loose [lose] every glimpse of hopes of a possibility of over taking them'. He regretted that he did not have better news, and that all the effort and hardship undergone by his troops had merely prevented them advancing to London or retiring to Wales. But the fact of the matter was ''tis impossible that regular forces should move with that expedition Rabble do, & who take by force whatever they want, which we cant al ways come at'.[9]

By late on 10 December the Duke of Cumberland was at Macclesfield, having marched fifty miles over 'dreadful Country', and confirmed that 'the thousand foot are now within an hours march of this place'.[10] The Duke of Richmond was also expected at Macclesfield with the remainder of the cavalry. While on the march, the Duke of Cumberland had received regular reports concerning the Jacobite army. He had hoped that they would remain some time at Manchester, for 'if they had halted there all yesterday I should have been in reach of them with my whole Cavalry & Volunteers'. But unfortunately, as the British army quartermasters arrived in the town, 'they quitted Manchester with the utmost hurry & confusion & went towards Wiggan & as yet I have no further accounts of them'. Regarding Manchester, the night before the duke had sent an order by express to the magistrates and inhabitants 'to enjoin them to seize all straglers of the Rebel Army or such as had abetted them, & to keep them in safe custody til further order'.

Colonel Conway had since returned with the letter from Marshal Wade and a copy of the council of war at Ferrybridge, to which the duke refers, in a surprisingly sanguine manner, that it 'gives me little hopes of His intercepting the Rebels'. On a happier note, the duke observes that he is finding 'the greatest zeal & affection express'd on the arrival of the Kings Troops here', and 'except at Manchester where the Rebels we[r]e joined by about sixty Persons, & the rising of the Papists at Ormskerk which the people of the Town suppress'd themselves, there have not been any marks of disaffection shewn since the Rebels came into England as they themselves ownd'. Moving on to the issue of rebel prisoners, the duke asserts, 'There are I believe to the number of about fifteen or sixteen of their straglers pick'd up who are sent to different Jayls: as they have so many of our Prisoners in their hands, I did not care to put them to death, but I have incouraged the Country People to do it, as they may fall into their way.' Admitting, in writing, that he had urged the local people to kill any stragglers from the Jacobite army is quite a statement, almost casually made. The mechanism may have been the 'Posse Comitatus', the conscription of any able-bodied men by a law officer to keep the peace or apprehend a felon, in concert with encouraging all civilians 'to attack & harry them' – as he had recommended in letters to the Earl of Derby and Lord Lonsdale (dated 12 December).[11]

One of the stragglers turned out to be a British army deserter of Colonel Murray's regiment, who had joined the Jacobite army after Prestonpans (he was not alone). Of him the duke states, again in a matter-of-fact manner, 'I had him tried this Morning, & He has been condemned & will be executed within this hour.' This might sound harsh, but in this instance death was the standard penalty for desertion and considered vital for maintaining discipline, particularly in such harsh conditions. The duke was well known to be a disciplinarian – consider the report that he had aimed a pistol at an officer attempting to flee during the Battle of Fontenoy – but he was also a considerate commander. If he had been otherwise, he would have marched his men the length and breadth of the country, with no thought at all of their welfare. Charles, too, cared for his men, but (as his own officers admitted) he was averse to punishment, even if it would have improved discipline within his army and therefore, in turn, his authority. Finally the duke observes, 'All that I am able to suggest to Marshal Wade is that if He shall find it impossible to intercept the Rebels before they can reach Westmoreland, it then appears to me that the best thing He can do, will be to post himself at Hexham, by which He may cover Newcastle [upon Tyne] & at the same time stop them on their return to Carlisle.'[12]

Marshal Wade's response to the duke's order, dated 12 December from Leeds, would not have encouraged him. Marching to Hexham was only feasible 'if the roads to that place were passable, but they are hardly so for a single horseman, much less for an Army with Artillery'. Taking the route via Newcastle would mean 'we could not reach Hexham under ten days march, besides the necessary halts, which would not answer the purpose Your Royal Highness proposes of meeting the Rebels in their return to Carlisle'. He states that he and his men have had to halt at Leeds to get vital provisions and equipment, but that he would proceed to Newcastle upon Tyne as soon as he could. He presumes his messenger, Captain Sebright, has informed the duke that 'our numbers diminish by sickness, occasioned from the rigour of the season, and badness of the roads, which will daily increase as we proceed Northwards; and if some means are not found to send us recruits, we shall soon be reduced to half our Complement'.[13]

Despite the fact that there was no support from Marshal Wade, for the immediate future at least, the following day (12 December) the Duke of Cumberland was almost buoyant (as he writes to the Duke of Newcastle), due to recent intelligence 'of the Pannick that has got among the Rebels which increases to such a degree that they are throwing away their Arms'. The duke continues, still unaware of the new orders decided at council in London, 'I have thought it would be unpardonable in me if I did not proffit of this Pannick & follow them with this Corps of Cavalry as I flatter my self we must infallibly destroy them.' Oglethorpe was now at Wigan with the St George's Regiment of Dragoons plus a detachment of 120 from Marshal Wade's Regiment of Horse. The duke, with the whole cavalry and the thousand mounted volunteers, would be at Wigan the following day, and Bligh's Regiment of Foot was moving on to Manchester. The Jacobite army 'have been forced to halt as this day at Preston' and therefore, 'I think in two or three days march We must come up wth them'.[14]

Lord Lonsdale had received his instruction to harry the retreating army, and confirmed in a letter to Sir Everard, dated midnight on the 12th (received the 14th), that in response he had sent orders to the deputy lieutenants and Justices of the Peace in Westmoreland and Cumberland to 'use their best Endeavours towards ritarding & interrupting the March of the Rebels by all Possible means', which he had absolutely no doubt they would endeavour to do. However, in reality, he considered there would be little that they could do, given 'the Country is mountainous . . . & very thinly inhabited', and 'it is generally so open that there are many different roads to the same place'. Furthermore, he considered the Duke of Cumberland advancing beyond Kendal (thirty-four miles south of Carlisle) as a serious issue in the increasingly hard winter season, because 'it will be difficult to have his army supplyed with Provisions, & what there is, will be either consumed or destroyed by the Rebels if they are before him'. Sickness and poor conditions were already laying waste to Wade's small army to the east. If the duke attempted such an advance, there was a very real prospect, and an unedifying one at that, of British Army soldiers dying of starvation on British soil. The nearest source of bread that Lord Lonsdale could think of was in Yorkshire, and to that end he had sent an express to Marshal Wade's commissary to organise it.[15]

Two days later (Saturday the 14th), Sir Everard writes to the Duke of Newcastle from Wigan, that they believed 'the first division of the Rebels went from Preston on Thursday [the 12th] but the rear only yesterday morning at ten'. Four hours later, 'the light horse his Royal Highness had detached, pass'd through that place, & about seven, the Corps of Cavalry detach'd from General Wades Army under Gen[era]l Oglethorpe arrived there'. These mounted regiments 'are advanced from thence this morning in the view of overtaking the rear of the Rebels, & the Duke will march in an hour to Preston'.[16] It appeared from the reports that the 'rear' was dragging back the swift advance of the Jacobite army, so much so that the duke's flying corps of cavalry had every chance of catching up with and even passing it.

This message was delivered to the Duke of Newcastle in London by the messenger 'Lamb' accompanied by an unnamed individual who, until recently, had been with the Jacobite army since Derby. The Duke of Cumberland had sent this individual to London to deliver a verbal message to the Principal Secretary of State. Sir Everard Fawkener confirms that 'the information He gives, agrees with the accounts He [the duke] has of the Rebels from all other parts'.[17] The exact identity of this person is confirmed in the next letter, sent from Sir Everard at Preston to the Duke of

Newcastle, in which he writes that he had dispatched with Messenger Lamb 'Mr Oliver Williams the Person from whom you had had some notices through the Canal [channel] of a Clergyman. The Messenger & He set out this afternoon from Wiggan.'[18] The 'notices', or information, Sir Everard is referring to must have been delivered to the Secretary of State only a day or so before, and came from a curate in Standish, Lancashire. The letter was written on 11 December 1745 and it concerned 'Mr. Oliver Williams' who, with the Jacobite cavalry, had quartered at Standish the night before.[19] Williams took the curate into his confidence 'so far as to inform me, that He left the Duke's Army at Litchfield on Thursday, 5th Inst[t]: & soon after on the same Day, arrived at Derby; where he threw himself into the Hands of the Rebels who were for marching within three Hours directly for London; wth a full Purpose to throw into Confusion & sack the City'. Williams, however, had informed them 'that there actually was an Army of 10000 men at Northampton, a Council was called, in wch thô their Prince was very urgent for advancing, it was at last resolv'd on to retreat'.

'Oliver Williams' was the code name for Dudley Broadstreet or Bradstreet, the man sent by the Duke of Newcastle to the Duke of Cumberland in early December. He was also the anonymous 'English Lord' who had joined the Jacobite army in Derby. Neither Sir Everard nor the Duke of Cumberland indicate in their correspondence that they had any idea why the Jacobite army had retreated, or had any notion of what had occurred during the Exeter House council of war. This letter was the first suggestion. It appears that Bradstreet, via Edward Smalley, curate at Standish, was attempting to take full credit for the Jacobite army's decision not to advance on London. Bradstreet, an Irish-born chancer, certainly had the brass neck to bluff his way into the Jacobite headquarters; as he later described it, 'I entered Derby, and displayed as much of my Lace as I conveniently could, and fretted my lovely and well-managed Charger, in order to create some Respect.' He was then, according to his own account, not only taken to Exeter House and interviewed by Lord Kilmarnock, the Duke of Perth and Colonel O'Sullivan, but having assured them of the eight or nine thousand men at Northampton – 'Observe,' says Bradstreet, 'there was not nine Men at Northampton to oppose them, which shews what mighty Events are often effected by the smallest Causes' – he was then ushered into the council of war, where he was told to repeat the information to the entire assembly. According to Bradstreet, when he mentioned the army at Northampton 'the Rebel Prince, who was in a Closet [a small room] just by, opened the Door, and pointed at me, saying "That Fellow will do me more Harm than all the Elector's Army"'. After this, a furious Charles 'directing himself to the Council, said, "You ruin, abandon, and betray me if you don't march on," and then shut the Door in a Passion'.[20]

Not one of the people who were present at the main council meeting at Exeter House, nor those who were party to any of the discussions and machinations afterwards, mentions such a scene, or specifically refers to intelligence concerning an army at Northampton. Lord George, as quoted before, refers to a third army near London – which could be the bogus army at Northampton, but more likely the troops mustering on Finchley Common. No one states that a single piece of information acted as the *coup de grâce* to the advance on London. Taken together, this makes Bradstreet's claims somewhat suspect. And yet the curate in his letter to the Secretary of State goes on, 'Mr. Williams did in my Hearing, I assure your Grace, appeal to several of the Rebel officers, if he was not the Cause of their present March towards the North, & they readily acknowledg'd that He was, much against their Inclinations, wch were strong for London.'[21] Bradstreet's published account of 1755, quoting Charles as saying his commanders aimed to 'betray me', does correlate with Lord Elcho's unpublished recollections of the same event. But until new information comes to light, it is difficult to establish what exactly happened at the Derby council of war, and whether Dudley Bradstreet had any influence on the decision to retreat. However, as previously observed, the news of the existence of yet another army would have simply confirmed what a vast majority of the council already believed: that to advance would have been suicide.

To the Duke of Cumberland, whether Bradstreet was lying or not was immaterial, as the Jacobite army was in retreat while he was in pursuit. The duke arrived in Preston on 15 December and later that day he received news that the 'main body of the rebels are stil at Lancaster. Some of our light horse have been within five miles of that Town, but found not any advanced partys.'[22] On this day he also, finally, received a letter from the Secretary of State (dated the 12th) which confirmed the new orders, as given at the cabinet meeting of 8 December. In addition, King George had received news from Admiral Edward Vernon who, with his fleet in the Channel, was dealing with an extremely difficult situation, 'that a considerable Number of Vessils, besides small Boats, are assembled at Dunkirk'. With an immediate invasion from France likely, Sir John Ligonier had been commanded to return 'with the utmost expedition to London, wth all the Battalions, your Royal Highness left with Him; Except those of Campbell and Sempil'. Further, the said 'Campbell, & Sempil and such Four Regiments of those, that are newly raised' plus one of the dragoon regiments, would join Marshal Wade, and the duke should return to London with the rest of the cavalry and the remainder of the foot. Newcastle concludes, 'The great Hurry, which, your Royal Highness will easily imagine, we are in at present hinders me from adding anything further.'[23]

The duke replied to this from Preston on the same day, stating with a hint of frustration (or sarcasm), 'I am very sorry that Mr. Vernon's frights should have saved the Rebel army now at Lancaster [whither] we had drove them. & where I hoped to have kept them at Bay, til I could have had the assistance of Marshall Wades army, utterly to have destroy'd them.' But, as 'I am not to be so fortunate as to be the instrument of destruction of those Villains, I am giving orders for obeying the Commands of his Majesty for the return of the Army.'[24]

Admiral Vernon, the hero of the Battle of Porto Bello (1739), was reading the urgency of the situation correctly, as Prince Henry had already left for Dunkirk (despite the rumours, he was definitely not the young man captured by HMS *Sheerness*) and on 17 December (OS, the 28th NS), the duc de Richelieu, commander of the French invasion, had also arrived. Only a day later, Richelieu received news of Prince Charles' retreat from Derby. But even then he had no immediate thoughts of abandoning the expedition. This continued activity around the north-west coast of France would keep Admiral Vernon, and therefore the British government, on constant alert for the time being.[25]

About the same time, Sir Everard Fawkener received a letter of condolence from Newcastle's brother, the Prime Minister Henry Pelham, for 'the unaccountable escape of the Rebels Northwards' despite the Duke of Cumberland's best efforts. But 'the irregular suddain and unus[u]al marches which these extraordinary Animals have taken, could not be forseen'. He understands that orders have already been issued to recall the greater part of the army to the south-east, and to place the rest under the command of Marshal Wade, which, he says, 'has arisen from the apprehensions the

King is under from the embarkation said to be carrying on att Dunkirk; and I can assure you giving perpetual alarms to His Majestys faithful subjects here'. Apparently 'the King was himself extremely desirous to have the Duke near him att this time', perhaps, in part, because he was receiving little moral support from the Prince of Wales. Furthermore, 'if your Army was to be running races this whole winter, I am afraid it would be the means of destroying that force which is almost the only security we have att present for all we hold dear to us'.[26] In fact, within days these orders to call off the pursuit were reversed. Unfortunately for the Duke of Cumberland, the main result was that Oglethorpe and his men were now several days behind the swiftly retreating Jacobite army.

John Pine, 'King's Own Regiment of Horse', from the
The Cloathing Book, 1742.

Clifton Moor

'a little affair'

On 16 December, the Duke of Cumberland arrived in Lancaster and immediately wrote to the Duke of Newcastle concerning some papers taken from the Duke of Perth's servant (Perth was in the Jacobite advance guard) by a mob in Kendal, and that 'all that is of consequence is the Cypher [code], which I send you'.[1] Presumably, this meant that the British government could now decipher any coded letters that fell into their hands. Details concerning this incident in Kendal were given to Sir Everard Fawkener in a letter dated 17 December from Lord Lonsdale, who states that 'as the Duke of Perth & 110 of the Rebels went out of Kendal the Mob rose upon them with Sticks and Stones, took two of his servants & his Portmanteau, that the Bell man was sent about ordering the Mob to desist, But this wou'd not restrain them from driving the Rebels out of the Town'. According to Lord Lonsdale, two people from the mob were killed, with one or two others wounded. As a result, as reported by Lonsdale, the Jacobite army 'threaten the utter destruction of the Town of Penrith, & I am very much afraid they will be as good as their word . . . It grieves me to think that these Poor People are to pay so dearly for their zeal.'[2] Evidently the Jacobite retreat was being hindered by the local people, as the Duke of Cumberland had requested. In turn, the Jacobite army no longer felt obliged to behave civilly. Penrith, however, was not destroyed.

The duke's advance guard finally caught up with the Jacobite rearguard on 18 December at Clifton Moor. The duke described it as 'a little affair . . . which tho but trifling of it self may I hope have good consequence, as it has increast that terror & pannick which was amongst the rebels before, to such a degree, that We have taken since the affair about seventy of their

People'.[3] In fact the affair was not as 'trifling' as the duke suggests. The village of Clifton was held by Lord George Murray with some cavalry, Glengarry's men, Roy Stuart's regiment, MacPhersons (under Cluny) and the Appin Stewarts (under Ardsheal): a total of about 1,000 men.[4] The King's Own Dragoons, Mark Kerr's and Cobham's regiments had moved forward during the early evening. First there was a firefight, with the two dismounted squadrons of the King's Own under Colonel Honeywood mistakenly firing from a distance of 150 yards. As the duke himself described it, Honeywood 'then giving way, the Rebels came out with their broad swords & wounded several of the Officers & some of the men but never dared make the least attempt upon Cobham & Mark Kerrs Regiments, who kept their fire the whole time & drove them out of the village with very little loss'. According to Lord George's recollection, he and Cluny led the charge, killing 'many of the enemy', and, once the firing ceased, Lord George waited until he was 'sure of no more trouble from the enemy' and 'ordered the retreat'.[5]

The main Jacobite army, which Lord George and his men were covering by their stand at Clifton Moor, had since moved on to Carlisle, but the Duke of Cumberland had not immediately pursued them, because 'our Men & horses were so fatigued with the forced marches we had made through an extreme bad country & with remaining all night upon the common in very cold & wet weather, that I was forc'd to halt them at Penrith to wait for the foot of whom the greater part came in last night & the remainder this morning'.[6] Regarding Carlisle, the duke writes that as far as he can tell, the Jacobite army is still there and that they aim to leave tomorrow. By which time, he hoped to be at Carlisle himself. In a postscript, the duke refers back to the skirmish at Clifton Moor, writing, 'When the officers of the Kings own Regiment were wounded, the Rebels cried no quarter murder them, & they received several wounds after they were knock[ed] down.'[7] This account may have come from Colonel Joseph Yorke, who was present and recalled these exact details in a letter to his father, Lord Chancellor Hardwicke.[8] It is the first specific mention of 'no quarter' from either side.

At this time the Duke of Cumberland had also received an offer 'from Gordon who acts as Quarter-master general to the Rebels, and Gordon, Colonel of Pitsligo's Horse' to 'come over to you, upon Promise of His Majestie's Pardon'. King George, as relayed by Newcastle, thought it would be very useful to accept such offers from 'Persons of Rank, and Consideration amongst the Rebels to leave them, at this Time . . . as It would not fail to create great Diffidence amongst them; and hinder others from engaging with them'.[9] Nothing seems to have come from this (the men the duke appears to be referring to remained with the Jacobite army) but it is a hint that the commitment to the campaign, among some of the officers at least, possibly as a result of the retreat, was wavering.[10]

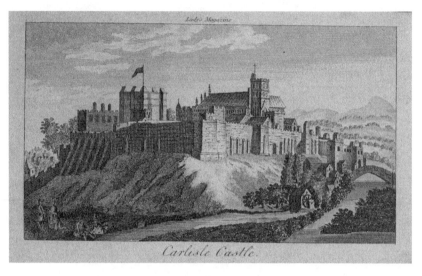

Anonymous, *View of Carlisle Castle from 'The Lady's Magazine'*, 1794.

Carlisle

'keep one of the keys'

The Jacobite army re-entered Carlisle at about midday on Thursday, 19 December, where John Hamilton had continued as governor during the five weeks that they had been in England. Contrary to the reports that the Duke of Cumberland had received, encouraging him to believe the army was retreating in complete disarray, the entire operation, despite the many hazards, had been in the main orderly and successful. According to James Maxwell, at Carlisle there were several old letters from Lord John Drummond and Lord Strathallan, both still in Scotland, the first informing the prince, once more, of the encouraging situation in France and the latter offering 'a very good account of the army assembled in that country [Scotland], which he said was certainly better than that which the Prince had along with him'. Lord John also advised Charles that King Louis wanted the prince to 'proceed with great caution, and, if possible, avoid a decisive action till he received the succours he intended to send him, which would be such as would put his success beyond all doubt'. In the meantime, Lord John 'had brought over a few troops and a train of artillery sufficient to reduce all the fortresses in Scotland'.[1]

With such encouraging, albeit old, news from France, Charles' mood must have lifted. Certainly, he would have been at his most optimistic since his overwhelming despair at the retreat from Derby. A council was called, during which it was unanimously decided to march into Scotland, where all the forces would be brought together. As James Maxwell observes, the 'encouragement given from France was an argument against all desperate measures'.[2] This was probably not the full council of war. Charles had declared, according to Lord Elcho, his intention not to take advice from that particular group ever again. Lord George, for one, was not present.[3] However, those who had argued for the retreat may have felt vindicated by the French king's reported advice for caution.

Another decision was made during this council meeting and it was one that caused some controversy among the Jacobite officers. The main decision was to retreat into Scotland in order to gather the entire army together. This was deemed eminently sensible. But the prince – and it does appear to have been his particular wish – insisted that a garrison be left at Carlisle. This garrison would include most of the Manchester Regiment, that is the core group of Englishmen who had joined the army during their march south through Lancashire, although by now the regiment was reduced from desertion. Captain Johnstone, who categorically refused that he or his men should be included in what he considered a suicidal action, offers a very extreme reason for Charles' decision: the garrison was simply bait to distract the Duke of Cumberland so that the main army could retreat 'at our ease'. Others suggested it was revenge against the English nation for not joining him, in particular 'the persons of distinction, in England, who invited the Prince to make a descent in Great Britain' yet had been conspicuous by their absence.[4] This is certainly a damning charge – it suggests a vindictive streak in the prince's character that had not, until now, presented itself.

In fact, the action can be explained in relatively straightforward terms. Charles had never displayed an interest in securing Scotland alone: whether he had declared it openly or not to his predominantly Scottish officers, his ultimate goal (as time revealed) had always been London and the combined thrones of England and Scotland. His despair at Derby, a mere 120 miles from his target, had been profound, stimulating a complete transformation in his behaviour, from a sober, vigorous, focused and inspirational leader, to a sullen, drunken, obstructive and decidedly uninspiring juvenile. As John Home summarised it: 'Charles was extremely averse to the retreat, and so much offended when it was resolved to return to Ashburn, that he behaved for some time as if he no longer thought himself commander of the army.' In contrast to his behaviour during the advance, 'in the retreat, though the rest of the army were on their march, and the rear could not move without him, he made them wait a long time; and when he came out, mounted his horse, rode straight on, and got to his quarters with the van'.[5] The blame for the delays in an otherwise well-ordered retreat (for which Lord George deserves great praise) lies with the prince, who insisted on spending longer in the various towns than was needed, almost to show who, nominally at least, was boss. His behaviour had been frustrating for all concerned, Lord George in particular.[6]

Yet, the news that the arrival of reinforcements and full French support was now imminent reignited the flame of hope that advancing to London was once again feasible. And almost as a visible pledge of this intention – as much to Lord George Murray and his supporters in the retreat, as to his enemies – Charles insisted that a Jacobite garrison should be left at Carlisle to act as an access point back into England.[7]

As the editor of Captain Johnstone's memoirs points out, there were in fact more Scots than English in this garrison, raising the obvious question, if Charles was exacting his revenge on the latter, why would he sacrifice Scotsmen to do it? After all the prince's reasoning may have been that the garrison would only be left for a short time. Besides which they would also have the guns – the very same which had been dragged so far into England and then almost back out again – to defend the town and castle. Maxwell (who was against the plan) admitted, 'It was, to be sure, much for the Prince's reputation, upon leaving England to keep one of the keys of it; and he was in hopes of returning before it could be taken.' However, 'he could not be absolutely sure of that; and the place was not tenable against a few pieces of battering cannon, or a few mortars'.[8] But Charles was convinced that he would return with his expanded army, en route to a second and more certain attempt to advance all the way to London. There was the added benefit that, without the guns, his retreating army would be lighter and even faster.

Few joined him in his optimism. Colonel Towneley – now the governor of the town, in addition to Hamilton as governor of the castle, and clearly in the 'garrison as sacrifice' camp – later stated, 'I knew that was a desperate Expedient to retard the Pursuit of our Enemies, and that those left in Garrison there, could not possibly avoid being cut to Pieces in the Place, or submitting to the Conquerors, from whom we had no Reason to expect the least Mercy.' Yet Towneley 'was willing to sacrifice my Life to the Safety of my [Prince] and his Friends.' Besides, had he refused to undertake such a dangerous post 'another would have accepted it, and I in that Case have been deemed a Coward, an Epithet which no one I believe ever yet tack'd to my Name'.[9] In addition to the Scots and English, the garrison now included a small contingent of Irishmen in the service of France under Captain Michael Brown of Lally's regiment. If the garrison successfully defended the castle, then they might be in a position to negotiate good terms, which the presence of 'French' troops (and thus prisoners of war) might facilitate. On this basis, the Jacobite army left Carlisle in the late morning on Friday, 20 December.

The British army began arriving in the vicinity of Carlisle only the following day. On the 22nd, from 'Blickhall' (that is Blackhall, where Charles had lodged) the duke writes to the Duke of Newcastle, 'I had heard on the march that the Rebels had quitted the Town the morning before & had left there between three & four hundred men, who according to the best accounts I could have, are most of them English recruits, & the rest Gordon of Glenbuckets men, commanded by one Hamilton.' These men 'endeavour to appear resolute, & have fired their Canon upon every body who has shewn Himself'. As he could not pursue the Jacobite army any further north, he considers 'it is better to wait the Canon which will arrive from Whitehaven in a day or two, than to expose our selves to any considerable loss against such an Enemy as this'. He lacked engineers, but with what he had to hand, the battery would be raised by the morning of the 24th and 'then in twenty four hours the Town will be ours, by Storm I hope, that We may at least have some revenge on these fellows, for the trouble they & the rest have given us'.[10] From this there is a suggestion that, for the duke, defeating the Jacobite army had now become personal.

The attack on Carlisle commenced a week after the British army's arrival. According to a later newspaper report, it stopped temporarily on the 29th for want of shot, until 'a fresh supply arriving, it was renewed very briskly for two Hours, which shook the Walls very much'. That night a new battery was raised of three eighteen-pounders, the guns from Whitehaven, which was ready for action by the morning. But 'on the first Platoon of the old Battery firing, the Rebels hung out the White Flag, whereupon the Battery ceased'. The castle governor, Colonel John Hamilton, sent a message asking what terms 'his Royal Highness will be pleased to give them, upon Surrender', to which the duke tersely responded, 'All the Terms his Royal Highness will or can grant to the Rebel Garrison of Carlisle, are, That they shall not be put to the Sword, but be reserv'd for the King's Pleasure.' If they agreed to these conditions 'the Governor and principal Officers are to deliver themselves up immediately, and the Castle, Citadel, and all the Gates of the Town, are to be taken Possession of forthwith by the King's Troops'. Small arms should be lodged in the Town Guard Room 'and the rest of the Garrison are to retire to the Cathedral, where a Guard is to be placed over them'. Finally, 'No Damage is to be done to the Artillery, Arms or Ammunition.'[11]

Not everyone agreed with Colonel Hamilton's decision to ask for terms of surrender. Colonel Towneley stated, 'I would have defended the City to the last Extremity, but Colonel *Hamilton*, God forgive him, counter-wrought my Resolutions, and giving up the Citadel, forced me also to surrender the Town.'[12] No doubt Towneley considered an honourable fight to the death preferable to the misery of a rebel's execution. The Duke of Cumberland, too, was disappointed by the ease with which the garrison surrendered, writing, 'I wish I could have blooded the soldiers with these Villains but it would have cost us many a brave man and it comes to the same end, as they have no sort of claim to the Kings mercy, & I sincerely hope will meet with none.'[13] He continues, regarding the surrender of Carlisle the previous month to the Jacobite forces, that it was the cause of all the troubles in 'this part' of the kingdom, meaning England, and is 'of so scandalous a nature, that it deserves the strictest enquiry & punishments'. Indeed, it would be to the benefit and future 'repose of the Kingdom', and His Majesty's current and future service, if 'some Examples were made in it'. To which end 'I have taken it upon myself to seize both the Mayor & Town Clerk of Carlisle, upon information that they both met the Pretenders Son, & proclaimed his Father'. He concludes, 'whether they did it out of fear or disaffection seems to me to be of the same bad consequence'.[14] Carlisle had allowed the Jacobite army to gain a foothold in England, and therefore Carlisle would be held up as an example.

Soon after, the duke must have received a letter from the Duke of Newcastle stating that 'His Majesty leaves it to your Royal Highness, if you think proper, and should judge it necessary to treat, and capitulate with Them, on condition of their being, all to be transported to the West Indies: For if they should all be made Prisoners of Discretion, The greatest Part of them must be disposed of in that manner.'[15] But events had obviously moved on. For now, though, the officers, including Colonel Towneley and Colonel Hamilton, were kept under guard in the castle, while the remainder were taken to the cathedral. James Miller, who had joined the Jacobite army at Preston during the retreat, states that he and his fellows imprisoned in the cathedral 'were barbarously treated, the souldiers rifling us and taking every thing of value from us both Money and Cloaths, they did not allow us any Provisions for three days, and on the fourth but one small Bisket a Man'. For sustenance, their guard 'broke open a well in the Body of the Church which had not been used for upwards of an hundred years. We was oblig'd to drink that or die of thirst, after we had been there five days, which I realy believe was for want of natural subsistence.'[16] It was clear that for rebels there would be no basic care or provisions, much less sympathy. After Carlisle's capture, the Duke of Cumberland returned to London to assist in the defence of the south-east from the expected French invasion.

An inventory of items left behind by the Jacobite army included 217 tents 'for private men', 226 tent poles, two officers' field bedsteads, three officers' mattresses, 414 drink canteens, 114 targets, 14 firelocks of which four 'want locks', one halberd, a weapon combining an axe blade and a long spear, one case of pistols, one Highland short coat, seven buff-coloured Dragoon Housings (protective cover for a saddle) and a 'bleu Velvet d[itt]o w[it]h Fringe', three red waistcoats, one 'Trunk wh Surgeons books & Medicins', four breeches and '4 Womens Gowns'. The list ends with '5 Shirts whereof one is to be broke to mend ye rest'.[17] The detritus of a hastily retreating army.

Unknown artist, *Lord George Murray*, c. 1745.
(BLAIR CASTLE, PERTHSHIRE)

38

Scotland

'on seeing their country again'

Prince Charles and his army reached the Esk, the main watery borderline between England and Scotland, at mid-afternoon on 20 December: his twenty-fifth birthday. After heavy rain, the normally shallow river had swollen, so that it was now four feet deep and the current dangerously strong. Lord George Murray recalled, 'I was this day in my philibeg [short kilt] . . . nothing encouraged the men more, than seeing their officers dressed like themselves, and ready to share their fate.'[1] The army also had to contend with the cold, rainy weather and the dwindling daylight. The cavalry was ordered to stand in the river to break the power of the current, while just downstream the infantry moved slowly through the water in groups of ten men abreast with arms linked. The entire manoeuvre took an hour. Captain Johnstone writes that fires were lit to dry the men 'and the bagpipers having commenced playing, the Highlanders began all to dance, expressing the utmost joy on seeing their country again; and forgetting the chagrin which had incessantly devoured them, and which they had continually nourished ever since their departure from Derby'.[2] Echoing this, Lord George recalled that 'the pipes began to play so soon as we passed, and the men all danced reels, which in a moment dried them, for they held the tails of their short coats in their hands in passing the river, so when their thighs were dry, all was right. It was near night.'[3] However, for those who had joined the army in England and had not been left at Carlisle, such as Captain John Daniel, this was not a homecoming; in fact the reverse.

The army then divided into two columns: the one led by Lord George travelled towards Moffat via Ecclefechan, and the other, with Prince Charles, marched to the north-west. Lord George recalled that those 'who went to Ecclefechan, had a very bad march, mostly through mossy ground, and our guides led us off the road. I found out that it was to shun houses, that our men might not go into them, and when they did not pass near them they could not see them.' They arrived late and exhausted. Lord George had caught 'a most violent cold and cough', not having changed his clothes since standing for several hours in the rain at Kendal followed by wading through freezing water and 'mid-thigh deep in moss'. But 'when I got myself washed with warm water, and oat meal and water – what the Highlanders call a brochin – in bed, at Ecclefechan, I was next day almost cured, and the day thereafter quite free of my cold and cough'.[4]

Lord Elcho and the cavalry moved directly to Dumfries, described by Captain Johnstone as 'a considerable town, full of fanatical Calvinists'.[5] Charles arrived here on 22 December. They had marched all night in driving rain, as Captain Daniel describes 'on excessive bad roads, all of us being very wet and cold, without any refreshment, except what we had before we left Carlisle'. However, on arriving in the town, they were 'as merry and gay as if they had only marched that morning'.[6] The reception from the 'fanatical Calvinists' was hardly welcoming. Captain Daniel noted the candles and bonfires, which had been lit in response to a reported Jacobite defeat. Indeed, some inhabitants of the town had taken some of the Jacobite army's ammunition waggons as they were passing south en route to England. As a result, in Captain Johnstone's words, 'We punished the inhabitants by levying a considerable fine on them.'[7] In addition, as reported in *The Scots Magazine*, the Jacobite army demanded '1000 pairs of shoes; seized about nine casks of gun-powder, all the arms publick and private, horse-furniture, boots, &c. every horse that could be found in town or country, and took free quarters'. As not all the money demanded had been paid, 'Provost Crosbie and Mr Walter Riddel were carried off as hostages, till the remainder should be remitted.' It was circulated that these men would be killed if anyone raised a finger against the Jacobite stragglers. *The Scots Magazine* continued that the Jacobite army 'were guilty of great outrages, having robbed and plundered several houses; and they told the people, they had reason to think themselves gently used, that their town was not laid in ashes. The damage done in the town cannot be repaired for 4000 l. but that done in the country is much greater.'[8]

Moving on northwards from Dumfries, the prince arrived at Drumlanrig Castle, the seat of the Douglas Dukes of Queensberry, on the night of 23 December. The family were Whigs and Unionists. The 2nd duke had not only supported William III, but had also been instrumental in steering the Articles of Union through the Scottish Parliament. The current duke, Charles, was then away. According to the nineteenth-century historian Robert Chambers, the prince 'occupied the state-bed, while a great number of his men lay upon straw in the great gallery'. Before departing, according to Chambers, 'the Highlanders took that opportunity of expressing their love of King James by slashing with their swords a series of portraits representing King William, Queen Mary, and Queen Anne, which hung in the grand staircase – a present from the last of these sovereigns to James, Duke of Queensberry, in consideration of his services at the Union'.[9] Having left Drumlanrig, Charles proceeded to Hamilton, staying at the magnificent palace of the Dukes of Hamilton. On Christmas Day, Charles occupied himself by shooting in the park 'in which he behaved to the admiration and surprise of all present, killing or hitting every thing he shot at, so that, without flattery, he was looked upon to be the best marksman in the army'.[10] For Christmas Day, the prince's household accounts note the purchase of 'a Turkie' at three shillings and two dozen pints of ale.[11]

An anonymous account, written by a resident of the nearby town of Hamilton, states that all was quite peaceful after the prince's arrival with an advance party of the clans, but specifically accuses 'the *Camerons, MacPhersons*, and *MacDonalds* of *Clan-Ronald's*', who arrived later, of being 'an undisciplin'd ungovernable Army of *Highland* Robbers, who took no more Notice of their nominal Prince, or Commanders, than a Pack of ill-bred Hounds'. The author was unimpressed by Charles, whom he saw dining, for he could not 'find out this Angel-like Prince amongst the whole Rabble, till he was pointed out to me'. There is the familiar complaint of citizens being robbed in the street – particularly being divested of their shoes – and although the author admits 'Amongst this Set of Ruffians there were some civil People', some of whom were lodged with his Aunt, he, on the other hand, 'had no less than 33 of them . . . of the worst Kind besides Horses and naked Whores'. In a description reminiscent of the angry citizen of Derby, on quitting the town on 27 December, the Highlanders are described as having 'left us nothing but an innumerable Multitude of Vermin, and their Excrements; which they left not only in our Bed-Chambers, but in our very Beds'. Indeed, the 'civilest Kind held their Doups over the Stock of the Beds, like Crows shiting over the Nest'. The letter is dated 6 January, but 'Our Town smells of them yet'. However, 'the Peoples Spirits are getting up, for while they were here, they look'd like dead Corps. They stop'd us from a merry Christmas, but God be thanked, we were bless'd with a merry New Year's Day. I wish you a happy New-Year, and Peace, which we now begin to learn to value.'[12]

Meanwhile, Lord George had reached Moffat on the 23rd and, rather than continuing to Edinburgh due north (as appeared to be his purpose), he turned north-west towards Glasgow, entering the city on Christmas Day. Captain Johnstone observed that 'Glasgow is the second city of Scotland, from the number of its inhabitants, and the extent of its commerce.'[13] In the late 1720s Captain Edmund Burt described the city as 'the prettiest and most uniform Town that I ever saw . . . I believe there is nothing like it in *Britain*.'[14] John Macky was even more impressed, declaring it 'the beautifullest little City I have seen in *Britain*', standing 'deliciously on the Banks of the River *Clyde*'. The four main streets, lined with houses of free stone, were 'spacious and well pav'd' and formed a cross or 'carrefour' with the Town House and Market Place at the centre.[15] As Captain Johnstone states, Glasgow was a wealthy trading town 'especially,' notes Macky, 'to the *Plantations*' of Maryland, Virginia and the West Indies from where their ships returned laden with tobacco and sugar.[16] This was 'an Advantage,' Macky continues, 'this Kingdom never enjoy'd till the Union'. By 1745, Glasgow's wealth was reflected by its major expansion to the west.

Macky also observes that Glasgow 'is strictly *Presbyterian*, and the best affected to this Government of any in *Scotland*'.[17] Aside from trade, the Provost of Glasgow, Andrew Cochrane, set out the city's allegiance to the House of Hanover, and thus the broadly held antagonism towards the Stuarts, in the following manner. Glasgow had long supported the principles that gave rise to the Glorious Revolution 'and for that adherence many of their inhabitants were confiscated, banished, and even murdered during the reigns of Charles II. and James VII'. The knowledge of this usage had been handed down from father to son, and as a result 'has created in them such a rooted and unconquerable aversion to the Pretender and his family, that there is almost nothing in life which they would not forgo to prevent their mounting the throne of Great Britain'.[18]

According to James Maxwell, Charles entered this decidedly anti-Jacobite town on 26 December 'on foot, at the head of the Clans'.[19] It seems his high spirits and urge to lead by example had returned. Captain Daniel recalled that 'we continued our march to one of the prittiest (but most whiggish) towns in all Scotland, viz., Glasgow. Here we arrived . . . much to their confusion.'[20] As Lord George had entered Glasgow the day before, it was resolved to rest the entire army here, 'which really stood in need of it, after such a long march performed in the severest season'. Yet, despite the fatigues, 'few complaints were ever heard. The Prince's example contributed not a little to the alacrity and cheerfulness the common men expressed on all occasions.'[21] Provost Cochrane's recollection was somewhat less enthusiastic, stating, 'On Friday the clans with the P—ce came to town. They attempted to huzza two or three times as he went to his lodgings, but fell through it, our mob with great steadiness declining to join in it. Our people of fashion kept out of the way; few or none at the windows; no ringing of bells, and no acclamation of any kind.'[22] The Provost is clearly establishing a contrast between the prince's reception in Glasgow and what he had enjoyed in Edinburgh.

Whether cheerful or not, the army had suffered greatly during the retreat. As described by Robert Chambers, 'the necessities of the army are described as having been at this time greater than at any other period of the campaign. It was now two months since they had left the land of tartan; their clothes were of course in a dilapidated condition.' Many were 'not only barefooted, but barelegged', with overgrown beards, their 'hair hung wildly over their eyes', and with exposed limbs 'tanned red with the weather'. 'Altogether,' he continues, 'they had a wayworn, savage appearance, and looked rather like a band of outlandish vagrants than a body of efficient soldiery. The pressure of want compelled them to take every practicable measure of supplying themselves; and, in passing towards Glasgow, they had stripped such natives as they met of their shoes and other articles of dress.'[23] To fit out his troops, Charles demanded from the magistrates 12,000 linen shirts, and 6,000 each of coats, pairs of stockings, bonnets, shoes and tartan hose. As Glasgow had also raised a militia via subscription from the local merchants and civic leaders, according to *The Gentleman's Magazine*, Charles demanded that the provost produce the list of subscribers on pain of execution.[24] Perhaps his recent experiences and the disappointment at Derby had made him impatient and less forgiving. Therefore, with good reason, Provost Andrew Cochrane later described the Jacobite occupation as 'our late unhappy Highland visit'.[25]

Charles took up residence at Shawfield Mansion, 'a house of unprecedented magnificence, surrounded by spacious gardens', located off the Trongate, then on the north-western edge of the city. During his stay, Charles apparently dined in public twice a day in the company of his officers.[26] From the household accounts kept by James Gib, we have some idea of what fare was served at these suppers. The purchases at Glasgow between 28 December and 4 January included forty-two dozen eggs, a dozen lemons, 'Spiceries' at ten shillings and four pence, fourteen pounds of sugar, fish, pickled oysters, cucumbers, twenty-three pounds of cheese, sausages, two pounds of rice, fifty-one pounds of butter, two partridges, eight 'fowls', five woodcocks, two hens, two geese, three ducks, six pigs, four gallons of ale and ten dozen apples.[27]

But most of the locals were decidedly unfriendly, a fact that Provost
Cochrane, writing to Mr Patrick Crawford in January 1746, considered to
be the real reason why Charles exacted such a heavy penalty on Glasgow:
his vanity. The prince 'appeared four times publickly on our streets, without acclamations or one huzza; no ringing of bells, or smallest respect or
acknowledgement paid him by the meanest inhabitant'. The ladies, in the
main, 'had not the curiosity to go near him, and declined going to a ball
held by his chiefs. Very few were at the windows when he made his appearance, and such as were declared him not handsome. This no doubt fretted.'
Cochrane states it had been suggested that if the magistrates and other
principal citizens would pay him a visit, the demands on Glasgow would
be lessened. This they declined. 'You see by this,' continues Cochrane,
'what was our unhappy situation under a government worse than French,
yea, even Turkish.'[28] In a similar vein, Provost Cochrane also observed that
when the magistrates refused to send a delegation 'their Prince was heard
to say, "That it was indeed a fine town, but he had no friends in it; and
what was worse, they were at no pains to hide it from him"'.[29]

Despite the retreat back into Scotland, the situation for the Jacobite
cause was hopeful. A review of Charles' troops on Glasgow Green revealed
that there had been few desertions. In fact, the whole adventure into
England and back was now billed as a public relations triumph. As James
Maxwell observed, previously Charles had carefully concealed the smallness of his army, 'but now thinking himself sure of doubling his army in
a few days, he was not unwilling to let the world see with what a handful
of men he had penetrated so far into England, and retired almost without
any loss'.[30] Captain John Daniel believed the review on Glasgow Green
was timed for the day after the men had been fed and provided with the
new clothing. They would therefore undoubtedly make a far better show
to the people of Glasgow than when they had first arrived. Fed and newly
kitted out, they marched 'with drums beating, colours flying, bag-pipes
playing, and all the marks of a triumphant army to the appointed ground,
attended by multitudes of people, who had come from all parts to see us,
[and] were now, charmed at the sight of the Prince, become most loyal'.[31]
The army gathered on the Green, in form, 'and every one putting himself
out for the best, the Prince rode through the ranks, greatly encouraging
and delighting all who saw him'.[32]

A bystander offers a different idea of the prince's manner while at
Glasgow: 'I managed to get so near him that I could have touched him
with my hand; and the impression which his appearance made upon my

mind shall neer fade from it as long as I live.' Charles 'had a princely aspect; and its interest was much deepened by the dejection that appeared in his pale countenance and downcast eye. He evidently wanted confidence in his own cause.'[33] In reality, Charles required no further confidence in his cause – he was very clear and robust on this. What he now lacked was complete confidence in his officers. For the events at Derby, from Charles' perspective, had made it abundantly clear that there was a limit to what these men, collectively, would be willing to do. The prince's personal desires, as well as his judgement, had not only been queried, but over-ruled. Furthermore, Charles would now be aware that the idea for a Stuart restoration, among a majority of his Scottish officers, was less ambitious than his. Essentially there was, perhaps had always been, a disjuncture of aim and purpose. It might be useful here to contrast the behaviour of the duke of Cumberland's officers. Of course, officers in a regular army obeyed orders whether they liked them or not. But not one of them queried the duke's methods; indeed, they followed him with absolute confidence and very cheerfully, too. Seasoned commanders like Sir John Ligonier openly stated their admiration and even love for him. No matter how loyal his officers were to the Stuart cause, Charles did not have complete, unerring and unquestioning personal loyalty and obedience.

Charles also behaved differently on his return to Scotland. Unlike his rather distant behaviour in Edinburgh towards the women, who, as a result, had to content themselves with a glimpse of him, at Glasgow he took part in dancing, being very conspicuous in his lavish behaviour, and, crucially, wore fine French clothes of silk, rather than Highland garb. As Lord Elcho states, 'The Prince sometime after his arrival at Glasgow road through the town dress'd in the French dress attended by his Guards', and 'Supp'd every night in publick and their was always a great deal of Company came to See him'.[34] James Gib noted that the 'Prince dressed more elegantly when in Glasgow that he did in any other place whatsomever'.[35] It has been suggested that the change of dress indicated Charles' acceptance that his warrior stance had failed. But the prince had already been seen on many occasions in fashionable 'English' or European, rather than 'Highland' dress. Rather, the extravagant dress and behaviour declared to the world that all was far from lost.

Provost Cochrane stated that Charles appeared 'twice in all his mock majesty, going and coming from a review at our green, without the small-est acclamation, or lest respect or acknowledgement paid by the mean-est inhabitant'.[36] However, his presence had been very much felt by the demands made on the town, for 'beside free quarters to there whole army for ten days, which cost the inhabitants £4000, and the £5500 formerly extorted from us. By there own confession all the money they got in England, including Taxes, was not above £7300; so that we have suffered by far more than any other place in Brittan.' In addition to the direct losses, the period of occupancy had an impact 'by stop of trade, sales, payments, bad debts and otherwise'.[37] For the time being, some individual livelihoods as well as local and regional economies – rural and urban – had clearly been affected north and south of the border.

Having now arrived at Scotland's second major town, Charles had time to consider his current position. Edinburgh had been retaken within days of the Jacobite army leaving for England; however, a second Jacobite army was gathering around Perth. Lady Anne MacIntosh had raised her husband's clan under MacGilvray of Dunmaglas, and Lady Fortrose had gathered together a regiment from the Mackenzies, though both were wives of men loyal to King George. Lord John Macleod and Lord Cromartie had brought in the main Mackenzie regiment, plus reinforcements from the west with MacDonald of Barisdale and young Glengarry. Lord Lovat had finally, openly, sided with the prince (he had been working behind the scenes all along), after being captured by Lord Loudoun and taken to Inverness. The reason for his arrest was that, in mid-October, James Fraser had at Lovat's request attempted to kidnap Lord President Forbes from Culloden House. After this failure there was no turning back, and on Lovat's escape on 19 December he immediately raised his clan. So, now one option for this expanded Jacobite army was to march to Edinburgh and recapture the city, which would have the effect of forcing a battle with the British army, something the prince was not keen to do just yet. He still hoped that a return to England was imminent, as soon as there was a report of his brother landing in the south-east.

While at Glasgow, news arrived which reduced the likelihood of a return south: the fall of Carlisle. James Maxwell states that it was delivered by 'two officers of the garrison, who had made their escape over the walls after the capitulation was signed'.[38] One of these officers was Captain Michael Brown of Lally's. John Daniel recalled that it 'was at first hard to be believed amongst us: but it appearing but too true, the Prince was exceedingly troubled, and lamented much the loss of his subjects, especially the English, who were to be made sacrifice of'.[39] However, Maxwell continues that this news would have hit the morale of the army harder, if it had not been for a previous report of a Jacobite victory near Inverurie a few days before.[40]

This was an encounter, on 23 December, between Norman MacLeod of Macleod and some newly raised companies of MacLeod clansmen from Skye, plus two Monro companies under the command of Captain George Monro of Culcairn, against a Jacobite force from Aberdeen of predominantly Lowlanders plus two companies of Lord John Drummond's Royal Ecossais under Lord Lewis Gordon. Men from Clan Grant had initially accompanied MacLeod and his detachment, but, prior to the battle, they had been ordered back to their lands to protect them. As reported, it was a Jacobite victory and in fact it was an important one, because the MacLeod and Monro companies fled across the Spey to the west, some deserting, and Lord Loudoun was forced to abandon the entire area around Aberdeen to Lords Lewis Gordon and John Drummond, who, for the time being, were able to range around as they liked.[41] As Maxwell concludes, 'the reputation of a victory is always of great consequence, particularly in civil wars'.[42] Lord Loudoun, with Lord President Forbes, remained at Inverness.

Thus recharged, on 3 January 1745/6 (OS) Charles and his men marched out of Glasgow. Meanwhile, the December issue of *The Scots Magazine* summarised the current situation in the following manner: 'Towards the end of December, the highland army at Glasgow were repairing to march Northward, their friends in the North to march South to join them, and the troops in England were in motion in Scotland.' The article concludes, 'so that we have the mortification to see our native country likely to be made again the seat of the war'.[43]

Louis Surugue, *Prince Charles Edward Stuart, c.* 1746.
(NATIONAL PORTRAIT GALLERY, LONDON)

Falkirk

'My heart is broke'

The Jacobite army left Glasgow in two columns. The first, commanded by Lord George, took the route to Cumbernauld and the second, with Charles, marched to Kilsyth.[1] Lord Elcho with the cavalry advanced to Falkirk to the north-west of Edinburgh, so giving the impression that the Scottish capital was once more the Jacobite army's destination. On 4 January the two columns joined near Stirling. One reason for rendezvousing here, according to Captain Johnstone, was to 'accelerate his junction with Lord John Drummond, whom he had ordered to repair to Alloa with the three thousand men under his command, and the artillery and military stores which he had brought from France'.[2] It should be noted that Lord John had been in Scotland for over a month and had shown no inclination to advance into England. Nor indeed had Lord Strathallan, despite having been ordered to do so. However, a day after Charles and his men had arrived at Stirling, Lord John wrote to Colonel John Roy Stuart (from Alloa, to the east of Stirling), stating, 'your returne has put us prety much in the Dumps here may heaven direct you and preserve the prince'.[3] This was largely because the opposition were turning the retreat to their psychological advantage, 'which is to intimidat and dispirit the princes frends here as much as possible and as wee have no newes but thro that channel youll easely imagen the situation wee are in'. As a result, he continues, 'for god sake if you have any good newes fall upon some way to let us know it, I wold be the faithfull publisher of evry thing thats dear to me could it be of the least use to my prince, and may never any friend of mine experience so money [many] uneasy moments as I have had since you left Edinburgh'.[4] With luck, Stirling would provide the happy news.

The aim was to capture the castle, an action that had arguments for and against it. On the one hand, the mighty castle of Stirling, like its neighbour at Edinburgh, had yet to be taken during this campaign and therefore its capture now would be a significant boost to overall morale and the army's reputation. At the same time, its loss would be a major blow to the British army and government. Stirling was the gate to the Highlands and therefore would act as a strategic base for operations to the north and south – potentially, despite the loss of Carlisle, their march back into England.

Captain Johnstone considered the whole endeavour futile because of the temperament and outlook of the Highland contingent, which was built for the swift battle charge rather than a slow, laborious siege. And, as previously seen, they were prone to wander off and even head home if inactive. But despite this, a siege was decided upon and Charles took up residence at Bannockburn House, the residence of Sir Hugh Paterson two miles from Stirling. Part of the army was cantoned in the villages of St Dennis and St Ninian, which were 'within cannon-shot of the town'.[5] Lord George travelled immediately to Alloa to organise the swift advance of the French artillery (which was needed to penetrate the formidable castle walls), as well as the men under Lord John Drummond's command, after which Lord George retired with the clans to nearby Falkirk. Lord Elcho was now stationed with the cavalry at Linlithgow.[6] While at Falkirk, Lord George entertained the clansmen by organising a sortie to plunder the large food stores the townspeople of Linlithgow had been gathering for the British army.[7]

Meanwhile, in Newcastle upon Tyne, Lieutenant General Henry Hawley had taken command of the army from Marshal Wade. Wade had written to the Duke of Newcastle asking that he should not be honoured with the command in Scotland: partly because he was too old and exhausted after recent events, but, in addition, quite frankly, because he was in despair that all the work he had overseen after the '15, specifically to prevent another rebellion, had been frittered away over the subsequent decades by a high-handed administration in London. 'Your Grace knows very well,' he wrote, 'the pains I took for many years in the Highland's to prevent the mischiefs which have now happned; but my opinion was not followed.'[8] He believed he was disliked north of the border and did not have the heart or stomach to get involved. The Duke of Cumberland was no doubt relieved. The new commander immediately moved his troops northwards. They arrived in Edinburgh in two columns on 2 and then 10 January, during an increasingly bitter winter. From the intelligence of the Jacobite army's advance, there had been every potential that Edinburgh would once again be their target. But it was now known that they had occupied Glasgow before moving to Stirling to besiege the town and castle.

As a result, Lieutenant General Hawley and his men, who included the Glasgow volunteers, marched towards Falkirk.

On 6 January, on the arrival at Stirling of Lord John Drummond (the French artillery arrived later on the 14th) the trenches were opened in front of the town under the direction of the comte Mirabel de Gourdon, who had arrived from France with Lord John. He soon proved of little use. Captain Johnstone said of him that 'he had not the shadow of judgment, discernment, or good sense; his figure being as ridiculous as his spirits',[9] while Lord George declared that he was 'so volatile, that he could not be depended upon'.[10] The outer defences of the town of Stirling were in a dilapidated state and after assurances that no harm would come to them or their property, the officials opened the gates on 8 January. But the garrison within the castle, consisting of several hundred men and still under the command of Major General William Blakeney, manned a fortress in a good state of repair and refused to surrender. While the siegeworks were under way, Charles lay ill at Sir Hugh Paterson's house with what Lord George dismissed as a 'bad coald'[11] and was nursed by Sir Hugh's niece, Clementina Walkinshaw. Clementina had been named after Charles' mother, the Princess Sobieska, an indication of the family's loyalties. It is not surprising that after all the stresses of the campaign so far, and in the middle of a bitter winter, Charles should now succumb to exhaustion and illness.[12]

Meanwhile, the prince's army had been significantly augmented. Captain Johnstone lists the new troops, aside from Lord John Drummond, his regiment the Royal Ecossais and five picquets of the Irish brigade, as: Lord Lewis Gordon and 600 'vassals of his brother' the Duke of Gordon (the supporter of King George); Simon Fraser, the eldest son of Lord Lovat, accompanied by 600 of the Clan Fraser; the Earl of Cromartie; his eldest son John; and Lord Macleod with men from the Mackenzies. There were also the members of the clans Mackintosh and Farquharson under 'Colonel' Lady Mackintosh. As a result, 'by this reinforcement our army was suddenly increased to eight thousand men, the double of what it was when we were in England'.[13] James Maxwell also observes that 'Lord Ogilvie had got a second battalion much stronger than the first' commanded by Sir James Kinloch. As Maxwell continues, all 'looked mighty well, and were very hearty' and that 'In fine, all were at hand in high spirits, and expressed the greatest ardour upon the prospect of a battle.'[14] The overall strategy was to consolidate and expand their gains in Scotland (both in regard to territory and manpower), and to defeat and then push the British army back out of the country – as they had done at Prestonpans – while awaiting support from France.

Learning that the British army was on the move, Lord George marched his men away from Falkirk to Stirling. A field of battle was reconnoitred on 15 January and the following day Charles (now recovered) reviewed his army. On the evening of the 16th they received word that Lieutenant General Hawley was at Falkirk and had 'encamped his whole army on the plain betwixt that town and the river Carron'.[15] During a council of war, it was decided to march the next day towards the British army encampment. As Hawley had not advanced to meet them, the battlefield previously chosen was now redundant. Instead it was decided, on Lord George's recommendation, to take Falkirk Hill lying to the south-west of the town and overlooking the British camp – as Lord George recalled, 'a thing they did not expect. I knew the ground well, and thought there was no difficulty of taking it before they could.' Battle lines were drawn up and agreed to and Charles was 'much pleased with the design'.[16] There is some debate as to the actual numbers in the Jacobite army at this time. Captain Johnstone's claim of 8,000 in total agrees with James Maxwell's comment that the army advancing east from Stirling 'did not amount to seven thousand fighting men, but they were all in fine spirits, and confident of victory',[17] if, that is, a thousand men were left to continue the siege. The muster-master, Henry Patullo, states that 'at the battle of Falkirk, there were 8000 men, besides about 1000 left to continue the blockade of Stirling Castle'.[18] The army, as observed almost double that at Derby, began its march towards Falkirk at about midday. The 1,000 men left at Stirling were commanded by the Duke of Perth.

As James Maxwell continues, it was 'the Prince's intention to gain the summit of the hill, and thence march directly down upon the enemy, if there remained enough of day-light; if not, the army was to remain there under arms all night, and begin the attack at day break next morning'.[19] Lord John Drummond, with some cavalry and foot, was sent out to distract Lieutenant General Hawley.

The British army troops in the encampment, roughly equal to the Jacobite army (i.e. 9,000), had no idea what was advancing towards them on the other side of Falkirk Hill. On hearing of the approach of Lord John Drummond and his small detachment, Hawley at his quarters in Callendar House (Lord Kilmarnock's residence) is stated by John Home (who was still a volunteer with the British army) to have said, and with no hint of urgency, that 'the men might put on their accoutrements, but there was no necessity for them to be under arms'.[20] At this point, no one was sent to see if the main body was following Lord John's detachment. However, between one and two o'clock in the afternoon, scouts patrolling the area suddenly 'came in upon the spur, and reported that the rebel army was advancing'.[21] There was then a scramble to form up the British army troops, during which 'one might hear the officers saying to one another, where is the General? what shall be done? we have no orders', while the commanding officers led by Major General John Huske improvised and 'formed their regiments upon the ground in the front of their camp'.[22] When Hawley, who was still at Callendar House, received word of the Jacobite army's approach, he leapt on his horse and rode straight for the top of Falkirk Hill to view the situation for himself, ordering that the dragoons commanded by Colonel Francis Ligonier (Sir John's brother who had taken command of Colonel Gardiner's regiment) should be brought up immediately, with the infantry and artillery forming behind them as soon as possible. The order was delivered to Colonel Ligonier by his close friend Stuart Mackenzie (brother to Lord Bute), who was Hawley's aide-de-camp. Later Mackenzie could not recall whether the colonel said that it was the most extraordinary order that was ever given, or whether he simply 'looked as if he thought so'.[23] After all, the dragoon regiments had not covered themselves in glory during the campaign so far and had proved completely ineffectual against a Highland charge. General Hawley on the other hand, himself an experienced cavalry officer, had been overheard saying after Prestonpans (by Lieutenant Colonel Hepburn), that he believed the Highanders were 'good milita', yet 'he was certain that they could not stand against a charge of dragoons who attacked them well'.[24] Hawley had led a successful attack by dragoons at Sheriffmuir in 1715.

Brigadier General James Cholmondeley, who was commanding infantry, recalled marching towards Falkirk Hill 'to the Left near half a mile, but as we had hollow roads, and very uneven Ground, to pass, we were in a great Confusion. Here we formed again, in my Opinion a very good Situation', but 'we were no sooner form'd but order'd a second time, to take Ground to the Left, and as we march'd, all the way up the hill, and Over very uneven Ground our men were greatly blown'.[25] As Cholmondeley's description suggests, after a dull and cloudy start a storm was now brewing. John Home wrote that 'by and by a storm of wind and rain beat directly in the face of the soldiers, who were marching up the hill with their bayonets fixed, and could not secure their pieces [guns] from the rain'.[26]

The battle proper began at just before four o'clock. In reality it was a muddled affair, fought predominantly in the dying daylight and in this increasingly fierce storm. Lord George believed that the Jacobite army had 'infinite advantage' from their position on Falkirk Hill, that is 'the nearness of the attack, the descent of a hill, the strong wind and rain which was in their backs, and directly in the enemy's face'. Also, that the Jacobite army 'had some mossy ground upon their right, which prevented the enemy's horse from being able to flank them' and finally, for the British army, 'that by reason of the badness of the road, and steepness of the hill, their cannon were of no use to them'. In Lord George's opinion 'the Highland army had all the advantages that nature or art could give them'.[27]

John Home recalled Colonel Francis Ligonier with the cavalry 'was a good way before the infantry, and for some time it seemed a sort of race between the Highlanders and the dragoons, which of them should get first to the top of the hill'.[28] The Jacobite right wing led by Lord George – his wig in his pocket and his bonnet 'scrogged'[29] – consisting of MacDonalds with the Athollmen behind, were 'a full quarter of an hour in sight of the enemy's horse, and within musket shot'. This right wing 'advanced very slowly, both that they might keep their ranks (which they did perfectly well) and to give time to the left to come up and form'. This was done in great order, as later recalled by Lord George, who went 'alongst the line all the time, and desiring them to keep their ranks, and not to fire till he gave the order'. The dragoons (Ligonier's, Cobham's and Hamilton's) moved to engage the Jacobite right wing, and when 'they came at last at the full trot, in very good order, within pistol shot of the first line' Lord George gave the order to fire. This halted the dragoons' charge in its tracks, after which all three regiments turned about and fled, Hamilton's back down the hill and crashing through the Glasgow volunteers located directly behind them. Meanwhile, Lord George could not prevent the MacDonalds from pursuing the dragoons, with the remaining front line following the MacDonalds. In the ensuing confusion, most of the British army infantry – blindly marching uphill with the wind and rain in their faces – panicked and fled back downhill. As Home described the scene, 'it seemed a total rout; and for some time General Hawley did not know that any one regiment of his army was standing'. But the British army infantry on their right wing, including Barrell's and Ligonier's foot under Brigadier General Cholmondeley (with Captain James Wolfe) and Lieutenant Colonel George Stanhope held fast, firing at the charging Highlanders 'by our Front Rank's kneeling, and the Center and Rear Ranks firing continually upon them'.[30] As seen at Fontenoy, this was the British army's standard form of firing at an enemy: usually, of course, a regular army advancing methodically, rather than charging. According to Home, 'the stand which these regiments made put a stop to the pursuit' and 'recalled the pursuers; who, when they heard so much fire behind them, turned back, and made what haste they could to the ground where they stood before the battle began, expecting to find their second line; but when they came there, the second line was not to be found'.

In the middle of all this was the British Army fusilier captain George Fitzgerald, who described later how he

> was knock'd down by a Muskett ball wch went thorow my hatt & wig & graz'd my head but I rose again being only stunn'd by it, and perceiv'd the left wings of both lines broke & retreating down the Hill, I observ'd the army still form'd on the right and was endeavouring to make that way, but was surrounded again by a party of the Rebells who cut me in the head & knock'd me down a 2[n]d time when they began to rob me, & as I immagin'd wou'd have afterwards murder'd me, but I call'd out to a French soldier going by and desir'd he wou'd not suffer those Villains to kill me, and he immediatly came to my assisstance & prevented their doing me any further mischief.

Captain Fitzgerald was now, however, a prisoner and was carried 'over a Muir that was, as I thought 2 miles from the field of Battle where the Pretender's son was, with a number of Horsemen abt him standing with his backe to an Hutt to shelter them from the weather, it raining & blowing excessively hard'.[31]

On the battlefield, Brigadier General Cholmondeley's men were still holding firm and, according to Colonel O'Sullivan, in support of John Home, took the Jacobite left 'in flanc & oblidged them to retire in disorder'. At this, as he continues, there 'was no remedy nor succor to be given them' as the second line 'went off, past the river & some of them even went to Banocburn, & Sterling, where they gave out [that] we lost the day'.[32] Lord George had continued the advance with the Athollmen, and observed the disorder among the British army infantry 'running off by forties and fifties to the right and left to get into Falkirk', excepting 'those in the rear', that is, the troops under Cholmondeley and Stanhope, with Howard's and other regiments led by Major General Huske. Lord George hoped to attack the retreating men, but having discovered 'that there were three or four regiments of the enemy at the rear, in better order than the rest' and considering 'as he had not about six or seven hundred men with him, the rest being all scattered on the face of the hill, he judged it would be risking all the advantages they had gained'.[33] John Home recalled, 'At this moment the field of battle presented a spectacle seldom seen in war, who great events Fortune is said to rule. Part of the King's army, much the greater part, was flying to the eastward, and part of the rebel army was flying to the westward.'[34]

The remainder of the British army had rallied in front of their camp, but the 'storm of wind and rain continued as violent as ever: night was coming on'.[35] Lieutenant General Hawley abandoned the Falkirk camp, setting fire to the tents, as 'the weather was so severe' and fearing 'to destroy the Men by lying on their Arms all Night, wet to the Skin, subject to continuall Alarms'.[36] After which the general and his men withdrew to Linlithgow, 'leaving behind him seven pieces of cannon, with a great quantity of provision, ammunition, and baggage'.[37]

At Linlithgow that same day, Hawley wrote a distraught letter to the Duke of Cumberland which opened with the line 'My heart is broke' and then continued, at times illegibly, with an outpouring of emotion that swings between shock, anger and despair: 'I cant say wee are quite beat to day, but our left is beat and theyr left is beat, wee had [two?] thousand men more than they but [suche?] scandalous cowardice I never saw before the whole second line of foot ran away without firing a shott'. With reference to the dragoons, 'three squadrons did well the others as usuall'. He then writes, with greater control, 'I must beg leave to refer youre Royall Highness to my nexte for particulars', although 'I muste say one thinge, that every Officer did theyr duty and what was in the power of man to do in trying to stop and rally the men and they led them on with as good a countenance till a halloo began before a single shott was fired, and at five hundred yards distance, then I owne I began to give it over.' He concludes, 'wee were niether surprised nor attacqued wee met them halfe way, and rather attacqued them, tho they were still in motion'. He signs off as 'the most unhappy but moste dutifull' Henry Hawley.[38]

As John Home observes, 'In this ill-conducted battle, many brave officers of the King's army fell.'[39] Twenty officers were killed out of seventy losses in total, and these from only five regiments (Ligonier's, Wolfe's, Blakeney's, Cholmondeley's and Monro's), including Lieutenant Colonel Shugborough of Ligonier's Dragoons, Lieutenant Colonel Maurice Powell of Cholmondeley's Foot and Colonel Sir Robert Monro of Monro's. Sir Robert's death was described in a letter to the Lord President by his distressed son Harry:

My father, after being deserted, was attacked by six of Locheal's Reg^t, & for some time defended himself w^t his half Pike [or spontoon]. Two of the six, I'm inform'd, he kill'd; a seventh, coming up, fired a Pistol into my father's Groin; upon wch falling, the Highlander w^h his sword gave him two strokes in the face, one over the Eyes & another on the mouth, wch instantly ended a brave Man.[40]

Harry had also lost his uncle Duncan, a doctor, who was shot in the chest while assisting his brother. Both were buried in Falkirk churchyard at the direction of the Earl of Cromartie with the clan chiefs in attendance. The casualties among the rank and file were far fewer because, frankly, they had run away before they had been in any danger. Thus abandoned and exposed, as seen at Prestonpans and as described by Sir Harry Monro, the officers disproportionately took the brunt.

The Jacobite army held the field and some of their troops had entered Falkirk, allowing Prince Charles to declare it a victory. However, Captain Johnstone believed the 'honour of remaining masters of the field was of little avail to us', and that 'we considered it, at most, as undecided, and expected a renewal of the combat next morning'.[41] To put it another way, the Jacobite army had not decisively won. As Colonel O'Sullivan had recounted, some of the Jacobite infantry had also fled the field and, in choosing not to pursue the British army troops, Charles' men did not behave like a victorious army. This failure to pursue was explained by a Jacobite broadsheet printed at Bannockburn (dated the day of the battle), which stated, 'Had not the Night come on, and so stormy, his Royal Highness's Army would have got betwixt them and Linlithgow, and would have utterly destroy'd them.'[42] This account also declares (erroneously) that in addition to officers, the Jacobite army had taken 700 rank and file prisoners, with 600 killed on the battlefield, besides 'what we are told were drowned in fording the River Carron. We had not above forty Men killed on our Side.'[43] The final casualties on the Jacobite side were fifty killed and up to eighty wounded.

Lord George later queried the broadsheet account, stating that it omitted mistakes that were the actual reason why the battle was not as decisive as it should have been.[44] As an example, Lord George believed that had 'the MacDonalds on the right, either not broke their ranks or rallied soon after, they, with the Athollmen, would have cut the whole enemy's foot to pieces, for they were close at them. And must have drove them down the hill before them; and by speed of foot, not a man of them could have got off from them.' Lord George also blamed Colonel O'Sullivan for not appointing an officer to command the left wing (if correct, it does seem a rudimentary error) and which, if well commanded, in his opinion 'would have had a complete victory'. But, 'most of the officers were with his Royal Highness in the reserve'[45] as Captain Fitzgerald could verify, and they did not advance until much later. Lord Macleod stated that after the battle, he found Charles 'in a little hutt on the top of the hill, where he was sitting by the fireside' in the company of Sir Thomas Sheridan and Colonel O'Sullivan.[46] He also observes, 'Had our army been disciplin'd or', more damningly, 'had we been commanded by experience'd generals, I am fully convinc'd that we wou'd have cut the King's army to pieces.'[47] According to John Home, Lord John Drummond and others blamed Lord George for not unleashing the MacDonald regiments on to the fleeing British army infantry, while Colonel O'Sullivan was blamed, in turn, for 'keeping out of harm's way'.[48] Whatever the truth of it, Charles entered Falkirk that evening, with the army following the next day. The general expectation would have been to pursue Hawley and his men as quickly as possible and finish them off. But even so, the Jacobite army had gained a considerable success at what was only their second full-scale confrontation with the British army: a success not against predominantly raw recruits as seen at Prestonpans, but against seasoned veterans, and (like the previous battle) under an experienced commander.

The day of 18 January was spent in the vicinity of Falkirk and here, despite his later misgivings, Lord George wrote to his brother, Tullibardine, of the prince's 'totall Victory over his Enemys', although he concludes his note with the urgent line, 'For God's sake send up our Recrutes.'[49] News that courts-martial were being set up in Edinburgh was taken as proof of the disarray of the British army command after the battle. One clansman stated that 'we were all in top spirits, and, I believe, had certainly followed Mr Hally [Hawley]'. But that day Glengarry's son Colonel Angus MacDonell was accidentally shot and killed by a Clanranald clansman, who had been, as Lord Elcho recalled, 'working with his Gun, Car[e]lesly, which the highlanders are too apt to do . . . The fellow was order'd immediately to be Shot in order to prevent mischeif happing between the two Clans.'[50] Donald MacDonell of Lochgarry described it as a 'melancholy and misfortunate accident' and that Angus was 'ador'd and regretted by H.R.Hs. and the whole army. His death really dispirited the whole Highlanders very much.' Angus was buried at Falkirk church alongside Sir Robert and Dr Duncan Monro. Far from quieting any unrest, however, the execution was followed by 'a general desertion in the whole army'.[51] Despite this, according to Lord Elcho several chiefs wanted to advance to Edinburgh and drive Hawley out. But Charles was determined to take Stirling Castle, and so, on 19 January, the Jacobite army returned to continue the siege, and took up their previous billets in the surrounding area.

However, the discord within the Jacobite command had clearly begun to leak out, in particular the idea propagated by Sir John Macdonald and others, that Lord George was, indeed always had been, a traitor in their midst. The retreat from Derby had certainly done nothing to improve Lord George's relationship with Charles. In response to a letter dated 18 January sent by an unnamed individual, George Colville, who had accompanied the Marquess of Tullibardine to Blair Castle 'to raise all the Men he possibly can in this country and to carry them over as fast as possible for our Dear Princes service', mentions a 'bad Report' concerning 'a near Friend of the marquess'. If, Colville writes, 'you mean Ld. George, I can assure you from my personal knowledge that it is a most malicious & villainous Aspersion hatched by some envious Person'. Not only has Lord George 'most justly acquired great Honour and Reputation on account of his Conduct, Valour and Intrepidity as well as sincere attachment to our king and country's cause', but he 'has acquired such Esteem and Respect amongst the Clans that I heard, very lately, some of their Chiefs declare they would never wish for a better General, and that they would chearfully follow wherever Ld. George would lead them'. Colville had himself 'heard some such malicious Innuendos since I came to this Country. What Pity it is that so deserving a Man should be so scandalously misrepresented? But the best of Men have Enemies, and much better be envied as pitied.'[52] As John Home wrote in conclusion to his description of the Battle of Falkirk, 'Altercation, contention, and animosity, prevailed in this irregular and undisciplined army, which it was not an easy matter to command.'[53]

Although far from disastrous, overall, neither can the Battle of Falkirk be described as a great day for the British army. A large force of predominantly seasoned regulars had failed to defeat 'a rabble'. And one predictable consequence was the return of the Duke of Cumberland, now as commander-in-chief in Scotland.

J. Harvie, *Stirling from St. Ninians*, before February 1745/6.
(STIRLING SMITH ART GALLERY AND MUSEUM)

Stirling

'have I lived to see this'

From Carlisle, Major General Howard wrote to Sir Everard Fawkener in late January, offering his condolences to the Duke of Cumberland, who was now preparing to travel to Scotland as a result of 'this last misfortune'. He also observes, 'I hear Court Martials are going on at Edinburgh, & that our men have promist to do well the next time, which I heartily hope they will.'[1] At about the same time, Horace Walpole wrote to Horace Mann that the 'great dependence is upon the Duke; the soldiers adore him; and with reason: he has a lion's courage, vast vigilance and activity; and, I am told, great military genius'.[2] Meanwhile, as Major General Howard had observed (and the Jacobites had since learned), Lieutenant General Hawley was busy organising courts-martial in the wake of Falkirk. On 19 January, he had written to the duke regarding the infantry (his second letter since the battle), stating, 'I cant helpe thinking they ought to be decimated [one in ten executed], I will proceed towards it at least, and as to the Dragoons I mean Hamiltons particularly, if there was some marke of ignomony put on the men till they regained theyr caracter, I thinke it might have some effect, your Royal Highness is a better judge.'[3] The duke eventually responded to Hawley's first, harassed letter of 17 January (from St James's on 23 January) saying that he had deferred writing until another account confirmed the situation, '& to day the desired account arrived which has eased people's minds vastly. I sincerely congratulate you on the King's being entirely satisfied with your conduct on that disagreeable occasion. I can assure you that I think that you have done wonders in coming off so after such a Pannick was struck in the Troops.'[4]

Regarding the behaviour of the dragoons, he says, 'I am not surprised. For, escaping the first time made them like safe methods,' and then states that 'for the future Officers should especially be made examples of'. He also shows empathy for Hawley 'having felt such a distress myself' (at Fontenoy), and then says, 'For God's sake, purge the Foot; for, they did not use to run away formerly.' It is not clear whether he is advocating something like 'decimation', pre-empting Hawley's later suggestion, or simply hard punishment such as flogging. He begs Hawley to 'continue your correspondence with me, as the times are so interesting', an elegant understatement, and then signs off 'your affectionate friend, William'.[5]

At Stirling the siegeworks continued, with General Blakeney, who was still refusing to surrender, continually firing on Charles' men. The prince visited the trenches only once, which was unlikely to encourage them. Provisions were also low. By 28 January the comte de Mirabel had raised a battery of three guns on Gowan Hill near the castle and was firing at it, causing some damage to the exterior wall. But General Blakeney responded with well-aimed fire from nine nine-pounders, which demolished the Jacobite battery in a few hours. No one could work out whether Mirabel was just incompetent or had been bribed.[6] Meanwhile on 21 January, Charles wrote a letter to King Louis, informing him of his recent victory at Falkirk:

> This victory removes my difficulties for the present, but your Majesty will recognise that the contest will be very unequal if I do not receive much more help soon. The troops and officers commanded by Lord John Drummond which have been sent me have distinguished themselves and it is plain to see from this what a greater number might achieve. If the invasion which I have been expecting for so long now takes place, all will soon be over; otherwise each day will see me forced to risk my life and all my hopes with an enemy who will soon have all the resources he needs.

He concludes, 'In the meantime I am in dire need of money.'[7] The officer entrusted with delivering the letter was Captain Michael Brown of Lally's. He sailed to Dunkirk in the former Royal Navy sloop *Le Prince Charles*, to the delight of the French court. Brown also delivered a letter from Sir Thomas Sheridan to Daniel O'Brien in which he describes the Battle of Falkirk and then the Jacobite army's current condition: 'We are like the old man who said, I am feeling very well, thank God, but I am going to die soon. The difference is that we depend solely on our allies to change the end of that sentence and to put paid to all our fears. But no time should be lost, particularly in sending us money.'[8] The duc de Richelieu had finally called a halt to the full invasion by the end of January, but, on receiving news of the Battle of Falkirk, some privateers were now preparing to transport the French cavalry regiment, the Fitz-James Horse, to the north-east coast of Scotland, with yet more transports (gathering at Ostend and Dunkirk) to follow, carrying more regiments, including Clare's and Berwick's, the latter under the command of Charles' cousin, James Fitz-James Stuart, duc de Berwick.[9]

The Duke of Cumberland had left London on the morning of 25 January. En route, he received another letter from Lieutenant General Hawley, dated 28 January, which refers to the duke's of the 23rd, and the 'goodness to me, there expressed, has rejoiced my grateful soule, and your coming here has given the greatest pleasure to every body, but in the strongest manner to me'.[10] Here was a man full of contrition. He continues, 'I sollemly protest, that the sincer desyr of allways serving under you by farr out weighs all the vanity that could have crept into my thoughts, I hope I never had muche that unfortunate day was enough to cure all I had. twas a rough remedy, but I hope will do me good.' The duke's support may well have saved Hawley from the ignominy of a court martial himself, but, beyond the expected flattery, the sentiments in Hawley's letter offer another example of the heartfelt admiration and faith that these seasoned soldiers had for their commander, who was still only twenty-four years old. In fact, despite the unsatisfactory outcome of the recent battle, which none the less many in the British army did not consider a defeat, the situation at Edinburgh was optimistic. Reinforcements had been arriving over the subsequent weeks, including Sempill's regiment, Campbell's fusiliers, Lord Mark Kerr's dragoons and a detachment from the Royal Artillery.[11] Hawley concludes his letter on more practical issues: 'There's ane apartment ready in the Abby, I hope to have a letter from some[one?] of your attendance, of every thinge you want.'[12] The apartment concerned was that of the Duke of Hamilton.

The Duke of Cumberland arrived in Edinburgh early on the morning of 30 January. According to Andrew Henderson, the city 'in Expectation of him the Night before, expressed their Joy, for the coming of their deliverer, by the most splendid Illuminations, Ringing of Bells, and other Demonstrations of Gladness'.[13] Also, according to the same source, the duke went to bed until eight o'clock the same morning (in the Duchess of Hamilton's crimson damask bed, as his cousin Charles had done before him), and then rose to write letters to his father and the Duke of Newcastle. Whatever damage the mob had done to the palace, after the Stuart prince had vacated it, had clearly been dealt with. Presumably George I and II's portraits were prominently displayed, although the duke's very presence reestablished his father's authority, while reflecting how far Stuart fortunes had plunged. However, too busy to muse on such twists of fate, the duke writes that he arrived at 3 a.m., 'having met on ye road all manner of civilities &

respect. Every thing here was in a readiness to move & after the state of things had been well consid[e]red I thought it of the utmost importance to move to the relief of Sterling-castle . . . thô the Rebells have as yet mounted but three guns.' He confirms that he will have fourteen battalions, plus the dragoons, which is 'enough to drive them off the face of the earth if they'll do their duty which we must expect'. He also sends 'a copy of our new order of batle & of Mr Hawley's [late one?] in the last unhapy affair. I put all the Cavallry in third line [the reserve] because by all accounts the Rebells don't fear that, as they do our fire & on that allone I must depend.' In the light of what he knew of the Jacobite army's tactics, the duke had sensibly modified the manner in which his troops would form up on any future battlefield, and, in so doing, was playing to his army's strengths. He concludes with reference to the recent court martial, 'As Hawley communicated to me copies of the infamous sentences that are passed on our cowardly Officers I thought it better to pardon all the private men to give a sort of mark of favour to the corps. if I might venture to give my opinion on the Officers I wish the King superceded them all since They are not hanged.'[14] In fact only four men were executed after the battle (at the Grassmarket) and they were far from the most reliable anyway: three had deserted after Fontenoy and had been captured aboard *Le Louis XV*, and the other, Henry MacManus of Hamilton's Dragoons, had joined the Jacobite army after Prestonpans.[15]

His official duties over, the duke then received visitors. Firstly, the General Officers with an account of the battle. Then 'the Soldiers, much disheartened at the late Disaster, crowded to him; his very Presence raised them almost from despair, to a Confidence of Victory'. After which, 'No sooner had he got rid of the Compliments of the Nobility, Gentry and Clergy, than, unable to stay a Moment from Action, he walked down Stairs, and viewed 16 Pieces of Cannon in the Close. As he came out of the Gate, the Drums ruffed, and a loud and continued Huzza ensued.' Following in the duke's no-nonsense, brisk approach, the army was ready to leave at four o'clock the next morning and, according to Andrew Henderson, there were no crowds, because it had been made known that all 'except such as brought Provision and Forage, or Information, for the Army, should be fired upon, if they presumed to approach within a Mile of it without a Pass'. In addition, 'the Dragoons of Hamilton and Ligonier were ordered to patrole along the Roads leading Westward from Edinburgh, to prevent any Intelligence coming to the Enemy'. An hour later, the British army set off towards Falkirk via Linlithgow (where they quartered), the duke riding at the head of the Royal Scots.[16]

At Stirling, the news arrived that the Duke of Cumberland was marching to the aid of Stirling Castle and would be at Linlithgow by 31 January.

All work on the siege ended. It appeared that a battle with the Duke of Cumberland was finally at hand, and Charles was keen to prepare for it. Since the unresolved battle at Falkirk, it was generally presumed that another would occur soon after. But the Jacobite army was suffering from a familiar lack of discipline. A week after the battle, Charles, now returned to Bannockburn, wrote to Lord George (still at Falkirk), displaying bemusement at officers as well as soldiers absenting themselves without permission from either the prince or Lord George, and that 'I desire you woud signify to every body concern'd that I expect they shou'd exactly comply with this so necessary a part of Military Disciplin'.[17] Three days later, Lord George was writing to his brother, 'I am quite dispirited by [your] men's goeing off and deserting their coullers; For God's sake make examples or we shall be undone.' Despite this, he also states that at a review that day, the army 'made a fine appearance' and that the 'enemy say they will be soon with us again'.[18] Meanwhile, hearing that the British army was preparing to march towards them, Charles had also written to the Marquess of Tullibardine, stating that he required him 'to hasten up all the men you can possibly send me without a moment's loss of time, for the thing presses and will in all appearance decide the fate of Scotland'.[19] In anticipation of the imminent and crucial encounter, John Hay states that Lord George drew up a plan of battle which the prince agreed to, and that night 'Charles was unusually gay, and sat up late at Bannockburn'.[20]

But unbeknown to the prince, a council of the clan chiefs was held at Lord George's Falkirk headquarters on 29 January. According to Lord George, the issue of desertion and wandering off could not be prevented, as 'many of the men went home from all the different corps, and this evil was daily increasing'. In the light of the Duke of Cumberland's advance with an augmented army, the principal officers from the clans 'were persuaded that we were in no condition to fight them, and that there was not the least hopes of taking Stirling Castle'.[21] They believed the siege would take weeks, or even months, and this was time they just did not have. Less than two hours after the council had commenced, a recommendation to Prince Charles to retreat, or rather 'retire', to the Highlands had been written and signed by all present who 'were unanimously of the same opinion'.[22] According to Lord George they believed that in the Highlands they could spend the rest of the winter 'taking and mastering the forts of the North', and he was certain 'we can keep as many men together as will answer that end, and hinder the enemy from following us in the mountains at this season of the year'. By spring 'we doubt not but an army of 10,000 effective Highlanders can be brought together, and follow your Royal Highness wherever you think proper'. This might include, by inference and sweetening the pill, England or even London. The petition concludes, 'The hard marches which your army has undergone, the winter season, and now the inclemency of the weather, cannot fail of making this measure approved of by your Royal Highness's allies abroad as well as your faithful adherents at home.'[23] No one was party to this petition except the subscribers, Lord George, Lochiel, Keppoch, Clanranald, Ardsheal, Lochgarry, Scothouse and Simon, son of Lord Lovat.[24]

According to one account, the petition arrived in Bannockburn late in the evening and, having read it, Secretary Murray and Colonel O'Sullivan decided not to trouble the prince (who had retired to bed) until the morning – fearing the response. The prince was, after all, preparing for a battle, possibly the deciding encounter of the entire campaign, with the added frisson that this time it was against a British army led by his Hanoverian cousin, the usurping Elector's favourite son. This was dynastic and personal. In another indication of his bias against Lord George, Secretary Murray is quoted as saying (referring to Charles) that 'this will set him mad, for he'l see plainly, [that] it is a Caballe & [that] Ld George has blinded all those peoples'.[25] At daybreak, they handed the document to Charles who read it and then, according to John Hay, 'struck his head against the wall till he staggered, and exclaimed most violently against Lord George Murry', saying, 'Good God! have I lived to see this.'[26] In response, once he had recovered his composure, the prince sent a letter to the chiefs, dated 30 January, stating: 'Is it possible that a Victory and a Defeat shou'd produce the same effects, and that the Conquerors should flie from an engagement, whilst the conquer'd are seeking it? Shou'd we make the retreat you propose, how much more will that raise the spirits of our Ennemys and sink those of our own People?' The army would be obliged to 'continue our flight to the Mountains, and soon find our selves in a worse condition than we were in at Glenfinnan'. What would France and Spain think? What about our friends closer to home? He asked them to reconsider.[27]

Sir Thomas Sheridan was sent to Falkirk with the letter, and then returned to Bannockburn with Keppoch (among others) to explain their position. After this Charles wrote another letter to the chiefs. In it he observes that they have no doubt 'heard great complaints of my Despotick temper' and therefore, to explain himself, he states: 'Wherever we go the Ennemy will follow, and if we now appear afraid of them their spirits will rise and those of our men sink very low.' He feared greater desertions but, worse still, if they crossed the Forth 'we shall be utterly undone and lose all the fruits of ye success providence has hitherto granted us'. To conclude, 'why we shoud be so much afraid now of an Enemy that we attacked and beat a fortnight ago when they were much more numerous I cannot conceive'. He asked them, again, to reconsider. But if they pursued this line and knowing he had 'an Army [that] I cannot command any further than the chief Officers please', he acknowledged that 'I must yield' and concluded: 'I take God to witness that it is with the greatest reluctance, and that I wash my hands of the fatal consequences wch I forsee but cannot help.'[28] If Lord George Murray and the prince had developed (or been allowed to develop) a better personal rapport, inevitably their professional/military relationship would have been vastly improved, to the benefit of the cause. The prince clearly believed that his opinion no longer counted at all and Lord George Murray was not even pretending that it did. Charles was surrounded by people he trusted, who had consistently told him that Lord George was a traitor. Ignoring the perfectly rational arguments for such an action, by advising a retreat, rather than driving home their advantage after Falkirk (as the prince would see it), Lord George's actions here would simply confirm this opinion. But, with no French battalions to act as a counterbalance to the clans, if the clan chiefs wanted to retreat then Charles was at their mercy: he was effectively impotent.

The retreat was ordered for 1 February but, prior to the march, expected to begin at ten o'clock, there was to be a general review between Bannockburn and Stirling. As James Maxwell recalled, 'if desertion was found to be as considerable as was supposed, the army would march off leisurely and in good order'.[29] As expected, the prince continued to hope, until the very last moment, that a retreat could be avoided. At Bannockburn, Lord George recollected: 'I continued at the Prince's quarters till betwixt twelve and one at night, where it was agreed upon that we were to rendezvous at nine near St Ninians, and appoint a rear guard, &c.' After which 'a message was ordered to be sent to Stirling to the Duke of Perth and Lord John Drummond, to be ready betwixt nine and ten, but not to evacuate the town till they received farther orders'.[30] Lord George 'went then to my quarters at Easter Green Yards, having the horse patrols, and several other things, to order'.[31] However, the news of a retreat had already spread among the men 'who,' as Maxwell recalls, 'imagining the danger much greater and nearer than it really was, had begun at day-break to take the road to the Frews'. Officers were immediately sent to stop them 'but it was to no purpose, the thing was already gone too far; even the troops that were quartered in the town of Stirling had taken the alarm too, and marched out of the town before the hour appointed'. The result was that at the review, 'There was hardly the appearance of an army'.[32] Lord George believed that new orders had been issued, without his knowledge, 'to evacuate it [the town] by break of day. I never got so much as a message, nor knew nothing of any change.'[33] Either way, as James Maxwell observed, 'Lord George Murray, who was quiet in quarters there waiting the hour, and several others, might have been taken had the garrison of the castle sallied out immediately.'[34] There was nothing to be done but to march on, with the few men left, towards the Ford at Frew.

The church at St Ninian's, located about a mile south of Stirling, had been used by the Jacobite army to store gunpowder. On the morning of the retreat, the church spectacularly blew up. As James Maxwell states, 'whether this happened by accident or design, I can't positively affirm'.[35] If by design, then the action was a very curious one, since, as Maxwell goes on to observe, 'no warning was given to any body to get out of the way. The Prince himself was within reach of being hurt when the thing happened, and some of the Highlanders, as well as several of the inhabitants of the village, were killed.'[36] One account recalls that Lochiel, injured at Falkirk, was driving past the church in a carriage with Secretary Murray's wife when 'some of the stones came very near them, the Horses startled, threw Mrs. Murray on the Street, where she lay speechless, 'till she was taken up by some of the soldiers'.[37] Captain George Fitzgerald (still a prisoner) was being held at a building nearby and stated, soon after, 'On the morning of their flight . . . The Pretender's son came att that time and satt on horseback att the door . . . till abt five minnetts before the Church of St Ninians was blown up, when he & his whole rabble gallop'd away.'[38] Lord George, apparently still at his lodgings in Bannockburn, 'heard the great noise made when the church of St Ninians was blown up, but thought it firing from the castle, and came not there [St Ninian's] till an hour after every body was gone'.[39] A local journal, *Stirling Neuse*, recorded that, 'They marched all in a body, out of toun, leaving their whole artillery and amonition behind them, excepting some which they had lodged in the church of St Ninian's, which they maliciously blew up, killing severall of themselves, and people of the toun.'[40] The event continues to be steeped in controversy.

The army crossed the Forth at the Ford of Frew. The prince lodged at Drummond Castle and the army at Dunblane, Doune and neighbouring villages.[41] On 2 February, the army arrived near Crieff where there was another review and, according to James Maxwell, it was discovered that the actual number of desertions had not been as bad as it had appeared at Stirling. His explanation is that the restless Highlanders had 'sauntered about all the villages in the neighbourhood of their quarters, and abundance of them had been several days absent from their colours'. The officers presumed that all the missing had gone home, but in fact 'all the stragglers had got to Crieff and appeared at the review there'.[42]

This muddled retreat was not likely to improve relations between Lord George and the prince. A council of war was called and, again according to Maxwell, 'there never had been such heats and animosities as at this meeting'[43] – quite a claim, considering what must have occurred at Derby. By his own admission, Lord George 'complained much of the flight, and entreated we should know who advised it. The Prince did not incline to lay the blame on any body, but said he took it on himself.'[44] However, as Maxwell continues, 'after a great deal of wrangling and altercation'[45] it was decided to divide the army into two, according to Alexander MacDonald, 'this measure being necessary for the armys easier march and better subsistence'.[46] Prince Charles and the clans were to take the Highland road to Inverness in order to drive Lord Loudoun and his now 2,000 Highland volunteers out of the town, while Lord George and Lord John Drummond, with the horse and Lowland regiments, were to march via Perth and the eastern coastal route to Aberdeen. The two were to assemble again at Inverness. On 4 February, Charles marched to Dunkeld and then on to Blair Atholl, remaining there over a week hunting and shooting. Lord George had arrived in Perth the evening after the council of war at Crieff, and remained there for almost two days. He recalled, 'we could not makeup any considerable body, for the way we had left Stirling had much discouraged the men', while Lord Ogilvie, knowing his men would wander as they passed near their homes, 'had asked leave the day before to go home with his men, and promised to join us at Aberdeen, or on our march'. The sooner they went home, the sooner they would rejoin the army.[47]

A Spanish ship had arrived at Peterhead (on the east coast) with 'a vast many carriages of arms and military stores'. The cargo was sent to Aberdeen, which Lord George and his troops entered soon after.[48] Lord George then marched out of Aberdeen on 11 February, leaving behind a small detachment of men who were ordered to retire as and when the British army approached. A great snowstorm hindered their first day's march and forced the French picquets and Lord John Drummond's regiment to halt at Kintore and Inverurie. Lord George waited two days at Strathbogie for them and then advanced to Speyside. While at Strathbogie he issued a threat to Clan Grant, stating, 'The Gentlemen and others of the name of Grant whose Country is most exposed by the present position of our army will do well to consider what the consequences may be if they appear in arms against us.' Lord George considered it his duty 'to apprise them of their danger both as to their persons houses and effects and they will have only themselves to blame if harsh measures should be used, and they are to know that we use nobody as Enemys but those who appear such and carry arms against us'.[49] He then pushed on towards Inverness, leaving garrisons in Elgin and Nairn to prevent Lord Loudoun's forces from venturing east and joining up with the remainder of the British army under the Duke of Cumberland, who by now was advancing north from Edinburgh.[50]

John Pine, 'Forty-third Regiment of Foot' [known as the Black Watch],
from *The Cloathing Book*, 1742.

41

Perth

'their holles & hiding places'

Having departed Edinburgh, the Duke of Cumberland's next letter to the Duke of Newcastle was dated the following day at Falkirk, and refers to the previous letter and the relief of Stirling Castle, where 'I hoped that the Rebells flush'd with their later success would have given us an opertunity of finishing this affair at once & which I am morally sure would have been in our favour as the troops in Generall show'd all the spirit that I could wish & would have retreaved whatever slips are pass'd.' However, this was not to be, for, to his great astonishment, the Jacobite army had blown up their powder magazine and retired, leaving behind their cannon, and 'a number of their sick & wounded, besides twenty of our wounded prisoners taken at the late affair which I have found here'.[1] The duke's next letter to the Secretary of State was dated from Stirling itself, only a day after the Jacobite army had evacuated. Here he reports on the incident at St Ninian's Church 'where their powder & ball was, & when the country people came to fetch it away they attempted to fire the magazine but fortunately the first train miss'd so that severall escaped but the second was so soon fired that many poor people were blown up and are buried in the ruins'. He continues, that he will move on swiftly to Perth to keep up with them as a body, 'but when they once are got into their holles & hiding places it will be impossible to follow them in a body'. He planned to leave troops to guard the entrances to the defiles, but 'litle parties can only be sent in to burn & destroy that nest of robbers & orders should be given to kill all that have arms in their houses as that will now be the only trace of treason left now they are got back &

I shant be surprized to hear it affirmd that there never was a rebellion as this is the situation here'.[2]

Three days later and only two days after the acrimonious Jacobite council of war, the duke writes from Crieff, 'We arrived here this day, & tomorrow shall march to Perth.' Regarding the 'rebels', who are known to have divided and are advancing further into Scotland in two columns, he says, 'to amuse us they pretend they are to joyn again, & to attack my Lord Loudon or Inverness' but he continues, indicating that he believes the rebellion all but over, 'I am firmly of [the] opinion that is only a feint, & that the Pretenders Son is making off, either by Montrose or the way He came. I rather think the latter tho I can have no certain intelligence.' Regarding the current march 'through some of the Drummonds Strathallan, & other disaffected Persons Estates', the duke 'thought fit to let the Soldiers a little loose with proper precautions, that they might have some sweets with all their fatigues'. This would include the plundering of property, seen as a soldier's perquisite. The duke concludes, confirming it was his belief that nothing but a degree of mopping up was now required, 'As the Rebellion is now crush'd & nothing left but the Punishment due to their crimes, I congratulate you, that our Credit will once more be re-established & the Kings hands free, to take what share He may think proper in the affairs of Europe.'[3]

On 10 February the duke reported from Perth, 'It is not quite certain whether the Pretenders Son is actually at Blair or incognito, with this other Party that is gone from Montrose', the latter including Captain Brown en route to France with the most recent good news. He continues, 'but whatever the reason of it is, the Rebels give out that He [is] every day hunting & hawking at Blair'.[4] The duke then indulges in a little humour (or sarcasm) when he says, that this 'dos not seem at all suited to his inclinations, for he can hardly sit on horse back, & therefore made all his marches on foot'. While here, the duke sent out two detachments to secure Atholl: one, under Lieutenant Colonel Webster, marched towards Castle Menzies and the other, commanded by Sir Andrew Agnew, Lieutenant Colonel of the Royal Scots Fuseliers and chief of the Lowland Clan Agnew, to Blair Castle. The duke had some misgivings regarding the people in the area, as he does not 'find the same zeal for totally supressing the Rebellion as there seem'd to be for driving the Rebels Northward' which he appears to be putting down to local economics and security, as he continues, 'this Kingdom gaining immensely by so large a body of Troops being kept here, which will amply make amends for all the harm done by the marches of the Rebels'. He praises the Lord Justice Clerk, Andrew Fletcher, 'who is of the utmost service to us here not only in obliging the Country to find us every thing that may be necessary; but with his advice, & being indefatigable in doing whatever may be expedient for the service of the troops'.

He then moves on to another subject, namely Major General John Campbell of Mamore, who arrived the day before '& has brought with Him four companys of Western Highlanders. He assures me that they will shew no favour or partiality to the other Highlanders, as He knows them best He must answer for it.' Yet the duke was very unsure, 'for those who were here with us before He came, almost absolutely refused to plunder any of the rebels houses which is the only way We have to punish them. & bring them back'. In other words, the policy was to attack the lands of those who had joined the rebellion (as a punishment in itself) and, further, to encourage desertion from within the Jacobite army. The harassing of 'soft' non-military targets – women, the elderly – aimed to undermine the resolve of the Jacobite troops through psychological means. Although civil wars and rebellions were not unheard of in Britain, it was still rare for such activity to occur on this scale within the British Isles and against British citizens.[5] However, despite his issues with the major general, the duke concludes by saying, 'I shall send Major Genl. Campbell to the Western Highlands & keep with me here his son with about six hundred Highlanders to go upon Partys as they are better qualified to that service here than our Troops.'[6] The duke remained at Perth for several days rather than immediately continuing his pursuit of the retreating Jacobite army, partly because of the bad weather and partly to see whether his instincts concerning the dispersal of the Jacobite army were correct.

On 8 February, six battalions of Hessian troops, commanded by the Duke of Cumberland's brother-in-law, Prince Frederick, landed at Leith. They had been called from Flanders to replace the Dutch troops, now rendered unable to fight with 'France's enemy', but who were, in any case, considered unmanageable and something of a liability. Among the welcoming party was Colonel Charles Whitefoord, who had been on parole, at Perth and later Glamis, since being made a prisoner of war at Prestonpans. Thomas White had written to Whitefoord congratulating him on his 'Great delivery from the Hands of those Canibals'[7] and the official report after their release notes that 'the prisoners were frequently insulted by the Rebel Soldiers, and fir'd at when they went to take the air in the fields, without any redress when complain'd of'.[8] By now, there were also rumours (unfounded) that prisoners were being executed.[9] Understandably, after all these months, Colonel Whitefoord was very relieved to be back in action. Prince Frederick took up residence in Holyroodhouse – the third prince to do so in almost as many months. Presumably he too occupied the Hamilton apartments. While at Edinburgh, the Hessian prince proved a bit of a favourite among the locals, as Sir John Clerk recalled: 'I found him to be a Comely young Man of about 25 years of Age, of a middle stature, and of great benevolence and humanity. He behaved exceedingly well towards everybody, and went to our Musick meetings and balls wherever he chanced to be invited.'[10]

A week later, Captain Alexander Campbell wrote from Fort William to Sir Everard Fawkener, concerning an event that had occurred the previous Saturday (13 February). Captain James Campbell and Lieutenant George McFarland having 'walked a musket shot from this Garrison, The Tunman of Inverlochy (one of Lochiels Captains) concealed himself behind a Rock and shot Poor Lieut. Mc. Farline Dead on the spot'. As a result of this 'barbarous Murder' Captain Alexander Campbell, in concert with the other officers, had sent out a party to apprehend the shooter, and 'to Burn the Village of Inverlochy, which place was the common Receptacle of the Rebells and being within a mile of the Fort was consiquently a very great Nuscence and there was not ten Inhabitants belonging to it but was in the Rebellion'. The party was unable to capture Lochiel's captain, but the burning of the village 'they Punctualy Obey'd, and brought in some of the Rebells Cattle, which I Orderd to be Distributed Equally between the Regular and Irregular Troops'. Such actions left the villagers destitute.

He then provides intelligence on the movement of the local clans. Many of the Camerons and MacDonalds 'are Returnd to this Country And some of their Chiefs have followed them with the Pretenders Orders to bring them back again to their Body at Badenough [near the garrison of Ruthven], and on their Refusal to Return to Destroy their Houses Cattle &c'. Such threats had the desired effect, as 'large Bodys are assembled in our Neighbourhood, some of which Marches of this day, and the whole will follow this week'. His intelligence confirms that they intend 'to take in this Garrison and Lochiel has Declared that whilst it is in our hands, Neither the Camerons nor Mc.Donalds will be kept to their Duty, as they apprehend being Destroy'd by us, and therefore insists that we should be destroy'd'. Meanwhile, information from Fort Augustus 'tells us the Rebells are on their March to Inverness from thence they Intend to proceed to Fort Augustus and this place'.[11] It is quite clear from the timing of the intelligence that this movement en masse of the Camerons and MacDonalds is part of the 'desertion' that occurred just before the Jacobite army retreated from Stirling on 1 February, quickly followed by the allowing of some clan chiefs to accompany their people back to their lands, on the proviso that they must force them to regather for the advance on Inverness. The threats of destruction to property and person appear to be common fare, whether from the Jacobite or the British army. Only a few days prior to receiving this news, it had been decided at a council at Edinburgh that the duke and his army would continue as far as Aberdeen, leaving Hessian units at Stirling and Perth, dragoon regiments at Bannockburn and loyalist regiments at Edinburgh.[12] In the event the Hessians would have little involvement in the campaign in the months ahead.

Three days later, Sir Everard was writing to the Duke of Newcastle, relaying his horror at the news of the recent resignation of both the principal Secretary of State and his brother, the Prime Minister, Henry Pelham: a dramatic situation which was as quickly reversed.[13] King George, who had always preferred Lord Granville to the Pelhams and had never attempted to hide his dislike of them, had been casting around for many months (even as the rebellion raged to the north) for someone to establish an alternative administration.[14] When the king refused to allow William Pitt to join the government (Pitt had vocally opposed the British subsidies sent to assist Hanover during the War of the Austrian Succession) and in order to address the situation head on, Newcastle, Pelham and Harrington resigned en masse, with Hardwicke agreeing to stand down when the legal term had ended. King George then encouraged Granville and his associates William Pulteney, 1st Earl of Bath, and the Marquess of Tweeddale to step into the breach. However, when they suggested it would take a sizable Tory contingent, supported by his son, Prince Frederick, in order to form an administration (neither of which was an attractive prospect) the king grudgingly accepted the return of the Pelhams, now in a much stronger position. Granville and Tweeddale were left out of the reorganised government, and the office of Secretary of State for Scotland was abolished. Lord Harrington, however, never returned to the King's favour. Sir Everard states that he had been 'under the most sensible concern for the effects of this very unexpected & thorough change, wch seem'd to be made at a time of all others the most delicate for such an experiment'. But, very soon after, he had received 'an express with the advice of his Majestys having been pleas'd to recall the old Ministers to the exercise of their former Employments: I hope this cloud in the Heaven's will be follow'd by a long course of serene fair weather.' A strange time indeed for such experiments.

He then returns to the business of the rebellion, which he appears to be very weary of, although, 'I persuade my self all in effect is over here & that our March forward, which We are now seting about is only for the total dissipation of thes[e] scoundrels & for setting good form of things.' He observes, 'I have been so long an inhabitant of much softer climes, I am not at all afraid of winds & snow, which We are yet to expect these three months. but I own I am a little affected with the view of marching northward.' Scotland, in the depths of winter, is a far cry from the Eastern Mediterranean. He then writes that the 'Highlanders are almost universally a nest of thieves & they are always ready to rise in order to rob'. In addition, 'many of them are also Papists', and 'they have been poison'd by that connexion which has been kept up with France by that mischievous practice of inlisting men, under which pretence ill affected People have been constantly going backwards and forward & by some Money & the employment of a few People in the French Service, Jacobitism, which in effect is a dependence on France has been propagated.'[15] It is certainly true that since 1688 the hope of achieving the one thing that united all Jacobites, the restoration of the Stuarts in Great Britain, had been nurtured, maintained and exploited by France.

A week later Archibald Campbell at Inveraray (probably writing to Major General John Campbell) sets out the recent activity among the rebels in the area: 'the greatest and most Universal preparation is making for taking the field again as if they intended to Dye or Conquer, may the wise Providence direct our Army & give them success. Our Accounts from every quarter are that they are to make the last push now, & that the greatest severities are exercised to Levy their Men.'[16]

James Macardell after Allan Ramsay, *Lady Anne MacKintosh, c.* 1748.
(NATIONAL PORTRAIT GALLERY, LONDON)

Moy Hall

'approaching danger'

From Blair Castle, Prince Charles had continued on towards Inverness, making a detour to Ruthven of Badenoch where, meeting up with Cluny MacPherson, Lochiel and others, they besieged the barracks, forcing the surrender of the small garrison. The garrison was allowed to leave, after which the buildings were torched. On Sunday, 16 February, about the time that Lord George was at Speyside, Charles arrived at Moy Hall, eight miles south-east of Inverness. James Maxwell observes, 'He was very ill attended when he got to Moy, most of his men were straggling behind, and some at a considerable distance; he had divided them for the convenience of quarters, and was now obliged to wait some days their arrival.'[1] At Moy he was entertained not by Angus Mackintosh, who was a captain in the British army, but by his wife, Lady Anne, the twenty-three-year-old daughter of the staunch Jacobite Chief of Clan Farquharson. She had personally raised a regiment that arrived at Bannockburn before the Battle of Falkirk. From the accounts of the prince's stay at Moy Hall, the extent of his personal household (which had accompanied him since Edinburgh) and the arrangements required for feeding him, as well as his combined domestic and military entourage, is revealed. According to James Gib on the first evening Lady Mackintosh wanted 'to compliment the Prince and his houshold with a supper that night, so that his cooks had the play for one night'. The entourage included 'the servants (the household consisting of about seventy at least)' and 'there were always ten coveres upon the Prince's own table, and eight covers upon another table in the same room for the aid de camps. Lady Mackintosh's supper was exceedingly genteel and plentifull.'[2]

Captain Malcolm MacLeod (cousin to the clan chief of Raasay) confirms that while Charles was staying at the hall, he did not have many men to guard him 'and these too dispersed up and down for proper quarters, there being no apprehension at all of any danger'.[3] Lady Mackintosh clearly thought otherwise. Because of her 'great care and anxiety about the Prince' she ordered a blacksmith called Donald Fraser, 'who happened to be there by chance, having a desire to see the Prince',[4] along with four servants to arm themselves with muskets. They then, unbeknown to the prince's men, patrolled the area beyond them. In this way 'they would prove a check upon the guards, and would be ready to discover approaching danger'. Accordingly, when it became dark, the blacksmith and his comrades moved off to about a two-mile distance from the house and patrolled. By this means, they came across a group of about thirty of Lord Loudoun's troops silently moving towards the house. This was the advance party from a detachment of 1,500 men of the Independent Companies and 64th Highlanders that Loudoun had marched out of Inverness to capture the prince. The blacksmith fired, as did his four companions, after which 'the blacksmith huzzaed and cried aloud, "Advance, Advance my lads, Advance! (naming some particular regiments) I think we have the dogs now"'.[5] The idea was to give the impression that there was a sizable guard present. According to James Gib they were so successful that Loudoun's men were 'struck with such a panick' and 'instantly they beat a retreat', throwing the main body of Loudoun's troops into some disarray, 'and made ther way back to Inverness in great disorder, imagining the Prince's whole army to be at their heels'.[6] In fact, despite the initial confusion, Lord Loudoun had managed to maintain some order among the majority of his troops and, having waited for an hour in the darkness, eventually recognised that surprise was no longer on his side and retreated. MacLeod of MacLeod's piper, Donald Ban MacCrimmon, the most famous in Scotland, had been killed and another man wounded.[7] However in the wake of this attempt, hundreds of Loudoun's troops deserted.

Just prior to this, Anna Duff of Drummuir, widow of Lachlan, 20th Laird of Mackintosh and called Old Lady Mackintosh, who was resident in Inverness, had heard of Lord Loudoun's plan to capture the prince and sent a young lad, Lachlan Mackintosh, to Moy Hall to warn him. Having hidden in the undergrowth while Loudoun's men passed by, Lachlan took a different road and arrived at the Hall at about five o'clock in the morning. One of the prince's footmen, Alexander Stewart, recalled that 'he came into the kitchen, where I was lying on the table-head asleep, and awakened me by pulling and hauling at my great coat, and desired me, for God's sake, to go and awaken the Prince'.[8] James Gib conjures up a slightly farcical scene when he recollects that he, 'upon the alarm, having been sleeping in his cloaths, stept out [side] with his pistols under his arm, and in the close he saw the Prince walking with his bonnet above his night-cap, and his shoes down in the heels', while Lady Mackintosh was 'in her smock petticoat running through the close, speaking loudly and expressing her anxiety about the Prince's safety'.[9]

Alexander Stewart recalled that Lady Mackintosh 'and her sister, and me, went to the room where he [the prince] slept, and took all the most valuable things that were in the room where he lay, and went up to the garrets, and hid them in the feather-stands, that were almost full of feathers; and my lady was always calling at me to follow with the canteens', no doubt the fine silver gilt items Charles had brought from France.[10] Meanwhile Charles, still partially dressed, had run through a wood and arrived over a mile away at the south-west end of Loch Moy where he was joined by Lochiel and his men. Here, they had resolved to make a stand if pursued. While they were waiting around in the freezing night 'taking a dram',[11] a message arrived announcing the all-clear. So ended the 'Rout of Moy'.[12]

The prince continued at Moy until 17 February where, James Maxwell recalled, he was joined by two or three thousand men.[13] The following day Charles marched to Inverness. According to Captain Malcolm MacLeod 'when they were approaching that town he drew them up in order of battle, expecting, as was given out, that Lord Loudon was to march out of the town to fight'. But, 'when they came near Inverness they saw Lord Loudon and his men making all the haste they could out of it, betaking themselves to ships and boats to carry them off. The Prince and his army entered the town without opposition or violence of any kind.'[14] In fact, after seeking the advice of Lord President Forbes and Norman MacLeod, Lord Loudoun was convinced that Inverness could not be defended with his now reduced troops and had ordered a strategic retreat, accompanied by the Lord President, initially to the Black Isle (the peninsula across the Moray Firth from Inverness), eventually stopping some twenty-eight miles away.[15]

Inverness is 'generally esteemed', as observed by Captain Edmund Burt, 'to be the Capital of the Highlands'.[16] The town sits at the north-

east edge of the Great Glen, where the River Ness enters the Firth of
Moray. The ancient castle and modern Fort George are located on rising
ground on the east bank close to the town's stone bridge (a vault within
one arch housed the town jail), from which Captain Burt was diverted 'to
see the *Seals* pursue the Salmon as they come up the River'.[17] Walking east
from the bridge (and north of the castle) is the market place and cross,
'the Exchange of the Merchants, and other Men of Business'.[18] According
to Captain Burt the houses in Inverness were mainly built of stone and
low 'because of the violent Flurries of Wind which often pour upon the
Town from the Openings of the adjacent Mountains'.[19] The roofs were
thatched. However, the houses of the gentry and aristocracy were on a
grander scale. Those on Church Street are later described as 'in the old
Flemish style, with large courts and arched gateways, and gables turned
towards the street'.[20]

Fort George was under the command of Major George Grant with 200
men left behind by Lord Loudoun to cover his retreat. After a short siege it
eventually surrendered on 25 February. Within, as Captain John Maclean
recalled, 'we found a Good store of Arms and Ammunition, Meall, Beef,
Cheese & Coals, and when all was taken out the Castle was Demolished'.[21]
The capital of the Highlands had fallen with barely a struggle. The
prince was now in residence at Culloden House and occupying the Lord
President's bedchamber, with those splendid views of the Moray Firth, and
a tester bed furnished with red tartan fabric.[22] The day before Fort George
surrendered, Charles was joined at Culloden by Lord George. He gave the
prince an account of the march via Aberdeen, saying, 'it is inconceivable
the fatigue and trouble we had undergone' and then informing him of a
plan he had discussed with Lord Pitsligo 'to get five thousand bolls of meal
in Banff, Murray, and Nairne shires', and then send 'most of the meal to
the Highlands, that if we were obliged to retreat there, so as to draw the
Duke of Cumberland to the hills with his army, we might have subsistence'. This plan, and particularly the mention of retreat, did not appeal
to the prince who 'would have it brought to Inverness'.[23] Where provisions were stored in order to feed an army – particularly one preparing for
imminent battle – was always important. During a winter campaign, when
forage was in very short supply, it was vital.

On about 21 February another French ship arrived at Peterhead with
men, money and arms, including Berwick's regiment, and the following

day a detachment of 121 of Fitz-James' Regiment of Horse arrived at Aberdeen but without horses.[24] Two of the accompanying French transports, the *Bourbon* and the *Charité*, were captured by the Royal Navy.[25] Due to the success of the Royal Navy blockade, it was becoming clear that getting French ships to the east coast of Scotland was now extremely difficult. On 23 February, Aberdeen was evacuated in expectation of the imminent arrival of the Duke of Cumberland, and this Jacobite detachment marched to Elgin and the surrounding neighbourhood. Their orders were to defend the passage of the River Spey against the British army.[26]

John Pine, 'Tenth Regiment of Dragoons', from *The Cloathing Book*, 1742.
(ROYAL ARMOURIES)

43

Aberdeen

'such seeds of Rebellion'

The Duke of Cumberland advanced with his troops on the east coast road to Aberdeen, with the Royal Navy cruising nearby to provide supplies. He arrived on 27 February, and then he and his army settled in for the remainder of the winter. The duke's infantry were mainly quartered in Aberdeen itself, with outposts further afield. Major General Humphrey Bland had already moved forward from Aberdeen with four battalions and two cavalry regiments.[1] By the 17th he was at Huntly where a Jacobite detachment was also located. On hearing of Bland's advance they retreated, while Bland remained at Gordon Castle and its environs. Patrols were sent out to reconnoitre but one, under Lieutenant Alexander Campbell, decided to exceed orders and attempt to surprise the Jacobite stronghold at Fochabers. Lying at Keith, en route to their target, they were surprised themselves by Major Nicholas Glasgoe of Lord Ogilvie's regiment. After a gun battle in the middle of the town, the Campbells firing from their position in the church, Major Glasgoe's men were victorious. In addition to ten dead and many wounded, ninety were taken to Speymouth as prisoners. In the meantime, Major General Bland was joined by two further battalions and, on the 23rd, William Anne van Keppel, 2nd Earl of Albemarle, arrived as the new commander of this 1st division. They were to remain at Huntly until 10 April to cover the movement of the other divisions still at Aberdeen.

On 19 March, the Duke of Cumberland, writing from Aberdeen to the Principal Secretary of State, observes that 'I have not heard any thing fresh from the West', that is, from Inverness, 'so I suppose all go[e]s on in the same way there'. He also states that the French are having difficulties landing troops on the nearby coast, 'so I must stil continue, of the opinion, that when France shall have duly considerd the situation of affairs here, they will not choose to throw away any troops here, as they must fall into our hands before they can join the Rebels if they should land'. He then observes, 'as we go further up into the Hills, our wants of Bread & Provision will increase'. He therefore requests that 'two hundred & eighty thousand weight of Biscuit & fifty thousand weight of cheese (which must be sound & entire, as broken ones leave great waste) could be shipped for Inverness, where if it should not be used for his Majesty's Troops, it would not be lost, as the remainder might serve for the fleet'.[2] This illustrates the crucial role of the Royal Navy in not only thwarting the movement of French ships, but in maintaining a constant flow of food and other supplies to the British army. The Jacobite army had no such support. It also reveals how close an eye the duke was keeping on all aspects of his campaign.

The Duke of Cumberland received intelligence from Mr John Scrogy of Tullich, dated 27 March, stating that the Jacobite troops around Elgin and at the River Spey were 4,000-strong and that 3,000 more commanded by Charles, plus 1,500 returning from Atholl, would soon arrive to support them. Further, that 'on the 26th 3000 of the Clans were arrived at Elgin which looks as if they intended to make a stand if the Dukes Army should approach nigh Fochabers in separate Bodies'. Yet the Jacobite army 'seem to have but small hopes from a General action, but place their hopes chiefly in what they call the laziness & Luxury of the Kings Troops with their ignorance of the Country, & the Friends they themselves have in it'. Their plan was 'to Cutt off all the Army by stolen marches on separate Parties and allways travel in the night Time'. The sender admits that 'most of this account he [Scrogy] had from one whom he sent among the Rebels and a Beggar'.[3]

On 31 March, the duke sent another update to the Duke of Newcastle stating that the 'continued ill weather which We have had here for this Month, has raised the Waters of Spey so high, that I fear it will retard me stil a week longer, tho I propose now to march on to Inverness without halting as soon as ever the Waters will allow us'.[4] He continues, setting out his current understanding of the state of the Jacobite army, 'I believe the desertion is pretty general, throughout their Highlanders and Lowlanders.' He then observes, through intelligence obtained via deserters recently picked up, that 'the Rebel Army have had no pay for these last seven days, & that tharre was no more money amongst them'. As a result he feared 'their dispersion is nigh at hand, for should this Rebellion end any way but by the Sword, I apprehend that from the lenity of our

Government, & from the ill placed Compassion which will be had, when our frights are over, the authors & actors of & in this Rebellion, will not be sufficiently punished to prevent another'. Indeed, he felt compelled to say, 'I see such seeds of Rebellion, & so much disaffection to any Government established upon an English foot' that 'there is little to flatter our selves but that We shall have other scenes of this kind wherever an opportunity may present except the whole Government & constitution in these parts of the Kingdom shall be changed.'⁵ This is an early hint that the duke considered military activity a short-term measure. In his opinion, in order to prevent another Jacobite rebellion, new laws and a new form of government would be required.

On 1 April, Major John Lafausille sent a copy of his recent journal entries to Colonel Napier, updating the colonel, and by extension the Duke of Cumberland, on his and his men's recent activities in the lands of the Ogilvy family around Glen Prosen and Cortachy in Angus. This is only one example of what was being done to the property and people of the Jacobite leadership by these small raiding parties. The entries are matter-of-fact: 31 March, 'March'd to the Center of Glen Prosen, set fire to Storman's house but extinguish'd it being certy'd the Wife was a good & loyal woman & that he did not care for her.' Then, 'Detach'd Lt. Carleton & 20 men to surprise Dav[i]d Ogilvy Laird of Poole 5 miles from this.' The 1st of April was particularly busy, including the burning of 'the Nonjuring Meeting House at Cortichy. Lt Carleton brought in Davd. Ogilvy Laird of Poole Prisonr Plunder'd & burnt his House – Plunder'd the House of Dougal a noted Rebel burnt the nonjuring meeting house at Kirkmayr', 'Detach'd Capt Cosbie wth 100 men to Jam[es] Ogilvy new Miln of Inshuren. Plunder'd the house burnt the Barns & 2 Stacks of Corn, then he march's Lindsay of Glenquick Plunder'd & burnt the Goods', after which 'Capt [Caroline] Scott March'd wth 50 men to Jam[e]s Ogilvy of Inshuren sav'd the House for His Majesty it being a neat one but burnt & Plunder'd the rest.' The levels of human suffering caused by such activity can be imagined.

Major Lafausille then states that, after this, all of David Ogilvy, Lord Airly's tenants arrived at his headquarters, declaring they had no arms and were now willing to swear the oath of loyalty to King George, and 'I swore nigh one hundred my self as also not to assist the Rebels wth men or money I refer'd the rest to a Justice' whom he would compel to complete the taking of oaths before the major left. Major Lafausille observes in conclusion, 'I think the Country is quiet & terryfy'd' and that 'I wish my Earnest endeavours to put His Royal Highness's orders in execution for quieting this Country may have the desir'd effect'. On the matter of David Ogilvy, 'the Laird of Poole', he asks that he might be favoured with orders and adds that the laird was arrested 'very cleverly' while in bed enjoying 'the Embraces of His Doxy'.[6]

Despite the duke's directives for such plunder and destruction to occur, it was still required to be practised under orders and in an orderly manner. As complaints had been made to Lord Albemarle 'that Small partys of the Campbles [Campbells] Stowll at night and plunder the Country', Colonel Campbell was ordered to collect his men every night for patrol duty, and 'the men to take the Rest in the Day'.[7] On 26 March, Lord Albemarle issued general orders that 'Any man that is found morading will be hang'd without a Court Martial'.[8] Soon after, a court martial was held at Strathbogie where four men from Cholmondeley's regiment were tried, described by Lord Albemarle as 'famous rogues and great plunderers'. His lordship writes to Colonel Napier, 'I make no doubt of their condemnation and if H:R:H should approve of the Sentence I beg you'll send a proper person to put it in execution, for wee have no hangman here or in ye neighbourhood.'[9]

However, the following day, Lord Albemarle states, again in a letter to Colonel Napier, 'The soldier's of Cholmondeley's Regiment ye Duke pardonn'd was releas'd last night, & ye other three received this morning 300 lashes each well laid on. I think ye Court Martial shewed lenity, and H:R:H clemency.'[10] Harsh measures extended to civilians assisting the Jacobite army. At Strathbogie Elizabeth Williams was convicted of 'endeavouring to inveigle men into the French Service'. She was seated in a cart facing backwards, towards her accomplice Peter M'Conachy, who was tied to the rear (stripped to the waist) with 'a Libel tyed about his Neck specifying his Crime', and then flogged 'for Spreading false Intelligence' while the cart trundled the entire length of the town. After which they were to be set free, but 'if they are ever seen amongst his Majesty's Troops it is H.R.H. Pleasure that they be Hanged imediatly without a Court Martial'.[11]

While at Aberdeen, the duke drilled his men in preparation for any future encounter with the Jacobite army. Discipline and cool heads would be crucial to their success. In consideration of the style of fighting favoured by the Highlanders in particular, he also introduced some new manoeuvres, which his troops practised and perfected. James Ray recalls, 'His Royal Highness had spared no Pains or Trouble to put every Thing in readiness to have been in Motion sooner, but bad Weather and contrary Winds have hitherto prevented him; but now a few Days of dry South Wind have brought up our Transports with Bligh's Regiment, our Firing and Provisions.'[12] Officers were sent to inspect the Spey and, on their advice that it was fordable, the duke ordered that the army begin advancing towards the river on 7 April.

John Slezer, *The Prospect of ye Town of Innerness
[Inverness] from 'Theatrum Scotiae'*, published 1693.

44

Inverness

'all these misfortunes'

By the beginning of March, having established himself at Inverness and its environs, the prince's key immediate objectives were to reduce Fort William and Fort Augustus, to disperse Lord Loudoun's army and to keep possession of the coast towards Aberdeen for supplies.[1] Lord Loudoun had retreated, with Lord President Forbes and a majority of his men (excepting the garrison at Fort George), to Dornoch, taking all the available boats with him (as Captain MacLeod had stated) and therefore making pursuit extremely difficult. Once at Dornoch he was able to successfully defend himself against an attack by Lord George. He and his party eventually withdrew to Skye. At the same time Lieutenant General Walter Stapleton of Berwick's regiment, accompanied by the Royal Ecossais, three Irish picquets and, crucially, the chief engineer Colonel James Grant of Lally's (who had been mysteriously absent at Stirling) advanced to Fort Augustus, then under the governorship of Major Hu Wentworth. The siege began on 3 March. After some well-aimed shelling, which set fire to the powder magazine and eventually blew a breach in the outer wall, Major Wentworth surrendered on the 5th.

From the end of February until the beginning of March, the prince had stayed either at Castlehill or Culloden House. But on 3 March he moved to Inverness and lodged at the house of Old Lady Mackintosh in Church Street.[2] A week later Charles travelled to Elgin where he became very ill, as Colonel O'Sullivan described it, with 'a spotted favor [fever]'.[3] O'Sullivan continues, 'The Prince happily recover'd a most viollent & dengerous favour & got up the ninth or tenth day, against the Docters advise.'[4] Unfortunately, in the meantime Secretary Murray, who had been the most proficient of all of Charles' administrators, had also fallen ill. Lord John Drummond, entrusted with the defence of the Spey, was initially headquartered at Gordon Castle, about nine miles east of Elgin. The Duke of Gordon had left on foot to join the Duke of Cumberland at Aberdeen, leaving behind his heavily pregnant wife, only two days before Charles had made a visit.[5] The Duke of Cumberland makes reference to a doctor he had sent to assist the duchess in the last stages of her confinement,[6] while the Duke of Gordon later confirmed a 'Dr. Donaldson' had been forced against his will to travel to Elgin to attend to Secretary Murray instead.[7] Meanwhile, the Jacobite cavalry were at Cullen and Strathbogie with the infantry at Strathbogie, Keith, Fochabers, Elgin and neighbouring places.

On 21 March Colonel O'Sullivan recalls 'the Prince arrived at Ivernesse, as well as cou'd be expected, after such a sicknesse, but very low'.[8] Lord Elcho observed that by now the army 'consisted of 10,000 men [who] occupied a circle of country whose diameter was 100 miles'.[9] During this time, according to Colonel O'Sullivan, the marquis d'Eguilles had been able to provide some pay for troops 'but the Prince had hardly where withal to pay the officers'.[10] O'Sullivan continues, 'The Contry of Ross furnished us meal, wth the little we had before, to give two pecks a week to each man.' However, the scarcity of cash 'made a great many grumble, & discouraged furiously every body'.[11] So the Duke of Cumberland's intelligence concerning the desperate lack of money and food was absolutely correct. Indeed, lack of money may explain an incident, later reported by Lord George, where an unnamed officer, having raised a new corps of men who were 'very ill clothed', began stripping the British army prisoners held in the church at Inverness 'to clothe his own men'. Lord George immediately informed the prince, who ordered it to stop and the clothes were returned. 'What possessed him,' Lord George observes of the Jacobite officer, 'I cannot tell.'[12]

It is not surprising, then, that the prince began to contemplate the most unlikely remedies to his financial plight. The engraver Robert Strange had joined the prince at Edinburgh and was serving in the Life Guards with Lord Elcho. He later recalled that one evening he had retired to bed at his billet, Culloden House, when he received an express summoning him to Inverness. On arrival he was shown into the prince's bedchamber, where he soon discovered that, for want of cash, the prince was actually contemplating printing his own money. Strange readily took on the challenge of designing and printing it.[13] The design proposed included a Stuart rose and the Scottish thistle and Charles 'seemed much pleased with the idea'. The mechanism of how the person receiving the note would redeem the value was discussed, with Strange presuming that the 'properest' time for payment would be the Stuart restoration. This comment, so simple and so optimistic, 'produced a general smile'.[14] Strange then proceeded to organise the construction of a rolling printing press and to engrave the copper plates.

Although the taking of Inverness had been a major boost to the Jacobite campaign, the frayed relations that had been evident before (in some instances throughout the campaign) between the senior administrators, in particular Secretary Murray, and some of the Scottish army commanders simply got worse. This is an indication of the strain they were all under, in addition to the usual clash of personalities and their differing ideas regarding how the campaign had been managed so far and, more importantly, how it should proceed. Lord Elcho sincerely believed that by this time Charles 'was entirely under the influence' of Secretary Murray, and the treasurer and undersecretary John Hay of Restalrig. As Colonel O'Sullivan's recollections reveal, feeding the army from Inverness alone was a challenge, and there was now very little money to pay the men or officers. Worse still, after Secretary Murray had fallen ill, he was succeeded to the positions of both chief secretary and quartermaster by John Hay. According to Lord Elcho, 'People had a low opinion of the honesty of Mr. Murray, and had no opinion at all of the capacities of Mr. Hay, who, although honourable, was a man of very limited intelligence.'[15] An officer (a Major Kennedy) is reported to have approached John Hay to offer a similar suggestion to the one Lord George had made to the prince about the dispersal of provisions. He thought as it was 'probable there would be a Battle; and, as the Event was very uncertain, it was Prudence to guard against the worst'. The provisions then at Inverness should be sent into different parts of the country, so that 'scattered Troops might join & have wherewithal to subsist' until the army was brought together again. But if this was not done, 'all must disperse, the Cause given up, & the Prince's Person in Danger: for, the Neighbourhood of that Country could not supply the smallest number of men for one week'.[16] Unfortunately, according to this report, 'Mr. Hay said nothing; nor, do I believe he ever mentioned it to the Prince.'[17] If all went well, then the caution displayed by Major Kennedy would have been prudent but unnecessary. But at this time the outcome of any battle was difficult to predict. As Major Kennedy had advised, if the outcome was defeat, then feeding the men would be even more sporadic should the army be forced to retire from Inverness where the provisions remained.

In the meantime, Lord George and Cluny MacPherson, accompanied by more than 700 men, had ventured to Blair Atholl in order to retake the area, which, early on 10 March, they succeeded in doing. Only Blair

Castle, with its garrison of 300 regulars from Campbell's and under the command of Lieutenant Colonel Agnew, remained and was besieged. The garrison was ordered to fire if attacked. However, Lord George was hampered in his task by poor equipment. In his opinion, the cannon he had been given (two four-pounders) were not only too small to penetrate the seven-foot-deep castle walls, but one gun 'seldom hit the Castle, though not half-musket shot from it'.[18] Yet the siege continued, with Lord George and his men constantly harassed by a detachment of Hessians and St George's Dragoons under Major General John Lindsay, Earl of Crawford.

On 25 March the sloop *Le Prince Charles*, returning from France with vital money and stores for the prince's army, was pursued by the Royal Navy (HMS *Sheerness* once again, commanded by Captain Lucius O'Brien) and ran aground at Tongue on the most northern coast of the Scottish mainland (in the old County of Sutherland) about eighty-five miles due north of Inverness. Captain George Mackay, son of the local chief, Lord Reay of Clan Mackay, and Lord Reay's men, along with Captain Sir Henry Monro and others from Loudoun's regiment, captured all the men and arms that had been on board, along with £12,000 sent to support the Jacobite campaign. The Earl of Cromartie and his son were immediately sent north to recover them.

Meanwhile, after the successful siege of Fort Augustus, Lieutenant General Stapleton had left Lord Lewis Gordon in command and marched on to Fort William accompanied by the Camerons and MacDonalds of Keppoch, who 'were particularly interested in the success of it, as Fort William commands their country; and during the Prince's expedition to England, the garrison made frequent sallies, burnt their houses, and carried off their cattle'.[19] The garrison was commanded by Captain Caroline Scott. Colonel Grant began raising the batteries on 20 March and proceeded to pound the fort for over a week, during which he was injured. The comte de Mirabel took over and 'succeeded no better . . . than he had done at Stirling'.[20] On 31 March two parties sallied out from the fort to attack the batteries and succeeded in spiking the guns in one battery and taking prisoners from both. A few days later the siege was abandoned and the Jacobite troops retired back to Inverness. At about the same time, Lord George and his men were also ordered to return to Inverness, allowing Major General Crawford the opportunity to relieve the starving garrison at Blair Castle.

Despite all the issues, including the constant concern over money and food and bouts of illness, Charles maintained – outwardly at least – a

strong, confident manner. As James Maxwell recalls, 'Amidst all these misfortunes, the Prince kept up his spirits wonderfully – he appeared gayer
even than usual.'[21] This was by far the longest period that the army had
rested in one area since Edinburgh and it was here, as Maxwell continues,
'he gave frequent balls to the ladies of Inverness, and danced himself, which
he had declined doing at Edinburgh in the midst of his grandeur and
prosperity'.[22] We might wonder how such extravagances were funded –
no doubt on promises of reimbursement after the restoration. But such a
display of princely poise was surely better than appearing withdrawn, nervous or anxious. However, it certainly caused some mutterings within the
Jacobite ranks. Maxwell observes that his 'conduct was censured by some
austere-thinking people', yet 'I believe it had a good effect in the main.
The greatest part of those that saw him cheerful and easy concluded he had
resources which they did not know; those, indeed, that knew the true state
of his affairs, had a very bad opinion of them.'[23] Considering the contrast
with the prince's behaviour at Edinburgh where, as James Maxwell says, he
was in the 'midst of his grandeur and prosperity', it cannot be dismissed
that Charles was responding to his less than favourable circumstances with
forced high spirits. Either he felt that all was lost, so why not? Or, he was
ignoring the severity of his situation. Perhaps it was simply his way of
keeping sane under such extraordinary pressure.

Thomas Bakewell, *An Exact representation of ye army passing the River Spey*, 1746.
(PRIVATE COLLECTION / BRIDGEMAN IMAGES)

The Spey

'to seek the Rebels'

The Duke of Cumberland and his division, six battalions of foot and Lord Mark Kerr's dragoons, finally left Aberdeen on 8 April as James Ray writes, 'in order to seek the Rebels'. Before the march, news came via Captain George Mackay and Captain Sir Henry Monro of the recent capture of the *Hazard* sloop (or *Le Prince Charles*). James Ray observed that 'the Rebels long expected Succours happily fell into our Hands, which undoubtedly must be a great Disappointment to them'.[1] It was. As the British army marched, the weather was fine and 'our Transports, at the same Time, moved along Shore, with a gentle Breeze and fair Wind'. They arrived at Oldmeldrum where 'the Army quarter'd the first Night, after 12 Miles March'.[2] The next day they marched on to Banff 'where his Royal Highness gave the Army a Day's Rest'. Here also two spies were taken, the first 'hanged on a Tree in the Town; and the other a little out of Town, and for want of a Tree, was hanged on what they call the Ridging-Tree of a House, which projected out from the End, and on his Breast was fixt in Writing, *A Rebel Spy*'.[3] On the onward march, a great fire could be seen in the distance to the south and, as no one knew what it was, James Ray investigated. He 'found it to be a Nonjuring Meeting-House, set on Fire by a Party of Kingston's, that were reconnoitring the Hills'.[4]

On the 11th they encamped at Cullen where Lord Albemarle and his men joined them. The duke's army was now gathered together. At Cullen, the duke quartered at James Ogilvy, 5th Earl of Findlater's house.[5] While here his lordship gave a guinea to every troop and company, 'tho', as the Duke of Cumberland recalled a few days later, 'his Estate & house have been extremely plundered by the Rebels'. In addition, 'Lord Braco has also given two hundred & fifty Guineas to be divided among the private men.'[6] The following day they marched on towards the Spey, the final barrier between the two armies.

As ordered, the Duke of Perth and his brother Lord John Drummond with 2,000 men had been located around Speymouth. The intention was either to prevent the British army from passing the river, or to delay their crossing for as long as possible, in order to allow the Jacobite army, now spread out over a large area of land (as Lord Elcho had stated) to gather strength and then regroup. According to Captain Johnstone 'nearly the half had gone home to see their families, along with the chiefs, who intended to order every vassal, without exception, capable of bearing arms'. The scarcity of provisions at Inverness was 'an additional motive for permitting them to return home, as the Prince was convinced that they would cheerfully join his army the moment they received orders for that purpose'.[7] As preventing the British army's crossing or, failing that, delaying it was crucial, Alexander MacDonald with the Clanranalds, Ardsheal's men, Pitsligo's Horse and French picquets were ordered to join the Duke of Perth and his brother in the defence of the Spey.[8] About this time Colonel O'Sullivan recalls being sent out to report on whether 'it was practicable to defend that River', but he believed the water level was so low that it was now fordable in several places and therefore 'saw it was needlesse to pretend to defend the passage of it'.[9] In O'Sullivan's opinion, the Duke of Perth and Lord John did what they could in a less than ideal situation, that is 'to have postes at the other side, [that] is the south side of the River, & watch the enemy as closely as possible'.[10]

Colonel O'Sullivan returned to Inverness to offer his report on the situation to the east. While in the vicinity of the Spey, he had heard that the British army numbered 18,000 men (a gross exaggeration) and if this was the case, declared O'Sullivan, 'the Prince was not in a Condition to measure himself wth them'.[11] Meanwhile, Alexander MacDonald with his fellow troops were marching to join Lord John and the Duke of Perth, when 'we found the guard on the Spey in full march back to Elgin, who gave out that they were neither able to guard the river nor fight the enemy after they had passed; the latter was true, but,' he continues, countering O'Sullivan's assessment, 'to guard the Spey was ane easy matter'. However, as the Duke of Cumberland's army was within a short distance of the now undefended river and would therefore soon cross it, they considered making a stand nearer Inverness, 'but it was thought more advisable to retreat till we should be joined by the rest of our army, as the Dukes whole army was comeing upon us and more numerous than we formerly understood them to be'.[12]

Now that the worst of the winter weather was over, and the crucial watery hurdle reportedly low and therefore fordable, the Duke of Cumberland and his army had begun their move towards the west and Inverness. Regarding the crossing, the Duke of Cumberland wrote on 13 April, 'they passed through, the foot soldiers up to their waists' and 'with no other loss than of one Dragoon & four Women who all were drown'd'.[13] Some Jacobite cavalry were seen observing their progress and in James Ray's opinion, 'In this Situation, had the Rebels stood us here, it might have been of bad Consequence to our Army; they having a great Advantage over us, and might have defended this important Pass a long Time, to our great loss.'[14] Yet they retired on seeing the British army cross and were immediately pursued by Kingston's Horse. 'But,' as the duke continues, 'the Rebels were already got out of their reach before they could pass.'[15] He then observes it 'is a very lucky thing We had to deal with such an Enemy, for it would be a most difficult undertaking to pass this River before an Enemy who should know how to take all advantages of the situation'. He thought their number in total between two and three thousand. The plan now was 'to march this morning for Elgin, & if We find it practicable shall trie to reach Forres, from whence there will be but two marches to Inverness'.[16]

The infantry, meantime, encamped on the north side of the river 'and Straw being wanting to bed the Tents, they were obliged to use Barley unthresh'd, which was very bad to lye upon; the Horse were ordered to repass the River and quarter in the Town of Fochabers'.[17] The duke quartered at the minister's house at Speymouth (on the north side of the river) which had been, since 18 March, Lord John Drummond's quarters, hastily abandoned during breakfast when a messenger burst in and announced that 'the Enzie was all in a vermine of Red Quites'.[18] From here, the duke wrote to the Duke of Newcastle with a summary of the march from Aberdeen, including the description of the Spey crossing (quoted above) and then observes, 'As our accounts of the Pretender's Son & the Clans are so various, I dont think it worth while to trouble his Majesty with them. Thank God We have had the finest weather that could be wish'd for our first incampments, & have hitherto found Plenty of Straw & Forage.'[19] On 13 April the Duke of Cumberland and his men continued the march west, reaching Elgin later that same day.

Robert Strange, Notes engraved for Prince Charles at Inverness April 1746.
(NATIONAL LIBRARY OF SCOTLAND)

Culloden

'a clap of thunder'

In Inverness, and in anticipation of an imminent battle, the Orders for the period of 14–15 April were issued under the signature of Lord George Murray and read:

> It is His Royall Highness posetive Orders that evry person atach themselves to some Corps of the Armie & to remain with that Corps night & day till the Batle & pirsute be finally over; This regards the Foot as well as the Horse. The Order of Batle is to be given to evry Ginerall officer & evry Commander of Regiments or Squadrons. It is requierd & expected that each individual in the Armie as well officer as souldier keeps their posts that shall be alotted to them, & if any man turn his back to Runaway the nixt behind such man is to shoot him. No body on Pain of Death to strip the slain or plunder till the Batle be over. The Highlanders all to be in kilts, & no body to throw away their Guns,
> by H:R:H Command George Murray.[1]

On 14 April, Prince Charles was informed that the Duke of Perth had been obliged to retire from defending the Spey some days before. This meant that, in all likelihood, the British army would have already passed the river. Captain Johnstone says that the 'astonishment which prevailed at Inverness, when the information came upon us like a clap of thunder, that the Duke of Cumberland had forded the river Spey, without experiencing the least opposition, may be easily conceived'.[2] Robert Strange had spent two weeks preparing the copper printing plates for the new Jacobite money and was in a position to commence production when the news arrived. He recalled that the town 'was in a general alarm, and even in confusion. Nothing was heard but the noise of bagpipes, the beating of drums, and the clash of arms. The field of Culloden was the following day to be the general rendevous' and, as ordered by Lord George, 'every individual betook himself to his corps'.[3] Colonel Ker recalled that the prince mounted up and rode at their head to Culloden House, while Lord George was left behind to gather those quartered around Inverness, 'which made it pretty late before he join'd the P. at Culloden'. Orders were also sent to the Duke of Perth and Lord John Drummond to assemble at Lord President Forbes' estate.[4]

Lord Elcho later recorded that that night the army 'lay out upon their arms' and, although there was meal at Inverness, 'by the mismanagement of the people that were Charged with it there was none of it Baked'. With no provisions, the men were forced to find what they could in the environs of Culloden.[5] Captain John Daniel describes arriving at the rendezvous and having 'accordingly encamped as well as we could on the heath that grew upon the common, which served us both for bedding and fuel, the cold being very severe, we were soon after joined by the Prince and several of his Clans. Finding that the enemy did not pursue us we rested ourselves all night upon the Common.'[6] Lord Elcho calculated that only 7,000 of the 10,000 men 'had time to assemble' and they were drawn up 'together in a plain near the Castle of Culloden'.[7] Both figures are certainly inflated, with closer to 5,000 likely to have been in the vicinity at this time.[8] The Camerons returned from Fort William that night, but among the missing regiments were the MacPhersons under Cluny MacPherson, Keppoch's MacDonalds, Cromartie's detachment (still pursuing the £12,000 and arms), the Frasers, and some reinforcements for Glengarry's.[9]

Lord Elcho continues that at supper in Culloden House, the prince was very optimistic about the outcome of a battle and that all those 'that spoke of a retreat and of waiting for the 3,000 men of his army that were away, were not listened to'. In addition, when a place of rendezvous in the event of defeat was mentioned, the prince 'answered that only those that were afraid could doubt his coming victory'.[10] Lord George observed, 'Many of our people, as it was seed time, had slipt home; and as they had no pay for a month past, it was not an easy matter to keep them together.' In support of Lord Elcho's recollection, he also says that 'many were for retiring to stronger ground till all our army was gathered; but most of the baggage being at Inverness, this was not agreed to'.[11] Colonel O'Sullivan, offering a more positive impression of the prince, states that on the 14th Charles 'continued the rest of the day in seeing the troops accomodated in the Parks, & inclosiors as well as they cou'd', for 'he never went to bed upon those occasions'.[12]

At daybreak on 15 April, Charles 'drew up his army in order of Battle upon a Spacious moor to the South of Culloden with some park walls to their right, and their left towards the descent That goes down to Culloden'.[13] The ground had been selected by Colonel O'Sullivan but Lord George had disagreed with the choice, believing that an area near Dalcross Castle, on the other or south side of the Water of Nairn was preferable. The ground they were now gathering on 'was certainly not proper for Highlanders'; that is, it was too flat and open and therefore, in his opinion, good for regular cavalry and artillery. He proposed that Brigadier Stapleton and Colonel Ker 'should view the ground on the other side of the water of Nairn, which they did. It was found to be hilly and boggy; so that the enemy's cannon and horse could be of no great use to them there. Mr O'Sullivan had gone to Inverness, so he was not with them when they reconnoitred the ground.'[14] If the battle went against them, this area would also offer a covered path for retreat to Inverness. Stapleton and Ker's report 'was entirely conformable to what I had said'.[15]

In contrast, Colonel O'Sullivan – hardly Lord George's greatest supporter – considered this 'famiouse' battlefield 'the worst [that] cou'd be chossen for the highlanders' and, worse still, 'the most advantagiouse for the enemy'. The reason for his disdain of Lord George's choice, aside from habitual antipathy, was that there was a ravine running between the proposed Jacobite line and the British army's – a great natural defence against an advancing army as it was 'impracticable for man or horse'. But in O'Sullivan's opinion, knowing the natural style of fighting among the Highland foot 'to go directly sword in hand on the enemy', to 'fire but one shot, & abandonne their firelocks after. If there be any obstruction, [that] hinders them of going on the enemy, all is lost; they don't like to be expos'd to the enemys fire, nor can they resist it, not being trained to charge [load] as fast as regular troops.'[16] Further, according to O'Sullivan, on Lord George's field the British army would have occupied rising ground and therefore would have been in a commanding position; the Jacobite troops, if they had managed to overcome the ravine, would have been running uphill against an army famed for its firing power. The prince was therefore presented with two very differing opinions as to where he should fight. Despite Lord George, Stapleton and Ker plus the clan chiefs that were present agreeing on the ground to the south of the Water of Nairn, in Lord George's words 'it was determined not to take that ground, as perhaps the enemy might pass on to Inverness without attacking us'.[17] O'Sullivan's proposed field of battle, located just south of the route from

Speymouth to Inverness, was therefore accepted, in O'Sullivan's opinion
much to Lord George's chagrin. Charles, however, was 'parfectly well satisfied wth what past'.[18]

While forming battle lines, Charles ordered biscuit to be brought from
Inverness, as the men had not eaten since the previous day, but only one
biscuit per man arrived. Colonel Ker recalled that the army 'were all drawn
up in order of battle, to wait the Duke of Cumberland's coming. Keppoch's
men joined in the field, from Fort William, and the whole was reviewed
by the Prince, who was very well pleased to see them in so good spirits,
though they had eaten nothing that day but one single biscuit a man, provisions being very scarce, and money too.'[19] Regarding the supplies, Lord
George Murray states, 'It was also said, that there was no provisions; this
last was indeed a great article, which had been unaccountably neglected;
and yet I was convinced there was enough at Inverness, which might even
then have been brought out.'[20] John Hay is usually blamed for the poor
organisation of what little rations they had, Secretary Murray being still
incapacitated through illness. This was a particularly desperate time to
mismanage the army's supplies, for, as Ker states, the Jacobite army was not
simply rehearsing the battle order. It was assembled to await the imminent
arrival of the British army with every expectation of fighting.

As a further indication of the fracturing relations among some of the
commanders, during the forming up for battle Lord George is reported
to have insisted that his Athollmen should be placed on the right of the
front line – a position traditionally held by the MacDonald regiments,
Glengarry's, Clanranald's and Keppoch's. According to the commander of
Glengarry's, Donald MacDonell of Lochgarry, when Charles gave the right
to Lord George 'Clanronald, Keppoch and I . . . begg'd he wou'd allow us
our former right, but he intreated us for his sake we wou'd not dispute it,
as he had already agreed to give it to Lord George and his Atholmen; and
I heard H.R.Hs say that he resented it much, and should never doe the
like if he had occasion for it.'[21] Sir John Macdonald confirms that there
had been 'a great dispute' between Lord George 'and Clan Ranald who
maintained hotly that the Macdonalds have always had the right hand,
and Lord George said that some times his people had had it'. Sir John
Macdonald thought the prince should be warned 'that it was most important not to offend the Clans which formed, as all the world knows, excellent
soldiers, by depriving them of their ancient right'.[22] But Lord George was
given his way and the Athollmen took their position at the furthest right of
the front line. The MacDonalds grudgingly occupied the far left.

It was around this time that, according to Colonel O'Sullivan, news arrived that the Duke of Cumberland and his men were encamped near Nairn, and Charles ordered Lord Elcho to ride out with a party of horse to gain intelligence. Lord Elcho left around ten o'clock, remained watching the British army for about three hours and then returned, advising the prince that they 'were quiet in their Camp at Nairn, and by all appearance they did not intend to move that day'.[23] According to Colonel O'Sullivan, Charles declared that 'If so, they'l starve us hear, if we don't march to them, & not give them time to retrinch themselfs'.[24] Charles then called a war council with the principal officers and asked their opinion. According to Lord George it was at this time that a discussion about a night attack occurred: 'Our reason being for this attempt, was, that as his Royal Highness had declared two days before, he was resolved to attack the enemy without waiting for those who were to join us; (the expression was, had he but a thousand men he would attack them).'[25] Lord George also recalled, 'His Royal Highness and most others were for venturing it, amongst whom I was; for I thought we had a better chance by doing it, than by fighting in so plain a field.'[26] He later writes, 'I was . . . of the same opinion, with many others, for a night attack; but that was only, of two evils to choose what we thought the least.'[27]

Arguing, therefore, for the lesser of two evils, the greater being O'Sullivan's open 'plain field', Lord George is credited by Lord Elcho with making a speech, where he considered the advantages of a surprise attack at night-time, rather than in daylight, 'for as regular troops depend intirely upon their discipline, and on the Contrary the Highlanders having none, the Night was the time to putt them most upon an Equality, and he Concluded that his Opinion was that they Should march at dusk of ye Evening'. To maintain the element of surprise, Lord George recommended that he and the right wing of the first line would march around Nairn itself and then attack the encampment in their rear, while the Duke of Perth with the left wing should attack them from the front. Charles would support Perth with the second line.[28] Lord George stressed that the attack needed to have taken place under darkness to have a hope of success: no later than one o'clock in the morning, two at a push. No one, he says, 'ever imagined we could attempt it later'.[29] This would require a swift, orderly march over rough terrain in the pitch darkness – no easy feat. Both Lord George and Lord Elcho recall that there was universal agreement to this plan, although the latter states that the proposal to wait until dusk before commencing the march was queried 'as Culloden was Eight miles from Nairn' and 'it was to be fear'd the Army would not Accomplish that march before day light'.[30] Lord George apparently answered the query by stating that he would take responsibility for it: 'So the march was resolved upon.'[31]

The date of the night attack was auspicious and it was hoped that this would contribute to the success of the plan: for 15 April was the Duke of Cumberland's twenty-fifth birthday. The plan was to march as discreetly as possible across the eight miles of moorland, rather than use the Inverness–Nairn road. Then – although not explicitly defined, but inevitable considering the covert manner of the attack – they were to kill as many of the British army soldiers in their beds as they could 'with Sword & Pistol'.[32] This would be made easier by the fact that, as Lord George is reported to have said, 'This is Cumberlands birth day, they'l all be as drunk as beggers.'[33] Colonel O'Sullivan recalled that everyone, and particularly the prince, 'was full of the good success of [that] project, & looked upon it to be the finishing stroke to restor the King, as in all likelyhood it wou'd'. However, as it was too early still to begin the march, it was decided that the plan should be kept secret until the final moment.[34]

This general secrecy may have had unforeseen consequences, for as Lord George recollected, between six and seven at night, and just before the night march was due to start, 'the men went off on all hands, and in great numbers, to shift for themselves, both for provisions and quarters: many officers were sent after them, but all to no purpose'. Lord George believed that as many as 2,000 men had wandered off before the night march began. As a result 'I do not know of one officer who had been made acquainted with the resolution of surprising the enemy, but declared in the strongest terms for laying it aside; much was spoken by them all for not attempting it then.'[35] But Charles 'was extremely bent upon it, and said that, whenever we began the march, the men would be all hearty, and those that had gone off would return and follow'.[36] Lord George was not convinced. Despite having argued for the night march 'which I did at first heartily concur, till the men went off, and then I was against it'.[37] It is believed that, prior to the march, Charles gave orders for Irish officers to keep a watch on Lord George – the prince clearly fearing, with the British army so near, that he might still betray him. According to Lord Elcho, 'Lord George knew of all these rumours, and so had simply confined himself to doing his duty as a soldier without offering any advice to the Prince.'[38]

Through the existence of a document in the Royal Archives, it is a possibility that just before the army marched, revised orders were issued dated 'Calodon April 15th 1746' and with the 'parol' or password 'Roy James' or King James. This possible revision to the previous orders issued at Inverness – dated 14–15 April in Lord George's hand and also with the code name 'Rie James (in English King James)'[39] and therefore prior to the decision to mount a night attack – follows these earlier orders precisely, except with an additional line inserted: 'And to give no Quarter to the Electors Troops, on any Account what so ever.'[40] The anonymous author of the 'Journal of the Young Pretender before, at and after the Battle of Cullooden' states that 'Betwixt eight & nine, orders were given for their marching, with an intention to surprise the Enemy in their Camp. The word was, K- James. The attack was to be made with Sword & Pistol.'[41] Captain John Daniel states that at dusk it was made known that they were going to attack the British army 'that night in their camp' and that 'Orders were accordingly given to that effect, which were obeyed with the greatest pleasure and alacrity by the whole army'.[42] Alexander MacDonald recalled that they were given 'express orders to observe the profoundest silence in our march' and that the code word 'was King James the Eighth'. In addition, and contrary to the anonymous author quoted above, they were 'forbid in the attack to make any use of our firearms, but only of sword, dirk and bayonet, to cutt the tent strings and pull down the poles, and where we observed a swelling or bulge in the falen tent there to strick and push vigorously'.[43] Through these means the Jacobite command was clearly aiming to annihilate the Duke of Cumberland's army. Killing your enemy in their beds could indeed be described as giving them 'no Quarter'.[44]

Thomas Sandby, *A British Camp*, 1748.

47

Nairn

'to give us battle'

On 15 April at his new encampment the Duke of Cumberland wrote his usual update to the Duke of Newcastle, covering the movement of his troops and any recent intelligence of the Jacobite army. The British army had reached the town of Nairn after two forced marches from Speymouth, and here had 'found tolerable Plenty of every thing for our encampments'. The only issue was crossing 'several broad Waters, which the men were forced to wade, & they were mid thigh, but they all went on with great cheerfulness, which they have shewn, ever since our setting out'. The day before, the quartermasters with their escort, while marking out the camp, had to halt 'for fear of being intercepted by the Rebels, a large body of Whom, were endeavouring to cut in between them & us'. But now, the foot were all gathered and encamped on the west side of the Water of Nairn, with the Campbells at the front and the cavalry at the rear. In the duke's opinion it was 'necessary to give our men a halt, after four hard days march'.

Intelligence had come that Charles was at Inverness the day before, but 'upon our driving this body of the Rebels towards Inverness', that is Lord John Drummond, the Duke of Perth and their men, 'He had marchd out a mile on this side [of] it, with what Intent I know not, tho I cant bring my self to believe that they propose to give us battle.' The main reason for his incredulity was that 'All accounts agree that they cannot assemble all their Clans & should they have them all together, I flatter my self the affair would not be very long.'[1] On the same day the duke writes again to the Secretary of State, revealing that Flanders and the war on the Continent had never been far from his thoughts. He thanks Newcastle for acknowledging 'the disagreeableness of the service I am now employed in, & which must be doubly so, if it is to be the cause of my not being employed in Flanders'. But if the king needs him here 'it is my inclination as well as my Duty as a soldier to prefer that which may be thought most for the advantage of his Majestys affairs'.[2]

Michael Hughes also recalls that during the day, encamped at Nairn, a boy of seventeen was to be hanged for a spy, but a local minister of the Kirk, on hearing this, told the Duke of Cumberland that 'he had not lately been with the Rebels, and was naturally but a poor simple Youth whom they deluded away'. Whereupon the duke spared his life. Unfortunately, by the time the reprieve reached the place of execution, the boy had already been hanging for ten minutes and 'the Executioner in cutting him down, carelessly let him fall to the Ground, the Gallows being very high'. But, 'he came to Life, though disordered in his Senses when the Army went away'.[3]

Aside from what could be foraged locally, the British army had the support of the Royal Navy, which continued to follow them along the coast. On the evening of Tuesday the 15th, as it was his twenty-fifth birthday the duke gave each battalion a half anker of brandy, just over 4 imperial gallons, to drink his health. Hughes recalls that 'every Man had a sufficient Quantity of Biscuit, Cheese and Brandy allowed him at the sole Expense of the Duke our glorious Leader'.[4] In an age when beer was considered a healthier drink than water, this was a small but well-received gesture. However, ever the disciplinarian (even on his birthday) and with an important battle ahead, drunkenness would not have been tolerated.

The Duke of Newcastle received the duke's letter (dated the 13th) with the 'welcome news of your having passed The Spey' and immediately responded by saying that he had no new command from the king but that 'His Majesty has the greatest Hopes, that your Royal Highness will be soon able to put an End to this unnatural Rebellion'.[5]

The letter was dated Whitehall, Thursday, 17 April 1746.

John Pine, 'Eighth Regiment of Dragoons', from *The Cloathing Book*, 1742.
(ROYAL ARMOURIES)

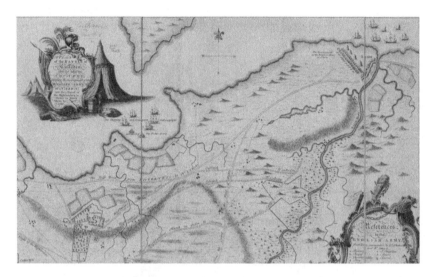

N. Carrington, *A Plan of ... Culloden and the Adjacent Country*, 1753. In this pro-Jacobite map, Culloden House is seen bottom left, with the Bristish army encampment at Nairn top right.

(AKG IMAGES)

Culloden to Nairn

'this will Crown all'

At dusk on Tuesday, 15 April, the Jacobite army left Culloden marching in two columns – one led by Lord George, the other by the Duke of Perth and Lord John Drummond – according to John Daniel, 'leaving great fires burning in our camp', to give the impression, from a distance, that they had not stirred. Lord George and the first line were to attack the cavalry, while the Duke of Perth with the second was to attack the infantry. Colonel O'Sullivan describes an extraordinary scene, which, he states, occurred just after the army had moved off. According to O'Sullivan, the prince put his arm about Lord George's neck declaring, '"yu cant imagine, nor I cant expresse to yu how acknowledging I am of all the services yu have rendred me, but this will Crown all. You'l restore the King by it, you'l deliver our poor Contry from Slevery, you'l have all the hon[ou]r & glory of it, it is your own work, it is yu imagined it, & be assured"', Charles apparently continued, '"that the King nor I, will never forget it. I speake to yu D[ea]r Ld George", the prince now squeezing him in a friendly manner, "from the bottom of my soul, & I am sure [that] it is to yu we'l owe all, so God Blesse yu."'[1] This heartfelt speech (as reported by O'Sullivan) establishes that Charles not only appreciated the cunning of the idea and Lord George's plan to execute it, but considered this surprise attack the deciding stroke in favour of the current campaign and the Jacobite cause. He had therefore placed this single, improvised action under an enormous burden to succeed.

Lord George simply states that having agreed to continue with the march (despite the disappearance of upwards of 2,000 men) the prince 'embraced me at the same time'.[2] Lord George may well have appreciated the prince's comments and physical signs of friendship, of deep feeling, but he was not one for outward displays of emotion or pretty speeches, no matter how heartfelt. According to O'Sullivan, Charles continued to walk beside Lord George for some time, the latter silent, until 'the Prince took leave of him, saying "well God blesse yu. Il go & see if all follows"'.[3] Lord George took off his bonnet, made a stiff bow and the prince walked off.

Charles returned to the rear among the French troops. But covering such marshy terrain and at night proved even more difficult than anticipated. Lord George's column arrived within two miles of the British army camp – he was close enough to hear the sentries calling out to each other – but an hour behind schedule. The second column, meanwhile, was even further behind, so that the entire army was effectively marching as a somewhat disjointed single column spread out over a large distance. One author stated, 'Many were so much fatigued, that they slept on their march; Others to a great number, wandered.'[4]

Hinting at not only the distances between the columns of this army, but the resulting confusion in the darkness, John Daniel recalls that 'the Prince's Aides-de-Camp in riding from rank to rank, and asking, for God's sake! what has become of His Lordship, and telling that the Prince was in the utmost perplexity for want of him'.[5] As dawn began to break, it was clear the element of surprise had gone. Inevitably there are differing opinions as to what then happened. Lord George could no doubt see that they had lost the initiative and that the only option was to retreat before the encamped army began to stir. One author states:

> a Person of Distinction, observing the State of the Army, & fearing all there, would be cut off, told Lord George Murray the Condition the Army was in; and, to prevent the loss of so many gallant men, wished He would retreat in time. Lord George was of his opinion; but, for Reasons he gave him, desired he might inform the Prince of their situation & bring him orders: which he undertook. But, before he could return with the Prince's Orders, Lord George Murray observing Day coming on, began to retreat.

This decision to retreat, before orders from Charles had been received, 'occasioned some Reflections, & confirmed several in their former opinion of him, tho', I believe, without any just Foundation'.[6]

According to Lord Elcho the 'Person of Distinction' was Lochiel, who found the prince somewhere between the centre and the rear, and informed him that it was the opinion of the officers at the front of the column that the surprise attack had failed and a retreat was the only option. But the 'Prince was not for going back, and said it was much better to march forward and attack, than march back and be attack'd afterwards, when the men would be all fatigued with their nights march. During the time of this Conversation the army, by what means I know not, began to move back.'[7] Another version states that about two o'clock in the morning,

> the Duke of Perth came galloping up . . . and ordered the officers to wheel about and march back to Culloden. They had not gone above one hundred yards back when they met the Prince, who called out himself, 'Where the devil are the men a-going?' It was answered, 'We are ordered by the Duke of Perth to return to Culloden House.' 'Where is the Duke of Perth?' says the Prince. 'Call him here.' Instantly the Duke came up, and the Prince, in an angry tone, asked what he meant by ordering the men back. The Duke answered that Lord George with the first line was gone back three-quarters of an hour agoe. 'Good God!' said the Prince, 'what can be the matter? What does he mean? We were equal in number, and would have blown them to the devil. Pray, Perth, can't you call them back yet? Perhaps he is not gone far yet.'

Perth begged leave to speak to the prince alone and they stood talking in hushed tones to one side. Then the 'Prince returned and call'd out, "There is no help for it, my lads; march back to Culloden House"'.[8]

In Colonel O'Sullivan's not unbiased opinion, 'About two hours before day', the real reason Lord George had been so unresponsive to Charles earlier in the evening, 'was discovered, at least it was judged so. Being within a mil[e] of the Camp, he sends Locheil to the Prince to let him know [that] he did not think proper to continu his march, because he cou'd never be strong enough for them, & besides it would be day.'[9] O'Sullivan also recorded that he had been ordered by the prince to stop the retreat and when he came up with Lord George, he reaffirmed to him that all the prince's 'confidence is in yu, [that] the losse or the gain of the cause is in your hands & depends entirely on yu'. As a result, Lord George should advance to the enemy, whom 'it is morrally sure you'l distroy'. The prince had no money or supplies, so a retreat would simply 'give all over to yr enemy', and, 'if they come upon yu in battle, superior as they are in horse & foot, & their Artillery, can yu resist them?' If not, 'Yu have nothing for it then, but to profit of the advantage yu may have over them in surprising them, & profit of the sperits your men are in.'¹⁰ Lord George apparently refused to listen to O'Sullivan.

Even if O'Sullivan had not actually made this speech to Lord George, this is certainly what he felt: firstly, that the plan to surprise the British army in its camp was their greatest hope of success and, secondly, that in retreating and therefore effectively ruining the Jacobite army's chances of success, Lord George was demonstrating that he was a traitor to the prince and the cause. Indeed, in O'Sullivan's opinion, Lord George had not simply pulled back from executing the final stages of the night attack plan, but in forcing the Jacobite army to march almost to the British army's camp, only then to retreat, he was putting them in the worst possible condition to fight a battle. Treachery indeed. Of course, this would only be an issue if a battle were to be fought later that day, which no one at this moment could have predicted with any certainty. But such an opinion clearly existed beyond O'Sullivan: note the comment from the anonymous author that Lord George's abandoning of the surprise attack 'confirmed several in their former opinion of him'. Lord George's recollection of this exchange (unsurprisingly) differs. O'Sullivan 'came up to the front, and said His Royal Highness would be very glad to have the attack made; but as Lord George Murray was in the van, he could best judge whether it could be done in time or not'. 'Perhaps,' Lord George continues, 'Mr. O'Sullivan may chuse to forget this, but others are still alive who heard him.'¹¹ Lord George was certainly more cautious than Charles, and although the plan for the night march was his, the manner in which it was executed was certainly not. Robert Strange, with Lord Elcho's Life Guards, supported the decision to retreat, for even though 'We saw, as it were before us, the glorious prize . . . we durst not encounter it, for there is almost a moral certainty that we should have been cut off to man.'¹²

Whether by design, accident or mismanagement, an army already under immense strain had been made, through the failure of this plan, almost catatonic with fatigue and hunger. Yet even though this impromptu exercise had failed, they were still able to fight another day, preferably when up to full strength, rested and fed, having chosen a well-appointed field of battle and applied a well-thought-out battle strategy. Lord George certainly believed that there were other options available to the prince and his army, whereas Charles considered their best chance was attacking the

British army in their camp; whether at night or in broad daylight made little difference to him.

On the retreat back to Culloden, the army was not required to avoid houses by marching over marshland. Now, on the main road, they managed the journey in a shorter time than the previous evening. Even so, some of the Horse Guards, Robert Strange included, were so 'overpowered by fatigue, and ready every instant to drop from our saddles' that they stopped at a barn only a few miles into the retreat and 'threw ourselves down upon some straw, tying our horses to our ankles, and the people assuring us that, in case of any danger, they should awake us'.[13] When Charles eventually arrived back at Culloden House 'after ordering and earnestly recommending to everybody to do their utmost to get provisions to his men', he 'went into the house, threw himself upon the top of a bed, books, etc., upon him'.[14] Lord Elcho states that the army 'return'd to the parks of Culloden, where Every body seemed to think of nothing but Sleep. The men were prodigiously tired with hunger and fatigue, and vast numbers of them went into Inverness, and the Villages about, both to Sleep and to pick up what little nourishment they Could gett.' Meanwhile, the principal officers made their way to Culloden House and 'were so much tired that they never thought of Calling a Councill what was to be done, but Every one lay'd himself down were he Could, some on beds, others on tables, Chairs, & on the floors, for the fatigue and the hunger had been felt as much amongst the officers as Soldiers'.[15] However, Lord Elcho also states that Charles was now so suspicious of Lord George 'that he engaged two officers to watch his conduct, and to shoot him in case they discovered that he wished to betray him'.[16]

According to James Maxwell the 'Prince was incensed beyond expression at a retreat begun in direct contradiction to his inclination and express orders; in the first moments he was convinced he was betrayed, and expressed himself to that purpose; he was confirmed in this opinion by those who never missed an opportunity of leading Lord George Murray.' However, knowing that Lochiel and others, whom he trusted, were also involved, 'he did not know what to think, nor what to do: Thus perplexed he arrived with the army at Culloden.'[17] Maxwell also tells us that, rather than simply collapsing with exhaustion, Charles and his principal officers returned to Culloden House, 'where, instead of deliberating about what was proper to be done at this critical juncture, they

stared at one another with amazement; every body looked sullen and
dejected; those that had taken it upon themselves to begin the retreat,
as well as those that had not any share in it.' Maxwell agrees with Lords
George and Elcho, that 'Nothing was easier than to avoid an action for
several days; the Prince had only to retire beyond Inverness, or beyond
the river of Nairn'. But Charles saw these options as 'an argument of
fear, an acknowledgement of the Duke of Cumberland's superiority, and
[would] discourage the army'. He continues that this 'was the first time
the Prince ever thought his affairs desperate'.[18] A much reduced army,
exhausted and hungry: the situation was desperate indeed. Yet 'he would
not think of a retreat, which he had never yielded to but with the greatest reluctancy, and which on this occasion he imagined would disperse
the few men he had, and put an inglorious end to his expedition. He
resolved to wait for the enemy.'[19]

The marquis d'Eguilles later reported that at this time he requested an
audience with Charles and, kneeling before him, begged the prince not
to fight that day but, again in tandem with Lord George, Lord Elcho and
James Maxwell, either to retire to Inverness or to fall back further into the
Highlands. But 'defied by enemies whom he thoroughly despised, seeing
at their head the son of the rival of his father', 'proud and haughty as he
was, badly advised, perhaps betrayed, forgetting at this moment every
other object', Charles 'could not bring himself to decline battle even for
a single day'. D'Eguilles, fearing the worst, immediately left Culloden
House for Inverness and, on arrival at his lodgings, began burning his
papers.[20]

Less than two hours after Charles had reportedly collapsed on to his
bed, a party of horse, which had been observing the Duke of Cumberland's
army at Nairn, arrived at Culloden House in great haste and 'brought word
that their was a party of his horse within two miles, and that his whole army
was not above four miles off'. In fact the British army had started moving
not long after Lord George had called the retreat. On this news the prince,
the Duke of Perth, Lord George and Lord John Drummond 'mounted
their horses, ordered the drums to beat & the pipes to play which Alarm
Caused great hurry & Confusion amongst people half dead with fatigue'.
With very little time, they 'Endeavoured to gett the men together as fast as
possible' but 'they were dispersed all over the Country as far as Inverness'.[21]
James Maxwell states that the 'men were scattered among the woods of

Culloden, the greatest part fast asleep. As soon as the alarm was given, the officers ran about on all sides to rouse them, if I may use that expression, among the bushes, and some went to Inverness to bring back such of the men as hunger had driven there.' Despite this, 'there were several hundreds absent from the battle, though within a mile of it: some were quite exhausted and not able to crawl, and others asleep in coverts that had not been beat up.'[22] John Daniel, ever the optimist, recalled, 'Those, however, who staid, put the best face on the affair they could, and all of us presently appeared surprisingly courageous, who only seemed to survive and [be] animated by the spirit of loyalty and love for our dear Prince.'[23]

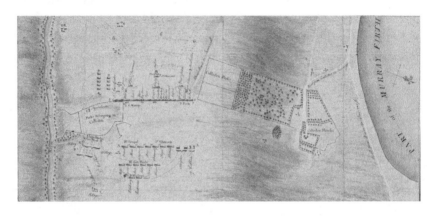

Thomas Sandby, *Plan of the Battle of Culloden*, dated Inverness
23 April 1746.
(ROYAL COLLECTION TRUST / BRIDGEMAN IMAGES)

Drummossie Muir

'our time was come'

The morning of Wednesday, 16 April was dark, cold, wet and windy: dreich. Colonel O'Sullivan says that the 'Prince got a horse-back, & went up upon the Moor', accompanied by Lochiel's Cameron regiment, all the while 'Not the least concern appear'd on his face.'[1] Lord Elcho recounts that on the call to arms 'their was near two thousand of them that was not at the Battle, so all The Prince Assembled was about five thousand men, which he march'd up the hill from Culloden, & drew them up in the same place they were drawn up in the day before with their right to Some park walls'.[2] Among the missing, although en route, were Cluny and his MacPhersons, and Simon, Master of Lovat, with some of the Frasers. Robert Strange, asleep in a barn some miles away, was awoken by a local woman on the appearance of the British army vanguard. He sped to the field with his fellow Horse Guards and, on arrival, found the prince 'engaged in holding a council of war, deliberating whether we should give battle to the Duke, or, circumstanced as the army was, retire and wait the arrival of our reinforcements'. 'The former,' states Strange, 'was determined on', which, in his opinion and no doubt shared by others present, was the wrong decision.[3] Strange wistfully continues, 'But our time was come. We were at variance within ourselves: Irish intriguers and French politics were too predominant in our councils,'[4] implying that, even at this time, the eleventh hour, if the Scottish officers had had their way, the depleted Jacobite army would have retired.

In fact, contrary to Lord Elcho's statement, the original location chosen by Colonel O'Sullivan was not the place where the Jacobite army now hastily drew up in battle order. According to Colonel Ker, O'Sullivan's ground had been some distance east: 'As there was no time to march to the ground they were on the day before, they were drawn up a mile farther westward, with a stone enclosure on the right of the first line, and the second at a proper distance behind.'[5] Considering the men were required to gather in haste, many coming back to the area around Culloden House from as far as Inverness (five miles to the west), then Ker's statement that the army assembled further to the west than the previous day makes absolute sense. Lord George himself recalled, 'When the enemy was approaching, betwixt ten and eleven o'clock, we drew up in the muir, a little back from where we had been the day before.'[6] The final word on this matter should go to Colonel O'Sullivan. In his memoir he states, 'The enemy was drawing near [from the north-east], & were very near the ground we occupyed the day before',[7] that is, just to the east of where the Jacobite army was now awaiting them.

The entire area was formed of boggy marsh, with patches of drier ground covered in rough grass, used by the local farmsteads for grazing. Two buildings called Culchunaig and Leanach, the latter a cottage with a heather-thatched roof, and several stone walls (as recalled by both Lord Elcho and Colonel Ker) were the key man-made features within the immediate landscape. Culloden House itself lies some distance to the north. Beyond the Lord President's house was the main road between Nairn and Inverness and further still, the Moray Firth.

Despite being in a different location, their new position had some advantages. The Jacobite army, facing in an easterly direction towards Nairn, was broadly arranged following the textbook French battle order, namely, a long first or front line, with a smaller second line or 'reserve' behind.[8] The first line stretched (left to right) from the bottom right tip of the walled parks adjoining Culloden House, across the moor, to the left tip of two connected stone-walled enclosures called the Culwhiniac enclosures to their right. The order of the first line was (again from left to right): the Glengarry MacDonells; then five smaller MacDonald regiments (Clanranald, Keppoch, Chisolm, Maclachlan, Monaltrie); then Mackintosh followed by Frasers at the centre; next, the smaller Appin Stewarts regiment; then Lochiel and the Camerons, and finally the Athollmen with their right against the first enclosure's wall. In this position, with the small second line located behind (picquets to the left; Perth, Glenbucket, Kilmarnock, Stuart, Ogilvy and Gordon located left to right centrally, and the Royal Ecossais to the right) and behind them, the cavalry (Strathallan's Horse, Scotch Hussars to the left, O'Shea at the centre, Fitz-James and Elcho to the right), the Culloden park walls and Culwhiniac enclosures, positioned either side of the Jacobite army, appeared to offer protection for both the left and right flank – particularly as the Culwhiniac enclosures, to the immediate right of the Athollmen, stretched all the way down the sloping ground to the Water of Nairn itself (to the far right). The river was a natural hindrance for any attempt to outflank them on this side. Behind and to the right of the Athollmen (a short distance from the left wall of the enclosures) was the Culchunaig farm building.

Throughout, as Colonel O'Sullivan recalled with evident admiration, Charles was very calm, cheerful and encouraging as his men watched, in the drizzle and wind, the British army advance over the miles of moorland before them. Charles' manner was 'very essential for a Prince or a General, [that] incourages very much the army, for every body examins them on those occassions'. Charles rode up and down, declaiming in a rousing manner to officer and private man alike, '"here they are comeing, my lades, we'l soon be wth them. They dont forget, Glads-mur, nor Falkirk, & yu have the same Armes & swords, let me see yours," takeing one of the men's swords. "Il answer this will cut of[f] some heads and arms to-day. Go on my Lads, the day will be ours & we'll want for nothing after."' O'Sullivan concludes, 'This & the like discource heartened very much our men' but then, less optimistically, 'tho' the Prince in the bottom had no great hopes'.[9]

Lord Elcho's recollections in his *Journal* of the prince's conversation at supper on 14 April challenge Colonel O'Sullivan's perception that the prince 'had no great hopes', prior to the failed night attack at least. According to Lord Elcho, Charles 'had no doubts as to the issue of the conflict with the Duke of Cumberland: he had the most exalted ideas as to the justice of his cause: he believed that the English soldiers would with difficulty be got to attack him, and was persuaded that his presence would of itself make the enemy afraid.'[10] This could have been Charles putting on a confident front for the benefit of his officers. It might also be evidence of the prince falling back on the irresistible power of his 'divine right', when all else, including luck, had apparently failed him. The inspired idea of the night march had clearly given the prince an enormous morale boost. But it had failed. Perhaps now – even before the first real battle with his cousin and enemy – Charles had accepted the total failure of this current attempt, and, psychologically, had already moved on to a future, undoubtedly more successful (i.e. better resourced) campaign. Without doubt, he had forced the present issue to a crisis, and against the advice of many of his officers. If it succeeded, then all was well. If it failed, then, he might say, there is always the next time.

Lord Elcho states that, in addition, as they all waited in the rain and wind, 'Their was no manner of Councill held upon the Field'.[11] This is not strictly true, as earlier that morning Robert Strange had encountered some form of council between the prince and (presumably) some of his officers, where the issue of whether they should fight now or delay was discussed. Yet, although the army had problems enough – lack of sleep, nourishment and, more importantly, depleted ranks – bickering and even disputes were again openly aired between some of the officers. A form of council, at this precise moment, might have forced some unity and discipline on them, while avoiding these dispiriting public outbursts. According to Colonel O'Sullivan, Lord George complained that this new field of battle had not been properly reconnoitred. This was hardly surprising, given the haste in which the army had gathered. Lord George in turn recalls,

> I told Mr O'Sullivan, who was placing the men in the order of battle, that I was convinced it was wrong ground; but he said that the muir was so interspersed with moss and deep ground that the enemy's horse and cannon could be of little advantage to them. We had still time to cross the water and take up the ground which Brigadier Stapleton and Colonel Ker had viewed the day before; for our right was within three hundred paces of the water, and the banks were very steppe, which was nothing to hinder Highlanders, and our horse and cannon could have crossed at a small ford, a mile farther back; but I reckon the belief that the enemy would have marched straight to Inverness was the occasion that we did not quit that plain muir.[12]

In another account Lord George states that if they had moved to the other side of the river, the Duke of Cumberland might not have attacked them, leaving the Jacobite army the option of drawing him 'up afterwards to passes in the mountains', where they could harass his troops and 'cut off some of his convoys', thus providing them with a chance of defeating him, or, rather, a greater chance than that currently presented by a battle on O'Sullivan's 'plain muir'. But some were 'against a hill campaign', Sir Thomas Sheridan was certainly too frail to survive one, and 'so we were obliged to be undone for their ease'.[13]

By his own admission, Colonel O'Sullivan responded to Lord George's concerns in a cocky manner, saying that 'here is as good a possition as yu cou'd desir':

> 'Yu see [that] Park before yu wch continues to the river wth a wall six foot high, & them houses near it, wch yu can fill wth men, & pierce the walls, [that] is your right. Yu see this Park here is to be our left, & both in a direct ligne. If there be not ground enough, we'l make use of the Parks & Il warant yu my Ld . . . the horse wont come to yu there.' He went off grumbling.[14]

But despite O'Sullivan's confident – almost provocative – riposte, there was an important proviso. As Colonel Ker later observed, the Culwhiniac enclosures were only secure and a protection to the Jacobite right flank, if the British army was not given the opportunity to create an entry point into the enclosures by pulling down part of the walls.[15] According to Colonel O'Sullivan's description, some of the walls were six feet high and could therefore obscure any movement behind them. The two Gordon battalions from the reserve were moved across to the right to keep watch on the enclosures. But in addition, O'Sullivan later suggested to Lord George that he might place some of his men inside the enclosure and use it as cover to fire at the British army. According to O'Sullivan, Lord George ignored this suggestion.[16]

There was another dispute. The Athollmen were still located on the right of the first line, as reportedly demanded by Lord George the previous day. The replacing of the MacDonald regiments (who were now standing on the left, as before) in the position they considered their ancient privilege since the days of the Bruce, continued to be an issue. Sir John Macdonald noted, 'On the way to the battle I talked to some of the Macdonald officers who told me that they would fight wherever they were placed but that few of their men would be there after this affront.'[17] But despite the discord that this had caused the previous day – indeed, continued to cause – and even as the British army was approaching, it was now, as O'Sullivan recalled, with a battle looming, that Lord George demanded that the Athollmen be moved from the right. As O'Sullivan observed 'there is nothing more dangerouse, then to change Regim[en]ts from one ground to another in presense of the enemy' besides which, the Athollmen had not actually fought on the right, as there had been no battle the previous day. To which '"Gad Sr," says Ld George swearing, "it is very hard [that] my Regim[en]t must have the right two days running".' O'Sullivan correctly observes that Lord George was now complaining of a situation which he himself had insisted upon.[18] Lord George's behaviour, as viewed through the hardly disinterested perception of Colonel O'Sullivan, does appear erratic and even self-destructive: if true, an indication of how exhausted and frustrated he was. There is no doubt that Lord George would have been against the decision to stand and fight that morning, particularly in that location. However, in his collective comments regarding Lord George, O'Sullivan is in reality suggesting that his lordship was completely incompetent in matters of war. In this instance Lord George was certainly acting like a regimental commander rather than the commander of the entire army. But O'Sullivan was hardly a thorough expert in military matters either.

Despite this reported disagreement, the Jacobite army remained, for a while, in the original formation. But as they watched the British army advance, Lord George's concern shifted to a low horseshoe-shaped turf wall (called the Leanach enclosure) which jutted out at an angle into the open moor, just beyond the stone wall of the Culwhiniac enclosures to Lord George's immediate right. It therefore formed an obstruction precisely where the Athollmen would move forward to meet the British army's front line. To avoid this, Lord George brought his men forward and then reformed them into three columns.

Colonel O'Sullivan, meanwhile, was near the left flank ensuring that the front line was battle-ready when, as he recalled, he 'was hardly at the left when he hears a cry of "close, close," he cant imagine what it means. He returns to the right finds intervals, [that] he had not seen before, goes to Ld George, finds his Regimt & those [that] were near him six deep [ie a column], instead of three [that] they are commonly upon.'[19] O'Sullivan says that he informed Lord George of the bad effect of this reordering on the remainder of the front line, but Lord George 'wont hear him nor even anser him': an indication, if one were needed, of how bitter and obstructive their relationship had become. O'Sullivan's concern was that Lord George's 'changement' – i.e. the unilateral forward move of the Athollmen to avoid the Leanach enclosure, while forming the men from three lines, three men deep, to three columns, six men deep – had not only shifted the axis of the whole front line, but, as the MacDonald regiments (on the far left) had refused to move to the right and thus away from the Culloden park walls (an action which would have exposed their left), it had also overstretched the front line, so that gaps appeared within it. In response O'Sullivan 'went of[f], as fast as he cou'd, for there was no time to be lost, to fill up the vecansy [that] was left (by Ld Georges changemt)'.[20] Perth and Glenbucket were brought out of the reserve second line and placed to the left of the MacDonald regiments, while the Stuart regiment was put between the Frasers and Appin Stewarts. This left the picquets, Kilmarnock, Ogilvy and the Royal Ecossais in reserve.

While these changes were being made, the Duke of Cumberland and his troops had been moving methodically forward. These men (according to the official account) consisted of 6,410 infantry and 787 cavalry, other sources put the army's total number as greater.[21] In Captain John Daniel's words, when the British army was in full view 'we began to huzza and bravado them in their march upon us . . . But, notwithstanding all our repeated shouts, we could not induce them to return one', rather, 'they continued proceeding, like a deep sullen river; while the Prince's army might be compared to a streamlet running among stones, whose noise sufficiently shewed its shallowness'.[22]

Until 15 April the Duke of Cumberland admitted, 'I never expected they would have had the impudence, to risk a general engagement'. However, hearing that Fort Augustus had been attacked and burnt, this 'convinced me that they intended to stand'.[23] On the early morning of 16 April scouts had also informed the duke that the Jacobite army had attempted a surprise attack on his encampment only hours earlier, and had come within a few miles before turning back.[24]

The British army had begun their march from Nairn between 4 and 5 a.m. in columns, three made up of infantry, with another column to the left of dragoons and light horse. For sustenance the men were 'allowed no Liquor, and no Provision but a piece of Amunition Bread'.[25] Lord Cathcart recalled after marching five or so miles in this manner, intelligence came that the Jacobite army was nearby 'and the ground being extreamly broken before us [we] thought proper to order the army to form [into battle lines]: This was instantly executed without [the] smallest confusion [the] different Corps wheeling up at once into their respective lines.'[26] Having wheeled from four columns into the three battle lines, a party was sent out to check the precise location of the Jacobite army. Alexander Taylor, a private in the Royal [Scots] Regiment, recalled that they 'marched that Way for two Miles with our Arms secoured and, Bayonet's fixed (a very uneasy Way of Marching)'.[27] Cathcart continues, 'The Country being further reconnoitred we found the Ennemy was not so near as we had had reason to believe: The Army was again reduced into Columns and the March continued.'[28] From this description it is clear that the months awaiting the change in weather at Aberdeen had not been wasted. The conditions over Drummossie Muir were still very windy and it was now raining hard. But unlike Falkirk, as Private Edward Linn (of Campbell's 21st or the Royal North Britain [Scots] Fusiliers) recalled, 'Thank God it was straight upon our Backs.'[29] Even so, as Alexander Taylor observed, 'We had also great Difficulty in keeping our Locks of our Firelocks dry.'[30]

Finally, the Jacobite army came into view, as James Wolfe, then aide-de-camp to Lieutenant General Hawley, recounted: 'The rebels had posted themselves on a high boggy moor, where they imagined our cannon and cavalry would be useless.'[31] The duke's recollection was that, 'We found them posted behind some old walls & huts in a line with Culloden House.'[32] The British army manoeuvred once more into the three battle lines.[33] The order as they were facing the Jacobite army (from left to right) and with the Water of Nairn lying to their left was: the front or first line commanded by Lord Albemarle comprising six battalions totalling 2,213 rank and file, beginning with Barrell's 4th Foot on the left, followed by Monro's (still named after their former commander, despite Sir Robert's death, but now commanded by Lieutenant Colonel Louis Dejean), Campbell's, Price's, Cholmondeley's and through to the Royal Regiment on the right. Directly in front of Barrell's regiment was the horseshoe-shaped Leanach enclosure (which had caused Lord George's changement) with the opening in the wall facing towards them. Behind the front line was the second, comprising six battalions and commanded by Major General John Huske from left to right, Edward Wolfe's 8th Foot (located behind Leanach cottage, with its heather-thatched roof, which lay between Wolfe's and Barrell's), Ligonier's, Sempill's (Edinburgh Regiment), Bligh's, Fleming's, Howard's; and behind them, the third or reserve (a much shorter line) from left to right: a squadron of Kingston's 10th Horse (behind Ligonier) then Brigadier Sir John Mordaunt's 5th Brigade in three battalions, i.e. Blakeney's, Battereau's, Pulteney's and the second squadron of Kingston's 10th Horse to the right (behind Howard's).[34] The British army's right flank was protected by a 'morass', as the duke described it, and Cobham's Horse was patrolling near by.

The Duke of Cumberland recalled, 'As we thought our right entirely secure, General Hawley and General Bland went to the left with the two Regiments of Dragoons to endeavour to fall upon the Rebels right flank.'[35] So, to the immediate left of Barrell's and therefore partially obscured from the Jacobite army by the horseshoe-shaped Leanach enclosure and the first Culwhiniac enclosure, were now located the two dragoon regiments, Kerr's 11th and Cobham's 10th under Major General Bland, accompanied by a half battalion of Highlanders made up of four companies: the first from the 64th Highlanders under Captain Colin Campbell of Ballimore, the second Captain Dugald Campbell of Auchrossan's Black Watch company, and two Argyll Militia companies under Captain John Campbell of Achnaba and Captain Duncan Campbell. The Duke of Cumberland observed that 'all our Highlanders (except about one hundred & fourty, which were upon the left with General Hawley) . . . were left to guard the baggage'.[36] Lieutenant General Hawley with his Highlanders broke through the first or eastern wall of the first Culwhiniac enclosure and, in company with the two dragoon squadrons, moved across the enclosed ground. Meanwhile, as the Duke of Cumberland continues, when 'we were within five hundred yards of the Rebels, I found the Morass upon our right was ended, which left our right Flank quite uncovered to them'. He moved Kingston's Horse from the reserve '& a little squadron of about sixty of Cobhams . . . to cover our Flank & Pulteney's Regiment was ordered from the reserve to the Right of the Royals. We spent above half an hour after that, trying to [see?] which should gain the Flank of the other.'[37]

The Jacobite left flank of the front line, to which, having passed the natural protection of the 'morass' and on to dryer ground, the British army's right flank had become exposed, had about this time been strengthened with the additional regiments, to the left of the MacDonalds, after Lord George's changement. The duke's last statement obviously refers to this sequence of moves and counter-moves – such as the deploying of regiments from the reserve to the front line – while each army attempts to gain the initiative over the other, or to reduce their vulnerability or exposure, before the battle proper begins. Finally, the Royal Artillery was dispersed along the front line within the intervals between each of the battalions. Each artillery detachment was operating two three-pounder cannon. In addition, there were two batteries of three coehorn mortars (a light, easily transportable bomb-firing weapon) located at either end of the second line. The artillery was commanded by Captain Lieutenant John Godwin and Colonel William Belford.

Before the battle began, the Duke of Cumberland rode up the line addressing his troops:

Gentlemen and Fellow Soldiers, I Have but little Time to address myself to you, but I think proper to acquaint you, that you are instantly to engage in the Defence of your King and Country, your Religion, your Liberties and Properties, and through the Justice of our Cause, I make no Doubt of leading you to certain Victory. Stand but firm, and your Enemies will soon flee before you. But if there be any amongst you, who thro' Timidity, are diffident of their Courage or Behaviour, which I have not the least Reason to suspect; or any others, who through Conscience or Inclination, cannot be zealous or alert in performing their Duty; it is my Desire, that all such would immediately retire; and I further declare, that they shall have my Pardon for so doing; for I had much rather be at the Head of one Thousand brave and resolute Men, than ten Thousand amongst whom there are some, who, by Cowardice or Misbehaviour, may dispirit or disorder the Troops, and so bring Dishonour and Disgrace on an Army under my Command.[38]

The duke wanted to be as confident as possible that his men would stand firm. According to Michael Hughes, this speech was welcomed 'by a full Acclamation of the Soldiers, testifying their intire Satisfaction and Loyalty'.[39] There is no reference to any one taking him up on his generous offer. The duke then positioned himself 'upon the right', where he imagined 'the greatest push would be'.[40]

Meanwhile, Lieutenant General Hawley was breaking down an exit in the western wall of the first Culwhiniac enclosure. The dragoons passed

through and then around on to an area of open ground behind a long
depression or ditch, at some distance to the right of Lord Elcho's Life
Guards, while Ballimore with his Highlanders remained within the enclosure walls. Lord Cathcart states that Hawley and his men were 'covered by
[the] brow of the hill . . . which slopes from the Plain [i.e. the open moor]
towards the river . . . and marched his squad[ron]s unperceived through
[the] Park'.[41] As James Maxwell later observed, with this manoeuvre Hawley
had come 'round the right of the Prince's army, and formed in the rear of
it'.[42] Seeing this, as he himself later wrote, Colonel O'Sullivan (although
Maxwell says it was Lord George) suggested deploying regiments from the
reserves and cavalry, including Gordon's, Elcho's and O'Shea, to cover any
attack from Hawley's dragoons by forming up along the crest above where
Hawley and his men were gathered.[43] Having done this, the order of the
Jacobite army had now changed significantly from the original battle lines.
They also had the disadvantage of hail and rain blowing into their faces.

With the wind and rain battering down, about 14,000 men in all now
faced each other on this open, boggy moor awaiting the signal.

Lord George later wrote, 'It is not an easy task to describe a battle':

> Springs and motions escape the eye, and most officers are necessarily taken up
> with what is immediately near themselves; so that it is next to impossible for
> one to observe the whole: add to this, the confusion, the noise, the concern
> that the people are in, whilst in the heat of action. The smallest oversights
> and most minute incidents, are often the cause of the loss or gain of the day;
> an opportunity, once missed, cannot be recalled; and when a commanding
> officer commits a mistake, it may perhaps not be perceived but by very few, if
> by any, and yet prove fatal. And there is not any part so trying for a General,
> as the immediate laying hold of opportunities, either in improving advan-
> tages, or giving immediate succour where it is necessary. This requires a quick
> eye, a good judgment, and great composure of mind.[44]

Unsurprisingly, then, there is some conflicting opinion among the participants regarding the precise course of the battle. Indeed, and as already
illustrated, such were the internal divisions and open hostility displayed
by some of the Jacobite commanders, before, during and after the battle –
Lord George, Lord Elcho and Colonel O'Sullivan in particular – that their
retrospective accounts must be approached with a little caution. There is
even debate over when exactly the first cannon was fired – somewhere
between twelve and one o'clock – but it is almost universally agreed that it

was a Jacobite gun. The Duke of Cumberland wrote that he had ordered 'Lord Bury forward within a hundred yards of the Rebels, to reconnoitre somewhat that appeared like a battery to us', but 'they began firing which was extremely ill served & ill pointed'.[45] Lord Cathcart states that 'we were saluted by some pieces of Cannon from the right of the Rebels which did very little damage. Our artillery being brought in to our Intervals, and between ye lines answered them to better purpose.'[46]

Captain John Daniel, who was located at the centre rear of the Jacobite army with Prince Charles, Lord Balmerino and Balmerino's Life Guards, stated that 'the whole fury of the enemy's Artillery seemed to be directed against us . . . as if they had noticed where the Prince was. By the first cannon shot, his servant, scarcely thirty yards behind him, was killed.'[47] Indeed, according to John Home, Colonel William Belford (of the Royal Artillery) 'observing the body of horse with Charles, ordered two pieces of cannon to be pointed at them; several discharges were made'.[48] A number of the prince's Horse Guards were wounded, and the hind leg of one officer's horse 'was shot, and hanging by the skin'.[49] The prince's face was 'bespattered with dirt'[50] from the explosions. This 'made some about the Prince desire, that he would be pleased to retire a little off; but this he refused to do, till seeing the imminent danger from the number of balls that fell about him, he was by the earnest entreaties of his friends forced to retire a little, attended only by Lord Balmerino's corps.'[51] The bombardment continued for a few minutes, after which, as described by Joseph Yorke, 'When our cannon had fired about two rounds, I could plainly perceive that the Rebels fluctuated extremely, and could not remain long in the position they were in without running away or coming down upon us' and accordingly, 'in two or three minutes they broke from the centre in 3 large bodies, like wedges, and moved forward'.[52] Alexander Taylor, with the Royals on the right flank of the front line, wrote, 'our Gunners galling their Lines, they betook them to their small Arms, Sword and Pistol, and came running on our Front-Line like Troops of Hungry Wolves'.[53]

One of the great strengths of the Highland charge was its speed and ferocity, the effects greatly augmented if the entire line ran forward together. But the Jacobite front line was not standing at an equal distance its entire length from the British army front line. Rather, it was angled, so that Lord George and his Athollmen were much closer than Perth's regiment to the farthest left. According to James Maxwell, Lord George held his men back for as long as he could (despite Charles' order to advance) but eventually the men 'grew very impatient, called aloud to be led on'.[54] Colonel Ker had been entrusted with delivering the orders for the charge forward, and apparently

did so moving from the left to the right, in the hope that the staggered timing of the order would allow the left to cover the greater distance and 'catch
up' with the right.[55] But according to James Maxwell, the right advanced
immediately, leaving the centre and left behind. Add to this the wind in their
faces, and all 'buried in a cloud of smoke'[56] from the British army's cannon-
ade, confusion ensued with some of the troops breaking rank and charging
sword in hand without firing. The three Atholl regiments made straight for
Barrell's, 'running on', as the Duke of Cumberland described it, 'in their Wild
manner',[57] but meanwhile the Camerons were forced against the walls of the
Leanach enclosure by a sudden swing to the right from the Mackintosh and
Fraser regiments. It is possible that this was the result of the quick fire from
the small three-pounder guns which, as Michael Hughes described, 'made
open Lanes quite through them, the Men dropping down by Wholesale',[58]
coupled with the need to avoid a particularly boggy area of marsh. The result
was that these Jacobite regiments were forced together in a 'mob'. Barrell's,
Monro's and Campbell's (and possibly Price's, too) on the front line, numbering well over a thousand men, opened fire all together, rather than in a
sequence (as was the usual method), because a Highland charge was faster
than the advance of a regular army, and so killing or wounding as many as
possible, and as fast as possible, was crucial: another lesson learned.[59]

   While the two rows of British army troops behind reloaded, the front row
fixed their bayonets ready to receive the charge. This was the moment for a
new drill, which had been practised while the army had been at Aberdeen. As
described by one British army officer, 'the alteration was mightily little but of
the last consequence'.[60] It was the usual practice to thrust at the man in front,
by which the attacking clansman would be protected by his shield or targe.
With the new manoeuvre, the soldier thrust his bayonet into the side of the
man attacking the soldier to his immediate right, expecting the soldier to his
left to do the same to the man directly in front of him. Such manoeuvres are
never that smooth in practice, but it certainly improved overall confidence
and increased the resolve of the British army front line to stand firm.

   Meanwhile, on the British army right flank, where the Duke of
Cumberland was positioned, the Jacobite left 'came down three several
times within a hundred yards of our men, firing their Pistols & brandishing
their swords; but', as he continues, 'the Royals & Pulteneys hardly tooke
their firelocks from their shoulders'.[61] As the duke's comment, that they
'came down three several times' suggests, the advance of the Jacobite left
may have been hampered by another boggy and sunken area of ground
lying between the two armies on this side. Captain Johnstone, located

on the left with Glengarry's, later described it as waterlogged up to the knee.[62] Some of the Jacobite regiment leaders, advancing with their men, were wounded or killed. Captain Donald Roy MacDonald saw Keppoch fall twice, and the second time heard him say, 'O God, have mercy on me. Donald, do the best for yourself, for I am gone.'[63] However, on the British army left flank, Barrell's and Monro's, but particularly the former who had been outflanked, were under great pressure and ferocious hand-to-hand fighting ensued. Alexander Taylor recalled the clansmen here 'fought with intrepidity'[64] while Henderson writes that 'in a stooping Posture, with their Targets in their left hand, covering their Head and Breast, and their glittering Swords in their Right, they ran swiftly upon the Cannon, making a frightful Huzza'. At some point during this fierce struggle, Captain Lord Robert Kerr of Barrell's, son of the Marquess of Lothian and brother of Lord Ancram, was brought down by a sword cut to the head 'from the Crown to the Collar Bone' and was then, according to Andrew Henderson, 'cut to Pieces'.[65] Lieutenant Colonel Sir Robert Rich was also attacked while defending the regimental colours, receiving sword cuts to his head and right forearm, and his left hand (possibly holding the colours) was cut off.[66] In fact both Barrell's and Monro's had had to give ground and some Jacobite troops, as Henderson suggests, managed to overrun the cannon. At which the Duke of Cumberland ordered Huske to bring up the second line and reserves on the left, that is Sempill's, Bligh's and Wolfe's, to surround the clansmen on three sides. The duke reported that,

Bligh's & Sempill's giving a fire upon those who had outflanked Barrels, soon repulsed them, & Barrels whole Regiment & the left of Monro's fairly beat them with their Bayonets, & I dare say, There was neither soldier nor officer of Barrels & that part of Monros which engaged who did not kill their one or two men with their Bayonets, & spontoons, & they so fairly drove them back, that they could not make any impression upon the Battalions, they threw stones at them, for at least a minute or two before their total rout began.[67]

Lieutenant Loftus Cliffe of Monro's recalled, 'in the midst of the Action, the officer that led the Camerons, called to me to take Quarters, which I refused, and bid the Rebel Scoundrel advance; he did and fired at me, but providentially missed his mark: I then shot him dead, and took his Pistol and Dirk, which are extremely neat.'[68] Meanwhile, Lord George had attempted to gather men from the dwindling second line to bolster the Jacobite right, but by this point he believed 'nothing could be done – all was lost'.[69]

Still advancing under fire on the left of the Jacobite front line, the MacDonalds saw the Athollmen, Camerons and the Appin Stewarts fall back and, with their leadership collapsing, followed suit. 'What a spectacle of horror!' cried James Johnstone; 'The same Highlanders, who had advanced to the charge like lions, with bold, determined countenances, were, in an instant, seen flying like trembling cowards, in the greatest disorder.'[70] William Home, a cornet in Balmerino's Horse and who is named as having carried Charles' standard during the battle, stated later that the 'rout became general and the confusion inexpressible'.[71] The Duke of Cumberland wrote of the Jacobite left flank, 'after those faint attempts they made off, and the three little squadrons [of cavalry] on our right were sent to pursue them'. This cavalry division, under the command of Lord Ancram, pursued the MacDonalds, as Edward Linn observed, 'with Sword & pistol & Cutt a great many of them down So that I never Saw a Small field thicker of Dead'.[72] On the other side of the battlefield, there was a brief firefight between Ballimore's men (located within the enclosure) and the Royal Ecossais, during which Ballimore was killed.[73] Meanwhile, Hawley and Bland with the dragoons were still positioned behind the Jacobite reserve on their right flank, but were unable to see what exactly was going on due to the downward slope from the battlefield. James Wolfe recalled that when 'the Rebels began to give way and the fire of the Foot slacken'd' they advanced. Lord Cathcart observed that Fitz-James' Horse, 'on G.l Bland appearing . . . fled towards Inverness with most of the French Infantry'.[74] In fact some of the Royal Ecossais and Irish brigade had stood their ground, providing the only screen against total disaster for the Jacobite command. However Bland then, as the Duke of Cumberland recounted, 'fell upon the right flank of their second line; & the horse on our right charging their left our Cavalry met in their centre', after which 'the rout was universal'.[75]

The Gentleman's Magazine later reported that the 'battle was so desperate, that the soldiers bayonets were stain'd and clotted with the blood of the rebels up to the muzzles' and, in another reference to Barrell's regiment, 'after the battle there was not a bayonet in this regiment but was either bloody or bent'.[76] Lieutenant Cliffe of Monro's, who was unwounded but his 'Coat had six Balls thro' it', considered 'Our Regiment had ample Revenge for the Loss of our late Colonel, Sir Robert; and the rest of our Officers, whom the Scoundrels murdered in cold Blood; but . . . we had ample Revenge in hot: For I can with great Truth assure you, not one that attacked us escaped alive; for we gave no Quarters, nor would accept of any.'[77] Andrew Henderson considered the manner by which officers such as Colonel James Gardiner, Sir

Robert Monro and now Captain Robert Kerr had been killed, 'slaughtered as by a bungling Butcher', goes some way to explain, rather than excuse, the behaviour of the victorious troops, who, 'when they found Vengeance in their Power . . . violated the stricter Rules of Humanity'.[78] In a similar manner, Colonel Yorke recalled, 'The remembrance of former wrongs, the barbarity with which our prisoners had in general been used, and the glorious desire of recovering lost reputation, infused such spirits in the breast of all, that had not fear added wings to their feet, none would have escaped the edge of the sword.'[79] This general desire to regain the dignity and reputation of the British army, in tatters after Prestonpans and Falkirk, is clear from a letter also quoted in *The Gentleman's Magazine*, in which the author states that they had now convinced the Highland 'boasters' that 'the broad sword and target is unequal to their musket and bayonet, when in the hands of veterans, who are determined to use them'.[80] Andrew Henderson concludes, that the 'Field was clear, and the Victory being compleat, the Soldiers, warm in their Resentment, did Things hardly to be accounted for; several of the wounded Men were stabbed, yea, some who were lurking in Houses, were taken out and shot upon the Field', although, he continues, 'others were saved, by those whose Compassion was raised at the Sight of so many Victims'.[81]

The Duke of Cumberland recorded that 'the Cavalry pursued & made a great slaughter, for three miles'.[82] Their commander, Lord Ancram, had been ordered to continue 'as far as He could, & wch He did with so good effect that a very considerable number were killed in the pursuit . . . Bland had also made great slaughter, & gave quarter to none but about fifty French Officers & soldiers He pick'd up in his pursuit.'[83] Following and attacking soldiers fleeing in disarray was a standard action of any victorious army, as seen at Prestonpans. In addition, one key role of the cavalry (as these accounts illustrate) was to pursue well beyond the field of battle. Without doubt the pursuit from Drummossie Muir to Inverness and beyond was a terrible and bloody slaughter.[84] Civilians, too, were caught up in it. *The Gentleman's Magazine* reported that the cavalry 'continued quite thro' the town of *Inverness*, where the streets ran with blood'.[85] Colonel Charles Whitefoord, in turn, wrote to an unnamed friend, 'You know the pursuit was very bloody, and are no stranger to the other circumstances that followed.'[86] Perhaps unsurprisingly, he does not go on to detail what those 'circumstances' were. Alexander Taylor, writing to his wife the following day, confirmed the cavalry in pursuit 'made a most dreadful Havock', while a 'great Number was slain in Field' – so much so that 'I may say, there's two thousand fewer Rebels than was Yesterday Morning'.[87]

Anonymous, *Tandem Triumphans*, 1746.

Ruthven

'rallying again'

Prince Charles left the battlefield, but there are differing reports as to how he exited. William Home (positioned nearby) states he was made to leave 'with the utmost reluctance, the bridle of his horse having been seized and forcibly turned about'.[1] Colonel O'Sullivan recalled seeing a regiment of British army cavalry appear to move across the field to cut off the prince's retreat 'and tels him [that] he has no time to loose, [that] he'l be surrounded imediatly if he does not retir. "Well," says the Prince, "they wont take me alive."'[2] However, as all immediate hope had gone, he was eventually persuaded to leave for his own safety and the future of the cause. Others say he refused to lead a last heroic charge, and instead galloped away with a bitter jibe from Lord Elcho ringing in his ears: 'There you go for a damned cowardly Italian!'[3]

Charles certainly left accompanied by a guard, about sixty men from Fitz-James' Horse. According to Edward Burke, a local man who knew the countryside well, the prince turned to him and said, 'If you be a true friend, pray, endeavor to lead us safe off',[4] which he duly did, accompanied by Colonel O'Sullivan, Sir Thomas Sheridan, Alexander MacLeod (one of Charles' aides-de-camp), Peter MacDermit (footman), Captain Felix O'Neil (an Irish officer who had recently arrived from France) and James Gib. A document in the prince's own hand recalls (in the third person) that 'their hero (so wee Shall call Charles) was forced off the fild, by the People about him, as their was then nothing more remaining for him but to consult his safety. Charles exchanged his horce, which had been shot through the sho[u]lder by a Musket Ball and retre[a]ted with a few chosen friends.'[5] Colonel Ker observed that the 'Prince retired in good order, with some few of his men, and crossed the water of Nairn at the ford, on the highway between Inverness and Corribreigh, without being pursued by the enemy, where he parted with them, taking only a few of Fitzjames's horse and some gentlemen along with him up that river'.[6]

John Hay either accompanied the prince off the field or joined him soon after, while a badly wounded Lochiel, in the company of some of his men, rode the sixty miles south-west to his house at Achnacarry. Lord Elcho left the field with Lord Balmerino who was determined to surrender to the Duke of Cumberland if the prince's army did not regroup. William Home, who followed Balmerino to a mill some twelve miles from the field where they remained that night, recalled his lordship was resolved 'not to outlive the misfortunes of that day, his duty [protecting Charles] had prevented him from doing it where he wished, on the field'.[7] Meanwhile, Lord Elcho describes how 'the Prince made a halt four miles from the field of battle and I found him in a deplorable state'.[8] Lord Elcho does not mention the 'cowardly Italian' taunt in either of his accounts – as bitter and anti-Charles as they undoubtedly are – which suggests that this is a later elaboration. According to Captain Johnstone, Lord Elcho found Charles 'surrounded by Irish, and without a single Scotsman near him, in a state of complete dejection'. Charles 'having given himself altogether up to the pernicious counsels of Sheridan and the other Irish, who governed him as they pleased' had now 'abandoned every other project, but that of escaping to France, as soon as possible'. Lord Elcho encouraged Charles to consider the battle as a setback, to rally the army 'putting himself at its head, and trying, once more, the fortune of war, as the disaster might be easily repaired'. But Charles 'was insensible to all that his Lordship could suggest, and utterly disregarded his advice'.[9] This is almost identical to Lord Elcho's own recollection, confirming he must be Johnstone's source and, as will become clear, there is evidence to suggest that here, at least, he is a particularly unreliable witness.

The Irishmen mentioned would inevitably show concern for Charles' personal safety to the exclusion of anything else, while the Scots, with family, property and lands now in even greater jeopardy than ever before, would want Charles to continue the fight. Johnstone, via Lord Elcho, does not explain Charles' desire to escape to France as soon as possible, beyond implying it was at the insistence of the Irish for the prince's preservation, with the additional inference that Charles was now so completely in their power that he was capable of abandoning to its fate (apparently with little or no regard) what was left of the Jacobite army. And what was left, despite the carnage inflicted on them during and after the battle, was a sizable body of men, some of whom had not even been present at the fateful hour.

However, Charles and his companions continued on, stopping briefly on entering the strath or valley of Stratherrick which lies midway along the eastern side of Loch Ness (south-west from Culloden) where other officers and men joined them. Lord Elcho states that here the prince 'neither Spoke to any of the Scots officers present, or inquired after any of the Absent'; in fact, 'He appeared very Uneasy as long as the Scots were about him, and in a Short time order'd them all to go to Ruthven of Badenoch, where he would Send them orders'. But, according to Lord Elcho, 'before they had rode a mile, he Sent Mr. Sheridan after them, to tell them that they might disperse and every body Shift for himself the best way he Could'.¹⁰ This account is repeated by James Maxwell.¹¹ That Charles suspected that there was a traitor within the Jacobite army (which was, excluding the Irish and French troops, predominantly Scottish) is evident from his correspondence and the recollections (in his hand) previously quoted: 'Varios Causes, (not to say tre[a]chery) paved the way for the rout of the Hi[gh]landers at Culloden.'¹² But what Lord Elcho is suggesting is that Charles was keen to remove all Scots from his entourage, fearing that any one of them might now be tempted to act the Judas: partly to save their own hides and partly for those 30,000 pieces of silver which remained unclaimed.

Given the prince and his officers were still reeling from the failed night march when the news arrived of the British army's approach, it is unsurprising that there is confusion over the place of rendezvous in the event of a defeat. It is also possible that no such location had been officially defined, given Charles' antipathy to any consideration of what he saw as failure. James Gib recalled that after travelling about four miles from the battlefield, John Hay 'desired him to go off and shift for himself in the best manner he could'. Gib protested, saying that he did not know the country and did not wish to leave his master. John Hay replied that he too would be leaving the prince, 'therefore your best is to go to Ruthven, the place of rendezvous, where you shall either see me or hear from me'. So under duress James Gib left for Ruthven.¹³ Yet according to Lord Elcho's memoir already quoted, Charles had, within hours of the battle, effectively told his army to disperse, which again (as we shall see) runs counter to other information. It is easy to see how, in the tumult of emotion after such a terrible event, potentially a catastrophic and definitive defeat – from confusion and anger, to despair and terror – a man might act illogically or rashly, or misremember dates and the precise sequence of events. It is also understandable why there are such differing perceptions as to what happened, particularly as the hours and days passed by, and the personal as well as collective ramifications of the defeat at Culloden hit home.

Having now entered Fraser country, Charles dismissed his horse guard and, with Lord Elcho still in attendance along with Sheridan, O'Sullivan, Burke, Alexander MacLeod, Peter MacDermit and Captain O'Neil, the prince immediately made for the house of Thomas Fraser at the small hamlet of Gorthleck (Gortleg or Gorthlic) some twenty miles south-west of Inverness. Here they remained for supper in the company of Lord Lovat himself. This was the first time that the two had met. According to Lord Elcho, along with Lovat, here Charles found himself among 'a great many other Scots Gentlemen, who advised him not to quit the Country, but Stay and gather together again his Scatter'd forces'.[14] But as Lord Elcho continues, Charles apparently refused. However, the prince himself records that he had made for the house at Gorthleck 'as it was near the place he intended for to assemble the scattard Hilanders'.[15] As the prince and his party were moving in a south-westerly direction, he cannot have meant Ruthven (mentioned as the rendezvous by both Lord Elcho and John Hay via James Gib), which is located due south of Culloden. The prince left Gorthleck soon after, with only O'Sullivan, O'Neil, Burke, Alexander MacLeod and Allan MacDonald (a priest) in attendance.[16] Sheridan, too weak to maintain the pace, was left behind.

This smaller party advanced to Fort Augustus, as Captain O'Neil recalled, where the prince remained some time 'in expectation his troops would have join'd him'.[17] No troops arriving, Charles continued to Castle Invergarry, which he had been advised 'was the surest and safest place . . . and a great conveniency for concealment'.[18] He arrived at Invergarry early on the morning of the 17th and probably rested here until 3 p.m. There was no food, so Edward or Ned Burke was sent to catch some salmon 'which the guide made ready in the best manner he could; and the meat was reckoned very savoury and acceptable'.[19] After his meal, Charles was keen 'to be quit of the clothing he had on, and Ned gave him his own coat'.[20] Having refreshed himself 'he took a resolution to proceed still further, fearing to stay long in one place'.[21] In one of the accounts of the flight from Culloden (in the Stuart Papers) it states that at Invergarry 'he remain'd for some time, but hearing none of his troops assembled at fort augustus where the rendezvous was given, and being assur'd the enemy was approaching, he sett forward into the Mountains'.[22] So according to both Captain O'Neil and Charles himself, the ruined Fort Augustus (not Ruthven) was the place of rendezvous. Certainly he and those with him in these first hours and days after the battle all testify that he maintained an interest in knowing if his troops had gathered and where. Whether he intended joining them and continuing the fight, perhaps waging some sort of guerrilla-style war from the Highlands (as Lord George had favoured), or simply wanted to inform them en bloc what his intentions were, will become clear.

Charles moved on with O'Sullivan, Allan MacDonald and Ned Burke along Loch Arkaig, arriving at 2 a.m. on the 18th at Glenpean. O'Neil had been left behind at Invergarry to direct those of the army that passed by to follow the prince.[23] Charles and his companions stayed at the house of Donald Cameron and here he reportedly slept for the first time in five days and nights. At five o'clock in the afternoon – two days after the battle – he continued on foot to the Glens of Morar 'over almost inaccessible mountains'[24] and arrived at the braes of Morar at four o'clock on the morning of the 19th. Here he was entertained at 'a small sheal house' of Angus MacEachine, Borrodale's son-in-law, although apparently Charles 'was so much fatigued that night, that he could neither eat nor drink, and required the help of a man to support him to his bed'.[25] The following day the prince 'ventured to pass the whole day in a wood near the house, in order to recruit more strength for a night walk'.[26] Thus rested, Charles then walked by night to Borrodale via Glenbeasdale and arrived at Angus MacDonald's house on Lochnanaugh – the very same house he had occupied eight months earlier – at four o'clock in the afternoon:

> At his arrival here, he found a great many Mack Donalds assembled together, who had lately escaped out of the battle of Colloden . . . During the eight days he stayed in that country, he had daily conferences with young Clanranald, Colonel MacDonald of Barisdale, and several others of both families, treating which was the safest place, and the surest method for his concealment. After they had satisfied him as to that, they protested, and assured him he should have nothing to fear, that they would stand by him if he only would stay among them to the last man.[27]

That the MacDonalds 'protested' that Charles would be safe in their country and in their midst, does suggest that at this moment the prince appeared fearful of being betrayed. However, here the prince 'got a sute of new Highland cloaths' from Angus MacDonald's wife, Catriona, 'the better to disguise him and to make him pass for one of the country'.[28] While at this house, Charles met Donald MacLeod, tenant of Gualtergill (on Loch Dunvegan in Skye) who had been sent to him to act as a guide by Aeneas MacDonald. Captain O'Neil also arrived from Invergarry, 'and gave him an account of the little or no appearance there was of assembling his troops'.[29]

In his recollections, Charles writes that he

> toke the resolution to go to ye Western Isles, where he might find more easily a Chip [ship] to carry him over to France as he expected that his presence there wou'd precipitat[e] that Government to Give him the succors he so much wanted and that had been so often promised without execution, for that Effect he chose to Carry with him on[e?] Onel [O'Neil] & O sulivan t[w]o Irish officers.[30]

So we can now suppose that Charles had indeed refused to stay and fight in Scotland, as the gathering at Gorthleck had begged him to do, not through cowardice or lack of any interest in the fate of his army, but thinking instead that he could better serve the cause, that is the Stuart cause in general, rather than the immediate issue of the defeated army in Scotland, by a quick dash to France to plead in person for the long-promised battalions from King Louis. The sooner he could leave, the sooner these troops would arrive, the sooner the campaign could be resurrected and the more likely, this time, it would succeed. By insisting on fighting at Culloden, Charles had forced this episode of his campaign to a swift resolution, rather than having to endure it staggering on from crisis to crisis through lack of both money and troops. Now another chapter could begin.

Between 22 and 25 April, while Donald made the necessary arrangements to get the prince off the mainland, Charles remained in the vicinity of Borrodale, still awaiting news of his army and reports of the wider effects of the battle. O'Neil states that the prince's decision to leave the mainland arose from what appeared (from the isolation of Borrodale) to be his abandonment by the remnants of his army: a situation that had left him vulnerable to attack and capture.[31] Charles was certainly vulnerable, but his main aim in travelling to the islands was to find a ship to take him to France. If the prince was beginning to fear that he had indeed been abandoned, then O'Neil was hardly discouraging the idea. It is likely that at this time Charles received a letter written by Lord George Murray dated from Ruthven (Thursday) 17 April.

At Culloden, Lord George is described as having 'behaved with great Gallantry, lost his Horse, his Per[i]wig & Bonnet; was amongst the last that left the Field; had several Cuts with Broadswords in his Coat & covered over with Blood & Dust'.[32] He then, along with almost two thousand

members of the Jacobite army (including some of those who had been
absent, such as Cluny MacPherson and his men), had made his way to the
village near the recently burnt-out Ruthven barracks, lying thirty miles due
south of the battlefield and thirty miles to the east of Invergarry (where
Charles was on the 17th). The letter he penned to the prince the day after
the battle is by turns angry, pompous, bitter, accusatory and despairing.
Lord George opens with the following:

> As no person in these kingdomes ventured more franckly in the cause than
> myself and as I had more at stake than almost all the others put together, so
> to be sure I cannot but be very deeply affected with our late loss and present
> situation, but I declare that were your R. H. person in safety, the loss of the
> cause and the misfortunate and unhappy situation of my countrymen is the
> only thing that grieves me, for I thank God, I have resolution to bear my
> own and family's ruine without a grudge.[33]

Lord George continues by setting out some 'truths which all the
Gentlemen of our army seem convinced of'. Firstly, that the royal standard
should never have been raised without the certainty that the King of France
would provide his full support and assistance; secondly, that Charles' absolute faith and trust in Colonel O'Sullivan in 'the most essential things
with regard to your operations' was undeserved, he being 'exceedingly
unfit for it, and committed gross blunders on every occasion of moment'.
Lord George is particularly scathing of O'Sullivan's inexperience on the
battlefield (as Lord George sees it), declaring, 'I never saw him in time of
action neither at Gladsmuir, Falkirk nor in the last, and his orders were
vastly confused.' O'Sullivan 'did not so much as visit the ground where
we were to be drawn up in line of battle' and further, which was 'the fatal
error yesterday', he should not have allowed 'the enemy those walls upon
their left which made it impossible for us to break them, and they with
their front fire and flanking us when we went upon the attack destroyed us
without any possibility of our breaking them'. He wished that O'Sullivan
had been left to look after the baggage which, by all accounts, was what
'he had been brought up to and understood'. Lord George then moves
on to a third issue: provisions, or lack of them, 'which had the most fatal
consequence', blaming John Hay for neglecting his duty and by whose
incompetence during 'the three last days which were so critical our army
was starved'. In fact, he blames the mismanagement of provisions as 'the
reason our night march was rendered abortive when we possibly might

have surprized and defeat the enemy at Nairn, but for want of provisions a third of the army scattered to Inverness and the others who marched had not spirits to make it so quick as was necessary being really faint for want of provisions'. Then, referring to the day of the battle, he believed with well-organised provisions 'we might have crossed the water of Nairn and drawn up so advantageously that we would have obliged the enemy to come to us, for they were resolved to fight at all hazards, at prodigious disadvantage, and probably we would in that case have done by them as they unhappily have done by us'.[34] He concludes by reiterating that, 'In short Mr O'Sulivan & Mr. Hay had rendered themselves odious to all our army and had disgusted them to such a degree that they had bred mutiny in all ranks that had not the battle come on they were to have represented their grievance to Y[our]. R[oyal]. H[ighness]. for a remedy.'[35] Finally, he resigns his commission – which he says he would have done earlier, on returning from the siege of Blair Castle, but was persuaded to continue – while still swearing loyalty to the cause.

On first reading, Lord George's letter appears to be the thoughts of a man who either has no expectation of seeing the prince again – suggesting that Charles had indeed sent orders to disband his army within hours of the battle – or, at this emotionally heightened time, was simply well beyond caring what the prince now thought of him, whether he saw him again or not. However, the letter does not read as one written in the knowledge that the prince had definitely abandoned the current campaign. Lord George does state that *were* the prince safe, then his main concern was for the army etc. Rather, it is Lord George's opinion as to why the night march failed and then why they lost the battle. According to the account in Charles' own hand, the prince had no idea where the army was gathering. And Captain Johnstone states that Ruthven 'happened, by chance, to become the rallying point of our army, without having been previously fixed upon'.[36]

Among these men gathering at Ruthven was Captain John Daniel. He had fled the battlefield on horseback with Lord John Drummond and six others, riding nonstop until one o'clock the next morning. After a fitful rest, they marched on 'we knew not whither, through places it would be in vain to describe; for we saw neither house, barn, tree, or beast nor any beaten road, being commonly mid-leg deep in snow, till five o'Clock that afternoon; when we found ourselves near a village called Privanna a Badanich'.[37] Fortunately for Captain Daniel and his companions, none of whom knew where the place of rendezvous was, this was the village currently occupied by a sizable contingent of the Jacobite army, the chief of whom were Lord George Murray and the Duke of Perth. The relief of finding so large a group of their fellows was tinged with concern for their leader, 'but we heard no news where the poor Prince was'.[38] Captain Johnstone says he arrived at Ruthven the following day (Friday the 18th) where he found 'the Duke of Athol, Lord George Murray, the Duke of Perth, Lord John Drummond, Lord Ogilvie, and many other chiefs of clans' plus several thousand troops 'all in the best possible dispositions for renewing hostilities and taking their revenge'. Johnstone believed the village was easily defendable, something he recalled Lord George was also convinced of, as the latter had set up guards to defend the passes. Lord George then ordered his aide-de-camp, 'Mr MacLeod', to go out and find the prince (no easy matter at this juncture) to inform him that 'a great part of his army was assembled at Ruthven' including those who had been absent at the time of the battle. If this is true, then it was surely the aide-de-camp who also delivered Lord George's letter to the prince. It was Johnstone's belief that clans which had remained neutral during the campaign so far were now ready to declare for the cause. Johnstone's assessment was overly optimistic, but he was not the only Jacobite officer to report willingness among the command to rally and continue the campaign: Lord Elcho for one.

According to Johnstone, Saturday the 19th passed without any word from Prince Charles, during which the men remained 'cheerful, and full of spirits'.[39] But on the 20th, again according to Johnstone, MacLeod returned with the 'laconic answer' from their prince, 'Let every man seek his safety in the best way he can.'[40] Captain Daniel supports, in part, Johnstone's account, saying that 'at first we had great hopes of rallying again; but they soon vanished, order coming for every one to make the best of his way he could'.[41] William Home had reluctantly left Lord Balmerino, after his lordship had bid him 'an eternal adieu', and made his way to Ruthven. He recollects, albeit several decades later, that Lord George arrived at Ruthven on the Saturday, and 'drew us all out, made a short speech, which he concluded by telling us to shift for ourselves as there was no more occasion for our services'.[42] James Gib arrived at Ruthven the day after the battle, and was persuaded to remain there until Saturday the 19th by Colonel John Roy Stuart, who assured him 'that against next morning they would certainly receive some account from or about the Prince'. However, 'they received no accounts whatsomever about the Prince, and then Colonel Roy Stewart said it was high time for every one of them to do the best he could for himself'.[43]

Captain Johnstone recalls, 'Our separation at Ruthven was truly affecting. We bade one another an eternal adieu. No one could tell whether the
scaffold would not be his fate. The Highlanders gave vent to their grief in
wild howlings and lamentations.'[44] Johnstone decided to risk making his
way to Edinburgh, rather than head further into the Highlands.[45] John
Daniel records that 'some went one way, some another: those who had
French Commissions surrendered; and their example was followed by my
Colonel, Lord Balmerino, tho' he had none. Many went for the mountains, all being uncertain what to do or whither to go.'[46]

Apparently still unaware of what exactly was happening to the east
(although by now he may have read Lord George's letter), Charles wrote
a formal farewell to the clan chiefs from Borrodale, in which he sets out
what they should do for now and what his own plans were.[47] It was left
with John Hay, who was to take it to Sir Thomas Sheridan (with whom
the prince had been in recent correspondence) for delivery to the chiefs.
The covering letter addressed to Sheridan and dated 23 April (a full week
after the battle) states that the prince is 'still of the same opinion that we
have traitors among us' and that as a result, he has taken himself off 'for
the good of the cause altho [risking?] in itself'.[48] Charles advises Sheridan
to delay announcing his departure for as long as possible, and signs off
'Follow me as soon as you think it convenient – Adieu Charles P.R.' Here
is the prince's letter to the chiefs in its entirety:

When I came into this Country, it was my only view to do all in my power
for your good and safety. This I will allways do as long as life is in me, But
alas! I see with grief I can at present do little for you on this side [of] the
water, for the only thing that can now be done, is to defend your selves, 'till
the French assist you. If not, to be able to make better terms;- To effectuate
this, the only way is to assemble in a body as soon as possible, and then take
measures for the best, which you that know the Country are only judges
of: This makes me be of little use here, whereas by my going into France
instantly, however dangerous it be, I will certainly engage the French Court
either to assist us effectually and powerfully, or at least to procure you such
terms as you would not obtain otherways :- My presence there, I flatter my
self, will have more effect to bring this sooner to a determination than any
body else, For several reasons, one of which I will mention here, vizt., It is
thought to be a Politick, 'tho a false one, of the French Court, not to restore
our Master, but to keep a continual civil war in this Country, which renders
the English government less powerful and, of consequence, themselves

more; This is absolutely destroyed by my leaving this Country, which nothing else but this will persuade them, that this Play cannot last, and, if not remedied, the Elector will soon be as despotick as the French King, which I should think will oblige them to strike the great stroke, which is always in their power, how ever averse they may have been to it for the time past. Before leaving off, I must recommend to you, That all things should be decided, by a Councill of all you Chiefs, or, in any of your absence, the next Commander of your several corps, with the assistance of the Duke of Perth and Lord George Murray, who, I am persuaded, will stick by you to the very last. My departure should be kept as long private and concealed as possible, on one pretext or other, which you will fall upon. May the Almighty bless and direct you.[49]

This letter confirms that Charles did not consider that he was abandoning the clans and, by extension, his army or his supporters. Rather, he wished them to maintain themselves as best they could, while he travelled to France to get the money and troops he needed to resurrect the campaign. He also acknowledges the true, self-serving motivation behind French support so far and, while seeking more from Louis, believes that his swift removal from Britain now, with the immediate effect of terminating the current 'civil war', will convince France that they can no longer use Jacobitism to make the British state (to reprise the marquis d'Argenson's phrase) 'a little tottering': they must resolve for nothing short of a Stuart restoration.

Lord George, meanwhile, in the prince's absence, could have attempted (despite resigning his commission) to keep the army massing at Ruthven together for days, or even weeks. In that time, as Johnstone argues, it might even have expanded, making it a more formidable force than that which had gathered, exhausted and hungry, on Drummossie Muir. But this reinvigorated army would still need to be fed, and no supplies had been dispersed from Inverness in the event of such a scenario. This army would also have needed Charles at its head sooner not later and, in the meantime, Lord George evidently did not have the energy, or the will, to fill the void.

Anonymous, *Satire on the Duke of Cumberland*, 1746.

Church Street, Inverness

'no quarter'

On the morning of 16 April, HMS *Shark* had been anchored in the Firth of Moray only two miles from Culloden. Her captain, Christopher Middleton, noted in his journal that about noon, he could observe the first stirrings of the battle from the deck of his ship. An hour later he weighed anchor and sailed towards Inverness. The distant cannon blasts and gunfire had finished by two o'clock, and seeing some British army cavalry on the shore, Captain Middleton sent a boat to find out what had happened. He was informed that 'they had got a complete victory over the rebels'. Judging that the Duke of Cumberland would be entering Inverness at four o'clock, at this exact hour the *Shark* fired a twenty-one-gun salute in his honour. Three hours later, Captain Middleton went ashore to congratulate the duke in person, and was ordered to immediately carry Lord Bury south, to get word to King George of the victory.[1]

The duke had entered Inverness, 'bespattered with dirt, covered in dust and with sweat', sword in hand at the head of a squadron of dragoons. His path from the battlefield to the town centre was strewn with bodies. The remainder of the army reportedly drank a 'Glass of Spirits upon the Field' and then forming up, marched into town behind their leader. Initially, according to Andrew Henderson, the bells were ringing in honour of the victory but the duke 'moved his Hand for them to forbear'. His first act was to release the British army prisoners with the words 'Brother Soldiers you are free'.[2]

As the bloody pursuit of the fleeing Jacobite troops was occurring, British army soldiers scouring the woods around Culloden picked up a number of prisoners including Lord Kilmarnock. The day after the battle the duke, now occupying Old Lady Mackintosh's house in Church Street (as his cousin before him), issued the order that a captain and fifty men were 'to march immediately to the field of battle and search all cottages in the neighbourhood for rebels. The officers and men will take notice that the publick orders given yesterday were to give us no quarter.'³ This statement, the most controversial of the entire campaign, was in response to an order, allegedly discovered on a prisoner, which stated under 'Parole Roy James', or the password 'King James', 'Its H.R.H positive orders that every person attach themselves to some Corps of the Army, and remain with that Corps Night and Day until the Battle and pursuite be finally over, And to give no Quarter to the Electors Troops, on any Account what so ever.'⁴ The content of this document, with some variation, including the password King James in Gaelic or French 'Righ Shemuis' and 'Roy Jaques', was widely circulated in the press and journals, *The Gentleman's Magazine* included.⁵ Some believed it to be a forgery. The version quoted above, which is among the Duke of Cumberland's papers, is not signed by or in the hand of Lord George Murray, although it could have been a copy taken from a now lost original.

However, the scramble to reach the field on the morning of the battle, so soon after they arrived back from the aborted night attack, suggests that Lord George had no time to issue new written orders for the 16th. This document (as already argued) may in fact relate to revised orders circulated late on 15 April before the night march. As previously noted, 'King James' was the password during that attempt and, by the nature of the attack, no quarter would have been in the offing. In addition, the manuscript in the Duke of Cumberland's papers (again as already stated) has the date 'Calodon April 15ᵗʰ 1746', which can only relate to either the forming-up for battle on that day, which was later abandoned and for which, in any case, orders already existed (i.e. those of 14–15 April issued in Inverness) or the night march. Orders for the latter, if written, would have been issued to the officers from Culloden House late afternoon or early evening on the 15th.⁶ There is also the evidence of Lieutenant Loftus Cliffe of Monro's Regiment, who recalled the day after the battle, as previously quoted, that an officer leading the Camerons had 'called to me to take Quarters' but Cliffe refused.⁷ If the order to offer 'No Quarters' was still current on the 16th, why did the Jacobite officer do so? So one scenario is that the manuscript is a copy of an order issued by Lord George Murray specifically for the night march, which was found on a Jacobite prisoner after the battle the following day, and wrongly assumed by the British army commanders to refer to that later event.

If we now consider the possibility that this order is in fact a fake, was it created with the agreement of the Duke of Cumberland? The duke's attitude throughout, more than evident in his extensive correspondence – he is equally candid in his official as well as private letters – does not suggest that he would have stooped to such desperate and shameful measures in order to justify punishing people he considered rebels and traitors, and therefore deserving of the severest treatment, whether on the battlefield, on the run, or, once caught, under the law. This does not cast doubt on the possibility that this 'No Quarter' document is bogus but rather, if so, the duke's complicity in its creation.

Two days later, the Duke of Cumberland began to deal with a backlog of urgent correspondence. To Lord Loudoun he highlighted 'our Highlanders' who had assisted the breaking down of the enclosure walls and 'who behaved very well'.[8] He computes the Jacobite losses at 2,000 killed and about 600 prisoners. He then observes that the 'great loss is fallen upon the Clans who, formed the first line, and many of their chiefs are said to be killd, as Lochiel, Stuart of Appin, Keppoch, Lord Nairn, & Lord Strathallan. Kilmarnock & other are prisoners'. His information about Lochiel, Charles Stewart of Ardsheal who led the Appin Stewarts and Lord Nairn is incorrect. All were alive and on the run, the former (as stated earlier) badly wounded. Moving on to the British army, at the current calculation the loss was sixty killed and about 250 wounded (of which some would die later) and 'of the Officers those of Chief note are Ld Robert Kerr kill'd, & Col.[l] Rich has lost a hand'. In addition, 'We have all their Canon, ammunition & their baggage which is a good deal plunderd, nine colours & a great number of arms.' Regarding the immediate future, he orders Lord Loudoun to

> use all diligence to land with what men you have & can get on some part of the Coast where some of those Clans inhabit, who have been in the Rebellion, whence you will march to Fort Augustus, & in good way drive the Cattle burn the Ploughs & destroy what you can belonging to all such as are or have been in the rebellion, & burning the houses of the Chiefs. You will let me know when you propose being at Fort Augustus, that I may have Provisions ready for you there.[9]

To the Duke of Newcastle he writes, 'I had the honor to acquaint his Majesty the 16, by Lord Bury, of the compleat Victory we gaind that day over the Rebels.' He continues, 'as we were on our march on to Inverness & were near arrived there . . . I immediately receivd the French Officers & soldiers as Prisoners of War', one of whom was the marquis d'Eguilles.[10]

Regarding the Jacobite army death toll, he repeats the figures he had given
to Lord Loudoun of 2,000 killed 'upon the field of Battle & in the pursuit
As few of their wounded could get off & we have here 222 French, & 326
Rebel Prisoners'.[11] That 'few of their wounded could get off' may corroborate the accusations made from the time of the battle to the present, that
the British army troops, in response to the reminder of the 'No Quarter'
order allegedly issued by the Jacobite command for the 16th, killed rather
than took prisoner wounded men on the field and beyond. The *Westminster
Journal* justified the killing of wounded men in the following manner:

> We are assured, that the great Slaughter made of the Rebels in the last Battle,
> was owing not only to the Knowledge which the King's Forces had of the
> Pretender's Orders to the Rebels, not to give Quarter, but to the Obstinacy
> of the Rebels, who, as they lay wounded on the Ground, fired many Pistol-
> Shot at the Soldiers, as they passed them, which obliged the latter, for their
> own Security, to dispatch them out of the Way; notwithstanding which,
> and the treacherous Behaviour of some of the Rebels, who, after Quarters
> given, fired at the Officers who had given it, many were spared, and above
> 500 made Prisoners.[12]

In support of the fact that hundreds were made prisoner, rather than
methodically slaughtered en masse, Lieutenant Cliffe recalled the day after
the battle that 'Our Goals [jails] are full of them, and they still continue to
bring them in by hundreds'.[13] Colonel Whitefoord believed 'the kill'd and
prisoners' amounted to 'upwards of 3,000 besides numbers that crauld off
and died in the woods'.[14]

One accusation, repeated by Captain Johnstone and many others, is
particularly damning. It involves the Duke of Cumberland issuing a specific order that a barn full of wounded rebels should be set alight. As the
men attempted to escape, so the report goes, British army soldiers pushed
them back into the furnace with their bayonets, so that every man was
burnt alive.[15] A sadistic officer on the ground, who happened to find these
members of the Jacobite army gathered in a barn, may indeed have ordered
his men to do this, although the military historian Jonathan Oates argues
that there is no concrete evidence that it happened at all. But a query must
remain against the duke *specifying* such an action.[16]

The duke observes that he will continue to make the distinction between
French prisoners of war and rebels, 'endeavouring to find out who are

native born subjects of the King, not looking upon them as Prisoners of War but as Rebels'.[17] He confirms that Lord Strathallan had been killed by Colonel Howard and then lists what items have been taken, including 'the Pretenders & all their Baggage but it was so plunderd that I am afraid I shall be able to render but an indifferent account of it'. On the subject of Charles, he says that the 'Pretenders son it is said lay at Lord Lovats house at Aird the night after the affair. Brigadier Mordaunt is detached with nine hundred volunteers this morning into the Fraziers Country to destroy all the Rebels He finds there.' The duke's intelligence is certainly accurate here. He also states that Lord Cromartie and his son (both absent from the battle) had been taken. While attempting to recover the arms and money from the beached *Le Prince Charles* (taken by troops led by Captain George Mackay and Captain Sir Henry Monro), they had been surprised by the Earl of Sutherland's militia at Dunrobin (the day before Culloden) and later taken prisoner. Regarding what is left of the Jacobite army the duke says, 'They continue as yet dispers'd, & their own accounts make their loss greater by two thousand that I have ventured to state it.' He had also arrested Major Grant, the Govenor of Fort George, while enquiries were made as to how the fort was allowed to surrender, '& as I fear He will not have any good ones to give, I shall order a Court Martial for his trial'.

He then recommends that 'It will be absolutely necessary that new Forts be erected here & where Fort Augustus stood, & whoever his Majesty may think proper to order to inspect their construction, should be sent down immediately as the season is now come for works of that kind.'[18] While at Inverness, the duke and his engineers reconnoitred a new location for Fort George. They found an excellent one, a promontory jutting out into the Moray Firth at Ardersier, eight miles from Culloden. Here a mighty fortress would be built by William Adam's sons to designs by Lieutenant General William Skinner, accommodating an artillery detachment manning eighty guns and 1,600 infantry. Another important and connected development, again encouraged by the duke soon after Culloden, was the Military or Ordnance Survey of Scotland. According to the chief surveyor, William Roy, the rebellion had 'convinced the Government of what infinite importance it would be to the State, that a country, so very inaccessible by nature, should be thoroughly explored and laid open'.[19] Commencing in 1747, as the teams of engineers, surveyors and draftsmen, including the brothers Paul and Thomas Sandby, roamed the length and breadth of the country, measuring and drawing, no more could it be said that the distant lands of India and the Far East were better known than the Highlands of Scotland.

The duke next turns to a letter to Lord President Forbes, of whom he writes, in regard to the recent victory, 'your known affections & Zeal for his Majesty his family & the common cause, leave no room to doubt but the news of it will be extremely agreeable & wellcome to you'. He even states, 'I dare say it will be some additional satisfaction to you, that the Battle was fought so near your house of Colloden that it takes its name from thence.' It is extremely unlikely that the Lord President, who had worked tirelessly for decades to prevent such a catastrophe befalling his friends and neighbours, would have found this particular irony worthy of any satisfaction at all. On the subject of the current state of the Lord President's house, the duke continues,

> I am apprehensive least from the resort of the Pretender & some of the Chiefs of the Rebels for some time before the action to your house our people may have been drawn that way. & that from the licence of such a time some excesses may have been committed there which I shall be sorry for, but at all Events the House will have farred better from our Victory than it would otherwise, for the Rebels had vowed it for bonfire, in case of success. I hope this event will soon restore tranquility to the Country, & put an end to your long fatigues.[20]

A few days after the battle, the official return of the killed and wounded was signed by Robert Napier. Of the officers, Captain Lord Robert Kerr and Ballimore were confirmed killed on the battlefield, with Captain Grosset, Captain John Campbell of Lord Loudoun's Regiment and Captain Colin Campbell of the Argyllshire Militia 'wounded & dead since', while 44 rank and file were listed as killed and 233 wounded. The return for Barrell's and Monro's was unsurprisingly high in comparison with the other regiments: rank and file Barrell's, 14 killed and 101 wounded, and Monro's, 13 killed and 60 wounded.[21]

Over the subsequent days the news gradually filtered out. From Edinburgh, Lord Justice Clerk Andrew Fletcher wrote to Sir Everard Fawkener that he had received the tidings 'of his Royal Highness haveing obtained a compleat victory over the Rebells' initially about eleven o'clock in the evening from James, Duke of Atholl, which was then confirmed via a message from Aberdeen:

> I beg leave in name of all his Majesty's faithfull subjects here, all the good Freinds of our happy Constitution, to congratulate his Royall Highness, on

so glorious and happy an Event, which has at once freed us of all the torment-
ing anxietys we were in, and fulfilled our wishes, by a glorious and happy
Deliverance, so unexpectedly obtained, and at so small an expence of Blood.[22]

To the Duke of Newcastle (at midnight on the 19th) he had written,
'God be thanked our tedious Troubles now draw to a Speedy and happy
conclusion in a word His Royal Highness The Duke of Cumberland is safe
and victorious.'[23] Sir John Ligonier, writing from London to the Duke of
Cumberland on 25 April, gleefully states that 'this town has been in a Blaze
these two days. Return as soon as you Please' for, apparently, his victory has
made him the great hero among the ladies, none of whom 'will refuse you'.
But, he continues, Flanders beckons and 'the Duke must be at the head of
the allyed army, and the king was yesterday saying some thing of His son
and ten Brittish Batt[alio]ns and if that should be the case I want, I desire
to have, may Glory and Victory ever attend your steps.'[24]

On 23 April the duke writes again to the Secretary of State, concerning
the arrival of more French Jacobite army prisoners, which he has 'ship'd off',
and that the Laird of Grant has promised to deliver a list of all the members of his clan who signed and agreed to neutrality (after Lord George's
demand several weeks before): after which, 'I shall immediately have them
committed as Traitors for corresponding with the Rebels.' However, the
Grants had apparently 'deliverd to me Lord Balmerino who fel into their
hands by accident'. Furthermore, almost all of Charles' servants had surrendered and 'as they were all French & had not been with Him before He
came to France, according to their desire I have given them Passports to
go home'. He reports that Lord Sutherland with eight or nine hundred of
his men were now in Fraser country hunting down rebels in general, and
specifically Charles and Lord Lovat. He also confirms that Lord Findlater,
who 'has behaved with the greatest zeal & activity for the Kings service' is
en route to London '& is thoroughly apprised of the bad constitution of
this part of the Kingdom, & appears to me to have just notions of what
would be proper to amend it'. He concludes,

I hope that whatsoever Resolutions his Majesty may come to about the
new modeling this Government [in Scotland], they may be fixt as soon as
conveniently may be, as it will be of absolute necessity, that the new laws
take place before his Majestys forces quit this Country, & I flatter my self
that within a month or six weeks at longest, We shall have done all that can
be done by the military.[25]

As noted before, the duke believed that the military could only do so much and its actions were, in any case, a short-term measure: new laws and a revised form of government in Scotland was required to stamp out any potential for another rebellion. For even if 'we had destroyed every man of them, such is the very soil that rebellion would sprout out again'.[26]

On 30 April Joseph Yorke wrote from Inverness to his brother Philip, hoping 'this is the last time blood will be shed in the field by fellow subjects of this island'. He continues, 'Since the battle our time has been taken up in hunting out the Rebels who made their escape from our fury that day', and, regarding Charles, 'When we move, we shall do our best to ferret him out, and if we can't send him to his long home, endeavour at least to rid the island of him.'[27] Having read through the correspondence retrieved from the Jacobite army's baggage, as well as that found on the Jacobite officers, dead and alive (much of which has been quoted in the current history), Joseph observes that the Jacobite army appeared to have no formed plan, were 'guided wholly by events', 'the circumstances arising from daily occurences' and 'accidents', while 'Disputes, jealousies, doubts of one another are on all sides plain which, with the total want of order, discipline and economy, must have made a hell upon earth',[28] a fair assessment.

On 5 May, Sir Everard Fawkener confirmed in a letter to the Duke of Newcastle that 'the Person calling Himself Marquis of Tullibardin is taken or has given himself up'. By this time the marquess was extremely ill. He goes on, 'I imagine that those who have surrendered themselves have done it merely to avoid the fatigues, hardships & continual Terrors of sculking & hiding.' Finally,

> I think I may upon the best & surest grounds rejoice with your Grace, that the Head of that Monster Rebellion was quite crush'd on the glorious field of Collodden, the dispers'd Members will by degrees be quite pickd up, so that nothing may remain of that Fury let loose from Hell upon us to disturb these Kingdoms any more.[29]
> 'Augusto prebente Deos'

Four days later, Lord Ancram sent in a report of his activities around Aberdeen: 'Since I left Inverness I have burnt two Roman catholick meetings Houses & five Episcopal . . . not forgetting two librarys of Popish and Jacobite Books, in the house of one Gordon a Priest I found several hundred volumes all upon that Religion. Major la fousille would have been pleased with the blaze.'[30]

In the meantime, Lord President Forbes had arrived in Inverness. After months of wandering in 'bad weather, forced marches, through mountains almost impassable, lying on roots or straw or heather, and a low diet from mere necessity', the Lord President now described himself as 'absolutely naked: soled shoes, darned stockings, ragged shirts, fragments of boots are my apparel'. However, the sixty-year-old considered himself 'rather improved than impaired' from his difficulties, and observes, with more than a hint of dark humour, that a cure for the vapours was 'A Rebellion, if the patient can stand it'.[31] Although Culloden House itself (excluding the interiors) had largely survived intact, the same could not be said of the surrounding country. The people and their property within the Lord President's lands had suffered greatly from both Jacobite and British army assaults.[32]

In mid-May, Henry Pelham congratulated the Duke of Cumberland, writing, 'Every day bring us fresh advices of the great success of your Royal Highness att Culloden, and we are no less happy in the accounts we receive of the almost total submission of the rebellious crew; which in justice is attributed to your Royal Highnesses civil conduct, as well as to your military execution.' He then confirms that the House of Commons are likely to confer on the duke and his male heirs an annuity of £25,000, in addition to the £15,000 a year already settled.[33] The duke's prize for Culloden.

By or after Francesco Ponzone, *James Francis Edward Stuart, c.* 1741.

52

Albano

'great anxiety & pain'

June 6th 1746 [27 May OS][1]

God knows where or when this will find you, My Dearest Carluccio, but still I cannot but write to you in the great anxiety & pain I am in for you from what the publick news mentions from Scotland. I know nothing else, & I doubt not but those accounts are exagerated, considering from whence they come. But still it is but too plain to see that affairs with you don't go as I could wish; I am thò still in hopes you may be able to keep your ground in Scotland, till you can have assistance from France. But if you really cannot ma[i]ntain yourself in Scotland, Do not for Gods sake drive things too far, but think of your safety, on which so much depends; Thò your Enterprize should miscarry, the honor you have gaind by it will always stick by you, it will make you be respected & consider[e]d abroad, & will, I think I may answer for it, always engage The French to protect & assist you, & to renew in time another project in your favor. So that you should really have no temptation to pursue rash or desperate measures at this time, for should you do so, it would be the ruin of all, & even a drawback from the honor you have already gained. En fin, My Dear Child, never separate prudence & courage. Providence has wonderfully assisted you hitherto, & will not abandon you for the time to come. This I firmly hope, while I shall not cease to beseech God to bless & direct you.

Adieu my dearest child I tenderly embrace you & am all yours, once more God bless you & protect you

James R.

Detail from *The Pretender's Flight*, 1747, published by J. Cole.

53

Coradale

'well concealed'

Charles left the mainland for the Hebrides as planned. After being continually harassed by the Royal Navy – spending eight days on an island 'in the greatest misery', feeding off fish that had washed up on the shore and dried – some time around 10 May, the prince and his small party arrived in Benbecula (between North and South Uist) where he sent a messenger to the clan chiefs, Secretary Murray and John Hay 'requiring an exact account how affairs stood'.[1] They then retired to Coradale on South Uist on 14 May to await the response, and remained there for three weeks, living in a small house in the forest.[2] Here Captain Alexander MacDonald (of Clanranald) noted that Charles was accompanied by O'Sullivan, O'Neil, the clergyman Allan MacDonald, several officers from the Clanranald regiment and 'a dozen of other sturdy clever fellows that served as guard, and running several incident errands back and forward'.[3] After the prince's ordeal thus far, life at Coradale was almost pleasant. Alexander MacDonald observes the area was the 'best for game in all Scotland' and Charles, the crack shot, 'was pretty oft at his diversion through the mountain, papping down perhaps dozens in a day of muircocks and hens'.[4] Charles himself recalled (less romantically) that he 'had a tolerable hut at Coradell' but complains that for food, there was 'mostly nothing else but Milck, which as a nourishment [is] always contrary to him' and 'so it proved', as the prince 'got a moste violent Bludy flux, which lasted afornet [a fortnight]' and was only alleviated, as he continues, by regular doses of brandy.[5]

Hugh MacDonald of Baleshare (south-west of North Uist) recalled meeting Charles at the house in early June in the company of Alexander MacDonald of Boisdale, the half-brother to the Chief of Clanranald and who, the previous August, had told Charles to go home. Both had refused to join the prince, but neither wanted him harmed so, for safety, the latter arrived separately and a little later. Baleshare had been sent by Lady

Margaret MacDonald (wife of Sir Alexander of Sleat) with letters and copies of recent newspapers, as requested by the prince himself.[6] Baleshare
recalls arriving at 'Glen Coridile, in South Uist, where (being a mist day)
I cam near them before they discover'd me, which surpriz'd them'.[7] Not
knowing who the stranger was, the prince was given a warning by Colonel
O'Sullivan and had hurried inside the small house. But Captain Allan
MacDonald vouched that Baleshare was trustworthy and, once he had
entered the house, Charles greeted his visitor saying he 'was heartily glade
to see the face of an honest man in such a remot corner'.

Baleshare later described the prince's grubby appearance: 'His dress was
then a tartan short coat and vest of the same, got from Lady Clanranald,
his night cape linen, all patched with [soot] drops, his short [shirt], hands
and face patchd with the same, a short kilt, tartan hose and Highland
brogs, his upper coat being English cloath.' As he was in company, Charles
called for a dram 'being the first article of a Highland entertainment' and
food, namely 'half a ston of butter' and 'near a leg of beef . . . all patchd
with suit [soot] drops'.[8] Boisdale (having now also arrived) informed the
prince that parties of Sir Alexander of Sleat's MacDonalds as well as some
MacLeods were searching for him on Barra, and, still fearing that they were
putting the prince in danger, Baleshare suggested leaving. In response, the
'young gentleman told us as it was but seldom he met with friends he coud
enjoy himself with, he wou'd not on any account part with us that night'.[9]
On hearing this, Boisdale turned to Baleshare and in 'Highland' said that
it would be bad-mannered to leave now. Baleshare responded that if the
prince was willing to risk it, then so was he. Still among the company
was Ned Burke whom Charles ordered to serve the drink – Alexander
MacDonald recalled it was 'only cold brandy out of a clean shell without
any mixture at all'[10] – but Boisdale insisted on changing his shirt and being
shaved before commencing. 'Then,' says Baleshare, 'we began with our
boul [bowl] frank and free; as wee were turning merry, wee were turning
more free.'

Emboldened by the brandy, Baleshare asked if the prince would have
any objection to being told what, in Baleshare's opinion, were the most
significant issues against the prince in Britain. Charles apparently replied
that he had no objection, at which Baleshare observed that 'Popery' and
arbitrary government were the greatest. Charles responded that this was
simply the hostile interpretation of his enemies. Then, as Baleshare relays
it, the prince continued, '"Do you 'no, Mr. M'Donald," he says, "what
religion are all the princes in Europe of?" I told him I imagin'd they were

of the same establish'd religion of the nation they liv'd in. He told me they had litle or no religion at all.'[11] This cynical or, perhaps, simply realistic statement seems to suggest that Charles understood of religion and religious affiliation as being something that princes, in his experience, did not particularly believe in. Indeed, it was a cloak that they put on and took off as and when the situation required it. If the statement derived from recent bitter experience, Charles may have had Louis XV in mind. Through such comments it is clear that Charles was less wedded to Catholicism than either his father or his brother. It is the prince's personal tragedy that a major bar to what he most desired was a thing he seemed to care so little about.

Then the conversation took a less theological, more personal turn, due to the unusual intimacy that this convivial episode had brought about between the prince and his companions of circumstance. Boisdale informed Charles that his predecessor, Donald Clanranald, had fought many battles for the prince's family yet when Charles II returned after the restoration, his ancestor was not acknowledged at court. In reply the prince reportedly said, 'Boystill [sic], Dont be rubbing up old sores, for if I cam home the case woud be otherwise with me.'[12] In a similar vein, Baleshare observed 'that notwithstanding of what freedome wee enjoy'd there with him, wee coud've no access to him if he was setled at London', to which Charles replied, 'if he had never so much ado, he'd be one night merry with his Highland freinds'. It seems the cause was far from over in Charles' mind. According to Baleshare, they continued drinking or partaking of the 'boul' for three days and nights, during which time Charles 'still had the better of us, and even of Boystill himself, notwithstanding his being as able a boulman, I dare say, as any in Scotland'.[13]

Some days later, Baleshare recalled that Major General John Campbell was known to have marched to South Uist. Concerned for the prince's safety, Baleshare crossed over to where Charles was then hiding, and found him next to a loch in very different circumstances from their last meeting. Still in a kilt, his face was 'black weather beaten' due to 'night and day in the open fields'. Although in good health he had not eaten for a day. Yet despite all this he 'was very canty and jockose'. Eventually, Ranald MacDonald of Torlom arrived 'with bread, butter, and a rosted hen'. The butter, half salt, was the type 'prepared for cureing their scabbed horses; no man cou'd 've tasted it but a starving man'. Charles spread the butter on the hot bread and 'devoured the whole'. He then ate the chicken and, taking his bonnet to the loch, he filled it with water and drank from it. Baleshare

recalled, 'His hose was all brunt betuixt his ankle and garter. I ask'd him
what befell his hose. He told me he threw it of[f] that morning and was
drying it to a heather fire, and as he was falling asleep it took fire.'[14]

It may have been at this time that Baleshare sent a letter to his brother
Donald Roy MacDonald, who had seen Keppoch fall at Culloden and
was himself injured making his escape, stating that Charles intended leaving the Long Isle for a grassy island called Fladda Chuain, Sir Alexander
MacDonald of Sleat's land, which had a single tenant. Clearly shocked
by the prince's physical condition, Baleshare urged his brother to deliver
'necessities' along with the newspapers that Lady Margaret MacDonald
continued to supply. Understandably Charles was keen to keep abreast of
events beyond South Uist. Baleshare 'complained that the Prince wanted
almost all necessities, particularly shirts, and therefore desired his brother
might do his best to procure him some shirts and blankets, for that the
Prince had lain hitherto only in his plaid'.[15] According to Baleshare, Sir
Alexander had contrived not to call upon his people to assist in the hunting
down and capture of the beleaguered prince, 'as it did not lay in his way to
do him good, he had no inclination to do him hurt'.[16] This would explain
why Sir Alexander's wife, Margaret, was aiding Charles. It is about this
time that the messenger had returned with a letter from Secretary Murray
who, having avoided the carnage at Culloden through illness, was now
aiming to escape to the Netherlands via Leith. Murray reported, according
to Felix O'Neil, 'that almost all the clans had delivered up themselves and
arms, and consequently they were no more to be depended upon'.[17]

If that was not devastating enough, the prince was also informed that
two Nantes privateers, the *Mars* and the *Bellona*, had arrived off the mainland some weeks before carrying a small fortune (42,000 louis d'ors) and
arms. These ships had been sent from France, on the recommendation of
Antoine Walsh, well before the Battle of Culloden. Walsh had persuaded
the French Court that if the prince's affairs were going well, then the money
and arms would support his ongoing campaign. If it was not going well
and Charles 'would have no alternative to seeking refuge in the hills', then
these ships would bring him back to France.[18] It was also Walsh who had
specified that, whatever the prince's circumstances, any French ship would
have to steer for the west coast, as he rightly feared the worst regarding the
fate of the ships that had recently sailed to the north-east. On the arrival of
the *Mars* and the *Bellona*, a message had been sent out and the members of
the Jacobite army, who had been lying low in the neighbourhood, gradually emerged from their hideouts and gathered on the coast. The money,

subsequently known as Loch Arkaig treasure (where it was eventually hidden), was brought onshore at Loch nan Uamh. Initially at least, Secretary Murray knew its whereabouts. But he was arrested on 27 June at his sister's house, after which he was transported to London for interrogation. The care of the treasure then passed to Lochiel. The presence of so much money (after such a long period with no pay) encouraged some, including Lochiel, to continue the struggle for a while longer. But what exactly happened to it remains a mystery to this day.

However, with no news of Charles and after a vicious battle with the Royal Navy, the ships embarked for France, carrying with them (among others) the Duke of Perth, Lord John Drummond, Sir Thomas Sheridan, John Hay and John Daniel. After ten days at sea, with disease sweeping through the passengers and crew, Daniel recalled, 'I saw the body of my friend and patron the Duke of Perth, thrown over-board'.[19] The ships arrived back in Nantes on 27 May (NS). That Charles was not on board caused great consternation at the French Court. France had openly (if at times a little half-heartedly) supported the prince's campaign, so it was a matter of national honour that they get him back alive. But as the comte de Maurepas observed to his cousin, 'It seems certain that the Stuart Prince is in one or other of the small islands of the north of Scotland. But he is so well concealed from his enemies and from those who would help him, that both seek him with the same lack of success.'[20]

Thomas Sandby, *Fort Augustus*, 1746.

Fort Augustus

'burn & destroy'

A t the end of May, from his new base at Fort Augustus (in a dilapidated state since the Jacobite attack), the Duke of Cumberland updated the Duke of Newcastle on recent activity.[1] The Duke of Cumberland had moved here partly to signal that the British army and King George's authority could easily penetrate into the Highlands. Lord Loudoun, with his Highland force, had successfully dispersed the hundreds of Camerons and MacDonalds gathered at Lochiel and Barrisdale, and who were eventually ordered by Lochiel (who was in hiding in the area) to shift for themselves. After which the Camerons sent a messenger to request that they surrender their arms and give themselves up to the king's mercy. This had been agreed to. Lord Loudoun had since ventured into Badenoch 'to burn & destroy that Country which has not yet laid down their Arms; but I believe they immediately will, the McPhersons having already in great measure done it'. Orders to destroy the property of those who had been in the rebellion were left to the officers on the ground to carry out as they saw fit – some more enthusiastically than others – but what was not allowed was indiscriminate plunder. After one particular incident, an order was issued by the duke that there should be 'No plundering nor Moroding on pain of hanging', that 'no man on any pretence after Tatoo to goe out of the camp', and 'Patroles to goe instantly from the picquet during the Night & take up & search all soldiers they find out of camp'.[2]

Regarding the pacification of the Highlands, even the Lord President believed (as indicated in a memorandum sent to the duke dated 20 May) that 'No severity that is necessary, ought to be Dispensed with', considering that 'Omitting such severitys, is Cruelty to the King, and to the Kingdom' and that those of the leaders who had abused the lenity shown them after the '15 should be dealt with by the full and swift due process of law. Yet, he also counselled, 'Unnecessary Severitys create Pity' and such pity is 'the most Dangerous', because it is a 'nurse to Disaffection'. The government should consider 'whether, and how far, it is consistent with the Future tranquillity of the Kingdom, to restrain merited Punishment, and to extend Unmerited mercy'.[3] Lord Justice Clerk Andrew Fletcher was also pondering who to make examples of, whether to include 'Advisers Assisters Receptors and harborers Clerks and Servants as well as those who have actually carried arms' in order that 'the Country may be apprised what acts do amount to Treason', while considering 'at the same tim the leniety of the Government may appear in punishing so few of so great a multitude of Criminals'.[4]

That the Duke of Cumberland was paying any attention to the Lord President's measured advice in particular is unlikely, for despite the fact that 'as yet we are vastly fond of one another', as he wrote to the Duke of Newcastle, 'I fear it wont last as he is as arrant Highland mad as L. Stair, or Crauford [John Lindsay, Earl of Crawford]', 'wishes lenity if it can be with safety' and believes that 'once they are dispersed, it is of no more consequence then [than] a London mob'.[5] The duke profoundly disagreed with this optimistic assessment. As he continues in his letter of 27 May to the Duke of Newcastle, 'I hope his Majesty will not imagine, that by these people laying down their Arms, the Country is a jot surer from any fresh rising'. Not only was each Highlander in possession of two or three arms, which remain hidden, but 'tho I know that every single Person in the Country has been in the Rebellion, yet unless I could get each Person sworn against it, there is no taking them up, so that in appearance all that can be done, purely military, is now over, therefore I dont propose to stay here above a week longer unless any thing extraordinary should happen.' He concludes, 'I hope that when ever the situation of this Country shall be considered, that some expedient may be found for transplanting several of there Clans to some part of the Indies where they will be much happier, & without which this Island will never be free from commotions.'[6]

The idea of transportation to the West Indies or the American colonies, rather than execution, as had also happened, for example, after Monmouth's rebellion in 1685, had occurred to others. In his notes dated 20 May, Lord President Forbes considered (regarding the Highlanders) whether they might 'transport the most active & dangerous, to America, where they might be of use to the Crown, & to the Kingdom'.[7] He observes, 'it would probably be to the Taste of all that Part of Scotland that borders with them; could be complained of by no Body, & would, in some Degree yield the Security proposed'.[8] Andrew Fletcher too was pondering whether 'Transportation be thought expedient for any number of privat men.'[9] In this instance, then, the duke seems to have taken on board the Lord President's advice.

Over a week later, on hearing that Charles was around South Uist, Sir Everard Fawkener issued a command from the Duke of Cumberland that two sloops, including HMS *Furnace*, which had been in the vicinity for some weeks, should cruise this area, landing as and when 'to enquire after and search for, all strangers who may have resorted there since the Battle of Culloden, & to seize all such of them as they can lay hands on'. Locals who they suspect of knowing about or harbouring such strangers 'should be menaced' and threatened with military execution, 'in order to oblige them to a discovery where such strangers may be, or at least which way they tooke'. The order closes by reminding the sloop captains that particular care should be taken that no 'excesses or disorders' are committed on the island of South Uist, being the territory of Sir Alexander MacDonald 'from whose Factors or Agents you will meet all friendly treatment & assistance'.[10] On the same day Sir Everard writes to Major General John Campbell, informing him that the duke was extremely approving of his diligence 'in the enquirys after & search for the Pretenders Son', as well as regarding 'the effects & Arms [recently] landed from the French Ships'. It is clear that Aeneas MacDonald had been captured, as Sir Everard continues, Major General Campbell should 'draw what you can from the Paris Banker either with regard to the Young Pretender, or the Money transactions', although he should stop short of offering a pardon in return for such information.[11]

Meanwhile, local ministers, at the behest of the Duke of Cumberland, were sending in lists of those from within their parish who had either joined the rebellion, or had assisted the Jacobite army by (for example) the collecting of taxes. William Carlyle of Prestonpans confirmed that none from a total of 1,500 inhabitants above the age of ten years old 'have been concerned in this detestable Rebellion', excepting seven named men who had collected, often in a menacing manner, customs and salt duties.[12] The Reverends James Fraser and Andrew Robertson of Allness in Ross believed that they should be better employed in encouraging repentance for 'the wickedness of any of our people who were concerned in this Rebellion', rather than have them punished, albeit deservedly so in their opinion, 'by our Information'.[13]

On 11 June the captain of the *Furnace* sloop, John Ferguson, completed his journal of activity for the previous month. On 18 May he landed 120 men at the Bay of Morar and burnt a small village. The following day, having moved on to Loch Novay in Arisaig, he once more landed 120 men 'and burnt the house the young Pretender lodg'd att, with two or three Villages, & brought off two Prisoners' along with some ammunition and arms. On this occasion there had been some resistance, 'the Hills being crouded with Men In Armes, they had buried some Barrals of Powder with Trains which they sett fire too & blew up three of my men, one of which is since dead'. On the 23rd the *Furnace* arrived at Stornoway, where, they were informed, Charles had been only days before, but had since escaped. On the 29th he and his men burnt the house of Kinlochmoidart and then, two days later, having heard that Lord Lovat and several clan chiefs were at Morar, he marched his men the six miles, arriving about six o'clock in the evening. He eventually caught up with Lord Lovat at night on 7 June, the Old Fox 'conceal'd in the Trunk of a Tree in a wood with only four of his Guard & a Woman'. By the 8th, Lord Lovat was on board the *Furnace* and Captain Ferguson completes his report by stating that he has burnt all the houses in and around Morar.[14]

Detail from Thomas Sandby, *Fort Augustus*, 1746.

J. Williams, *Charles Edward Stuart ['Betty Burke']*, after 1746.

Skye

By mid-June Charles and his companions had reached Loch Boisdale, where he had hoped Alexander MacDonald of Boisdale would assist him. But on arrival they discovered that Boisdale had been arrested.[1] Here the prince 'stayed 8 days upon a rock, making a tent of the sail of the boat, and lived upon fish and fowl of his own killing'. He had now been a fugitive for over two months. Danger had stalked him for most of this time, but now he 'found himself in the most terrible situation'.[2] He received intelligence that the Lowlander Captain Caroline Scott, formerly of Fort William and keen for revenge, had landed at Kilbride less than two miles away. On 20 June, the prince left Colonel O'Sullivan with the boat crew, and, accompanied by Captain O'Neil and his new guide Neil MacEachain, he made for the mountains. Soon after, he heard that Major General John Campbell was at Berneray, an island between North Uist and Harris, and as a result the prince was now close to being trapped, having troops nearby on two sides, with the sea on the other and no boat.

The prince, O'Neil and MacEachain arrived at a hut near Ormaclett at midnight on the 21st. According to one account, 'In this perplexity Captain O'Neil accidentally met with Miss Funivella or Flora MacDonald, to whom he proposed assisting the Prince to make his escape'.[3] In his own account, O'Neil also says he met Flora by chance and told her that he had 'brought a friend to see her, and she, with some emotion, asked if it was the Prince. I answered her it was, and instantly brought him in.'[4] Flora was a year younger than the prince, a modest, honourable young woman. But asking for Flora's assistance came with risks. She was the stepdaughter of Hugh 'one-eyed' MacDonald of Armadale (on Skye), who was the captain of a militia raised by Sir Alexander MacDonald and therefore, technically, hunting the fugitive prince. However, as the stepdaughter of a militia captain, Flora could get the necessary passports, which would give the prince a chance to slip past the advancing troops and on to a place of relative safety.

In the event, O'Neil's apparently improvised plan may not have been as risky or as improvised as it appeared. According to one witness, Donald MacLeod, it was Hugh MacDonald himself (a former officer in the French army) who sent word to the prince's party of Captain Scott's arrival nearby, and who then recommended, with his aid – including the escort of his stepdaughter – that the prince make his way to Skye to the east.[5] The island had remained isolated from the impact of the rebellion because of Sir Alexander MacDonald of Sleat's refusal to join on the Jacobite side. Here the prince would be under the protection of Lady Margaret MacDonald. Either way, it was Flora who would have the hazardous task of accompanying Charles to Skye, the prince travelling in the guise of her servant. Despite initially refusing (as recalled by O'Neil) through loyalty to Sir Alexander, her chief, whom she feared would be punished if the plan was discovered, 'she at last consented to, on condition the Prince would put on women's cloaths, which he complied with. She then desired they would goe to the mountain of Corradale and stay there till they heard from her, which should be soon.' Flora then left to make the necessary arrangements, which included the swift construction of a convincing maid's outfit to be worn by a young man almost six feet tall. According to Flora the garments were provided by Lady Clanranald.[6] They included a floral-pattern gown of 'stamped linen with a purple sprig'[7] and a white apron.

After both Flora and then MacEachain had been arrested by militia, only to be freed by Captain Hugh MacDonald, MacEachain returned to the prince and together they rowed to Benbecula, eventually arriving at the house of Clanranald's principal tenant. On the 27th the prince was joined for supper by Lady Clanranald, her daughter Peggy, Flora MacDonald, her brother Milton, Neil MacEachain and Captain O'Neil. Flora recalled, 'they all dined very heartily' on roasted 'heart, liver, kidneys, etc., of a bullock or sheep' which Charles assisted in preparing.[8] The party were then warned that Major General Campbell, Captain Scott, and Captain Ferguson of HMS *Furnace* were closing in, and early on the 28th they took a boat across Loch Uskevagh.[9] Lady Clanranald was summoned back to her house at Nunton and both she and her husband were taken prisoner shortly after. On Flora's insistence, Captain O'Neil did not accompany the prince to Skye, and so it is here that Charles, 'With much difficulty and after many intreaties', bade O'Neil a sad farewell.[10]

In the evening, Charles disguised himself as Flora's Irish maid, 'Betty Burke' – 'the character C-s was too assume'[11] as the prince later wrote – and sailed for Skye in the company of Flora, Neil MacEachain and four boatmen.[12] During the rough crossing Flora awoke to find the prince covering her head, while the boatmen adjusted the sails.[13] He is even reported to have sung songs to keep their spirits up: 'The King shall enjoy his own again' was a particular favourite.[14] On 29 June they arrived near Monkstadt House. The traditional beach landing is named *Alt a Chuain*, north of Kilbride. The boatmen were sent back to Uist, while Flora made her way to Monkstadt to warn Lady Margaret of their arrival. Sir Alexander was then at Fort Augustus. Lady Margaret in turn sent the estate steward, Alexander MacDonald of Kingsburgh, to the prince with refreshment. As Kingsburgh approached, the prince (still in his frock, petticoat, mop cap and apron) advanced towards him with a cudgel aloft, and demanded to know whether he was Mr MacDonald of Kingsburgh. Once he had confirmed it, the prince replied, 'Then all is well; come let us be jogging on.'[15] Before they did, the two sat on a rock while Charles ate the bread and drank the wine that Kingsburgh had brought him. As they made their way across the countryside to Kingsburgh's house, 'the Prince lifted the petticoats too high in wading the rivulet . . . and that honest MacKechan hastily called to him to beware . . . "For God's sake, Sir, take care what you are doing, for you will certainly discover yourself;" and that the Prince laughed heartily, and thanks him kindly for his great concern.'[16]

According to a later account, when the group arrived at the house and Charles, still in his disguise, was pacing manfully up and down in the hallway, Kingsburgh's daughter ran to her mother and said, 'Mama! Mama! my Father has brought hither a very odd, muckle, ill-shaken-up Wife as ever I saw.'[17] Like her daughter, Mrs MacDonald was frightened to see such a 'muckle Trollop of a Carling make sick lang Strides through the Hall'. Eventually the muckle trollop was introduced and as 'she' kissed her hostess' hand, Mrs MacDonald felt the bristles of a beard brush against her, and realised that this was a man in disguise – although she was apparently still ignorant of exactly who he was. A little later Mrs MacDonald's husband told her the truth, upon which she exclaimed (indicating this was no game), 'then we are a'ruined; we will a' be hanged now'. To which Kingsbrugh replied, 'if we are hanged for this, we die in a *good cause*, doing only an Act of Humanity and Charity. But go make haste with Supper.'[18] Charles ate the supper, smoked a pipe and then spent the night at Kingsburgh House.[19]

The prince slept well into the following day, causing an already nervous Flora considerable anxiety. When he finally awoke, Mrs MacDonald
'behoved to employ her daughter as handmaid to the Prince for putting on
his womens cloaths.' But when her daughter was dressing him 'he was like
to fall over with laughing. After the peenes, gown, hood, mantle, etc., were
put on, he said, "O, Miss, you have forgot my apron. Where is my apron?
Pray get me my apron here, for that is a principal part of my dress."'[20] As
this anecdote suggests, and both Kingsburgh and his wife later declared,
'the Prince behaved not like one that was in danger, but as cheerfully and
merrily as if he had been putting on women's cloathes merely for a piece
of diversion'.[21] Indeed Kingsburgh felt the female disguise was ridiculous,
exclaiming when he first saw the prince, 'Your enemies call you a pretender, but if you be, I can tell you, you are the worst of your trade I ever
saw!'[22] As a result Kingsburgh advised Charles,

> to take from him a suite of Highland cloaths with a broadsword in his hand,
> which would become him much better. But in the meantime that he should
> go out of his house in the female dress, lest the servants should be making
> their observations, and stop at the edge of a wood upon the side of a hill,
> not far from the house, where he and others should come to him with the
> Highland cloathes, broadsword, etc.[23]

When Charles removed his 'female rags' as planned, they were hidden
within a bush 'till a proper opportunity should offer of taking them up;
for these that were present resolved to preserve them all as valuable tokens
of distress'.[24]

Charles was then met by Donald Roy MacDonald (the brother of
Baleshare) who made arrangements to take him to Raasay, an island
between Skye and the mainland. He walked to the coastal town of Portree
with Neil MacEachain while Flora travelled on horseback on the main
road nearby. The group spent two hours in a public house, possibly Charlie
MacNabb's Inn.[25] At last, Flora left the prince at Portree, Charles reportedly saying, 'For all that has happened I hope, Madam, we shall meet in
St. James's yet'.[26] She was arrested less than two weeks later.[27] The boatmen who had carried her and the prince to Skye had since been detained,
confessed to the whole enterprise and named her as the accomplice. On
examination, she explained that Betty Burke was an Irish woman who had
escaped transportation and had asked for her assistance, but that 'she never

saw the young Pretender, tho she often heard of that person'.[28] However, a militia captain, 'Mac Niel', had already confirmed that Flora and 'her Bettie Bourk were traced to Portree where Bettie appeared in man's Cloaths and parted from Miss MacDonald'.[29] Flora was then sent to Edinburgh en route to the Tower of London.

At about the same time Captain O'Neil, who after leaving Charles had been initially rescued along with Colonel O'Sullivan by another French ship, *Le Hardi Mendiant*, was sent ashore to find the prince. He was captured and then interrogated aboard the *Furnace*.[30] All too aware of the danger they were now in, Lady Margaret MacDonald wrote to the Lord President: 'Your Lordship can't yet be a Stranger to the trouble which has been lately brought upon this Island by the indiscretion of a foolish Girl, with whom the unhappy disturber of this Kingdom landed at this place.' He was in disguise, she declared, so they knew nothing about it until after he had left. She concludes, 'I must, at the same time, not only look upon myself, but the whole Country, as greatly suffering from the hurt it is likely he has done to the Man into whose House he intruded himself that night; I mean Kingsborrow.'[31] About the same time Captain Ferguson arrived at Kingsburgh House and arrested Kingsburgh and his daughter.

Anonymous, *Satire on the executions of Townley and Fletcher after the Jacobite rebellion*, 1746.

Kennington Common

'dying in so just and so glorious a cause'

When news of the victory arrived in London, as one resident, Gertrude Savile, recalled,

> The Guns of the Tower and Park were fired twice. At night such rejoycing, so many Bonfires, such illuminations were never seen. Scarce the meanest house that had not some candles – nay, some Hackney Coaches and Chairs, Cellars and Bulks [shopfronts and stalls]. Some Houses had Flamboys on the outside as well as Candles. 'Twas a Glorious sight.[1]

At his Mayfair home, George Frideric Handel was already composing an oratorio in celebration, on the subject of the great Jewish warrior-hero Judas Maccabaeus.

The Jacobite army had failed to reach the British capital but, as noted by the compiler of the *State Trials*, 'During the rebellion . . . an act [19 Geo. 2. C. 9.] passed empowering his majesty to issue commissions for trying the rebels in any county of the kingdom', including Surrey where Southwark was located, 'in the same manner as if the treasons had been committed in that county.'[2] This avoided the need for any trials in Scotland – with its separate legal system, and where sympathy and lenity, it was feared, would prevail – although hundreds of examinations were held across Scotland to determine who would be fit for trial. As a result, all of those captured and imprisoned at any point during or after the rebellion would be tried in England, with the trials and executions occurring in York, Carlisle and London. In Carlisle alone over three hundred prisoners were tried. Kinlochmoidart, a prisoner at Edinburgh Castle since his arrest in late 1745, was convicted and executed at Gallows Hill in nearby Harraby.[3] The marquis d'Eguilles had been captured and imprisoned after Culloden and then marched to Carlisle. Here he sent a letter to Sir Everard Fawkener, begging to be allowed to return to his estate in Provence, and lead a quiet life among his vines and fig trees. Sir Everard had also received a letter from Voltaire on the same mission, but, alas, as Sir Everard had responded, it was beyond his and the Duke of Cumberland's power to intervene in the court's deliberations.[4] The marquis was eventually sent home. Hundreds of men and some women were sent south and then held for months on prison hulks on the Thames and Thames estuary, where conditions were so terrible that many died before trial.[5] Important prisoners, including the Marquess of Tullibardine, Secretary Murray and Sir Hector Maclean, the latter still languishing a year on, were held in the Tower: an unpleasant experience, but a far cry from the filth and squalor of Newgate Prison, where some of the lower ranks were incarcerated.

The set-piece trials focused on the higher ranks: the four captured nobles, Lords Balmerino, Kilmarnock, Cromartie and Lovat (the latter trial delayed), of which Kilmarnock was the highest ranking, and the officers of the Manchester Regiment. Other Jacobite commanders including Lochiel, Cluny and Lord George Murray were still in hiding. As was Charles, of whom Horace Walpole wrote, 'We know nothing certainly of the young Pretender, but that he is concealed in Scotland, and devoured with distempers: I really wonder how an Italian constitution can have supported such rigours!' In the same letter Walpole observes that Sir John Cope is to stand trial for Prestonpans, yet Hawley, 'who is fifty times more culpable', is not: in his opinion 'Cope miscarried by incapacity: Hawley, by insolence and carelessness'.[6] In the event, the Board of General Officers, presided over by Marshal Wade and the Duke of Richmond among others, found Sir John's behaviour 'unblameable', and that 'there is no Ground for Accusation against the said Sir *John Cope*'.[7]

On 25 and 26 June 1746 the Grand Inquest found bills of indictment for High Treason 'committed against his Majesty's Person and Government, in levying and carrying on a cruel and destructive War, &c. in these Kingdoms' against thirty-four prisoners, including the officers of the Manchester Regiment. Peter Moss, who had persuaded James Dawson to join Prince Charles at Manchester, and Charles Holker managed to escape from Newgate Prison on 26 June. On that day, William Deacon, uncle to Charles and Thomas (Robert having died on the journey to London), 'who were so foolish as to engage in the Rebellion', wrote a desperate letter to Sir Everard Fawkener, hoping that the Duke of Cumberland would see fit to intercede on their behalf: 'Their youth perhaps may plead somewhat for them, when they were taken at Carlisle, one was not quite 16, & the other between 21 & 22.' However, he feared his letter, written in London to Sir Everard several hundred miles away at Fort Augustus, would arrive too late. As a result you 'will easier think the Affliction I am in, than I can tell you'.[8]

William Deacon wrote again three days later, updating Sir Everard on the swift progress of the trials. On Thursday, 3 July, the prisoners were brought to the bar of St Margaret's courthouse in Southwark to hear the indictment and to plead. The judges included Lord Justice Willes, who had commanded the law volunteers and drilled them around Lincoln's Inn the previous December. Three of the prisoners pleaded guilty, the remainder not guilty and the latter were committed to trial. But as the trial was at such a distance from where the alleged crimes had occurred, as well as distant from where many witnesses for their defence resided, the court agreed to delay the trial of the English prisoners until Tuesday, 15 July and the Scottish prisoners until 25 July.

On 15 July, the most significant of this group, Francis Towneley, colonel of the Manchester Regiment and Jacobite governor of the town of Carlisle, duly stood trial.[9] Almost half of those being tried in July were officers of this regiment. Twelve members of the jury were chosen from the one hundred men put forward and included Daniel Ponton of Lambeth, a starch-maker, Michael Cuffe of Battersea, a gardener, Robert Wood of Epsom, a baker, and William Taylor of St Saviour in Southwark, a brewer.[10] Towneley was accused of not only appearing in arms against the king and levying war, but specifically appearing on 10 November 1745 at Carlisle, along with 3,000 other persons, and 'with Drums beating, and Colours flying, Pipes playing, and there, being so array'd, did, in a warlike and hostile Manner, levy a cruel War, and took Possession of the City of *Carlisle* and the Citadel'.[11] This was demonstrably untrue, as Towneley had joined the Jacobite army at Preston several weeks later. Towneley again pleaded not guilty, and the witnesses for the prosecution were brought in one by one. These included Captain Vere, the spy whom Prince Charles had refused to execute, and Samuel Maddox, the apothecary's apprentice who had joined the Jacobite army at Manchester and was later imprisoned in Carlisle Cathedral. The latter confirmed that Towneley had been colonel of the Manchester Regiment (of which

Maddox was an ensign), had beaten up for volunteers, and had also been appointed governor of Carlisle, 'in consequence of which he ordered the guns to be mounted, chevaux de frize to be made, and an house to be burnt, from which the king's forces fired'.[12] Maddox also recalled that Towneley had argued with Colonel John Hamilton over the surrender of Carlisle, declaring *it was better to die by the Sword, than fall into the Hands of those damn'd* Hanoverians'.[13]

In Towneley's defence, his counsel argued that he still held a commission from the King of France and therefore should be treated as a prisoner of war, not a rebel.[14] John Hayward and Thomas Dickenson were then brought before the court to invalidate Maddox's evidence, by describing him as of very bad character and therefore not to be trusted to speak the truth under oath.[15] In response to the defence, the court considered the proof that Towneley was an officer in the French army would simply count against him anyway, for a natural-born British subject of King George should not be fighting for the nation's enemy.[16] And, in regard to Maddox, being a bad apprentice was not reason enough to discount his evidence under oath. The jury consulted, did not agree, left the court for ten minutes, returned, by which time they had unanimously found Francis Towneley guilty.

George Fletcher, Thomas Chadwick, Thomas Deacon, John Berwick and James Dawson then followed, Maddox acting as witness for the prosecution for each, and all were found guilty. John Hunter, also of the Manchester Regiment, was acquitted as Captain Vere could vouch that Hunter 'had run away 11 miles, in order to escape from the rebels, but was overtaken, and made to return, on pain of death; and that himself and the prisoner were tied together with a rope to a horse's tail, and obliged to run many miles without shoes in great torment'.[17] On the 18th, Andrew Blood changed his plea to guilty and then John Sanderson, Thomas Syddall, James Wilding, Charles Deacon and David Morgan were tried. Again, all were found guilty. On Tuesday, 22 July, the convicted prisoners were brought before the judges and sentence was pronounced. They were to be 'hang'd, drawn and quarter'd', the punishment for high treason.

The prisoners were moved to the New Prison in Southwark, where orders were received on 29 July, that the execution of Francis Towneley, George Fletcher, Thomas Chadwick, James Dawson, Thomas Deacon, John

Berwick, Andrew Blood, Thomas Syddall and David Morgan would occur the following day. The remaining eight, including Sanderson, Wilding and Charles Deacon, were reprieved for two weeks. While in prison, Francis Towneley had kept himself to himself, remaining in his room for most of the time. During a visit by an unnamed friend he admitted 'with tears in his eyes . . . My dear friend, I never thought it would come to this'.[18] The nine condemned were awoken in their cells at six o'clock on the morning of the 30th and, having dressed, they stood in the courtyard drinking coffee. They were all attired as gentlemen, Francis Towneley in a black suit made for the occasion. Only Tom Syddall was seen to tremble when the halter was put around his neck.[19] Their irons were removed and, with arms tied, they were placed on three sledges each pulled by three horses. The procession to Kennington Common was accompanied by troops from the Foot Guards.[20]

A large mob had assembled at the gallows on the common and began to jeer when the procession came into view. A pile of faggots and a block had been placed nearby. While they were removed from the sledges and then assisted on to the cart, from which they were to be hanged, the faggots were lit. There was no clergyman in attendance, so David Morgan read out prayers, to which the others responded. This took half an hour. On conclusion, they reportedly took some written papers out of the books they carried and threw them into the crowd. They were found to be declarations that they died for a just cause, that their deaths would be avenged and so on. They also delivered papers to the sheriff and then removed their hats – some of which were gold-laced – and threw them into the crowd. Apparently they too contained 'treasonable papers'. Tom Deacon's read:

> I am come here to pay the last debt to nature, and I think myself happy in having an opportunity of dying in so just and so glorious a cause. The deluded and infatuated vulgar will no doubt brand my death with all the infamy that ignorance and prejudice can suggest. But the thinking few who have not quite forsaken their duty to God and their king, will I am persuaded look upon it as being little inferiour to martyrdom itself, for I am just going to fall a sacrifice to the resentment and revenge of the Elector of Hanover and all those unhappy miscreants who have openly exposed the cause of a foreign German usurper and withdrawn allegiance from their only rightful, lawful and native sovereign, King James the 3d.[21]

Immediately after this, the executioner removed caps from their pockets and pulled them over their heads so that their eyes were covered, and then tightened the nooses around their necks. The cart moved gradually away and the men were 'turned off' one by one. Unlike a drop hanging, where their necks would have been broken from the fall, by this means the men were slowly strangled.

They were left hanging altogether for three minutes, while each was stripped of their clothes. Then the executioner cut down Francis Towneley and laid him on the block. It was usual, by this date, to suspend the condemned until dead, so that the degradations described in the punishment were inflicted on the corpse. In fact Towneley was discovered to be still alive, and so the executioner violently struck his chest several times. But this did not kill him, at which the executioner cut his throat. After this the 'verenda', his penis and testicles, were cut off and thrown into the fire and then his torso was sliced open. The executioner removed the bowels and heart and threw them into the fire. Then with a cleaver, he cut off the head. David Morgan's corpse followed and so it went on, until finally the body of James Dawson was cut down. After completing his task, splattered in blood, the executioner cried 'God save King George!' and the crowd responded. By this time the air must have been heavy with the sickening aroma of roasting human entrails.

The mutilated and headless bodies were then returned to the prison to the jeers of the crowd. The heads of Francis Towneley and George Fletcher were taken to Fleet Street and fixed on the spikes on top of Temple Bar, the western gate to the City of London. Those of Deacon, Berwick, Chadwick and Tom Syddall were preserved in spirits, so they could survive the journey to Manchester and Carlisle for similar display. The head of Colonel John Hamilton, former Jacobite governor of the town of Carlisle, who had been executed at Kennington soon after the officers of the Manchester Regiment, joined those sent to Carlisle a few months later. Charles Deacon, under sentence himself, was allowed to witness his brother's final moments.[22] And perhaps most famously, according to legend, James Dawson's fiancée followed the sombre cavalcade to Kennington Common, watched his grisly execution and then expired from grief.[23]

A month later, at five in the morning, the heads of Tom Syddall and Tom Deacon were fixed over the Exchange in the old Market Place of

Manchester, and, soon after, Dr Deacon stood in the square 'and looking up at the Heads, pull'd off his Hat, and made a Bow to them with great Reverence. He afterwards stood some time looking at them.'[24] He was later accused of worshipping his son's remains as the relic of a martyred saint.[25] Soon after Mrs Syddall, now a mourning widow with five young children, neglected to signal her joy at the crushing of the rebellion by the placing of candles in her windows. A mob, encouraged by some soldiers, forced her and her terrified children to flee to a neighbour's house, as they proceeded to break into and then destroy her home.[26]

Detail from *The Pretender's Flight*, 1747, published by J. Cole.

Glenmoriston

'romantic habitation'

By mid-July, Charles was in Borrodale under the protection of Angus MacDonald of Borrodale, his host in Lochnanuagh the previous year. John MacDonald, Angus' son, and his nephew Alexander MacDonald of Glenaladale were now the prince's guards. On 23 July, Charles had arrived at Strathclunie. It was calm and uncomfortably warm, and to deter the battalions of midges Charles was wrapped from head to toe in his plaid and then covered in long heather. John MacDonald recalls that as he lay in this manner, the prince 'uttered several heavy sighes and groands'.[1] The party then moved on, arriving in Glenmoriston the following day. Here they were met by a guide who invited the prince to join a small group of men, including Patrick Grant (known as Black Peter of Craskie), all of whom had served under Charles and were now lying low from the British army and militia raiding parties. These men had established a very comfortable hideout in a cave or structure made of huge stones lying within the glen, apparently large enough to accommodate thirty men. John MacDonald recalled that everyone 'marched all with cheerfulness in our countenance to this new unexpected mansion, and found ourselves as comfortably lodged as we had been in a Royal pallace'.[2] On his arrival, the Glenmoriston men made a new oath of loyalty to Charles: 'That their backs should be to God and their faces to the Devil; that all the curses the Scriptures did pronounce might come upon them and all their posterity if they did not stand firm to the Prince in the greatest dangers.'[3] A bed of heather was prepared and after a hearty meal of whisky, mutton, butter and cheese, the prince 'was lulled asleep with the sweet murmurs of the finest purling stream that could be, running by his bedside, within the grotto'. Charles remained under the protection of his companions in this 'romantic habitation' for three days. After months sleeping in the open, at the mercy of the elements, he declared himself so refreshed that he was now 'able to encounter any hardships'.[4]

Artist unknown, *Effigies of the late Earl of Kilmarnock
and the late Lord Balmerino, c.* 1746.

58

The Tower

'he died a Scotchman'

The Duke of Cumberland arrived in London on 25 July to the ringing of bells, gun salutes, illuminations, bonfires and 'all other demonstrations of the greatest of joy from people of all ranks'.[1] The programme of pacification of the Highlands had been handed over to Lord Albemarle, to whom the duke wrote that Scotland 'is in so unsteady a situation' that Albemarle should keep the troops 'in a Readiness to take the Field at a Day's Warning'.[2] Months on, he believed another battle was still possible. Horace Walpole reports that one of the duke's first acts was to attend the Prince of Wales at St James's Palace. Frederick's sole contribution to the war effort (not entirely his fault) had been the commissioning of a sugar 'Carlisle Castle' which his guests, during an entertainment, were encouraged to bombard with sugarplums in mocking imitation of the recent siege of the town.[3] However, now keen to bask in reflected glory, Frederick walked his brother to a large window overlooking St James's Park and embraced him, while the crowds below, awaiting such an appearance, cheered enthusiastically.[4]

Three days after the duke arrived, the trial of the 'rebel lords' (excepting Lord Lovat) began in Westminster Hall, before their fellow peers including Hardwicke, Newcastle, Richmond, Lonsdale and Tweeddale. No member of the royal family was present. The Marquess of Tullibardine was spared a trial, as he had died in the Tower on 9 July. Lord Cromartie and Lord Kilmarnock immediately pleaded guilty. Lord Balmerino, however, pleaded not guilty on a technicality: that contrary to the details of the indictment, he was not present at the taking of Carlisle. Witnesses testified, whether he was there at the taking or not, at some point he had certainly entered the town at the head of a regiment of horse, as part of the Jacobite army, and with sword drawn. After which, like his fellow prisoners, he was unanimously found guilty.

The second day, Wednesday, 30 July 1746 (the day Francis Towneley and his fellow officers met their fate), the prisoners returned to Westminster Hall, where they had the opportunity to address the assembled lords and, if they so wished, to ask for mercy. Lord Kilmarnock stated that after the Battle of Culloden he could have escaped, but had surrendered instead to Lord Ancram. All his published pronouncements, whether expressed in public or private, declared that he had joined the rebellion against his better judgement and against his upbringing, and that he was heartily sorry for it. He even confirmed that George II was the rightful and legitimate king. He asked for mercy. 'But,' he continued, 'if justice will not allow of mercy, my lords, I will lay down my life with patience and resignation: my last breath shall be employed in the most fervent prayers for the preservation and prosperity of his majesty, and his august house, and to beg his forgiveness, and the forgiveness of my country.'[5] Lord Cromartie, whose wife was (apparently) heavily pregnant, appeared equally contrite, observing, 'I have involved an innocent wife (no party to my guilt), and, with her, an unborn infant, to share its penalty.' Lord Balmerino remained unrepentant. All three were condemned to death in the same manner as Francis Towneley and his men.[6] However, unlike the officers of the Manchester Regiment, who had been shown no mercy or compassion whatsoever, the form of execution for the rebel Lords was commuted to beheading.

Meanwhile, in another part of the Palace of Westminster, laws were beginning to be passed which would alter the government of Scotland for ever. Jacobitism was not restricted to the Highlands, nor indeed was it universal there, but the area had been, once more, the crucible of rebellion. In contrast to what had occurred after previous risings, now the Highland way of life was directly and comprehensively targeted. As Joseph Yorke declared to his brother Philip soon after Culloden (possibly paraphrasing his commander-in-chief), 'You must never expect to see a total end to the rebellious spirit of this country till the Highlanders are unclanned, undressed, effectually disarmed and taught to speak English.'[7] To many beyond the Highlands, the dress and particularly tartan plaid was now firmly synonymous with the Jacobite cause. Lord President Forbes, however, considered disarming, rather than 'undressing', to be the crucial factor in preventing another rebellion, and argued that banning their garb – designed for the difficult terrain and severe weather – would simply hinder the common people from going about their lawful business. What was true in the

Highlands as a whole, was doubly the case within the areas already devastated by plundering armies (of either stripe) and raiding parties. Further, the Lord President continues, in punishing those who had come out for Charles, along with 'all the rest who have not, and who I will venture to say are the greatest Number, in so severe a manner, seems to me unreasonable'. However, he did not agree with the proposal that the loyal should be exempted, thereby highlighting those 'for the Pretender', causing even greater resentment between the clans; rather, that such a ban should be set aside completely.[8] Despite his plea, which was transmitted to the British government by a very supportive Lord Lyon, the Act of Proscription came into force on 1 August 1746, through which the wearing of Highland dress was prohibited. The only official exemption was within the British army, towards which Highland military fervour and prowess would now be channelled. Inevitably, this law also confirmed tartan as the covert and, in some instances, overt symbol of protest and resistance throughout the land.

After their sentencing, Lords Cromartie, Kilmarnock and Balmerino were held in comfortable surroundings at the Tower of London, while a date for their execution was settled on. Petitions were made on behalf of Cromartie and Kilmarnock, one by the Duke of Hamilton 'who has never been at Court' but 'designs to kiss the King's hand and ask for Lord Kilmarnock's life'. The Privy Council had recommended to the king that one of the three should be shown mercy, something King George was very inclined to do, but against the will of the Duke of Cumberland who, as Horace Walpole observed, 'has not so much of Caesar after a victory, as in gaining it' and 'is for the utmost severity'. In fact, by this time, as Lord President Forbes had predicted, severity against participants in the rebellion was beginning to be less tolerated, while sympathy with their plight was gaining ground. The bloodshed during and after the Battle of Culloden, and the duke's intransigence in regard to punishment, was well known. As Horace Walpole continues, 'It was lately proposed in the City, to present him with the freedom of some company; one of the alderman said aloud, "Then let it be of the *Butchers!*"'[9] The alderman's outburst may indicate a late flowering of Jacobite sentiment from within the City of London. But much like toasting the King over the Water, it was, at first glance, a hollow gesture: too little, too late. However, the duke had by this time became the particular focus for those who, now the danger had passed, were voicing opposition to the manner in which the rebellion had been suppressed: and this despite the fact that the duke had been very clear about his plans and methods and no one in the government had challenged it. Indeed, he was supported implicitly if not explicitly. The soubriquet 'the Butcher' captured the popular imagination, partly assisted by a sequence of engravings. There is even a suggestion that this popularity was fanned, covertly of course, by none other than the Prince of Wales.[10] However, of the three lords, Cromartie won the pardon (although he remained in the Tower) after his wife petitioned with the support of Augusta, Princess of Wales. Cromartie's father-in-law had been Frederick's private secretary. Walpole wrily observed, 'Duke Hamilton's intercession for Lord Kilmarnock has rather hurried him to the block.'[11]

On Monday, 11 August both Lord Balmerino and Lord Kilmarnock were informed by General Adam Williamson, deputy governor of the Tower of London, that they would die the following Monday: 'Lord Kilmarnock received this news with the outward behaviour of a man, that knew and felt the importance of the scene of death, but without any marks of disorder, without any unbecoming anxiousness or terror.'[12] Balmerino, meanwhile, had 'pressed extremely to have his wife, his Pretty Peggy, with him in the Tower' and, in Walpole's immortal words, 'the instant she came to him, he stripped her and went to bed'.[13] On the Saturday before, Lord Kilmarnock was told the form the day of execution would take, to which he 'without the least visible emotion, expressed his satisfaction', although he requested that the coffin be placed on the scaffold, rather than left in the hearse nearby, so that 'the bodies would be still sooner removed out of sight'. In addition, to prevent what he had heard from similar executions, he asked that four people would be present holding red cloth 'to receive the head', rather than allow it to 'roll about the scaffold, and be thereby mangled and disfigured', for 'he was not willing that his body should appear with any unnecessary indecency'. On being told that his head would then be raised up for all to see and declared 'the head of a traitor', Kilmarnock acknowledged that he knew this to be the case in such circumstances.[14]

To attempt to prepare him for the event (if such a thing were possible) the dissenting minister, Mr James Foster, who was in attendance and whose account of the event was later published in *State Trials*, advised him 'to think frequently on the outward apparatus and formalities that would attend his death', that is the scaffold, the block, axe and executioner, the tense excitement of the thousands gathered to witness him die, because 'these circumstances, striking to sense, might impress his mind with horror, and disarm him of part of his resolution, if he was not by reflection thoroughly prepared for the scene'.[15] Condemned men were expected to appear contrite, but, above all, they should be calm and resolute, not hysterical.

At six o'clock on the day of execution, 1,000 guardsmen accompanied by horse grenadiers marched from St James's Park to Tower Hill. They began forming lines from the entrance to the Tower to the scaffold located just to the west and then around the place of execution itself. At eight o'clock the sheriffs of London and Middlesex with their officers, who included the executioner, breakfasted at the Mitre Tavern in Fenchurch Street and then made their way to the Tower. At the same time, James Foster and the Revd Mr Hume were in attendance in Lord Kilmarnock's chamber and the chaplain of the Tower and an unnamed clergyman of the Church of England likewise with Lord Balmerino. As General Williamson had earlier explained, there was some flexibility in the timings, but in any event, both executions had to be completed by one o'clock in the afternoon. Kilmarnock appeared composed as he prepared himself for death. Just after ten o'clock, when the block with its black drape had been fixed upon the scaffold and sacks of sawdust brought up alongside, General Williamson arrived in Kilmarnock's rooms, stating that the sheriffs were now waiting to receive him at the gates of the Tower, to which Kilmarnock said, 'General, I am ready; I will follow you.'[16]

As he walked out, he met his fellow prisoner Lord Balmerino. They embraced and Balmerino said, 'My lord, I am heartily sorry to have your company in this expedition.' They walked to Tower Gate, where they were met by the sheriffs who said, as was the tradition, 'God bless KING GEORGE', to which Kilmarnock bowed and Balmerino replied, 'God bless King James'. According to one witness, Dudley Bradstreet – now a frustrated petitioner to the Dukes of Newcastle and Cumberland for financial reward after his activities in Derby – the lords were jeered and cursed by a mob.[17] The officers, sheriffs, prisoners and chaplains, followed by musketeers, two hearses and a mourning coach, processed to a house located thirty yards from the scaffold, which had been hired to allow the condemned men a private space to pray, to take refreshment and to say farewell to wives, friends and family. As the prisoners approached the house, spectators were heard to ask '*which is lord* Balmerino?', to which his lordship 'answer'd smiling, I am lord Balmerino, gentlemen, at your service'.[18] The two men were taken to different apartments within the house, both of which were draped in black fabric.

Having prayed, Lord Kilmarnock drank a glass of wine with a little bread. He told the sheriffs that he would not address the crowd, but had left with Mr Foster the words he intended for public consumption after his death. At eleven o'clock, Lord Kilmarnock received a request for a meeting with Lord Balmerino, which he agreed to. Balmerino was brought into Kilmarnock's apartment:

> *Balm.* My lord, I beg leave to ask your lordship one question.
> *Kilm.* To any question, my lord, that you shall now think it proper to ask, I believe I shall see no reason to decline giving an answer.
> *Balm.* Why then, my lord, did you ever see or know of any order, signed by the prince, [meaning the Pretender's son] to give no quarter at the battle of Culloden?
> *Kilm.* No, my lord.
> *Balm.* Nor I neither: and therefore it seems to be an invention to justify their own murder, or murderous scheme . . .
> *Kilm.* No, my lord, I do not think that this inference can be drawn from it; because, while I was prisoner at Inverness, I was informed by several officers, that there was such an order, signed George Murray; and that it was in the duke's custody.
> Lord George Murray! replied lord Balmerino, why then they should not charge it upon the prince.[19]

This meeting, contrived by Lord Balmerino, allowed this particular charge against Prince Charles to be publicly refuted and was widely reported in the more formal accounts of the execution, and in the newspapers. The blame for the 'No Quarter' order had now transferred to Lord George. The two men embraced once more, with Balmerino saying, 'My dear lord Kilmarnock, I am only sorry, that I cannot pay all this reckoning alone; once more, farewel for ever!' One observer states that Kilmarnock replied, 'It was exceedingly kind and generous in his lordship.' Balmerino was escorted from the room.

At 11.30, the assembly knelt for prayers. Lord Kilmarnock then drank another glass of wine and, at about midday, he took leave of those present 'in a very affectionate manner' and left the house, preceded by the sheriffs and accompanied by his friends. Newspaper reports state that the crowd was well behaved, that is no jeering, so it is likely that Kilmarnock's last journey was accompanied by relative silence – perhaps with only the distant sound of a boat passing along the Thames. The executioner, dressed not in black but in a blue coat and scarlet waistcoat, uncased an axe and awaited the arrival of the first rebel lord. Kilmarnock walked to the black-draped scaffold with all eyes fixed upon him and climbed the steps on to the stage. Here he was greeted with the paraphernalia of his own imminent death, and despite having tried to imagine the scene and therefore be less alarmed at the reality of it, he started and turning to Mr Hume said, '*Hume! this is terrible*'.[20] It was later reported that at this even the executioner burst into tears. Some time was taken in gathering up Kilmarnock's long hair into a cap and then tucking his shirt collar into his waistcoat, so that neither would obstruct the axe's blow. He gave the executioner five guineas and informed him that his signal would be the dropping of a handkerchief.

He then knelt on a black cushion in front of the block, prayed again and afterwards placed his hands on the block to steady himself. The executioner leant forward and gently asked him to let his hands drop down, 'lest they should be mangled, or break the blow'. It was then observed that the collar of his waistcoat was in the way, so Kilmarnock got up, with the assistance of Mr James Walkingshaw of Scotston removed the garment, returned to the block, knelt down, gave two minutes warning of his signal – the time seeming to his friends 'who were then upon the rack, appeared much longer' – during which he prayed. According to one account, Kilmarnock had in fact requested that his severed head should not be held up, and 'as the law does not require it', it had been agreed that this particular part of the ceremony would be put aside. However, in order to confirm that the execution had occurred, the sheriffs told everyone on the scaffold to kneel. As the block had been made taller (about two feet) the crowd could now witness the severing of the head. Kilmarnock finished his prayers and then, on his signal, the executioner raised the axe as high as he could and his lordship's head was taken off with one blow – excepting a small piece of skin that required a gentle cut – so that Mr Hume's servant could collect it in a red baize cloth (as Lord Kilmarnock had requested).[21] Dudley Bradstreet recorded that the main blow caused 'a Cloud of Blood'[22] to spray up. The body and the wrapped head were quickly placed in the coffin and handed over to the keeping of his lordship's family and friends for burial in the Tower.

All trace of this execution was then removed, with fresh sawdust scattered around the block to cover Kilmarnock's blood, in preparation for the arrival of Lord Balmerino. The executioner is described as having changed 'such of his cloaths as appeared bloody'.[23] Unlike Lord Kilmarnock, Balmerino was not regretting his allegiance to the Jacobite cause, which was, in any case, of a much longer standing. He seemed keen to get on with it and in as cheery a manner as possible. He too drank some wine and ate bread, but declared that the company should drink to him 'ain degrae ta haiven'. He then said, 'Gentlemen, I shall detain you no longer.' By all accounts he strode to the scaffold and climbed the steps in an 'undaunted' manner, which took the assembled spectators by surprise. He was wearing the uniform he had worn at the Battle of Culloden, a blue coat with red facing, and seemed to parade around the scaffold, inspecting the inscription on his coffin lid – which must have been a very peculiar sensation, given that it stated the date of his execution and his age at death, fifty-eight – nodded his approval, then looked over the block or, as he described it 'his pillow of rest', all the while bowing to the crowd.[24]

After this, Lord Balmerino put on his spectacles and took a speech from his pocket, which he read out and then gave to the sheriff to do with as he wished. The speech commenced, 'I was brought up in true loyal Anti-Revolution principles and I hope the world is convinced that they stick to me.' Having described his allegiance to King James and his participation in the '15, he turns to the events of the previous year. He joined Prince Charles at Edinburgh because, if he had not 'I could never have had peace of conscience if I had stayed at home when that brave Prince was exposing himself to all manner of dangers and fatigue both night and day'. He then turns to the subject of Charles, of the 'incomparable sweetness of his nature, his patience, and his courage', which 'are virtues, seldom all to be found in one person. In short, he wants no qualification requisite to make a great man.' As was evident from his conversation with Lord Kilmarnock less than an hour before, Balmerino refutes categorically that Charles had issued orders before the Battle of Culloden that 'no quarters should be given to the enemy'. He believed such orders to be 'unchristian' and 'so unlike that gallant Prince'. Indeed, he goes so far as to say that those who had circulated such a malicious accusation, the Duke of Cumberland for one, had done so 'to excuse themselves for the murders they were guilty of in calm blood after the battle'. Such accusations stuck. He ended on a short prayer for God 'to bless the King, the prince, and Duke of Yorke, and all the dutiful branches of the royal family!' asking the Almighty to 'enrich them with thy heavenly grace' and 'prosper them with all happiness'.[25] Such a defiantly Jacobite final speech was, inevitably, edited down for the newspaper and magazine reports.

Lord Balmerino then paid the executioner three guineas, for which he apologised, saying, 'I never was rich, this is all the money I have now' but offering in addition to this his coat and waistcoat. He removed these outer garments, throwing them casually over his coffin, leaving just a flannel waistcoat (made specially) over his shift and then replaced his wig with a plaid cap – another defiant gesture, given the recent Act prohibiting Highland garb. In this manner he declared 'he died *a Scotchman*'.²⁶ He told the executioner that his signal would be the dropping of his arms. He said his last farewells to his friends gathered about the scaffold – whether his wife Peggy was present is unclear – and then noted to all the assembled that his manner may seem bold to some, but 'it arises from a confidence in God, and a clear conscience'. He even took the axe from the executioner and checked the keenness of the blade's edge, indicating where the blow should strike and that it should be done 'with resolution', for 'in that, friend', said his lordship, 'will consist your mercy'.²⁷ He knelt down, held his arms out and, after a final quick prayer, dropped his arms as the signal to strike.

Unfortunately the executioner was so surprised at the swiftness of the signal that he fumbled a blow that did not sever the head. One account has the blow sufficient to 'deprive him of all sensation', although the head flopped back on the shoulders, requiring two further cuts to remove it completely, before placing it in the awaiting red baize. Another account, printed in *The Gentleman's Magazine*, offers a more harrowing scenario. The executioner's first blow was 'not given with strength enough to wound him very deep' after which, still conscious, Lord Balmerino appeared to try and turn his head towards the executioner, 'the under-jaw fell and returned very quick, like anger and gnashing the teeth; but it could not be otherwise, the part being convulsed'. The second blow followed quickly after, rendering him 'insensible', although still not dead and after this second blow, another witness describes taking hold of one of Balmerino's arms and drawing up the body, so that the head was in the correct position to allow the executioner to deliver the necessary final cut. As the magazine concluded, 'a third finish'd the work'.²⁸ In disgust, Dudley Bradstreet observed that the executioner had 'mangled him terribly'²⁹ but the head and corpse were likewise placed in the coffin, for burial alongside Lord Kilmarnock at the Tower.

Bradstreet then recalls that after the executions some of the crowd began to disperse, but others gathered into groups, discussing the rights and wrongs of the punishment. A fistfight broke out between two men, one arguing that the executioner had made a mess of Balmerino's execution on purpose, the other disagreeing. Bradstreet watched the two slug it out for a while and then left them, still landing blows on each other and 'besmear'd with Blood, to be of one Opinion before they parted'.³⁰

William Delacour, *Dr. Sir Stuart Threipland, c.* 1750.

59

Cluny's Cage

'very romantic comical habitation'

From 17 August (four months since the Battle of Culloden) to the 27th of that month, the prince stayed in the region of Loch Arkaig until he received a message from Lochiel to meet him at Badenoch. Lochiel's house, Achnacarry, had been torched by raiding parties and he was now, like the prince, 'skulking' in the hills. Charles travelled at night, accompanied by Lochiel's messenger, his brother Dr Archibald Cameron, John Cameron, Lochgarry and several servants. John Cameron described Charles at this time as 'bare-footed, had an old black kilt on, a plaid, philapeg and waistcoat, a dirty shirt and a long red beard, a gun in his hand, a pistol and durk by his side. He was very cheerful and in good health' and, in John Cameron's opinion, 'fatter than when he was at Inverness'.[1] Physically thicker-set and with his garb, weapons, long red beard and hair, for the first time Charles looked every inch the Highlander. His cheerfulness, as observed when he donned the guise of 'Betty Burke', hints once again at Charles' delight in acting a part.

The prince found Lochiel at Meall Mor in Ben Alder forest at the beginning of September, the latter still suffering greatly from the wound he had received at the battle. He had been tended by Dr Stuart Threipland. Lochiel's cousin, Cluny MacPherson, had also been hiding out since his own house, along with all the surrounding properties, had been destroyed. Cluny recalled, 'It was in this forrest where the Prince found Cluny with Lochiell in his wounds and other friends under his care.'[2] According to Donald MacPherson, Cluny's youngest brother, the 'joy at the meeting was certainly very great and much easier to be conceived than express'd'.[3] Lochiel was about to kneel before the prince but Charles grasped his shoulder, warning him that any such action, if seen, would signal his whereabouts. Lochiel and the prince then entered a hut which had served as the former's temporary home, Charles reportedly 'gay, hearty, and in better spirits than it was possible to think he could be'.[4] The party dined well on mutton, beef, bacon, cheese and an anker of whisky. Charles 'took a hearty dram, which he pretty often called for thereafter to drink his friends healths'.[5] The meal was served without decorum, although, despite his recent hardships, Charles still carried a silver spoon, which he used to eat his food straight from the saucepan. Lochiel recalled that even at this time he and some fellow unnamed chiefs 'were convinced that France would not leave them in the lurch' and that should the prince make it to France, he 'would soon return with the support that had so often been promised him'.[6]

But for now, Cluny feared that if the prince had to remain in hiding for the foreseeable future his 'constitution might not suit with lying on the ground or in caves', although in truth, he seemed to have survived such exposure and discomfort remarkably well so far. Even so, Cluny 'was solicitous to contrive a more comfortable habitation for him'. This he did 'upon the south front of one of these mountains, overlooking a beautiful lake of 12 miles long'.[7] After two days at Lochiel's hideout, the prince and his group were escorted by Cluny to another hut near Alder Water and after a few more days they moved on further up Ben Alder, to where the structure Cluny had built was located. This became known as the 'cage' and, even with detailed descriptions, it is still difficult to imagine.[8] Donald MacPherson stated that it was located 'in the face of a very rough high rockie mountain called Letternilichk' and 'within a small thick bush of wood'. It was oval-shaped with trees laid down to make a floor, which was then covered with gravel and earth. Branches intertwined with ropes of heath and birch twigs, all covered in moss, formed the walls and roof. There was a stone fire for heating and cooking. According to Donald MacPherson it 'was no larger than to contain six or seven persons, four of which number were frequently employed in playing cards, one idle looking on, one becking, and another firing bread and cooking'.[9] The following description was possibly written by Cluny himself:

> The uper room serv'd for *salle à manger* and bed chamber while the lower serv'd for a cave to contain liquors and other necessaries, at the back part was a proper hearth for cook and baiker, and the face of the mountain had so much the colour and resemblance of smock [smoke], no person cou'd ever discover that there was either fire or habitation in the place.[10]

Here Charles and his companions could hide out for days, weeks, perhaps even months.

Cluny placed guards at varying distances around the 'cage', 'who dayly brought them notice of what happened in the country, and even in the enemie's camps, bringing them likewise the necessary provisions, while a neighbouring fountain supplied the society with rural refreshment of pure rock water'.[11] Cluny's spies were even mingling with Lord Loudoun's troops. In regard to his ingenious cage of twisted trees and moss, Cluny continues, 'As, therefore, an oak tree is to this day rever'd in Brittain for having happily sav'd the grand uncle, Charles the Second, from the pursuits of Cromwell [after the Battle of Worcester, 1651] so this holly thicket will probablie in future times be likeways rever'd for having saved Prince Charles, the nephew, from the still more dangerous pursuits of Cumberland, who show'd himself on all occasions a much more inveterate enemy.'[12] Charles' great-uncle had been saved to return soon after in triumph. Here was another Charles Stuart who hoped to do the same.

From 6 to 12 September the prince dwelt in this 'very romantic comical habitation'[13] as Donald MacPherson described it, attended by Lochiel, Cluny, Lochgarry, Dr Archibald Cameron, Breakachie, Allan Cameron and four MacPhersons, servants of Cluny.[14] In the meantime, as the prince only had the one grubby shirt, Cluny's sisters German, Isobel and Christian set 'about making some for him in all haste'.[15]

On 6 September two French ships, Le Prince de Conti and L'Heureux, with Colonel Richard Warren and young Sheridan (Sir Thomas' nephew), arrived at Lochnanuagh, apparently on the advice of John O'Sullivan who had arrived in Paris by mid-August. Colonel Warren had written to Antoine Walsh just before departing on 29 August (NS, 18 August OS), 'I have great confidence that I will bring our hero back safe and sound.'[16] In retrospect, Charles may have regretted his decision to leave the mainland so quickly for the Western Isles after the Battle of Culloden. As the comte de Maurepas had observed, it had certainly hindered his rescue. However, news of the arrival of the ships reached the cage just a week later and so, on 13 September at one o'clock in the morning, the party began to move towards the coast. They were joined by Donald MacPherson of Breakachie and Colonel John Roy Stuart at Uiskchilra and then continued their journey at night.[17] On 19 September, the prince and his party reached Borrodale and before Charles boarded L'Heureux he turned to his escort, which included John MacDonald of Borrodale, and reportedly said, 'my lads be in good spirits, it shall not be long before I shall be with you, and shall endeavour to make up for all the loss you have suffered'.[18] After they had made their farewells, Cluny MacPherson returned to his cage.[19]

The following day, fourteen months since the landing at Eriskay, twelve months after the Battle of Prestonpans and five months on from the Battle of Culloden, the prince, accompanied by Lochiel, Dr Archibald Cameron and Colonel John Roy Stuart, finally left Scotland for France, leaving the Highlanders, as John MacDonald sardonically observed, 'in a worse state than he found us'.[20]

Detail from Luke Sullivan after William Hogarth, *A Representation of the March of the Guards towards Scotland in the year 1745*, 1750.

United Kingdom

'unfortunate princes'

On 10 October (NS), Captain Warren wrote from Roscoff, Brittany, to Antoine Walsh: 'I have only just arrived. I had the happiness to find H.R.H. in Scotland and to bring him back with me . . . He starts to-morrow for Paris.'[1] Charles stepped ashore, apparently still wearing his soiled and tattered Highland garb, and was immediately kitted out by local merchants. The prince, the most famous man in Europe, arrived in Paris to a hero's welcome. Madame de Pompadour recalled that Charles 'had been received with great joy and marks of consideration'.[2] He was greeted by his devoted brother and, true to his word, Charles immediately set about petitioning Louis for men and arms to embark on another attempt. And while France and Britain were still at war, he was a very real threat. On 27 October, Lord Albemarle reported to the Duke of Newcastle that Cluny MacPherson (still at large) was in possession of some money, possibly the Arkaig treasure, and it was circulating that 'the Pretender's Son and a considerable Force from France was to return soon to this Country'. To prevent this, Albemarle recommended a strong Royal Navy presence around the coast of Scotland.[3]

Meanwhile, Sir Thomas Sheridan had returned to Rome. James 'reprimanded him for persuading his son to undertake such an expedition without better grounds' and this 'reproof so far affected Sir Thomas that he fell ill and died of grief'.[4] In the December, Lord George Murray finally escaped to Holland and proceeded to Rome where he was welcomed by James and granted a pension.

On the other side of the Channel, laws continued to be passed which fundamentally altered the government of Scotland, and, specifically, the ability of the Jacobite clans ever to rise again. Most notable was the Heritable Jurisdictions (Scotland) Act, whereby the old clan system was effectively dismantled. All clan chiefs, regardless of their affiliation, no longer had the right to call their men to arms, and this despite the fact that a majority of Scots had not joined the rebellion, while only a portion of the Highland clans had actually risen in support of the Stuart cause. But the government was determined to stamp out the possibility of another rising, once and for all. As important, this Act extended royal jurisdiction throughout the whole of Scotland. Beyond the Highlands, the improving economy, as symbolised by major towns such as Glasgow, coupled with a more stable Hanoverian dynasty and British state, meant that disaffection towards the Union – a powerful source of recruitment to the Jacobite cause – was broadly in decline. However, conversely, sympathy for the Stuarts and Jacobitism thrived: even as Charles was sailing away from Scotland, the legend of the prince in the heather, the Highland Laddie 'Bonnie Prince Charlie', was taking root.[5]

Simon Fraser, Lord Lovat, was tried at Westminster Hall in early 1747. Secretary John Murray, confined since his arrest in the Tower of London and by all accounts an alcoholic, had now turned King's Evidence and provided the details that could finally condemn the Old Fox: a punishment for decades of skulduggery and 'shilly-shally' which many believed was long overdue. In Lord President Forbes' opinion Lovat's involvement in the rebellion 'proceeded from a deliberate and malignant purpose to ruin and subvert our present government, merely because they have not thought fit to gratify his ambitious and avaritious passions and desires'.[6] He was beheaded on 9 April 1747 at Tower Hill. John Murray was released after Lovat's execution, but was not pardoned until the following year.[7]

In June 1747, the Indemnity Act offered a general pardon (excluding certain individuals) and, soon after, Sir Hector Maclean and Flora MacDonald, among others, were released. Lord Elcho and Lord George Murray, who had been attainted in 1746, were among those who had been excluded. Horace Walpole observed, 'Lord Elcho has written from Paris to Lord Lincoln to solicit his pardon; but as he has distinguished himself beyond all the rebel commanders by brutality and insults and cruelty to our prisoners, I think he is likely to remain where he is.'[8] Lochiel, meanwhile, accepted the command of the Regiment d'Albanie in the French army, but died soon after, in October 1748, at Bergues.

Also in June 1747, on the advice of Cardinal Tencin, Prince Henry Benedict secretly left Paris for Rome, in order to take holy orders as the first step towards entering the College of Cardinals. On hearing the news,

Charles wrote to his father, 'had I got a Dager throw my heart it would not have been more sensible to me'.[9] His disgust, despair and sense of betrayal were acute. Henry had been sending letters to his brother throughout June with no response. In a typical letter, sent from Albano, he writes:

> Tho I have still the mortification to be without hearing from you I think it my duty to continue to write to you and to assure you of my most respectfull and tender love and affection, until you let me know more plainly then [than] by the silence of a few weeks that my letters will not be acceptable but I trust in God that will never happen and that you will never do me, and give me leave to say, yourself the wrong of breaking with a Brother, who you will be sensible at last is not unworthy of your kindness. I remain dear Brother with the utmost respect, your most loving Brother, Henry.[10]

Father Myles McDonnell, writing to James from Paris on 14 July (NS), reported that Charles 'I am told for I dont go near him . . . has shutt himself up for several hours alone upon his hearing that news, the Dukes health is no more drank nor his name mentioned at his table: he is teazed about his safety, & made to believe that his life will be in danger, being now alone and unmarry'd'. Henry's actions caused great consternation among many Jacobites, as Father McDonnell observes: 'The general distraction is only equal to the confusion your Majesty's subjects here are in', 'agreeing in nothing so unanimously as in thinking it a mortal deadly stroke to the Cause'. Meanwhile, in Britain 'the old bugbears of Popery, bigotry &c. will be renew'd with (I am afraid) too much success'.[11] In part, the intention was to consolidate the status of the Stuart court in Rome after another failed attempt, but it was certainly an own goal for the cause in Britain, and, as McDonnell predicts, a new source of anti-Stuart propaganda for the British government. Around this time, Lord George, now regretting the manner in which their relationship had soured, attempted to gain an audience with Charles in Paris. The prince, still convinced of his treachery, refused to see him.[12]

On 10 December 1747, Lord President Forbes died at his Edinburgh house on Cowsgate. The months of wandering, the great burden of work after Culloden, as well as concerns over enormous debts acquired by bankrolling government business throughout the rebellion, had taken their toll. In a letter to his son, John, he had written,

> I am very sorry for you, the great charges and expenses I have been at in supporting His Majesty in the Rebellion have far exceeded the sum I

thought it would have cost when I saw you last. I would advise you to go to London where I believe I may have some friends yet. Mr Scrope, Mr Littleton and Mitchell are kind-hearted, affectionate men and they will tell the King that his faithful servant Duncan Forbes has left you a very poor man, – Farewell. – May the God of Heaven and Earth bless you!

In the event John would spend many decades paying off these debts.[13]

By far the greatest impact on the immediate future of the Jacobite cause was the peace between France and Britain in May 1748. Ratified by the Treaty of Aix-la-Chapelle the following October, the terms included the stipulation imposed by the British government, as it had habitually done since 1688, that all Stuarts must be expelled from French land. Charles protested and, despite repeated requests by Louis and his ministers to comply, maintained a defiant and very public resistance – or 'an obstinacy beyond example'[14] as Pompadour phrased it – for months. He had absolutely no intention of returning to Rome. Pompadour recalled making overtures on the prince's behalf to Louis, 'who answered me with some heat, *What would you have me do, Madam? Should I continue the war with all Europe for Prince [Charles] Edward? England will not allow him to be in my dominions; it was only on this condition, that she came into the peace. Should I have broke off the conference at Aix-la-Chapelle, and distressed my people, more and more, because the Pretender's son is for living at Paris?'*[15]

At last, on 10 December (NS) Charles was arrested in broad daylight outside the Paris Opera, tied up and then bundled into a coach for Vincennes. Here he agreed to leave France, arriving at Avignon on 27 December (NS) to the surprise of the Vatican: it was a terrible humiliation for all concerned. Cardinal de Bernis observed, 'No event ever so vexed me for the kings sake.' Charles 'was inexcusable for wanting to lay down the law to France; he deserved to be arrested; but it aught to have been done at night, with the consideration due to his rank, and, above all, to his misfortunes'.[16] Indeed, those 'who advised the king on this occasion forgot to remind him that Prince [Charles] Edward was a grandson of Henry IV and that the French throne has ever been the support and shelter of unfortunate princes'. Madame de Pompadour recalled that when Charles' lodgings in Paris were searched 'it was found turned into an Arsenal'. He had gathered 'arms enough to stand a siege in form. It was talked at court that he had determined to fight singly himself against a whole regiment, and then set fire to a barrel of powder, which communicated with others, and thus blow up himself, with all that belonged to him':[17] proof of his increasing paranoia, while hinting that his grip on reality was loosening. Apparently Louis, on being told of this, declared it 'A very ill-timed bravery, indeed!'[18]

But with the Stuart prince safely out of France, the '45 was finally over.

The planned French invasion of 1743–4 had failed mainly through an intervention beyond anyone's control, the weather, while the early successes of Charles' improvised campaign of 1745–6 had caught everyone, including the French king, by surprise. The events of 1688–9 proved that a foreign invasion, supported by influential men within Britain, could topple a king. In the future, if France decided, unequivocally, to put her full weight behind a rebellion, not necessarily within Britain itself but in her colonies – America, for example – what impact might French support then have on Britain and the world? For the time being, France had already turned her attention back to Flanders and, further afield, to her colonial interests. It would not be very long before Britain and France were at war once again.

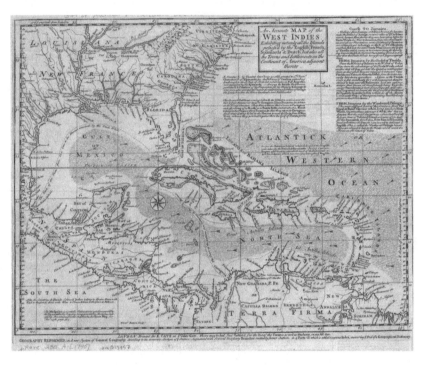

Emanuel Bowen, *An Accurate map of the West Indies*, 1740.

Epilogue

Richard Riding, a Lancastrian weaver, was probably one of the unemployed artisans who joined the Jacobite army in November 1745, and served as a private man under Colonel Francis Towneley in the Manchester Regiment. He was listed among the garrison who surrendered at Carlisle and was incarcerated, with more than one hundred of his companions, in the grim conditions within the cathedral.[1] Unlike some of his fellows, however, he was not executed at Carlisle, as he is named as a prisoner at Lancaster Castle in October 1746.[2] Eight months later, he appears on another list describing '150 Rebel Prisoners Ship'd at Liverpool on board the Veteran' in May 1747, with John Riley the captain, and heading for the Leaward Islands in the West Indies. Among the prisoners were labourers, shoemakers, millers and bakers from all over Scotland and the north of England: from Badenoch, Aberdeen and Edinburgh, to York, Preston and Wigan. The destination was Barbados and some of these men, with a few women, were to be sold as indentured servants on arrival. This was the punishment meted out to hundreds of 'rebel' prisoners. To speed up the judicial process, the lower ranks imprisoned in England drew lots, with one in twenty committed to trial.[3] As for the remainder, according to an order dated 3 October 1746, 'his Majesty is graciously pleas'd to declare his Intention to extend his Mercy to them, provided it shall be their own Request to be pardon'd on such Conditions as His Majesty shall think proper'.[4] The condition was transportation either with or without indenture.[5] Indeed, many of those tried and then condemned to death (rather than pardoned) were eventually transported to one of the British colonies instead. Charles Deacon is one such example. Condemned at Southwark like his brother, the jury later recommended mercy because of his youth, and he was shipped off to the West Indies. He died soon after arrival.

However, the Veteran had been captured by a French privateer on 28 June and arrived under escort at Martinique two days later. The prisoner list, including brief descriptions, was intended to identify them so that they could be returned to British custody. Mary McKenzie for example, number 144, aged twenty, a spinner from Lochaber, was five feet tall and 'lusty healthy'. While Richard Riding, number 127, is described as aged '24', a 'Weaver near Preston', five feet three inches tall, 'light brown hair' and 'sturdy'.[6]

However, the governor of Martinique not only refused to hand back the prisoners, he set them free. The British government continued to remonstrate with the French authorities well into 1748, but to no avail. At least one of these prisoners is known to have returned to Britain: Charles Hackett, a writer's clerk from Cess.[7] With his newfound freedom, Richard Riding may have stayed in the West Indies, travelled north to the British colonies in America to make a new life for himself there, or even found his way home to Lancashire. Unfortunately a volcanic eruption destroyed all the official records on the island. So, along with his fellow 'rebels', he simply disappeared.

Notes

Abbreviations

BL HP   British Library Hardwicke Papers
BL NP   British Library Newcastle Papers
HRO MP   Hampshire Record Office Malmesbury Papers
JSAHR   *Journal of the Society for Army Historical Research*
LM   Henry Paton, ed., *The Lyon in Mourning: or a Collection of Speeches Letters Journals etc, Relative to the Affairs of Prince Charles Edward Stuart by the Rev. Robert Forbes*, 3 vols, Edinburgh, 1896
ODNB   *Oxford Dictionary of National Biography* online edition
NA SP   National Archives State Papers
RA CP   Royal Archives Cumberland Papers
RA SP   Royal Archives Stuart Papers

Prologue

1   NA SP 36/67/1 f. 78 Owen Prichard to Newcastle, Liverpool 16 August 1745 and ff. 79–80 'Richard Robinson's Account', Liverpool 16 August 1745.
2   BL NP Add MS 32705, f. 90 Newcastle to Prichard, Whitehall 18 August 1745 OS.
3   *London Gazette*, 13–17 August 1745, p. 2.

Chapter 1: Rome

1   For a detailed description of the Stuart court see Edward Corp's groundbreaking *The Stuarts in Italy, 1719–1766*, Cambridge, 2011.
2   For summaries of Jacobitism and the risings see Daniel Szechi, *The Jacobites: Britain and Europe 1688–1788*, Manchester, 1994 and Bruce Lenman, *The Jacobite Risings in Britain, 1689–1746*, Dalkeith, 1995/2004.
3   See Christopher Whatley, *The Scots and the Union: Then and Now*, Edinburgh, 2nd edition, 2014, p. 355.
4   See Daniel Szechi, *1715: The Great Jacobite Rebellion*, New Haven, 2006.
5   See Eveline Cruickshanks, *Political Untouchables: The Tories and the '45*, London, 1979.
6   PG 2511 *The Baptism* by Antonio David dated 1725 and PG 2415 *The Marriage* by Agostino Masucci dated *c.*1735 are now at the Scottish National Portrait Gallery, Edinburgh.

7 For a full description of the Palazzo del Re see Corp, *The Stuarts in Italy*, Chapter 2.

8 Charles de Brosses, *Lettres historiques et critiques sur l'Italie*, 3 vols, Paris, 1799, Vol. 2, p. 361.

9 RA SP/MAIN/302/134 'Heads of a letter wrote from Rome in answer to one from London on enquiring into the Character education &c of a certain young Gentleman', possibly in James Edgar's hand, dated December 1749. 132 and 135 are versions in Charles' hand, but he was not in Rome at that time.

10 RA SP/MAIN/245/46 James Edgar to Balhady, Albano 1 October 1742 NS.

11 Katharine Prescott Wormeley, trans., *Journal and Memoirs of the Marquis d'Argenson*, 2 vols, Boston, 1902, Vol. I, p. 182.

12 RA SP/MAIN/259/64 James to Charles, [Albano?] 11 September 1744 NS.

13 RA SP/MAIN/249/128 James to Sempill, Rome 9 May 1743 NS.

14 For a full discussion see Corp, *The Stuarts in Italy*.

15 Brosses, *Lettres historiques*, 1799, Vol. 2, pp. 355–6.

16 John Russell, *Letters from a young painter abroad to his friends in England*, London, 1748, 'Letter XIX, To Mrs R., Rome, 2 December 1741 NS', pp. 72–5, p. 74.

17 Frank McLynn, *Bonnie Prince Charlie: Charles Edward Stuart*, London, 1988/2003, p. 69.

18 BL Egerton MS 2234 ff. 237–8, 237r–237v, Joseph Spence to his mother, Rome 13 January 1731 NS.

19 BL Add MS 47463 ff. 1–2 Samuel Crisp to Christopher Shute of Broadwell, Rome 15 February 1739 NS.

20 Russell, *Letters*, 'Letter XIII. To Mr. FBM, Rome 2 March 1741 NS', pp. 41–5, p. 45.

21 'Alexander Cunyngham's Travels' in A. Forbes, ed., *Curiosities of A Scots Charta Chest 1600–1800*, Edinburgh, 1897, pp. 99–123, p. 112. Cunyngham later changed his surname, becoming Sir Alexander Dick, Baronet.

22 Ibid.

23 Ibid., p. 113.

24 Thanks to Edward Corp for drawing my attention to this.

25 John M. Gray, ed., *Memoirs of the Life of Sir John Clerk of Penicuik*, Edinburgh, 1892, p. 176.

26 Extract from 'Lord Elcho's Journal' translated in Bruce Lenman and John S. Gibson, *The Jacobite Threat*, Edinburgh, 1990, pp. 189–90, p. 189.

27 Ibid., pp. 189–90.

28 Ibid., p. 190.

29 Anon., *Genuine Memoirs of John Murray, Esq*, Dublin, 1747, p. 9.

Chapter 2: Versailles

1 Jeanne Antoinette Poisson, Madame de Pompadour, *Memoirs of the Marchioness of Pompadour. Written by herself*, 2 vols, London, 1766, Vol. 1, p. 11.

2 For France in the long eighteenth century see Colin Jones, *The Great Nation: France from Louis XV to Napoleon*, London, 2002.

3 Pompadour, *Memoirs*, Vol. 1, pp. 11–12.

4 Katharine Prescott Wormeley, trans., *Memoirs & Letters of Cardinal de Bernis*, 2 vols, London, 1902, Vol. 1, Entry for 11 August 1739 NS, p. 118.

5 Wormeley, *Journal & Memoirs of the Marquis d'Argenson*, Vol. 1, p. 179.

6 Pompadour, *Memoirs*, Vol. 1, p. 24.

7 Annie E. Challice, *The secret history of the Court of France under Louis XV*, 2 vols, London, 1861, Vol. 1, p. 138.

8 Wormeley, *Journal & Memoirs of the Marquis d'Argenson*, Vol. 1, pp. 182–3.

9 Ibid., Vol. 1, p. 182.

10 Ibid., Vol. 1, p. 183.

11 See Jeffrey Stephen, 'Scottish Nationalism and Stuart Unionism: The Edinburgh Council, 1745', in *Journal of British Studies*, Vol. 49, No. 1, January 2010, pp. 47–72.

12 'Letter from the Associators to Cardinal Fleury' translated in W. B. Blaikie, *Origins of the 'Forty-Five*, Edinburgh, 1916, pp. xxxv–xxxvii.

13 RA SP/MAIN/245/46 James Edgar to Balhady, Albano 1 October 1742 NS.

14 Wormeley, *Journal & Memoirs of the Marquis d'Argenson*, Vol. 1, pp. 312–13.

15 My thanks to Julian Swann for this information.

16 Robert Fitzroy Bell, ed., *Memorials of John Murray of Broughton*, Edinburgh, 1898, p. 44.

17 Ibid., pp. 44–5.

18 Cruickshanks, *Political Untouchables*, pp. 41–2.

19 RA SP/MAIN/252/94 Sempill to James, [Versailles?] 9 September 1743 NS.

20 Ibid.

21 Copies were sent to James by Balhady RA SP/MAIN/253/51, 52 (in French) and 254/154 (in English). See also Cruickshanks, *Political Untouchables*, Appendices I and II.

22 RA SP/MAIN/253/154 Balhady to James, [Paris?] 13 November 1743 NS. See also Cruickshanks, *Political Untouchables*, p. 45.

23 L. L. Bongie, *The Love of a Prince: Bonnie Prince Charlie in France, 1744–1748*, Vancouver, 1986, p. 102.

24 See Frank McLynn, *France and the Jacobite Rising of 1745*, Edinburgh, 1981, pp. 19–20 and McLynn, *Bonnie Prince Charlie*, 1988/2003, pp. 80–2.

25 RA SP/MAIN/235/172.

26 RA SP/MAIN/255/6 James to Sempill, Rome 2 January 1744 NS.

27 RA SP/MAIN/255/30 James to Sempill, Rome 9 January 1744 NS.

28 RA SP/MAIN/255/60 James to Sempill, Rome 17 January 1744 NS.

29 RA SP/MAIN/255/76 James to Ormonde, Rome 21 January 1744 NS.

30 'Horace Mann to Horace Walpole, Florence 22 January 1744 NS' in W. S. Lewis, ed., *Horace Walpole's Correspondence*, 48 vols, London, 1937–83, Vol. 18 (1955), pp. 374–5.

31 'Horace Mann to Horace Walpole, Florence 28 January N.S' in Lewis, *Horace Walpole's Correspondence*, Vol. 18, pp. 376–81, pp. 378–9.

32 RA SP/MAIN/255/115 James to Sempill, Rome 30 January 1744 NS.

33 McLynn, *Bonnie Prince Charlie*, pp. 83–8.

34 'A portion of the diary of David, Lord Elcho' in H. Tayler ed., *A Jacobite Miscellany: Eight original papers on the Rising of 1745–6*, Oxford, 1948, pp. 127–171, pp. 132–3.

35 Cruickshanks, *Political Untouchables*, pp. 57–8.

36 RA SP/MAIN/256/128 Charles to James, Gravelines 13 March 1744 NS.

37 RA SP/MAIN/256/126–126a Earl Marischal to Charles, Dunkirk 13 March 1744 NS.

38 RA SP/MAIN/256/132 Charles to Earl Marischal, Gravelines 15 March 1744 NS.

39 Ibid.

40 RA SP/MAIN/256/134 Earl Marischal to Charles, Dunkirk 16 March 1744 NS.

41 RA SP/MAIN/256/135 intelligence from 'Dr Cooper' as enclosure to 256/134.

42 RA SP/MAIN/256/139 Earl Marischal to Charles, Dunkirk 17 March 1744 NS.

43 'Lord Elcho's Diary' in Tayler, *A Jacobite Miscellany*, p. 134.

44 RA SP/MAIN/256/169 Charles to James, Gravelines 26 March 1744 NS.

Chapter 3: Paris

1 RA SP/MAIN/256/194 James to Charles, Rome 15 April 1744 NS.

2 RA SP/MAIN/256/197 Charles to James, [no location] 16 April 1744 NS.

3 RA SP/MAIN/257/7 Charles to James, [no location] 24 April 1744 NS.
4 RA SP/MAIN/257/15 Charles to James, [no location] 29 April 1744 NS.
5 RA SP/MAIN/257/13 James to Charles, Rome 28 April 1744 NS.
6 RA SP/MAIN/257/22 James to Sempill, Rome 5 May 1744 NS.
7 RA SP/MAIN/257/34 Charles to James, 'Francfort' [Paris] 11 May 1744 NS.
8 Ibid.
9 RA SP/MAIN/257/48 Charles to James, 'Francfort' [Paris] 18 May 1744 NS.
10 Ibid.
11 RA SP/MAIN/257/116 Charles to James, Paris 14 June 1744 NS.
12 RA SP/MAIN/257/94 Sheridan to James, Paris 8 June 1744 NS.
13 RA SP/MAIN/258/133 James to Sempill, Rome 14 August 1744 NS.
14 'Lord Elcho's Diary' in Tayler, *A Jacobite Miscellany*, p. 138.
15 Ibid., pp. 138–9.
16 Bell, *Murray of Broughton*, p. 90.
17 Ibid., p. 93.
18 Ibid.
19 'John William O'Sullivan's Narrative . . . written 1747' in A. Tayler and H. Tayler, eds, *1745 and After*, London and Edinburgh, 1938, pp. 45–216, p. 46.
20 The aftermath was so bitter, with accusations and blame-dodging rife, that it is sensible to approach any account with caution, particularly those written in hindsight.
21 RA SP/MAIN/258/139 Charles to James, Paris 17 August 1744 NS.
22 Ibid.
23 Bongie, *The Love of a Prince*, p. 109.
24 RA SP/MAIN/259/64 James to Charles, Rome 11 September 1744 NS.
25 'Lord Elcho's Diary' in Tayler, *A Jacobite Miscellany*, p. 138.
26 Ibid., pp. 138–9.
27 RA SP/MAIN/260/62 Charles to James, Paris 16 November 1744 NS.
28 RA SP/MAIN/260/81 Charles to James, Paris 30 November 1744 NS.
29 RA SP/MAIN/260/150 Charles to Edgar, Paris 14 December 1744 NS.
30 RA SP/MAIN/261/11 Charles to James, Paris 21 December 1744 NS.
31 RA SP/MAIN/260/149 Charles to James, Paris 14 December 1744 NS.
32 RA SP/MAIN/261/118 Sheridan to Edgar, Paris 4 January 1745 NS.
33 RA SP/261/170 James to Sempill, Rome 12 January 1745 NS.
34 'Character of Mr. Sullivan' in Tayler and Tayler, eds, *1745 and After*, pp. 16–19, p. 18.
35 RA SP/MAIN/261/155 Charles to James, Paris, 11 January 1745 NS.
36 RA SP/MAIN/262/160 Charles to James, Fitz-James 14 February 1745 NS.
37 RA SP/MAIN/262/133 Charles to James, Fitz-James 7 February 1745 NS.
38 RA SP/MAIN/263/24 Charles to James, Paris 28 February 1745 NS.
39 RA SP/MAIN/264/95 Charles to James, [no location, Fitz-James?] 26 April 1745 NS.

Chapter 4: Fontenoy

1 For the Duke's early life see Evan Charteris, *William Augustus Duke of Cumberland: His Early Life and Times (1721–1748)*, London, 1913. For the most recent reassessments of the Duke's involvement in the '45 see W. A. Speck, *The Butcher*, Cardiff, 1981 and 1995 (revised edition imminent) and Jonathan Oates, *Sweet William or The Butcher?*, Barnsley, 2008.
2 Andrew Henderson, *The Life of William Augustus, Duke of Cumberland*, London, 1766, p. 10.

3 For the reign of George II see Andrew Thompson, *George II: King and Elector*, New Haven and London, 2011.

4 John Hervey, *Memoirs of the Reign of George the Second*, 2 vols, London, 1848, Vol. 2, p. 512.

5 Horace Walpole, *Memoirs of the last ten years of the reign of George the Second*, 2 vols, London, 1822, Vol. 1, p. 88.

6 T. McCann, ed., *The correspondence of the Dukes of Richmond and Newcastle, 1724–1750*, Lewes, 1984, pp. 103–4.

7 T. Smollett and T. Franklin, *The Works of M. de Voltaire*, 25 vols, London, 1761–6, Vol. 19 (Vol. 14 of Prose Works), 1762, p. 131.

8 Henderson, *Duke of Cumberland*, pp. 397–8.

9 BL NP Add MS 32704 ff. 233–234, f. 233 Cumberland to Newcastle, Lessines Camp 22 May NS.

10 See Norma Perry, *Sir Everard Fawkener, friend and correspondent of Voltaire*, Banbury, 1975 and Haydn Mason 'Sir Everard Fawkener', *ODNB* online, article 9228, 2004.

11 Archibald Ballantyne, *Voltaire's visit to England 1726–1729*, London, 1893, p. 245.

12 RA CP/MAIN/2/110 Fawkener to Pelham, Brussels 19/30 April 1745 OS/NS.

13 BL HP Add MS 35354 ff. 98–99 Hardwicke to Joseph Yorke, [Powis House?] 15 April 1745 OS.

14 BL HP Add MS 35354 ff. 96–97, f. 96 Hardwicke to Joseph Yorke, [Powis House?] 24 April 1745 OS.

15 Ibid.

16 BL HP Add MS 35354 ff. 96–97, f. 97 Hardwicke to Joseph Yorke, [Powis House?] 24 April 1745 OS.

17 Wormeley, *Journal & Memoirs of the Marquis d'Argenson*, Vol. 1, p. 218.

18 Smollett and Franklin, *The Works of M. de Voltaire*, Vol. 19 (Vol. 14), p. 228.

19 Wormeley, *Memoirs & Letters of Cardinal de Bernis*, Vol. 1, p. 154.

20 Smollett and Franklin, *The Works of M. de Voltaire*, Vol. 19 (Vol. 14), p. 222.

21 Ibid.

22 Ibid., pp. 231–2.

23 Ibid., p. 232.

24 Ibid., pp. 232–3.

25 Philip Yorke, *Life and Correspondence of Philip Yorke Earl of Hardwicke*, 3 vols, Cambridge, 1913, Vol. 1, p. 405.

26 Ibid., p. 408.

27 'Letter from James Wolfe to his Father, Ghent 4 May 1745 NS' in Beckles Willson, *The Life and Letters of James Wolfe*, London, 1909, p. 5.

28 'Letter from Philip Yorke to Horatio Walpole, London 16 May 1745' quoted in William Coxe, *Memoirs of the Administration of the Right Honourable Henry Pelham*, 2 vols, London, 1829, Vol. 1, pp. 235–7, p. 236.

29 Wormeley, *Memoirs & Letters of Cardinal de Bernis*, Vol. 1, p. 156.

30 'Horace Walpole to Thomas Mann, Arlington Street, London, 24 May 1745 OS' in Lewis, *Horace Walpole's Correspondence*, Vol. 19 (1955), pp. 52–3, p. 52.

31 *A full and particular account of a bloody battle, fought between the English and French, in Flanders under the command of his Royal Highness William Duke of Cumberland*, BL Cup 21 g.31/48.

32 BL HP Add MS 35354 ff. 104–5 Joseph Yorke to Hardwicke, Camp at Ath 12 May 1745 NS [1 May OS].

33 As seen in Sir Joshua Reynolds' portrait of *c.*1753–5, Manchester City Art Gallery (Acc. No. 1981.36).

34 BL HP Add MS 35354 f. 100–01, f. 100 Hardwicke to Joseph Yorke, Powis House 5 May 1745 OS.

35 Ibid., f. 101.

36 BL NP Add MS 32704 ff. 233–234 Cumberland to Newcastle, Lessines Camp 22 May NS.

37 BL NP Add MS 32704 ff. 235–236 Fawkener to Newcastle, Lessines Camp 23 May 1745 NS.

Chapter 5: Brittany

1 RA SP/MAIN/265/73 'to Barclay' with a note 'shortly before 20 June 1745'. RA SP/MAIN/265/72 is in several hands, including Charles' who writes re. code names 'Barclay for Murrey'.

2 RA SP/MAIN BOX 1/210 'Copy of letter from Charles to the Chiefs' via Hector Maclean about May 1745.

3 RA SP/MAIN/268/8 Abbé Butler to Ormonde, 20 September 1745 NS.

4 RA SP/MAIN/266/174 Charles to James, 'Loughaylort' 4 August 1745 OS.

5 RA SP/MAIN/265/135 Charles to Edgar, 'Navar' 12 June 1745 NS.

6 Ibid.

7 'Dutillet' is the spelling used by Captain Darbé in his journal, see 'Captain Darbé's Journal' in Murray MacGregor, trans., *A Royalist Family: Irish and French (1689–1789) and Prince Charles Edward*, Edinburgh, 1904, pp. 17–31, although it was probably named after M. Du Teillay (see Translator's Appendix A, p. 109, n. 2). Revd John Jardine, in his manuscript for his unpublished history of the rebellion, calls the ship the 'Du Tilly'; see NRS Papers of Dr John Jardine GD1/1440/2/4 Section marked 'D' of John Jardine's draft history of the 1745 rebellion *c.*1746–8.

8 RA SP/MAIN/265/135 Charles to Edgar, Navarre 12 June 1745 NS.

9 'O'Sullivan's Narrative' in Tayler and Tayler, *1745 and After*, p. 47.

10 'Character of Mr. Sullivan' in Tayler and Tayler, *1745 and After*, pp. 16–19, p. 18.

11 For example RA Captured Stuart Papers CP/MAIN/2/328, 330, 331 and 340.

12 RA Captured Stuart Papers CP/MAIN/2/354 and 363.

13 RA Captured Stuart Papers CP/MAIN/2/321 Sheridan to O'Sullivan, Fitz-James 2 May 1745 NS [21 April OS].

14 RA Captured Stuart Papers CP/MAIN/2/349–352. The chandeliers alone are 24 livres.

15 RA Captured Stuart Papers CP/MAIN/2/364.

16 RA Captured Stuart Papers CP/MAIN/2/336 Sheridan to O'Sullivan, Fitz-James 14 May 1745 NS. O'Sullivan's address is 'l'Hotel de Condé Rue des tous Enfans aupres du Palais Royal a Paris'.

17 The sword was made by Charles Frederick Kandler of London between 1740 and 1741 and is now in the National Museums Scotland, Edinburgh (Acc. No. H.MCR 2).

18 This beautiful canteen is also in the National Museums Scotland (Acc. No. H.MEQ 1584.1).

19 RA Captured Stuart Papers CP/MAIN/2/325 and 327.

20 'O'Sullivan's Narrative' in Tayler and Tayler, *1745 and After*, pp. 47–8.

21 RA SP/MAIN/265/129 Charles to James, 'Navar' 12 June 1745 NS.

22 Ibid.

23 Ibid.

24 Ibid.

25 The letter is translated in Lenman and Gibson, *The Jacobite Threat*, pp. 200–1. The original in French is transcribed in Bell, *Murray of Broughton*, p. 507.

26 RA SP/MAIN/265/129 Charles to James, 'Navar' 12 June 1745 NS.

27 RA SP/MAIN/265/155 Sempill to James, [Versailles?] 14 June 1745 NS.

28 RA Captured Stuart Papers CP/MAIN/2/367 Sheridan to O'Sullivan, Navarre 30 May 1745 NS.

29 RA SP/MAIN/265/155 Sempill to James, [Versailles?] 14 June 1745 NS.

30 RA SP/MAIN/266/33 Sempill to James, [Versailles?] 28 June 1745 NS.

31 See Tayler and Tayler, *1745 and After*, p. 6.

32 RA Captured Stuart Papers CP/MAIN/2/370 Sheridan to O'Sullivan, Navarre 3 June 1745 NS.

33 'John Macdonald's Account' included as footnotes in Tayler and Tayler, *1745 and After*, pp. 46–162, p. 46, n. 2.

34 'Aeneas MacDonald's Journal' in *LM*, Vol. 1, pp. 281–296, p. 282.

35 Ibid.

36 RA SP/MAIN/266/36 James to Ormonde, Albano 28 June 1745 NS.

37 The former is dated from 'Navar'.

38 RA SP/MAIN/265/156 Charles to O'Brien, 'Navar' 14 June 1745 NS.

39 O'Sullivan says Charles arrived in Nantes 'about the 10th of June' and left two or three days later; see 'O'Sullivan's Narrative' in Tayler and Tayler, *1745 and After*, p. 48. This does not fit with the dating of the prince's letters from Navarre, although Charles may have post-dated them to further cloak his movements.

40 'O'Sullivan's Narrative' in Tayler and Tayler, *1745 and After*, p. 48.

41 Ibid.

42 RA SP/MAIN/266/34 Sempill to James, [Versailles?] 28 June 1745 NS.

43 RA SP/MAIN/266/86 Sir Richard Holmes' transcription of Charles' letter to James dated 2 July 1745 NS, the original removed on the order of Queen Victoria, 29 March 1873.

44 'Captain Darbé's Journal' in Murray MacGregor, *A Royalist Family*, pp. 17–31, p. 17.

45 RA SP/MAIN/266/102 Charles to Edgar, St Lazaire [sic] 2 July 1745 NS.

46 'Captain Darbé's Journal' in MacGregor, *A Royalist Family*, p. 18.

47 'Aeneas MacDonald's Journal' in *LM*, Vol. 1, p. 285.

48 RA SP/MAIN/266/102 Charles to Edgar, Saint-Nazaire 2 July 1745 NS, postscript Belle-Île 12 July 1745 NS.

49 'Captain Darbé's Journal' in MacGregor, *A Royalist Family*, p. 18.

Chapter 6: Flanders

1 RA Captured Stuart Papers CP/MAIN/4/299 James Hay to Alexander Baillie, 'Aalst', 6 August 1745 NS.

2 RA SP/MAIN/266/184 Drummond to Edgar, Aalst 9 August 1745 NS.

3 RA CP/MAIN/3/320 Trevor to Fawkener, The Hague 3 August NS.

4 RA CP/MAIN/2/340 Newcastle to Cumberland, Newcastle House 26 July 1745 OS.

5 RA CP/MAIN/3/341 Newcastle to Cumberland, Whitehall 26 July 1745 OS.

6 RA CP/MAIN/4/17 Fawkener to Harrington, Vilvoorde 9 August 1745 NS [29 July 1745 OS].

7 RA CP/MAIN/4/16 Fawkener to Newcastle, Vilvoorde 9 August 1745 NS [29 July 1745 OS].

8 RA CP/MAIN/4/17 Fawkener to Harrington, Vilvoorde 29 July/9 August 1745 OS/NS.

9 RA CP/MAIN/4/26 Trevor to Fawkener, The Hague 10 August 1745 NS [30 July 1745 OS].

10 RA CP/MAIN/4/43 Newcastle to Cumberland, Whitehall 2 August 1745 OS.

11 RA CP/MAIN/4/48 Newcastle to Fawkener, Whitehall 2 August 1745 OS.

12 RA CP/MAIN/4/57 Harrington to Cumberland, Hanover 2/13 August 1745 OS/NS.

Chapter 7: Edinburgh

1 Francis H. Groome, ed., *Ordnance Gazetteer of Scotland*, 2 vols, Edinburgh, Vol. 2, 1884, p. 317.
2 George Menary, *The Life and Letters of Duncan Forbes of Culloden*, London, 1936, p. 5. For Forbes see also John S. Shaw, 'Duncan Forbes' in *ODNB* online, article 9822, 2006.
3 For an in-depth analysis of this see Christopher Whatley, 'Reformed Religion, Regime Change, Scottish Whigs and the Struggle for the "Soul" of Scotland, *c.*1688–*c.*1788', *Scottish Historical Review*, XCII, 1, No. 233 (April 2013), pp. 66–99.
4 'Letter from Colonel John Munro [Monro] to Lord President Forbes, the Camp near Ath 2 May 1745 NS' in H. R. Duff, ed., *Culloden Papers comprising an Extensive and Interesting Correspondence from the year 1625 to 1748*, London, 1815, No. 208, pp. 200–1.
5 Duncan Warrand, ed., *More Culloden Papers*, 5 vols, Inverness, 1927–30, Vol. 3, p. 211.
6 'Letter from Lord President Forbes to Henry Pelham, 2 August 1745 OS' in Duff, *Culloden Papers*, No. 245, p. 203.
7 Ibid.
8 'Lord President Forbes to the Marquis of Tweeddale, Edinburgh 8 August 1745 OS' in Duff, *Culloden Papers*, No. 247, pp. 204–5, p. 204.
9 Ibid., p. 205.
10 Ibid.

Chapter 8: Eriskay

1 Captain Darbé's account of this engagement is in MacGregor, *A Royalist Family*, pp. 9–20.
2 'O'Sullivan's Narrative' in Tayler and Tayler, *1745 and After*, p. 50.
3 'Aeneas MacDonald's Journal' in *LM*, Vol. 1, p. 286.
4 *Caledonian Mercury*, 29 July 1745, p. 2.
5 'Aeneas MacDonald's Journal' in *LM*, Vol. 1, p. 286.
6 'Journal of Prince's embarkation . . . taken from Duncan Cameron' in *LM*, Vol. 1, pp. 201–11, p. 204.
7 'Captain Darbé's Journal' in MacGregor, *A Royalist Family*, p. 22.
8 Edmund Burt, *Letters from a Gentleman in the North of Scotland to His Friend in London*, 2 vols, London, 1754, Vol. 1, p. 5.
9 Ibid., p. 6.
10 For a full discussion see Murray G. H. Pittock, *The Invention of Scotland*, London, 1991 and *The Myth of the Jacobite Clans*, 2nd revised edition, Edinburgh, 2009.
11 John Gibson describes the Keppoch MacDonells as 'cattle-thieves par excellence'; see John S. Gibson, *Lochiel of the '45*, Edinburgh, 1994, p. 51.
12 This included attempts to eliminate cattle thieving; see Gibson, *Lochiel of the '45*, pp. 50–1.
13 'Aeneas MacDonald's Journal' in *LM*, Vol. 1, p. 288.
14 'Captain Darbé's Journal' in MacGregor, *A Royalist Family*, p. 23.
15 Martin Martin, *A description of the Western Islands of Scotland*, London, 1703, p. 87.
16 Ibid., pp. 87–8.
17 Ibid., p. 88.
18 Ibid., p. 67.
19 'Duncan Cameron's Journal' in *LM*, Vol. 1, pp. 201–11, p. 205.

20 'Aeneas MacDonald's Journal' in *LM*, Vol. 1, pp. 288–9.
21 Ibid.
22 'Captain Darbé's Journal' in MacGregor, *A Royalist Family*, p. 23.
23 'O'Sullivan's Narrative' in Tayler and Tayler, *1745 and After*, p. 53.
24 'Duncan Cameron's Journal' in *LM*, Vol. 1, p. 205.
25 'O'Sullivan's Narrative' in Tayler and Tayler, *1745 and After*, p. 53.
26 'John Macdonald's Account' in Tayler and Tayler, *1745 and After*, p. 53, n. 1.
27 'Aeneas MacDonald's Journal' in *LM*, Vol. 1, p. 289.
28 'Captain Darbé's Journal' in MacGregor, *A Royalist Family*, p. 24.
29 'Hugh MacDonald's Narrative' in *LM*, Vol. 3, pp. 50–3, p. 50.
30 Ibid., p. 50.
31 Alexander MacDonald, 'Journall and Memoirs of P. C. Expedition into Scotland . . . By a Highland Officer in his Army' in *The Lockhart Papers*, 2 vols, London, 1817, Vol. 2, pp. 479–510, p. 479. For the identification of the author of the anonymous account by a 'Highland Officer' published in the *Lockhart Papers* see Hugh Cheape, 'The '45 and its Aftermath: the Moidart Kinsmen's View' in Camille Dressler and Domhnall Uilleam Stiùbhart, eds, *Alexander MacDonald Bard of the Gaelic Enlightenment*, Lewis, 2013, pp. 37–8.
32 MacDonald, 'Journall and Memoirs' in *The Lockhart Papers*, Vol. 2, pp. 479–510.
33 'Hugh MacDonald's Narrative' in *LM*, Vol. 3, p. 51.
34 Ibid.
35 John Home, *The History of the Rebellion in the year 1745*, London, 1802, pp. 39–40.
36 Home, *The History of the Rebellion*, pp. 44–5, n.
37 'Narrative of a Conversation with Young Glengary' in *LM*, Vol. 3, pp. 119–121, pp. 120–21.
38 Donald Cameron of Lochiel, 'Mémoire d'un Ecossais, April 1747' translated in Gibson, *Lochiel of the '45*, pp. 173–85, p. 173.
39 'Captain Darbé's Journal' in MacGregor, *A Royalist Family*, p. 26.
40 'Charles' letter to Walsh, Borrodale 16 August 1745 NS' in MacGregor, *A Royalist Family*, p. 31.
41 RA SP/MAIN/266/174 Charles to James, 'Loughaylort' 4 August 1745 [OS].

Chapter 9: Culloden House

1 RA CP/MAIN/4/138 Enclosures sent to Cumberland by Newcastle within letter 4/136 dated Whitehall 13 August 1745 OS.
2 RA CP/MAIN/4/137 Copy of letter from Argyll to Newcastle, Rosnath 7 August 1745.
3 'Letter from Norman MacLeod to Lord President Forbes, Dunvegan 3 August 1745 OS' in Duff, *Culloden Papers*, No. 246, pp. 203–4.
4 Ibid., p. 204.
5 'Lord Elcho's Diary' in Tayler, *A Jacobite Miscellany*, pp. 138–9.
6 Ibid., p. 141.
7 'Letter from Sir Alexander MacDonald to Lord President Forbes, Tallisker 11 August 1745' in Duff, *Culloden Papers*, No. 250, p. 207.
8 'Letter from Lord President Forbes to Sir John Cope, Culloden 15 August 1745' in Duff, *Culloden Papers*, No. 401, pp. 371–3, p. 372.
9 'Letter from Lord President Forbes to the Duke of Gordon, Culloden 14 August 1745' in Duff, *Culloden Papers*, No. 400, pp. 370–1, p. 371.

10 'Lord President Forbes to Sir John Cope, Culloden 15 August 1745' in Duff, *Culloden Papers*, No. 401, pp. 371–2, p. 372.

11 John Struthers, *The History of Scotland from the Union to the Abolition of the Heritable Jurisdictions in 1748*, 2 vols, Glasgow, 1828, Vol. 2, p. 231.

12 For a recent and excellent biography of Lord Lovat see Sarah Fraser, *The Last Highlander: Scotland's most notorious clan chief, rebel & double agent*, London, 2012.

13 'Letter from the Marquis of Tweeddale to Lord President Forbes, Whitehall 17 August 1745' in Duff, *Culloden Papers*, No. 253, pp. 208–9, p. 209.

14 Ibid.

Chapter 10: Glenfinnan

1 MacDonald 'Journall and Memoirs' in *The Lockhart Papers*, Vol. 2, pp. 479–510, p. 482.

2 'O'Sullivan's Narrative' in Tayler and Tayler, *1745 and After*, p. 58.

3 RA Captured Stuart Papers CP/MAIN/4/316 Charles to Glenbucket, 'Kinloch' 14 August 1745 OS.

4 A. N. Campbell Maclachlan, *William Augustus, Duke of Cumberland*, London, 1876, p. 243.

5 Bell, *Murray of Broughton*, p. 169.

6 'O'Sullivan's Narrative' in Tayler and Tayler, *1745 and After*, p. 60.

7 'John Macdonald's Account' in Tayler and Tayler, *1745 and After*, p. 59, n.

8 John Home mentions blue elements as well; see *The History of the Rebellion*, p. 50, n. See also Hilary Horrocks, ed., *Glenfinnan Monument*, The National Trust for Scotland, Edinburgh, 2006.

9 Home, *The History of the Rebellion*, p. 50, n.

10 'Aeneas MacDonald's Journal' in *LM*, Vol. 1, p. 292.

11 Bell, *Murray of Broughton*, p. 169.

12 'O'Sullivan's Narrative' in Tayler and Tayler, *1745 and After*, p. 60.

13 Stuart Reid observes that a lack of 'discipline' in an eighteenth-century military context meant training; see Stuart Reid, *Like Hungry Wolves: Culloden Moor 16 April 1746*, London, 1994, p. 58.

14 'O'Sullivan's Narrative' in Tayler and Tayler, *1745 and After*, p. 60.

15 'John Macdonald's Account' in Tayler and Tayler, *1745 and After*, p. 60, n.

16 'O'Sullivan's Narrative' in Tayler and Tayler, *1745 and After*, p. 61.

17 'Letter from Cluny MacPherson to Lord President Forbes, Cluny 19 August 1745' in Duff, *Culloden Papers*, No. 405, pp. 375–6, p. 375.

18 'Letter from Lord Lovat to the Lord Advocate, Beaufort 23 August 1745' in Duff, *Culloden Papers*, No. 255, pp. 210–1.

Chapter 11: Auld Reekie

1 Daniel Defoe, *A Tour thro' the Whole Island of Great Britain*, 4 vols, 3rd edition, London, 1742, Vol. 4, p. 65.

2 Home, *The History of the Rebellion*, p. 66.

3 Defoe, *A Tour thro' the Whole Island*, Vol. 4, p. 63.

4 Ibid., p. 65.

5 Burt, *Letters from a Gentleman in the North of Scotland*, Vol. 1, pp. 23–4.

6 Defoe, *A Tour thro' the Whole Island*, Vol. 4, p. 63.

7 Ibid., p. 66.

8 Home, *The History of the Rebellion*, p. 66.
9 Quoted in John Anderson, *A History of Edinburgh*, Edinburgh and London, 1856, p. 172.
10 *Caledonian Mercury*, 20 August 1745.
11 Ibid., 22 August 1745, p. 3.
12 Ibid., 27 August 1745.
13 Ibid., 3 September 1745.
14 Ibid., 6 September 1745, p. 3.
15 Bruce A. Hedman, 'Colin Maclaurin's Journal of the 'Forty-Five', in *Miscellany XIII of the Scottish History Society*, 5th series, Vol. 14, Edinburgh, 2004, pp. 312–22, p. 317.
16 *Woodhouselee Manuscript. A narrative of events in Edinburgh and district during the Jacobite occupation, September to November 1745*, London and Edinburgh, 1907, pp. 14–15. This document is generally accepted to have been written by Patrick Crichton and quoted accordingly here.
17 James Kinsley, ed., *Alexander Carlyle: Anecdotes and Characters of the Times*, London, 1973, p. 10.
18 Ibid., p. 58.
19 Ibid.
20 *Woodhouselee MS*, pp. 13–14.
21 Ibid., p. 14.
22 Kinsley, *Alexander Carlyle: Anecdotes and Characters*, p. 59.
23 Hedman, 'Colin Maclaurin's Journal of the 'Forty-Five', p. 321.
24 *Woodhouselee MS*, p. 16.
25 Kinsley, *Alexander Carlyle: Anecdotes and Characters*, p. 60.
26 Ibid.
27 *Woodhouselee MS*, p. 14.
28 Kinsley, *Alexander Carlyle: Anecdotes and Characters*, p. 60.
29 Ibid., pp. 60–1.
30 Ibid., p. 61.
31 Ibid., pp. 61–2.
32 *Woodhouselee MS*, p. 17.
33 David Daiches, *Charles Edward Stuart: The Life and Times of Bonnie Prince Charlie*, London, 1973, p. 126.
34 *Woodhouselee MS*, p. 19.
35 Ibid.
36 Ibid., p. 20.
37 Home, *The History of the Rebellion*, p. 88.
38 This statement was recalled by Lord Mark Kerr, quoted in Daiches, *Charles Edward Stuart*, p. 127.
39 Ibid.
40 *Woodhouselee MS*, p. 18.
41 Home, *The History of the Rebellion*, pp. 88–9.
42 Ibid., p. 89.
43 Ibid.
44 'Copy of the Prince's Summons to the City of Edinburgh to Surrender' in *LM*, Vol. 1, p. 249.
45 Kinsley, *Alexander Carlyle: Anecdotes and Characters*, p. 64.
46 Home, *The History of the Rebellion*, p. 91.
47 Ibid.
48 Ibid., p. 91, n.
49 Kinsley, *Alexander Carlyle: Anecdotes and Characters*, p. 65.

Chapter 12: Perth

1   Christopher Duffy, *The '45: Bonnie Prince Charlie and the Untold Story of the Jacobite Rising*, London, 2003, p. 180.

2   'Thomas Fraser to Lord President Forbes, Gortuleg 29 August 1745 OS' in Duff, *Culloden Papers*, No. 262, pp. 216–17, p. 216.

3   The various meetings John Roy Stuart had prior to travelling to Scotland are described in a letter to James Edgar dated Ghent 16 August 1745 transcribed in H. Tayler, ed., *Jacobite Epilogue*, London and Edinburgh, 1941, pp. 250–2.

4   RA Captured Stuart Papers CP/MAIN/4/302 Bouillon to Charles, [no location] 10 August 1745 NS [30 July 1745 OS].

5   RA Captured Stuart Papers CP/MAIN/4/303 Campo Florida to Charles, [no location] 30 July 1745 NS.

6   Charles Sanford Terry ed., *The Albemarle Papers: being the Correspondence of William Anne, Second Earl of Albemarle, Commander in Chief in Scotland, 1746–1747*, 2 vols, Aberdeen, Vol. 1, p. 237.

7   'Thomas Bisset to Duke James, Blair Castle 31 August 1745 OS' in J. H. Stewart-Murray and Jane Anderson, eds, *Chronicles of the Atholl and Tullibardine Families*, 5 vols, Edinburgh, 1908, Vol. 3, pp. 12–13, p. 12.

8   Ibid.

9   Ibid., p. 13.

10 Ibid.

11 'Duncan Cameron's Journal' in *LM*, Vol. 1, p. 208.

12 Terry, *The Albemarle Papers*, Vol. 1, pp. 257–8.

13 'Duncan Cameron's Journal' in *LM*, Vol. 1, p. 209.

14 'Tullibardine to Baron Reid, Dunkeld 4 September 1745 OS' in Stewart-Murray and Anderson, *Atholl Chronicles*, Vol. 3, p. 21.

15 'Lady Amelia Murray to Duke James, Tullibardine 5 September 1745 OS' in ibid, p. 22.

16 'Lord George Murray to Duke James, Tullibardine "Six at night" 3 September 1745 OS' in ibid., pp. 19–20.

17 Yorke, *Hardwicke Life and Correspondence*, Vol. 1, p. 455.

18 'John Murray to Duke James, Eton [September] 1745 OS' in Stewart-Murray and Anderson, *Atholl Chronicles*, Vol. 3, pp. 51–2.

19 James Johnstone, *Memoirs of the Rebellion in 1745 and 1746*, 2nd edition, London, 1821, p. 26.

20 Ibid., pp. 27–8.

21 Ibid., p. 27.

22 'Lord President Forbes to Lady Cluny, Culloden 31 August 1745 OS' in Duff, *Culloden Papers*, No. 263, p. 217.

23 'Narrative of Young Glengarry' in *LM*, Vol. 3, p. 120.

24 *The York Courant*, 17 September 1745. Letter from Gent in Dundee to friend in Newcastle, 13 September 1745 and 24 September 1745.

25 'O'Sullivan's Narrative' in Tayler and Tayler, *1745 and After*, p. 69.

26 Ibid., p. 67.

27 Ibid.

28 'Copy of a letter from the Prince to his father, Perth September 10 1745' in *LM*, Vol. 2, pp. 58–61, pp. 58–9. It was sent to Robert Forbes by Dr John Burton of York in March 1747–8 OS.

29 Ibid., p. 61.

30 Some finessing during transcription by the editor of the manuscripts within *Lyon in Mourning*, i.e. Robert Forbes or John Burton, is a possibility.
31 'John Macdonald's Account' in Tayler and Tayler, *1745 and After*, p. 68, n. 1.
32 Stewart-Murray and Anderson, *Atholl Chronicles*, Vol. 3, pp. 25–6.
33 Bell, *Murray of Broughton*, p. 191.
34 'Lord George's account of the march from Perth to Edinburgh' in Stewart-Murray and Anderson, *Atholl Chronicles*, Vol. 3, pp. 25–8, p. 27.
35 Evan Charteris, ed., David, Lord Elcho, *A Short Account of the Affairs of Scotland in the Years 1744, 1745, 1746*, Edinburgh, 1907, pp. 227–448, pp. 254–5.
36 Home, *The History of the Rebellion*, p. 88.
37 Bell, *Murray of Broughton*, p. 193.
38 Home, *The History of the Rebellion*, p. 86, n.

Chapter 13: Gray's Mill

1 Johnstone, *Memoirs of the Rebellion*, p. 24.
2 W. B. Blaikie, *Itinerary of Prince Charles Edward Stuart from his landing in Scotland July 1745 to his Departure in September 1746*, Edinburgh, 1897, p. 14, n.
3 'Lord Elcho's Diary' in Tayler, *A Jacobite Miscellany*, p. 144.
4 Ibid., p. 144.
5 Ibid.
6 Ibid., p. 145.
7 Bell, *Murray of Broughton*, pp. 193–4.
8 Ibid., p. 194.
9 Lord Elcho, *A Short Account*, p. 256.
10 'Copy of the Prince's Summons to the City of Edinburgh to surrender' in *LM*, Vol. 1, pp. 249–50.
11 'Lord Elcho's Diary' in Tayler, *A Jacobite Miscellany*, p. 144.
12 Bell, *Murray of Broughton*, p. 194.
13 'Copy of the Prince's Summons to the City of Edinburgh to surrender' in *LM*, Vol. 1, p. 250.
14 Kinsley, *Alexander Carlyle: Anecdotes and Characters*, p. 65.
15 Ibid.

Chapter 14: Netherbow Port

1 Bell, *Murray of Broughton*, p. 194.
2 'O'Sullivan's Narrative' in Tayler and Tayler, *1745 and After*, p. 72.
3 Bell, *Murray of Broughton*, p. 195.
4 RA CP/MAIN/5/163 'Particulars relating to what preceded the Battle of Preston Pans, & some account of it; by Mr. Rich[ar]d Jack', October 1745 OS.
5 'O'Sullivan's Narrative' in Tayler and Tayler, *1745 and After*, p. 73.
6 Bell, *Murray of Broughton*, p. 197.

Chapter 15: Canongate

1 *Woodhouselee MS*, p. 23.
2 Ibid., pp. 23–4.

3 Lord Elcho, *A Short Account*, p. 257.
4 *Woodhouselee MS*, p. 24.
5 Ibid., p. 17.
6 Ibid., p. 20.
7 Ibid., p. 24.
8 Lord Elcho, *A Short Account*, pp. 257–8.
9 'O'Sullivan's Narrative' in Tayler and Tayler, *1745 and After*, p. 73.
10 *Woodhouselee MS*, p. 24.
11 Ibid.
12 Lord Elcho, *A Short Account*, pp. 258–9.
13 Andrew Henderson, *The History of the Rebellion*, 5th edition, London, 1753, p. 50.
14 Ibid.
15 Ibid., pp. 50–1.
16 Ibid., p. 51. The description of Charles' voice is not in the 1st edition of Henderson's history.
17 Ibid.
18 Andrew Henderson, *The History of the Rebellion*, 1st edition, London, 1748, pp. 25–6.
19 Home, *The History of the Rebellion*, p. 99.
20 Ibid., n.
21 Ibid., pp. 99–100.
22 Lord Elcho, *A Short Account*, p. 259.
23 'Lord Elcho's Diary' in Tayler, *A Jacobite Miscellany*, p. 145.
24 MacDonald, 'Journall and Memoirs' in *The Lockhart Papers*, Vol. 2, p. 489.
25 Defoe, *A Tour thro' the Whole Island*, Vol. 4, p. 86.
26 Ibid.
27 Home, *The History of the Rebellion*, p. 101.
28 Ibid., p. 100.
29 Ibid.

Chapter 16: The Mercat Cross

1 Lord Elcho, *A Short Account*, pp. 259–60.
2 Home, *The History of the Rebellion*, p. 102.
3 'O'Sullivan's Narrative' in Tayler and Tayler, *1745 and After*, p. 74.
4 *Woodhouselee MS*, p. 25.
5 Ibid., p. 26.
6 'Extract of a Letter from Edinburgh, dated 1 November', published in *Newcastle Courant*, 9–16 November 1745, p. 2.
7 James Steuart noted under 26 May 1746 'The carpet that laid upon the Cross at the proclamations Lyes upon the Exchequer Table' in A. Francis Steuart, *The Plenishing of Holyrood House in 1714*, Reprinted from the Proceedings of the Society of Antiquaries of Scotland, 1928, p. 195.
8 *Woodhouselee MS*, p. 27.
9 'Two Letters from Magdalen Pringle' in Tayler, *A Jacobite Miscellany*, Oxford, 1948, pp. 37–42, p. 39.
10 'Extract of a Letter from Edinburgh, dated 1 November', published in *Newcastle Courant*, 9–16 November 1745, p. 2.
11 An example is in the British Library, C.115.i.3(62).

12 *Woodhouselee MS*, p. 28.
13 Ibid., p. 29.
14 Lord Elcho, *A Short Account*, p. 259.
15 *Caledonian Mercury*, Wednesday 18 September 1745.
16 Ibid.
17 'Magdalen Pringle's Letters' in Tayler, *A Jacobite Miscellany*, p. 39.
18 James Maxwell of Kirkconnell, *Narrative of Charles Prince of Wales' Expedition to Scotland in the Year 1745*, Edinburgh, 1861, p. 46.
19 'Magdalen Pringle's Letters' in Tayler, *A Jacobite Miscellany*, p. 39.
20 *Woodhouselee MS*, p. 32.
21 'Extract of a Letter from Edinburgh, dated 1 November', published in *Newcastle Courant*, 9–16 November 1745, p. 2.
22 Bell, *Murray of Broughton*, p. 198.
23 'Lord Tweeddale to Lord Milton, Whitehall, 21 September 1745 OS' transcribed in Home, *The History of the Rebellion*, Appendix No. XX, pp. 308–10.

Chapter 17: Prestonpans

1 *Woodhouselee MS*, p. 23.
2 Bell, *Murray of Broughton*, p. 200.
3 'O'Sullivan's Narrative' in Tayler and Tayler, *1745 and After*, p. 75.
4 Kinsley, *Alexander Carlyle: Anecdotes and Characters*, p. 69.
5 *The Gentleman's Magazine*, Vol. 15, October 1745, p. 520.
6 Kinsley, *Alexander Carlyle: Anecdotes and Characters*, p. 71.
7 Ibid.
8 *The Gentleman's Magazine*, Vol. 15, October 1745, p. 520.
9 Kinsley, *Alexander Carlyle: Anecdotes and Characters*, p. 72.
10 *The Gentleman's Magazine*, Vol. 15, October 1745, p. 519.
11 *The Report of the Proceedings and Opinion of the Board of General Officers, on their Examination into the Conduct, Behaviour, and Proceedings of Lieutenant-General Sir John Cope*, London, 1749, p. 38.
12 Johnstone, *Memoirs of the Rebellion*, p. 33.
13 Kinsley, *Alexander Carlyle: Anecdotes and Characters*, p. 73.
14 *The Gentleman's Magazine*, Vol. 15, October 1745, p. 520.
15 Lord George Murray, 'The March of the Highland Army' in Robert Forbes and Robert Chambers, eds, *Jacobite Memoirs of the Rebellion of 1745*, Edinburgh, 1834, p. 38.
16 Johnstone, *Memoirs of the Rebellion*, p. 33.
17 Ibid., p. 34.
18 Bell, *Murray of Broughton*, p. 202.
19 Johnstone, *Memoirs of the Rebellion*, p. 35.
20 Ibid.
21 Ibid.
22 Ibid., p. 26.
23 Ibid., p. 35.
24 See W. A. S. Hewins, ed., *The Whitefoord Papers*, Oxford, 1898, pp. xviii–xix.
25 *The Gentleman's Magazine*, Vol. 15, October 1745, pp. 519–20.
26 Kinsley, *Alexander Carlyle: Anecdotes and Characters*, pp. 73–4.
27 Johnstone, *Memoirs of the Rebellion*, p. 39.

28 Kinsley, *Alexander Carlyle: Anecdotes and Characters*, p. 74.
29 Ibid.
30 Johnstone, *Memoirs of the Rebellion*, p. 38.
31 Henderson, *History of the Rebellion*, 1748, p. 44.
32 Ibid., p. 43.
33 James Ray, *A Compleat History of the Rebellion*, York, 1749, pp. 52–3.
34 Bell, *Murray of Broughton*, p. 204.
35 Philip Doddridge, *Some Remarkable Passages in the Life of Colonel James Gardiner*, London, 1747, pp. 194–5.
36 Henderson, *History of the Rebellion*, 1748, p. 44.
37 Bell, *Murray of Broughton*, p. 205.
38 Kinsley, *Alexander Carlyle: Anecdotes and Characters*, p. 75.
39 Ibid., p. 77. Captain Blake recovered and when Carlyle visited him some time later 'complain'd of nothing but the pain of a little Cut he had Got on one of his Fingers'. The two were briefly in correspondence before Blake's death in 1802; see Kinsley, *Alexander Carlyle: Anecdotes and Characters*, p. 80.
40 Ibid., pp. 76–7.
41 Ibid., p. 77.
42 Lord Elcho, *A Short Account*, p. 277.
43 Bell, *Murray of Broughton*, p. 205.
44 'Lord Elcho's Diary' in Tayler, *A Jacobite Miscellany*, p. 147.
45 'Letter from Prince Charles to his father, 21 September 1745' in *LM*, Vol. 1, p. 211.
46 *Woodhouselee MS*, p. 39.

Chapter 18: Holyroodhouse

1 Clarissa Campbell Orr, 'Introduction' in Clarissa Campbell Orr, ed., *Queenship in Britain, 1660–1837: Royal Patronage, Court Culture and Dynastic politics*, Manchester, 2002, pp. 1–52, p. 25.
2 See Whatley, *The Scots and the Union*, p. 14 and p. 354.
3 Sir Walter Scott, *Waverley; or 'Tis Sixty Years Since*, 3 vols, Edinburgh, 1814, Vol. 2, p. 302.
4 *Caledonian Mercury*, 22 August 1745, p. 3.
5 Corp, *The Stuarts in Italy*, p. 369.
6 NRAS Hamilton Papers 2177 Bundle 1053 Duke of Hamilton's Correspondence, Letter from the Duke of Hamilton to George II *c*.1740.
7 'Lord Elcho's Diary' in Tayler, *A Jacobite Miscellany*, p. 138.
8 Sent with RA SP/MAIN/265/73 Charles to John Murray, [no location] June 1745.
9 *Caledonian Mercury*, 5 August 1745, p. 4. On 20 August 1745, p. 2, the paper reported that on 10 August the duke had just arrived in London 'and will soon set out on his Travels'.
10 Steuart, *The Plenishing of Holyrood House*, p. 196.
11 'Copy of the Accompts of James Gib, who served the Prince in station of Master Household and provisor for the Prince's own Table' in *LM*, Vol. 2, pp. 115–52, p. 115.
12 Defoe, *A Tour thro' the Whole Island*, Vol. 4, p. 87. The portraits were originally framed and hung on the walls, but were later fixed into the panelling.
13 My thanks to Deborah Clarke for her help in the description of the Hamilton/prince's apartments. See also John S. Gibson, *Edinburgh in the '45: Bonnie Prince Charlie at Holyrood*, Edinburgh, 1995, pp. 32–3.

14 Duchess of Northumberland, 7 August 1760, 'The lodgings very good and handsome; our Drawing Room, the Place where the young Pretr. kept all his Plans' in James Greig, ed., *The Diaries of a Duchess*, London, 1926, p. 20.

15 This wing is described as having been 'lately pulled down' in *Finance Accounts, &c. of the United Kingdom . . . for the year 1831*, Vol. 26, Royal Palaces and Buildings, London, 1832, p. 561. It was done on the orders of George IV after his visit to Edinburgh in 1822, the first such visit by a reigning monarch since 1650.

16 For example see NRAS 2177 Hamilton Papers, Bundle 872 'Letters to William Adam concerning Holyroodhouse', Bundle 873 'Accounts regarding William Adam's work at Holyrood', Bundle 876 1733–1746 'Accounts of repairs to Holyrood Abbey' and NRAS 332 Hamilton Papers, F/1/908 'Accounts etc. of William Adam', F/21123 'Estimates of repairs to Holyroodhouse' and F/2/853 'Account Book 1743–6'.

17 Samuel Boyse, *Impartial History of the Late Rebellion*, Reading, 1747, p. 89.

18 Steuart, *The Plenishing of Holyrood House*, p. 188.

19 A 'limner' had been charged with cleaning and restoring the paintings and is named as 'Mr Chalmers' in William Adam's accounts (see Hamilton Papers F/1/908 Accounts etc. of William Adam) which is possibly an error for 'James Chambers' as seen in the inventory, Hamilton Papers F/1/1064 Account of pictures at Holyroodhouse. Further details can be found in NRAS 332 M/4 Inventories Holyroodhouse 1740–1781.

20 Scott, *Waverley*, Vol. 2, pp. 315–16.

21 Steuart, *The Plenishing of Holyrood House*, p. 181.

22 Ibid., p. 194.

23 Lord Elcho, *A Short Account*, p. 306.

Chapter 19: The Abbey: Part One

1 *Woodhouselee MS*, p. 39.

2 Ibid., p. 40.

3 Ray, *A Compleat History of the Rebellion*, p. 59.

4 *Caledonian Mercury*, 25 September 1745, p. 1.

5 'Extract of a Letter from Edinburgh dated 1 November' published in *Newcastle Courant*, 9–16 November 1745, p. 3.

6 Henry Paton ed., 'Leaves from the Diary of John Campbell, an Edinburgh Banker, in 1745' in *Scottish History Society Publications*, Vol. 15, Miscellany, Vol. 1, Edinburgh, 1893, pp. 537–59, p. 540.

7 Yorke, *Hardwicke Life and Correspondence*, Vol. 1, p. 470.

8 Declaration, Holyroodhouse 10 October 1745 OS, British Library C.115.i.3(66).

9 Proclamation, Holyroodhouse 23 September 1745 OS, British Library C.115.i.3(69).

10 For example at the National Museums Scotland (H. UI 3), British Museum and West Highland Museum, Fort William.

11 Gray, *Memoirs of the Life of Sir John Clerk*, p. 186.

12 Thomas Lumisden and John Robertson, *The Whole Prophecies of Scotland, England, France, Ireland and Denmark; prophesied by Thomas Rymer . . .* Edinburgh, 1745, dedicated to 'Sacra & Augusta Monarcho, Jaccobo, Magnae Britanniae, Galliae, & Hiberniae, Regi, &c.', p. 13.

13 James Miller, *The Lamp of Lothian or, the History of Haddington*, Haddington, 1844, p. 272, n.

14 *The Scots Magazine*, Edinburgh, Vol. 7, November 1745 p. 521.

15 Proclamation, Holyroodhouse 24 September 1745 OS, British Library C.115.i.3.(63) and *Caledonian Mercury*, 25 September 1745, pp. 1–2.

16 Kinsley, *Alexander Carlyle: Anecdotes and Characters*, pp. 79–80.

17 'O'Sullivan's Narrative' in Tayler and Tayler, *1745 and After*, p. 86, p. 88.

18 Lord Elcho, *A Short Account*, p. 289.

19 Ibid.

20 Ibid., pp. 289–90.

21 'Lord Elcho's Diary' in Tayler, *Jacobite Miscellany*, p.149.

22 Maxwell of Kirkconnell, *Narrative*, pp. 54–5.

23 Henderson, *History of the Rebellion*, 1753, p. 92.

24 'O'Sullivan's Narrative' in Tayler and Tayler, *1745 and After*, p. 88.

25 'Magdalen Pringle's Letters' in Tayler, *A Jacobite Miscellany*, p. 37.

26 Ibid., p. 40.

27 Ibid., pp. 40–1.

28 Lord Elcho, *A Short Account*, p. 306.

29 'O'Sullivan's Narrative' in Tayler and Tayler, *1745 and After*, p. 88.

30 For the vow of chastity see Bongie, *The Love of a Prince*, pp. 176–7.

31 NRS Papers of Dr John Jardine GD1/1440/2/10 Section marked 'G' of John Jardine's draft history of the 1745 rebellion *c.*1746–8.

32 Christian Threipland, *Copy of a Letter from a Lady to the Lady G—dd-s, at K-l-v-ck, to the Care of Mr. James R----- Merchant in Inverness. Dundee, November 20th 1745*, British Library C.115.i.3.(77.).

33 Christian Threipland, *Copy of a Letter*.

34 Robert Chambers, *The Threiplands of Fingask: A Family Memoir*, London and Edinburgh, 1880, p. 44.

35 Lord Elcho, *A Short Account*, p. 261.

36 Kinsley, *Alexander Carlyle: Anecdotes and Characters*, p. 80.

Chapter 20: The Abbey: Part Two

1 Gibson, *Edinburgh in the '45*, p. 39.

2 *Woodhouselee MS*, pp. 53–4.

3 Proclamation, Holyroodhouse 2 October 1745 OS, British Library C.115.i.3.(64).

4 *Woodhouselee MS*, p. 55.

5 Ibid.

6 'Magdalen Pringle's Letters' in Tayler, *A Jacobite Miscellany*, p. 40.

7 BL Add MS 39923/59 Archibald Hart to William Innes, Edinburgh 10 October 1745 OS.

8 Proclamation, Holyroodhouse 5 October 1745 OS, British Library C.115.i.3.(65).

9 Declaration, Holyroodhouse 9 October 1745 OS, British Library C.115.i.3.(66).

10 'Hardwicke to Herring, Powis House, 12 September 1745' in Yorke, *Hardwicke Life and Correspondence*, Vol. 1, pp. 449–50, p. 450.

11 Thomas Herring, *A sermon preach'd at the cathedral church of York, September the 22nd 1745; on occasion of the present rebellion in Scotland*, York, 1745.

12 Proclamation, Holyroodhouse 10 October 1745 OS, British Library C.115.i.3.(67) and *Caledonian Mercury*, 14 October 1745.

13 Paton, 'John Campbell's Diary', p. 553.

14 'Walsh to James, Paris 14 September NS' in MacGregor, *A Royalist Family*, pp. 31–2, p. 31.

15 'Magdalen Pringle's Letters' in Tayler, *A Jacobite Miscellany*, p. 42.

16 'Letter from O'Sullivan to O'Bryen dated Holyroodhouse 6 and 7 October 1745' transcribed in Tayler and Tayler, *1745 and After*, pp. 34–5.

17 'O'Sullivan's Narrative' in Tayler and Tayler, *1745 and After*, p. 90.
18 See John S. Gibson, *The Diary of John Campbell: A Scottish Banker and the 'Forty-Five*, Edinburgh, 1995, pp. 1–19 and Paton, 'John Campbell's Diary', pp. 541–57, p. 541. Gibson writes (pp. 18–19) that John and his fellow directors gained access to the Castle on 3 October under false pretences 'hiding the fact, it seems, that their purpose . . . was to "bank-roll" the Highland Army.' See also Gibson, *Edinburgh in the '45*, pp. 40–1.
19 RA SP/MAIN/269/74 Louis XV to Charles, 24 September 1745 NS.
20 RA SP/MAIN/266/11 James to Charles, [no location] 26 June 1745 NS.
21 The letter in the original French transcribed in Bongie, *The Love of a Prince*, p. 124.
22 RA SP/MAIN/269/122 Charles to James, Edinburgh 15 October 1745 OS.
23 RA SP/MAIN/269/122 Enclosing 269/123 dated Edinburgh 7 October 1745 OS.
24 RA SP/MAIN/269/123 Charles to James, Edinburgh 7 October 1745 OS.
25 There is no letter from Charles filed in the Stuart Papers, Vol. 268 covering 13–30 September 1745 or among the Captured Stuart Papers in the Cumberland Papers under September in CP/MAIN/5.
26 Robert Chambers, *History of the Rebellion in Scotland in 1745, 1746*, 4th edition, 2 vols, Edinburgh, 1830, Vol. 1, p. 214.
27 Boyse, *Impartial History of the Late Rebellion*, p. 83.
28 RA Captured Stuart Papers CP/MAIN/6/269 John Roy Stuart to Allan Ramsay, Holyroodhouse 26 October 1745 OS.
29 The connection was brought to light by Dr Bendor Grosvenor. It has been listed in the family inventory as an Allan Ramsay of the prince since the 1760s.
30 Possibly from this portrait, the local engraver Robert Strange, who joined the prince, took a slightly crude image, which proved extremely popular. Less than three years after the portrait and engraving were completed, Dr John Burton wrote to Robert Forbes, dated York 17 September 1748, saying 'I shall be glad to know in your next whether the picture of the Prince which was drawn by a young man in Edinburgh, and was very like, be yet done on a copper plate. If it be finished, and like the original, pray send me some, with the charge.' The letter in return from Forbes, dated 5 November 1748, states that 'The copper plates you mention were all sold off long before you writ me. One cannot be had for any price.' See *LM*, Vol. 2, p. 320.

Chapter 21: Vilvoorde

1 RA CP/MAIN/5/29 Harrington to Cumberland, Whitehall 4 September 1745 OS.
2 RA CP/MAIN/5/77 Newcastle to Cumberland, Newcastle House 11 September 1745 OS. A copy in the Newcastle Papers 32705 f.135 is dated 4 September 1745 OS.
3 'Horace Walpole to Horace Mann, Arlington Street, 20 September 1745 OS' in Lewis, *Horace Walpole's Correspondence*, Vol. 19, pp. 108–12, p. 109.
4 'Hardwicke to Herring, Powis House, 12 September 1745' in Yorke, *Hardwicke Life and Correspondence*, Vol. 1, pp. 449–50, p. 450.
5 RA CP/MAIN/5/174 Ligonier to Cumberland, London 24 September 1745 OS.
6 RA CP/MAIN/5/179 Harrington to Cumberland, Whitehall 25 September 1745 OS.
7 BL NP Add MS 32705 f. 213–14, f. 213 Newcastle to Cumberland, Newcastle House 25 September 1745 OS.
8 RA CP/MAIN/5/205 Harrington to Robert Trevor, Whitehall 27 September 1745.
9 RA CP/MAIN/5/214 Ligonier to Fawkener, London 27 September 1745 OS [8 October NS].
10 Ibid.

11 Ibid.
12 Yorke, *Hardwicke Life and Correspondence*, Vol. 1, p. 459, London 28 September 1745 OS.
13 'Charles Yorke to Joseph Yorke, Bellbar 30 September 1745 OS', ibid., p. 462.
14 RA CP/MAIN/6/18 Cumberland to Harrington, Vilvoorde 12 October 1745 NS [1 October OS].
15 BL NP Add MS 32705 ff. 248–249 Newcastle to Earl of Chesterfield, Newcastle House 9 October 1745 OS.
16 RA CP/MAIN/6/30 Cumberland to Harrington, Vilvoorde 14 October 1745 NS [3 October OS].
17 RA CP/MAIN/6/58 Cumberland to Harrington, Vilvoorde 18 October 1745 NS [7 October OS].
18 RA CP/MAIN/6/101 Cumberland to Harrington, Vilvoorde 21 October 1745 NS [10 October OS].
19 RA CP/MAIN/6/61 Harrington to Cumberland, Whitehall 8 October 1745 OS [19 October NS].

Chapter 22: South

1   RA Captured Stuart Papers CP/MAIN/6/229 'Warrant sent to Lord Lewis Gordon to apprehend Lord President Duncan Forbes, Holyroodhouse 17 October 1745 OS'.
2   Duffy, *The '45*, p. 214.
3   A full list of attendees is given in Stephen, 'Scottish Nationalism and Stuart Unionism' in *Journal of British Studies*, p. 47, n. 2.
4   Bell, *Murray of Broughton*, p. 231.
5   Lord Elcho, *A Short Account*, p. 304.
6   Bell, *Murray of Broughton*, pp. 231–2; 'Lord Elcho's Diary' in Tayler, *A Jacobite Miscellany*, p. 149.
7   Lord Elcho, *A Short Account*, pp. 301–2.
8   Ibid.
9   Johnstone, *Memoirs of the Rebellion*, pp. 47–52.
10 Ibid., p. 53.
11 'John Macdonald's Account' in Tayler and Tayler, *1745 and After*, pp. 88–9, n. 1.
12 John Roy Stuart described the plan proposed after Prestonpans as an alternative to entering England in 'John Roy Stuart's Account sent to James Edgar, Boulogne [1747]' in Tayler, *Jacobite Epilogue*, pp. 252–5, pp. 253–5. The attitude and aims of the Scottish commanders at this time are summarised in Stephen, 'Scottish Nationalism and Stuart Unionism' in *Journal of British Studies*, pp. 53–6.
13 Lochiel, 'Mémoire d'un Ecossais' in Gibson, *Lochiel of the '45*, p. 178.
14 Lord Elcho, *A Short Account*, p. 304.
15 Ibid., p. 305; Bell, *Murray of Broughton*, p. 233.
16 'John Roy Stuart's Account' in Tayler, *Jacobite Epilogue*, p. 253.
17 'O'Sullivan's Narrative' in Tayler and Tayler, *1745 and After*, p. 88.
18 'Lord Elcho's Diary' in Tayler, *A Jacobite Miscellany*, p. 148.
19 Maxwell of Kirkconnell, *Narrative*, p. 59.
20 Donald Nicholas, ed., *Intercepted Post*, London, 1956, p. 48.
21 'Queries sent to Mr. Patullo . . . Muster-Master of the Rebel Army' in Home, *The History of the Rebellion*, Appendix No. XXX, pp. 329–33, p. 331.
22 'James Murray to Duke James, Foulden 1 November 1745 OS' in Stewart-Murray and Anderson, *Atholl Chronicles*, Vol. 3, p. 83.

23 RA Captured Stuart Papers CP/MAIN/7/379 Charles to Strathallan, Dalkeith 2 November 1745 OS.

24 Paton, 'John Campbell's Diary', p. 558.

25 John Campbell noted under Thursday 14 November, '2000 foot and dragoons enterd the City this evening'; see Paton, 'John Campbell's Diary', p. 559.

Chapter 23: Fontainebleau

1 RA SP/MAIN/255/147 Henry to Charles, Rome 5 February 1744 NS.

2 RA SP/MAIN/266/194 James to Sempill, Rome 11 August 1745 NS.

3 RA SP/MAIN/268/43 James to Ormonde, Rome 20 September 1745 NS.

4 RA SP/MAIN/269/177 Balhady to James, Fontainebleau 19 October 1745 NS.

5 'The Treaty of Fontainebleau' 24 October 1745 (NS) translated in Lenman and Gibson, *The Jacobite Threat*, pp. 208–10, p. 209.

6 RA SP/MAIN/270/89 Henry to James, Bagneux 1 November 1745 NS.

7 RA SP/MAIN/270/142 Balhady to James, Fontainebleau 8 November 1745 NS.

8 RA SP/MAIN/270/143 Clancarty to James, Paris 8 November 1745 NS. Harrington joined Charles after the Prince returned to Paris in 1746, see Bongie, *The Love of a Prince*, p. 192, p. 252.

9 RA SP/MAIN/ 270/187 Graeme to James, Paris 25 November 1745 NS.

10 Quoted in McLynn, *France and the Jacobite Rising*, p. 114.

11 RA SP/MAIN/270/187 Graeme to James, Paris 25 November 1745 NS.

12 NA SP 36/73/3 ff. 74–75, Copy of a letter from Henry to Charles, Bagneux 26 November 1745 NS.

13 John S. Gibson, *Ships of the '45: The Rescue of the Young Pretender*, London, 1967, p. 20, and MacGregor, *A Royalist Family*, pp. 36–8.

14 NA SP 36/73/3 ff. 74–75, Copy of a letter from Henry to Charles, Bagneux 26 November 1745 NS.

15 See McLynn, *France and the Jacobite Rising*, Appendix III, 'Voltaire's manifesto on behalf of Charles Edward Stuart, December 1745' and L. L. Bongie, 'Voltaire's English, high treason and a manifesto for Bonnie Prince Charlie' in *Studies on Voltaire and the eighteenth century*, Vol. 171 (1977), pp. 7–29.

Chapter 24: England

1 For Carlisle Castle see English Heritage Archaeological Report No. 18, *Carlisle Castle: a survey and documentary history*, 1990 and for eighteenth-century Carlisle see Sydney Towill, *A History of Carlisle*, Chichester, 1991, pp. 63–9.

2 Jonathan Oates, *The Jacobite Campaigns: The British State at War*, London and New York, 2011, p. 102.

3 NA SP 36/67/2 f. 54 Lonsdale to Newcastle, Byram 9 September 1745 OS.

4 'Dr Waugh's Narrative' in George Gill Mounsey, ed., *Authentic Account of the Occupation of Carlisle in 1745 by Prince Charles Edward Stuart*, London, 1846, pp. 57–70, p. 58.

5 'Proceedings of the General Court Martial, held for the Trial of Lieutenant Colonel James Durrand, The 15th and 16th September, 1746' in Mounsey, *Carlisle*, pp. 71–5, p. 72.

6 The gates were named after the countries towards which each faced.

7 'Waugh to Bettesworth, Carlisle 17 October 1745' in Mounsey, *Carlisle*, pp. 33–4.

8 'Waugh to Bettesworth, Carlisle 2 November 1745' in Mounsey, *Carlisle*, p. 35.

9 'Intelligence received by John Waugh from Scotland' in Mounsey, *Carlisle*, pp. 36–8, p. 38.

10 'Provost of Dumfries to Waugh, Dumfries 5 November 1745, 8 at Night' in Mounsey, *Carlisle*, pp. 39–40, p. 39.

11 'Waugh to Bettesworth n.d.' in Mounsey, *Carlisle*, p. 40.

12 Johnstone, *Memoirs of the Rebellion*, p. 55.

13 'O'Sullivan's Narrative' in Tayler and Tayler, *1745 and After*, p. 92.

14 Bell, *Murray of Broughton*, p. 238.

15 'A Journall of the Travells and Marches of John Maclean in his Highness's Army 1745' transcribed in Iain Gordon Brown and Hugh Cheape, *Witness to Rebellion: John Maclean's Journal of the 'Forty-Five and the Penicuik drawings*, East Linton, 1996, pp. 21–40, p. 23.

16 Johnstone, *Memoirs of the Rebellion*, p. 56.

17 Bell, *Murray of Broughton*, p. 239.

18 J. A. Wheatley, *Bonnie Prince Charlie in Cumberland*, Carlisle, 1903, p. 14.

19 'O'Sullivan's Narrative' in Tayler and Tayler, *1745 and After*, p. 95.

20 Ibid., pp. 95–6.

21 Ibid., p. 95. This anecdote is repeated in Bell, *Murray of Broughton*, p. 239.

22 *Westminster Journal or New Weekly Miscellany*, Saturday 5 October 1745, p. 2.

23 'O'Sullivan's Narrative' in Tayler and Tayler, *1745 and After*, p. 96.

24 Ibid., p. 92.

25 Ibid.

26 Ibid.

27 Ibid., pp. 92–3.

28 NA SP 36/73/3 f. 40 Charles to the Mayor of Carlisle, 'Two in the afternoon' 10 November 1745 OS.

29 'O'Sullivan's Narrative' in Tayler and Tayler, *1745 and After*, p. 93.

30 Bell, *Murray of Broughton*, p. 240.

31 'O'Sullivan's Narrative' in Tayler and Tayler, *1745 and After*, p. 93.

32 NA SP 36/73/2 f. 94. This is how Peter Pattinson recalled the wording of the letter 'thinking Himself obliged to declare the Contents of it to Lord Barrymore'. SP 36/73/2 f. 95 is another version, incomplete, in faded pencil on a small piece of paper and with more erratic spelling e.g. 'stright', 'disine'. In other quoted versions 'Cheshire' is replaced with 'Lancashire' and 'now or for ever' with 'now or never'; see Rupert C. Jarvis, *Collected Papers on the Jacobite Risings*, 2 vols, Manchester, Vol. 2, p. 85 and Frank McLynn, *The Jacobite Army in England 1745*, Edinburgh, 1998, pp. 38–9.

33 'O'Sullivan's Narrative' in Tayler and Tayler, *1745 and After*, p. 93.

34 Ibid.

35 NA SP 36/73/3 f. 39 Pattinson to Lonsdale, Carlisle 12 November 1745 OS.

36 NA SP 36/73/3 f. 85 Newcastle to Pattinson, Whitehall 15 November 1745 OS.

37 Ibid.

38 Bell, *Murray of Broughton*, p. 240.

39 'Lord George to Tullibardine, Harbery "four of the morning" 14 November 1745 OS' in Stewart-Murray and Anderson, *Atholl Chronicles*, Vol. 3, pp. 89–90, p. 90.

40 'Secretary Murray to Lord George, Brampton 14 November 1745' in Stewart-Murray and Anderson, *Atholl Chronicles*, Vol. 3, p. 91.

41 RA CP/MAIN/7/44 Durrand to Folliot, 18 November 1745 OS.

42 Ibid.

43 Johnstone, *Memoirs of the Rebellion*, p. 58.

44 RA CP/MAIN/7/44 Durrand to Folliot, 18 November 1745 OS.

45 Ibid.

46 Ibid.
47 Ibid.
48 'O'Sullivan's Narrative' in Tayler and Tayler, *1745 and After*, p. 94.
49 RA CP/MAIN/7/44 Durrand to Folliot, 18 November 1745 OS.
50 Ibid.
51 Ibid.
52 Ibid.
53 Quoted in Stewart-Murray and Anderson, *Atholl Chronicles*, Vol. 3, p. 89.
54 RA Captured Stuart Papers CP/MAIN/7/422 Strathallan to Gordon, Perth 23 November 1745 OS.
55 'Lord George to Charles, [Harbery?] 14 November 1745 OS' in Stewart-Murray and Anderson, *Atholl Chronicles*, Vol. 3, p. 91.
56 'O'Sullivan's Narrative' in Tayler and Tayler, *1745 and After*, p. 94.
57 NA SP 36/76/2 ff. 24–5, f. 24 Intercepted letter from Alexander Blair to his wife, Derby 5 December 1745 OS.
58 Mounsey, *Carlisle*, p. 50.
59 Lord George Murray, 'Marches of the Highland Army' in Forbes and Chambers, *Jacobite Memoirs*, pp. 48–9.

Chapter 25: Newcastle upon Tyne

1 NA SP 36/70/1 f. 151 Copy of the message from Charles found in Hixon's glove, 5 October 1745.
2 RA CP/MAIN/6/161 Proclamation by Field Marshal Wade, Newcastle 30 October 1745 OS.
3 RA CP/MAIN/6/160 Wade to Cumberland, Newcastle 31 October 1745 OS.
4 RA CP/MAIN/7/100 Cholmondeley to Fawkener, Chester 23 November 1745 OS.
5 RA CP/MAIN/7/151 Wade to Cholmondeley, Newcastle 23 November 1745 OS.
6 RA CP/MAIN/7/28 Loudoun and Forbes to Wade, Culloden 13 November 1745 OS.

Chapter 26: Lancashire

1 W. Brockbank and F. Kenworthy, eds, *The Diary of Richard Kay, 1716–51 of Baldingstone, near Bury: A Lancashire Doctor*, Manchester, 1968.
2 'Entry for 24 September 1745 OS' in Brockbank and Kenworthy, *The Diary of Richard Kay*, p. 101.
3 'Entry for 25 September 1745 OS', ibid.
4 After the entry for 26 September, the next time Kay mentions the rebellion is in the entry for 21 November, where he notes the arrival of the Jacobite army in Penrith; see ibid., pp. 101–2.
5 BL Add MS 39923 f. 57 Richard Shepherd to John Nourse, Preston 7 October 1745 OS.
6 RA CP/MAIN/7/13 Cholmondeley to Fawkener, Chester 8 November 1745 OS.
7 Ibid.
8 RA CP/MAIN/7/21 Cholmondeley to Fawkener, Chester 11 November 1745 OS.
9 RA CP/MAIN/7/38 Douglas to Cumberland, Chester 18 November 1745 OS.
10 Ibid.

11   NA SP 36/74/1 f. 84 Lord Buttevant's Examination of Pattinson and Newby signed by R Leyster and G Legh, Northwich 19 November 1745 OS. See also NA SP 36/74/1 ff. 79–81 Peter Pattinson's Examination, 10 November 1745 OS.

12   NA SP 36/74/1 f. 84 Lord Buttevant's Examination of Pattinson and Newby.

13   RA CP/MAIN/7/86 Enclosure Mr. Cowper to Mr. Lamb at Brough, Penrith 20 November 1745 OS.

14   RA CP/MAIN/7/88 Enclosure Mr. Cowper to Mr. Lamb at Brough, Penrith midnight 20 November 1745 OS.

15   RA CP/MAIN/7/102 Copy of a letter from Mr. Cowper to the Post Master at Brough.

16   RA CP/MAIN/7/107 Enclosures from P.O. Liverpool to Ligonier, 24 November 1745 OS.

17   RA Captured Stuart Papers CP/MAIN/7/416 Order to the High Constable of Penrith, Penrith 2 November 1745 OS.

18   RA CP/MAIN/7/57 Intelligence from Walter Chambers, Recorder at Kendal, Kendal 21 November 1745 OS.

19   See also McLynn, *The Jacobite Army in England*, p. 61.

20   Nicholas, *Intercepted Post*, pp. 142–3.

21   Ibid.

22   Ray, *A Compleat History of the Rebellion*, p. 138.

23   'A True Account of Mr. John Daniel's Progress with Prince Charles Edward in the Years 1745 and 1746 written by himself' in Blaikie, *Origins of the 'Forty-Five*, pp. 165–224, p. 168.

24   Ibid., p. 169.

25   Ibid.

26   Brown and Cheape, *John Maclean's Journal*, p. 26.

27   Bell, *Murray of Broughton*, pp. 245–6.

28   Lord Elcho, *A Short Account*, p. 327.

29   Bell, *Murray of Broughton*, p. 246.

30   'O'Sullivan's Narrative' in Tayler and Tayler, *1745 and After*, p. 98.

31   Lord Elcho, *A Short Account*, p. 329.

32   Ibid., p. 328.

33   Ibid.

34   Ibid., pp. 328–9.

35   Bell, *Murray of Broughton*, p. 246.

36   *Authentic Copies of the Letters and other Papers delivered, at their Execution, by the Nine REBELS who suffer'd Death on Wednesday, July 30, 1746, on Kennington Common*, London, 1746, p. 8.

37   Henry Fielding, *The True Patriot: and History of Our Own Times*, 10 December 1745, p. 2.

38   'John Macdonald's Account' in Tayler and Tayler, *1745 and After*, p. 98, n. 1.

39   Edward Jeffery, *The history of Preston in Lancashire*, London, 1822, pp. 58–9, n.

40   Johnstone, *Memoirs of the Rebellion*, pp. 63–4.

Chapter 27: Manchester

1   First noted in the publication of 1724–1727 and repeated in every subsequent edition, see Defoe, *A Tour through the Whole Island of Great Britain*, 1748, Vol. 3, p. 243.

2   John Parkinson-Bailey, *Manchester: An architectural history*, Manchester, 2000, pp. 4–5.

3   Maxwell of Kirkconnell, *Narrative*, p. 69.

4 Richard Parkinson, ed., *The Journal of Elizabeth Byrom*, reprinted from Vol. II, Part II of 'Remains of John Byrom', Chetham Society, Manchester, 1857.

5 Ibid., p. 4.

6 Ibid.

7 Ibid.

8 Ibid., pp. 4–5.

9 Ibid., p. 5.

10 Ibid.

11 Ibid., pp. 5–6.

12 Ibid., p. 6.

13 The letter dated 29 November 1745 and quoted in Lord Mahon, *The Forty-Five*, London, 1851, p. 81. A search in NA SP 36/75 for 29 November 1745 did not uncover this letter.

14 J. P. Earwaker, *The Constables' Accounts of the Manor of Manchester*, 3 vols, Manchester, 1892, Vol. 3 (1743–76), p. 21. Under expenses for 26 November. Walley and Fowden were reimbursed £1 and 6 shillings each.

15 'Thomas Walley's diary' quoted in Earwaker, *The Constables' Accounts of the Manor of Manchester*, Vol. 3, pp. 21–22, p. 21, n. 4.

16 Parkinson, *Elizabeth Byrom's Journal*, p. 7.

17 Ibid.

18 'Lord Elcho's Diary' in Tayler, *A Jacobite Miscellany*, p. 150.

19 Parkinson, *Elizabeth Byrom's Journal*, p. 6.

20 Ibid., pp. 7–8.

21 'John Byrom to Mr. Vigor, Manchester 1 March 1745/6 OS' in Richard Parkinson ed., *The private journal and literary remains of John Byrom*, 4 vols (32, 34, 40, 44), Chetham Society, Manchester, 1854–7, Vol. 44, pp. 411–14, p. 411.

22 Johnstone, *Memoirs of the Rebellion*, pp. 64–5.

23 Ibid., pp. 65–6.

24 Lord Elcho, *A Short Account*, pp. 331–2.

25 NA SP 36/75/2 f. 30 dated 28 November 1745; also quoted in Mahon, *The Forty-Five*, p. 81.

26 Ray, *A Compleat History of the Rebellion*, pp. 148–9.

27 *Derby Mercury*, 29 November–13 December 1745, p. 1.

28 *Authentic Copies of the Letters and other Papers delivered, at their Execution, by the Nine REBELS*, p. 18.

29 Ibid., pp. 19–20.

30 Parkinson, *Elizabeth Byrom's Journal*, p. 9.

31 Ibid., pp. 9–10.

32 John Byrom, *Miscellaneous Poems*, 2 vols, Manchester, 1773, Vol. 2, p. 342.

33 'Brief for the defendant in the suit of the King v. William Fowden' in HMRC, *The Manuscripts of Lord Kenyon, Royal Commission on Historical Manuscripts*, 14th Report, Appendix, Part 4, London, 1894, pp. 478–86, p. 480.

34 Ibid.

35 Parkinson, *Elizabeth Byrom's Journal*, p. 10.

36 Lord Elcho, *A Short Account*, p. 330.

37 Beatrice Stott, 'The informations laid against certain townsmen of Manchester in 1746', in *Transactions of the Lancashire & Cheshire Antiquarian Society*, Manchester, 1927, Vol. XLII, pp. 25–52, pp. 30–1.

38 The letter dated 29 November 1745 and quoted in Mahon, *The Forty-Five*, p. 81.

39 'Byrom to Vigor' in Parkinson, *Remains of John Byrom*, Vol. 44, pp. 411–12.
40 Charles Henry Timperley, *Annals of Manchester*, Manchester, 1839, p. 41. It is noted here that the building became known as 'Palace Inn' and later 'Palace Buildings'.
41 RA CP/MAIN/7/180 Intelligence from Manchester, 29 November 1745 OS.
42 John Marchant, *The History of the Present Rebellion*, London, 1746, p. 199.
43 Parkinson, *Elizabeth Byrom's Journal*, pp. 10–11.
44 'John Daniel's Account' in Blaikie, *Origins of the 'Forty-Five*, p. 171.
45 Maxwell of Kirkconnell, *Narrative*, p. 70.
46 Marchant, *The History of the Present Rebellion*, pp. 198–9.
47 'John Macdonald's Account' in Tayler and Tayler, *1745 and After*, p. 98, n. 1.
48 'Brief for the defendant in the suit of the King v. William Fowden' in HMRC, *The Manuscripts of Lord Kenyon*, p. 480.
49 Ibid.
50 Ibid., p. 481.
51 'Byrom to Vigor' in Parkinson, *Remains of John Byrom*, Vol. 44, p. 411.
52 Parkinson, *Elizabeth Byrom's Journal*, p. 11.
53 Lord Elcho, *A Short Account*, 1907, p. 332.
54 James Gib, 'The Prince's Household Accounts' in Chambers and Forbes, *Jacobite Memoirs*, p. 151.
55 Parkinson, *Elizabeth Byrom's Journal*, p. 11.
56 'John Byrom's Memorandum' in Parkinson, *Remains of John Byrom*, Vol. 44, pp. 410–11, p. 410.
57 Parkinson, *Elizabeth Byrom's Journal*, p. 11.
58 Ibid.
59 RA Captured Stuart Papers CP/MAIN/7/444 Order by Prince Charles, Manchester 30 November 1745 OS.
60 Bell, *Murray of Broughton*, p. 247.
61 'Byrom to Vigor' in Parkinson, *Remains of John Byrom*, Vol. 44, p. 412.
62 Marchant, *The History of the Present Rebellion*, p. 199.
63 Parkinson, *Elizabeth Byrom's Journal*, p. 11.
64 Ibid., p. 12.
65 NA SP 36/76/2 ff. 24–5, f. 24 Alexander Blair to his wife, Derby 5 December 1745 OS.
66 'John Daniel's Account' in Blaikie, *Origins of the 'Forty-Five*, p. 171.
67 Alastair Livingstone, Christian Aikman and Betty Stuart Hart, eds, *No Quarter Given: The Muster Roll of Prince Charles Edward Stuart's Army, 1745–46*, Glasgow, 2001, pp. 206–10.
68 Ray, *A Compleat History of the Rebellion*, p. 149.
69 'Lord Elcho's Diary' in Tayler, *A Jacobite Miscellany*, p. 150.
70 'O'Sullivan's Narrative' in Tayler and Tayler, *1745 and After*, p. 99.
71 McLynn, *The Jacobite Army* in *England*, p. 61.
72 'Letter from marquis d'Eguilles to the *minister des affaires étrangères*' in *Revue Rétrospective: Recueil de pièces intéressantes et de citations curieuses*, Paris, 1886, pp. 116–9. D'Eguilles writes p. 119, 'M. Townly, qui aura l'honneur de vous remettre mes dépêches, est l'homme, de ceux qui sont icy auprès du Prince, qui a le plus d'intelligence et de prudence'. Translation quoted from McLynn, *The Jacobite Army in England*, p. 99.
73 RA CP/MAIN/9/16 'List of prisoners . . . at Carlisle', December 1745 OS.
74 'John Daniel's Account' in Blaikie, *Origins of the 'Forty-Five*, p. 174.
75 Maxwell of Kirkconnell, *Narrative*, p. 70.

Chapter 28: Lichfield

1 RA CP/MAIN/7/95 Richmond to Fawkener, Lichfield 23 November 1745 OS.
2 BL NP Add MS 32705 f. 362 Richmond to Newcastle 'To yourself secret' enclosed in ff. 360–361 dated Lichfield, 23 November 1745.
3 RA CP/MAIN/7/112 Derby to Richmond, Knowsley 24 November 1745 OS.
4 Ibid.
5 RA CP/MAIN/7/117 George II 'instructions' to Cumberland, Court of St. James's 25 November 1745 OS.
6 RA CP/MAIN/7/149 Bland to Richmond, Newcastle 27 November 1745 OS.
7 RA CP/MAIN/7/163 Cumberland to Newcastle, Lichfield 28 November 1745 OS.
8 Ibid.
9 RA CP/MAIN/7/164 Cumberland to Newcastle, Lichfield 28 November 1745 OS.
10 RA CP/MAIN/7/189 Wade to Cumberland, Ripon 30 November 1745 OS.
11 BL Add MS 32705 ff. 399–400, Richmond to Newcastle, Lichfield 30 November 1745 OS.
12 RA CP/MAIN/7/240 Rider to Cumberland, Congleton 1 December 1745 OS.
13 Ibid.
14 BL Add MS 32705 Hardwicke to Newcastle, Powis House 1 December 1745 OS, ff. 401–402, f. 401.

Chapter 29: Montrose

1 The whole episode is described in detail by Stuart Reid, *1745: A military history of the last Jacobite rising*, Staplehurst, 1996, pp. 82–3.
2 RA Captured Stuart Papers CP/MAIN/7/454 Lord John Drummond's Declaration, Montrose 2 December 1745 OS.

Chapter 30: Derbyshire

1 *Derby Mercury*, 27 September–4 October 1745, p. 4.
2 Ibid.
3 Quoted in Robert Simpson, *A collection of fragments illustrative of the history and antiquities of Derby*, Derby, 1826, p. 243.
4 Transcribed in Simpson, *History and Antiquities of Derby*, p. 243.
5 'Copy of a letter from a Clergyman near Derby, to his Brother in London, 9 December 1745' in *The Chester Miscellany. Being a collection of several pieces, both in prose and verse, which were in the Chester Courant from January 1745, to May 1750*, Chester, 1750, pp. 65–9, p. 65.
6 Ibid., p. 65.
7 Mahon, *The Forty-Five*, pp. 83–4.
8 Maxwell of Kirkconnell, *Narrative*, p. 71.
9 Lord George Murray, 'Marches of the Highland Army' in Forbes and Chambers, *Jacobite Memoirs*, p. 53.
10 Katherine Thomson, *Memoirs of the Jacobites of 1715 and 1745*, 3 vols, 1845, London, Vol. 3, p. 109.
11 Maxwell of Kirkconnell, *Narrative*, p. 72.

12 Lord Elcho, *A Short Account*, p. 336.
13 *Derby Mercury*, 29 November–13 December 1745, p. 3.
14 Ibid.
15 'Clergyman to his brother, 9 December 1745' in *The Chester Miscellany*, p. 65.
16 *Derby Mercury*, 29 November–13 December 1745, p. 3.
17 Ibid.

Chapter 31: Derby

1   Defoe, *A Tour thro' the Whole Island*, 1742, Vol. 3, p. 67.
2   Defoe, *A Tour thro' the Whole Island*, 1742, Vol. 3, pp. 68–9.
3   John Macky, *A Journey through England. In Familiar Letters from A Gentleman Here to His Friend Abroad*, 2nd Edition, 2 vols, London, 1724, Vol. 2, p. 173.
4   Ibid., p. 172.
5   Ibid.
6   Defoe, *A Tour thro' the Whole Island*, 1742, Vol. 3, p. 67.
7   Brown and Cheape, *John Maclean's Journal*, p. 27.
8   See Thomson, *Memoirs of the Jacobites of 1715 and 1745*, Vol. 3, p. 113.
9   'Hugh Bateman's letter' in W. Hutton, *The History of Derby; from the Remote Ages of Antiquity to the Year 1791*, 2nd edition, London, 1817, pp. 222–7, p. 222.
10 *Derby Mercury*, 29 November–13 December 1745, p. 3.
11 Ibid.
12 Ibid.
13 'Hugh Bateman's letter' in Hutton, *The History of Derby*, p. 222.
14 Ibid., p. 223. See also *Derby Mercury*, 29 November–13 December 1745, p. 3.
15 Thomas Drake, Constable at Derby, quoted in L. Eardley Simpson, *Derby and the Forty-Five*, London, 1933, p. 172.
16 Ibid., quoted in Eardley Simpson, *Derby and the Forty-Five*, p. 172. Eardley Simpson reveals his loyalties by describing the British army as 'the Elector's forces'.
17 'Clergyman to his brother, 9 December 1745' in *The Chester Miscellany*, p. 65.
18 *Derby Mercury*, 29 November–13 December 1745, p. 3.
19 'Hugh Bateman's letter' in Hutton, *The History of Derby*, p. 223.
20 Ibid.
21 *Derby Mercury*, 29 November–13 December 1745, p. 3.
22 'Hugh Bateman's letter' in Hutton, *The History of Derby*, p. 222.
23 Ibid., p. 223.
24 'O'Sullivan's Narrative' in Tayler and Tayler, *1745 and After*, p. 101.
25 Eardley Simpson, *Derby and the Forty-Five*, pp. 123–4.
26 'Hugh Bateman's letter' in Hutton, *The History of Derby*, p. 224.
27 Eardley Simpson, *Derby and the Forty-Five*, p. 147.
28 Thomson, *Memoirs of the Jacobites of 1715 and 1745*, Vol. 3, pp. 279–80.
29 *Derby Mercury*, 29 November–13 December 1745, p. 3.
30 'Hugh Bateman's letter' in Hutton, *The History of Derby*, p. 224.
31 Thomson, *Memoirs of the Jacobites of 1715 and 1745*, pp. 136–7.
32 *Derby Mercury*, 29 November–13 December 1745, p. 3.
33 NA SP 36/76/1 f. 107 Anonymous letter to 'Miss H', Derby 4 December 1745 OS.
34 This is recounted as 'a tradition' by Eardley-Simpson in *Derby and the Forty-Five*, p. 146.

Chapter 32: Stafford

1 RA CP/MAIN/7/262 Fawkener to Newcastle, Stafford 2 December 1745 OS.
2 RA CP/MAIN/7/238 Newcastle to Cumberland, Whitehall 1 December 1745 OS. There is a copy of this letter in SP 36/76/13 but it is incomplete; it ends at 'he shall have been able to make'.
3 RA CP/MAIN/7/287 Cumberland to Newcastle, Stafford 4 December 1745 OS.
4 RA CP/MAIN/7/288 Cumberland to Wade, Stafford 4 December 1745 OS.
5 Finchley Common lay between Finchley, Friern Barnet and Muswell Hill; see www.barnet.gov.uk.
6 RA CP/MAIN/7/287 Cumberland to Newcastle, Stafford 4 December 1745 OS.
7 BL Add MS 32705, ff. 403–404, f. 403 Cumberland to Newcastle, Stafford 4 December 1745 OS.
8 RA CP/MAIN/7/295 Fawkener to Newcastle, Lichfield 5 December 1745 OS.
9 BL NP Add MS 32705 ff. 421–424, Richmond to Newcastle, Coventry 'Fryday afternoon' 7 [6th?] December 1745.
10 Ibid.

Chapter 33: London

1 'Horace Walpole to Horace Mann, Arlington Street, London, 20 September 1745 OS' in Lewis, *Horace Walpole's Correspondence*, Vol. 19, pp. 108–12, pp. 109–10.
2 Frederick Maurice, *History of the Scots Guards*, 2 vols, London, 1934, Vol. 1, p. 133.
3 *General Advertiser*, 28 September 1745.
4 *Daily Advertiser*, 30 September 1745.
5 Percy Scholes, *God Save the Queen!*, Oxford, 1954, p. 7.
6 Slava Klima, Garry Bowers and Kerry S. Grant, eds, *Memoirs of Dr. Charles Burney, 1726–1769*, Lincoln and London, 1988, p. 55.
7 James Boaden, *The private correspondence of David Garrick*, 2nd edition, 2 vols, London, 1835, Vol. 1, p. xv.
8 'William Harris to Mrs James Harris, Grosvenor Square 31 October 1745' in James Howard Harris, *A Series of Letters of the First Earl of Malmesbury, his family and friends from 1745–1820*, London, 2 vols, 1870, Vol. 1, pp. 12–13, p. 13.
9 *St. James's Evening Post*, 31 October–2 November 1745.
10 HRO MP 9M73/G309/9 Thomas Harris to James Harris, Lincoln's Inn, 7 November 1745 OS.
11 'Shaftesbury to James Harris, London 7 November 1745' in Harris, *A Series of Letters of the First Earl of Malmesbury*, Vol. 1, pp. 14–16, p. 14.
12 HRO MP 9M73/G309/10 Thomas Harris to James Harris, Lincoln's Inn n.d.
13 William Coxe, *Memoirs of Horatio, Lord Walpole*, 2 vols, London, 1808, Vol. 2, p. 126.
14 Fielding, *The True Patriot: and History of Our Own Times*, 19 November 1745 OS.
15 HRO MP 9M73/G309/15 Thomas Harris to James Harris, Lincoln's Inn 19 November 1745 OS.
16 HRO MP 9M73/G309/15 Thomas Harris to James Harris, Lincoln's Inn 30 November 1745 OS.
17 'Charles Yorke to Warburton, London 23 November 1745 OS' in Yorke, *Hardwicke Life and Correspondence*, Vol. 1, pp. 466–7.

18 'Charles to Joseph Yorke, London end of November 1745 OS' in Ibid., p. 469.
19 BL NP Add MS 32705 Hardwicke to Newcastle, Powis House, 1 December 1745 OS, ff. 401–402.
20 Maurice, *History of the Scots Guards*, Vol. 1, Appendix VI, pp. 142–3.
21 See Nicholas Rogers, 'Popular Disaffection in London During the Forty-Five' in *The London Journal*, Vol. 1, No. 1, May 1975, pp. 5–27 and Paul Monod, *Jacobitism and the English People, 1688–1788*, Cambridge, 1989, pp. 161–94.
22 Maurice, *History of the Scots Guards*, Appendix VI, pp. 142–3.
23 Duffy, *The '45*, p. 304.
24 'William Harris to Mrs Harris, Grosvenor Square 5 December 1745 OS' in Harris, *A Series of Letters of the First Earl of Malmesbury*, Vol. 1, pp. 19–20.
25 *The Soldier's Companion or Martial Recorder*, London, 1824, pp. 292–3.
26 NA SP 36/76/2 ff. 41–4 Newcastle to Lord Mayor Richard Hoare, Whitehall 6 December 1745 OS.
27 HRO MP 9M73/G309/16 Thomas Harris to James Harris, Lincoln's Inn 7 December 1745 OS.
28 Maurice, *History of the Scots Guards*, Vol. 1, p.132.
29 Fielding, *The True Patriot: and History of Our Own Times*, 10 December 1745, p. 2.
30 F. W. Hamilton, *The origins and history of the First or Grenadier Guards*, 3 vols, London, 1874, Vol. 2, p. 134.

Chapter 34: Exeter House

1 Maxwell of Kirkconnell, *Narrative*, p. 73.
2 Johnstone, *Memoirs of the Rebellion*, p. 67.
3 See also those written by Bartholomew Sandilands and Nathan Ben Saddi, quoted in Eardley Simpson, *Derby and the Forty-Five*, pp. 169–70.
4 NA SP 36/76/2 f. 21 Letter from Peter Ouchterlony to his wife Jeanie, Derby 5 December 1745 OS. Once intercepted, the letter was sent by express to Lichfield, and received by Sir Everard Fawkener on 6 December.
5 NA SP 36/76/2 ff. 24–5 Alexander Blair to his wife, Derby 5 December 1745 OS.
6 *Derby Mercury*, 29 November–13 December 1745, p. 3.
7 'Hugh Bateman's letter' in Hutton, *The History of Derby*, p. 227.
8 *Derby Mercury*, 29 November–13 December 1745, p. 3.
9 'Hugh Bateman's letter' in Hutton, *The History of Derby*, p. 224.
10 Lord George Murray 'March of the Highland Army', in Forbes and Chambers, *Jacobite Memoirs*, p. 76.
11 Brown and Cheape, *John Maclean's Journal*, p. 27.
12 *The Gentleman's Magazine*, Vol. 16, July 1746, p. 337. The prosecution witness at Chadwick's trial, Maddox, refers to this happening at Lancaster.
13 Brown and Cheape, *John Maclean's Journal*, p. 27.
14 'Hugh Bateman's letter' in Hutton, *The History of Derby*, p. 225. Bateman's description is supported by the *Derby Mercury*.
15 Eardley Simpson, *Derby and the Forty-Five*, p. 122.
16 Johnstone, *Memoirs of the Rebellion*, pp. 68–9.
17 Lord Elcho offers a lengthy description, particularly of Lord George's argument for retreat, in *A Short Account*, pp. 336–41.
18 Johnstone, *Memoirs of the Rebellion*, p. 70.

19 See 'John Hay's Account of the Retreat of the Rebels from Derby' in Home, *The History of the Rebellion*, Appendix XXXII, pp. 337–9, p. 338.

20 'Lord Elcho's Diary' in Tayler, *A Jacobite Miscellany*, p.151.

21 Lord Elcho, *A Short Account*, p. 337.

22 Ibid.

23 'Lord Elcho's Diary' in Tayler, *A Jacobite Miscellany*, p. 152.

24 Lord George Murray, 'March of the Highland Army', in Forbes and Chambers, *Jacobite Memoirs*, p. 54.

25 'John Macdonald's Account' in Tayler and Tayler, *1745 and After*, p. 101, n. 1.

26 Lord Elcho, *A Short Account*, p. 339; Johnstone, *Memoirs of the Rebellion*, p. 71.

27 Lord George Murray, 'March of the Highland Army' in Forbes and Chambers, *Jacobite Memoirs*, pp. 54–5.

28 Maxwell of Kirkconnell, *Narrative*, p. 74.

29 Lord George Murray, 'March of the Highland Army' in Forbes and Chambers, *Jacobite Memoirs*, p. 55.

30 See in particular Lord Elcho, *A Short Account*, pp. 340–1.

31 Ibid., p. 340.

32 Johnstone, *Memoirs of the Rebellion*, pp. 70–1.

33 Lord Elcho, *A Short Account*, pp. 340–1.

34 Lord Elcho names the Duke of Perth and Sir William Gordon in *A Short Account*, p. 339, while Secretary Murray is quoted as saying during his examination that everyone except the Duke of Perth was for returning to Scotland, see 'Examination of John Murray of Broughton' in Bell, *Murray of Broughton*, Appendix 9, pp. 422–36, p. 434.

35 Lord George Murray, 'March of the Highland Army' in Forbes and Chambers, *Jacobite Memoirs*, p. 55.

36 Johnstone, *Memoirs of the Rebellion*, p. 71.

37 Lord Elcho, *A Short Account*, p. 340.

38 See 'Examination of John Murray of Broughton' in Bell, *Murray of Broughton*, Appendix 9, p. 434.

39 'Queries sent to Charles at Rome' in Home, *The History of the Rebellion*, Appendix No. XXXIII, pp. 339–40, p. 340.

40 Maxwell of Kirkconnell, *Narrative*, p. 75.

41 'O'Sullivan's Account' in Tayler and Tayler, *1745 and After*, p. 102.

42 Lord Elcho, *A Short Account*, p. 341.

43 Maxwell of Kirkconnell, *Narrative*, p. 75.

44 Lord George Murray, 'March of the Highland Army' in Forbes and Chambers, *Jacobite Memoirs*, pp. 57–8.

45 Ibid., p. 57.

46 'John Macdonald's Account' in Tayler and Tayler, *1745 and After*, p. 102, n. 2.

47 Quoted in McLynn, *The Jacobite Army in England*, pp. 129–30, n. 186 manuscript reference SP Dom 80 ff. 163–4.

48 Lord George Murray, 'March of the Highland Army' in Forbes and Chambers, *Jacobite Memoirs*, p. 58.

49 RA Captured Stuart Papers CP/MAIN/8/197 John Murray to Gordon, Dumfries 22 December 1745 OS.

50 'John Daniel's Account' in Blaikie, *Origins of the 'Forty-Five*, pp. 177–8.

51 Lord Elcho, *A Short Account*, p. 341.

52 *Derby Mercury*, 29 November–13 December 1745, p. 3.

53 Ibid.

54 Ibid.
55 Ibid., pp. 3–4.
56 Lord George Murray, 'The March of the Highland Army' in Forbes and Chambers, *Jacobite Memoirs*, p. 126.
57 'Clergyman to his brother, 9 December 1745' in *The Chester Miscellany*, p. 68.
58 Dudley Bradstreet, *The Life and Uncommon Adventures of Capt. Dudley Bradstreet*, Dublin, 1755, p. 128.
59 'O'Sullivan's Account' in Tayler and Tayler, *1745 and After*, p. 103.
60 *Derby Mercury*, 29 November–13 December 1745, p. 3.
61 'John Hay's Account of the Retreat of the rebels from Derby' in Home, *The History of the Rebellion*, Appendix XXXII, pp. 337–9, pp. 338–9.
62 *Derby Mercury*, 29 November–13 December 1745, p. 3.
63 Johnstone, *Memoirs of the Rebellion*, p. 73.
64 Ray, *A Compleat History of the Rebellion*, p. 172.

Chapter 35: Packington

1 RA CP/MAIN/7/324 Cumberland to Newcastle, Packington 6 December 1745 OS.
2 RA CP/MAIN/7/358 Intelligence from Theo. Levett to Fawkener, Lichfield 6 December 1745 OS.
3 RA CP/MAIN/7/351 Devonshire to Cumberland, Pontefract 8 December 1745 OS.
4 Ibid.
5 RA CP/MAIN/7/352 Furnivall to Cumberland, Congleton Sunday noon, 8 December 1745 OS.
6 RA CP/MAIN/7/357 Enclosure to 356, John Stephenson to Halifax, Stafford 8 December 1745 OS.
7 RA CP/MAIN/7/350 Council of War minutes, Ferrybridge 8 December 1745 OS.
8 RA CP/MAIN/7/346 Cabinet meeting minutes, Whitehall 8 December 1745 OS.
9 RA CP/MAIN/7/369 Cumberland to Newcastle, Lichfield 9 December 1745 OS.
10 RA CP/MAIN/8/6 Cumberland to Newcastle, Macclesfield 11 December 1745 OS.
11 RA CP/MAIN/8/25 Cumberland to Derby and Lonsdale, Macclesfield 12 December 1745 OS.
12 RA CP/MAIN/8/6 Cumberland to Newcastle, Macclesfield 11 December 1745 OS.
13 RA CP/MAIN/8/11 Wade to Cumberland, Leeds 12 December 1745 OS.
14 RA CP/MAIN/8/24 Cumberland to Newcastle, Macclesfield 12 December 1745 OS.
15 RA CP/MAIN/8/17 Lonsdale to Fawkener, Byram midnight 12 December 1745 OS.
16 RA CP/MAIN/8/35 Fawkener to Newcastle, Wigan 14 December 1745 OS.
17 RA CP/MAIN/8/36 enclosed in 8/35 Fawkener to Newcastle, Wigan 14 December 1745 OS.
18 RA CP/MAIN/8/37 Fawkener to Newcastle, Preston begun 14 finished 15 December 1745 OS.
19 NA SP 36/73/2 ff. 101–2 Smalley to Newcastle, Standish misdated 11 November [December] 1745 OS.
20 Bradstreet, *Life and Uncommon Adventures*, p. 127. See also NA SP 36/75/2 f. 50 Letter from Bradstreet to Newcastle, 29 November 1745 OS in which Bradstreet offers his services as a spy; and NA SP 36/76/1 f. 103 Bradstreet to Newcastle, 4 December 1745 OS where he reports on his activities since arriving in Dunstable.
21 NA SP 36/73/2 ff. 101–2 Smalley to Newcastle, Standish misdated 11 November [December] 1745 OS.

22 RA CP/MAIN/8/37 Fawkener to Newcastle, Preston 14–15 December 1745 OS.
23 RA CP/MAIN/8/9 Newcastle to Cumberland, Whitehall 12 December 1745 OS.
24 RA CP/MAIN/8/44 Cumberland to Newcastle, Preston 15 December 1745 OS.
25 McLynn, *France and the Jacobite Rising*, p. 143.
26 RA CP/MAIN/8/19 Pelham to Fawkener, [London?] 12 December 1745 OS.

Chapter 36: Clifton Moor

1 RA CP/MAIN/8/52 Cumberland to Newcastle, Lancaster 17 December 1745 OS.
2 RA CP/MAIN/8/57 Lonsdale to Fawkener, Byram 17 December 1745 OS.
3 RA CP/MAIN/8/80 Cumberland to Newcastle, Penrith 20 December 1745 OS.
4 See Reid, *1745*, pp. 76–8, and Lord George's description 'The March of the Highland Army' in Forbes and Chambers, *Jacobite Memoirs*, pp. 66–72.
5 Lord George Murray, 'The March of the Highland Army' in Forbes and Chambers, *Jacobite Memoirs*, p. 71.
6 RA CP/MAIN/8/80 Cumberland to Newcastle, Penrith 20 December 1745 OS.
7 Ibid. This was reported in the *London Gazette*, 24 December 1745, and *The Gentleman's Magazine*, Vol. 15, December 1745, p. 626.
8 Yorke, *Hardwicke Life and Correspondence*, Vol. 1, p. 486, n.
9 RA CP/MAIN/8/118 Newcastle to Cumberland, Whitehall 25 December 1745 OS. Newcastle states that he is responding to the information in a letter he had received from the Duke of Cumberland dated 20 December.
10 Possibly Francis Gordon of Kincardine Mill and Lieutenant Colonel Sir William Gordon of Park respectively; see Livingstone, Aikman and Stuart Hart, eds, *No Quarter Given*, p. 60 and p. 3.

Chapter 37: Carlisle

1 Maxwell of Kirkconnell, *Narrative*, p. 87.
2 Ibid., pp. 87–8.
3 Lord George Murray, 'The March of the Highland Army' in Forbes and Chambers, *Jacobite Memoirs*, p. 74.
4 Johnstone, *Memoirs of the Rebellion*, pp. 95–7.
5 Home, *The History of the Rebellion*, p. 147.
6 'Lord Elcho's Diary' in Tayler, *A Jacobite Miscellany*, p. 153. Elcho recalled Charles thought Lord George 'made him march too quickly before his enemy'.
7 Maxwell of Kirkconnell, *Narrative*, p. 88.
8 Ibid.
9 *Authentic Copies of the Letters and other Papers delivered, at their Execution, by the Nine REBELS*, London, 1746, pp. 10–11.
10 RA CP/MAIN/8/89 Cumberland to Newcastle, 'Blickhall' near Carlisle 22 December 1745 OS.
11 *Newcastle Courant*, 4–11 January 1746, p. 1. This was dated half past two, Blackhall.
12 *Authentic Copies of the Letters and other Papers delivered, at their Execution, by the Nine REBELS*, pp. 10–11.
13 RA CP/MAIN/8/161 Cumberland to Newcastle, Blackhall 30 December 1745 OS.
14 Ibid.
15 RA CP/MAIN/8/138 Newcastle to Cumberland, Whitehall 28 December 1745 OS.

16 'The Diary of James Miller', *JSAHR*, Vol. 3, No. 14, October 1924, pp. 208–26, p. 209.
17 Maclachlan, *Duke of Cumberland*, pp. 261–2.

Chapter 38: Scotland

1   Lord George Murray, 'March of the Highland Army' in Forbes and Chambers, *Jacobite Memoirs*, p. 75.
2   Johnstone, *Memoirs of the Rebellion*, pp. 99–100.
3   Lord George Murray, 'March of the Highland Army' in Forbes and Chambers, *Jacobite Memoirs*, p. 75.
4   Ibid., p. 76.
5   Johnstone, *Memoirs of the Rebellion*, p. 103.
6   'John Daniel's Account' in Blaikie, *Origins of the 'Forty-Five*, p. 190.
7   Johnstone, *Memoirs of the Rebellion*, pp. 103–4.
8   *The Scots Magazine*, December 1745, pp. 580–1.
9   Chambers, *History of the Rebellion*, p. 207.
10 'John Daniel's Account' in Blaikie, *Origins of the 'Forty-Five*, p. 191.
11 James Gib, 'The Prince's Household Accounts' in Chambers and Forbes, *Jacobite Memoirs*, p. 154.
12 *A Short Account of the Behaviour of the Rebel Army, while at Hamilton, in a Letter to a Friend at Edinburgh*, British Library C.115.i.3(91).
13 Johnstone, *Memoirs of the Rebellion*, p. 108.
14 Burt, *Letters from a Gentleman in the North of Scotland*, Vol. 1, p. 28.
15 John Macky, *A Journey through Scotland*, 2nd edition, London, 1729, p. 291.
16 See Christopher A. Whatley, *Scottish Society, 1707–1830: Beyond Jacobitism, Towards Industrialisation*, Manchester, 2000, pp. 102–4. Through such activity the Glasgow merchants, as elsewhere throughout Great Britain, were connected with the North Atlantic Slave trade.
17 Macky, *A Journey through Scotland*, pp. 294–5.
18 'Memorial stating the Facts relative to the Conduct of the Town of Glasgow during the present Rebellion' in James Dennistoun, ed., *The Cochrane Correspondence regarding the Affairs of Glasgow 1745–6*, Glasgow, 1836, pp. 80–5, p. 83.
19 Maxwell of Kirkconnell, *Narrative*, p. 89.
20 'John Daniel's Account' in Blaikie, *Origins of the 'Forty-Five*, p. 191.
21 Maxwell of Kirkconnell, *Narrative*, p. 90.
22 'Provost Cochrane to Mr. Maule, 4 January 1746 OS' in Dennistoun, *The Cochrane Correspondence*, pp. 65–7, p. 66.
23 Chambers, *History of the Rebellion*, pp. 209–10.
24 *The Gentleman's Magazine*, Vol. 16, January 1746, p. 43.
25 'Provost Cochrane to Mr. Maule, 4 January 1746 OS' in Dennistoun, *The Cochrane Correspondence*, pp. 65–7, p. 66.
26 Wallace Harvey, *Chronicles of Saint Mungo: or, Antiquities and traditions of Glasgow*, Glasgow, 1843, p. 123.
27 James Gib, 'The Prince's Household Account' in Chambers and Forbes, *Jacobite Memoirs*, pp. 154–6.
28 'Provost Cochrane to Mr. Patrick Crawford January 1746 OS' in Dennistoun, *The Cochrane Correspondence*, pp. 62–4, p. 63.
29 'Reasons for Compensation of the Losses sustained by Glasgow during the Rebellion' in Dennistoun, *The Cochrane Correspondence*, pp. 78–80, p. 79.

30 Maxwell of Kirkconnell, *Narrative*, p. 90.

31 'John Daniel's Account' in Blaikie, *Origins of the 'Forty-Five*, p. 191.

32 Ibid., p. 192.

33 Recalled during a conversation between Edward Hazelrigg and an unnamed man (b. 1733) in *The Attic Stories or the Opinions of Edward Hazelrig*, Glasgow, 1818, p. 290.

34 Lord Elcho, *A Short Account*, pp. 355–6.

35 'Copy of the Accompts of James Gib' in *LM*, Vol. 2, p. 125.

36 'Provost Cochrane to Mr. Maule, 4 January 1746 OS' in Dennistoun, *The Cochrane Correspondence*, pp. 65–7, p. 66.

37 Ibid., p. 67.

38 Maxwell of Kirkconnell, *Narrative*, p. 91.

39 'John Daniel's Account' in Blaikie, *Origins of the 'Forty-Five*, pp. 193–4.

40 Maxwell of Kirkconnell, *Narrative*, p. 91.

41 See Duffy, *The '45*, pp. 356–62.

42 Maxwell of Kirkconnell, *Narrative*, p. 91.

43 *The Scots Magazine*, December 1745, p. 590.

Chapter 39: Falkirk

1 Johnstone, *Memoirs of the Rebellion*, pp. 108–9.

2 Ibid., p. 109.

3 Presumably from Alloa; there is no location on the letter.

4 RA Captured Stuart Papers CP/MAIN/9/170 John Drummond to Roy Stuart, [no location] 5 January 1745/6 OS.

5 Johnstone, *Memoirs of the Rebellion*, p. 109.

6 Ibid., p. 110.

7 RA Captured Stuart Papers CP/MAIN/9/210 Lord George Murray to O'Sullivan, Falkirk 13 January 1745/6 OS.

8 RA CP/MAIN/7/286 Extract of a letter from Marshal Wade to Newcastle, [no location] 5 December 1745 OS.

9 Johnstone, *Memoirs of the Rebellion*, pp. 110–11.

10 Lord George Murray, 'March of the Highland Army' in Forbes and Chambers, *Jacobite Memoirs*, p. 96.

11 RA Captured Stuart Papers CP/MAIN/9/210 Lord George Murray to O'Sullivan, Falkirk 13 January 1745/6 OS.

12 Clementina would become Charles' mistress from 1752 to 1760. Their only child was Charlotte, Duchess of Albany in the Jacobite Peerage, 1753–1789.

13 Johnstone, *Memoirs of the Rebellion*, pp. 110–11.

14 Maxwell of Kirkconnell, *Narrative*, p. 98.

15 Ibid.

16 Lord George Murray, 'March of the Highland Army' in Forbes and Chambers, *Jacobite Memoirs*, p. 80.

17 Maxwell of Kirkconnell, *Narrative*, p. 99.

18 'Queries sent to Mr. Patullo' in Home, *The History of the Rebellion*, Appendix No. XXX, p. 332.

19 Maxwell of Kirkconnell, *Narrative*, p. 100.

20 Home, *The History of the Rebellion*, p. 166.

21 Ibid.

22 Ibid., p. 167.

23 Ibid., p. 176 and p. 176, n.

24 Ibid., p. 177.

25 Reid, *1745*, p. 99.

26 Home, *The History of the Rebellion*, p. 167.

27 Lord George Murray, 'March of the Highland Army' in Forbes and Chambers, *Jacobite Memoirs*, p. 83.

28 Home, *The History of the Rebellion*, p. 167.

29 Alexander MacNab (a captain in Keppoch's Regiment), 'A Vindication of the Conduct of Lord George Murray, 19 March 1795' in Stewart-Murray and Anderson, *Atholl Chronicles*, Vol. 3, p. 153.

30 Reid, *1745*, p. 101, n. 17.

31 RA CP/MAIN/9/110 Captain George Fitzgerald's Account of Falkirk, 18 January 1745/6 OS. The manuscript, or part of it, must be later because he describes the blast at St. Ninian's.

32 'O'Sullivan's Narrative' in Tayler and Tayler, *1745 and After*, p. 118.

33 Lord George Murray, 'March of the Highland Army' in Forbes and Chambers, *Jacobite Memoirs*, pp. 86–7.

34 Home, *The History of the Rebellion*, p. 173.

35 Ibid., p. 174.

36 Reid, *1745*, p. 102, n. 20.

37 Home, *The History of the Rebellion*, p. 175.

38 RA CP/MAIN/9/99 Hawley to Cumberland, Linlithgow 17 January 1745/6 OS.

39 Home, *The History of the Rebellion*, p. 177.

40 'Letter from Sir Harry Monro to Lord President Forbes, Edinburgh 22 January 1745/6 OS' in Duff, *Culloden Papers*, No. 311, pp. 267–8.

41 Johnstone, *Memoirs of the Rebellion*, p. 125.

42 RA Captured Stuart Papers CP/MAIN/9/267 A short narrative of the Battle of Falkirk, Bannockburn 17 January 1745/6 OS.

43 Ibid.

44 Lord George Murray, 'March of the Highland Army' in Forbes and Chambers, *Jacobite Memoirs*, pp. 88–9.

45 Ibid., p. 89.

46 'Narrative by John Lord Macleod, 1745–6' in William Fraser, *The Earls of Cromartie, their Kindred, Country and Correspondence*, 2 vols, Edinburgh, 1874, Vol. II, pp. 379–98, p. 393.

47 'Lord Macleod's Narrative' in Fraser, *The Earls of Cromartie*, Vol. II, p. 392.

48 Home, *The History of the Rebellion*, p. 179.

49 'Lord George to Tullibardine, Falkirk 18 January 1745/6 OS' in Stewart-Murray and Anderson, *Atholl Chronicles*, Vol. 3, p. 158.

50 Lord Elcho, *A Short Account*, pp. 380–1.

51 'Donald MacDonell of Lochgarry's narrative' in Blaikie, *Itinerary of Prince Charles Edward Stuart*, p. 74.

52 RA Captured Stuart Papers CP/MAIN/9/245 George Colville [to ?], Blair Castle 19 January 1745/6 OS.

53 Home, *The History of the Rebellion*, p. 179.

Chapter 40: Stirling

1 RA CP/MAIN/9/16 Howard to Fawkener, Carlisle 27 January 1745/6 OS.
2 'Horace Walpole to Horace Mann, Arlington Street, London, 28 January 1745/6 OS' in Lewis, *Horace Walpole's Correspondence*, Vol. 19, pp. 203–5, p. 204.
3 RA CP/MAIN/9/115 Hawley to Cumberland, Edinburgh 19 January 1745/6 OS.
4 RA CP/MAIN/9/141 Cumberland to Hawley, St. James's Palace 23 January 1745/6 OS.
5 Ibid.
6 Lord Elcho, *A Short Account*, p. 382.
7 Translation in Gibson, *Ships of the '45*, pp. 22–3. Original in French, Bell, *Murray of Broughton*, p. 515.
8 RA SP/MAIN/272/84 Sheridan to Colonel O'Brien, Bannockburn 21 January 1745/6.
9 Gibson, *Ships of the '45*, p. 23.
10 RA CP/MAIN/10/18 Hawley to Cumberland, Edinburgh 28 January 1745/6 OS.
11 Reid, *1745*, p. 104.
12 RA CP/MAIN/10/18 Hawley to Cumberland, Edinburgh 28 January 1745/6 OS.
13 Henderson, *History of the Rebellion*, 1748, p. 98.
14 RA CP/MAIN/10/28 Cumberland to Newcastle, Holyroodhouse 30 January 1745/6 OS.
15 Reid, *1745*, pp. 103–4 and *The Last Speech and dying Words of Henry MacManus*, 23 January 1745/6 OS, British Library C.115.i.3.(79).
16 Henderson, *History of the Rebellion*, 1748, pp. 98–9.
17 'Charles to Lord George, Bannockburn 24 January 1745/6 OS' in Stewart-Murray and Anderson, *Atholl Chronicles*, Vol. 3, p. 165.
18 'Lord George to Tullibardine, Falkirk 27 January 1745/6 OS' in Stewart-Murray and Anderson, *Atholl Chronicles*, Vol. 3, p. 167.
19 'Charles to Tullibardine, Bannockburn 28 January 1745/6 OS' in Stewart-Murray and Anderson, *Atholl Chronicles*, Vol. 3, p. 167.
20 'John Hay's Account of the Retreat from Stirling' in Home, *The History of the Rebellion*, Appendix No. XL, pp. 355–6, p. 355.
21 Lord George Murray, 'March of the Highland Army' in Forbes and Chambers, *Jacobite Memoirs*, p. 96.
22 Ibid., p. 99.
23 'Address from the Chiefs to Charles, after the Battle of Falkirk' in Home, *The History of the Rebellion*, Appendix No. XXXIX, pp. 352–4, p. 353.
24 Ibid., p. 354.
25 'O'Sullivan's Narrative' in Tayler and Tayler, *1745 and After*, pp. 122–3.
26 'John Hay's Account of the Retreat from Stirling' in Home, *The History of the Rebellion*, p. 355.
27 'Letter from the Prince to the Chiefs, Bannockburn 30 January 1745/6' in Blaikie, *Itinerary of Prince Charles Edward Stuart*, pp. 76–7 and the subsequent letter 'The Prince to the Chiefs' in ibid., pp. 78–9.
28 Ibid.
29 Maxwell of Kirkconnell, *Narrative*, p. 114.

30 Lord George Murray, 'March of the Highland Army' in Forbes and Chambers, *Jacobite Memoirs*, p. 99.
31 Ibid., p. 100.
32 Maxwell of Kirkconnell, *Narrative*, p. 114.
33 Lord George Murray, 'March of the Highland Army' in Forbes and Chambers, *Jacobite Memoirs*, p. 100.
34 Maxwell of Kirkconnell, *Narrative*, p. 114.
35 Ibid., p. 115.
36 Ibid.
37 RA CP/MAIN/69/XI.41.18 'Journal of the Young Pretender, Before, at, and after the Battle of Culloden. 1746. Copied from the Manuscript, found among the Papers of Mrs. Cameron, Wife of Doctor Cameron, when she was taken up at Breda, in her way to Paris, in January 1748.' See also 'John Cameron's Journal' in *LM*, Vol. 1, p. 86.
38 RA CP/MAIN/9/110 Captain George Fitzgerald's Account of Falkirk, 18 January 1745/6 OS.
39 Lord George Murray, 'March of the Highland Army' in Forbes and Chambers, *Jacobite Memoirs*, p. 100.
40 Ibid., p. 99, n.
41 Maxwell of Kirkconnell, *Narrative*, p. 115.
42 Ibid., pp. 115–16.
43 Ibid., p. 116.
44 Lord George Murray, 'March of the Highland Army' in Forbes and Chambers, *Jacobite Memoirs*, p. 100.
45 Maxwell of Kirkconnell, *Narrative*, p. 116.
46 MacDonald, 'Journall and Memoirs' in *The Lockhart Papers*, Vol. 2, p. 504.
47 Lord George Murray, 'March of the Highland Army' in Forbes and Chambers, *Jacobite Memoirs*, p. 101.
48 Lord George Murray, 'March of the Highland Army' in Forbes and Chambers, *Jacobite Memoirs*, p. 101.
49 RA Captured Stuart Papers CP/MAIN/10/370 Lord George Murray to 'The Grants', Strathbogie 12 February 1745/6 OS.
50 Lord George Murray, 'March of the Highland Army' in Forbes and Chambers, *Jacobite Memoirs*, p. 103.

Chapter 41: Perth

1   RA CP/MAIN/10/37 Cumberland to Newcastle, Falkirk 1 February 1745/6 OS.
2   RA CP/MAIN/10/43 Cumberland to Newcastle, Stirling 2 February 1745/6 OS.
3   RA CP/MAIN/10/74 Cumberland to Newcastle, Crieff 5 February 1745/6 OS.
4   RA CP/MAIN/10/168 Cumberland to Newcastle, Perth 10 February 1745/6 OS.
5   I am grateful to Jonathan Oates for his thoughts on this subject.
6   RA CP/MAIN/10/168 Cumberland to Newcastle, Perth 10 February 1745/6 OS.
7   Thomas White to Charles Whitefoord 'att his Lodging Edenbrowgh', Chatham 6 February 1745/6 in Hewins, *The Whitefoord Papers*, pp. 69–70, p. 69.
8   'State of the prisoners who were brought over to Ed[inbu[r]gh the 19[th] and 21[st] January 1746' in Hewins, *The Whitefoord Papers*, pp. 68–9.
9   Plank, *Rebellion and Savagery*, p. 44.
10 Gray, *Memoirs of the Life of Sir John Clerk*, p. 198.
11 RA CP/MAIN/10/266 Captain Alexander Campbell to Fawkener, Fort William 17 February 1745/6 OS.

12 Reid, *1745*, p. 105.
13 RA CP/MAIN/10/293 Fawkener to Newcastle, Perth 19 February 1745/6 OS.
14 See Thompson, *George II*, pp. 169–71
15 RA CP/MAIN/10/293 Fawkener to Newcastle, Perth 19 February 1745/6 OS.
16 RA CP/MAIN/11/5 Archibald Campbell to [General John Campbell?], Inveraray
    10 a.m. 20 February 1745/6 OS.

Chapter 42: Moy Hall

1 Maxwell of Kirkconnell, *Narrative*, p. 117.
2 'Copy of the Accompts of James Gib' in *LM*, Vol. 2, p. 137.
3 'Malcolm MacLeod's Account' in *LM*, Vol.1, pp.130–154, p. 149.
4 Ibid. James Maxwell of Kirkconnell states that it was six MacDonalds see *Narrative*,
   p. 117.
5 'Malcom MacLeod's Account' in *LM*, Vol. 1, p. 149.
6 'Copy of the Accompts of James Gib' in *LM*, Vol. 2, p. 136.
7 Quoted in Lord George Murray, 'March of the Highland Army' in Forbes and
   Chambers, *Jacobite Memoirs*, p.103, n.
8 Ibid., p.102, n.
9 'Copy of the Accompts of James Gib' in *LM*, Vol. 2, pp. 135–6.
10 Quoted in Lord George Murray, 'March of the Highland Army' in Forbes and
    Chambers, *Jacobite Memoirs*, pp. 102–3, n.
11 Ibid., p. 103, n.
12 'Malcom MacLeod's Account' in *LM*, Vol. 1, p. 149; 'Copy of the Accompts of James
    Gib' in *LM*, Vol. 2, p. 134, p. 245.
13 Maxwell of Kirkconnell, *Narrative*, p. 118.
14 'Malcom MacLeod's Account' in *LM*, Vol. 1, pp. 150–51.
15 Duffy, *The '45*, pp. 446–7.
16 Burt, *Letters from a Gentleman in the North of Scotland*, Vol. 1, p. 40.
17 Ibid., p. 47.
18 Ibid., p. 60
19 Ibid., p. 64.
20 George and Peter Anderson, *Guide to the Highlands and Islands*, Edinburgh, 1842, p. 91.
21 Brown and Cheape, *John Maclean's Journal*, p. 34.
22 A section of these tartan hangings was purchased for Culloden House from Bonham's
    Moy Hall Collection Sale in 2008 and are now displayed in the entrance hall of
    Culloden House (now a hotel).
23 Lord George Murray, 'March of the Highland Army' in Forbes and Chambers, *Jacobite
    Memoirs*, pp. 103–4.
24 Maxwell of Kirkconnell, *Narrative*, p. 121; Alexander MacDonald's 'Journall and
    Memoirs' in *The Lockhart Papers*, Vol. 2, p. 506.
25 *London Gazette*, 25 February–1 March 1746.
26 Alexander MacDonald's 'Journall and Memoirs' in *The Lockhart Papers*, Vol. 2, p. 506.

Chapter 43: Aberdeen

1 Reid, *1745*, p. 121.
2 RA CP/MAIN/12/198 Cumberland to Newcastle, Aberdeen 19 March 1745/6 OS.

3   RA CP/MAIN/13/25 Intelligence from several hands, Strathbogie 28 March 1746 OS.
4   RA CP/MAIN/13/88 Cumberland to Newcastle, Aberdeen 31 March 1746 OS.
5   Ibid.
6   RA CP/MAIN/13/104 Lafausille to Napier, Cortachy 1 April 1746 OS.
7   National War Museum of Scotland 355.486.242.34 (1746), Cholmondeley's Orderly Book (34th Regiment of Foot) entry for Aberdeen 26 March 1746 OS. My thanks to Darren Layne for drawing my attention to this document.
8   Maclachlan, *Duke of Cumberland*, p. 279.
9   RA CP/MAIN/13/129 Albemarle to Napier, Strathbogie 3 April 1746 OS.
10 RA CP/MAIN/13/149 Albemarle to Napier, Strathbogie 4 April 1746 OS.
11 National War Museum of Scotland Cholmondeley's Orderly Book, entry for Strathbogie 7 April 1746 OS.
12 Ray, *A Compleat History of the Rebellion*, p. 335.

Chapter 44: Inverness

1   Maxwell of Kirkconnell, *Narrative*, p. 118.
2   'Copy of Accompts of James Gib' in *LM*, Vol. 2, p. 139.
3   'O'Sullivan's Narrative' in Tayler and Tayler, *1745 and After*, p. 145.
4   Ibid., p. 146.
5   'Copy of Accompts of James Gib' in *LM*, Vol. 2, p. 138.
6   RA CP/MAIN/12/198 Cumberland to Newcastle, Aberdeen 19 March 1745/6.
7   RA CP/MAIN/13/112 Gordon to Fawkener, Haddo House 2 April 1746.
8   'O'Sullivan's Narrative' in Tayler and Tayler, *1745 and After*, p. 146.
9   'Lord Elcho's Diary' in Tayler, *A Jacobite Miscellany*, p. 159.
10 'O'Sullivan's Narrative' in Tayler and Tayler, *1745 and After*, p. 147.
11 Ibid.
12 Lord George Murray 'Marches of the Highland Army' in and Forbes Chambers, *Jacobite Memoirs*, p. 129.
13 James Dennistoun, *Memoirs of Sir Robert Strange and Andrew Lumisden*, 2 vols, London, 1855, Vol. 1, pp. 50–1.
14 Ibid., p. 53.
15 'Lord Elcho's Diary' in Tayler, *A Jacobite Miscellany*, p. 159.
16 RA CP/MAIN/69/XI.41.18 'Journal of the Young Pretender'.
17 Ibid.
18 Lord George Murray 'March of the Highland Army' in and Forbes and Chambers, *Jacobite Memoirs*, p. 108.
19 Maxwell of Kirkconnell, *Narrative*, p. 119.
20 Ibid., p. 121.
21 Ibid., pp. 135–6.
22 Ibid., p. 136.
23 Ibid.

Chapter 45: The Spey

1   Ray, *A Compleat History of the Rebellion*, pp. 335–6.
2   Ibid., p. 337.
3   Ibid., p. 338.

4   Ibid., p. 339.
5   Ibid., p. 340.
6   RA CP/MAIN/13/294 Cumberland to Newcastle, Nairn 15 April 1746 OS.
7   Johnstone, *Memoirs of the Rebellion*, pp. 168–9.
8   Alexander MacDonald's 'Journall and Memoirs' in *The Lockhart Papers*, Vol. 2, pp. 506–7.
9   'O'Sullivan's Narrative' in Tayler and Tayler, *1745 and After*, pp. 148–9.
10 Ibid., p. 149.
11 Ibid., pp. 149–50.
12 Alexander MacDonald's 'Journall and Memoirs' in *The Lockhart Papers*, Vol. 2, p. 507.
13 RA CP/MAIN/13/279 Cumberland to Newcastle, 'Spey Mouth' 13 April 1746 OS.
14 Ray, *A Compleat History of the Rebellion*, pp. 342–3.
15 RA CP/MAIN/13/279 Cumberland to Newcastle, 'Spey Mouth' 13 April 1746 OS.
16 Ibid.
17 Ray, *A Compleat History of the Rebellion*, pp. 343–4.
18 Marchant, *The History of the Present Rebellion*, p. 375.
19 RA CP/MAIN/13/279 Cumberland to Newcastle, 'Spey Mouth' 13 April 1746 OS.

Chapter 46: Culloden

1   RA Captured Stuart Papers CP/MAIN/13/404 Orders from the 14th to the 15th Ap.[l] 1748 in Lord George Murray's hand. There is also an order of battle dated 15 April 1746 RA Captured Stuart Papers CP/MAIN/13/406.
2   Johnstone, *Memoirs of the Rebellion*, p. 169.
3   Dennistoun, *Memoirs of Robert Strange*, Vol. 1, p. 55.
4   Colonel Henry Ker of 'Gradyne' or Graden, 'Battle of Culloden' in Forbes and Chambers, *Jacobite Memoirs*, pp. 131–44, pp. 137–8.
5   Lord Elcho, *A Short Account*, p. 422.
6   'John Daniel's Account' in Blaikie, *Origins of the 'Forty-Five*, p. 210.
7   'Lord Elcho's Diary' in Tayler, *A Jacobite Miscellany*, p. 161.
8   Stuart Reid calculates there were about 5,000 men on 15 April, prior to the night march, see Reid, *1745*, p. 132.
9   Ibid., p. 129.
10 'Lord Elcho's Diary' in Tayler, *A Jacobite Miscellany*, p. 161.
11 Lord George Murray, 'March of the Highland Army' in Forbes and Chambers, *Jacobite Memoirs*, pp. 120–1.
12 'O'Sullivan's Narrative' in Tayler and Tayler, *1745 and After*, p. 153.
13 Lord Elcho, *A Short Account*, p. 423.
14 Lord George Murray, 'March of the Highland Army' in Forbes and Chambers, *Jacobite Memoirs*, p. 121.
15 'Copy of a letter from Lord George Murray to William Hamilton, Emmerick, 5 August 1749 [NS?]' in Home, *The History of the Rebellion*, Appendix No. XLII, p. 362.
16 'O'Sullivan's Narrative' in Tayler and Tayler, *1745 and After*, pp. 151–2.
17 'Lord George Murray to William Hamilton' in Home, *The History of the Rebellion*, Appendix No. XLII, p. 362.
18 'O'Sullivan's Narrative' in Tayler and Tayler, *1745 and After*, p. 153.
19 Henry Ker, 'Battle of Culloden' in Forbes and Chambers, *Jacobite Memoirs*, p. 138.
20 'Lord George Murray to William Hamilton' in Home, *The History of the Rebellion*, Appendix No. XLII, pp. 362–3.

21 'Donald MacDonell of Lochgarry's narrative' in Blaikie, *Itinerary of Prince Charles Edward Stuart*, 1897, pp. 120–1.
22 'John Macdonald's Account' in Tayler and Tayler, *1745 and After*, p. 161, n. 1.
23 Lord Elcho, *A Short Account*, p. 426.
24 'O'Sullivan's Narrative' in Tayler and Tayler, *1745 and After*, p. 154.
25 'Lord George Murray to William Hamilton' in Home, *The History of the Rebellion*, Appendix No. XLII, p. 361.
26 Lord George Murray, 'March of the Highland Army' in Forbes and Chambers, *Jacobite Memoirs*, p. 121.
27 Ibid., p. 130.
28 Lord Elcho, *A Short Account*, p. 426.
29 'Lord George Murray to William Hamilton' in Home, *The History of the Rebellion*, Appendix No. XLII, p. 363.
30 Lord Elcho, *A Short Account*, p. 427.
31 Ibid.
32 RA CP/MAIN/69/XI.41.18 'Journal of the Young Pretender'.
33 'O'Sullivan's Narrative' in Tayler and Tayler, *1745 and After*, p. 155.
34 Ibid.
35 'Lord George Murray to William Hamilton' in Home, *The History of the Rebellion*, Appendix No. XLII, pp. 363–4.
36 Lord George Murray, 'March of the Highland Army' in Forbes and Chambers, *Jacobite Memoirs*, p. 122.
37 Ibid., p. 129.
38 'Lord Elcho's Diary' in Tayler, *A Jacobite Miscellany*, p. 162.
39 RA Captured Stuart Papers CP/MAIN/13/404.
40 RA Captured Stuart Papers CP/MAIN/13/405. The line is inserted between 'pursuite be finally over' and 'This regards the Foot'.
41 RA CP/MAIN/69/XI.41.18 'Journal of the Young Pretender'.
42 'John Daniel's Account' in Blaikie, *Origins of the 'Forty-Five*, pp. 210–11.
43 Alexander MacDonald's 'Journall and Memoirs' in *The Lockhart Papers*, Vol. 2, p. 508.
44 This document and the issue of the Jacobite army ordering that 'no quarter' should be given to the British army remain highly contentious; see Speck, *The Butcher*, 1981 and 1995, pp. 148–55. Speck's suggestion that the order now in the Cumberland Papers related to the night attack is followed here, as also by Jonathan Oates in *Sweet William or The Butcher?*

Chapter 47: Nairn

1 RA CP/MAIN/13/294 Cumberland to Newcastle, Nairn 15 April 1746 OS.
2 RA CP/MAIN/13/295 Cumberland to Newcastle, Nairn 15 April 1746 OS.
3 Michael Hughes, *A Plain Narrative and Authentic Journal of the late Rebellion*, 2nd edition, London, 1747, pp. 34–5.
4 Ibid, p. 35.
5 RA CP/MAIN/14/12 Newcastle to Cumberland, Whitehall 17 April 1746 OS.

Chapter 48: Culloden to Nairn

1 'O'Sullivan's Narrative' in Tayler and Tayler, *1745 and After*, pp. 155–6.
2 'Lord George Murray to William Hamilton' in Home, *The History of the Rebellion*, Appendix No. XLII, p. 364.

3 'O'Sullivan's Narrative' in Tayler and Tayler, *1745 and After*, p. 156.

4 RA CP/MAIN/69/XI.41.18 'Journal of the Young Pretender'.

5 'John Daniel's Account' in Blaikie, *Origins of the 'Forty-Five*, p. 211.

6 RA CP/MAIN/69/XI.41.18 'Journal of the Young Pretender'.

7 Lord Elcho, *A Short Account*, p. 428.

8 'A genuine and full Account of the Battle of Culloden . . . together with the young Prince's miraculous escape . . . from the mouths of the old Laird of MacKinnon, Mr. Malcolm MacLeod, etc' in *LM*, Vol. 1, pp. 66–7.

9 'O'Sullivan's Narrative' in Tayler and Tayler, *1745 and After*, p. 156.

10 Ibid., pp. 157–8.

11 'Lord George Murray to William Hamilton' in Home, *The History of the Rebellion*, Appendix No. XLII, p. 366.

12 Dennistoun, *Memoirs of Robert Strange*, Vol. 1, p. 58.

13 Ibid., p. 59.

14 'A genuine and full Account of the Battle of Culloden' in *LM*, Vol. 1, p. 67.

15 Lord Elcho, *A Short Account*, pp. 428–9.

16 'Lord Elcho's Diary' in Tayler, *A Jacobite Miscellany*, p. 160.

17 Maxwell of Kirkconnell, *Narrative*, p. 146.

18 Ibid., pp. 146–7.

19 Ibid., pp. 147–8.

20 'Extract from the marquis d'Eguilles' official report' translated in Blaikie, *Origins of the 'Forty-Five*, pp. lxviii–lxix.

21 Lord Elcho, *A Short Account*, p. 429.

22 Maxwell of Kirkconnell, *Narrative*, p. 148.

23 'John Daniel's Account' in Blaikie, *Origins of the 'Forty-Five*, p. 212.

Chapter 49: Drummossie Muir

1 'O'Sullivan's Narrative' in Tayler and Tayler, *1745 and After*, p. 160.

2 Lord Elcho, *A Short Account*, p. 430.

3 Dennistoun, *Memoirs of Robert Strange*, Vol. 1, pp. 59–60.

4 Ibid., p. 60.

5 Henry Ker, 'Battle of Culloden' in Forbes and Chambers, *Jacobite Memoirs*, pp. 140–1.

6 Lord George Murray, 'March of the Highland Army' in Forbes and Chambers, *Jacobite Memoirs*, p. 123.

7 'O'Sullivan's Narrative' in Tayler and Tayler, *1745 and After*, p. 160.

8 See diagram in Tony Pollard, ed., *Culloden: The History and Archaeology of the Last Clan Battle*, Barnsley, 2009, p. 107 and for the whole battle see Stuart Reid's chapter 'The Battle of Culloden: A Narrative Account' in Pollard, *Culloden*, pp. 103–29.

9 'O'Sullivan's Narrative' in Tayler and Tayler, *1745 and After*, p. 160.

10 'Lord Elcho's Diary' in Tayler, *A Jacobite Miscellany*, p. 161.

11 Lord Elcho, *A Short Account*, p. 430.

12 Lord George Murray, 'March of the Highland Army' in Forbes and Chambers, *Jacobite Memoirs*, p. 123.

13 'Lord George Murray to William Hamilton' in Home, *The History of the Rebellion*, Appendix No. XLII, p. 368.

14 'O'Sullivan's Narrative' in Tayler and Tayler, *1745 and After*, p. 161.

15 Henry Ker, 'Battle of Culloden' in Forbes and Chambers, *Jacobite Memoirs*, p. 141.

16 'O'Sullivan's Narrative' in Tayler and Tayler, *1745 and After*, p. 162.

17 'John Macdonald's Account' in Tayler and Tayler, *1745 and After*, p. 161, n. 1.

18 'O'Sullivan's Narrative' in Tayler and Tayler, *1745 and After*, pp. 160–1.

19 Ibid., p. 163.

20 Ibid.

21 RA CP/MAIN/14/7 Strength of the British army, 16 April 1746 OS. See also Reid, 'The British Army at Culloden' in Pollard, *Culloden*, pp. 62–86.

22 'John Daniel's Account' in Blaikie, *Origins of the 'Forty-Five*, pp. 213–14.

23 RA CP/MAIN/14/48 Cumberland to Newcastle, Inverness 19 April 1746 OS.

24 'Joseph Yorke to Hardwicke, Inverness, 18 April 1746 OS' in Yorke, *Hardwicke Life and Correspondence*, Vol. 1, p. 522.

25 Hughes, *A Plain Narrative*, p. 36.

26 RA CP/MAIN/14/4 Lord Cathcart 'Description of ye Order of March from Nairne to Inverness, and of the Battle of Culloden April 16th 1746'.

27 'Copy of a letter from Alexander Taylor to his wife, Inverness Camp 17 April 1746' in *JSAHR*, Vol. 35, No. 144, December 1957, pp. 183–5, p. 184.

28 RA CP/MAIN/14/4 Lord Cathcart 'Description of ye Order of March from Nairne to Inverness, and of the Battle of Culloden April 16th 1746'.

29 Quoted in Oates, *Sweet William or The Butcher?*, p. 79.

30 'Alexander Taylor's Letter' in *JSAHR*, Vol. 35, No. 144, December 1957, p. 184.

31 Willson, *Life and letters of Wolfe*, p. 65.

32 RA CP/MAIN/14/58 Cumberland to Newcastle, Inverness 19 April 1746 OS.

33 For a detailed description see Stuart Reid, 'The British Army at Culloden' in Pollard, *Culloden*, pp. 62–86.

34 See Reid, 'The Battle of Culloden' in Pollard, *Culloden*, p. 106, Fig. 12.

35 RA CP/MAIN/14/58 Cumberland to Newcastle, Inverness 19 April 1746 OS.

36 Ibid.

37 Ibid.

38 Quoted in Ray, *A Compleat History of the Rebellion*, pp. 356–7.

39 Hughes, *A Plain Narrative*, p. 39.

40 RA CP/MAIN/14/58 Cumberland to Newcastle, Inverness 19 April 1746 OS.

41 RA CP/MAIN/14/4 Lord Cathcart 'Description of ye Order of March from Nairne to Inverness, and of the Battle of Culloden April 16th 1746'.

42 Maxwell of Kirkconnell, *Narrative*, p. 151.

43 'O'Sullivan's Narrative' in *1745 and After*, pp. 162–3, and Maxwell of Kirkconnell, *Narrative*, p. 151.

44 Lord George Murray, 'March of the Highland Army' in Forbes and Chambers, *Jacobite Memoirs*, p. 82.

45 RA CP/MAIN/14/58 Cumberland to Newcastle, Inverness 19 April 1746 OS.

46 RA CP/MAIN/14/4 Lord Cathcart 'Description of ye Order of March from Nairne to Inverness, and of the Battle of Culloden April 16th 1746'.

47 'John Daniel's Account' in Blaikie, *Origins of the 'Forty-Five*, p. 214.

48 Home, *The History of the Rebellion*, p. 231.

49 Dennistoun, *Memoirs of Robert Strange*, Vol. 1, p. 63.

50 Home, *The History of the Rebellion*, p. 231.

51 'John Daniel's Account' in Blaikie, *Origins of the 'Forty-Five*, p. 214.

52 'Joseph Yorke to Hardwicke, Inverness, 18 April 1746 OS' in Yorke, *Hardwicke Life and Correspondence*, Vol. 1, pp. 521–5, p. 523.

53 'Alexander Taylor's Letter' in *JSAHR*, Vol. 35, No. 144, December 1957, p. 184.

54 Maxwell of Kirkconnell, *Narrative*, p. 152.

55 Henry Ker, 'Battle of Culloden' in Forbes and Chambers, *Jacobite Memoirs*, p. 142.

56 Maxwell of Kirkconnell, *Narrative*, p. 152.

57 RA CP/MAIN/14/58 Cumberland to Newcastle, Inverness 19 April 1746 OS.

58 Hughes, *A Plain Narrative*, p. 39.

59 See Reid, 'The Battle of Culloden' in Pollard, *Culloden*, pp. 115–16.

60 Ibid., p. 115.

61 RA CP/MAIN/14/58 Cumberland to Newcastle, Inverness 19 April 1746 OS.

62 Johnstone, *Memoirs of the Rebellion*, p. 188; see also Reid, 'The Battle of Culloden' in Pollard, *Culloden*, p. 120.

63 'Donald Roy MacDonald's Narrative' in *LM*, Vol. 2, pp. 3–35, p. 5.

64 'Alexander Taylor's Letter' in *JSAHR*, Vol. 35, No. 144, December 1957, p. 184.

65 Henderson, *History of the Rebellion*, 1748, p. 117.

66 See Reid, 'The Battle of Culloden' in Pollard, *Culloden*, p. 119.

67 RA CP/MAIN/14/58 Cumberland to Newcastle, Inverness 19 April 1746 OS.

68 'Extract of a letter from a Captain in the late Sir Robert Monro's Regiment, to a Captain at Newcastle, dated April 17' in *Westminster Journal: Or, New Weekly Miscellany*, 3 May 1746 OS.

69 Lord George Murray, 'The March of the Highland Army' in Forbes and Chambers, *Jacobite Memoirs*, p. 124.

70 Johnstone, *Memoirs of the Rebellion*, p. 190.

71 NRS Irvine Robertson Papers GD1/53/109 Letter to John Home from William Home, Broomhouse 28 February 1792. NA SP 36/88/1 f. 39 states that William 'Bore the Pretenders Standard at Falkirk and Culloden, but was at that time only 14 Years old'.

72 Quoted in Oates, *Sweet William or The Butcher?*, p. 85.

73 See Reid, 'The Battle of Culloden' in Pollard, *Culloden*, p. 123.

74 RA CP/MAIN/14/4 Lord Cathcart 'Description of ye Order of March from Nairne to Inverness, and of the Battle of Culloden April 16th 1746'.

75 RA CP/MAIN/14/57 Cumberland to Loudoun, Inverness 19 April 1746 OS.

76 *The Gentleman's Magazine*, Vol. 16, April 1746, pp. 221–2.

77 'Extract of a letter . . . dated April 17' in *Westminster Journal*, 3 May 1746, p. 4.

78 Henderson, *History of the Rebellion*, 1748, p. 117.

79 Yorke, *Hardwicke Life and Letters*, Vol. 1, p. 524.

80 *The Gentleman's Magazine*, Vol. 16, April 1746, p. 222.

81 Henderson, *History of the Rebellion*, 1748, p. 116.

82 RA CP/MAIN/14/57 Cumberland to Loudoun, Inverness 19 April 1746 OS.

83 RA CP/MAIN/14/58 Cumberland to Newcastle, Inverness 19 April 1746 OS.

84 For the time, however, Stuart Reid considers it was 'nothing out of the ordinary'; see Reid, 'The Battle of Culloden' in Pollard, *Culloden*, p. 128.

85 *The Gentleman's Magazine*, Vol. 16, April 1746, p. 222.

86 'Lieut.-Col. Whitefoord's Account of the Battle of Culloden' in Hewins, *The Whitefoord Papers*, pp. 76–80, p. 79.

87 'Alexander Taylor's Letter' in *JSAHR*, Vol. 35, No. 144, December 1957, p. 184.

Chapter 50: Ruthven

1 NRS Irvine Robertson Papers GD1/53/109 Letter to John Home from William Home, Broomhouse 28 February 1792.

2 'O'Sullivan's Narrative' in Tayler and Tayler, *1745 and After*, p. 164.

3   Sir Walter Scott, *The Complete Works*, 7 vols, New York, 1833, Vol. 7, p. 467. Scott certainly believed it. The information had come from Sir James Stewart Denham, Lord Elcho's nephew, and was noted by Scott in his diary.

4   'Journal of Ned Burke' in Forbes and Chambers, *Jacobite Memoirs*, pp. 362–73, p. 363.

5   RA SP/MAIN/307/173 continues 175/175a both documents (ten sides in total) in Charles' handwriting and entitled 'Manuscript found by some soldiers in a Quakers Lodging on ye 10th June 1750 A Plain authentick and impartiall account of ye adventures of a certain young & daring man, since ye Battle of Culloden to his safe arrival in France'. Written on unused f. 175, not in Charles' hand, 'Adventures of a young man after the battle of Culloden writ in the P's own hand in 1750'.

6   Henry Ker, 'Battle of Culloden' in Forbes and Chambers, *Jacobite Memoirs*, p. 143.

7   NRS Irvine Robertson Papers GD1/53/109 Letter to John Home from William Home, Broomhouse 28 February 1792.

8   'Lord Elcho's Diary' in Tayler, *A Jacobite Miscellany*, p. 163.

9   Johnstone, *Memoirs of the Rebellion*, p. 198.

10 Lord Elcho, *A Short Account*, p. 436.

11 Maxwell of Kirkconnell, *Narrative*, p. 158.

12 RA SP/MAIN/307/173 'A Plain authentick and impartiall account'.

13 'Robert Forbes' third meeting with James Gib' in *LM*, Vol. 2, pp. 159–63, p. 160.

14 Lord Elcho, *A Short Account*, p. 436.

15 RA SP/MAIN/307/173 'A Plain authentick and impartiall account'.

16 'Donald MacLeod's Journal' in *LM*, Vol. 1, pp. 154–186, p. 155.

17 'Felix O'Neil's Journal' in *LM*, Vol. 1, pp. 365–75, p. 367.

18 'Neil MacEachain's Narrative' in Blaikie, *Origins of the 'Forty-Five*, pp. 227–66, p. 228.

19 'Journal of Ned Burke' in Forbes and Chambers, *Jacobite Memoirs*, p. 364.

20 Ibid.

21 'Neil MacEachain's Narrative' in Blaikie, *Origins of the 'Forty-Five*, p. 229.

22 'A Short account of what happened [to] his royal Highness after the bat[t]le of Culloden', RA SP/MAIN/280/19 dated some time between 31 December 1746 and 26 January 1747 NS (not in Charles' hand, possibly Sheridan or O'Sullivan?). The account covers the whole period up to his setting off for France.

23 'Felix O'Neil's Journal' in *LM*, Vol. 1, p. 367.

24 'A genuine and full Account of the Battle of Culloden' in *LM*, Vol. 1, p. 69.

25 'Neil MacEachain's Narrative' in Blaikie, *Origins of the 'Forty-Five*, p. 229.

26 Ibid.

27 Ibid., pp. 229–30.

28 'Captain Alexander MacDonald's Journal' in *LM*, Vol. 1, pp. 321–351, p. 322.

29 'Felix O'Neil's Account' in *LM*, Vol. 1, pp. 367–8.

30 RA SP/MAIN/307/173 'A Plain authentick and impartiall account'.

31 'Felix O'Neil's Account' in *LM*, Vol. 1, p. 368.

32 RA SP/MAIN/69/XI.41.18 'Journal of the Young Pretender'.

33 RA SP/MAIN/273/96 Letter from Lord George Murray to Charles [copy], Ruthven 17 April 1746 OS.

34 Ibid.

35 Ibid.

36 Johnstone, *Memoirs of the Rebellion*, p. 198.

37 'John Daniel's Account' in Blaikie, *Origins of the 'Forty-Five*, p. 215.
38 Ibid., p. 216.
39 Johnstone, *Memoirs of the Rebellion*, p. 200.
40 Ibid., p. 201.
41 'John Daniel's Account' in Blaikie, *Origins of the 'Forty-Five*, p. 216.
42 NRS Irvine Roberton Papers GD1/53/109 Letter to John Home from William Home, Broomhouse 28 February 1792.
43 'Robert Forbes' third meeting with James Gib' in *LM*, Vol. 2, p. 161.
44 Johnstone, *Memoirs of the Rebellion*, p. 203.
45 He eventually made his way to London and, disguised as a servant of Lady Jane Douglas, ventured to the Netherlands. Later in 1746 he arrived in Paris. See J. G. Alger, revised James Jay Carafano, 'James Johnstone', *ODNB* online, article 14963, 2006.
46 'John Daniel's Account' in Blaikie, *Origins of the 'Forty-Five*, p. 216.
47 'Felix O'Neil's Account' in *LM*, Vol. 1, p. 368.
48 RA SP/MAIN/273/116 Charles to Sheridan, [Borrodale?] 23 April 1746. Enclosure SP/MAIN/273/117 written on the reverse of the letter in Charles' hand 'The Princes Letter to ye Chifs, in parting from Scotland'.
49 RA SP/MAIN/273/117 'The Prince's letter to ye Chifs, in parting from Scotland' dated 28 April 1746, surely in reality the 23rd, as per the letter to Sheridan 273/116, but postdated on purpose.

Chapter 51: Church Street, Inverness

1 Gibson, *Ships of the '45*, p. 26.
2 Henderson, *History of the Rebellion*, 1748, p. 118.
3 Charteris, *Cumberland*, p. 278.
4 RA Captured Stuart Papers CP/MAIN/13/405.
5 *The Gentleman's Magazine*, Vol. 16, April 1746, p. 220. Gertrude Savile certainly believed the reports, writing in her diary, 'They were not to give Quarter to Man, Woman, or Child (cruell wretches), and upon pain of death they were not to plunder before the Batle and their conquest was over ... These two orders were found in the Pocket of one of their officers.' See 'Diary entry for 28 April 1746 OS' in Alan Saville, ed., *Secret Comment: The Diaries of Gertrude Savile, 1721–1757*, Nottingham/Kingsbridge, 1997, p. 271.
6 To confuse the issue further, Colonel O'Sullivan states that on 15 April, in preparation for the night march, 'Sullivan was commanded to give orders, & explain what he said in them. Ld George answered yt there was no need of orders, yt every body knew what he had to do, yt he'd march wth the first ligne, & whom H.R.Hs. plais'd wth the second ; the order of Battle was sufficient.' See 'O'Sullivan's Narrative' in Tayler and Tayler, *1745 and After*, pp. 154–5. This presumably does not preclude the possibility that a verbal order for the night march was written down by someone other than Lord George or O'Sullivan.
7 'Extract of a letter ... dated April 17', *Westminster Journal*, 3 May 1746, p. 4.
8 RA CP/MAIN/14/57 Cumberland to Loudoun, Inverness 19 April 1746 OS.
9 Ibid.
10 'Translation of a Letter from the Officers in the Service of his most Christian Majesty, who were at Inverness the Day of the Battle of Culloden' in *Westminster Journal*, 3 May 1746, p. 2. The marquis was a signatory.
11 RA CP/MAIN/14/58 Cumberland to Newcastle, Inverness 19 April 1746 OS.
12 *Westminster Journal*, 3 May 1746.

13 'Extract of a letter from a Captain in the late Sir Robert Monro's Regiment, to a Captain at Newcastle, dated April 17' in *Westminster Journal*, 3 May 1746, p. 4. See also Reid, 'The British Army at Culloden' in Pollard, *Culloden*, pp. 83–5. Reid argues that 'vestry men' tasked with battlefield clearance and grave digging, rather than regulars, are likely to have murdered wounded and helpless men; Reid, 'The British Army at Culloden' in Pollard, *Culloden*, p. 85.

14 'Lieut.-Col. Whitefoord's Account of the Battle of Culloden' in *The Whitefoord Papers*, pp. 76–80, p. 79.

15 Johnstone, *Memoirs of the Rebellion*, p. 197.

16 See Oates, *Sweet William or The Butcher?*, pp. 89–91.

17 RA CP/MAIN/14/58 Cumberland to Newcastle, Inverness 19 April 1746 OS.

18 Ibid.

19 William Roy, *An Account of the Measurements of a Base on Hounslow-Heath*, London, 1785, p. 4.

20 RA CP/MAIN/14/56 Cumberland to Lord President Forbes, Inverness 19 April 1746 OS.

21 RA CP/MAIN/14/60 'Return of the Killed and Wounded at the Battle of Culloden'.

22 RA CP/MAIN/14/62 Fletcher to Fawkener, Edinburgh 20 April 1746 OS.

23 RA CP/MAIN/14/63 Fletcher to Newcastle, Edinburgh midnight 19 April 1746 OS.

24 RA CP/MAIN/14/114 Ligonier to Cumberland, London 25 April 1746 OS.

25 RA CP/MAIN/14/99 Cumberland to Newcastle, Inverness 23 April 1746 OS.

26 Ibid.

27 'Letter from Joseph Yorke to Philip Yorke, Camp of Inverness, 30 April 1746' in Yorke, *Hardwicke Life and Correspondence*, Vol. 1, pp. 528–9, p. 528.

28 Some of the manuscripts Joseph is describing, the Captured Stuart Papers now archived with the Cumberland Papers at the Royal Archives, have been quoted extensively in this history.

29 RA CP/MAIN/14/303 Fawkener to Newcastle, Inverness 5 May 1746 OS.

30 RA CP/MAIN/14/354 Ancram to Fawkener, Aberdeen 9 May 1746 OS.

31 Quoted in Menary, *Duncan Forbes of Culloden*, p. 280.

32 Ibid., p. 281.

33 RA CP/MAIN/14/397 Pelham to Cumberland, London 12 May 1746 OS.

Chapter 52: Albano

1 RA SP/MAIN/275/26 James to Charles, Albano 6 June 1746 NS.

Chapter 53: Coradale

1 'Felix O'Neil's Account' in *LM*, Vol. 1, p. 370.

2 'Alexander MacDonald's Journal' in *LM*, Vol. 1, pp. 321–51, p. 326.

3 Ibid.

4 Ibid., p. 327.

5 RA SP/MAIN/307/175a 'A Plain authentick and impartiall account'.

6 'Donald Roy MacDonald's Narrative' in *LM*, Vol. 2, p. 7.

7 'Hugh MacDonald of Baleshare's Account' in *LM*, Vol. 2, pp. 95–103, p. 95.

8 Ibid.

9 Ibid., p. 96.

10 'Alexander MacDonald's Journal' in *LM*, Vol. 1, p. 327.
11 'Hugh MacDonald of Baleshare's Account' in *LM*, Vol. 2, p. 97.
12 Ibid.
13 Ibid.
14 Ibid., p. 99.
15 'Donald Roy MacDonald's Narrative' in *LM*, Vol. 2, p. 7.
16 'Hugh MacDonald of Baleshare's Account' in *LM*, Vol. 2, p. 102.
17 'Felix O'Neil's Account' in *LM*, Vol. 1, p. 370.
18 Gibson, *Ships of the '45*, p. 29.
19 'John Daniel's Account' in Blaikie, *Origins of the 'Forty-Five*, p. 224.
20 Quoted in Gibson, *Ships of the '45*, p. 70.

Chapter 54: Fort Augustus

1 RA CP/MAIN/15/221 Cumberland to Newcastle, Fort Augustus 27 May 1746 OS.
2 Maclachlan, *Duke of Cumberland*, p. 323.
3 RA CP/MAIN/15/101. See also Duff, *Culloden Papers*, No. 326, pp. 284–5, p. 284.
4 NLS Fletcher of Saltoun Papers MS. 17523 ff. 1–2 'Memorial of the different sorts of prisoners in Scotland and Queries to be resolved concerning them', Edinburgh 23 July 1746 OS. My thanks to Darren Layne for drawing my attention to this document.
5 'Letter from Cumberland to Newcastle, Inverness 30 April 1746 OS' in Warrand, *More Culloden Papers*, Vol. 5, pp. 71–2, p. 71.
6 RA CP/MAIN/15/221 Cumberland to Newcastle, Fort Augustus 27 May 1746 OS.
7 'Lord President Forbes' Ideas' in Duff, *Culloden Papers*, No. 326, pp. 284–5, p. 285.
8 RA CP/MAIN/15/101. See also Duff, *Culloden Papers*, No. 326, p. 285.
9 NLS Fletcher of Saltoun Papers MS. 17523 ff. 1–2 'Memorial of the different sorts of prisoners in Scotland and Queries to be resolved concerning them' Edinburgh 23 July 1746 OS.
10 RA CP/MAIN/16/8 Fawkener to the commanding officers of His Majesty's ships, Fort Augustus 8 June 1746 OS.
11 RA CP/MAIN/16/9 Fawkener to Major General Campbell, Fort Augustus 8 June 1746 OS.
12 RA CP/MAIN/16/27 William Carlyle to Fawkener, Prestonpans 9 June 1746 OS.
13 RA CP/MAIN/16/43 James Fraser and Andrew Robertson to Fawkener, Alness in Ross 10 June 1746 OS.
14 RA CP/MAIN/16/59 Captain John Ferguson's Journal, 'Tobbermury' 11 June 1746 OS.

Chapter 55: Skye

1 'Donald MacLeod's Journal' in *LM*, Vol. 1, p. 268.
2 'A genuine and full Account of the Battle of Culloden' in *LM*, Vol. 1, p. 71.
3 Ibid.
4 'Felix O'Neil's Account' in *LM*, Vol. 1, p. 371.
5 'Donald MacLeod's Journal' in *LM*, Vol. 1, p. 176.
6 'Flora MacDonald's Journal' in *LM*, Vol. 1, pp. 296–306, p. 297. This is confirmed in Charles' document SP/MAIN/307/173,175, 175a, 'A Plain authentick and impartiall account'.

7 The fabric details were given to Robert Forbes by Alexander MacDonald of Kingsburgh; see *LM*, Vol. 1, p. 81.
8 'Flora MacDonald's Journal' in *LM*, Vol. 1, p. 297.
9 Ibid., p. 297; 'Felix O'Neil's Account' in *LM*, Vol. 1, p. 372.
10 'Felix O'Neil's Account' in *LM*, Vol. 1, p. 373.
11 RA SP/MAIN/307/175a 'A Plain authentick and impartiall account'.
12 'Copy of part of a Letter . . . from the Revd. Mr. James Hay' in *LM*, Vol. 3, pp. 21–2, p. 22.
13 'Flora MacDonald's Journal' in *LM*, Vol. 1, p. 299.
14 Ibid., p. 305.
15 'Kingsburgh's observations' in *LM*, Vol. 1, pp. 74–83, p. 77.
16 Ibid.
17 John Burton, *A Genuine and True Journal of the most miraculous Escape of the Young Chevalier, From the Battle of Culloden, to his landing in France*, London, 1749, p. 28.
18 Ibid., p. 29.
19 'Flora MacDonald's Journal' in *LM*, Vol. 1, p. 301.
20 'Kingsburgh's observations' in *LM*, Vol. 1, pp. 75–6.
21 Ibid., p. 75.
22 Mahon, *The Forty-Five*, p. 129.
23 'Kingsburgh's observations' in *LM*, Vol. 1, p. 75.
24 Ibid., p. 76; 'Flora MacDonald's Journal' in *LM*, Vol. 1, p. 302.
25 'Malcolm MacLeod's Account' in *LM*, Vol. 1, p. 130; 'Flora MacDonald's Journal' in *LM*, Vol. 1, p. 302; 'Donald Roy MacDonald's Narrative' in *LM*, Vol. 2, p. 22.
26 'Donald Roy MacDonald's Narrative' in *LM*, Vol. 2, p. 25.
27 'Flora MacDonald's Journal' in *LM*, Vol. 1, p. 303.
28 RA CP/MAIN/17/248 Donald MacDonald to Sir Alexander MacDonald, 'Keanlochdale' 11 July 1746 OS.
29 Ibid.
30 Gibson, *Ships of the '45*, pp. 78–80.
31 'Letter from Lady Margaret MacDonald to Lord President Forbes, Skye 24 July 1746' in Duff, *Culloden Papers*, No. 335, pp. 290–1.

Chapter 56: Kennington Common

1 'Diary entry for 24 April 1746 OS' in Saville, *Secret Comment: The Diaries of Gertrude Savile*, p. 271.
2 T. B. Howell, ed., *A Complete Collection of State Trials and Proceedings*, Vol. 18 (1743–1753), London, 1813, pp. 329–30.
3 On 18 October 1746 with eight others.
4 RA CP/MAIN/16/173 D'Eguilles to Fawkener, Carlisle 18 June 1746 OS and RA CP/MAIN/16/358 Everard to d'Eguilles, Fort Augustus 29 June 1746 OS.
5 NA Treasury Solicitor Papers 20/80/13 refers to '268 prisoners at Tilbury out of 300 sent from Inverness'. See also Bruce Gordon Seton and Jean Gordon Arnot ed., *The Prisoners of the '45*, 3 vols, Edinburgh, 1928, Vol. 1, pp. 6–7.
6 'Horace Walpole to Horace Mann, Arlington Street, London, 12 August 1746 OS' in Lewis, *Horace Walpole's Correspondence*, Vol. 19, pp. 293–7, p. 295.
7 *The Report on Sir John Cope*, p. 104.
8 RA CP/MAIN/17/128 William Deacon to Fawkener, London 25 June 1746 OS.

9   G. Griffith, *The Genuine Trial of Francis Townley*, London, 1746, pp. 11–32.
10 Ibid., p. 6.
11 Ibid., p. 13.
12 *The Gentleman's Magazine*, Vol. 16, July 1746, pp. 335–6.
13 Griffith, *The Genuine Trial of Francis Townley*, p. 21.
14 Ibid., pp. 26–7.
15 Ibid., pp. 29–30.
16 Ibid., p. 29.
17 *The Gentleman's Magazine*, Vol. 16, July 1746, p. 337.
18 Ibid, p. 398.
19 Ibid., p. 390.
20 The execution is described in ibid., p. 383.
21 'The Speech of Mr. Thomas Theodore Deacon' in *LM*, Vol. 1, pp. 22–6, pp. 22–3.
22 His uncle succeeded in saving him from his brother's fate but he was eventually sent as an indentured servant to Jamaica in 1749, where he died soon after.
23 See for example *The Scots Magazine*, Vol. 8, July 1746, p. 330.
24 'Whitworth's *Manchester Magazine*, 23 September 1746' in Anon [Thomas Deacon], *Manchester Vindicated*, Chester, 1749, p. 1.
25 Anon [Deacon], *Manchester Vindicated*, pp. v–vi.
26 '*Chester Courant*, 28 October 1746' in Anon [Deacon], *Manchester Vindicated*, p. 3.

Chapter 57: Glenmoriston

1   'John MacDonald's Narrative' in *LM*, Vol. 3, pp. 375–83, pp. 379–80.
2   Ibid., pp. 380–1.
3   'Narrative by Patrick Grant' in *LM*, Vol. 3, pp. 97–106, p. 98.
4   'Captain Alexander MacDonald's Journal' in *LM*, Vol. 1, pp. 321–54, p. 344.

Chapter 58: The Tower

1   *The Gentleman's Magazine*, Vol. 16, July 1746, p. 382.
2   NA SP 36/85/2 f. 51 Copy 'Instructions for the Earl of Albermarle' July 1746.
3   'Horace Walpole to Horace Mann, Arlington Street, London, 29 November 1745 OS' in Lewis, *Horace Walpole's Correspondence*, Vol. 19, pp. 172–7, pp. 174–5.
4   'Horace Walpole to Horace Mann, Arlington Street, London, 1 August 1746 OS' in Lewis, *Horace Walpole's Correspondence*, Vol. 19, pp. 280–9, p. 288.
5   Howell, *State Trials*, 1813, Vol. 18, p. 492.
6   Ibid., p. 502.
7   'Joseph Yorke to Philip Yorke, Camp at Inverness 30 April 1746 OS' in Yorke, *Hardwicke Life and Correspondence*, Vol. 1, p. 529.
8   'Letter from Lord President Forbes to Lord Lyon, Edinburgh 8 July 1746 OS' in Duff, *Culloden Papers*, No. 332, pp. 288–9, p. 289. According to a footnote 'the kilt or Pheliebeg was not the antient Highland garb, but was introduced into the Highlands about 1720 by one Thomas Rawlinson, an Englishman . . . The convenience of the dress soon caused it to be universally adopted in the Highlands.' The source quoted is a letter by Evan Baillie written in 1769 and published in the *Edinburgh Magazine* in 1785.
9   'Horace Walpole to Horace Mann, Arlington Street, London, 1 August 1746 OS' in Lewis, *Horace Walpole's Correspondence*, Vol. 19, pp. 280–9, pp. 287–8.

10 Matthew Kilburn, 'Frederick Lewis, prince of Wales', *ODNB* online, article 10140, 2004.

11 'Horace Walpole to Horace Mann, Arlington Street, London, 12 August 1746 OS' in Lewis, *Horace Walpole's Correspondence*, Vol. 19, pp. 293–7, p. 296.

12 Howell, *State Trials*, 1813, Vol. 18, p. 508.

13 'Horace Walpole to Horace Mann, Arlington Street, London, 1 August 1746 OS' in Lewis, *Horace Walpole's Correspondence*, Vol. 19, pp. 280–9, p. 281.

14 Howell, *State Trials*, 1813, Vol. 18, p. 510.

15 Ibid.

16 Ibid., p. 512.

17 Bradstreet, *Life and Uncommon Adventures*, p. 161. He was still petitioning in October, see NA SP 35/88/1 f. 13 Bradstreet to Newcastle, [no location] 2 October 1746 OS.

18 *The Gentleman's Magazine*, Vol. 16, August 1746, p. 392.

19 Howell, *State Trials*, 1813, Vol. 18, pp. 511–12.

20 *The Gentleman's Magazine*, Vol. 16, August 1746, p. 392.

21 Howell, *State Trials*, 1813, Vol. 18, p. 514.

22 Bradstreet, *Life and Uncommon Adventures*, p. 163.

23 *The Gentleman's Magazine*, Vol. 16, August 1746, p. 393.

24 Ibid.

25 'The Speech of the Right Honorable Arthur, Lord Balmerino, faithfully transcribed from his lordships own handwrit' in *LM*, Vol. 1, pp. 54–6.

26 *The Gentleman's Magazine*, Vol. 16 August 1746, p. 393.

27 Howell, *State Trials*, 1813, Vol. 18, p. 522.

28 *The Gentleman's Magazine*, Vol. 16, August 1746, p. 394.

29 Bradstreet, *Life and Uncommon Adventures*, p. 164.

30 Ibid.

Chapter 59: Cluny's Cage

1 'John Cameron's Journal' in *LM*, Vol. 1, pp. 83–101, p. 97.

2 *Manuscripts in the Charter-Chest at Cluny Castle Inverness-shire*, Edinburgh, 1879, p. 40.

3 'Account by Donald MacPherson, Cluny's youngest brother' in *LM*, Vol. 3, pp. 38–48, p. 40.

4 Ibid.

5 Ibid., p. 41.

6 Lochiel, 'Mémoire d'un Ecossais' in Gibson, *Lochiel of the 'Forty-Five*, p. 174.

7 The full description is in *Cluny Charter-Chest*, pp. 41–2.

8 'Account by Donald MacPherson' in *LM*, Vol. 3, p. 42.

9 Ibid.

10 *Cluny Charter-Chest*, p. 41.

11 Ibid.

12 Ibid., p. 42.

13 'Account by Donald MacPherson' in *LM*, Vol. 3, p. 41.

14 Ibid., p. 48.

15 Ibid., p. 47.

16 'Warren to Walsh, Matignon 29 August NS' in MacGregor, *A Royalist Family*, p. 45.

17 'Account by Donald MacPherson' in *LM*, Vol. 3, p. 44.

18 'Intelligence from the Hills' sent by Albemarle to Newcastle in mid-November 1746, in Terry, *The Albemarle Papers*, Vol. 1, p. 303.
19 He remained there for nine years until he joined Charles in Paris in 1755.
20 'John MacDonald's Narrative' in *LM*, Vol. 3, p. 382.

Chapter 60: United Kingdom

1 MacGregor, *A Royalist Family*, p. 45.
2 Pompadour, *Memoirs*, Vol. 1, p. 112.
3 NA SP 54/34 f. 61 Albemarle to Newcastle, Edinburgh 27 October 1746 OS.
4 'Aeneas MacDonald's Journal' in *LM*, Vol. 1, p. 284.
5 Evident from the wealth of Jacobite visual and material culture created post-1746; see Richard Sharp, *The Engraved Record of the Jacobite Movement*, Aldershot, 1996; Robin Nicholson, *Bonnie Prince Charlie and the Making of a Myth: A Study in Portraiture 1720–1892*, London, 2002; Neil Guthrie, *The Material Culture of the Jacobites*, Cambridge, 2013; Murray G. H. Pittock, *Material Culture and Sedition, 1688–1760: Treacherous Objects, Secret Places*, Basingstoke, 2013.
6 Duncan Forbes, *Memoirs of the Life of Lord Lovat*, London, 1746.
7 Murray, probably unfairly, became the focus of all Jacobite ire until he died in 1777.
8 'Horace Walpole to Horace Mann, Arlington Street, London, 20 June 1746 OS' in Lewis, *Horace Walpole's Correspondence*, Vol. 19, pp. 271–3, p. 272.
9 RA SP/MAIN/285/104 Charles to James, St Ouen 10 July 1747 NS.
10 RA SP/MAIN/284/162 Henry to Charles, Albano 20 June 1747 NS.
11 RA SP/MAIN/285/126 Myles McDonnell to James, Paris 14 July 1747 NS.
12 Lord George died in Medemblik, Holland, in 1760.
13 'Duncan Forbes to John Forbes, no date' transcribed in Menary, *Duncan Forbes of Culloden*, pp. 339–40.
14 Pompadour, *Memoirs*, Vol. 1, p. 114.
15 Ibid.
16 Wormeley, *Memoirs and Letters of Cardinal de Bernis*, 2 vols, Vol. 1, p. 158.
17 Pompadour, *Memoirs*, Vol. 1, p. 117
18 Ibid.

Epilogue

1 RA CP/MAIN/9/16 A list of prisoners [Castle and Cathedral] at Carlisle, December 1745.
2 Seton and Arnot, *Prisoners of the '45*, Vol. 3, pp. 272–3.
3 This was decided upon 'taking into Consideration the great Numbers of Prisoners detain'd in Custody on Account of the late Rebellion' see NA SP 36/88/1 f. 43 Council meeting 'At the Court at Kensington' 23 July 1746 OS; also Seton and Arnot, *Prisoners of the '45*, Vol. 1, p. 7.
4 NA SP 36/88/1 f. 42 Order dated Whitehall 3 October 1746 OS.
5 Seton and Arnot, *Prisoners of the '45*, Vol. 1, pp. 24–8.
6 NA SP 36/102 ff. 95–6 'An exact list & Discription of 150 Rebel Prisoners ship'd at Liverpool on board the Veteran', October 1747.
7 Livingstone, Aikman and Stuart Hart, *No Quarter Given*, p. 7.

Bibliography

Manuscripts

British Library
  Hardwicke Papers Add MS 35354
  Miscellaneous letters and papers principally relating to Jacobites 1668–1790, Add MS 39923
  Newcastle Papers Add MS 32704, 32705, 32706
  Samuel Crisp Letters and Papers, Add MS 47463
  Joseph Spence Letters 1731–41, Egerton MS 2234

Hampshire Record Office
  HRO Malmesbury Papers: Letters written to James Harris by his brother Thomas Harris
    1745–6, 9M73/G309

National Archives
  NA State Papers Domestic George II 1745–7, SP 36/65–104
  NA State Papers Scotland Series II 1747, SP 54/34
  NA Treasury Solicitor: Jacobite Rebellion (1745) Prosecution Papers TS 20

National Library of Scotland
  NLS Fletcher of Saltoun Papers MS 17523

National Register of Archives Scotland
  NRAS Hamilton Papers 332, 2177

National Records of Scotland
  NRS Irvine Robertson Papers GD1/53
  NRS Papers of Dr John Jardine GD1/1440

National War Museum Scotland
  NWMS 355.486.242.34 (1746), Cholmondeley's Orderly Book (34th Regiment of Foot)

The Royal Archives
  Cumberland Papers including the Captured Stuart Papers CP/MAIN/1–69
  Stuart Papers SP/MAIN/235–307
  (The Cumberland and Stuart Papers are quoted with the kind permission of Her Majesty
    Queen Elizabeth II)

Primary Sources (Printed)

Aeneas and His Two Sons. A True Portrait, London, 1746.

A Full and Authentic History of the Rebellion 1745 and 1746 . . . To which is Added, A Copy of what Dr. Archibald Cameron intended to have delivered to the Sheriff of Middlesex, at the Place of Execution . . . By an Impartial Hand, London, 1755.

A full and particular account of a bloody battle, fought between the English and French, in Flanders under the command of his Royal Highness William Duke of Cumberland, British Library Cup 21 g.31/48.

A Full and True Collection of All the Orders, Proclamations, and Papers etc. Published by Authority of Charles Prince of Wales, Regent of Scotland, England, France and Ireland . . . Since his Arrival in Scotland to the present Time, Glasgow, 1746.

A Letter from an English Traveller at Rome to his Father, Of the 6th of May, 1721. O.S., London, 1721.

Allardyce, James, ed., *Historical Papers relating to the Jacobite Period, 1699–1750*, 2 vols, Aberdeen, 1895–6.

An Account of the Conduct of the Young Chevalier: from his first Arrival in Paris, after his Defeat at Culloden, to the Conclusion of the Peace at Aix-la-Chapelle . . . In a Letter from a Gentleman residing at Paris, to his Friend in London, 2nd edition, London, 1749.

Anon. [Deacon, Thomas], *Manchester Vindicated: being a compleat Collection of the Papers lately published in defence of that Town in the Chester Courant*, Chester, 1749.

Anon., *Genuine Memoirs of John Murray, Esq, Late Secretary to the Young Pretender*, Dublin, 1747.

A Serious Address to the People of Great Britain. In which the Certain Consequences of the Present Rebellion are fully demonstrated, London, 1745.

A Short Account of the Behaviour of the Rebel Army, while at Hamilton, in a Letter to a Friend at Edinburgh, British Library C.115.i.3(91).

Authentic Copies of the Letters and other Papers delivered, at their Execution, by the Nine REBELS who suffer'd Death on Wednesday, July 30, 1746, on Kennington Common, London, 1746.

Bell, Robert Fitzroy, ed., *Memorials of John Murray of Broughton*, Edinburgh, 1898.

Blaikie, W. B., *Origins of the 'Forty-Five and other papers relating to that rising*, Edinburgh, 1916. Includes 'A True Account of Mr. John Daniel's Progress with Prince Charles Edward in the Years 1745 and 1746 written by himself', pp. 165–224.

Bland, Humphrey, *A Treatise of Military Discipline; In which is Laid down and Explained The Duty of the Officer and Soldier, Thro' the several Branches of the Service*, 5th edition, London, 1743.

Boaden, James, ed., *The private correspondence of David Garrick*, 2nd edition, 2 vols, London, 1835.

Boyse, Samuel, *Historical Review of the Transactions of Europe . . . To which is Added an Impartial History of the Late Rebellion*, Reading, 1747.

Bradstreet, Dudley, *The Life and Uncommon Adventures of Capt. Dudley Bradstreet*, Dublin, 1755.

Brockbank, W. and F. Kenworthy, eds, *The Diary of Richard Kay, 1716–51 of Baldingstone, near Bury: A Lancashire Doctor*, Manchester, 1968.

Brosses, Charles de, *Lettres historiques et critiques sur l'Italie*, 3 vols, Paris, 1799.

Burt, Edmund, *Letters from a Gentleman in the North of Scotland to His Friend in London*, 2 vols, London, 1754.

Burton, John, *A Genuine and True Journal of the most miraculous Escape of the Young Chevalier, From the Battle of Culloden, to his landing in France*, London, 1749.

Byrom, John, *Miscellaneous Poems*, 2 vols, Manchester, 1773.

Caledonian Mercury, 5 August; 20 August; 22 August; 18 September; 14 October 1745.

Coxe, William, *Memoirs of Horatio, Lord Walpole*, 2 vols, London, 1808.

— *Memoirs of the Administration of the Right Honourable Henry Pelham*, 2 vols, London, 1829.

Daily Advertiser, 30 September 1745.

Declaration, Holyroodhouse 9 October 1745 OS; Holyroodhouse, 10 October 1745 OS, British Library C.115.i.3.(66).

Defoe, Daniel, *A Tour thro' the Whole Island of Great Britain*, 4 vols, 3rd edition, London, 1742.

Dennistoun, James, ed., *The Cochrane Correspondence regarding the Affairs of Glasgow 1745–6*, Glasgow, 1836.

— *Memoirs of Sir Robert Strange and Andrew Lumisden*, 2 vols, London, 1855.

Derby Mercury, 29 November–13 December 1745.

Doddridge, Philip, *Some Remarkable Passages in the Life of Colonel James Gardiner*, London, 1747.

Duff, H. R., ed., *Culloden Papers comprising an Extensive and Interesting Correspondence from the year 1625 to 1748*, London, 1815.

Earwaker, J. P., *The Constables' Accounts of the Manor of Manchester*, 3 vols, Manchester, 1892.

Elcho, David, Lord, ed. Evan Charteris, *A Short Account of the Affairs of Scotland in the Years 1744, 1745, 1746*, Edinburgh, 1907.

Fielding, Henry, *The True Patriot: and History of Our Own Times*, 10 December 1745.

Finance Accounts, &c. of the United Kingdom . . . for the year 1831, Vol. 26, Royal Palaces and Buildings, London, 1832.

Forbes, A., ed., *Curiosities of A Scots Charta Chest 1600–1800*, Edinburgh, 1897. Includes 'Alexander Cunyngham's Travels', pp. 99–123.

Forbes, Duncan, *Memoirs of the Life of Lord Lovat*, London, 1746.

Forbes, Robert and Robert Chambers, eds, *Jacobite Memoirs of the Rebellion of 1745*, Edinburgh, 1834. Includes Lord George Murray, 'The March of the Highland Army', pp. 29–130, one version of James Gib 'The Prince's Household Book', pp. 145–206 and Colonel Henry Ker's 'The Battle of Culloden', pp. 131–44.

Foster, James, *An Account of the Behaviour of the Late Earl of Kilmarnock, after his Sentence and on the Day of His Execution*, London, 1746.

Fraser, William, *The Earls of Cromartie, their Kindred, Country and Correspondence*, 2 vols, Edinburgh, 1874.

General Advertiser, 28 September 1745.

Gray, John M., ed., *Memoirs of the Life of Sir John Clerk of Penicuik*, Edinburgh, 1892.

Griffith, G., *The Genuine Trial of Francis Townley*, London, 1746.

[Griffiths, Ralph], *Ascanius: or, The Young Adventurer; A True History*, London, 1746.

Harland, John, ed., *Ballads and Songs of Lancashire, Chiefly Older than the 19th Century*, London, 1865.

Harris, James Howard, *A Series of Letters of the First Earl of Malmesbury, his family and friends from 1745–1820*, London, 1870.

Hedman, Bruce A., 'Colin Maclaurin's Journal of the 'Forty-Five', in *Miscellany XIII of the Scottish History Society*, 5th series, Vol. 14, Edinburgh, 2004, pp. 312–22.

Henderson, Andrew, *The History of the Rebellion*, 1st edition, London, 1748; 5th edition, 1753.

— *The Life of William Augustus, Duke of Cumberland*, London, 1766.

Herring, Thomas, *A sermon preach'd at the Cathedral Church of York, September the 22nd 1745; On Occasion of the present rebellion in Scotland,* York, 1745.

Hervey, John, *Memoirs of the Reign of George the Second,* 2 vols, London, 1848.

Hewins, W. A. S., ed., *The Whitefoord Papers: being the correspondence and other manuscripts of Colonel Charles Whitefoord and Caleb Whitefoord from 1739 to 1810,* Oxford, 1898.

HMRC, *The Manuscripts of Lord Kenyon, Royal Commission on Historical Manuscripts,* 14th Report, Appendix, Part 4, London, 1894.

Home, John, *The History of the Rebellion in the year 1745,* London, 1802.

Howell T. B., ed., *A Complete Collection of State Trials and Proceedings,* Vol. 18 (1743–1753), London, 1813.

Hughes, Michael, *A Plain Narrative and Authentic Journal of the late Rebellion,* 2nd edition, London, 1747.

Johnstone, James, *Memoirs of the Rebellion in 1745 and 1746,* 2nd edition, London, 1821.

Kinsley, James, ed., *Alexander Carlyle: Anecdotes and Characters of the Times,* London, 1973.

Kirkconnell, James Maxwell of, *Narrative of Charles Prince of Wales' Expedition to Scotland in the Year 1745,* Edinburgh, 1861.

Klima, Slava, Garry Bowers and Kerry S. Grant, eds, *Memoirs of Dr. Charles Burney, 1726–1769,* Lincoln and London, 1988.

Lewis, W. S., ed., *Horace Walpole's Correspondence,* 48 vols, New Haven and London, 1937–83.

Lochiel, Donald Cameron of, 'Mémoire d'un Ecossais, April 1747', translated in J. S. Gibson, *Lochiel of the '45,* Edinburgh, 1994, pp. 173–85.

Lumisden, Thomas and John Robertson, *The Whole Prophecies of Scotland, England, France, Ireland and Denmark; prophesied by Thomas Rymer,* Edinburgh, 1745.

McCann, T., ed., *The correspondence of the Dukes of Richmond and Newcastle, 1724–1750,* Lewes, 1984.

MacDonald, Alexander, 'Journall and Memoirs of P. C. Expedition into Scotland . . . By a Highland Officer in his Army', in *The Lockhart Papers,* 2 vols, London, 1817, Vol. 2, pp. 479–510.

MacGregor, Murray, trans., *A Royalist Family: Irish and French (1689–1789) and Prince Charles Edward,* Edinburgh, 1904.

Macky, John, *A Journey through England: In Familiar Letters from A Gentleman Here to His Friend Abroad,* 2nd edition, 2 vols, London, 1724.

— *A Journey through Scotland: In Familiar Letters from A Gentleman Here to His Friend Abroad,* 2nd edition, London, 1729.

Maclean, John, 'A Journall of the Travells and Marches of John Maclean in his Highness's Army 1745', transcribed in Iain Gordon Brown and Hugh Cheape, *Witness to Rebellion: John Maclean's Journal of the 'Forty-Five and the Penicuik drawings,* East Linton, 1996, pp. 21–40.

Manuscripts in the Charter-Chest at Cluny Castle Inverness-shire, Edinburgh, 1879.

Marchant, John, *The History of the Present Rebellion,* London, 1746.

Martin, Martin, *A description of the Western Islands of Scotland,* London, 1703.

Miller, James, 'The Diary of James Miller 1745–50', in *JSAHR,* Vol. 3, No. 14, October 1924, pp. 208–26.

Mounsey, George Gill, ed., *Authentic Account of the Occupation of Carlisle in 1745 by Prince Charles Edward Stuart,* London, 1846.

[Murray, Lord George], *A Particular Account of the Battle of Culloden. April 16, 1746. In a letter from an officer of the Highland army, to his friend at London,* London, 1749. The letter is dated Lochaber 16 May 1746 and offers another description of the Night

March and the Battle of Culloden. It was published anonymously but attributed to Lord George Murray, whose accounts (in John Home's *History of the Rebellion* and Forbes and Chambers, *Jacobite Memoirs*) it closely follows, both in overall thrust and in detail.

Newcastle Courant, 9–16 November 1745; 4–11 January 1745/6.

Parkinson, Richard, ed., *The private journal and literary remains of John Byrom*, 4 vols (32, 34, 40, 44), Chetham Society, Manchester, 1854–7.

— *The Journal of Elizabeth Byrom*, reprinted from Vol. II, Part II of 'Remains of John Byrom', Chetham Society, Manchester, 1857.

Paton, Henry, ed., 'Leaves from the Diary of John Campbell, an Edinburgh Banker, in 1745', in *Scottish History Society Publications*, Vol. 15, Miscellany, Vol. 1, Edinburgh, 1893, pp. 537–59.

— *The Lyon in Mourning: or a Collection of Speeches Letters Journals etc, Relative to the Affairs of Prince Charles Edward Stuart by the Rev. Robert Forbes*, 3 vols, Edinburgh, 1896. Includes the recollections of Duncan Cameron, Aeneas MacDonald, Donald Roy MacDonald, Flora MacDonald, Hugh MacDonald, John MacDonald, Malcolm MacLeod, Felix O'Neil, and a version of James Gib, 'Prince's Household Accounts'.

Pompadour, Jeanne Antoinette Poisson, Madame de, *Memoirs of the Marchioness of Pompadour. Written by herself*, 2 vols, London, 1766.

Proclamation, Holyroodhouse 23 September 1745 OS. British Library C.115.i.3(69).

— Holyroodhouse 24 September 1745 OS, British Library C.115.i.3.(63).

— Holyroodhouse 2 October 1745 OS, British Library C.115.i.3.(64).

— Holyroodhouse 5 October 1745 OS, British Library C.115.i.3.(65).

— Holyroodhouse 10 October 1745 OS, British Library C.115.i.3.(67).

Ray, James, *A Compleat History of the Rebellion*, York, 1749.

Revue Rétrospective: Recueil de pièces intéressantes et de citations curieuses, Paris, 1886.

Roy, William, *An Account of the Measurements of a Base on Hounslow-Heath*, London, 1785.

Russell, John, *Letters from a young painter abroad to his friends in England*, London, 1748.

St. James's Evening Post, 31 October–2 November 1745.

Saville, Alan, ed., *Secret Comment: The Diaries of Gertrude Savile, 1721–1757*, Nottingham and Kingsbridge, 1997.

Scott, Sir Walter, *Waverley; or 'Tis Sixty Years Since*, 3 vols, Edinburgh, 1814.

— *Miscellaneous Prose Works: Tales of a Grandfather*, vols 22–8, Edinburgh, 1836.

Shenstone, William, *The Poetical Works of Will. Shenstone. With the Life of the Author*, London, 1787.

Simpson, Robert, *A collection of fragments illustrative of the history and antiquities of Derby*, Derby, 1826.

Smollett, T. and T. Franklin, *The Works of M. de Voltaire*, 25 vols, London, 1761–6.

Stewart-Murray, J. H. and Jane Anderson, eds, *Chronicles of the Atholl and Tullibardine Families*, 5 vols, Edinburgh, 1908.

Tayler, A. and H. Tayler, eds, *1745 and After*, London and Edinburgh, 1938. Contains the accounts of John William O'Sullivan and Sir John Macdonald.

Tayler, H., ed., *Jacobite Epilogue*, London and Edinburgh, 1941.

— *A Jacobite Miscellany: Eight original papers on the Rising of 1745–6*, Oxford, 1948. Includes the transcriptions of Magdalen Pringle's letters, pp. 37–42, and a translation of 'A portion of the diary of David, Lord Elcho', pp. 127–71.

Taylor, Alexander, 'Copy of a letter from Alexander Taylor to his wife, Inverness Camp 17 April 1746', in *JSAHR*, Vol. 35, No. 144, December 1957, pp. 183–5.

Terry, Charles Sanford, ed., *The Albemarle Papers: being the Correspondence of William Anne, Second Earl of Albemarle, Commander in Chief in Scotland, 1746–1747*, 2 vols, Aberdeen, 1902.

The Chester Miscellany. Being a collection of several pieces, both in prose and verse, which were in the Chester Courant from January 1745, to May 1750, Chester, 1750.

The Gentleman's Magazine, Vol. 15, 1745; Vol. 16, 1746; Vol. 17, 1747.

The Last Speech and dying Words of Henry MacManus, 23 January 1745/6 OS, British Library C.115.i.3.(79).

The Report of the Proceedings and Opinion of the Board of General Officers, on their Examination into the Conduct, Behaviour, and Proceedings of Lieutenant-General Sir John Cope, Dublin, 1749.

The Scots Magazine, Edinburgh, Vol. 7, 1745; Vol. 8, 1746.

The Soldier's Companion or Martial Recorder, London, 1824.

The York Courant, 17 September 1745; 23 September 1745.

Threipland, Christian, *Copy of a Letter from a Lady to the Lady G—dd-s, at K-l-v-ck, to the Care of Mr. James R----- Merchant in Inverness. Dundee, November 20th 1745*, British Library C.115.i.3.(77.).

Transactions of the Lancashire & Cheshire Antiquarian Society, Vol. 42, Manchester, 1927.

True Copies of the Papers wrote by Arthur Lord Balmerino, Thomas Syddall, David Morgan . . . and delivered by them to the Sheriffs at the Places of their Execution, London, 1746.

Walpole, Horace, *Memoirs of the last ten years of the reign of George the Second*, 2 vols, London, 1822.

Warrand, Duncan, ed., *More Culloden Papers*, 5 vols, Inverness, 1927–30.

Westminster Journal: Or, New Weekly Miscellany, 5 October 1745; 3 May 1746.

Willson, Beckles, *The Life and Letters of James Wolfe*, London, 1909.

Woodhouselee Manuscript. A narrative of events in Edinburgh and district during the Jacobite occupation, September to November 1745, London and Edinburgh, 1907. This manuscript is generally accepted to have been written by Patrick Crichton and quoted here accordingly.

Wormeley, Katharine Prescott, trans., *Journal and Memoirs of the Marquis d'Argenson*, 2 vols, Boston, 1902.

— *Memoirs & Letters of Cardinal de Bernis*, 2 vols, London, 1902.

Yorke, Philip, *Life and Correspondence of Philip Yorke Earl of Hardwicke*, 3 vols, Cambridge, 1913.

Secondary Sources

Alger, J. G., revised James Jay Carafano, 'James Johnstone', *ODNB* online, article 14963, 2006.

Anderson, George and Peter Anderson, *Guide to the Highlands and Islands*, Edinburgh, 1842.

Anderson, John, *A History of Edinburgh*, Edinburgh and London, 1856.

Ballantyne, Archibald, *Voltaire's visit to England 1726–1729*, London, 1893.

Black, Jeremy, *Culloden and the '45*, Stroud, 2010.

Blaikie, W. B., *Itinerary of Prince Charles Edward Stuart from his landing in Scotland July 1745 to his Departure in September 1746*, Edinburgh, 1897.

— 'Edinburgh at the time of the occupation of Prince Charles', in *The Book of the Old Edinburgh Club for the Year 1909*, 2 vols, Edinburgh, 1909, Vol. 2, pp. 1–60.

Bongie, L. L., 'Voltaire's English, high treason and a manifesto for Bonnie Prince Charlie', in *Studies on Voltaire and the eighteenth century*, Vol. 171 (1977), pp. 7–29.

— *The Love of a Prince: Bonnie Prince Charlie in France, 1744–1748*, Vancouver, 1986.

Bowditch, Lyndsey, Andrew MacKillop and Tony Pollard, *Culloden*, The National Trust for Scotland, Edinburgh, 2009.

Brown, Iain Gordon and Hugh Cheape, *Witness to Rebellion: John Maclean's Journal of the 'Forty-Five and the Penicuik drawings*, East Linton, 1996.

Browning, Reed, 'Thomas Pelham-Holles, Duke of Newcastle upon Tyne and first duke of Newcastle under Lyme', in *ODNB* online, article 21801, 2011.

Campbell Orr, Clarissa, ed., *Queenship in Britain, 1660–1837: Royal Patronage, Court Culture and Dynastic Politics*, Manchester, 2002.

Challice, Annie E., *The secret history of the Court of France under Louis XV*, 2 vols, London, 1861.

Chambers, Robert, *History of the Rebellion in Scotland in 1745, 1746*, 4th edition, 2 vols, Edinburgh, 1830.

— *The Threiplands of Fingask: A Family Memoir*, London and Edinburgh, 1880.

Charles, George, *History of the Transactions In Scotland, in the Years 1715–16 and 1745–46*, 2 vols, Leith, 1817.

Charteris, Evan, *William Augustus Duke of Cumberland: His Early Life and Times (1721–1748)*, London, 1913.

Cheape, Hugh, 'The '45 and its Aftermath: the Moidart Kinsmen's View', in Camille Dressler and Domhnall Uilleam Stiùbhart, eds, *Alexander MacDonald – Bard of the Gaelic Enlightenment*, Lewis, 2013, pp. 37–8.

Clark, J. C. D., *English Society 1660–1832: Religion, Ideology and Politics During the Ancien Régime*, 2nd edition, Cambridge, 2000.

Colley, Linda, *Britons: Forging the Nation 1707–1807*, New Haven and London, 1992, revised 2003.

Corp, Edward, *The Stuart Court in Rome: A Legacy of Exile*, Farnham, 2003.

— *A Court in Exile: The Stuarts in France, 1689–1718*, Cambridge, 2009.

— *The Stuarts in Italy, 1719–1766: A royal court in permanent exile*, Cambridge, 2011.

Craig, Maggie, *Damn' Rebel Bitches: The Women of the '45*, Edinburgh, 1997.

Cruickshanks, Eveline, *Political Untouchables: The Tories and the '45*, London, 1979.

Cruickshanks, Eveline and Jeremy Black, eds, *The Jacobite Challenge*, Edinburgh, 1988.

Cruickshanks, Eveline and Edward Corp, eds, *The Stuart Court in Exile and the Jacobites*, London, 1995.

Cruickshanks, Eveline and Howard Erskine-Hill, *The Atterbury Plot*, Basingstoke, 2004.

Daiches, David, *Charles Edward Stuart: The Life and Times of Bonnie Prince Charlie*, London, 1973.

Dalgleish, George and Dallas Mechan, *I am Come Home: Treasures of Prince Charles Edward Stuart*, Edinburgh, 1985.

Daniels, Stephen and John Bonehill, *Paul Sandby: Picturing Britain*, London, 2009.

Devine, T. M., ed., *Conflict and stability in Scottish Society, 1700–1850*, Edinburgh, 1990.

Devine, T. M., *The Scottish Nation: 1700–2000*, London, 1999.

Duffy, Christopher, *The '45: Bonnie Prince Charlie and the Untold Story of the Jacobite Rising*, London, 2003. Revised and republished as *Fight for a Throne: The Jacobite '45 Reconsidered*, Solihull, 2015.

Eardley Simpson, L., *Derby and the Forty-Five*, London, 1933.

Fraser, Sarah, *The Last Highlander: Scotland's most notorious clan chief, rebel & double agent*, London, 2012.

Gibson, John S., *Ships of the '45: The Rescue of the Young Pretender*, London, 1967.

— *Lochiel of the '45*, Edinburgh, 1994.

— *Edinburgh in the '45: Bonnie Prince Charlie at Holyrood*, Edinburgh, 1995.

— *The Diary of John Campbell: A Scottish Banker and the 'Forty-Five*, Edinburgh, 1995.

Gillis, Richard, *The History of Culloden House*, Culloden House, Inverness, 1996, revised 2014.

Glover, Katharine, *Elite Women and Polite Society in Eighteenth-Century Scotland*, Woodbridge, 2011.

Greig, James, ed., *The Diaries of a Duchess*, London, 1926.

Groome, Francis H., ed., *Ordnance Gazetteer of Scotland*, 2 vols, Edinburgh, 1884.

Guthrie, Neil, *The Material Culture of the Jacobites*, Cambridge, 2013.

Hamilton, F. W., *The origins and history of the First or Grenadier Guards*, 3 vols, London, 1874.

Harvey, Wallace, *Chronicles of Saint Mungo: or, Antiquities and traditions of Glasgow*, Glasgow, 1843.

Hazelrigg, Edward, *The Attic Stories or the Opinions of Edward Hazelrig*, Glasgow, 1818.

Horrocks, Hilary, ed., *Glenfinnan Monument*, The National Trust for Scotland, Edinburgh, 2006.

Hutton, W., *The History of Derby; from the Remote Ages of Antiquity to the Year 1791*, 2nd edition, London, 1817.

Jackson, Clare, *Restoration Scotland, 1660–1690: Royalist Politics, Religion and Ideas*, Woodbridge, 2003.

Jarvis, Rupert C., *Collected Papers on the Jacobite Risings*, 2 vols, Manchester, 1970–1.

Jeffery, Edward, *The history of Preston in Lancashire*, London, 1822.

Johnstone, J., *Historical and Descriptive Account of the Palace and Chapel-Royal of Holyroodhouse*, Edinburgh, 1826.

Jones, Colin, *The Great Nation: France from Louis XV to Napoleon*, London, 2002.

Kilburn, Matthew, 'Frederick Lewis, prince of Wales', *ODNB* online, article 10140, 2004.

Kulisheck, P. J., 'Henry Pelham', *ODNB* online, article 21789, 2008.

Lang, Andrew, *Prince Charles Edward Stuart*, London, 1903.

Lenman, Bruce, *The Jacobite Clans of the Great Glen, 1650–1784*, London, 1984.

— *The Jacobite Risings in Britain, 1689–1746*, Dalkeith, 1995/2004.

Lenman, Bruce and John S. Gibson, *The Jacobite Threat*, Edinburgh, 1990.

Livingstone, Alastair, Christian Aikman and Betty Stuart Hart, eds, *No Quarter Given: The Muster Roll of Prince Charles Edward Stuart's Army, 1745–46*, Glasgow, 2001.

McCarthy, M. R., H. R. T. Summerson and R. G. Annis, *Carlisle Castle: a survey and documentary history*, English Heritage Archaeological Report No. 18, 1990.

Maclachlan, A. N. Campbell, *William Augustus, Duke of Cumberland: Being a Sketch of His Military Life and Character, Chiefly as Exhibited in the General Orders of H.R.H., 1745–1747*, London, 1876.

McLynn, Frank, *France and the Jacobite Rising of 1745*, Edinburgh, 1981.

— *The Jacobite Army in England 1745*, Edinburgh, 1998.

— *Bonnie Prince Charlie: Charles Edward Stuart*, London, 1988/2003.

Mahon, Philip Stanhope, Lord, *The Forty-Five*, London, 1851.

Marshall, Rosalind K., 'The Palace of Holyroodhouse', in *The Court Historian: The International Journal of Court Studies*, Vol. 1, No. 3 (October 1996), pp. 2–6.

Mason, Haydn, 'Sir Everard Fawkener', *ODNB* online, article 9228, 2004.

Menary, George, *The Life and Letters of Duncan Forbes of Culloden*, London, 1936.

Miller, James, *The Lamp of Lothian or, the History of Haddington*, Haddington, 1844.

Monod, Paul, *Jacobitism and the English People, 1688–1788*, Cambridge, 1989.

Monod, Paul, Murray G. H. Pittock and Daniel Szechi, eds, *Loyalty and Identity: Jacobites at Home and Abroad*, London, 2009.

Murdoch, Alexander, 'Archibald Campbell, third duke of Argyll', *ODNB* online, article 4477, 2006.

Nicholas, Donald, ed., *Intercepted Post*, London, 1956.

Oates, Jonathan, *The Jacobite Invasion of 1745 in North West England*, Lancaster, 2006.

— *Sweet William or The Butcher?*, Barnsley, 2008.

— *The Jacobite Campaigns: The British State at War*, London and New York, 2011.

Parkinson-Bailey, John, *Manchester: An architectural history*, Manchester, 2000.

Perry, Norma, *Sir Everard Fawkener, friend and correspondent of Voltaire*, Banbury, 1975.

Petrie, Sir Charles, *The Jacobite Movement: The Last Phase 1716–1807*, London, 1950.

Pittock, Murray G. H., *The Invention of Scotland: the Stuart Myth and the Scottish Identity, 1638 to the present*, London, 1991.

— 'Lord George Murray', *ODNB* online, article 19605, 2006.

— *The Myth of the Jacobite Clans*, 2nd revised edition, Edinburgh, 2009.

— *Material Culture and Sedition, 1688–1760: Treacherous Objects, Secret Places*, London, 2013.

Plank, Geoffrey, *Rebellion and Savagery: The Jacobite Rising of 1745 and the British Empire*, Philadelphia, 2006.

Pollard, Tony, ed., *Culloden: The History and Archaeology of the Last Clan Battle*, Barnsley, 2009.

Prebble, John, *Culloden*, London, 1961.

Reid, Stuart, *Like Hungry Wolves: Culloden Moor 16 April 1746*, London, 1994.

— *1745: A military history of the last Jacobite rising*, Staplehurst, 1996.

— *Culloden, 1746: Battlefield guide*, Barnsley, 2005.

Rogers, Nicholas, 'Popular Disaffection in London During the Forty-Five', in *The London Journal*, Vol. 1, No. 1, May 1975, pp. 5–27.

Sankey, M. and D. Szechi, 'Elite Culture and the Decline of Scottish Jacobitism 1716–1745', in *Past and Present*, No. 173, Oxford, 2001, pp. 90–128.

Scholes, Percy, *God Save the Queen!: The history and romance of the world's first national anthem*, Oxford, 1954.

Seton, Bruce Gordon and Jean Gordon Arnot, eds, *The Prisoners of the '45*, 3 vols, Edinburgh, 1928.

Sharp, Richard, *The Engraved Record of the Jacobite Movement*, Aldershot, 1996.

Shaw, John S., 'Duncan Forbes', *ODNB* online, article 9822, 2006.

Smith, Hannah, *Georgian Monarchy: Politics and Culture, 1714–1760*, Cambridge, 2006.

Speck, W. A., *The Butcher: The Duke of Cumberland and the Suppression of the '45*, Cardiff, 1981 and 1995.

— 'Prince William Augustus, Duke of Cumberland', *ODNB* online, article 29455, 2008.

Stephen, Jeffrey, 'Scottish Nationalism and Stuart Unionism: The Edinburgh Council, 1745', in *Journal of British Studies*, Vol. 49, No. 1, January 2010, pp. 47–72.

Steuart, A. Francis, *The Plenishing of Holyrood House in 1714*, Reprinted from the Proceedings of the Society of Antiquaries of Scotland, Edinburgh, 1928.

Struthers, John, *The History of Scotland from the Union to the Abolition of the Heritable Jurisdictions in 1748*, 2 vols, Glasgow, 1828.

Szechi, Daniel, *The Jacobites: Britain and Europe 1688–1788*, Manchester, 1994.

— *1715: The Great Jacobite Rebellion*, New Haven and London, 2006.

Thomas, Peter D. G., 'Philip Yorke, first earl of Hardwicke', in *ODNB* online, article 30245, 2007.

Thompson, Andrew, *George II: King and Elector*, New Haven and London, 2011.

Thomson, Katherine, *Memoirs of the Jacobites of 1715 and 1745*, 3 vols, 1845, London.

Timperley, Charles Henry, *Annals of Manchester*, Manchester, 1839.

Towill, Sydney, *A History of Carlisle*, Phillimore, 1991.

Whatley, Christopher A., *Scottish Society, 1707–1830: Beyond Jacobitism, Towards Industrialisation*, Manchester, 2000.

— 'Reformed Religion, Regime Change, Scottish Whigs and the Struggle for the "Soul" of Scotland, *c*.1688–*c*.1788', in *Scottish Historical Review*, Edinburgh, XCII, 1, No. 233 (April 2013), pp. 66–99.

— *The Scots and the Union: Then and Now*, Edinburgh, 2nd edition, 2014.

Wheatley, J. A., *Bonnie Prince Charlie in Cumberland*, Carlisle, 1903.

Woosnam-Savage, R. C., ed., *1745: Charles Edward Stuart and the Jacobites*, Edinburgh, 1995.

Acknowledgements

I must begin by drawing attention to the extraordinary work undertaken by scholars, antiquarian societies and heritage organisations over several centuries, to make key contemporary sources for the '45 available to everyone, whether in hard copy or online.

Thank you to the staff at the British Library, Culloden House, Derby Museums Trust, Hampshire Record Office, Hamilton Archives (Lennoxlove House), Inverness Museum and Gallery, The London Library, The National Archives, National Library of Scotland, National Museums of Scotland, National Records of Scotland and The Royal Collection. My particular thanks and gratitude to Pamela Clark and her colleagues at the Royal Archives, Windsor, who, for a year and a half, cheerfully moved many dozens of weighty boxes and volumes, from the stores, to the reading room and back again for this troublesome researcher. During one visit, while gazing out of a Round Tower window, I was mistaken for Her Majesty the Queen by a group of school children gathered below. Apparently it happens all the time. I waved, elegantly, to the distant flash of smart phones, but I apologise now for the collective disappointment caused when, soon after, those images would have been closely inspected.

I am profoundly indebted to the following historians who generously read chapters and advised on the content, despite very busy schedules: Hugh Cheape, Edward Corp, Julian Swann, Andrew Thompson and Christopher Whatley. I must also acknowledge the invaluable scholarship of Eveline Cruickshanks, Sir Tom Devine, Christopher Duffy, John S. Gibson, Bruce Lenman, Frank McLynn, Paul Monod, Murray G. H. Pittock, Stuart Reid, William Speck and Daniel Szechi. My deep gratitude also to Jonathan Oates, who read and commented on an early draft, and to Darren S. Layne, who read the full manuscript just after submitting his PhD thesis on the '45: beyond the call of duty, but I am thrilled he did so. And to Mike Leigh, for inspiring me to think afresh about how history is presented, and for the opportunity to witness, close-to, the craft of story telling in action.

In the course of research, I attended many conferences, seminars and lectures, which sharpened my thinking on this complex subject. Thanks to the individual speakers, and to the Association of Art Historians, Blair Castle, Pitlochry, the British Society of Eighteenth-Century Studies, the Caledonian Club, London, Fairfax House, York, Gosford House, East Lothian, the Institute of Historical

Research, the Jacobite Studies Trust, Lyon and Turnbull, the National Army Museum, the National Portrait Gallery, National Trust for Scotland and the Society for Court Studies.

At the start of this journey, I received a grant from the Society of Authors, which not only supported, financially, a period of research, but also gave this author a very welcome fillip and, I like to think, validation for the project.

At Bloomsbury, heartfelt thanks to Michael Fishwick who has taken on this book, a subject not without its controversies, with sensitivity and intelligence, gusto and humour; to Anna Simpson who has guided me, serenely, through the intricacies of text and design fine tuning; and Marigold Atkey, for being an all-round good egg. To my agent Bill Hamilton, whose fault, sorry, idea this was. I particularly thank him for his enduring faith and infectious enthusiasm.

For their knowledge, help, support and, in some cases, cheerleading skills, I thank the following colleagues, friends and family: Tabitha Barber, Andrew Barclay, Tony Butler, Juliet Carey, Deborah Clarke, Tim Clayton, Viccy Coltman, George Dalgleish, Jane Darcy, Janet Dickinson, Emma Dowley, Susanna Eastburn, Matthew Fox, Sarah Fraser, Ruth Gill, Helen Grearson, Bendor Grosvenor, Mark Hallett, Sarah Heaton, Charlotte Higgins, Caro Howell, Linda Johnson, Anna Keay, Rachel Kennedy, Tim Knapman, Paul Lay, John Lloyd, Georgina Lowe, Anne Lyles, Ian Peter 'Peeps' MacDonald, Sarah McBryde, Caroline Meer, Keith Miller, Fran Moyle, Steven Parissien, Matthew Plampin, Sue Prichard, Eileen Reed, Kate Retford, Christine Riding, Duncan Riding, my parents John and Patricia Riding (to whom, with my grandparents and uncle, I dedicate this book), James Robinson, Hallie Rubenhold, Jennifer Scott, Martin Stiles, David Teather and Sarah Victoria Turner.

In the distant and not-so-distant past, histories on this subject could be described as, broadly speaking, pro-Jacobite or pro-Hanoverian: the former vastly outweighing the latter. There is now a general desire, among established and emerging scholars alike, to approach this extraordinary moment in British history in a balanced manner, presenting it in all its complexity, while placing it, correctly, in an international, as well as national and local context. It was in this spirit that the current history was written, and is now humbly presented.

London, February 2016

Index

A NOTE ON THE TYPE

The text of this book is set in Adobe Garamond. It is one of several versions of Garamond based on the designs of Claude Garamond. It is thought that Garamond based his font on Bembo, cut in 1495 by Francesco Griffo in collaboration with the Italian printer Aldus Manutius. Garamond types were first used in books printed in Paris around 1532. Many of the present-day versions of this type are based on the Typi Academiae of Jean Jannon, cut in Sedan in 1615.

Claude Garamond was born in Paris in 1480. He learned how to cut type from his father and by the age of fifteen he was able to fashion steel punches the size of a pica with great precision. At the age of sixty he was commissioned by King Francis I to design a Greek alphabet; for this he was given the honourable title of royal type-founder. He died in 1561.

31901059634438